L.A. BANKS'
VAMPIRE HUNTRESS

VOLUME ONE
DAWN AND DARKNESS

DYNAMITE
ENTERTAINMENT

L.A. BANKS' Vampire Huntress

VOLUME ONE
DAWN and DARKNESS

WRITTEN BY **L.A. Banks**

SCRIPTING BY **Jess Ruffner** (Issues 1-2)

ARTWORK BY **Brett Booth** (Issue 1), **Greg Titus** (Issues 2-3) **& N Steven Harris** (Issue 4)

COLORS BY **Rachelle Rosenberg & Steve Downer**

LETTERS BY **Bill Tortolini**

COLLECTION COVER BRETT BOOTH
CONSULTATION LES & ERNST DABEL
COLLECTION DESIGN BILL TORTOLINI
COLLECTION EDITS RICH YOUNG

ENTERTAINMENT

Dynamite Entertainment:

NICK BARRUCCI • PRESIDENT
JUAN COLLADO • CHIEF OPERATING OFFICER
JOSEPH RYBANDT • EDITOR
JOSH JOHNSON • CREATIVE DIRECTOR
RICH YOUNG • BUSINESS DEVELOPMENT
JASON ULLMEYER • SENIOR DESIGNER
JOSH GREEN • TRAFFIC COORDINATOR
CHRIS CANIANO • PRODUCTION ASSISTANT

www.dynamite.net

ISBN13: 978-1-60690-179-3   ISBN10: 1-60690-179-6

10 9 8 7 6 5 4 3 2

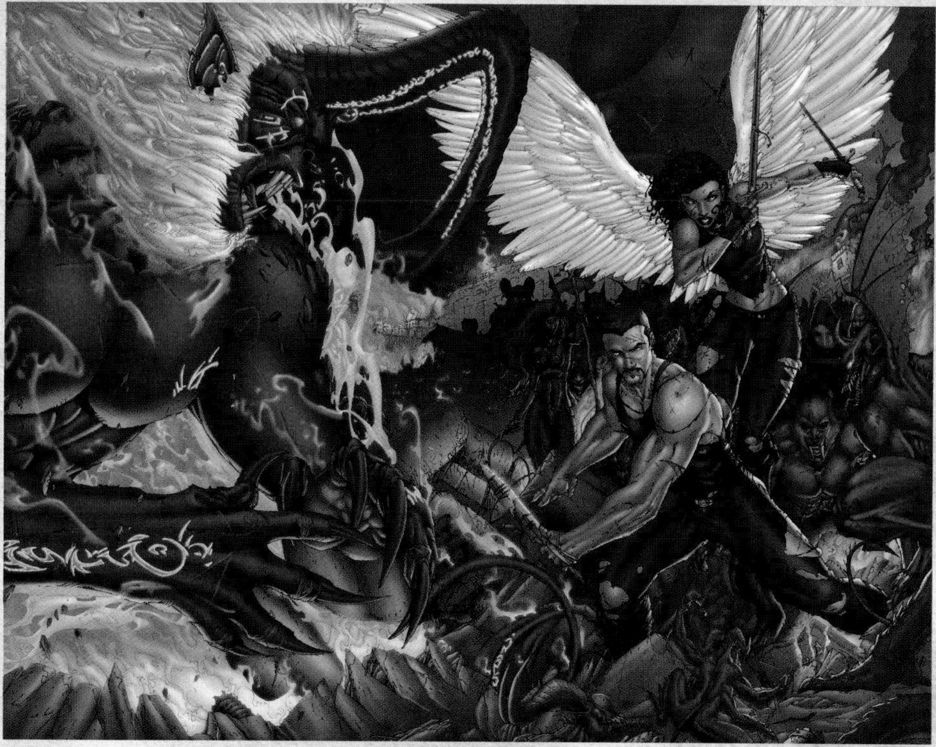

The Vampire Huntress Legend series is a twelve book series written by L.A. Banks. It centers around a young woman named Damali Richards, a spoken word artist who is also The Neteru (The Huntress), a human who is born every thousand years to fight the Dark Realms. Her most dangerous and most constant enemies from The Dark Realms are vampires.

Dawn and Darkness is an epilogue to the book series. It follows the aftermath of the Armageddon battle that took place at the thrilling conclusion of book 12.

Lucifier has been temporarily defeated, Lilith was vanquished, The Vampire Council was wiped out, the Anti-Christ was wounded—the Neterus and their Guardians are beat down and bloody, and half the team is pregnant. . . both sides have gone to their mutual corners to heal.

But the dark side is hardly ready to accept defeat, just as the Warriors of Light know full well that their temporary victory is a tenuous one.

For more information on the Vampire Huntress book series go to: http://www.vampire-huntress.com

AN INTRODUCTION BY
JONATHAN MABERRY

One of the running gags in genre review is that 'vampires are dead.'

The reviewers generally aren't talking about the undead state of the monsters. They are making a statement about the genre itself. Vampires are passé, they say. Vampires are a 'been there, done that, staked it to death' storytelling trope whose golden years are behind it.

They say that the legions of tweens embracing sparkly vampires was proof-positive that vampires have stopped being interesting to adult readers. Vampires, they say, are barely even scary anymore. And they're definitely not sexy.

They say.

The thing is, this is the same argument they've been trotting out since the era of Universal Pictures monsters began to fade in the late 1940s. Then Hammer Films proved them wrong a decade later when Christopher Lee proved that vampires could be scary and sexy all over again. And Richard Matheson proved that vampires were truly frightening with his novel **I Am Legend**.

The same rags predicted the death of the vampire genre again after a couple of those films were out…then **Dark Shadows** hit the airwaves in the sixties. In the seventies the genre not only refused to die, it spread like a blood-borne pandemic with the debut of **Stephen King's 'Salem's Lot**, the **Night Stalker** TV movies and series, Anne Rice's **Interview with the Vampire** (which sunk its fangs into the bestseller lists for over twenty-five years), and Chelsea Quinn Yarbro's series of Saint-Germain historical vampire romances. The Eighties added real heat to the whole 'are vampires sexy?' issue with **The Hunger**, and also gave us wicked-sexy fun with Grace Jones in **Vamp.**, and fused funny with scary in **Fright Night**. The Nineties gave us **Forever Knight**, **Buffy the Vampire Slayer**, **Angel** and **Blade**. And in the twenty-first century we have Laurell K. Hamilton's **Anita Blake, Vampire Hunter** series and the smoking hot HBO series **True Blood**, based on the Sookie Stackhouse novels by **Charlaine Harris**.

The new millennium also gave us the **Vampire Huntress** series by L. A. Banks. A dozen novels.

Wow. Talk about hot vampires. Talk about sexy, scary vampires. And sexy, scary vampire hunters. I burned my fingers reading those books. Hot blood pumped through every single page.

I've had the pleasure of knowing Leslie Banks since middle school. I could tell you stories. We've become colleagues since then, both of us New York Times bestsellers, both of us writing about the things that go bump in the night. But more importantly, I've been in awe of her since I picked up the first of her Vampire Huntress novels. When the series ended I went into withdrawal. Even **I** thought the era of scary, sexy vampire stories had finally come to an end.

Ah, ye of little faith.

Then Dynamite came out with **The Vampire Huntress** comic. Not a rehash…fresh stories, with stunning artwork by N. Steven Harris, Brett Booth and Gregory Titus and a script by L.A. Banks with Jess Ruffner. So delicious. Hot blooded. Incredibly sexy. And, yeah…scary as hell.

Now…settle back and turn the page and discover the fact that all those short-sighted critics completely missed…Vampires, my friend, are **immortal**.

Jonathan Maberry is a New York Times bestselling author, multiple Bram Stoker Award-winner, and Marvel Comics writer. His works include **The King of Plagues**, **Marvel Zombies Return**, **Rot & Ruin**, and **Patient Zero**.

BOOK ONE

ASHES to ASHES

VAMPIRE
HUNTRESS

COVER ONE ARTWORK BY: BRETT BOOTH

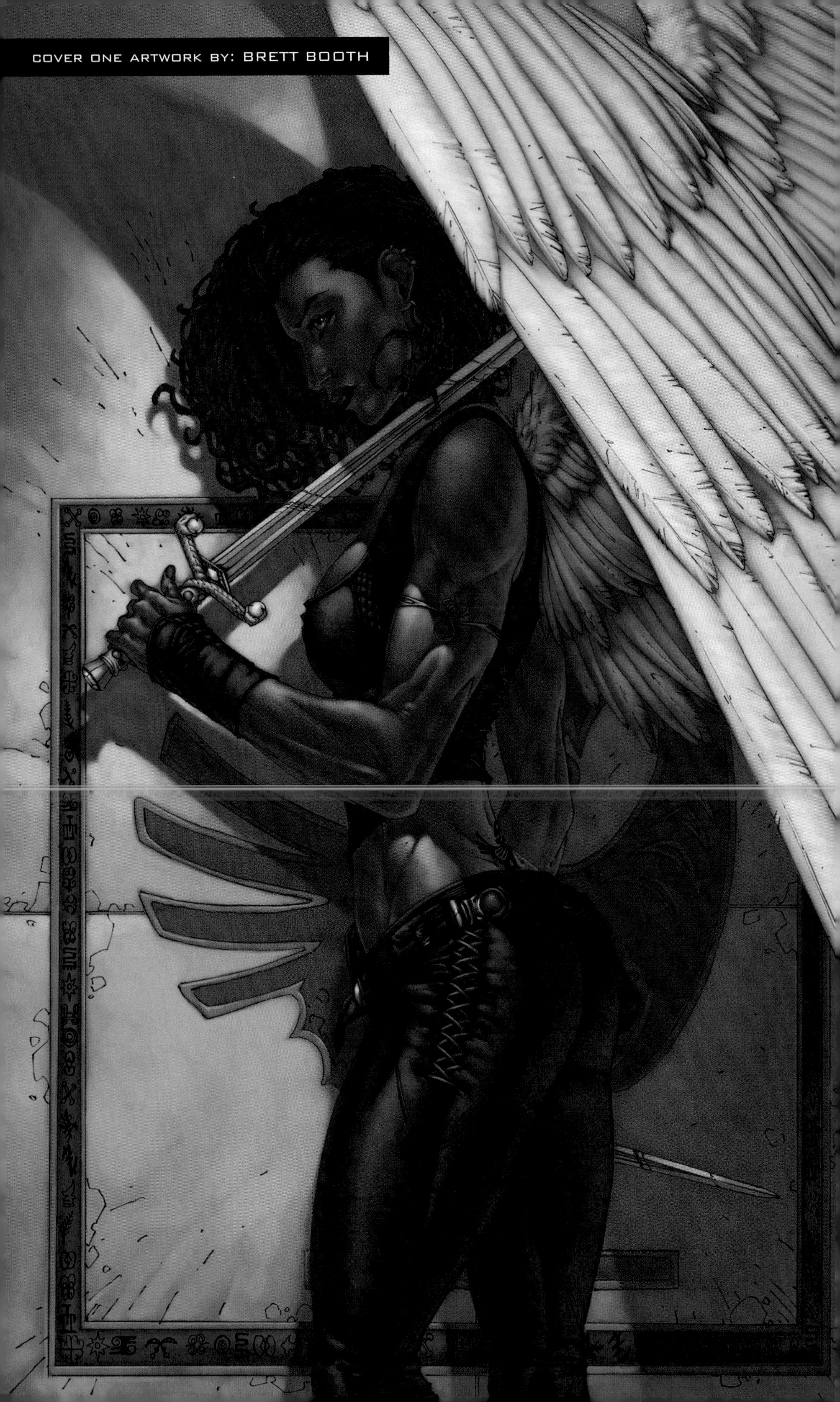

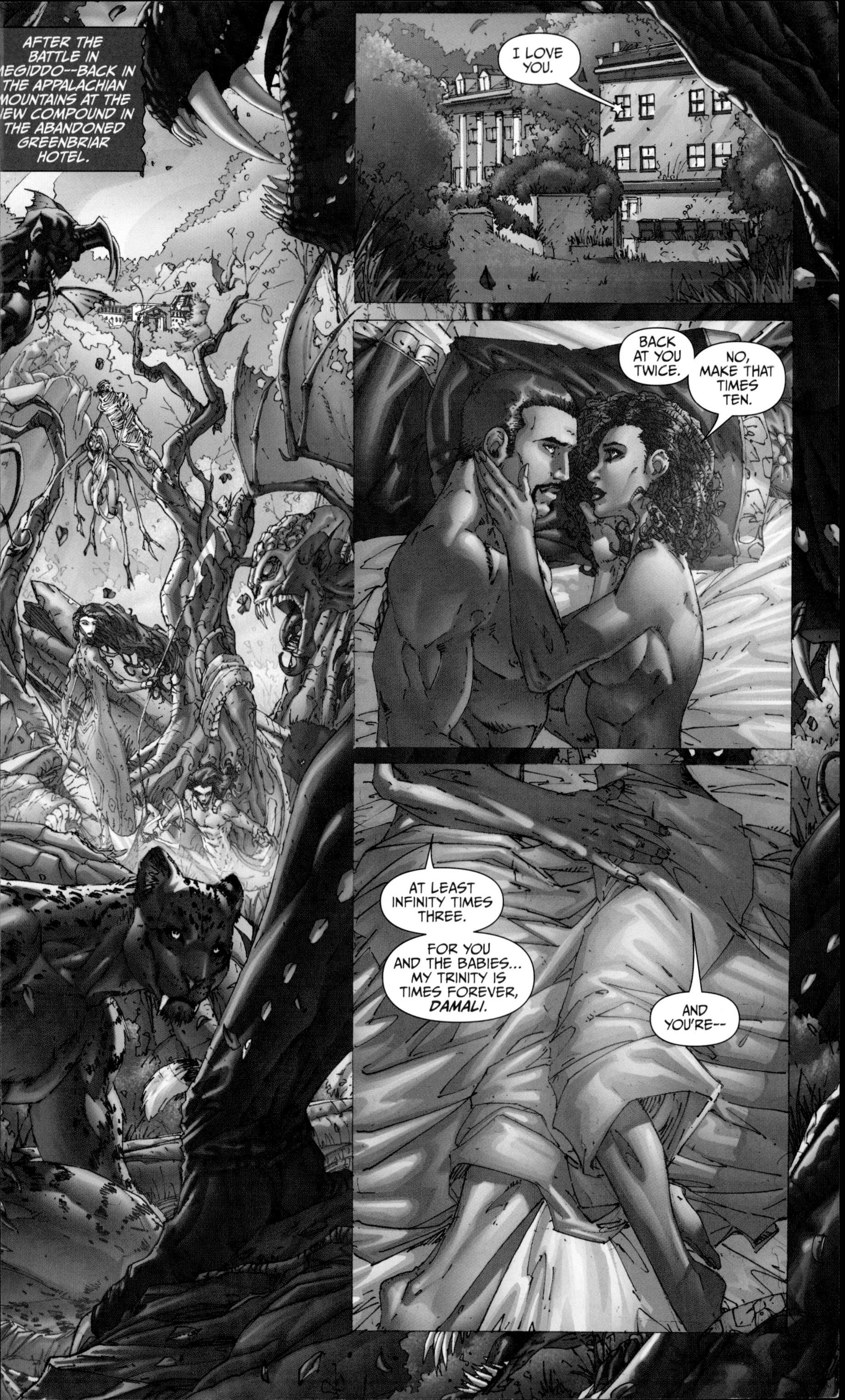
AFTER THE BATTLE IN MEGIDDO--BACK IN THE APPALACHIAN MOUNTAINS AT THE NEW COMPOUND IN THE ABANDONED GREENBRIAR HOTEL.
I LOVE YOU.
BACK AT YOU TWICE.
NO, MAKE THAT TIMES TEN.
AT LEAST INFINITY TIMES THREE.
FOR YOU AND THE BABIES... MY TRINITY IS TIMES FOREVER, *DAMALI*.
AND YOU'RE--

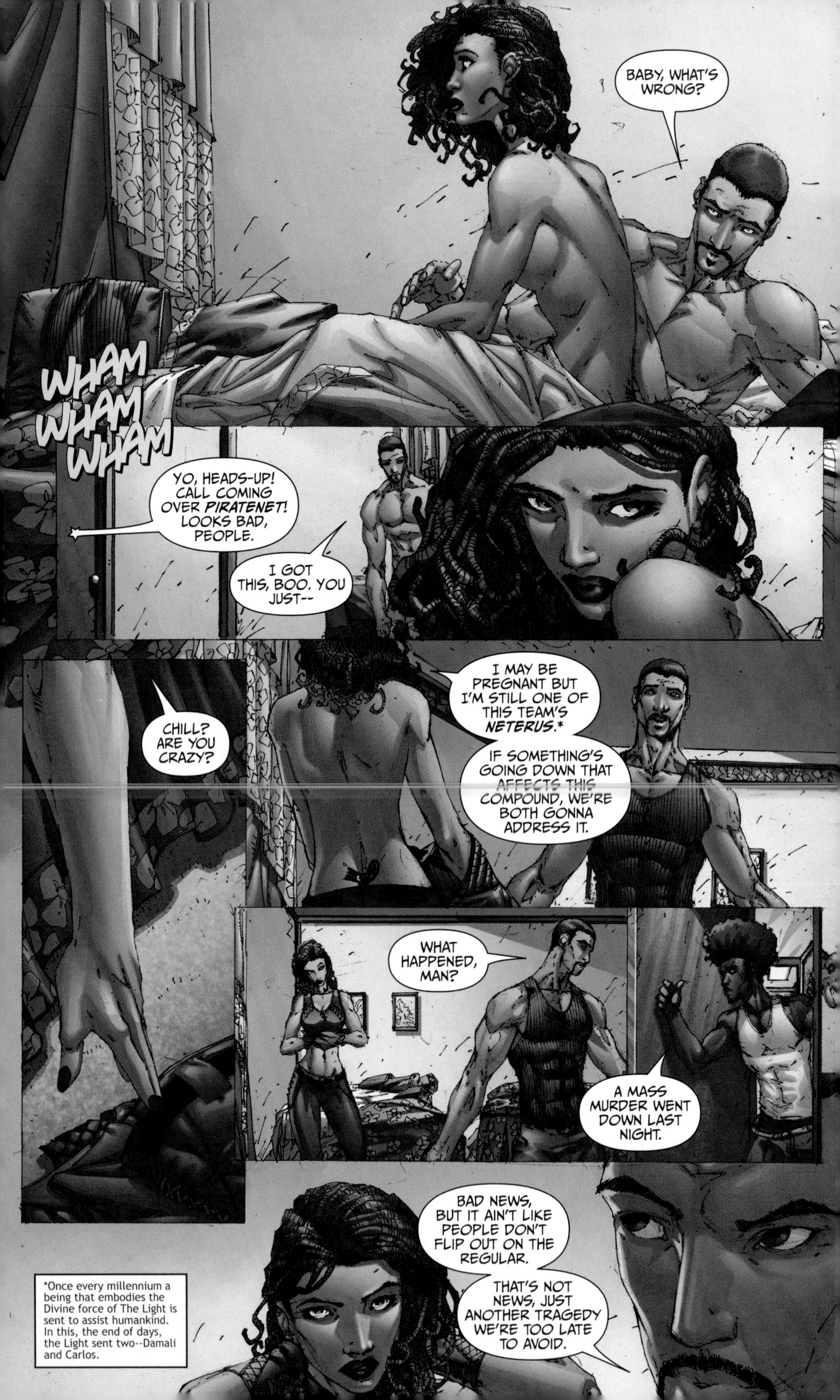
BABY, WHAT'S WRONG?
WHAM WHAM WHAM
YO, HEADS-UP! CALL COMING OVER PIRATENET! LOOKS BAD, PEOPLE.
I GOT THIS, BOO. YOU JUST--
CHILL? ARE YOU CRAZY?
I MAY BE PREGNANT BUT I'M STILL ONE OF THIS TEAM'S NETERUS.*
IF SOMETHING'S GOING DOWN THAT AFFECTS THIS COMPOUND, WE'RE BOTH GONNA ADDRESS IT.
WHAT HAPPENED, MAN?
A MASS MURDER WENT DOWN LAST NIGHT.
BAD NEWS, BUT IT AIN'T LIKE PEOPLE DON'T FLIP OUT ON THE REGULAR.
THAT'S NOT NEWS, JUST ANOTHER TRAGEDY WE'RE TOO LATE TO AVOID.
*Once every millennium a being that embodies the Divine force of The Light is sent to assist humankind. In this, the end of days, the Light sent two--Damali and Carlos.

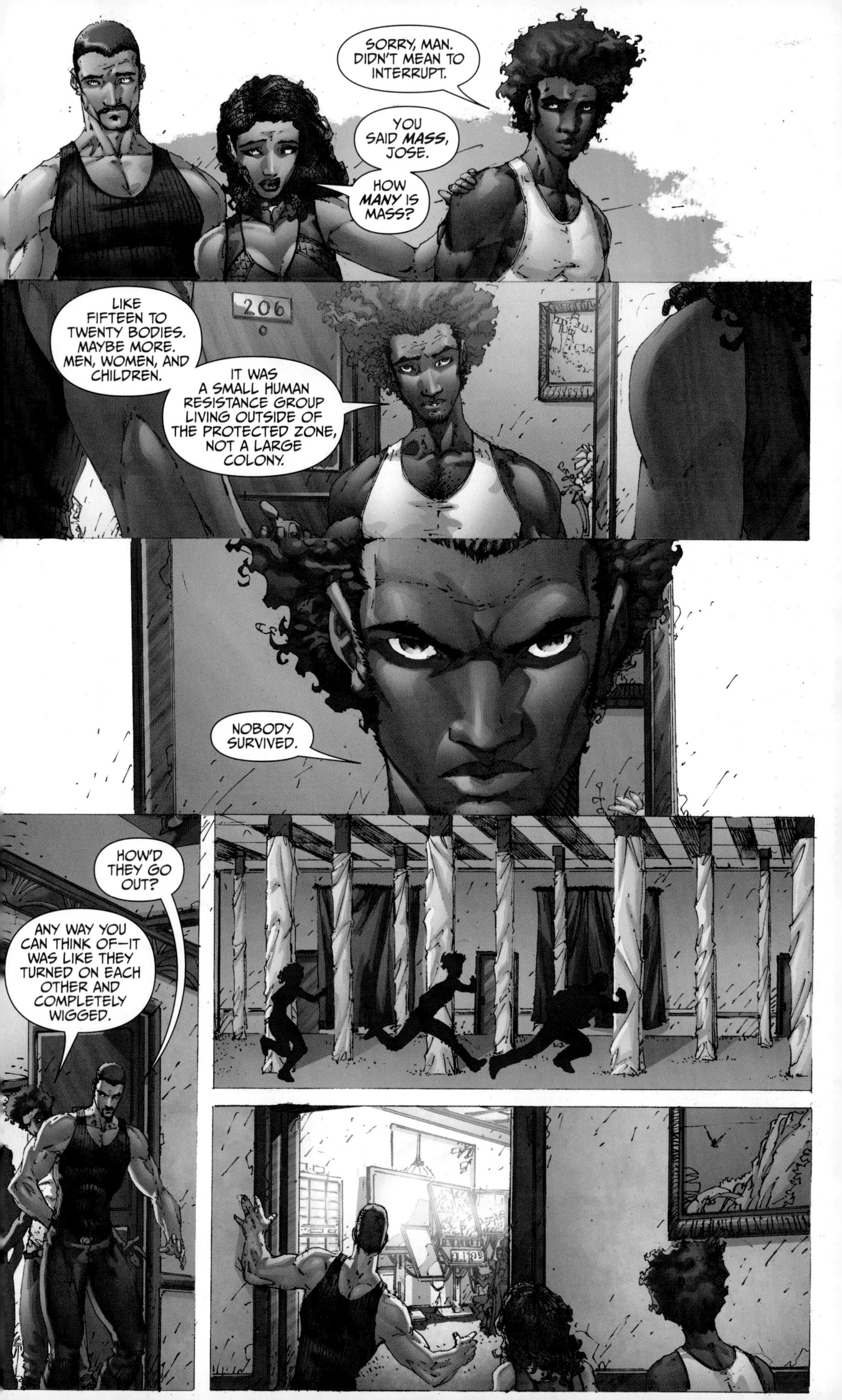
SORRY, MAN. DIDN'T MEAN TO INTERRUPT.
YOU SAID MASS, JOSE.
HOW MANY IS MASS?
206
LIKE FIFTEEN TO TWENTY BODIES. MAYBE MORE. MEN, WOMEN, AND CHILDREN.
IT WAS A SMALL HUMAN RESISTANCE GROUP LIVING OUTSIDE OF THE PROTECTED ZONE, NOT A LARGE COLONY.
NOBODY SURVIVED.
HOW'D THEY GO OUT?
ANY WAY YOU CAN THINK OF—IT WAS LIKE THEY TURNED ON EACH OTHER AND COMPLETELY WIGGED.

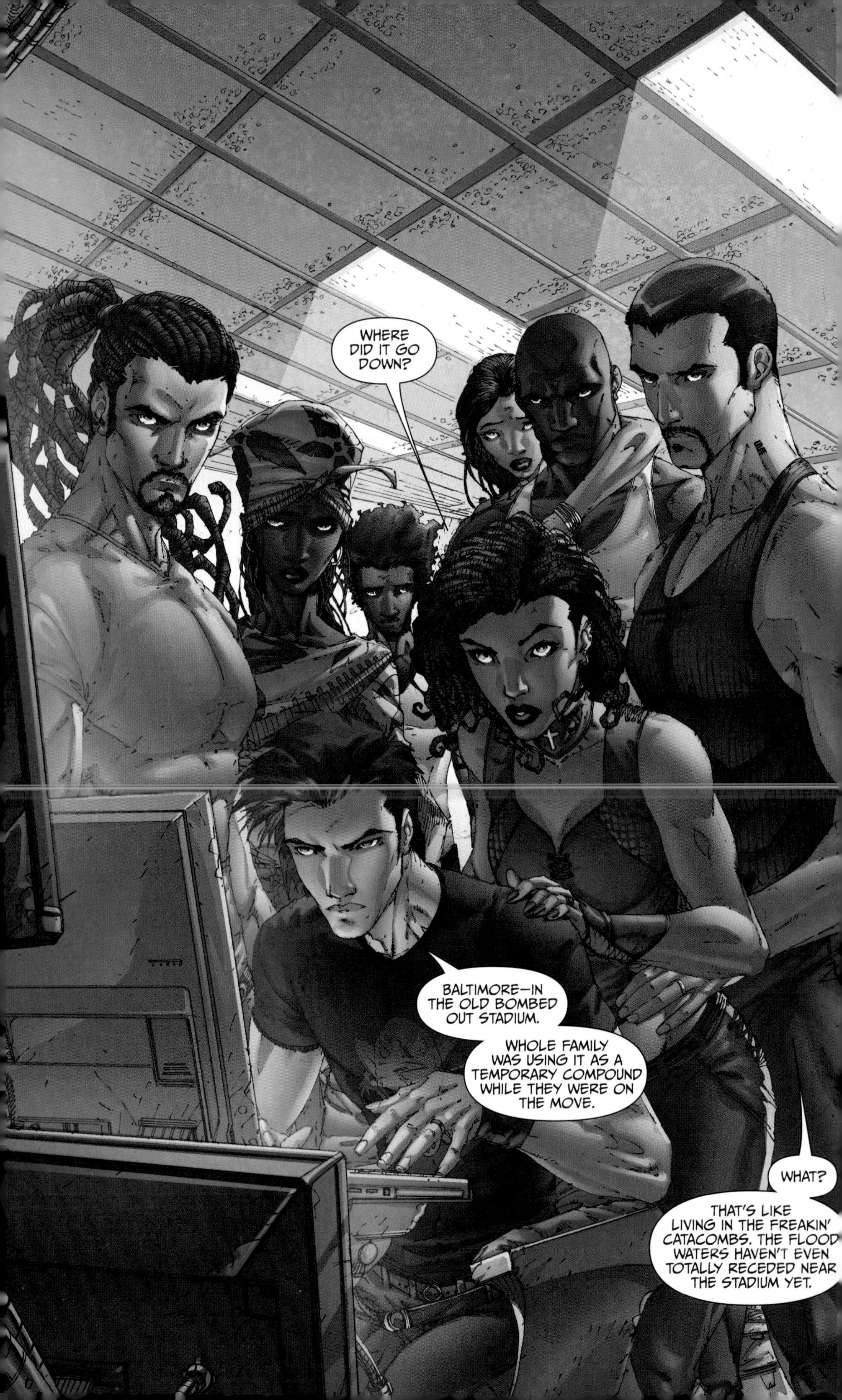
WHERE DID IT GO DOWN?
BALTIMORE—IN THE OLD BOMBED OUT STADIUM.
WHOLE FAMILY WAS USING IT AS A TEMPORARY COMPOUND WHILE THEY WERE ON THE MOVE.
WHAT?
THAT'S LIKE LIVING IN THE FREAKIN' CATACOMBS. THE FLOOD WATERS HAVEN'T EVEN TOTALLY RECEDED NEAR THE STADIUM YET.

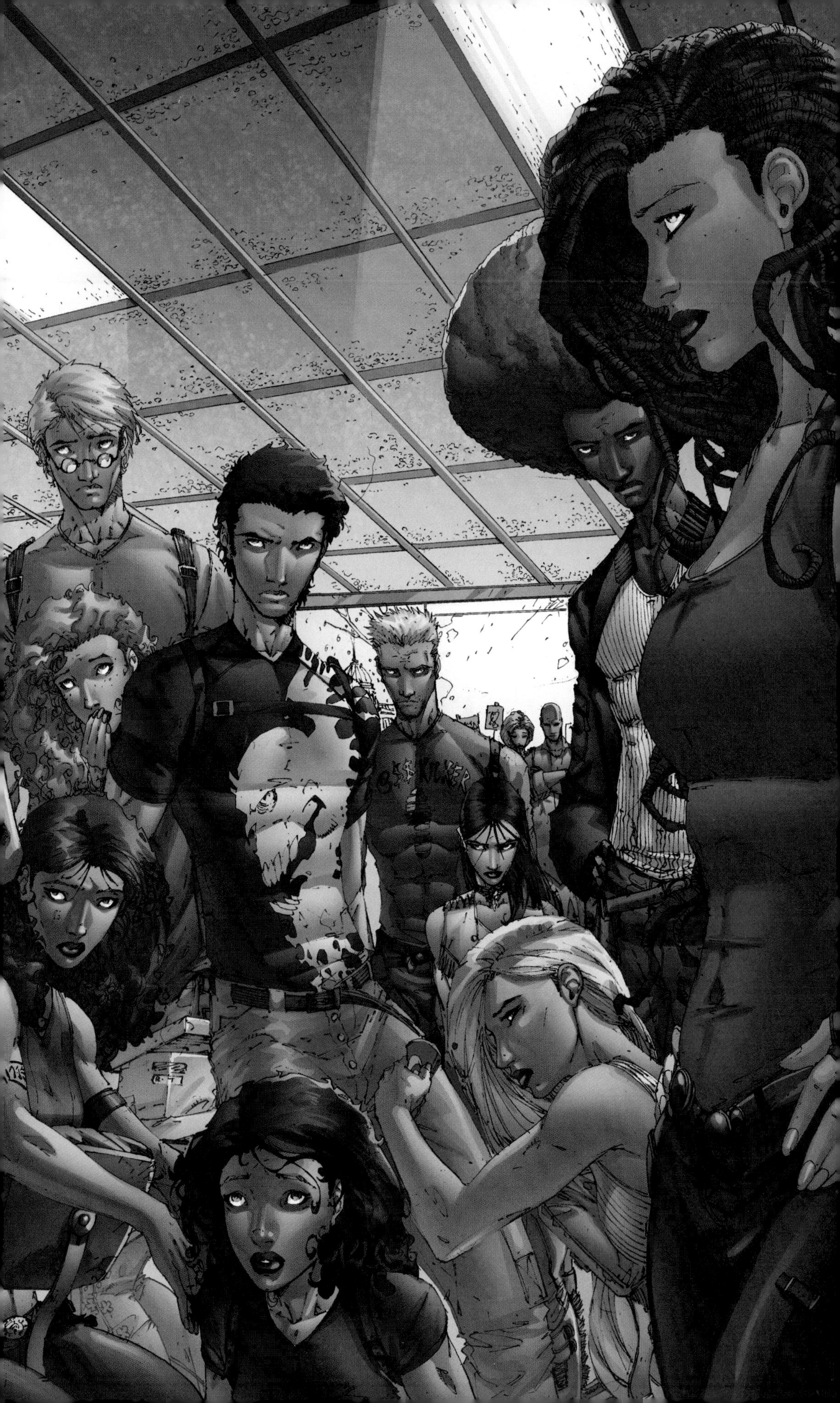

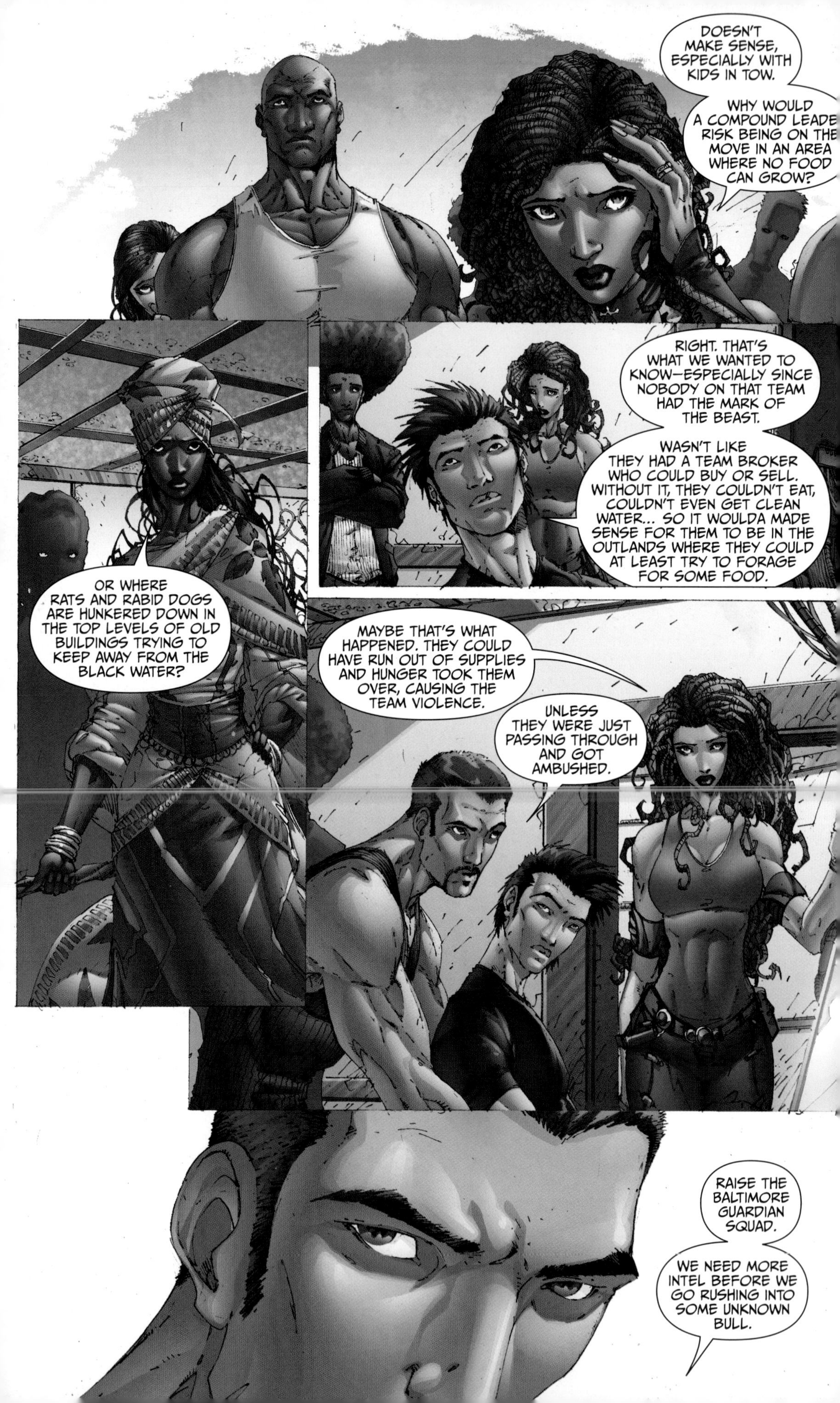

DOESN'T MAKE SENSE, ESPECIALLY WITH KIDS IN TOW.
WHY WOULD A COMPOUND LEADE RISK BEING ON THE MOVE IN AN AREA WHERE NO FOOD CAN GROW?
OR WHERE RATS AND RABID DOGS ARE HUNKERED DOWN IN THE TOP LEVELS OF OLD BUILDINGS TRYING TO KEEP AWAY FROM THE BLACK WATER?
RIGHT. THAT'S WHAT WE WANTED TO KNOW—ESPECIALLY SINCE NOBODY ON THAT TEAM HAD THE MARK OF THE BEAST.
WASN'T LIKE THEY HAD A TEAM BROKER WHO COULD BUY OR SELL. WITHOUT IT, THEY COULDN'T EAT, COULDN'T EVEN GET CLEAN WATER... SO IT WOULDA MADE SENSE FOR THEM TO BE IN THE OUTLANDS WHERE THEY COULD AT LEAST TRY TO FORAGE FOR SOME FOOD.
MAYBE THAT'S WHAT HAPPENED. THEY COULD HAVE RUN OUT OF SUPPLIES AND HUNGER TOOK THEM OVER, CAUSING THE TEAM VIOLENCE.
UNLESS THEY WERE JUST PASSING THROUGH AND GOT AMBUSHED.
RAISE THE BALTIMORE GUARDIAN SQUAD.
WE NEED MORE INTEL BEFORE WE GO RUSHING INTO SOME UNKNOWN BULL.

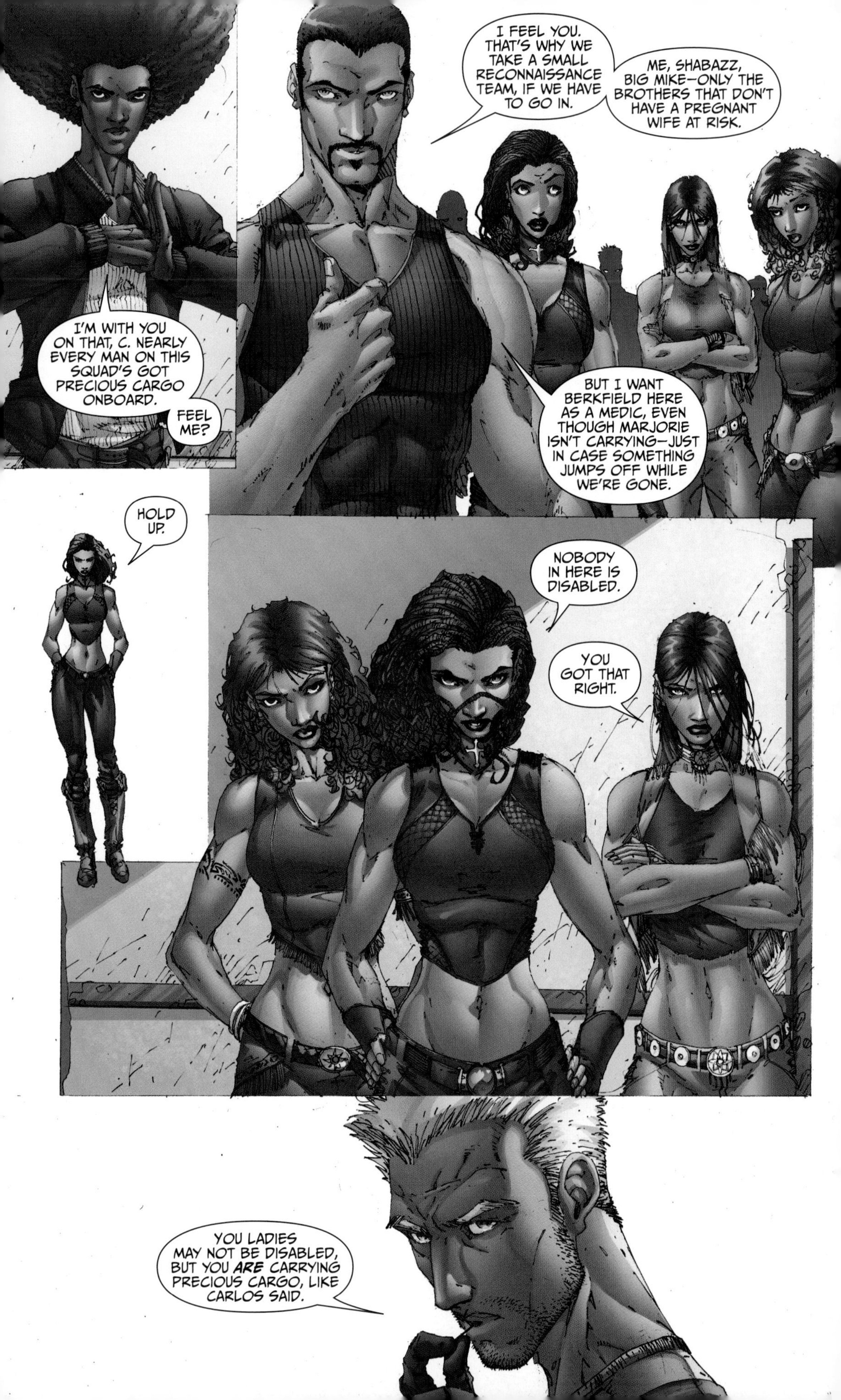
I'M WITH YOU ON THAT, C. NEARLY EVERY MAN ON THIS SQUAD'S GOT PRECIOUS CARGO ONBOARD.
FEEL ME?
I FEEL YOU. THAT'S WHY WE TAKE A SMALL RECONNAISSANCE TEAM, IF WE HAVE TO GO IN.
ME, SHABAZZ, BIG MIKE—ONLY THE BROTHERS THAT DON'T HAVE A PREGNANT WIFE AT RISK.
BUT I WANT BERKFIELD HERE AS A MEDIC, EVEN THOUGH MARJORIE ISN'T CARRYING—JUST IN CASE SOMETHING JUMPS OFF WHILE WE'RE GONE.
HOLD UP.
NOBODY IN HERE IS DISABLED.
YOU GOT THAT RIGHT.
YOU LADIES MAY NOT BE DISABLED, BUT YOU ***ARE*** CARRYING PRECIOUS CARGO, LIKE CARLOS SAID.

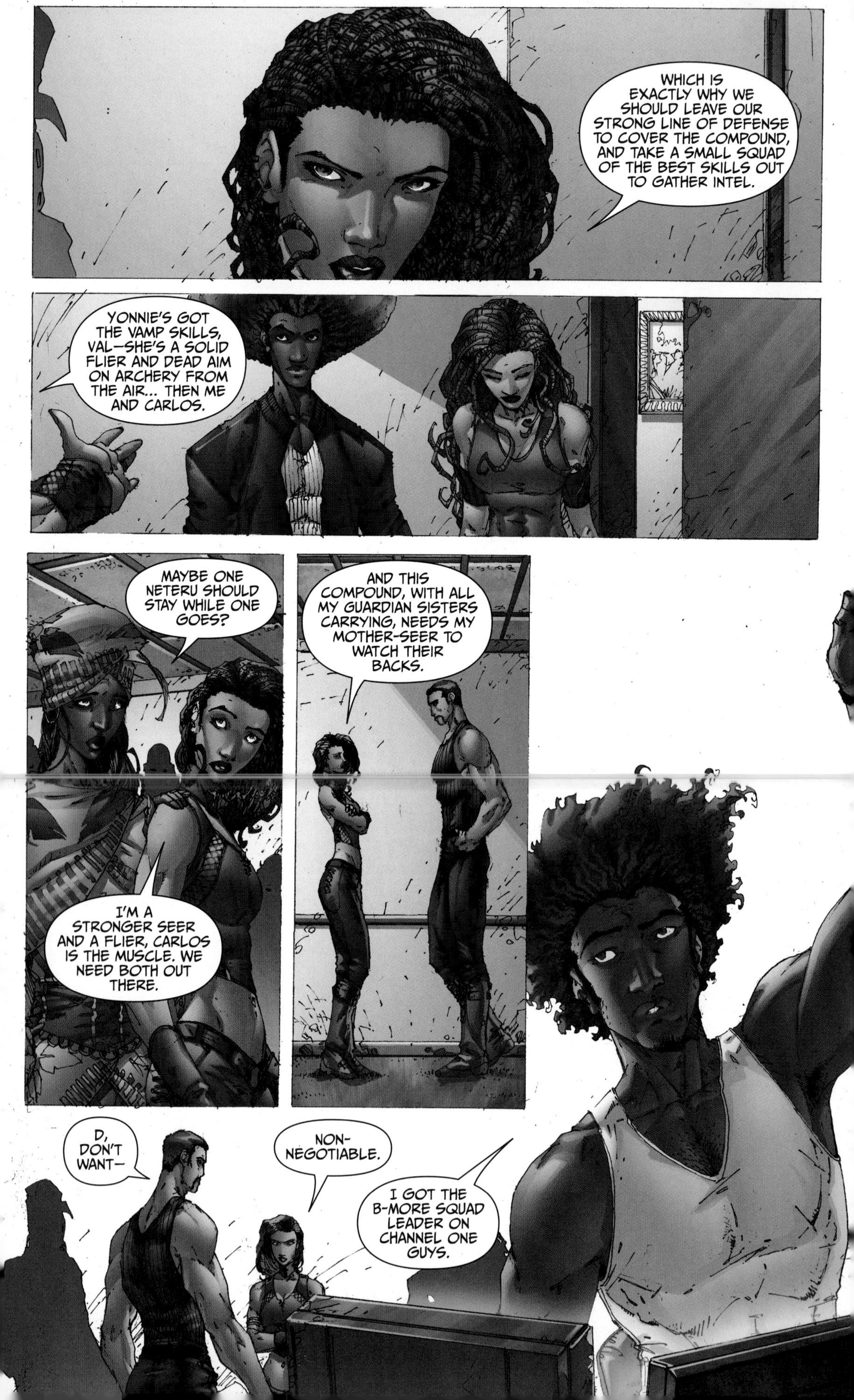
WHICH IS EXACTLY WHY WE SHOULD LEAVE OUR STRONG LINE OF DEFENSE TO COVER THE COMPOUND, AND TAKE A SMALL SQUAD OF THE BEST SKILLS OUT TO GATHER INTEL.
YONNIE'S GOT THE VAMP SKILLS, VAL—SHE'S A SOLID FLIER AND DEAD AIM ON ARCHERY FROM THE AIR... THEN ME AND CARLOS.
MAYBE ONE NETERU SHOULD STAY WHILE ONE GOES?
I'M A STRONGER SEER AND A FLIER, CARLOS IS THE MUSCLE. WE NEED BOTH OUT THERE.
AND THIS COMPOUND, WITH ALL MY GUARDIAN SISTERS CARRYING, NEEDS MY MOTHER-SEER TO WATCH THEIR BACKS.
D, DON'T WANT—
NON-NEGOTIABLE.
I GOT THE B-MORE SQUAD LEADER ON CHANNEL ONE GUYS.

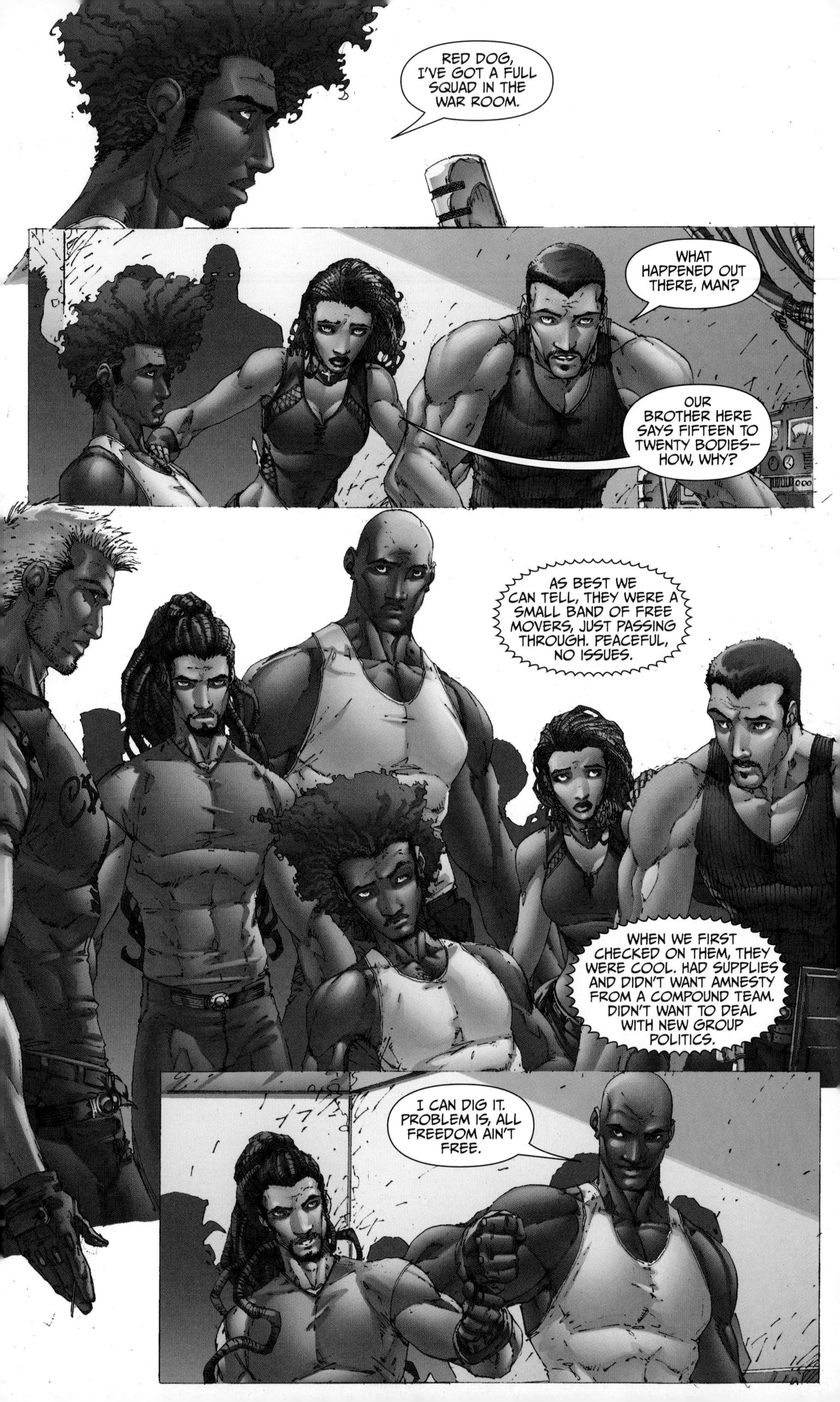
RED DOG, I'VE GOT A FULL SQUAD IN THE WAR ROOM.
WHAT HAPPENED OUT THERE, MAN?
OUR BROTHER HERE SAYS FIFTEEN TO TWENTY BODIES— HOW, WHY?
AS BEST WE CAN TELL, THEY WERE A SMALL BAND OF FREE MOVERS, JUST PASSING THROUGH. PEACEFUL, NO ISSUES.
WHEN WE FIRST CHECKED ON THEM, THEY WERE COOL. HAD SUPPLIES AND DIDN'T WANT AMNESTY FROM A COMPOUND TEAM. DIDN'T WANT TO DEAL WITH NEW GROUP POLITICS.
I CAN DIG IT. PROBLEM IS, ALL FREEDOM AIN'T FREE.

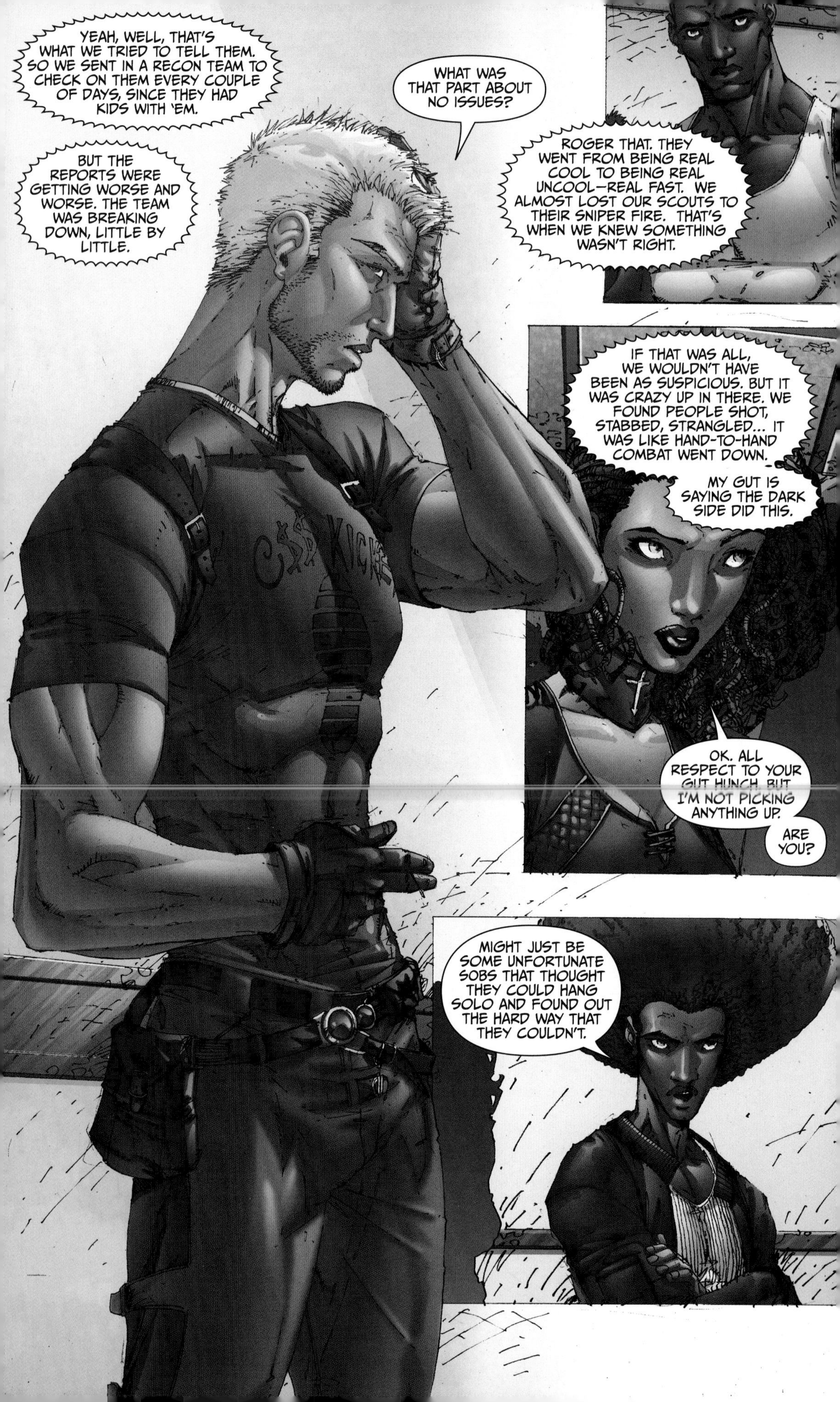
YEAH, WELL, THAT'S WHAT WE TRIED TO TELL THEM. SO WE SENT IN A RECON TEAM TO CHECK ON THEM EVERY COUPLE OF DAYS, SINCE THEY HAD KIDS WITH 'EM.
BUT THE REPORTS WERE GETTING WORSE AND WORSE. THE TEAM WAS BREAKING DOWN, LITTLE BY LITTLE.
WHAT WAS THAT PART ABOUT NO ISSUES?
ROGER THAT. THEY WENT FROM BEING REAL COOL TO BEING REAL UNCOOL—REAL FAST. WE ALMOST LOST OUR SCOUTS TO THEIR SNIPER FIRE. THAT'S WHEN WE KNEW SOMETHING WASN'T RIGHT.
IF THAT WAS ALL, WE WOULDN'T HAVE BEEN AS SUSPICIOUS. BUT IT WAS CRAZY UP IN THERE. WE FOUND PEOPLE SHOT, STABBED, STRANGLED... IT WAS LIKE HAND-TO-HAND COMBAT WENT DOWN.
MY GUT IS SAYING THE DARK SIDE DID THIS.
OK. ALL RESPECT TO YOUR GUT HUNCH, BUT I'M NOT PICKING ANYTHING UP.
ARE YOU?
MIGHT JUST BE SOME UNFORTUNATE SOBS THAT THOUGHT THEY COULD HANG SOLO AND FOUND OUT THE HARD WAY THAT THEY COULDN'T.

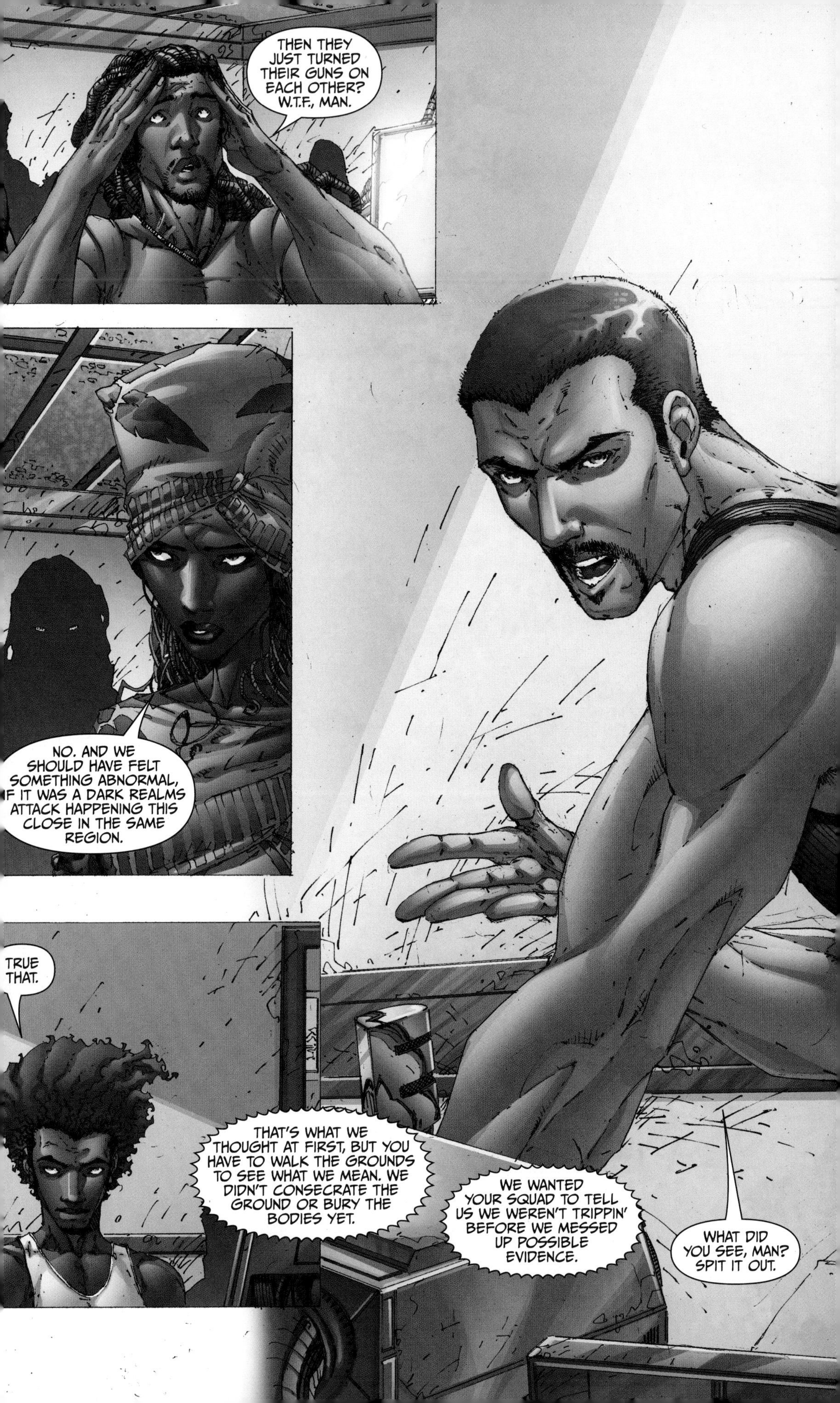
THEN THEY JUST TURNED THEIR GUNS ON EACH OTHER? W.T.F., MAN.
NO. AND WE SHOULD HAVE FELT SOMETHING ABNORMAL, IF IT WAS A DARK REALMS ATTACK HAPPENING THIS CLOSE IN THE SAME REGION.
TRUE THAT.
THAT'S WHAT WE THOUGHT AT FIRST, BUT YOU HAVE TO WALK THE GROUNDS TO SEE WHAT WE MEAN. WE DIDN'T CONSECRATE THE GROUND OR BURY THE BODIES YET.
WE WANTED YOUR SQUAD TO TELL US WE WEREN'T TRIPPIN' BEFORE WE MESSED UP POSSIBLE EVIDENCE.
WHAT DID YOU SEE, MAN? SPIT IT OUT.

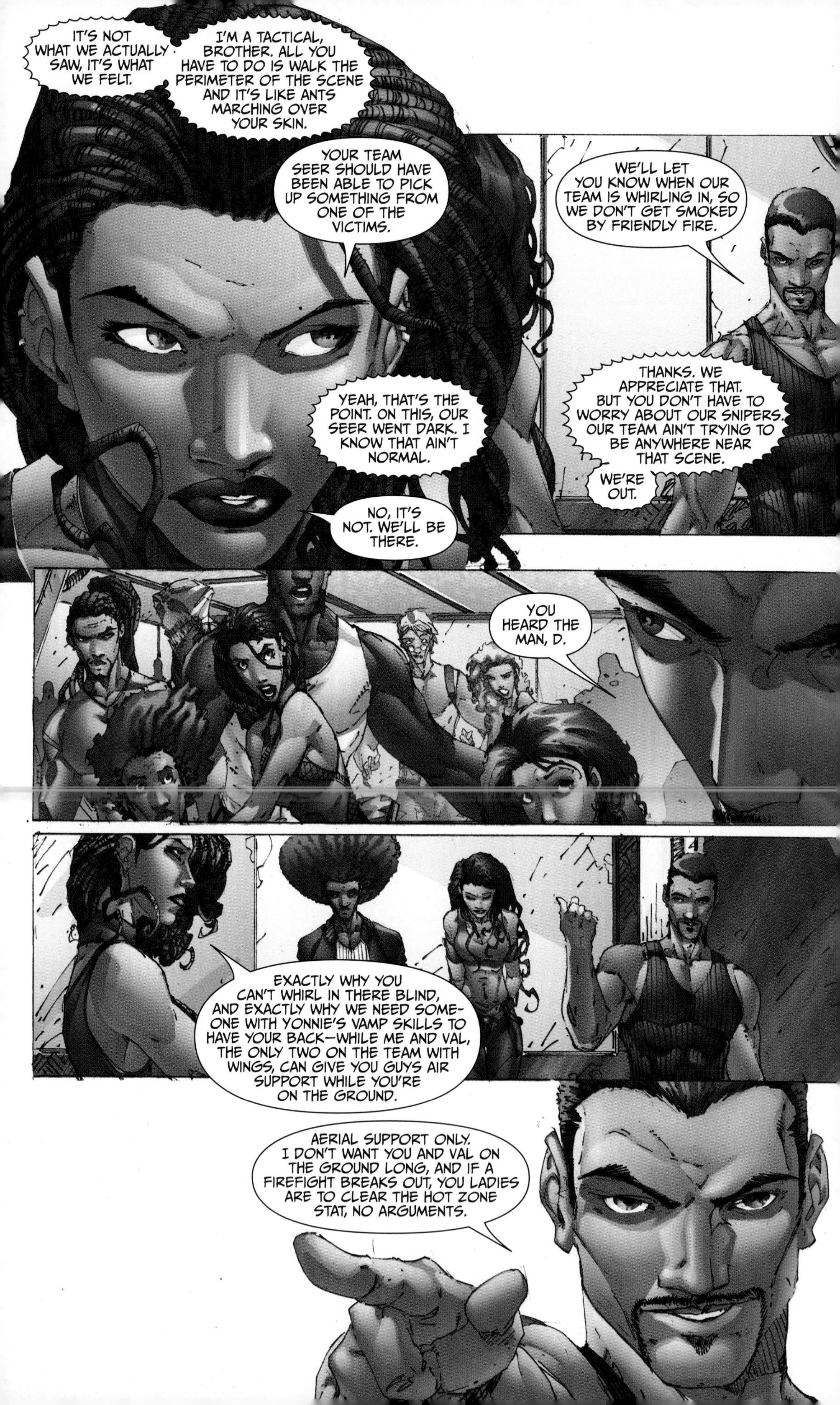
IT'S NOT WHAT WE ACTUALLY SAW, IT'S WHAT WE FELT.
I'M A TACTICAL, BROTHER. ALL YOU HAVE TO DO IS WALK THE PERIMETER OF THE SCENE AND IT'S LIKE ANTS MARCHING OVER YOUR SKIN.
YOUR TEAM SEER SHOULD HAVE BEEN ABLE TO PICK UP SOMETHING FROM ONE OF THE VICTIMS.
YEAH, THAT'S THE POINT. ON THIS, OUR SEER WENT DARK. I KNOW THAT AIN'T NORMAL.
NO, IT'S NOT. WE'LL BE THERE.
WE'LL LET YOU KNOW WHEN OUR TEAM IS WHIRLING IN, SO WE DON'T GET SMOKED BY FRIENDLY FIRE.
THANKS. WE APPRECIATE THAT. BUT YOU DON'T HAVE TO WORRY ABOUT OUR SNIPERS. OUR TEAM AIN'T TRYING TO BE ANYWHERE NEAR THAT SCENE.
WE'RE OUT.
YOU HEARD THE MAN, D.
EXACTLY WHY YOU CAN'T WHIRL IN THERE BLIND, AND EXACTLY WHY WE NEED SOME-ONE WITH YONNIE'S VAMP SKILLS TO HAVE YOUR BACK—WHILE ME AND VAL, THE ONLY TWO ON THE TEAM WITH WINGS, CAN GIVE YOU GUYS AIR SUPPORT WHILE YOU'RE ON THE GROUND.
AERIAL SUPPORT ONLY. I DON'T WANT YOU AND VAL ON THE GROUND LONG, AND IF A FIREFIGHT BREAKS OUT, YOU LADIES ARE TO CLEAR THE HOT ZONE STAT, NO ARGUMENTS.

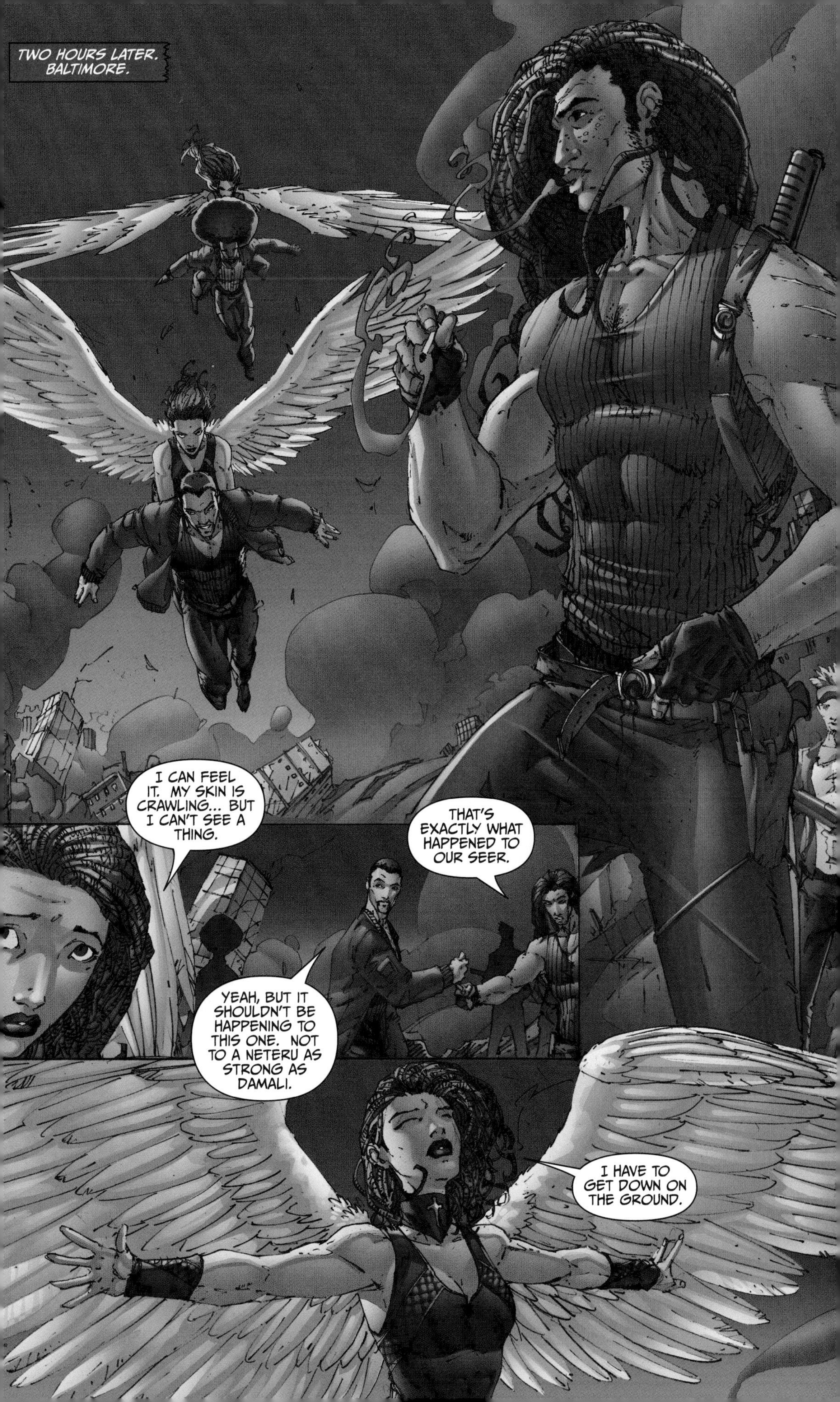
TWO HOURS LATER. BALTIMORE.
I CAN FEEL IT. MY SKIN IS CRAWLING... BUT I CAN'T SEE A THING.
THAT'S EXACTLY WHAT HAPPENED TO OUR SEER.
YEAH, BUT IT SHOULDN'T BE HAPPENING TO THIS ONE. NOT TO A NETERU AS STRONG AS DAMALI.
I HAVE TO GET DOWN ON THE GROUND.

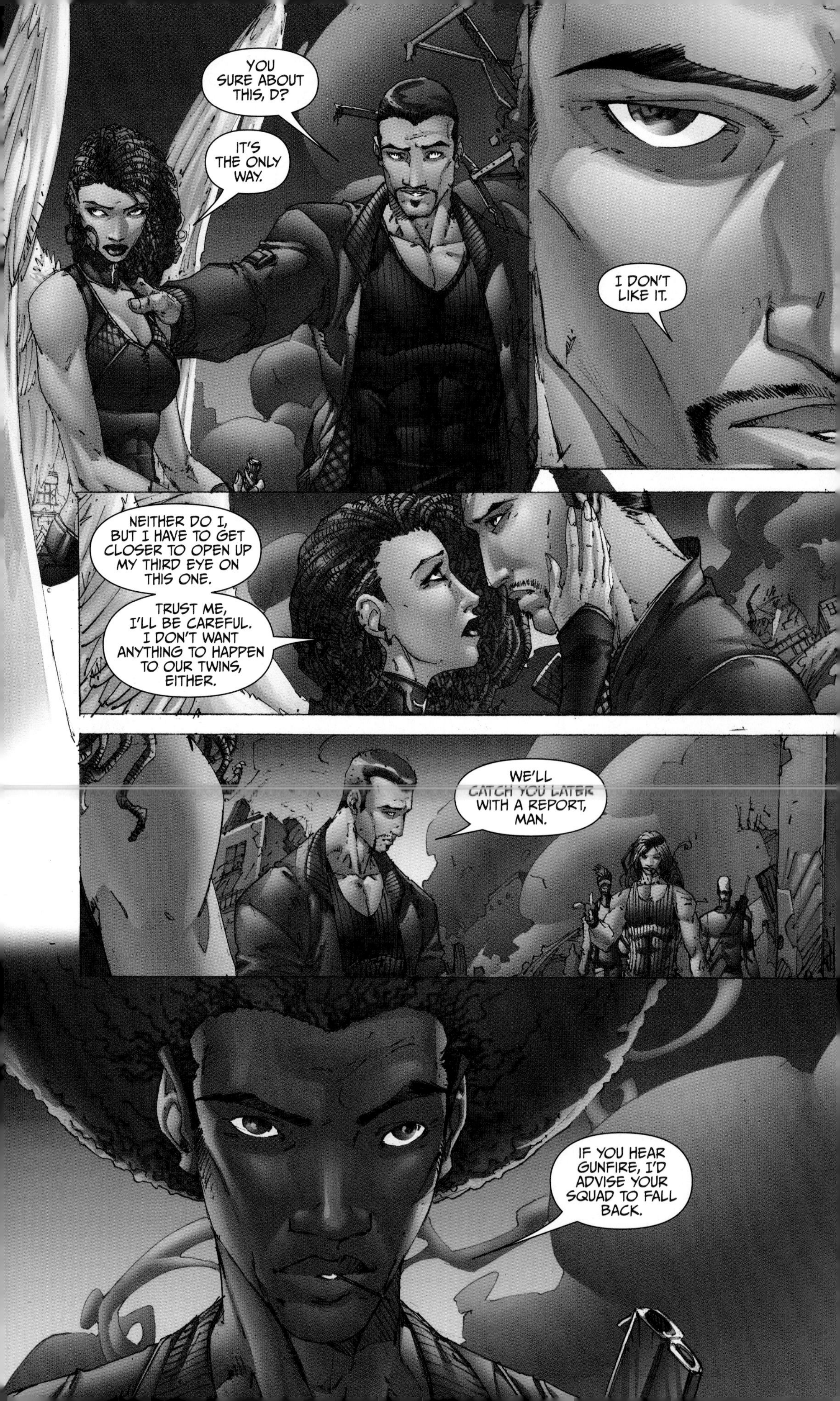

YOU SURE ABOUT THIS, D?
IT'S THE ONLY WAY.
I DON'T LIKE IT.
NEITHER DO I, BUT I HAVE TO GET CLOSER TO OPEN UP MY THIRD EYE ON THIS ONE.
TRUST ME, I'LL BE CAREFUL. I DON'T WANT ANYTHING TO HAPPEN TO OUR TWINS, EITHER.
WE'LL CATCH YOU LATER WITH A REPORT, MAN.
IF YOU HEAR GUNFIRE, I'D ADVISE YOUR SQUAD TO FALL BACK.

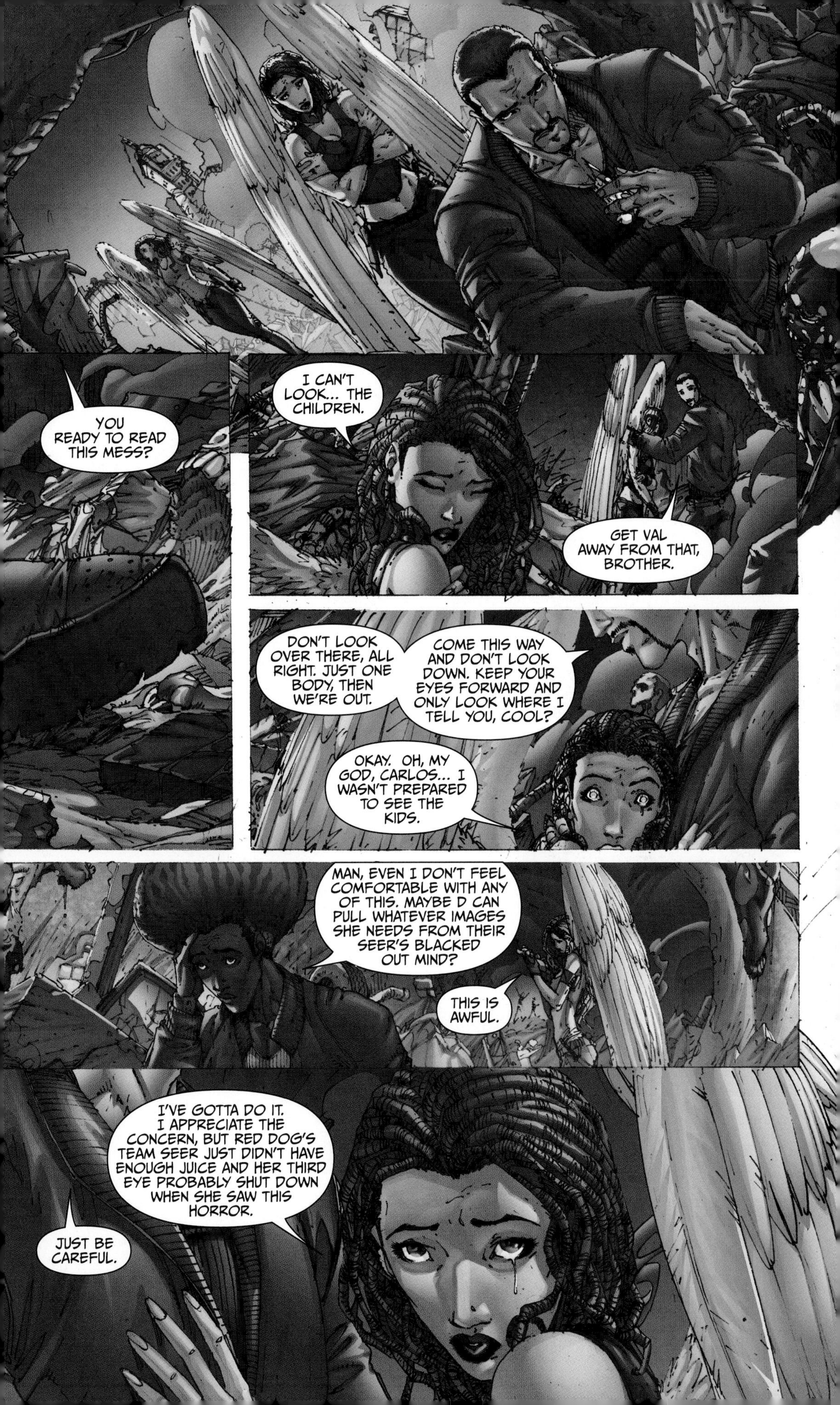
YOU READY TO READ THIS MESS?
I CAN'T LOOK... THE CHILDREN.
GET VAL AWAY FROM THAT, BROTHER.
DON'T LOOK OVER THERE, ALL RIGHT. JUST ONE BODY, THEN WE'RE OUT.
COME THIS WAY AND DON'T LOOK DOWN. KEEP YOUR EYES FORWARD AND ONLY LOOK WHERE I TELL YOU, COOL?
OKAY. OH, MY GOD, CARLOS... I WASN'T PREPARED TO SEE THE KIDS.
MAN, EVEN I DON'T FEEL COMFORTABLE WITH ANY OF THIS. MAYBE D CAN PULL WHATEVER IMAGES SHE NEEDS FROM THEIR SEER'S BLACKED OUT MIND?
THIS IS AWFUL.
I'VE GOTTA DO IT. I APPRECIATE THE CONCERN, BUT RED DOG'S TEAM SEER JUST DIDN'T HAVE ENOUGH JUICE AND HER THIRD EYE PROBABLY SHUT DOWN WHEN SHE SAW THIS HORROR.
JUST BE CAREFUL.

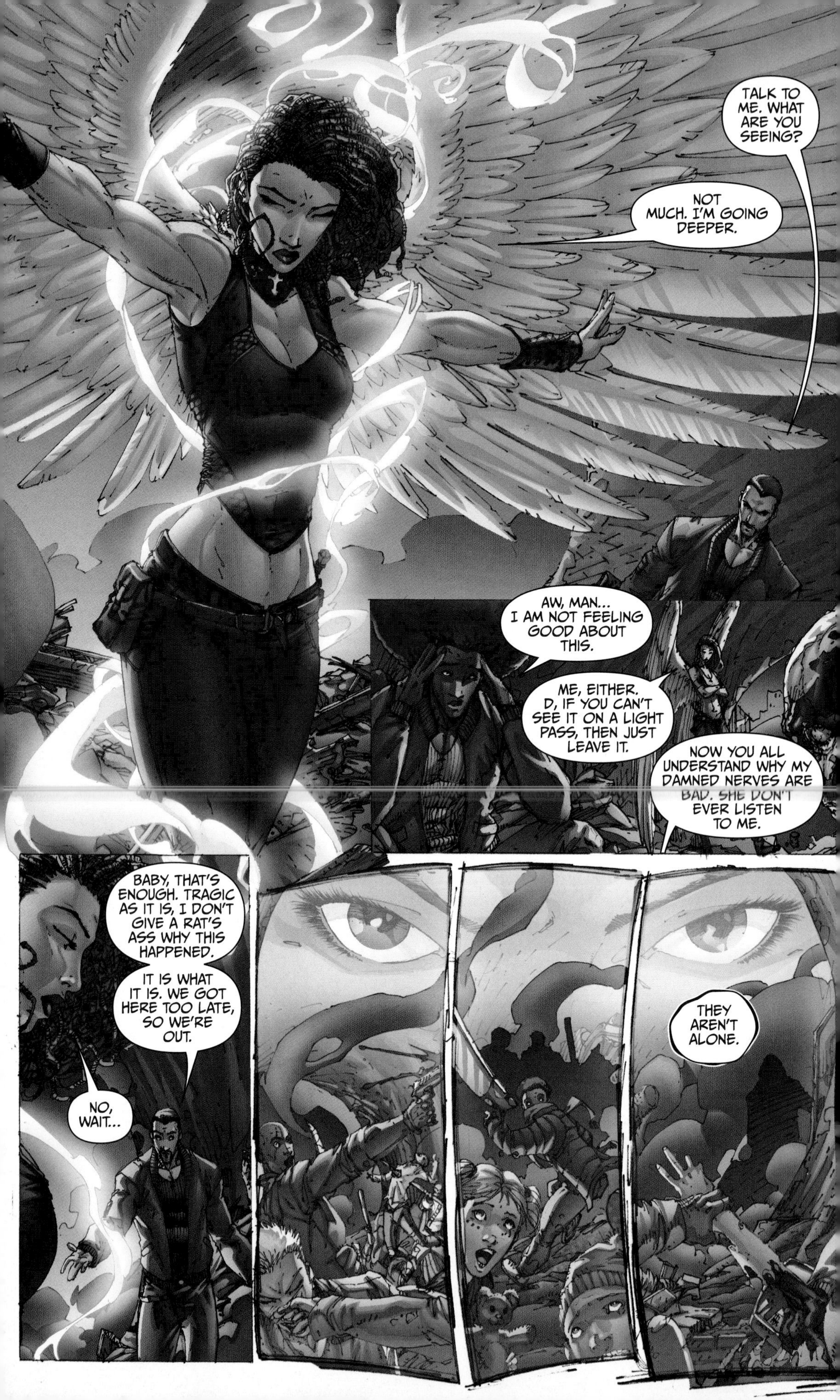
TALK TO ME. WHAT ARE YOU SEEING?
NOT MUCH. I'M GOING DEEPER.
AW, MAN... I AM NOT FEELING GOOD ABOUT THIS.
ME, EITHER. D, IF YOU CAN'T SEE IT ON A LIGHT PASS, THEN JUST LEAVE IT.
NOW YOU ALL UNDERSTAND WHY MY DAMNED NERVES ARE BAD. SHE DON'T EVER LISTEN TO ME.
BABY, THAT'S ENOUGH. TRAGIC AS IT IS, I DON'T GIVE A RAT'S ASS WHY THIS HAPPENED.
IT IS WHAT IT IS. WE GOT HERE TOO LATE, SO WE'RE OUT.
NO, WAIT...
THEY AREN'T ALONE.

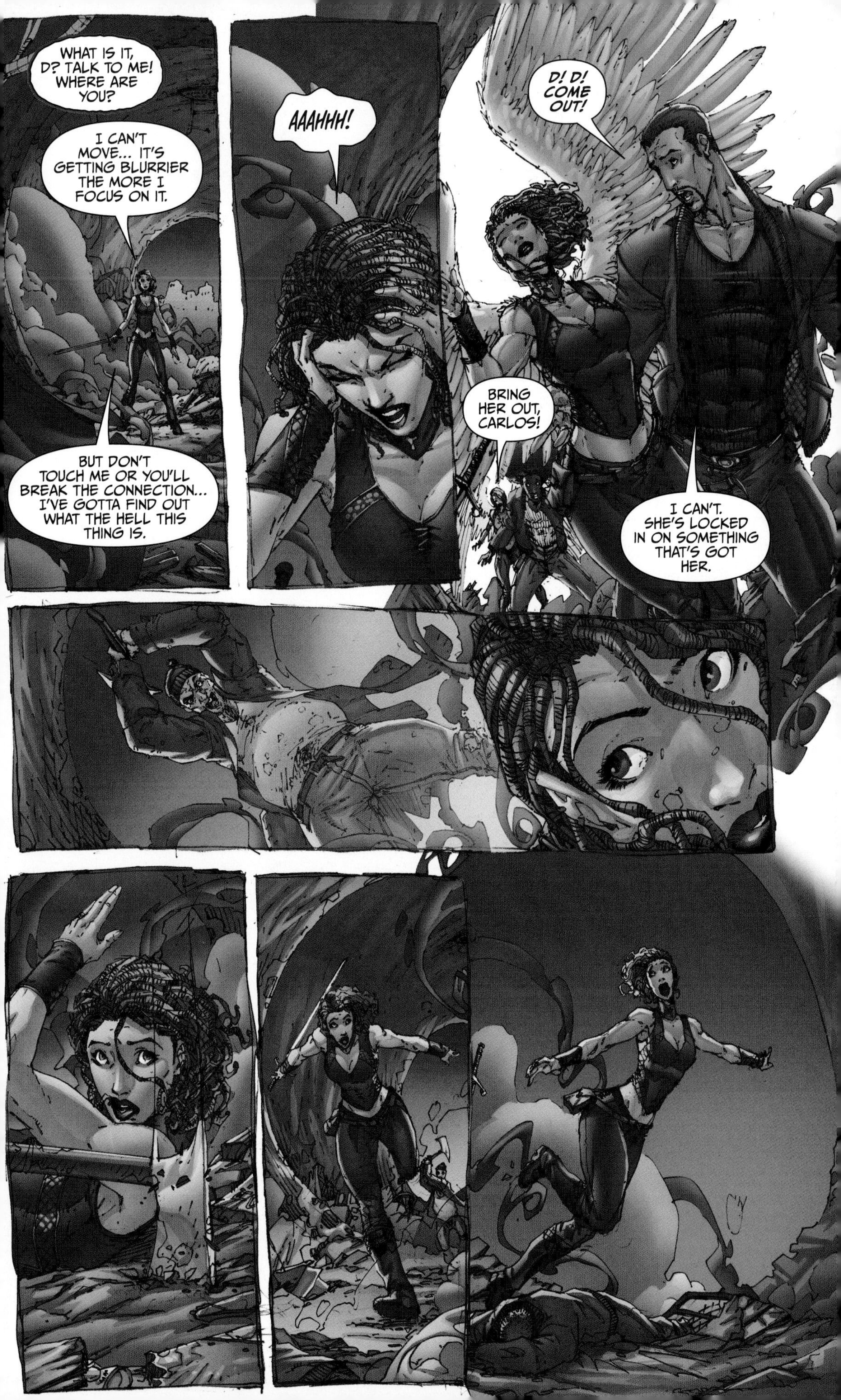
WHAT IS IT, D? TALK TO ME! WHERE ARE YOU?
I CAN'T MOVE... IT'S GETTING BLURRIER THE MORE I FOCUS ON IT.
BUT DON'T TOUCH ME OR YOU'LL BREAK THE CONNECTION... I'VE GOTTA FIND OUT WHAT THE HELL THIS THING IS.
AAAHHH!
D! D! COME OUT!
BRING HER OUT, CARLOS!
I CAN'T. SHE'S LOCKED IN ON SOMETHING THAT'S GOT HER.

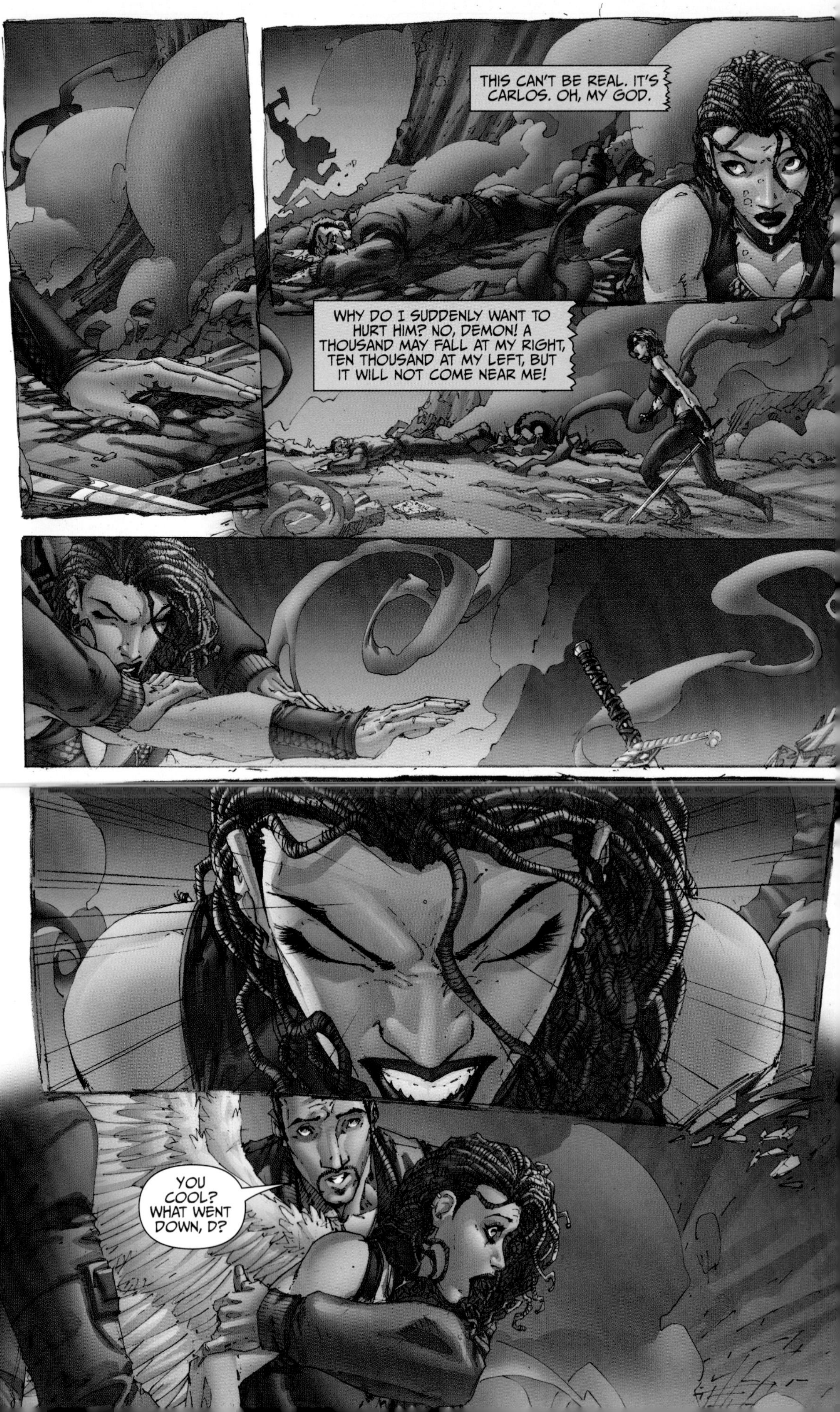
THIS CAN'T BE REAL. IT'S CARLOS. OH, MY GOD.
WHY DO I SUDDENLY WANT TO HURT HIM? NO, DEMON! A THOUSAND MAY FALL AT MY RIGHT, TEN THOUSAND AT MY LEFT, BUT IT WILL NOT COME NEAR ME!
YOU COOL? WHAT WENT DOWN, D?

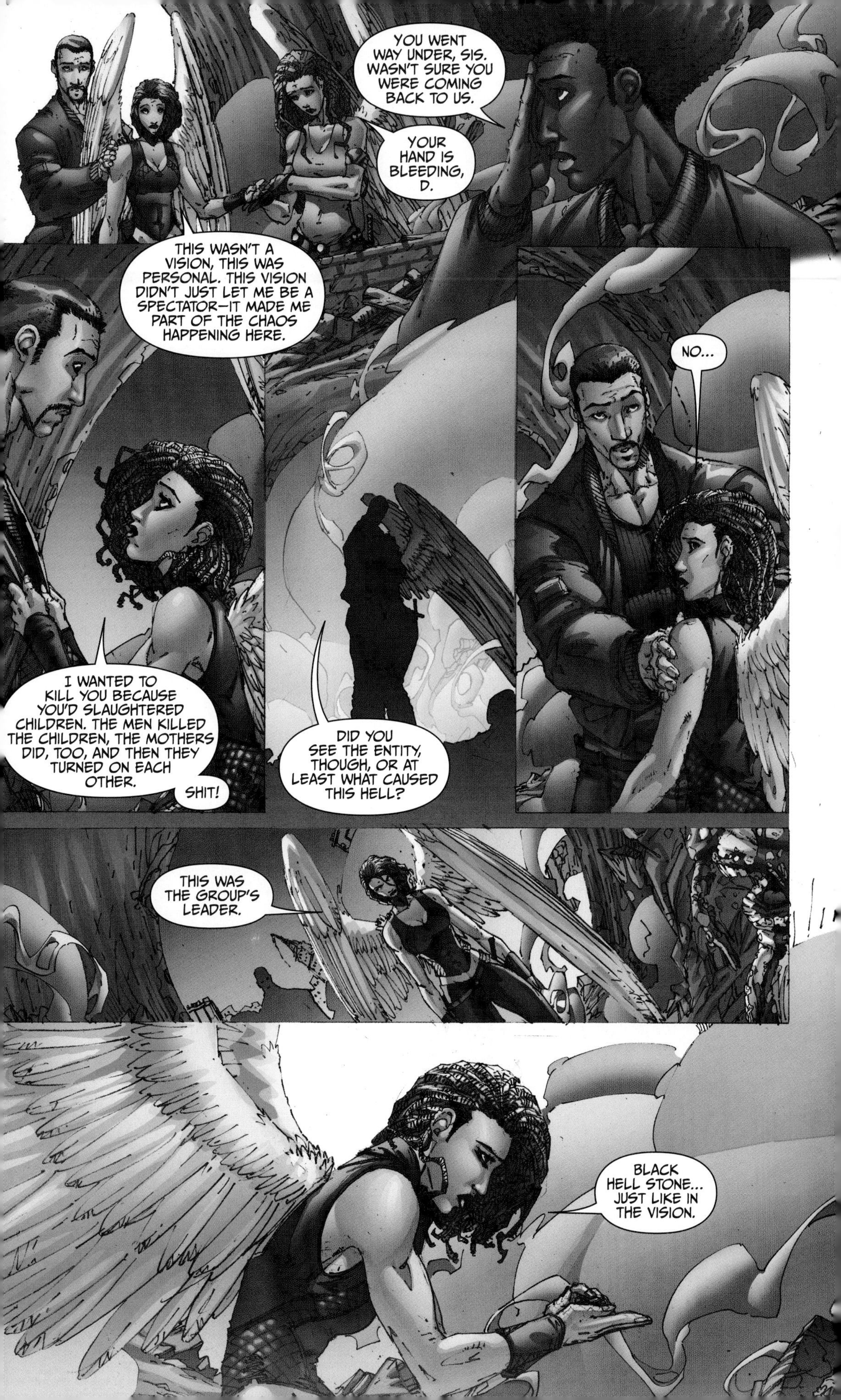

YOU WENT WAY UNDER, SIS. WASN'T SURE YOU WERE COMING BACK TO US.
YOUR HAND IS BLEEDING, D.
THIS WASN'T A VISION, THIS WAS PERSONAL. THIS VISION DIDN'T JUST LET ME BE A SPECTATOR—IT MADE ME PART OF THE CHAOS HAPPENING HERE.
I WANTED TO KILL YOU BECAUSE YOU'D SLAUGHTERED CHILDREN. THE MEN KILLED THE CHILDREN, THE MOTHERS DID, TOO, AND THEN THEY TURNED ON EACH OTHER.
SHIT!
DID YOU SEE THE ENTITY, THOUGH, OR AT LEAST WHAT CAUSED THIS HELL?
NO...
THIS WAS THE GROUP'S LEADER.
BLACK HELL STONE... JUST LIKE IN THE VISION.

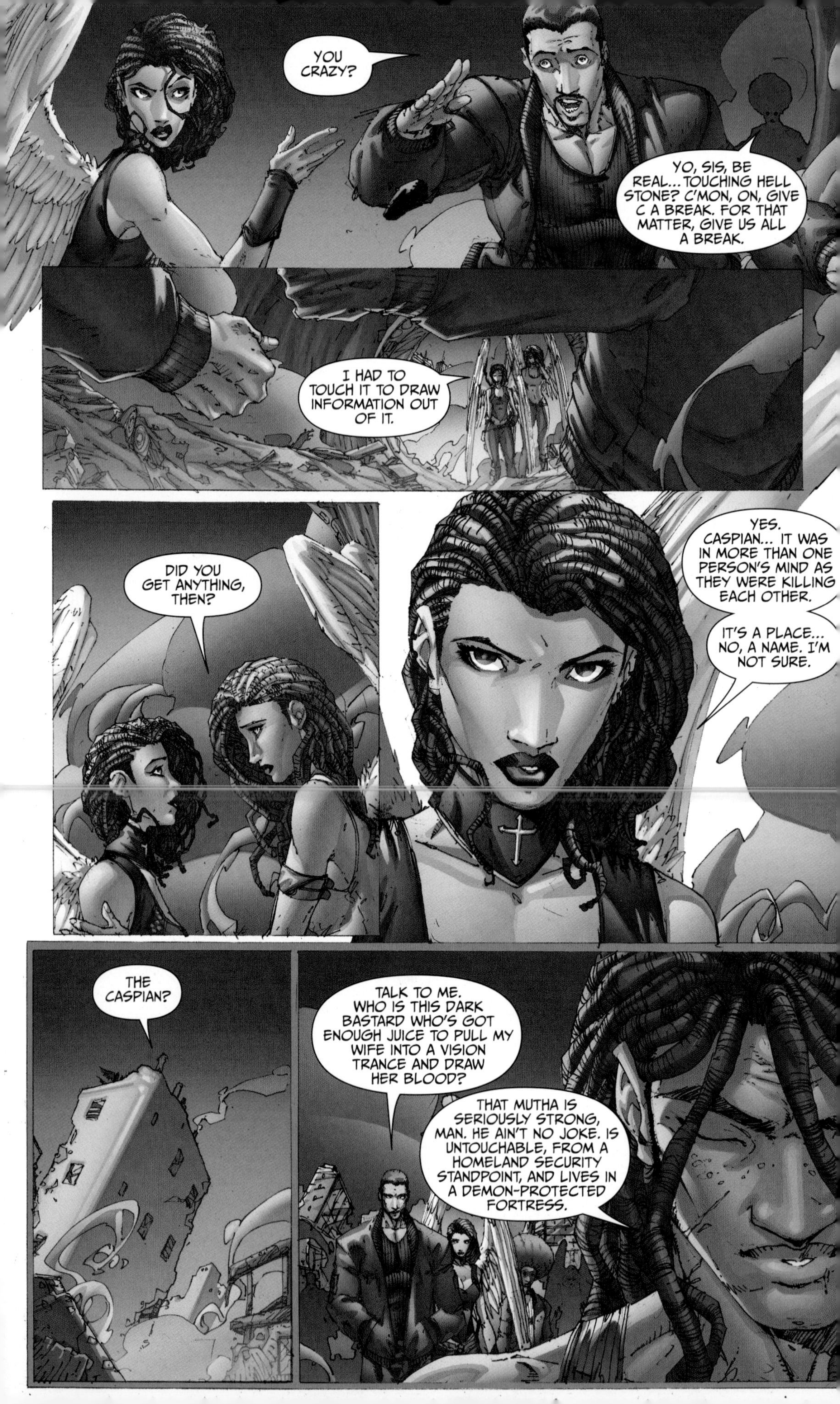

YOU CRAZY?
YO, SIS, BE REAL... TOUCHING HELL STONE? C'MON, ON, GIVE C A BREAK. FOR THAT MATTER, GIVE US ALL A BREAK.
I HAD TO TOUCH IT TO DRAW INFORMATION OUT OF IT.
DID YOU GET ANYTHING, THEN?
YES. CASPIAN... IT WAS IN MORE THAN ONE PERSON'S MIND AS THEY WERE KILLING EACH OTHER.
IT'S A PLACE... NO, A NAME. I'M NOT SURE.
THE CASPIAN?
TALK TO ME. WHO IS THIS DARK BASTARD WHO'S GOT ENOUGH JUICE TO PULL MY WIFE INTO A VISION TRANCE AND DRAW HER BLOOD?
THAT MUTHA IS SERIOUSLY STRONG, MAN. HE AIN'T NO JOKE. IS UNTOUCHABLE, FROM A HOMELAND SECURITY STANDPOINT, AND LIVES IN A DEMON-PROTECTED FORTRESS.

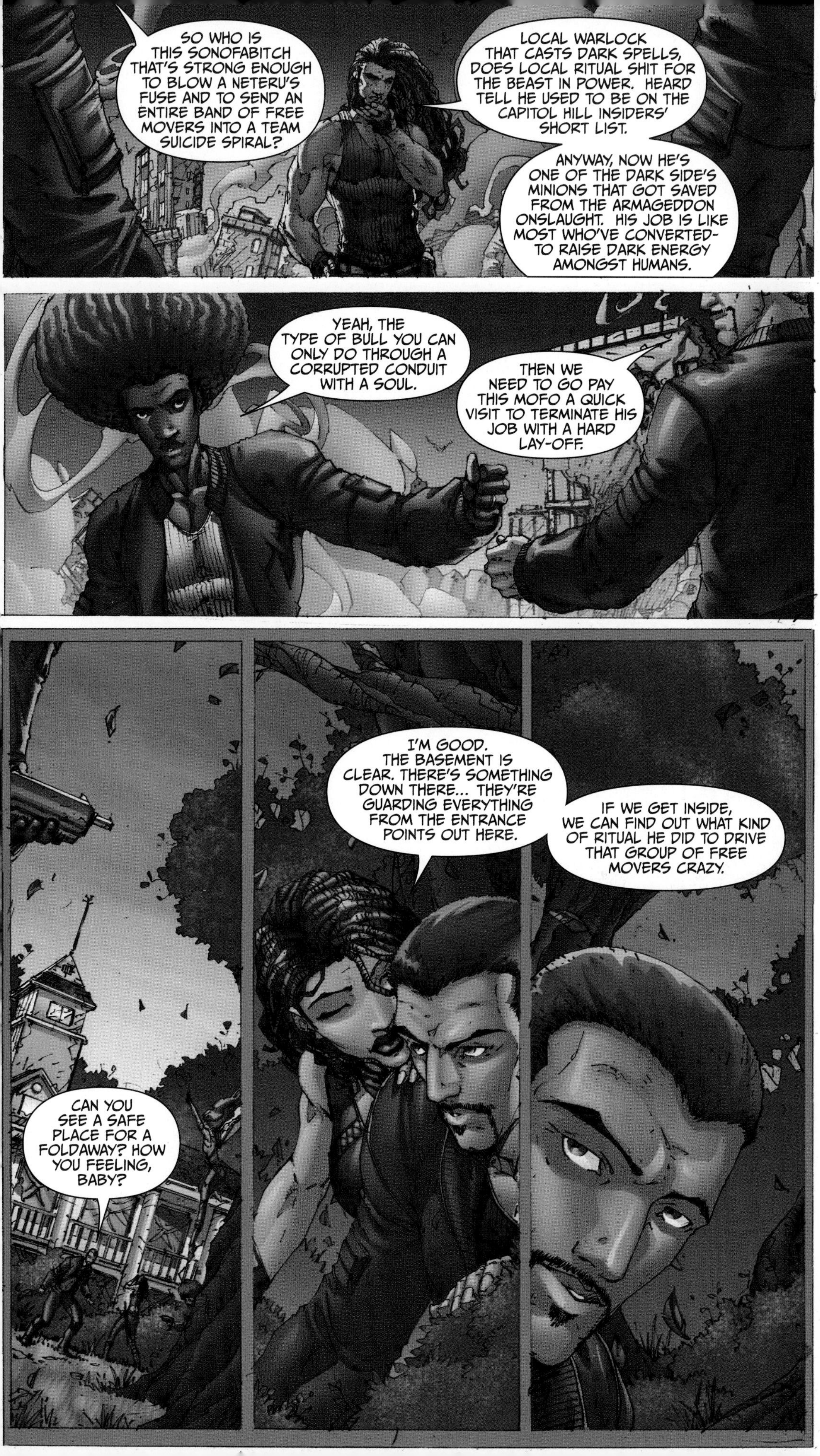
SO WHO IS THIS SONOFABITCH THAT'S STRONG ENOUGH TO BLOW A NETERU'S FUSE AND TO SEND AN ENTIRE BAND OF FREE MOVERS INTO A TEAM SUICIDE SPIRAL?
LOCAL WARLOCK THAT CASTS DARK SPELLS, DOES LOCAL RITUAL SHIT FOR THE BEAST IN POWER. HEARD TELL HE USED TO BE ON THE CAPITOL HILL INSIDERS' SHORT LIST.
ANYWAY, NOW HE'S ONE OF THE DARK SIDE'S MINIONS THAT GOT SAVED FROM THE ARMAGEDDON ONSLAUGHT. HIS JOB IS LIKE MOST WHO'VE CONVERTED-TO RAISE DARK ENERGY AMONGST HUMANS.
YEAH, THE TYPE OF BULL YOU CAN ONLY DO THROUGH A CORRUPTED CONDUIT WITH A SOUL.
THEN WE NEED TO GO PAY THIS MOFO A QUICK VISIT TO TERMINATE HIS JOB WITH A HARD LAY-OFF.
CAN YOU SEE A SAFE PLACE FOR A FOLDAWAY? HOW YOU FEELING, BABY?
I'M GOOD. THE BASEMENT IS CLEAR. THERE'S SOMETHING DOWN THERE... THEY'RE GUARDING EVERYTHING FROM THE ENTRANCE POINTS OUT HERE.
IF WE GET INSIDE, WE CAN FIND OUT WHAT KIND OF RITUAL HE DID TO DRIVE THAT GROUP OF FREE MOVERS CRAZY.

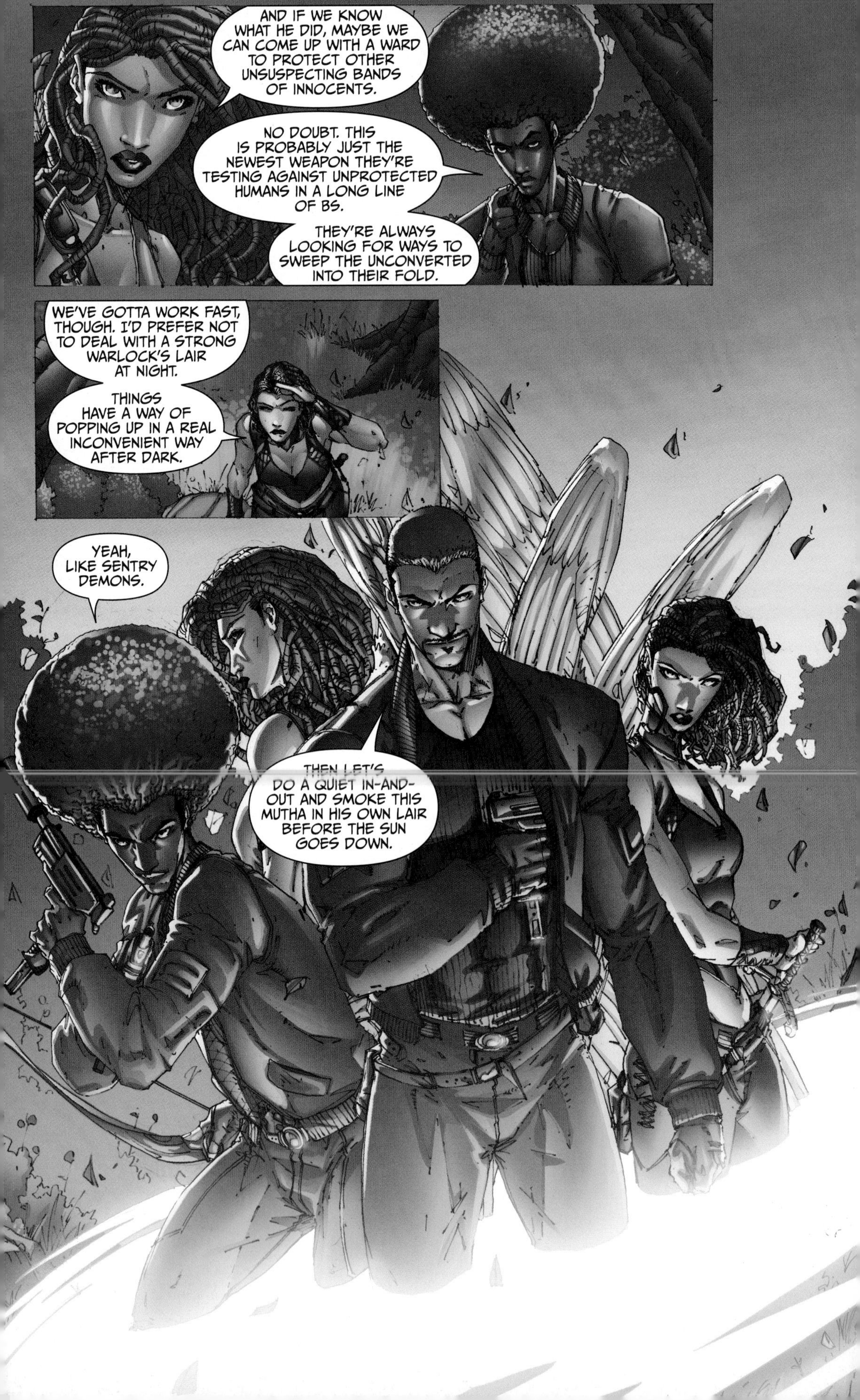

AND IF WE KNOW WHAT HE DID, MAYBE WE CAN COME UP WITH A WARD TO PROTECT OTHER UNSUSPECTING BANDS OF INNOCENTS.
NO DOUBT. THIS IS PROBABLY JUST THE NEWEST WEAPON THEY'RE TESTING AGAINST UNPROTECTED HUMANS IN A LONG LINE OF BS.
THEY'RE ALWAYS LOOKING FOR WAYS TO SWEEP THE UNCONVERTED INTO THEIR FOLD.
WE'VE GOTTA WORK FAST, THOUGH. I'D PREFER NOT TO DEAL WITH A STRONG WARLOCK'S LAIR AT NIGHT.
THINGS HAVE A WAY OF POPPING UP IN A REAL INCONVENIENT WAY AFTER DARK.
YEAH, LIKE SENTRY DEMONS.
THEN LET'S DO A QUIET IN-AND-OUT AND SMOKE THIS MUTHA IN HIS OWN LAIR BEFORE THE SUN GOES DOWN.

BOOK TWO

DUST to DUST

VAMPIRE
HUNTRESS

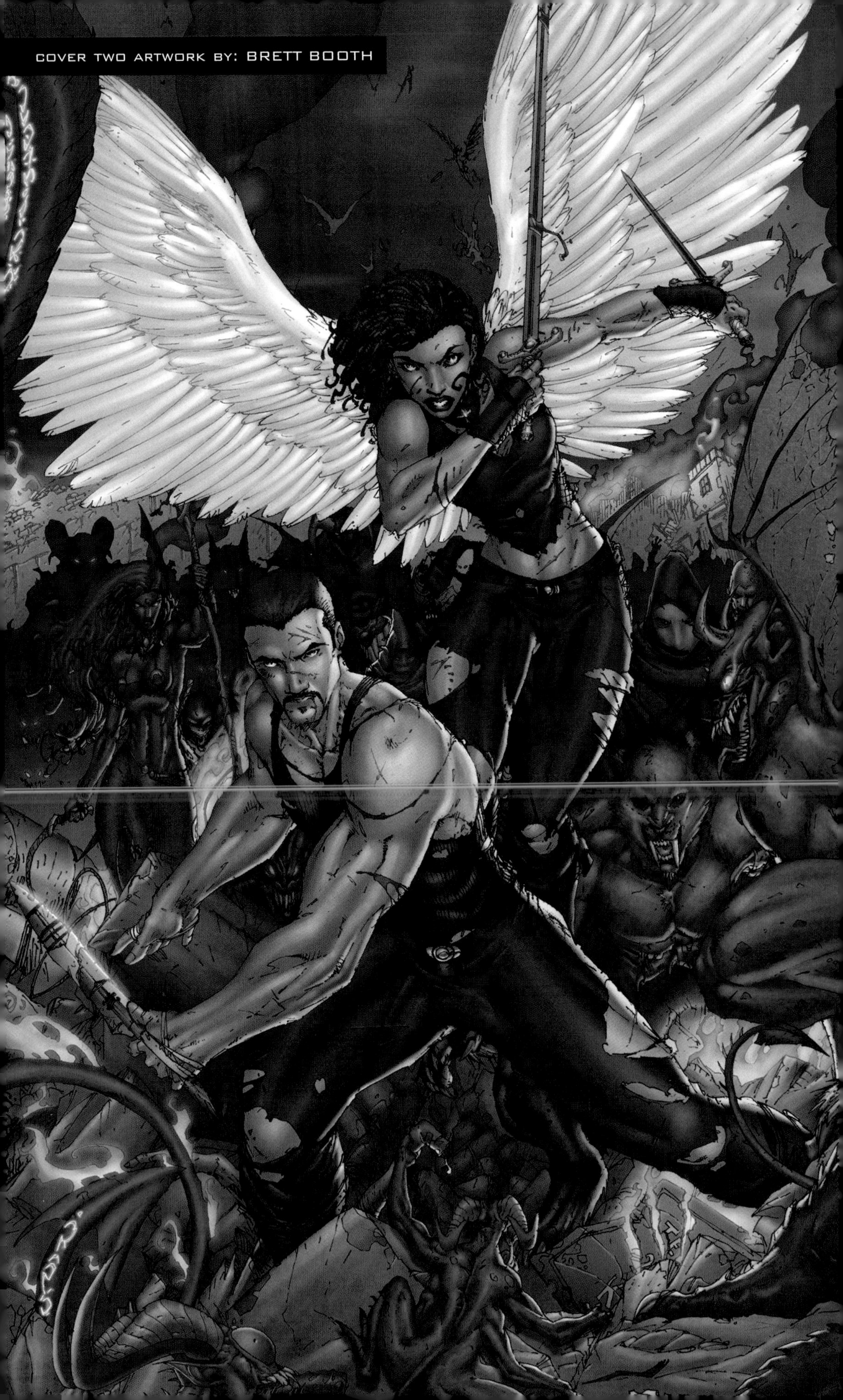

COVER TWO ARTWORK BY: BRETT BOOTH

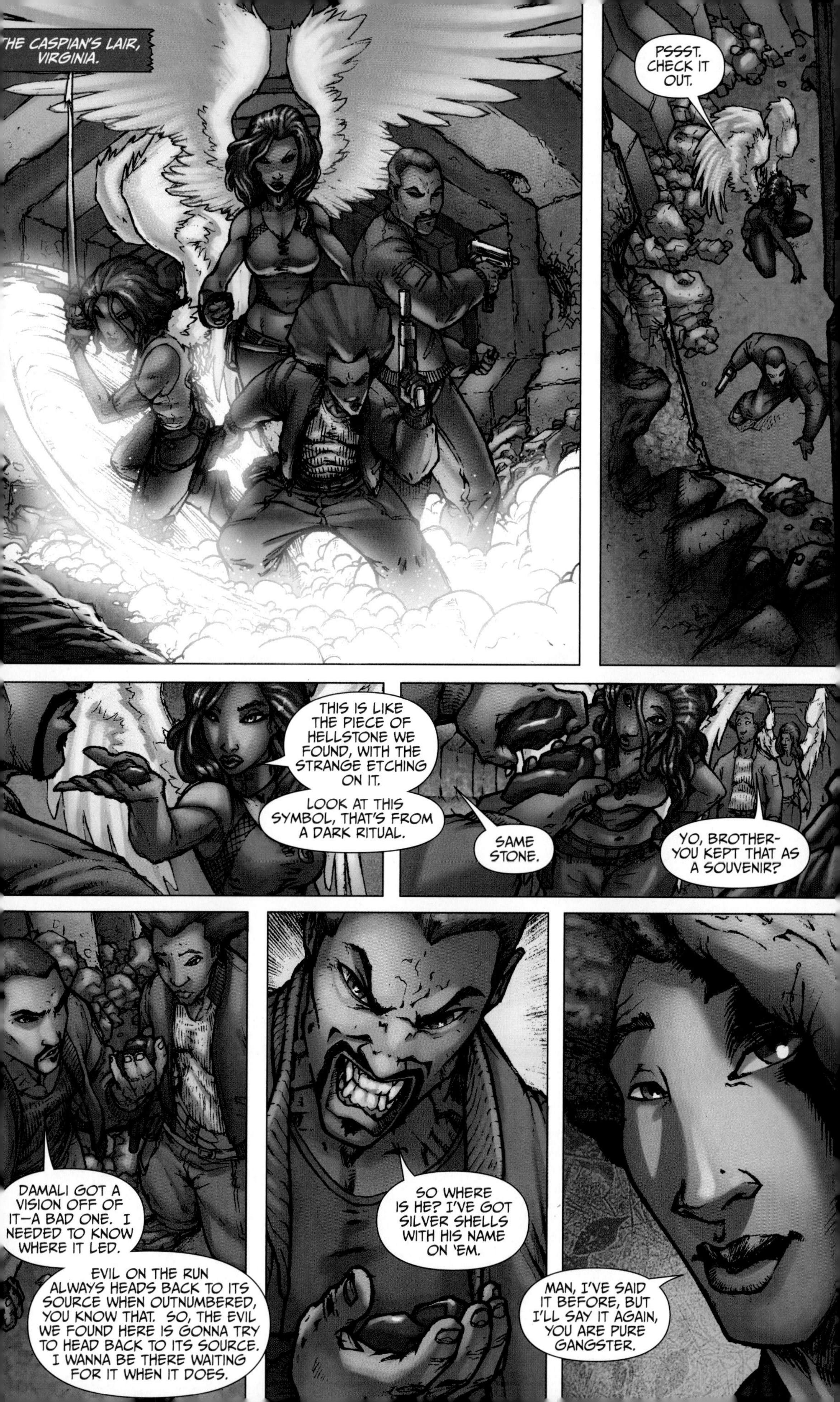
THE CASPIAN'S LAIR, VIRGINIA.
PSSST. CHECK IT OUT.
THIS IS LIKE THE PIECE OF HELLSTONE WE FOUND, WITH THE STRANGE ETCHING ON IT.
LOOK AT THIS SYMBOL, THAT'S FROM A DARK RITUAL.
SAME STONE.
YO, BROTHER- YOU KEPT THAT AS A SOUVENIR?
DAMALI GOT A VISION OFF OF IT—A BAD ONE. I NEEDED TO KNOW WHERE IT LED.
EVIL ON THE RUN ALWAYS HEADS BACK TO ITS SOURCE WHEN OUTNUMBERED, YOU KNOW THAT. SO, THE EVIL WE FOUND HERE IS GONNA TRY TO HEAD BACK TO ITS SOURCE. I WANNA BE THERE WAITING FOR IT WHEN IT DOES.
SO WHERE IS HE? I'VE GOT SILVER SHELLS WITH HIS NAME ON 'EM.
MAN, I'VE SAID IT BEFORE, BUT I'LL SAY IT AGAIN, YOU ARE PURE GANGSTER.

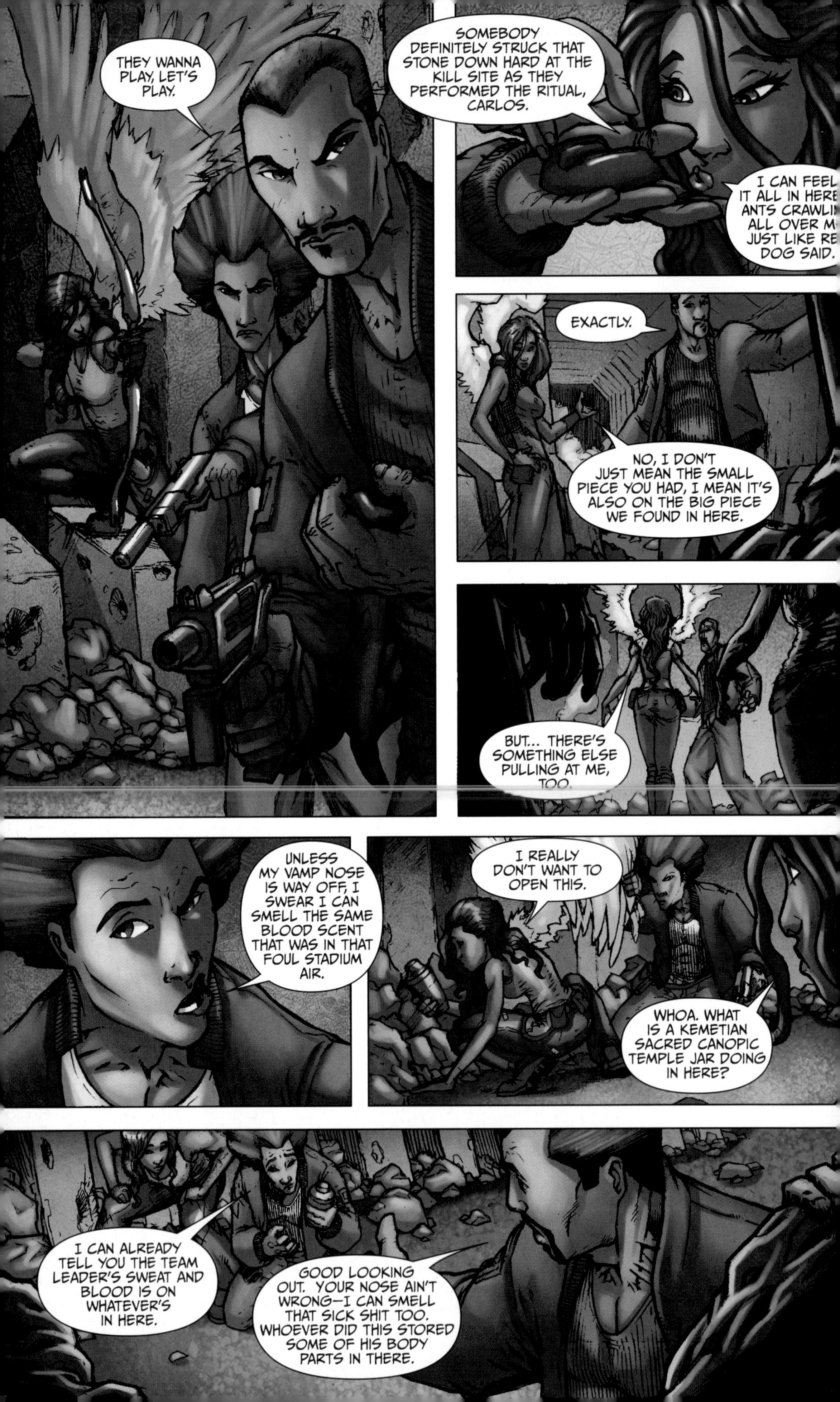
THEY WANNA PLAY, LET'S PLAY.
SOMEBODY DEFINITELY STRUCK THAT STONE DOWN HARD AT THE KILL SITE AS THEY PERFORMED THE RITUAL, CARLOS.
I CAN FEEL IT ALL IN HERE ANTS CRAWLI ALL OVER M JUST LIKE RE DOG SAID.
EXACTLY.
NO, I DON'T JUST MEAN THE SMALL PIECE YOU HAD, I MEAN IT'S ALSO ON THE BIG PIECE WE FOUND IN HERE.
BUT... THERE'S SOMETHING ELSE PULLING AT ME, TOO.
UNLESS MY VAMP NOSE IS WAY OFF, I SWEAR I CAN SMELL THE SAME BLOOD SCENT THAT WAS IN THAT FOUL STADIUM AIR.
I REALLY DON'T WANT TO OPEN THIS.
WHOA. WHAT IS A KEMETIAN SACRED CANOPIC TEMPLE JAR DOING IN HERE?
I CAN ALREADY TELL YOU THE TEAM LEADER'S SWEAT AND BLOOD IS ON WHATEVER'S IN HERE.
GOOD LOOKING OUT. YOUR NOSE AIN'T WRONG—I CAN SMELL THAT SICK SHIT TOO. WHOEVER DID THIS STORED SOME OF HIS BODY PARTS IN THERE.

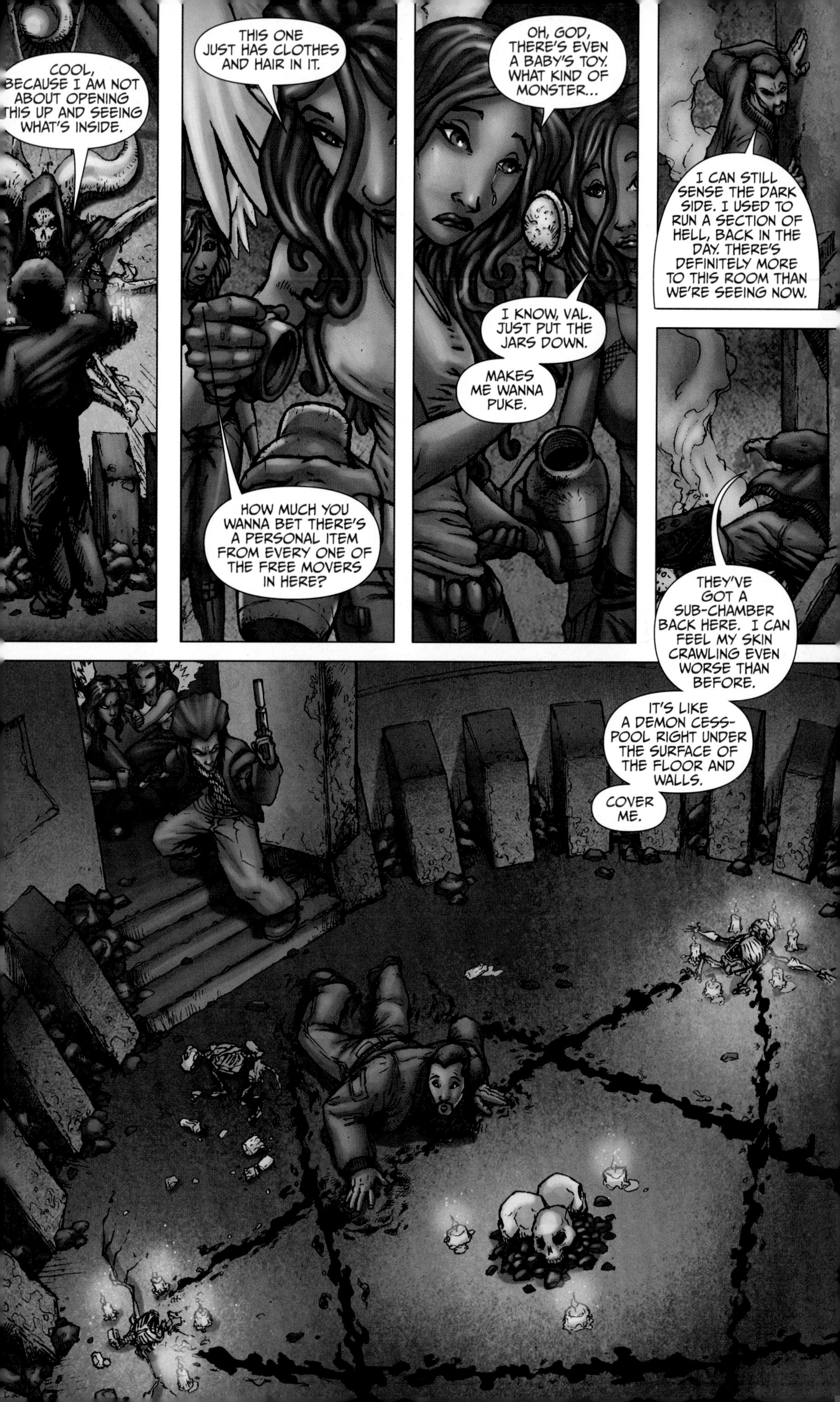
COOL, BECAUSE I AM NOT ABOUT OPENING THIS UP AND SEEING WHAT'S INSIDE.
THIS ONE JUST HAS CLOTHES AND HAIR IN IT.
HOW MUCH YOU WANNA BET THERE'S A PERSONAL ITEM FROM EVERY ONE OF THE FREE MOVERS IN HERE?
OH, GOD, THERE'S EVEN A BABY'S TOY. WHAT KIND OF MONSTER...
I KNOW, VAL. JUST PUT THE JARS DOWN.
MAKES ME WANNA PUKE.
I CAN STILL SENSE THE DARK SIDE. I USED TO RUN A SECTION OF HELL, BACK IN THE DAY. THERE'S DEFINITELY MORE TO THIS ROOM THAN WE'RE SEEING NOW.
THEY'VE GOT A SUB-CHAMBER BACK HERE. I CAN FEEL MY SKIN CRAWLING EVEN WORSE THAN BEFORE.
IT'S LIKE A DEMON CESS-POOL RIGHT UNDER THE SURFACE OF THE FLOOR AND WALLS.
COVER ME.

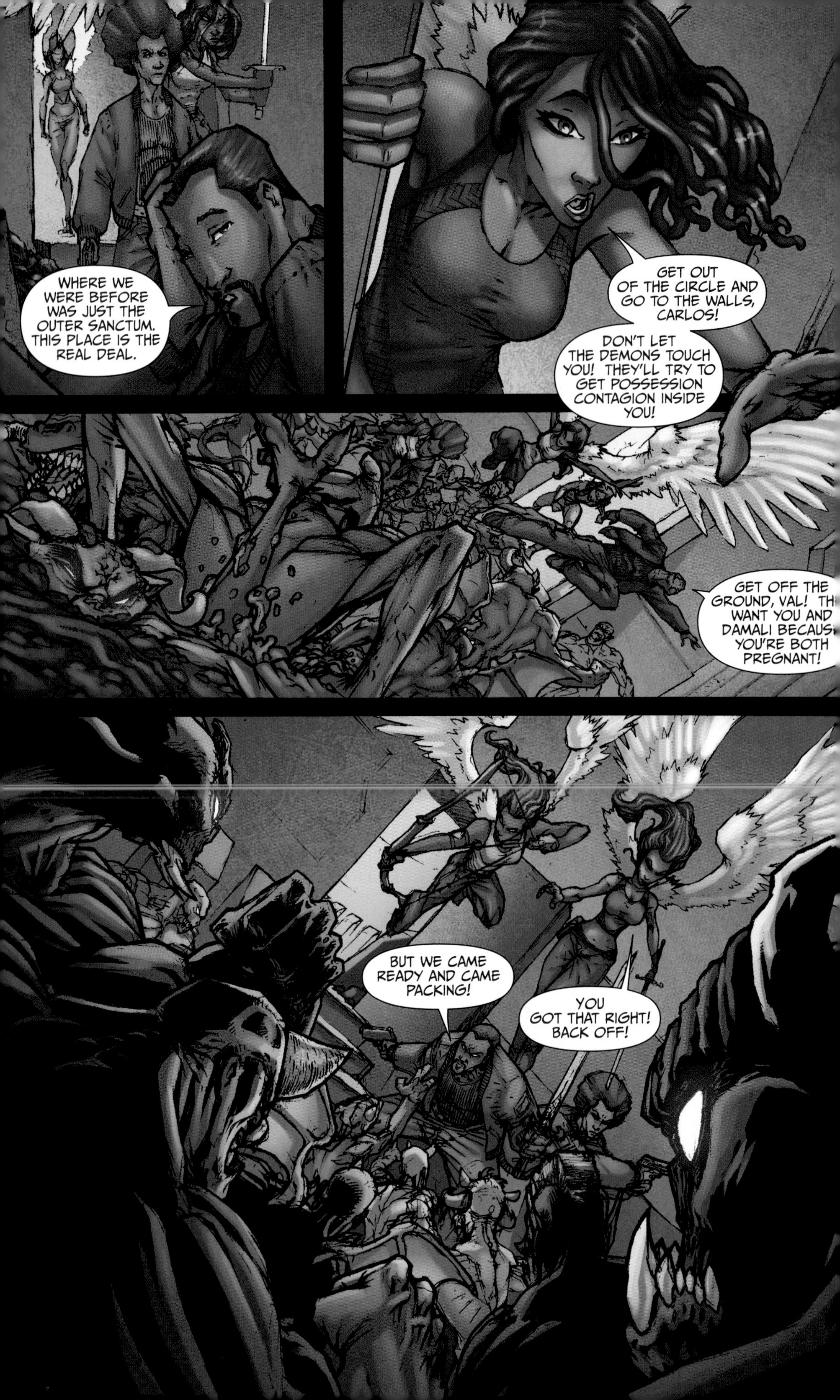

WHERE WE WERE BEFORE WAS JUST THE OUTER SANCTUM. THIS PLACE IS THE REAL DEAL.
GET OUT OF THE CIRCLE AND GO TO THE WALLS, CARLOS!
DON'T LET THE DEMONS TOUCH YOU! THEY'LL TRY TO GET POSSESSION CONTAGION INSIDE YOU!
GET OFF THE GROUND, VAL! TH
WANT YOU AND DAMALI BECAUS
YOU'RE BOTH PREGNANT!
BUT WE CAME READY AND CAME PACKING!
YOU GOT THAT RIGHT! BACK OFF!

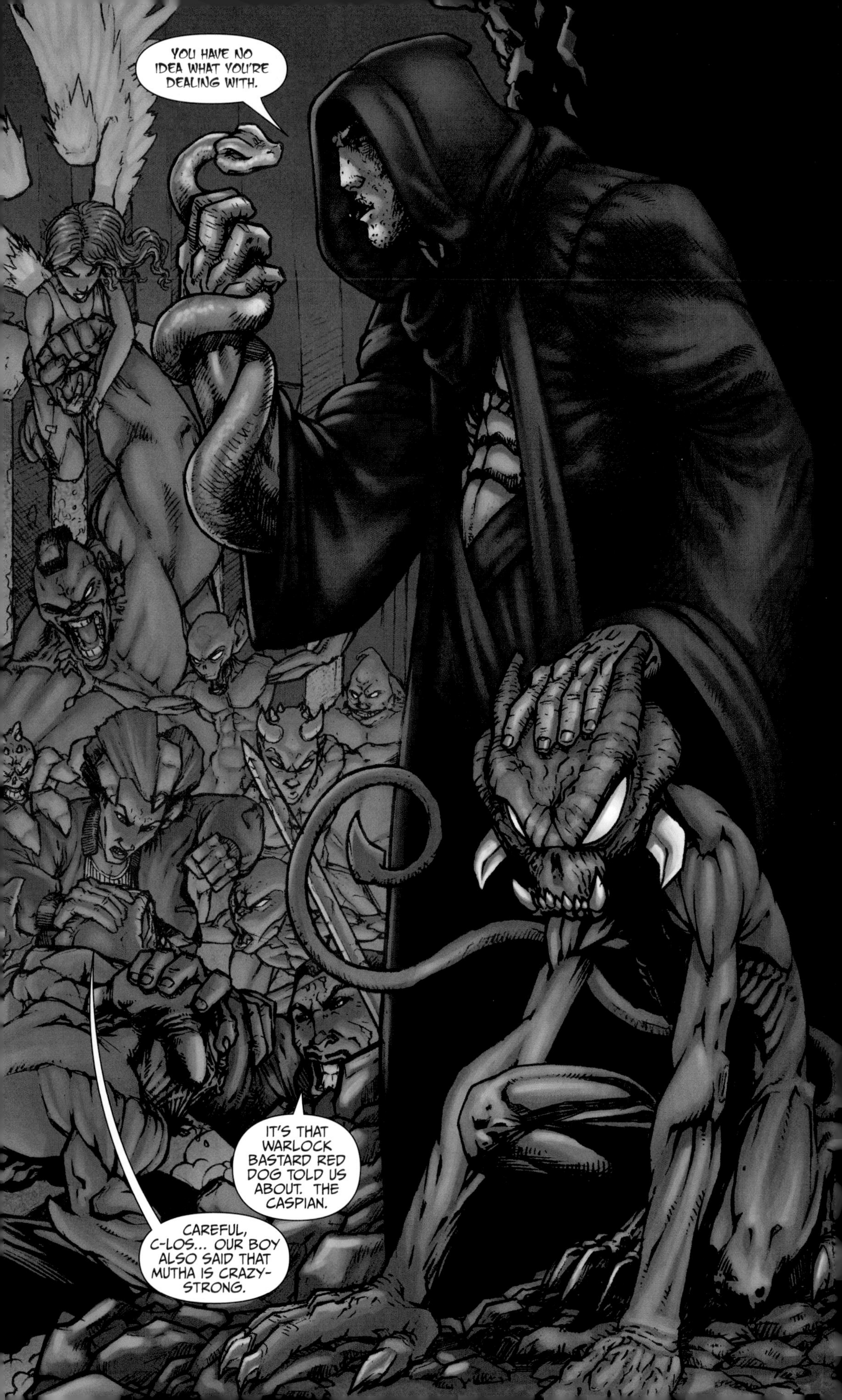
YOU HAVE NO IDEA WHAT YOU'RE DEALING WITH.
IT'S THAT WARLOCK BASTARD RED DOG TOLD US ABOUT. THE CASPIAN.
CAREFUL, C-LOS... OUR BOY ALSO SAID THAT MUTHA IS CRAZY-STRONG.

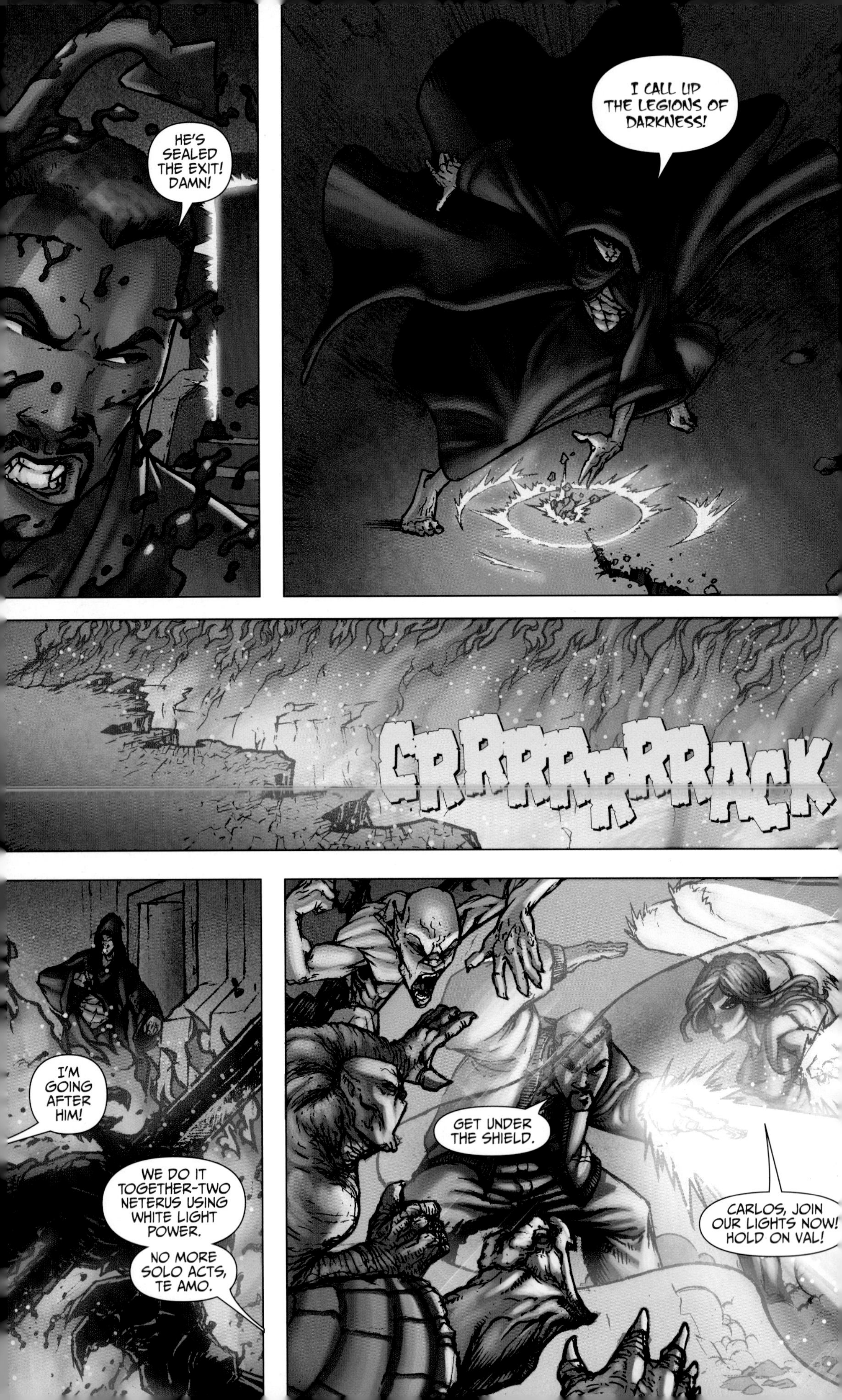
HE'S SEALED THE EXIT! DAMN!
I CALL UP THE LEGIONS OF DARKNESS!
CRRRRRRRACK
I'M GOING AFTER HIM!
WE DO IT TOGETHER-TWO NETERUS USING WHITE LIGHT POWER.
NO MORE SOLO ACTS, TE AMO.
GET UNDER THE SHIELD.
CARLOS, JOIN OUR LIGHTS NOW! HOLD ON VAL!

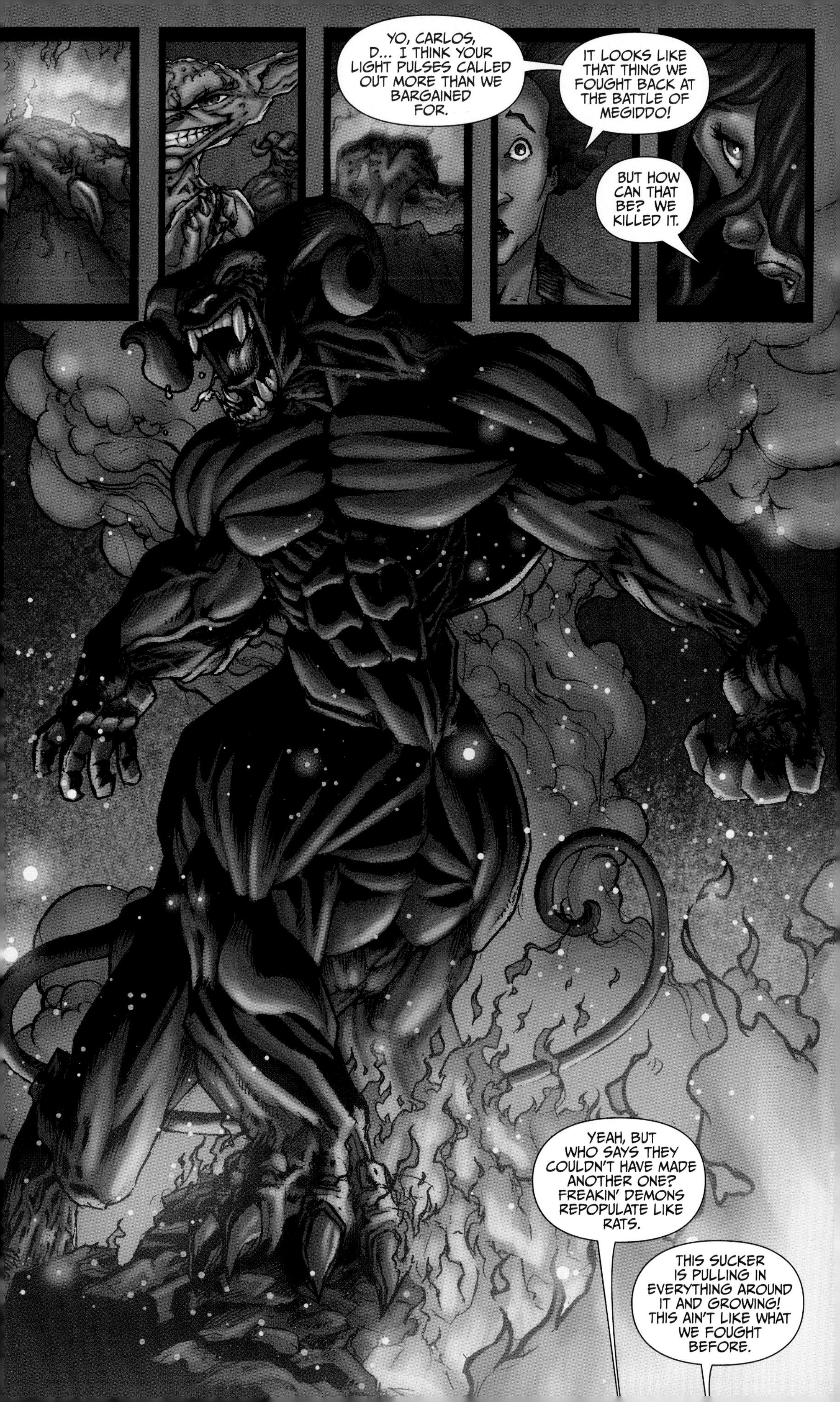
YO, CARLOS, D... I THINK YOUR LIGHT PULSES CALLED OUT MORE THAN WE BARGAINED FOR.
IT LOOKS LIKE THAT THING WE FOUGHT BACK AT THE BATTLE OF MEGIDDO!
BUT HOW CAN THAT BE? WE KILLED IT.
YEAH, BUT WHO SAYS THEY COULDN'T HAVE MADE ANOTHER ONE? FREAKIN' DEMONS REPOPULATE LIKE RATS.
THIS SUCKER IS PULLING IN EVERYTHING AROUND IT AND GROWING! THIS AIN'T LIKE WHAT WE FOUGHT BEFORE.

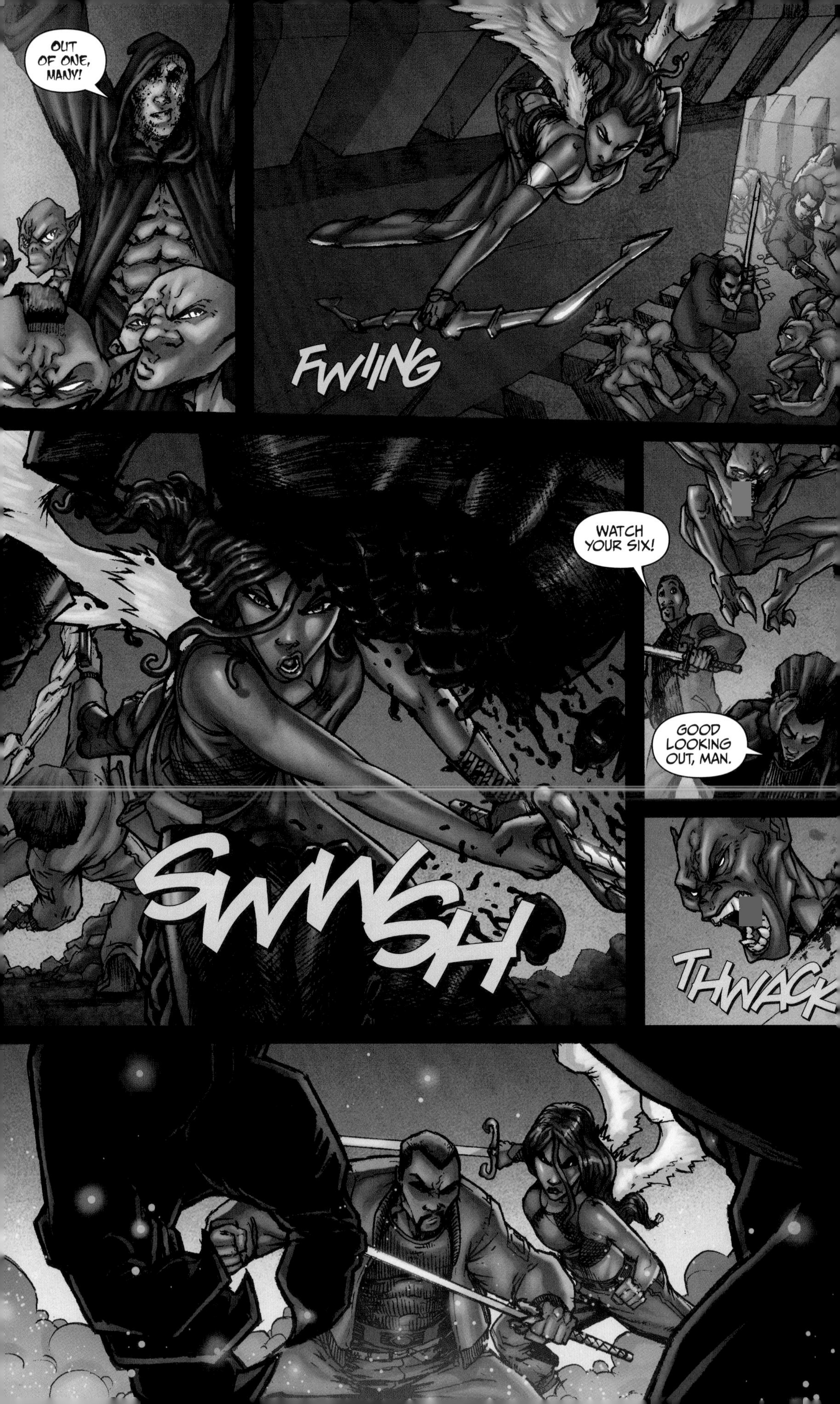
OUT OF ONE, MANY!
FWIING
WATCH YOUR SIX!
GOOD LOOKING OUT, MAN.
SWISH
THWACK

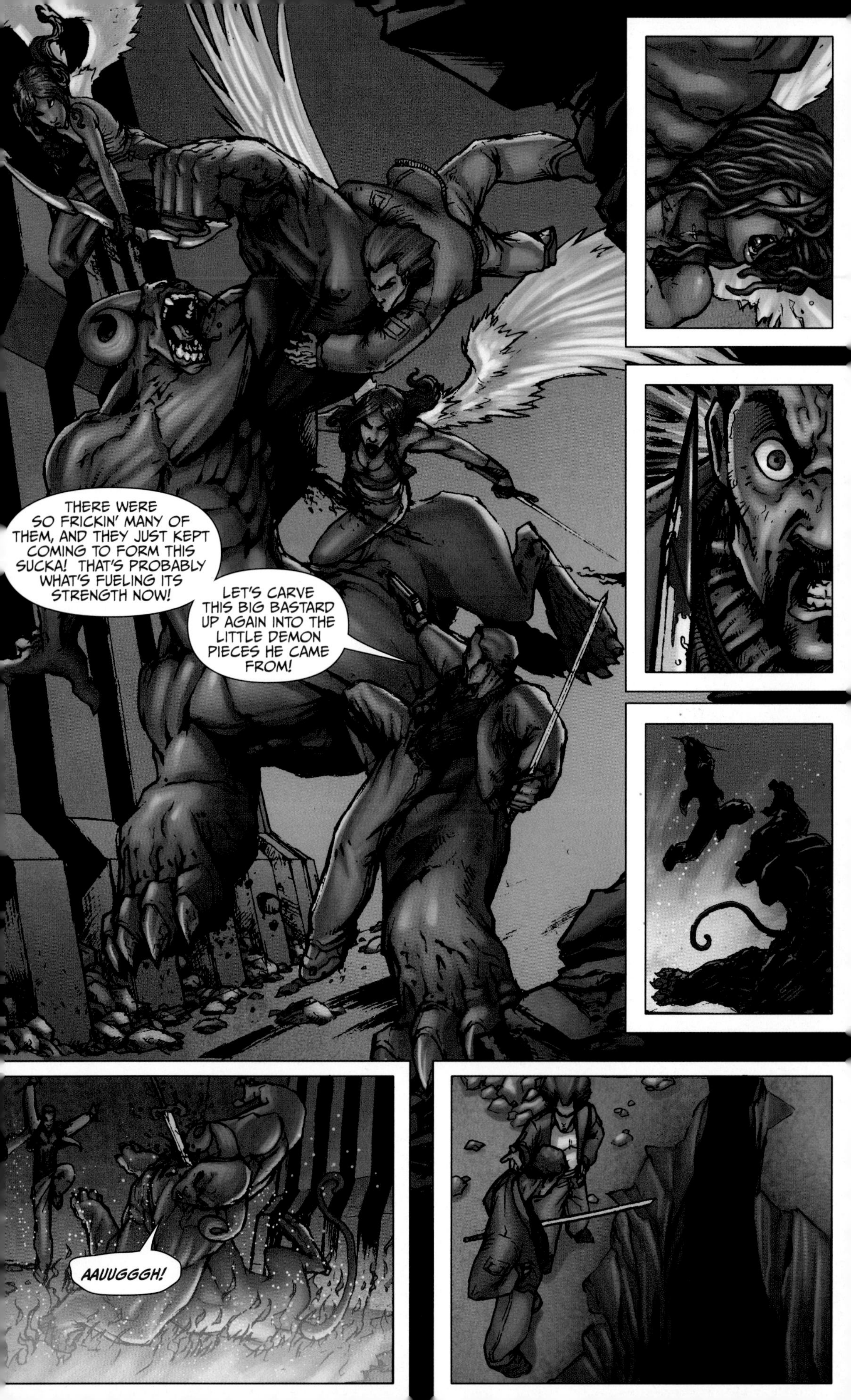
THERE WERE SO FRICKIN' MANY OF THEM, AND THEY JUST KEPT COMING TO FORM THIS SUCKA! THAT'S PROBABLY WHAT'S FUELING ITS STRENGTH NOW!
LET'S CARVE THIS BIG BASTARD UP AGAIN INTO THE LITTLE DEMON PIECES HE CAME FROM!
AAUUGGGH!

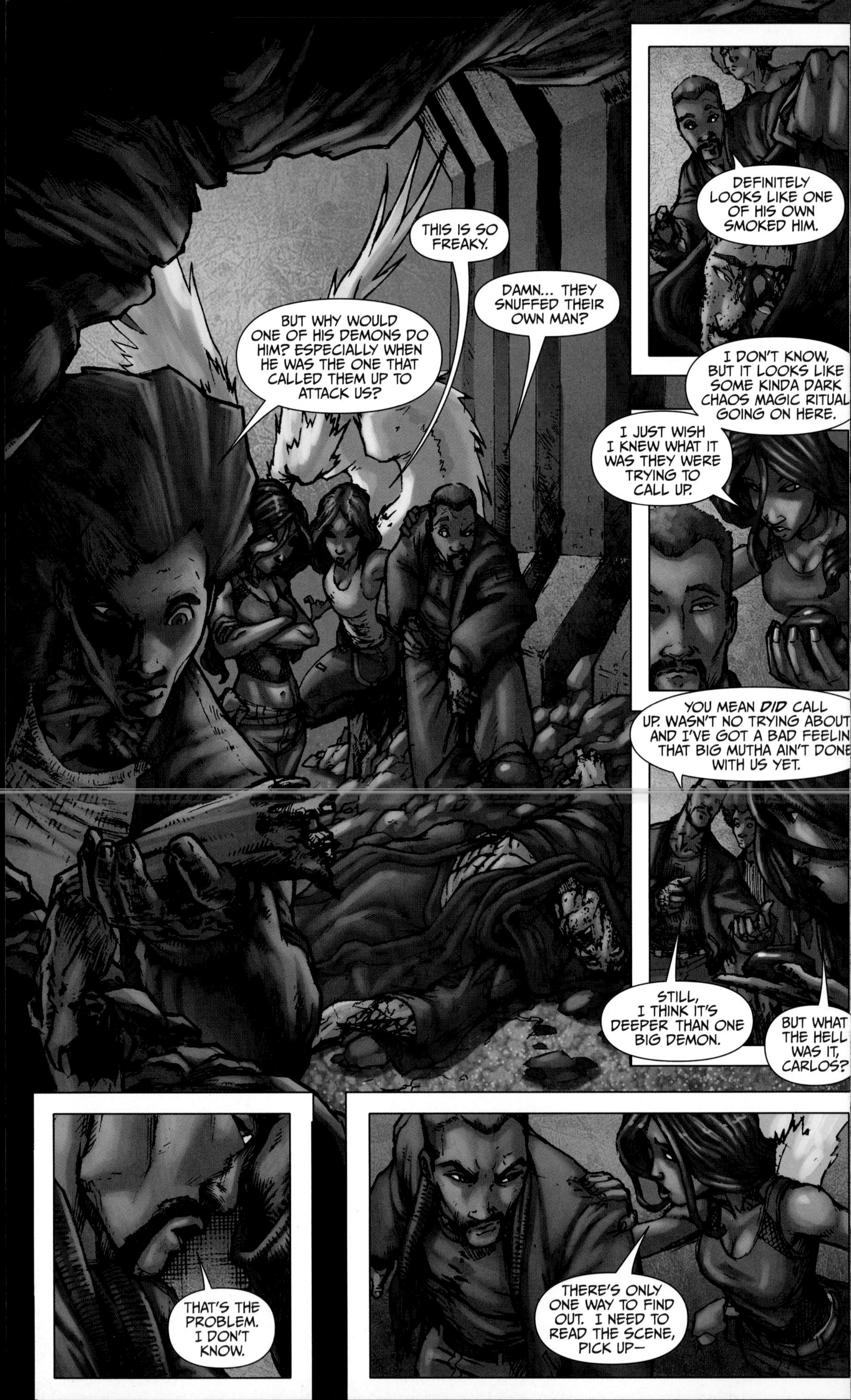
BUT WHY WOULD ONE OF HIS DEMONS DO HIM? ESPECIALLY WHEN HE WAS THE ONE THAT CALLED THEM UP TO ATTACK US?
THIS IS SO FREAKY.
DAMN... THEY SNUFFED THEIR OWN MAN?
DEFINITELY LOOKS LIKE ONE OF HIS OWN SMOKED HIM.
I DON'T KNOW, BUT IT LOOKS LIKE SOME KINDA DARK CHAOS MAGIC RITUAL GOING ON HERE.
I JUST WISH I KNEW WHAT IT WAS THEY WERE TRYING TO CALL UP.
YOU MEAN DID CALL UP. WASN'T NO TRYING ABOUT AND I'VE GOT A BAD FEELIN THAT BIG MUTHA AIN'T DONE WITH US YET.
STILL, I THINK IT'S DEEPER THAN ONE BIG DEMON.
BUT WHAT THE HELL WAS IT, CARLOS?
THAT'S THE PROBLEM. I DON'T KNOW.
THERE'S ONLY ONE WAY TO FIND OUT. I NEED TO READ THE SCENE, PICK UP—

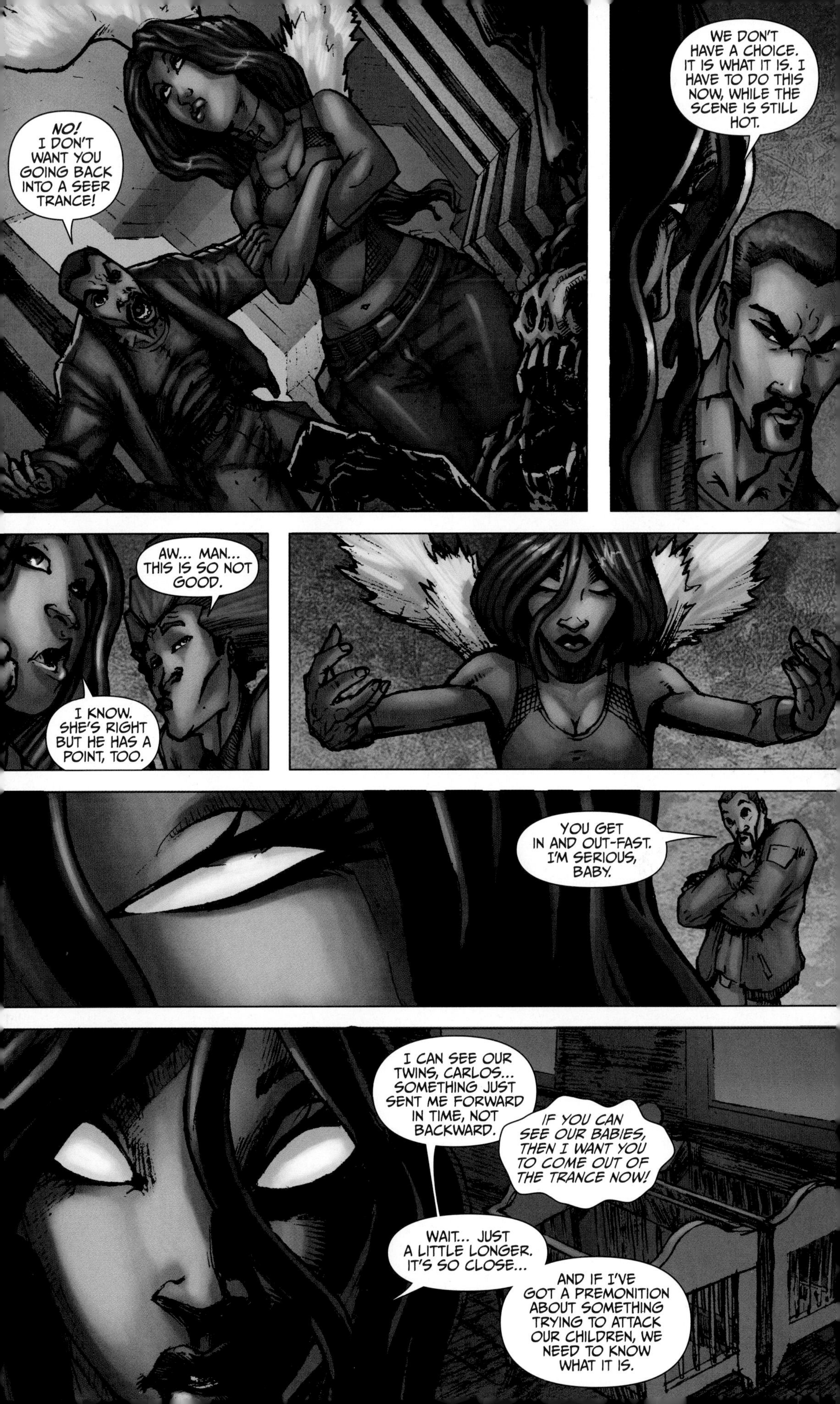
NO! I DON'T WANT YOU GOING BACK INTO A SEER TRANCE!
WE DON'T HAVE A CHOICE. IT IS WHAT IT IS. I HAVE TO DO THIS NOW, WHILE THE SCENE IS STILL HOT.
AW... MAN... THIS IS SO NOT GOOD.
I KNOW. SHE'S RIGHT BUT HE HAS A POINT, TOO.
YOU GET IN AND OUT-FAST. I'M SERIOUS, BABY.
I CAN SEE OUR TWINS, CARLOS... SOMETHING JUST SENT ME FORWARD IN TIME, NOT BACKWARD.
IF YOU CAN SEE OUR BABIES, THEN I WANT YOU TO COME OUT OF THE TRANCE NOW!
WAIT... JUST A LITTLE LONGER. IT'S SO CLOSE...
AND IF I'VE GOT A PREMONITION ABOUT SOMETHING TRYING TO ATTACK OUR CHILDREN, WE NEED TO KNOW WHAT IT IS.

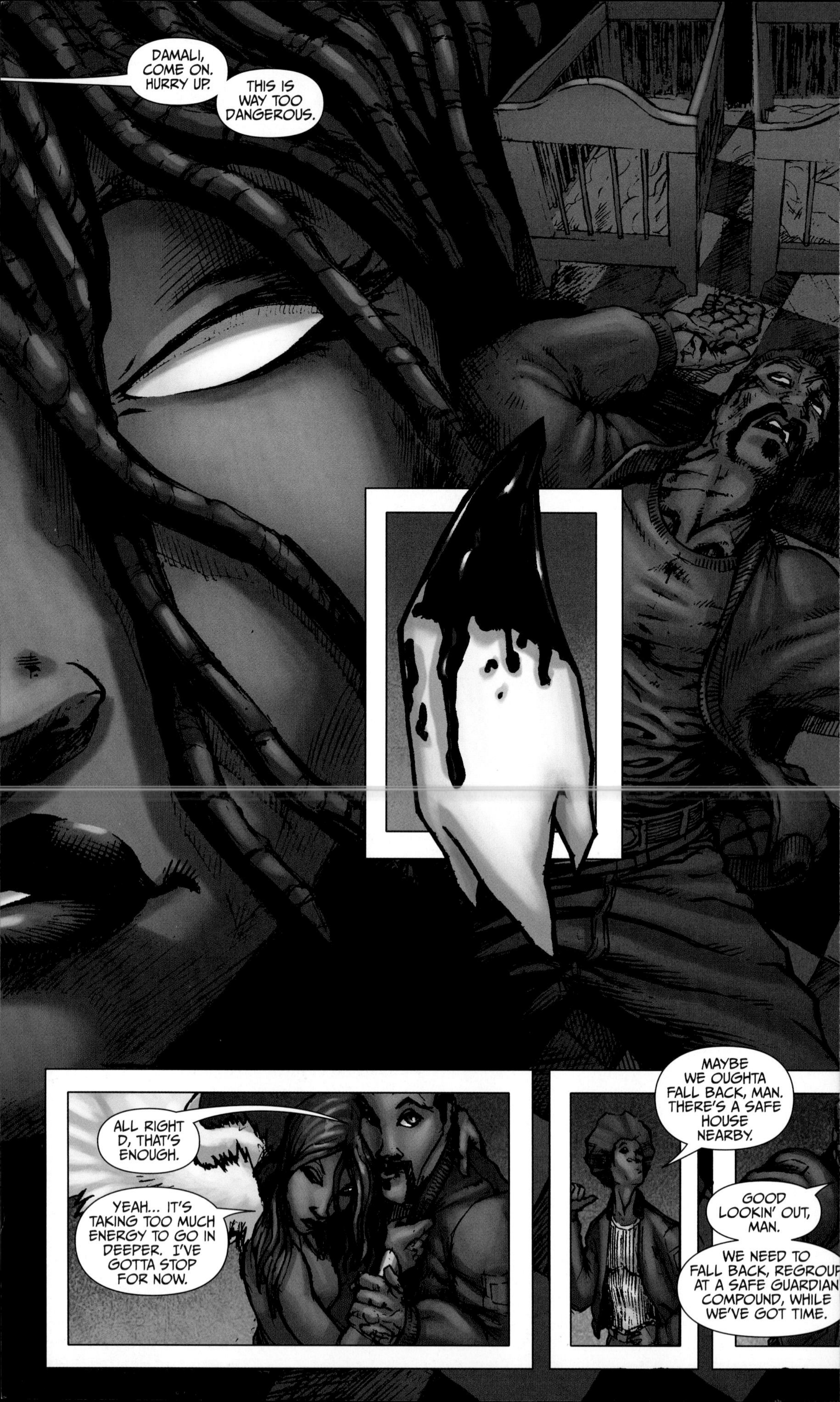
DAMALI, COME ON. HURRY UP.
THIS IS WAY TOO DANGEROUS.
ALL RIGHT D, THAT'S ENOUGH.
YEAH... IT'S TAKING TOO MUCH ENERGY TO GO IN DEEPER. I'VE GOTTA STOP FOR NOW.
MAYBE WE OUGHTA FALL BACK, MAN. THERE'S A SAFE HOUSE NEARBY.
GOOD LOOKIN' OUT, MAN.
WE NEED TO FALL BACK, REGROUP AT A SAFE GUARDIAN COMPOUND, WHILE WE'VE GOT TIME.

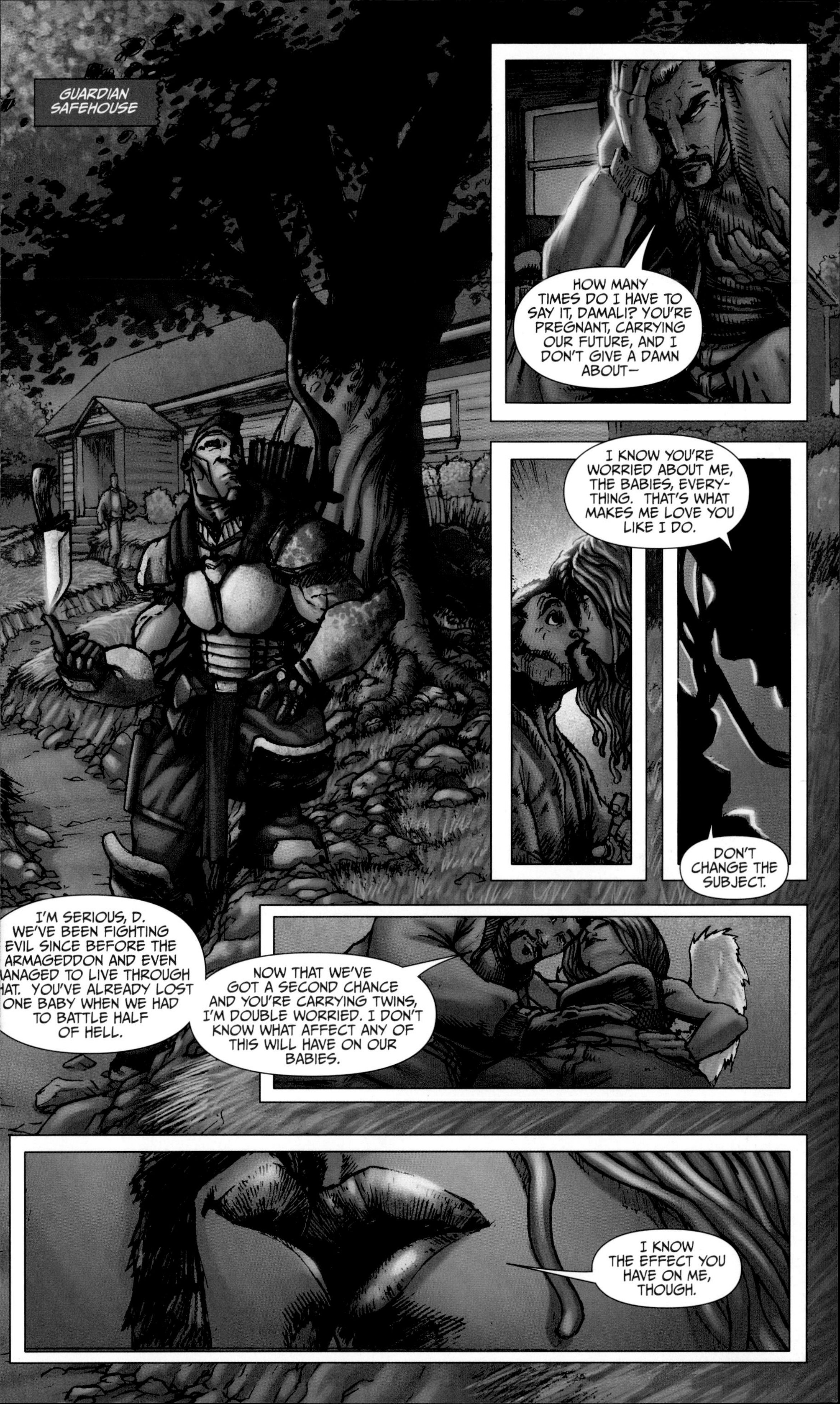
GUARDIAN SAFEHOUSE
HOW MANY TIMES DO I HAVE TO SAY IT, DAMALI? YOU'RE PREGNANT, CARRYING OUR FUTURE, AND I DON'T GIVE A DAMN ABOUT—
I KNOW YOU'RE WORRIED ABOUT ME, THE BABIES, EVERY-THING. THAT'S WHAT MAKES ME LOVE YOU LIKE I DO.
DON'T CHANGE THE SUBJECT.
I'M SERIOUS, D. WE'VE BEEN FIGHTING EVIL SINCE BEFORE THE ARMAGEDDON AND EVEN MANAGED TO LIVE THROUGH THAT. YOU'VE ALREADY LOST ONE BABY WHEN WE HAD TO BATTLE HALF OF HELL.
NOW THAT WE'VE GOT A SECOND CHANCE AND YOU'RE CARRYING TWINS, I'M DOUBLE WORRIED. I DON'T KNOW WHAT AFFECT ANY OF THIS WILL HAVE ON OUR BABIES.
I KNOW THE EFFECT YOU HAVE ON ME, THOUGH.

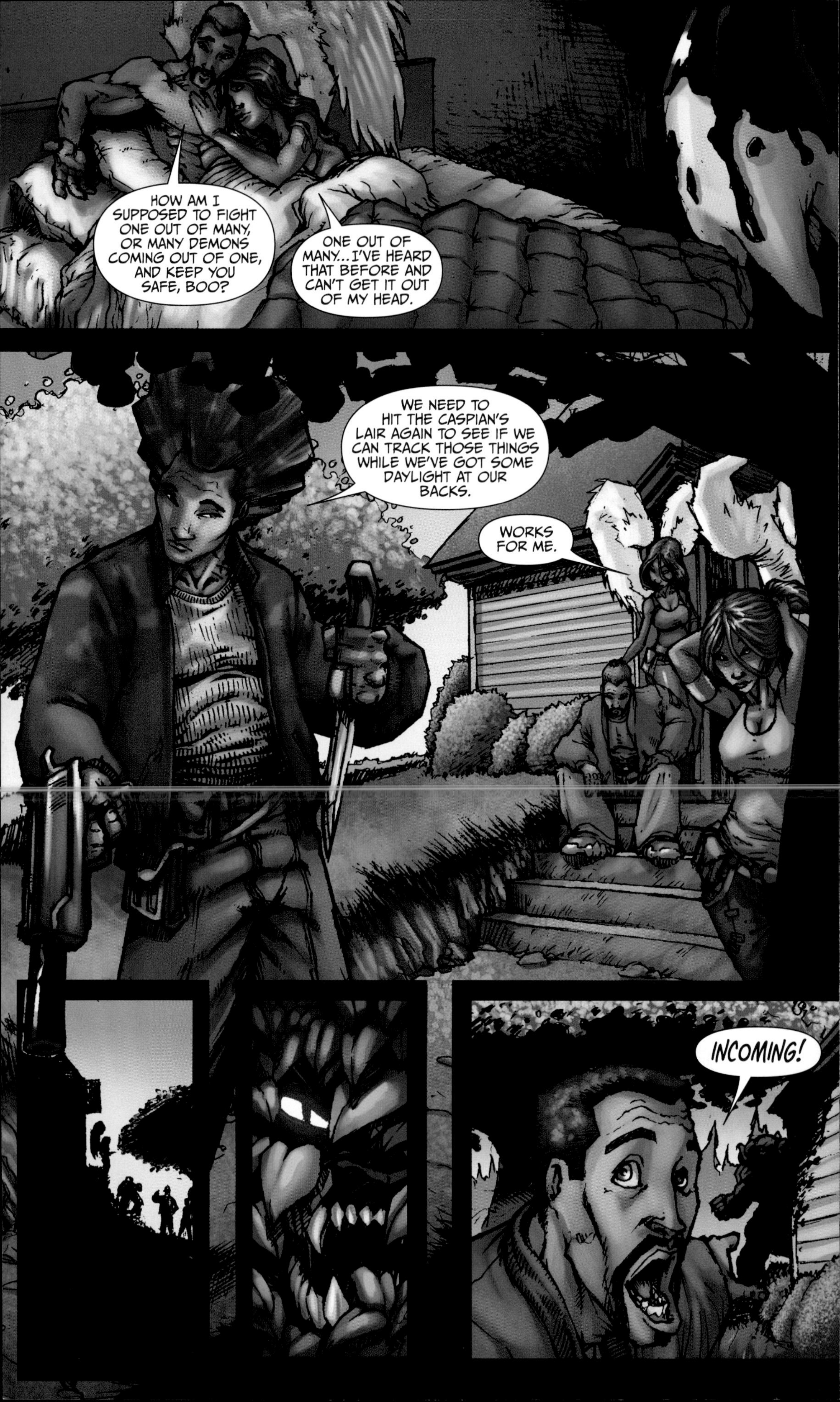
HOW AM I SUPPOSED TO FIGHT ONE OUT OF MANY, OR MANY DEMONS COMING OUT OF ONE, AND KEEP YOU SAFE, BOO?
ONE OUT OF MANY... I'VE HEARD THAT BEFORE AND CAN'T GET IT OUT OF MY HEAD.
WE NEED TO HIT THE CASPIAN'S LAIR AGAIN TO SEE IF WE CAN TRACK THOSE THINGS WHILE WE'VE GOT SOME DAYLIGHT AT OUR BACKS.
WORKS FOR ME.
INCOMING!

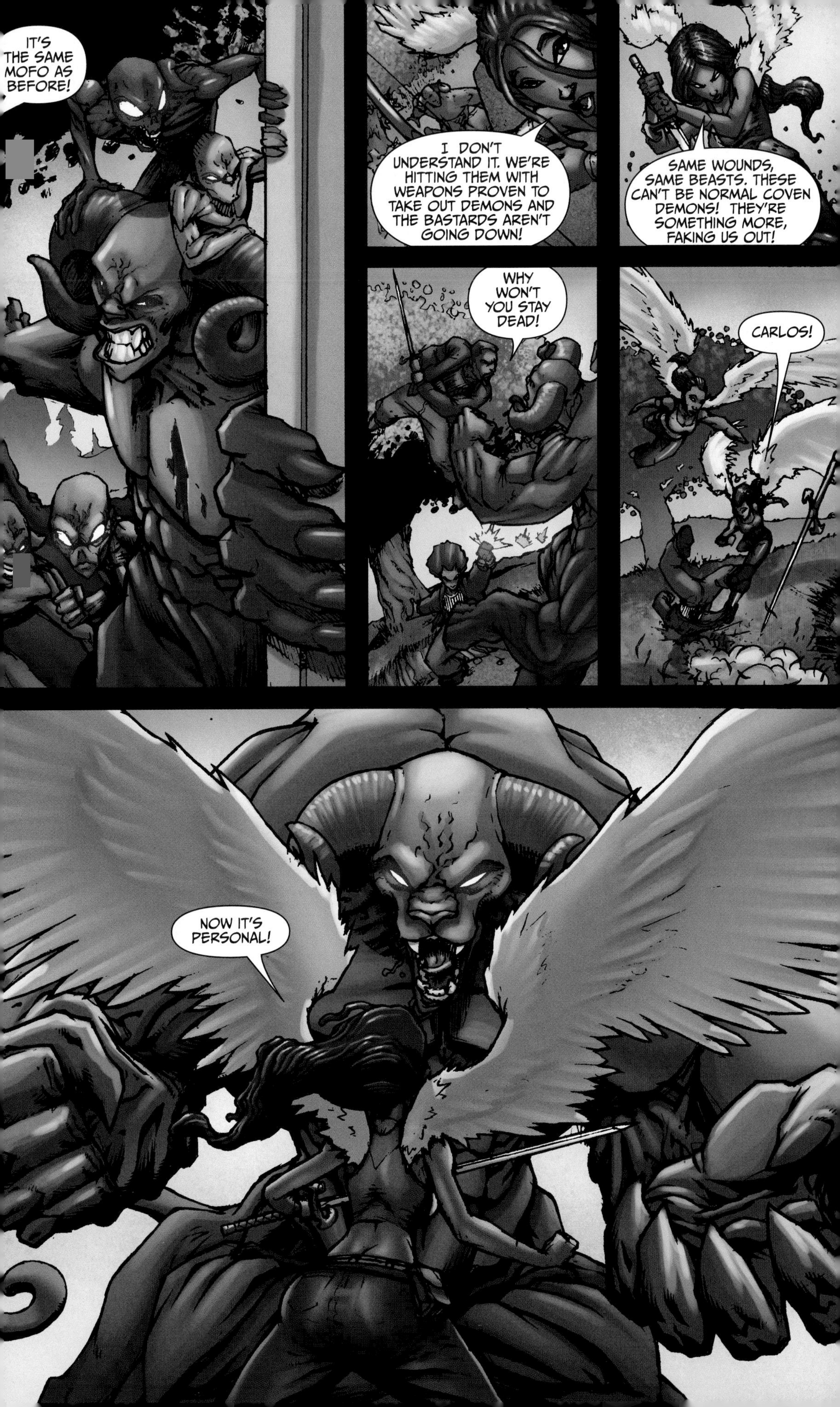
IT'S THE SAME MOFO AS BEFORE!
I DON'T UNDERSTAND IT. WE'RE HITTING THEM WITH WEAPONS PROVEN TO TAKE OUT DEMONS AND THE BASTARDS AREN'T GOING DOWN!
SAME WOUNDS, SAME BEASTS. THESE CAN'T BE NORMAL COVEN DEMONS! THEY'RE SOMETHING MORE, FAKING US OUT!
WHY WON'T YOU STAY DEAD!
CARLOS!
NOW IT'S PERSONAL!

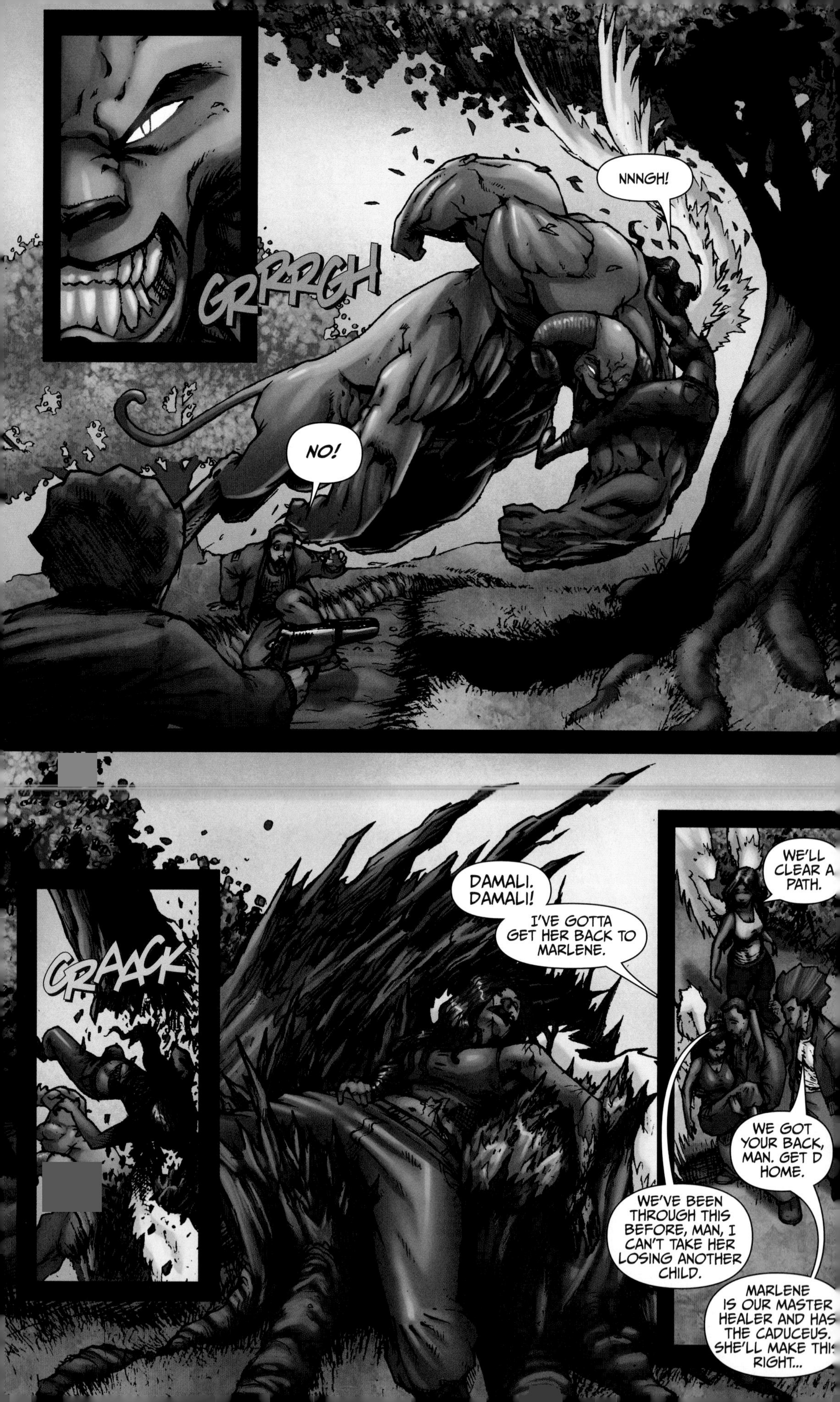
GRRRGH
NNNGH!
NO!
CRAAACK
DAMALI. DAMALI!
I'VE GOTTA GET HER BACK TO MARLENE.
WE'LL CLEAR A PATH.
WE GOT YOUR BACK, MAN. GET D HOME.
WE'VE BEEN THROUGH THIS BEFORE, MAN, I CAN'T TAKE HER LOSING ANOTHER CHILD.
MARLENE IS OUR MASTER HEALER AND HAS THE CADUCEUS. SHE'LL MAKE THIS RIGHT...

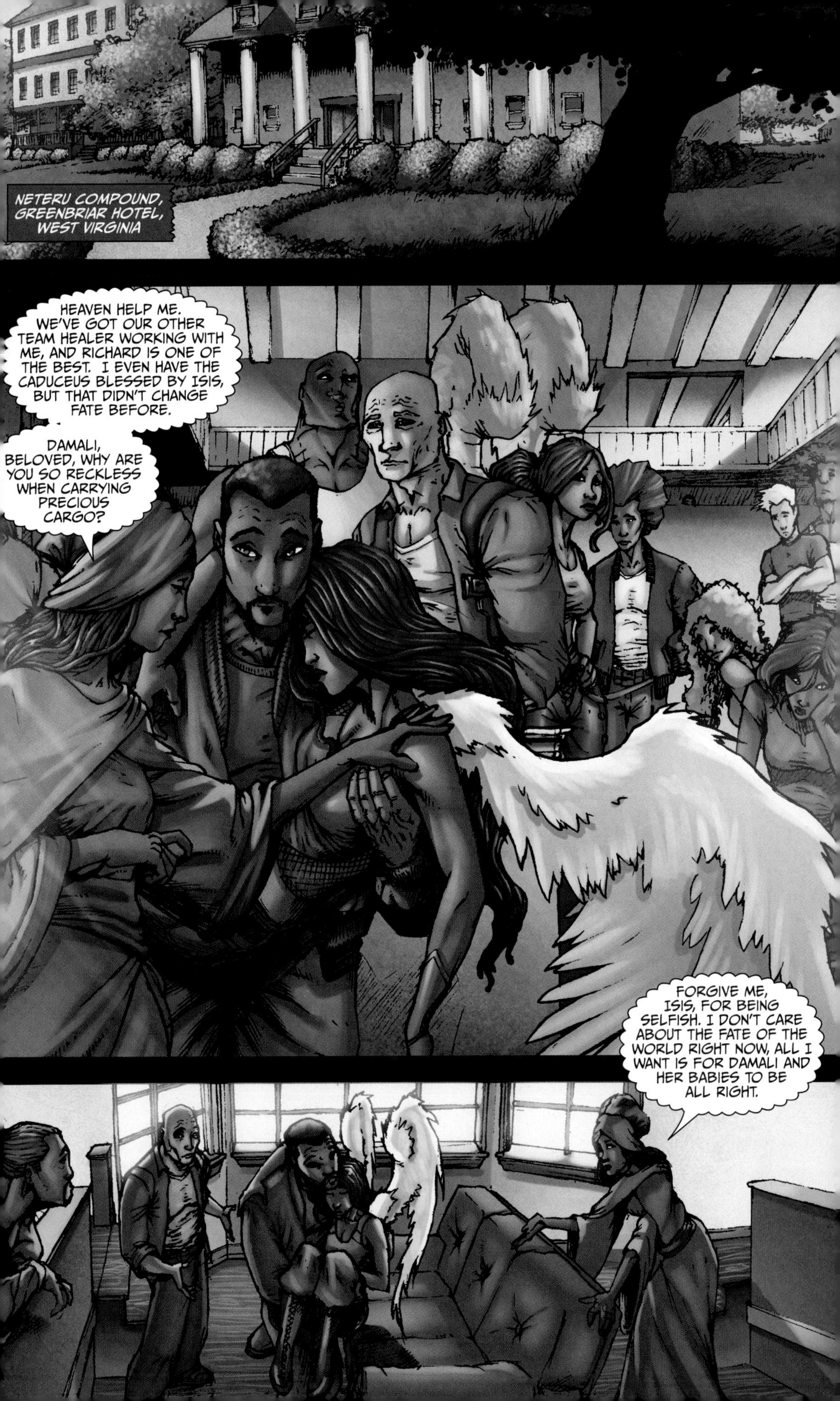
NETERU COMPOUND,
GREENBRIAR HOTEL,
WEST VIRGINIA
HEAVEN HELP ME. WE'VE GOT OUR OTHER TEAM HEALER WORKING WITH ME, AND RICHARD IS ONE OF THE BEST. I EVEN HAVE THE CADUCEUS BLESSED BY ISIS, BUT THAT DIDN'T CHANGE FATE BEFORE.
DAMALI, BELOVED, WHY ARE YOU SO RECKLESS WHEN CARRYING PRECIOUS CARGO?
FORGIVE ME, ISIS, FOR BEING SELFISH. I DON'T CARE ABOUT THE FATE OF THE WORLD RIGHT NOW, ALL I WANT IS FOR DAMALI AND HER BABIES TO BE ALL RIGHT.

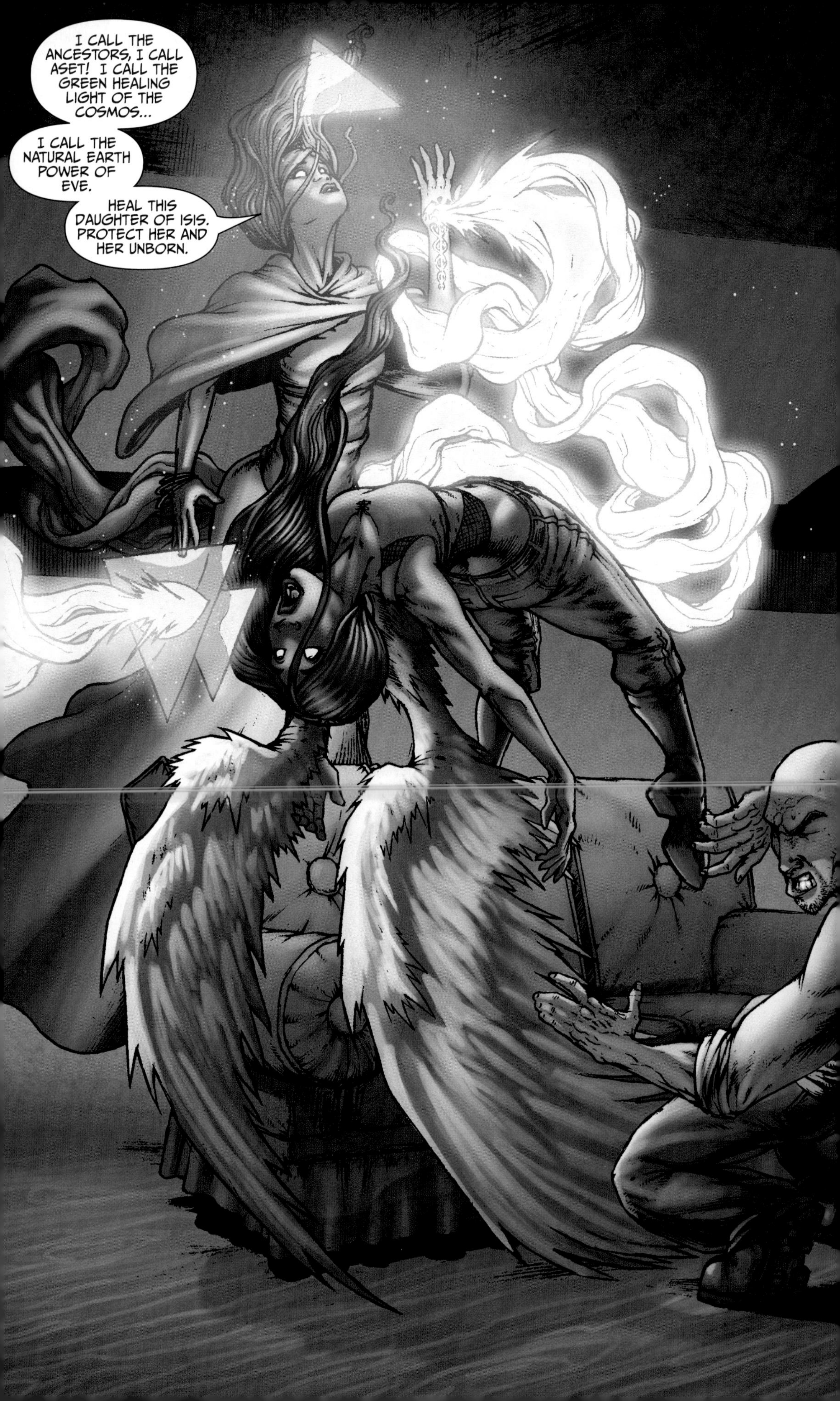
I CALL THE ANCESTORS, I CALL ASET! I CALL THE GREEN HEALING LIGHT OF THE COSMOS...
I CALL THE NATURAL EARTH POWER OF EVE.
HEAL THIS DAUGHTER OF ISIS. PROTECT HER AND HER UNBORN.

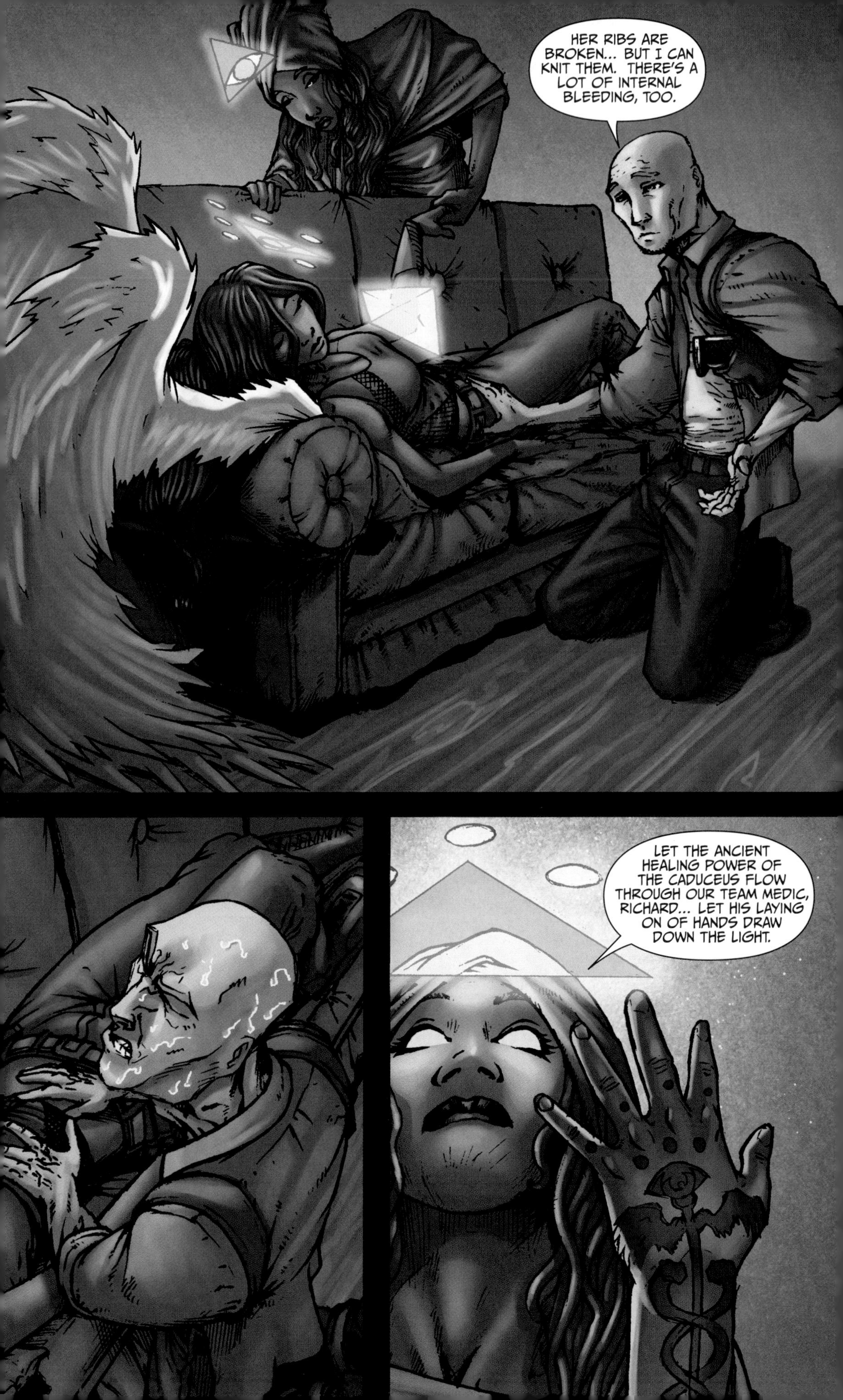
HER RIBS ARE BROKEN... BUT I CAN KNIT THEM. THERE'S A LOT OF INTERNAL BLEEDING, TOO.
LET THE ANCIENT HEALING POWER OF THE CADUCEUS FLOW THROUGH OUR TEAM MEDIC, RICHARD... LET HIS LAYING ON OF HANDS DRAW DOWN THE LIGHT.

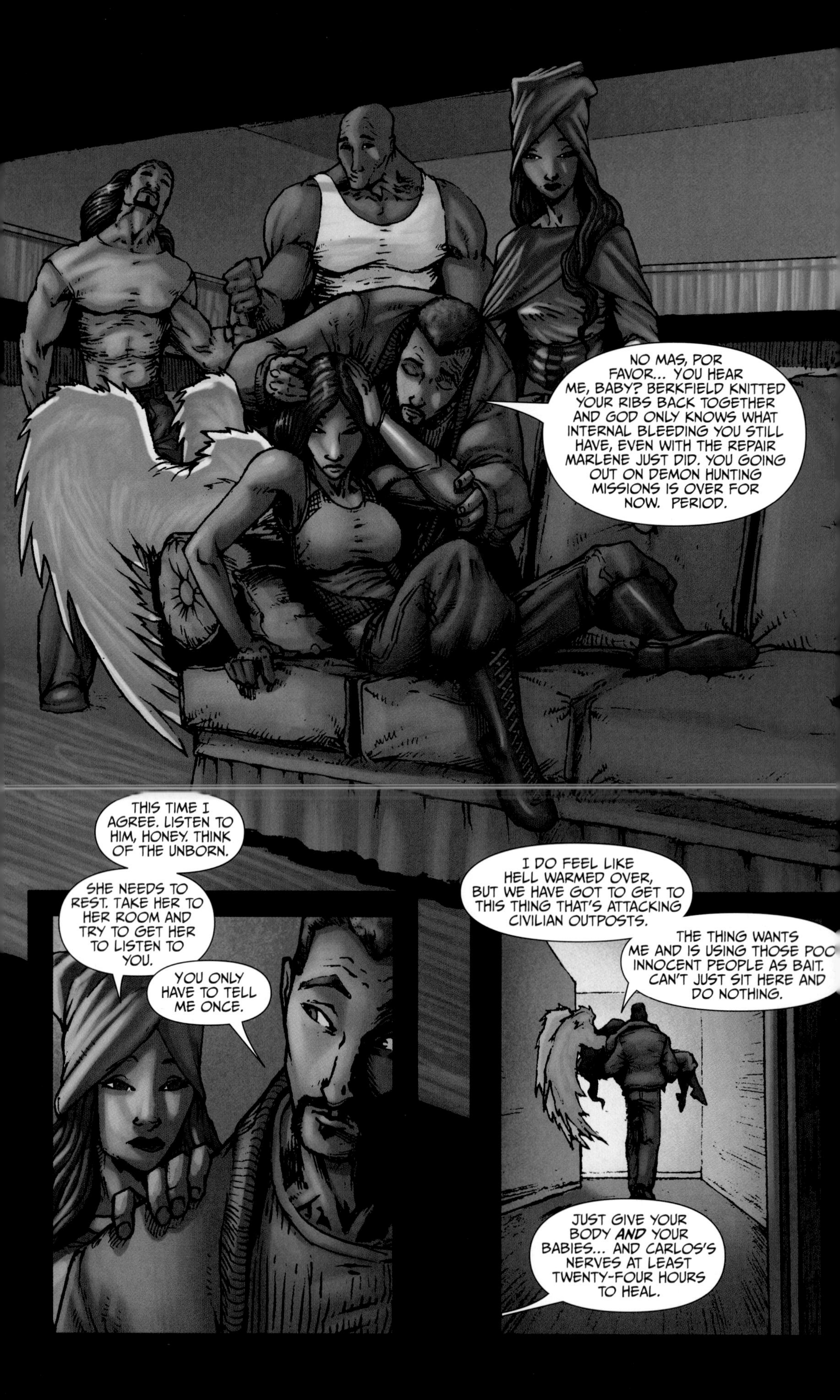
NO MAS, POR FAVOR... YOU HEAR ME, BABY? BERKFIELD KNITTED YOUR RIBS BACK TOGETHER AND GOD ONLY KNOWS WHAT INTERNAL BLEEDING YOU STILL HAVE, EVEN WITH THE REPAIR MARLENE JUST DID. YOU GOING OUT ON DEMON HUNTING MISSIONS IS OVER FOR NOW. PERIOD.
THIS TIME I AGREE. LISTEN TO HIM, HONEY. THINK OF THE UNBORN.
SHE NEEDS TO REST. TAKE HER TO HER ROOM AND TRY TO GET HER TO LISTEN TO YOU.
YOU ONLY HAVE TO TELL ME ONCE.
I DO FEEL LIKE HELL WARMED OVER, BUT WE HAVE GOT TO GET TO THIS THING THAT'S ATTACKING CIVILIAN OUTPOSTS.
THE THING WANTS ME AND IS USING THOSE POO INNOCENT PEOPLE AS BAIT. CAN'T JUST SIT HERE AND DO NOTHING.
JUST GIVE YOUR BODY *AND* YOUR BABIES... AND CARLOS'S NERVES AT LEAST TWENTY-FOUR HOURS TO HEAL.

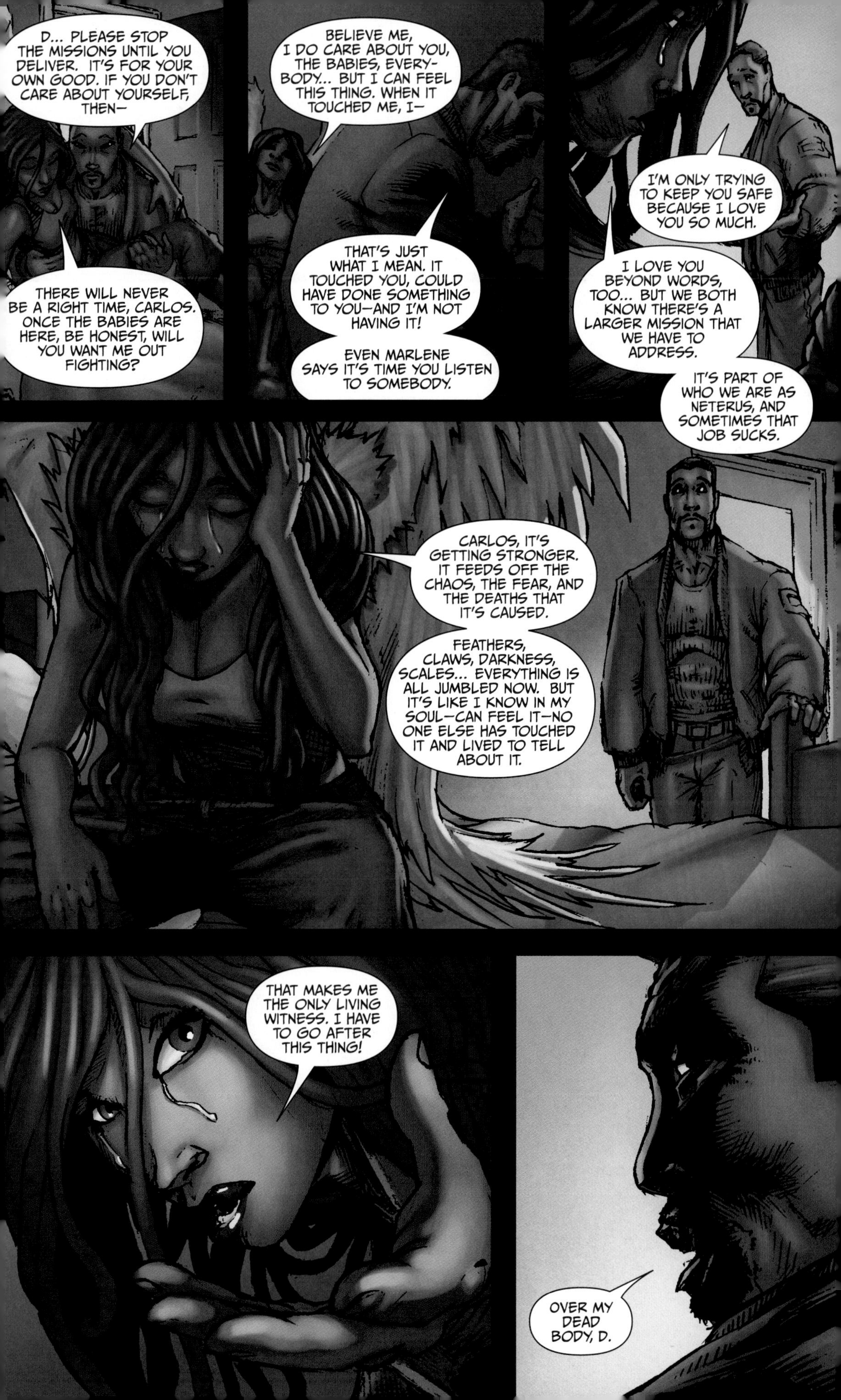
D... PLEASE STOP THE MISSIONS UNTIL YOU DELIVER. IT'S FOR YOUR OWN GOOD. IF YOU DON'T CARE ABOUT YOURSELF, THEN—
THERE WILL NEVER BE A RIGHT TIME, CARLOS. ONCE THE BABIES ARE HERE, BE HONEST, WILL YOU WANT ME OUT FIGHTING?
BELIEVE ME, I DO CARE ABOUT YOU, THE BABIES, EVERY-BODY... BUT I CAN FEEL THIS THING. WHEN IT TOUCHED ME, I—
THAT'S JUST WHAT I MEAN. IT TOUCHED YOU, COULD HAVE DONE SOMETHING TO YOU—AND I'M NOT HAVING IT!
EVEN MARLENE SAYS IT'S TIME YOU LISTEN TO SOMEBODY.
I'M ONLY TRYING TO KEEP YOU SAFE BECAUSE I LOVE YOU SO MUCH.
I LOVE YOU BEYOND WORDS, TOO... BUT WE BOTH KNOW THERE'S A LARGER MISSION THAT WE HAVE TO ADDRESS.
IT'S PART OF WHO WE ARE AS NETERUS, AND SOMETIMES THAT JOB SUCKS.
CARLOS, IT'S GETTING STRONGER. IT FEEDS OFF THE CHAOS, THE FEAR, AND THE DEATHS THAT IT'S CAUSED.
FEATHERS, CLAWS, DARKNESS, SCALES... EVERYTHING IS ALL JUMBLED NOW. BUT IT'S LIKE I KNOW IN MY SOUL—CAN FEEL IT—NO ONE ELSE HAS TOUCHED IT AND LIVED TO TELL ABOUT IT.
THAT MAKES ME THE ONLY LIVING WITNESS. I HAVE TO GO AFTER THIS THING!
OVER MY DEAD BODY, D.

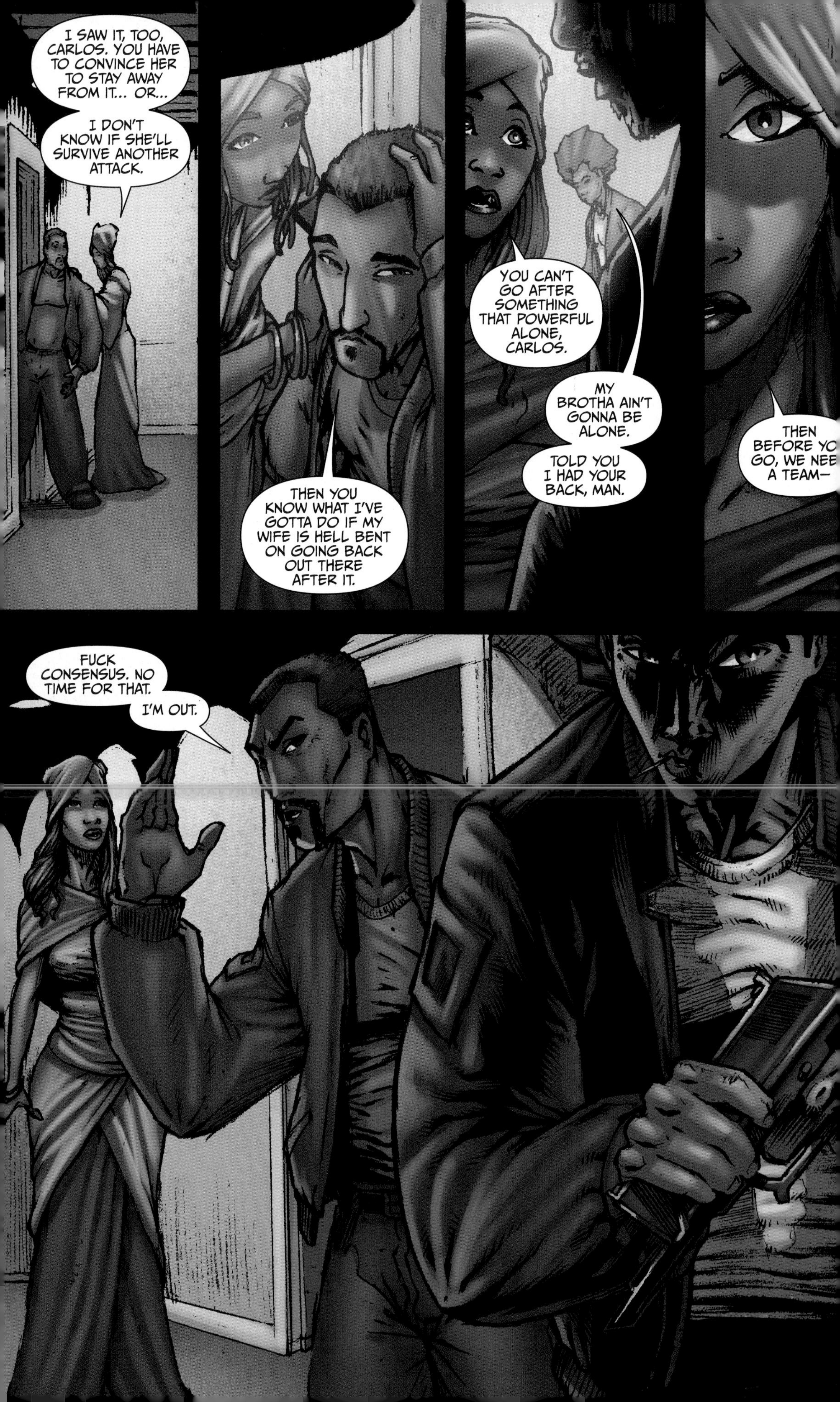

I SAW IT, TOO, CARLOS. YOU HAVE TO CONVINCE HER TO STAY AWAY FROM IT... OR...
I DON'T KNOW IF SHE'LL SURVIVE ANOTHER ATTACK.
THEN YOU KNOW WHAT I'VE GOTTA DO IF MY WIFE IS HELL BENT ON GOING BACK OUT THERE AFTER IT.
YOU CAN'T GO AFTER SOMETHING THAT POWERFUL ALONE, CARLOS.
MY BROTHA AIN'T GONNA BE ALONE.
TOLD YOU I HAD YOUR BACK, MAN.
THEN BEFORE YO GO, WE NEE A TEAM—
FUCK CONSENSUS. NO TIME FOR THAT.
I'M OUT.

BOOK THREE
BYGONES to BLOOD

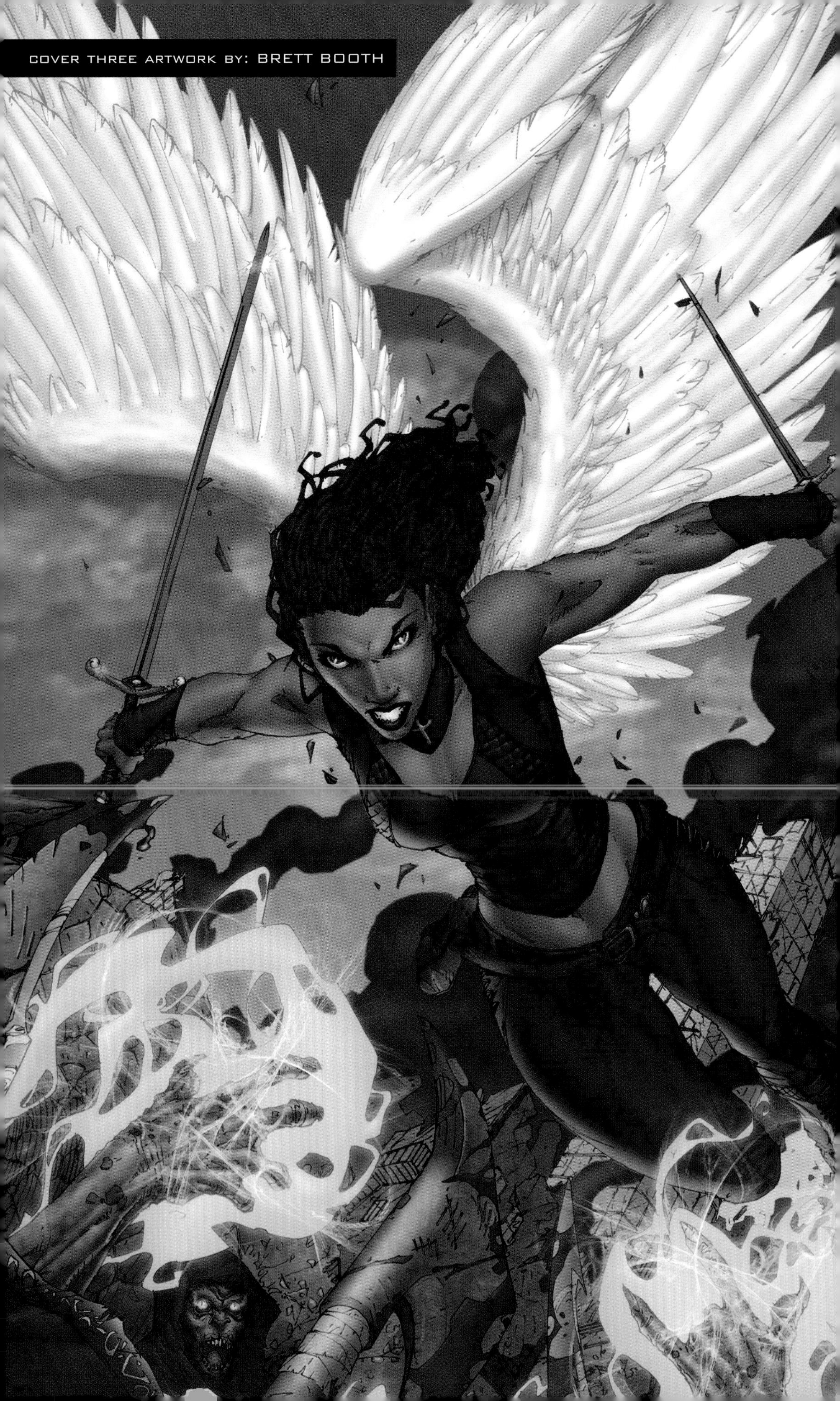

COVER THREE ARTWORK BY: BRETT BOOTH

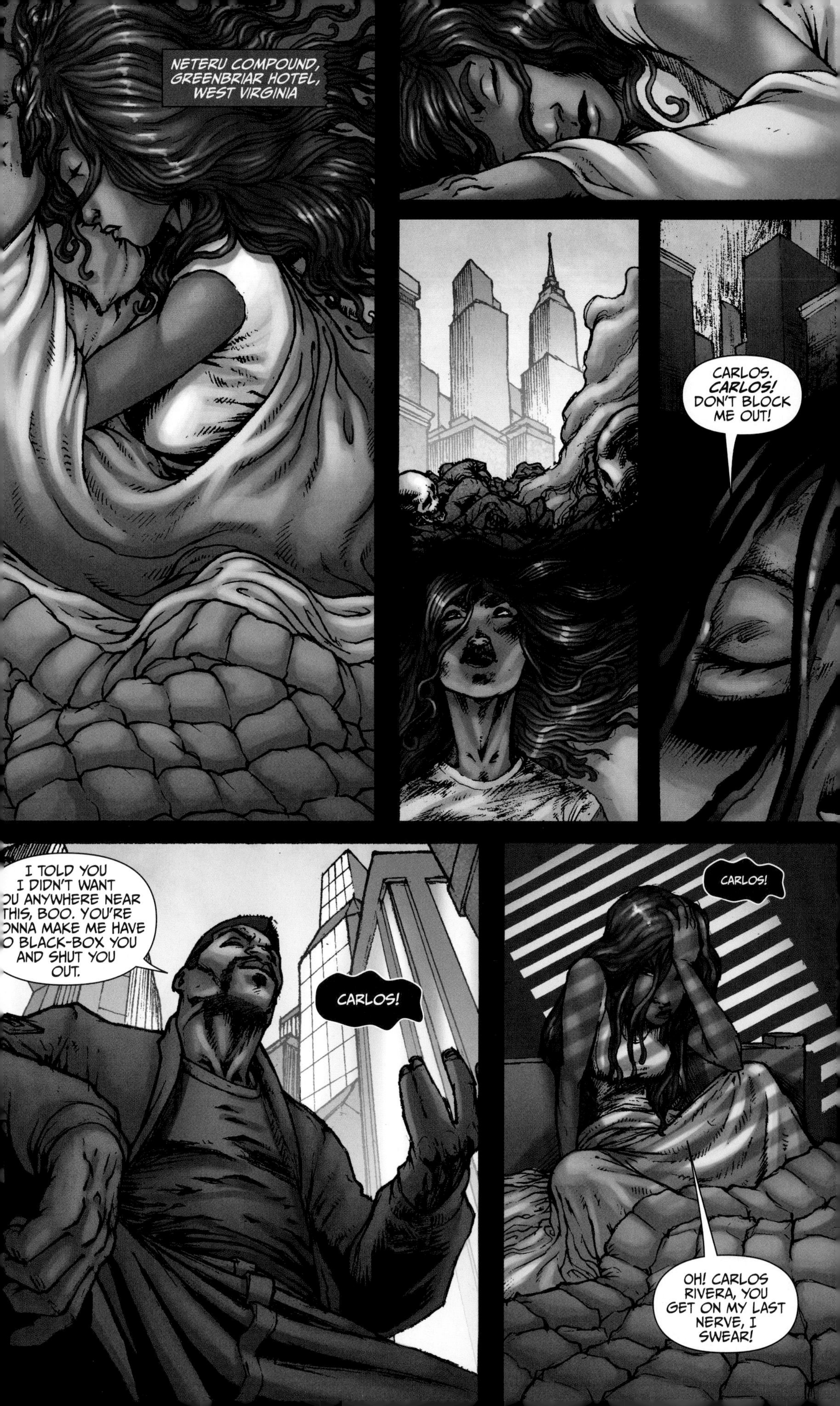
NETERU COMPOUND, GREENBRIAR HOTEL, WEST VIRGINIA
CARLOS. CARLOS! DON'T BLOCK ME OUT!
I TOLD YOU I DIDN'T WANT OU ANYWHERE NEAR THIS, BOO. YOU'RE ONNA MAKE ME HAVE O BLACK-BOX YOU AND SHUT YOU OUT.
CARLOS!
CARLOS!
OH! CARLOS RIVERA, YOU GET ON MY LAST NERVE, I SWEAR!

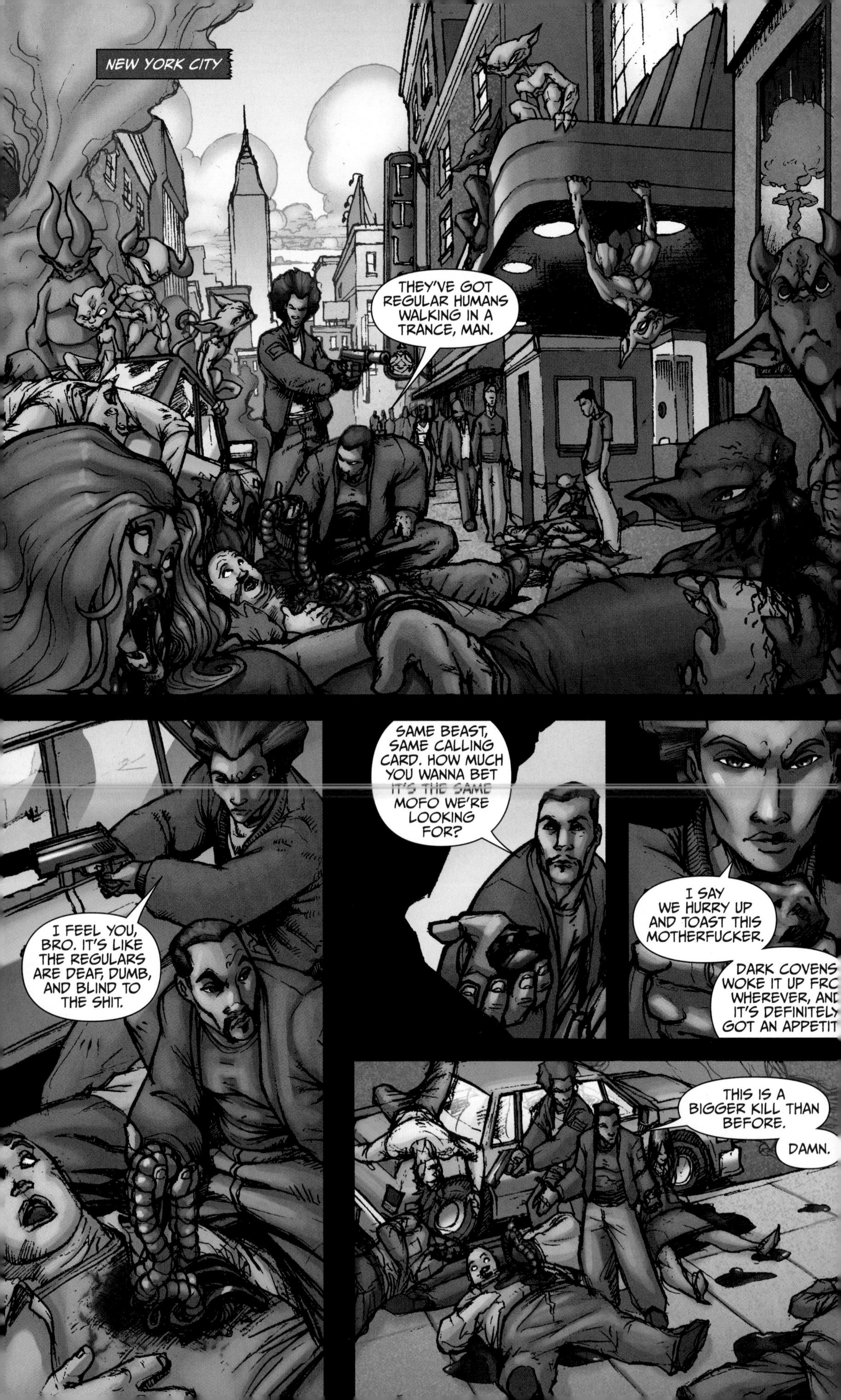

NEW YORK CITY
THEY'VE GOT REGULAR HUMANS WALKING IN A TRANCE, MAN.
I FEEL YOU, BRO. IT'S LIKE THE REGULARS ARE DEAF, DUMB, AND BLIND TO THE SHIT.
SAME BEAST, SAME CALLING CARD. HOW MUCH YOU WANNA BET IT'S THE SAME MOFO WE'RE LOOKING FOR?
I SAY WE HURRY UP AND TOAST THIS MOTHERFUCKER.
DARK COVENS WOKE IT UP FRC WHEREVER, ANC IT'S DEFINITELY GOT AN APPETIT
THIS IS A BIGGER KILL THAN BEFORE.
DAMN.

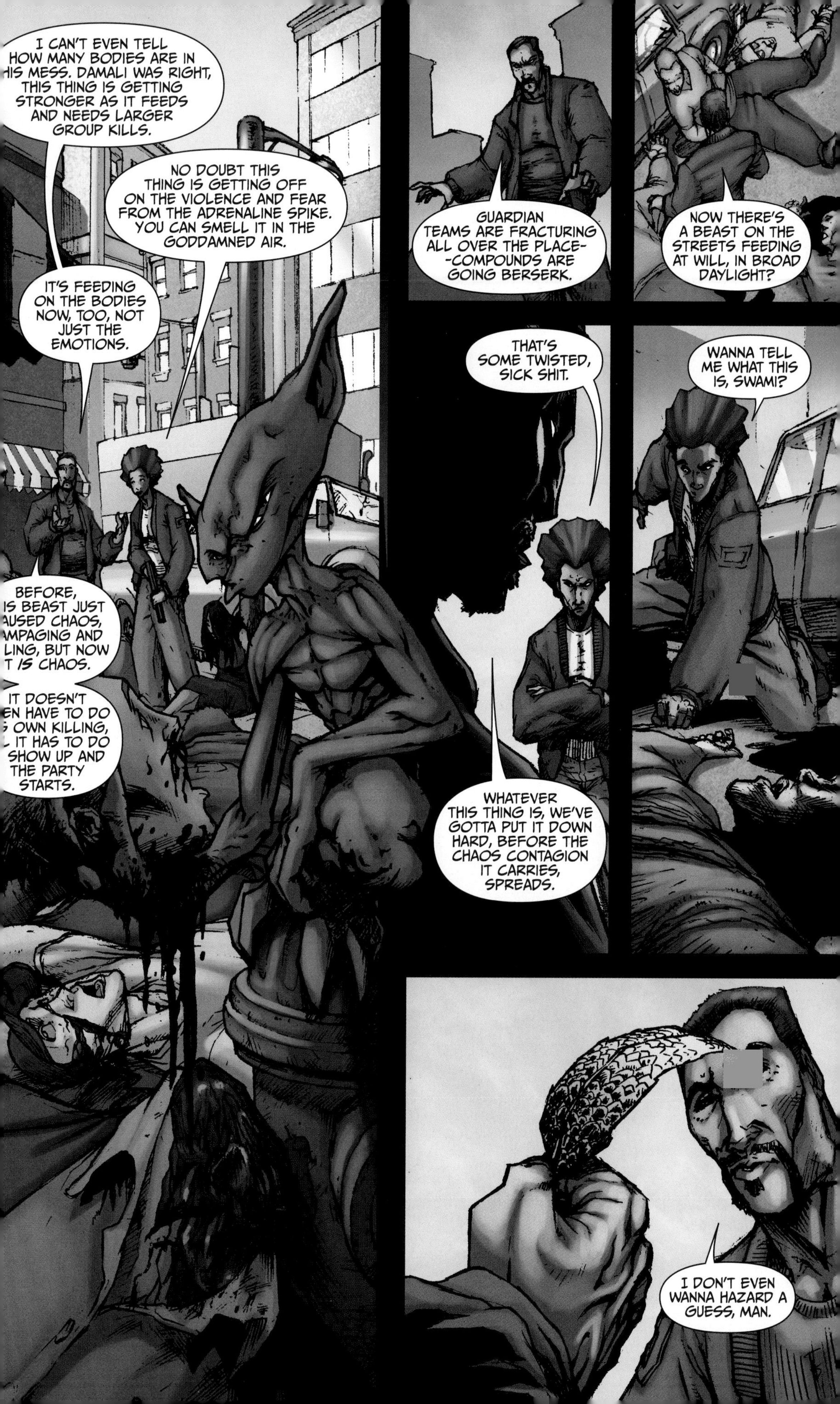
I CAN'T EVEN TELL HOW MANY BODIES ARE IN IS MESS. DAMALI WAS RIGHT, THIS THING IS GETTING STRONGER AS IT FEEDS AND NEEDS LARGER GROUP KILLS.
NO DOUBT THIS THING IS GETTING OFF ON THE VIOLENCE AND FEAR FROM THE ADRENALINE SPIKE. YOU CAN SMELL IT IN THE GODDAMNED AIR.
IT'S FEEDING ON THE BODIES NOW, TOO, NOT JUST THE EMOTIONS.
BEFORE, IS BEAST JUST AUSED CHAOS, AMPAGING AND LING, BUT NOW T *IS* CHAOS.
IT DOESN'T EN HAVE TO DO OWN KILLING, IT HAS TO DO SHOW UP AND THE PARTY STARTS.
GUARDIAN TEAMS ARE FRACTURING ALL OVER THE PLACE- -COMPOUNDS ARE GOING BERSERK.
NOW THERE'S A BEAST ON THE STREETS FEEDING AT WILL, IN BROAD DAYLIGHT?
THAT'S SOME TWISTED, SICK SHIT.
WANNA TELL ME WHAT THIS IS, SWAMI?
WHATEVER THIS THING IS, WE'VE GOTTA PUT IT DOWN HARD, BEFORE THE CHAOS CONTAGION IT CARRIES, SPREADS.
I DON'T EVEN WANNA HAZARD A GUESS, MAN.

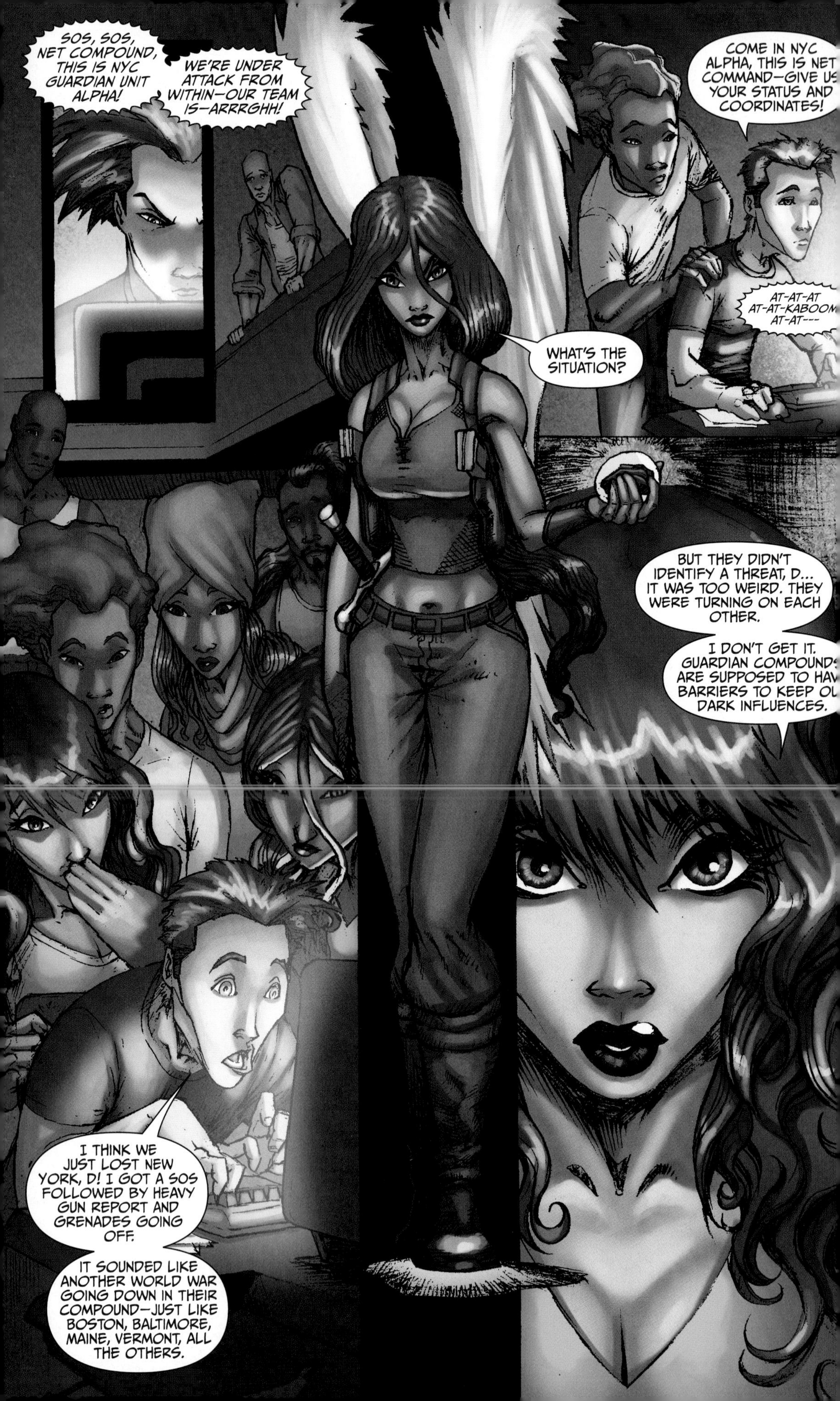
SOS, SOS, NET COMPOUND, THIS IS NYC GUARDIAN UNIT ALPHA!
WE'RE UNDER ATTACK FROM WITHIN—OUR TEAM IS—ARRRGHH!
COME IN NYC ALPHA, THIS IS NET COMMAND—GIVE US YOUR STATUS AND COORDINATES!
AT-AT-AT AT-AT-KABOOM AT-AT---
WHAT'S THE SITUATION?
I THINK WE JUST LOST NEW YORK, D! I GOT A SOS FOLLOWED BY HEAVY GUN REPORT AND GRENADES GOING OFF.
IT SOUNDED LIKE ANOTHER WORLD WAR GOING DOWN IN THEIR COMPOUND—JUST LIKE BOSTON, BALTIMORE, MAINE, VERMONT, ALL THE OTHERS.
BUT THEY DIDN'T IDENTIFY A THREAT, D... IT WAS TOO WEIRD. THEY WERE TURNING ON EACH OTHER.
I DON'T GET IT. GUARDIAN COMPOUNDS ARE SUPPOSED TO HAVE BARRIERS TO KEEP OUT DARK INFLUENCES.

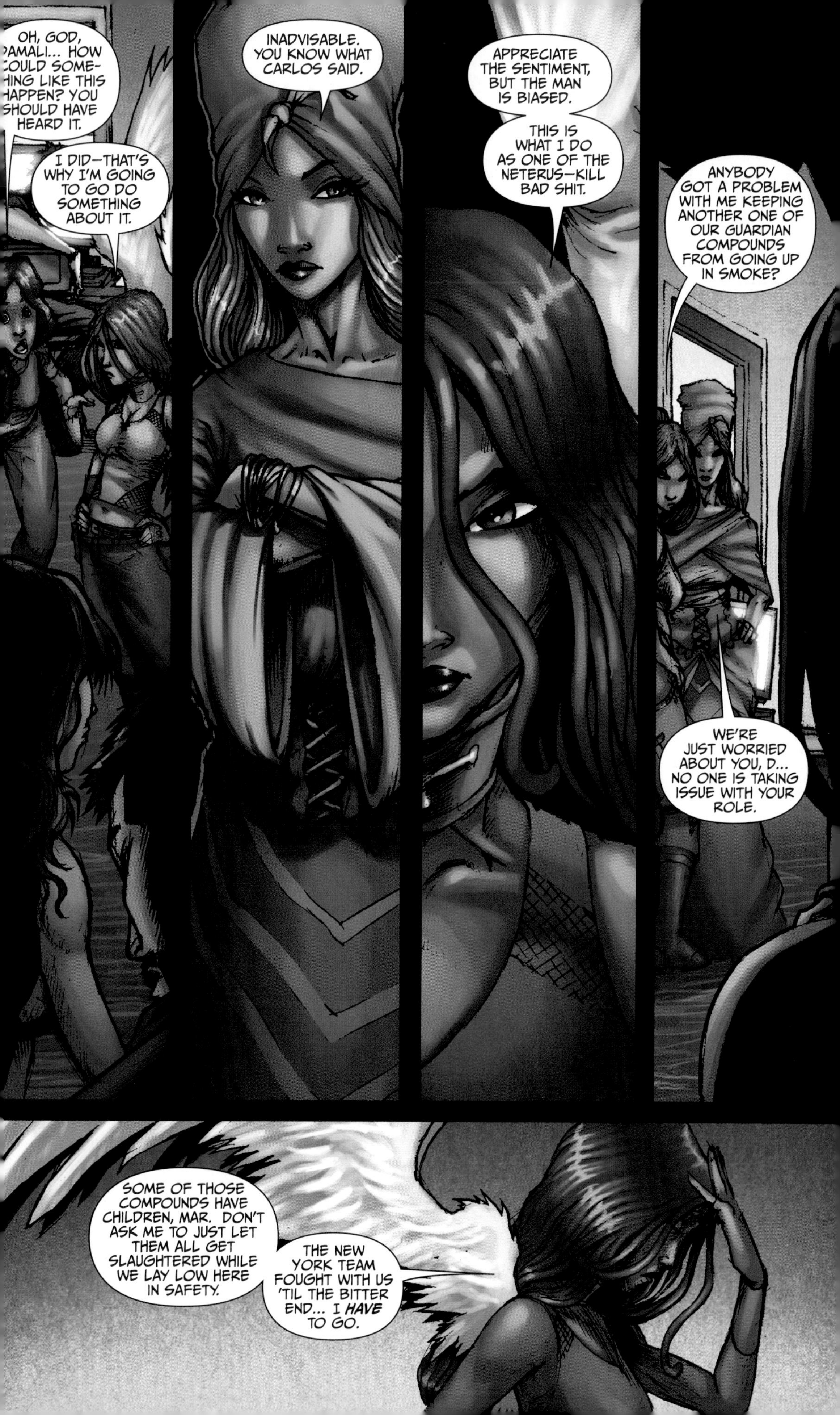
OH, GOD, DAMALI... HOW COULD SOMETHING LIKE THIS HAPPEN? YOU SHOULD HAVE HEARD IT.
I DID—THAT'S WHY I'M GOING TO GO DO SOMETHING ABOUT IT.
INADVISABLE. YOU KNOW WHAT CARLOS SAID.
APPRECIATE THE SENTIMENT, BUT THE MAN IS BIASED.
THIS IS WHAT I DO AS ONE OF THE NETERUS—KILL BAD SHIT.
ANYBODY GOT A PROBLEM WITH ME KEEPING ANOTHER ONE OF OUR GUARDIAN COMPOUNDS FROM GOING UP IN SMOKE?
WE'RE JUST WORRIED ABOUT YOU, D... NO ONE IS TAKING ISSUE WITH YOUR ROLE.
SOME OF THOSE COMPOUNDS HAVE CHILDREN, MAR. DON'T ASK ME TO JUST LET THEM ALL GET SLAUGHTERED WHILE WE LAY LOW HERE IN SAFETY.
THE NEW YORK TEAM FOUGHT WITH US 'TIL THE BITTER END... I *HAVE* TO GO.

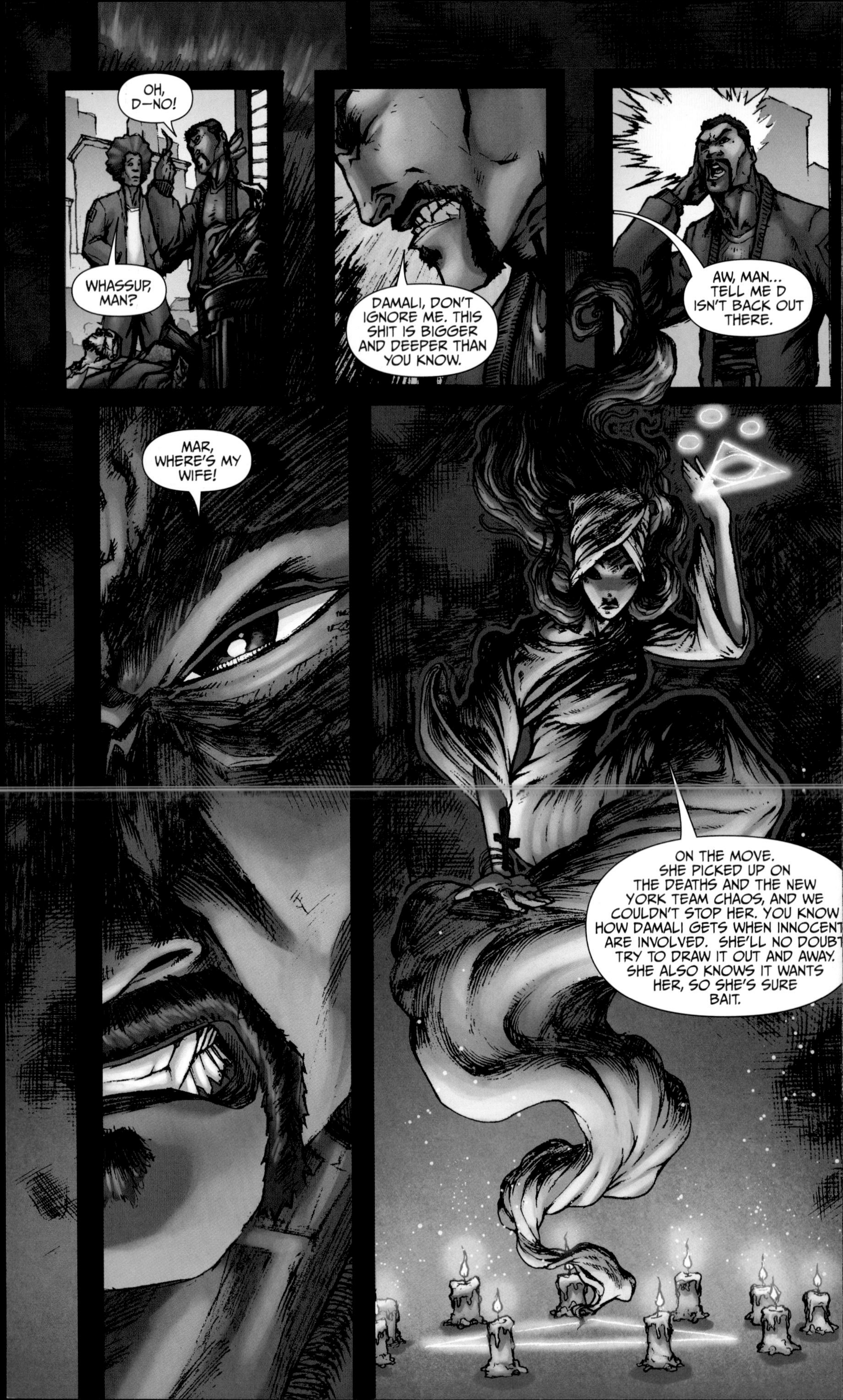
OH, D—NO!
WHASSUP, MAN?
DAMALI, DON'T IGNORE ME. THIS SHIT IS BIGGER AND DEEPER THAN YOU KNOW.
AW, MAN... TELL ME D ISN'T BACK OUT THERE.
MAR, WHERE'S MY WIFE!
ON THE MOVE. SHE PICKED UP ON THE DEATHS AND THE NEW YORK TEAM CHAOS, AND WE COULDN'T STOP HER. YOU KNOW HOW DAMALI GETS WHEN INNOCENTS ARE INVOLVED. SHE'LL NO DOUBT TRY TO DRAW IT OUT AND AWAY. SHE ALSO KNOWS IT WANTS HER, SO SHE'S SURE BAIT.

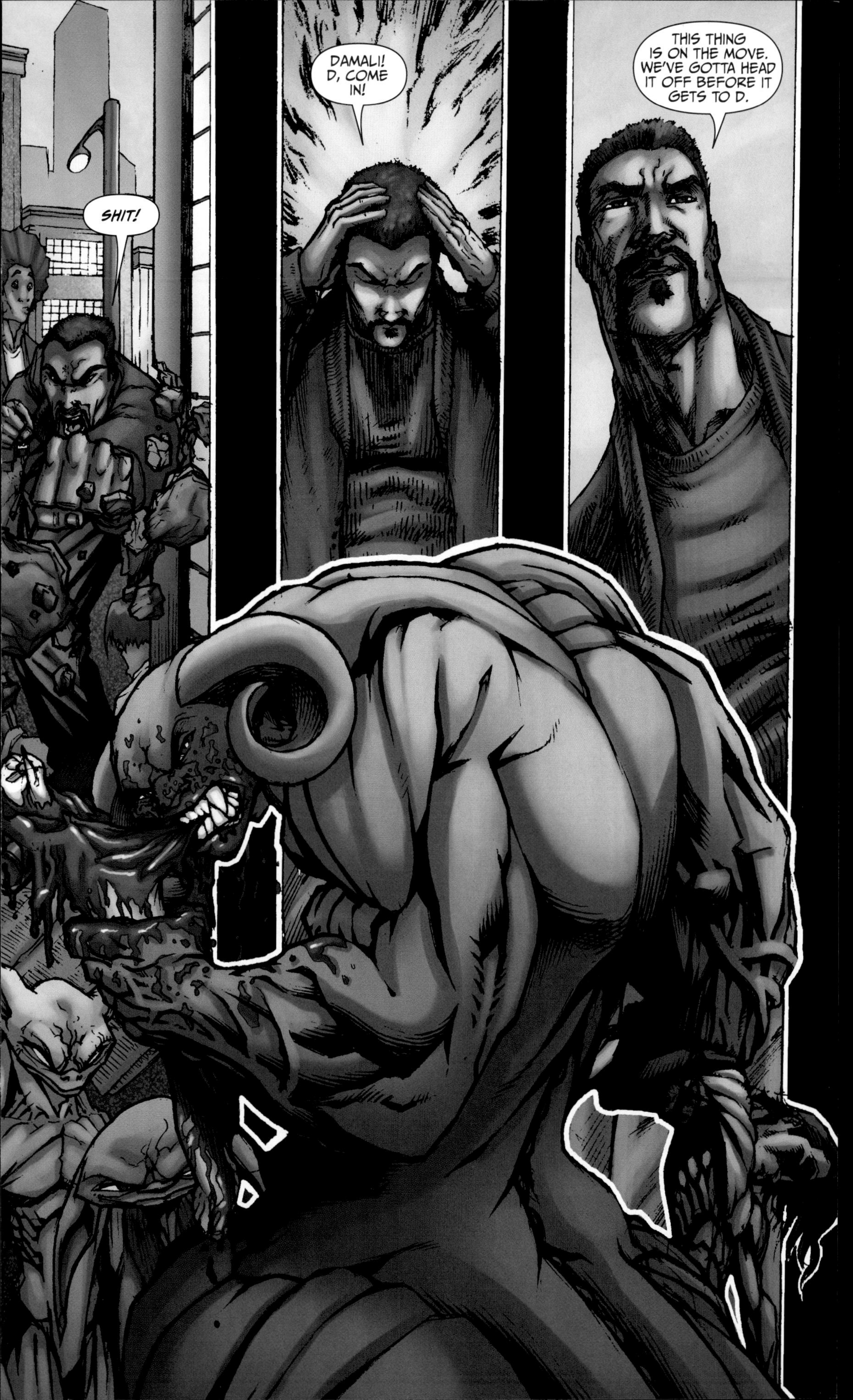
SHIT!
DAMALI! D, COME IN!
THIS THING IS ON THE MOVE. WE'VE GOTTA HEAD IT OFF BEFORE IT GETS TO D.

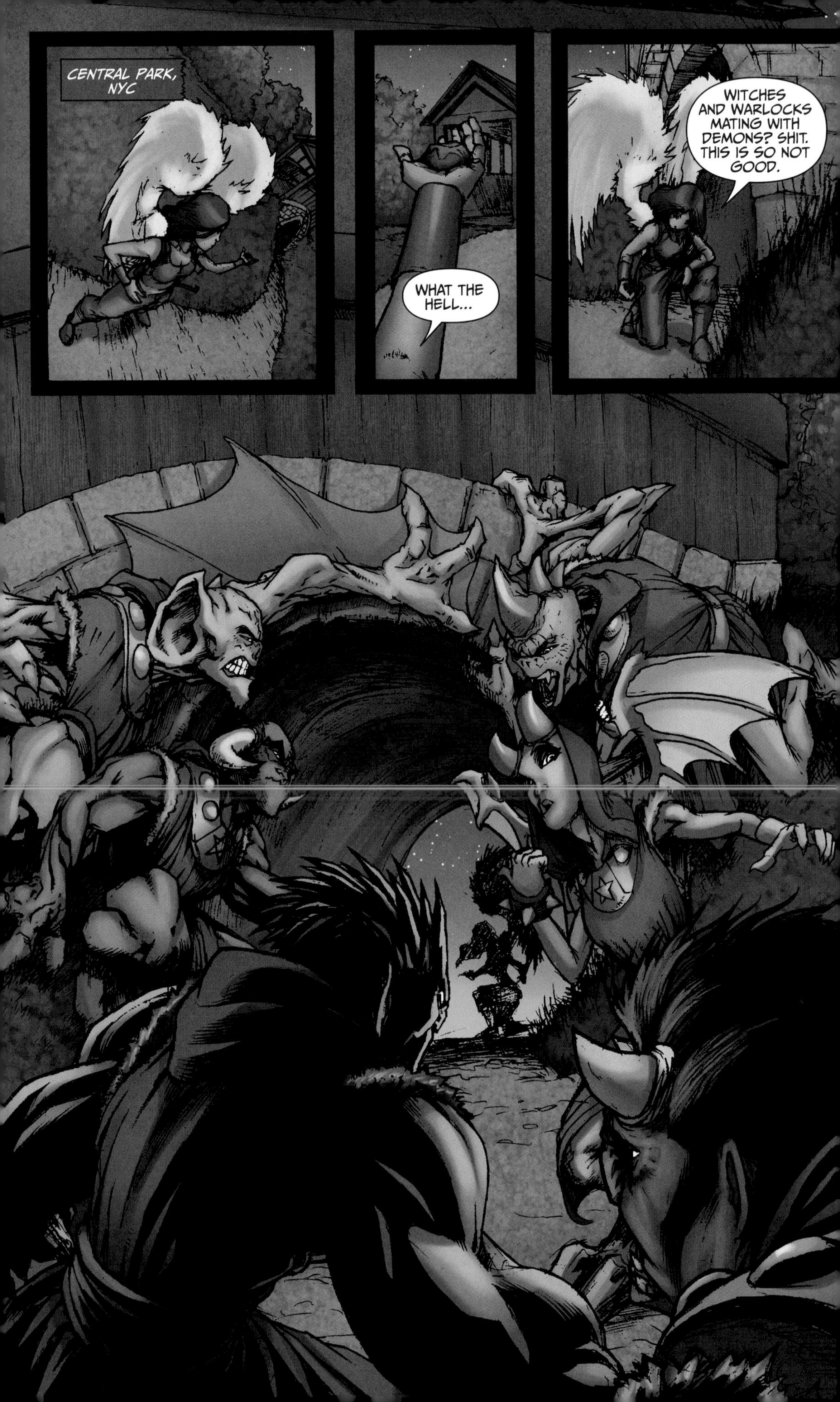

CENTRAL PARK, NYC
WHAT THE HELL...
WITCHES AND WARLOCKS MATING WITH DEMONS? SHIT. THIS IS SO NOT GOOD.

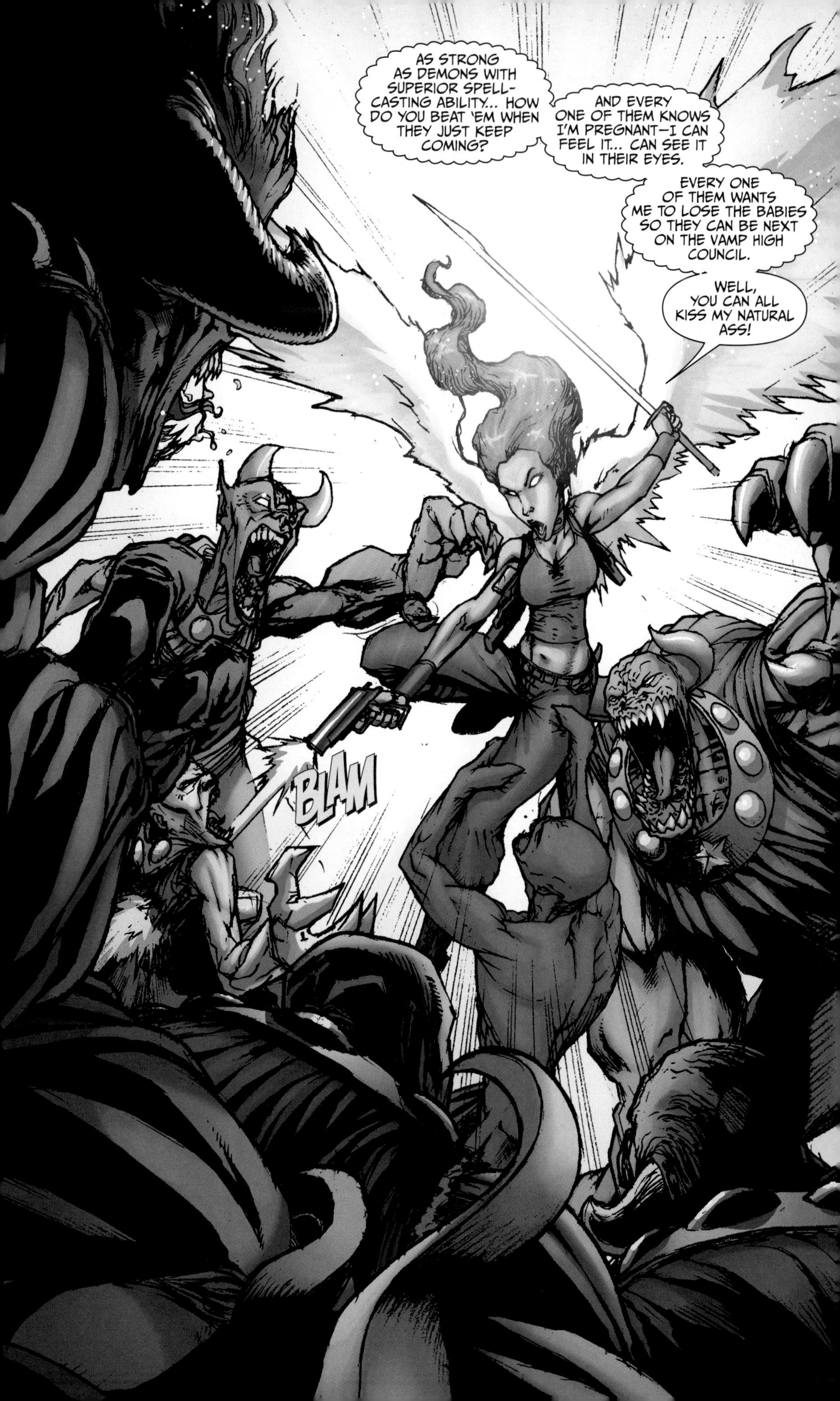
AS STRONG AS DEMONS WITH SUPERIOR SPELL-CASTING ABILITY... HOW DO YOU BEAT 'EM WHEN THEY JUST KEEP COMING?
AND EVERY ONE OF THEM KNOWS I'M PREGNANT—I CAN FEEL IT... CAN SEE IT IN THEIR EYES.
EVERY ONE OF THEM WANTS ME TO LOSE THE BABIES SO THEY CAN BE NEXT ON THE VAMP HIGH COUNCIL.
WELL, YOU CAN ALL KISS MY NATURAL ASS!
BLAM

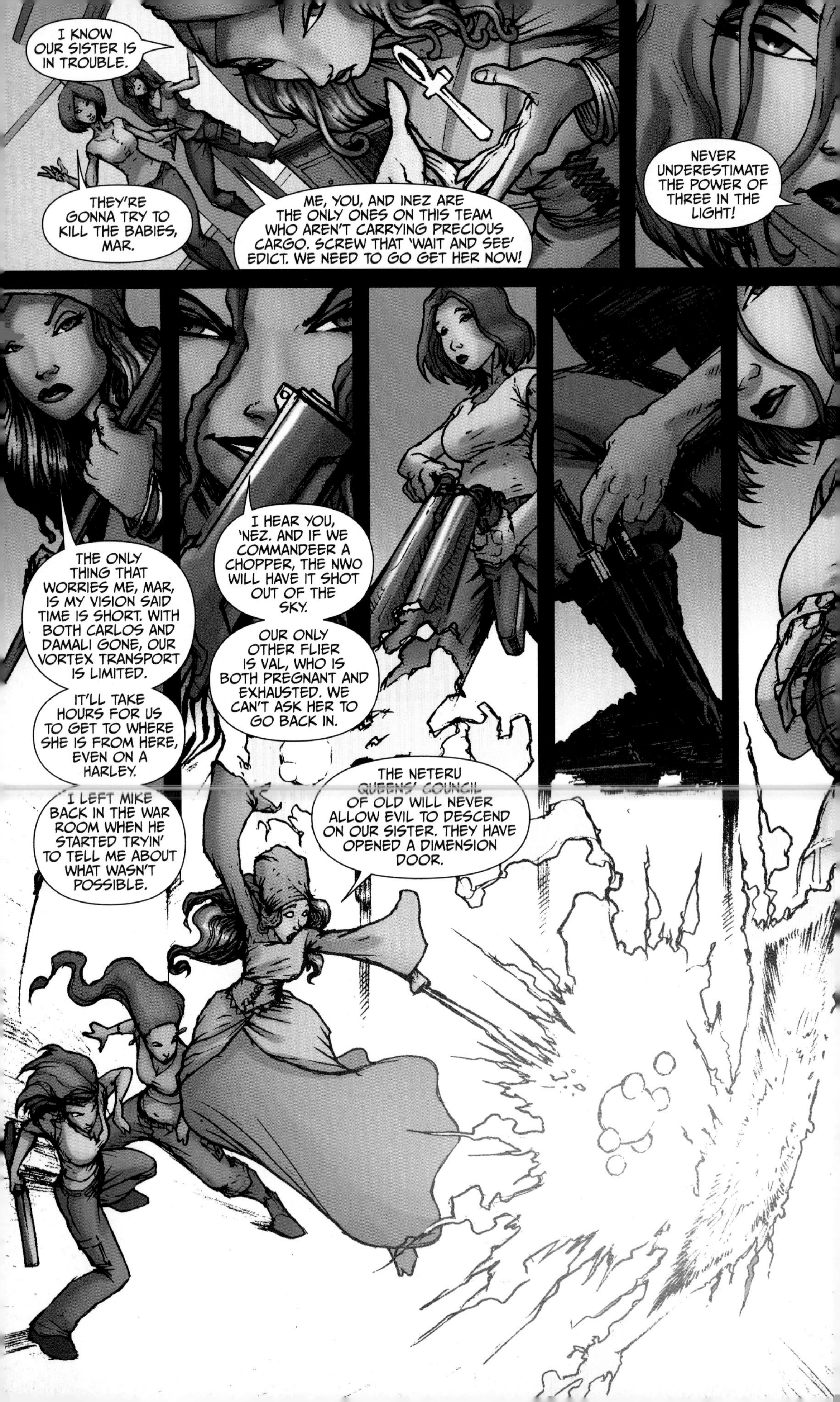
I KNOW OUR SISTER IS IN TROUBLE.
THEY'RE GONNA TRY TO KILL THE BABIES, MAR.
ME, YOU, AND INEZ ARE THE ONLY ONES ON THIS TEAM WHO AREN'T CARRYING PRECIOUS CARGO. SCREW THAT 'WAIT AND SEE' EDICT. WE NEED TO GO GET HER NOW!
NEVER UNDERESTIMATE THE POWER OF THREE IN THE LIGHT!
THE ONLY THING THAT WORRIES ME, MAR, IS MY VISION SAID TIME IS SHORT. WITH BOTH CARLOS AND DAMALI GONE, OUR VORTEX TRANSPORT IS LIMITED.
IT'LL TAKE HOURS FOR US TO GET TO WHERE SHE IS FROM HERE, EVEN ON A HARLEY.
I HEAR YOU, 'NEZ. AND IF WE COMMANDEER A CHOPPER, THE NWO WILL HAVE IT SHOT OUT OF THE SKY.
OUR ONLY OTHER FLIER IS VAL, WHO IS BOTH PREGNANT AND EXHAUSTED. WE CAN'T ASK HER TO GO BACK IN.
I LEFT MIKE BACK IN THE WAR ROOM WHEN HE STARTED TRYIN' TO TELL ME ABOUT WHAT WASN'T POSSIBLE.
THE NETERU QUEENS' COUNCIL OF OLD WILL NEVER ALLOW EVIL TO DESCEND ON OUR SISTER. THEY HAVE OPENED A DIMENSION DOOR.

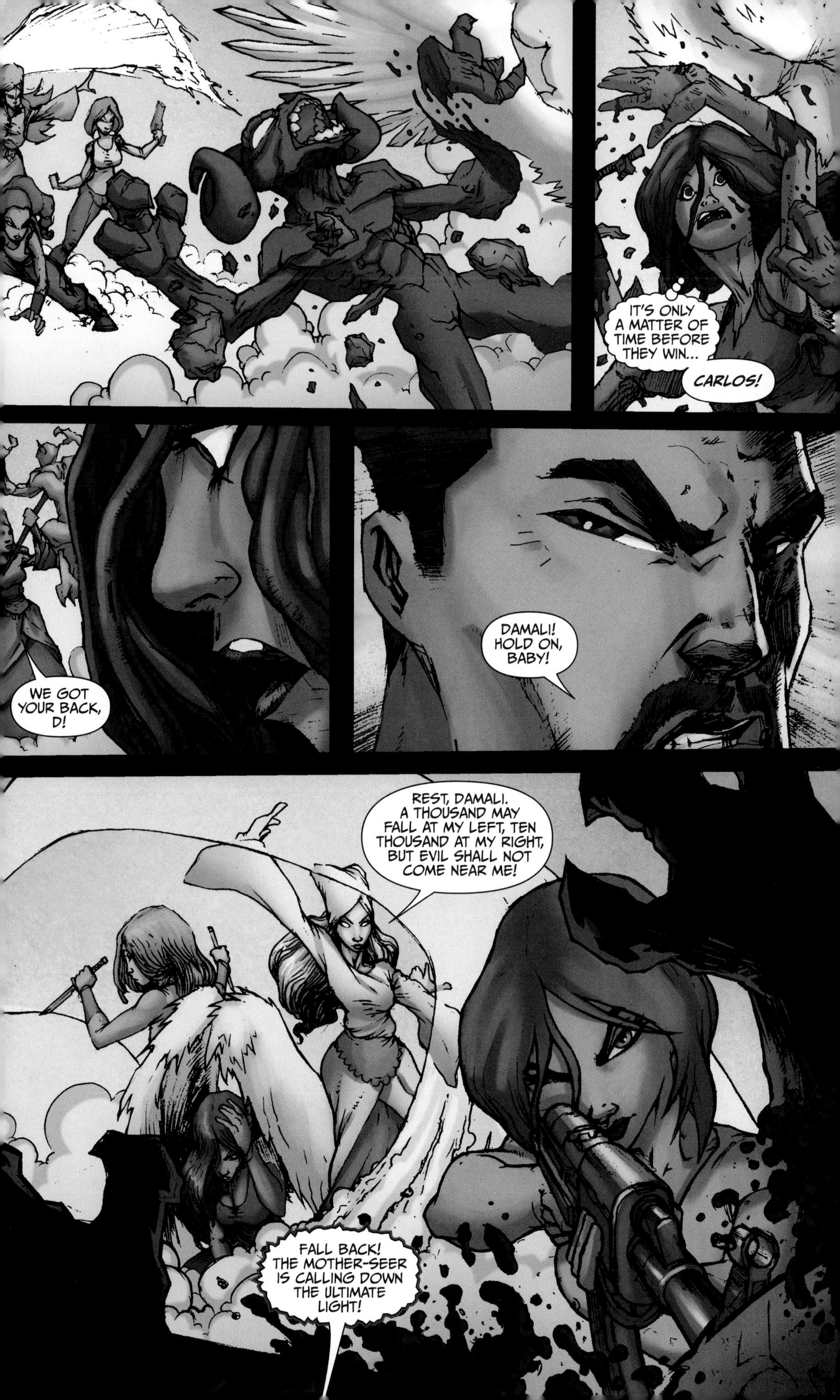
IT'S ONLY A MATTER OF TIME BEFORE THEY WIN...
CARLOS!
WE GOT YOUR BACK, D!
DAMALI! HOLD ON, BABY!
REST, DAMALI. A THOUSAND MAY FALL AT MY LEFT, TEN THOUSAND AT MY RIGHT, BUT EVIL SHALL NOT COME NEAR ME!
FALL BACK! THE MOTHER-SEER IS CALLING DOWN THE ULTIMATE LIGHT!

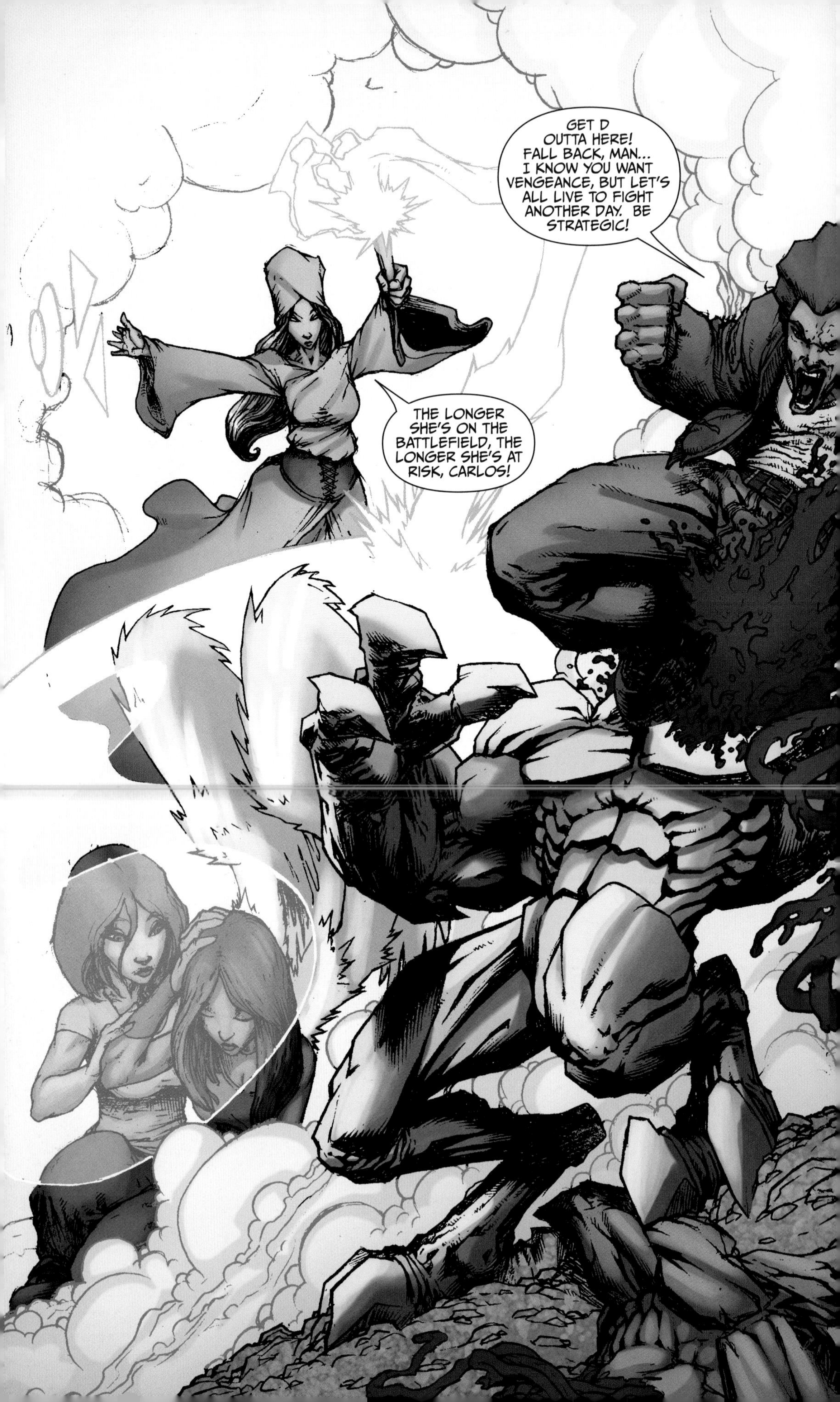
GET D OUTTA HERE! FALL BACK, MAN... I KNOW YOU WANT VENGEANCE, BUT LET'S ALL LIVE TO FIGHT ANOTHER DAY. BE STRATEGIC!
THE LONGER SHE'S ON THE BATTLEFIELD, THE LONGER SHE'S AT RISK, CARLOS!

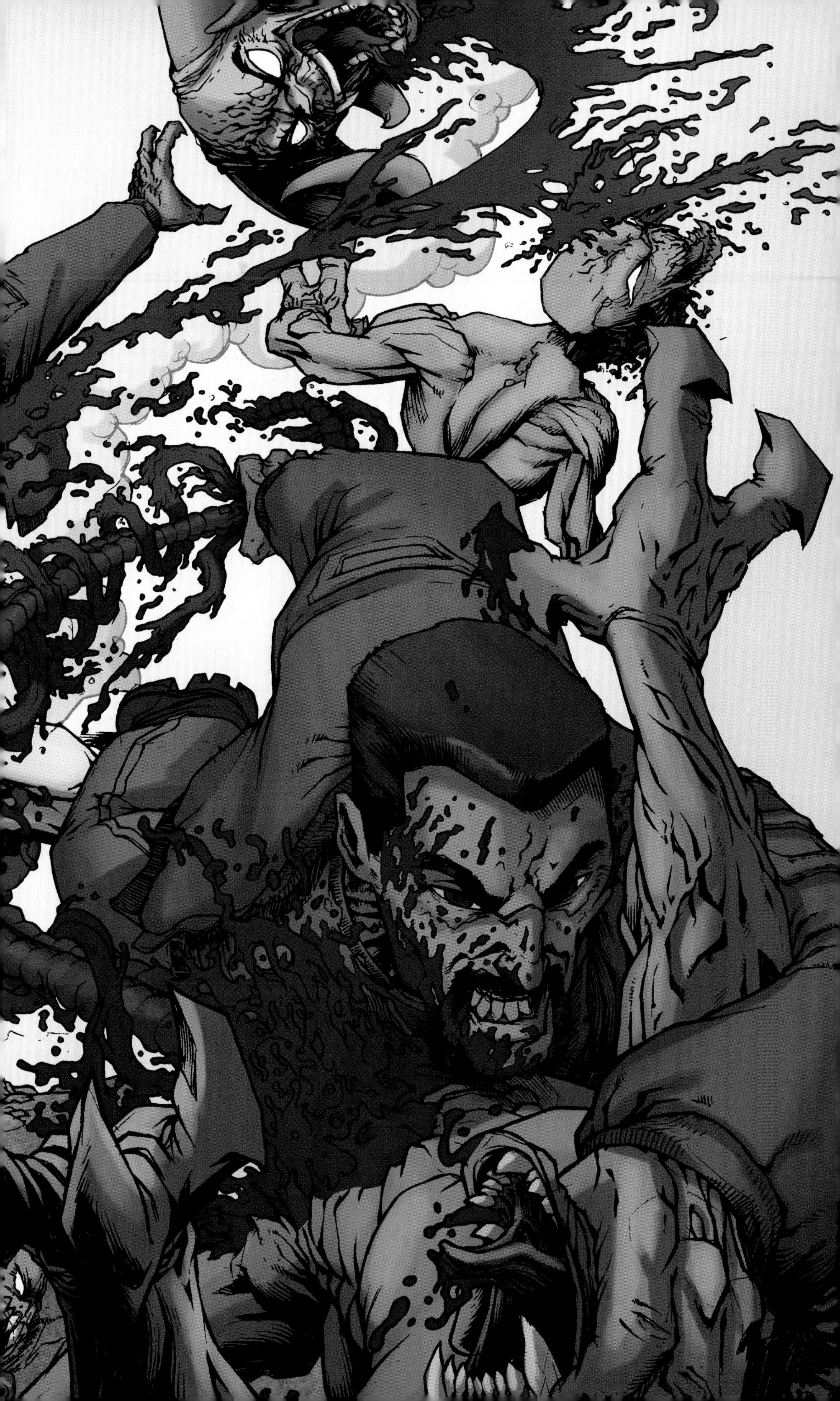

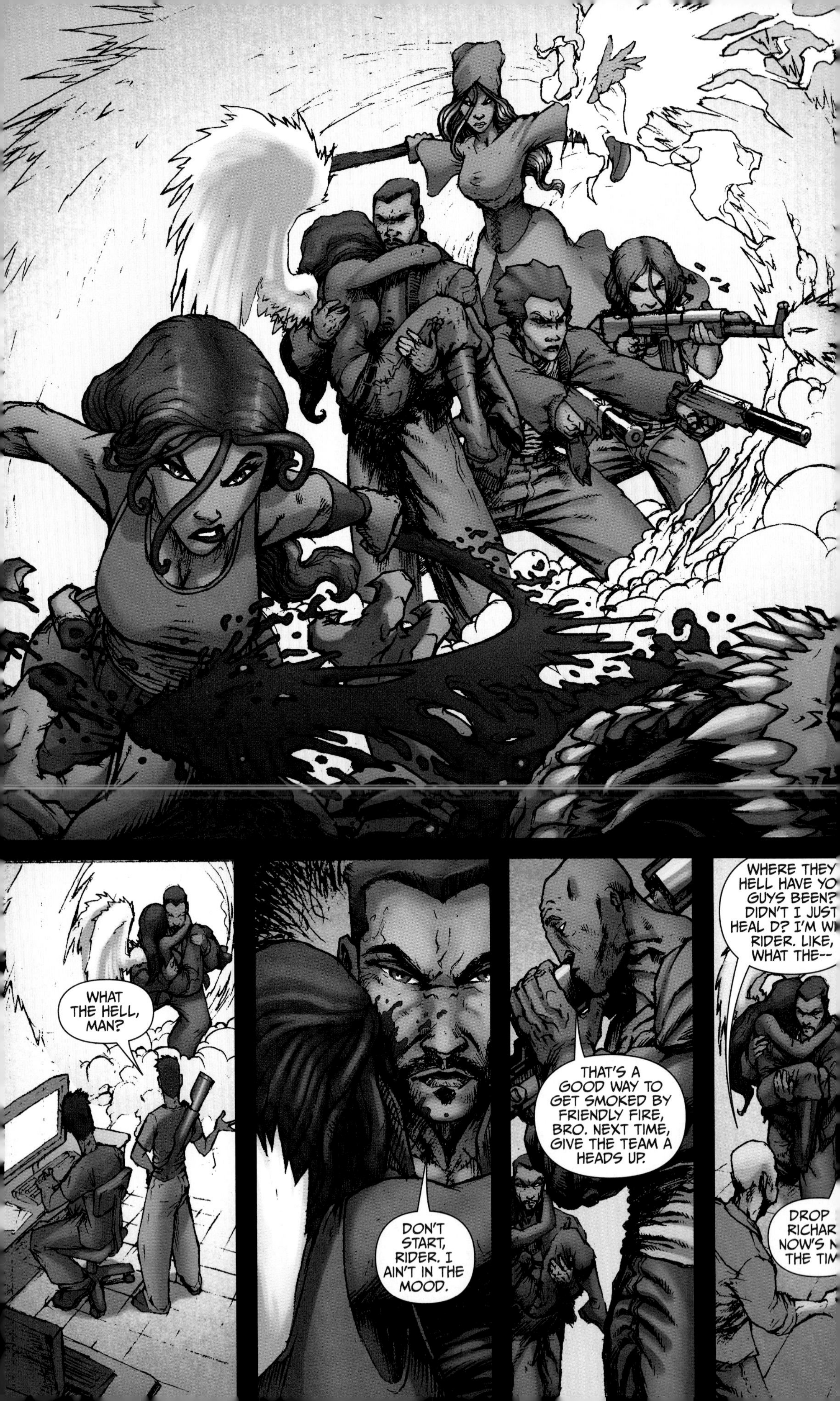
WHAT THE HELL, MAN?
DON'T START, RIDER. I AIN'T IN THE MOOD.
THAT'S A GOOD WAY TO GET SMOKED BY FRIENDLY FIRE, BRO. NEXT TIME, GIVE THE TEAM A HEADS UP.
WHERE THE HELL HAVE YO GUYS BEEN? DIDN'T I JUST HEAL D? I'M W RIDER. LIKE, WHAT THE--
DROP RICHAR NOW'S THE TIM

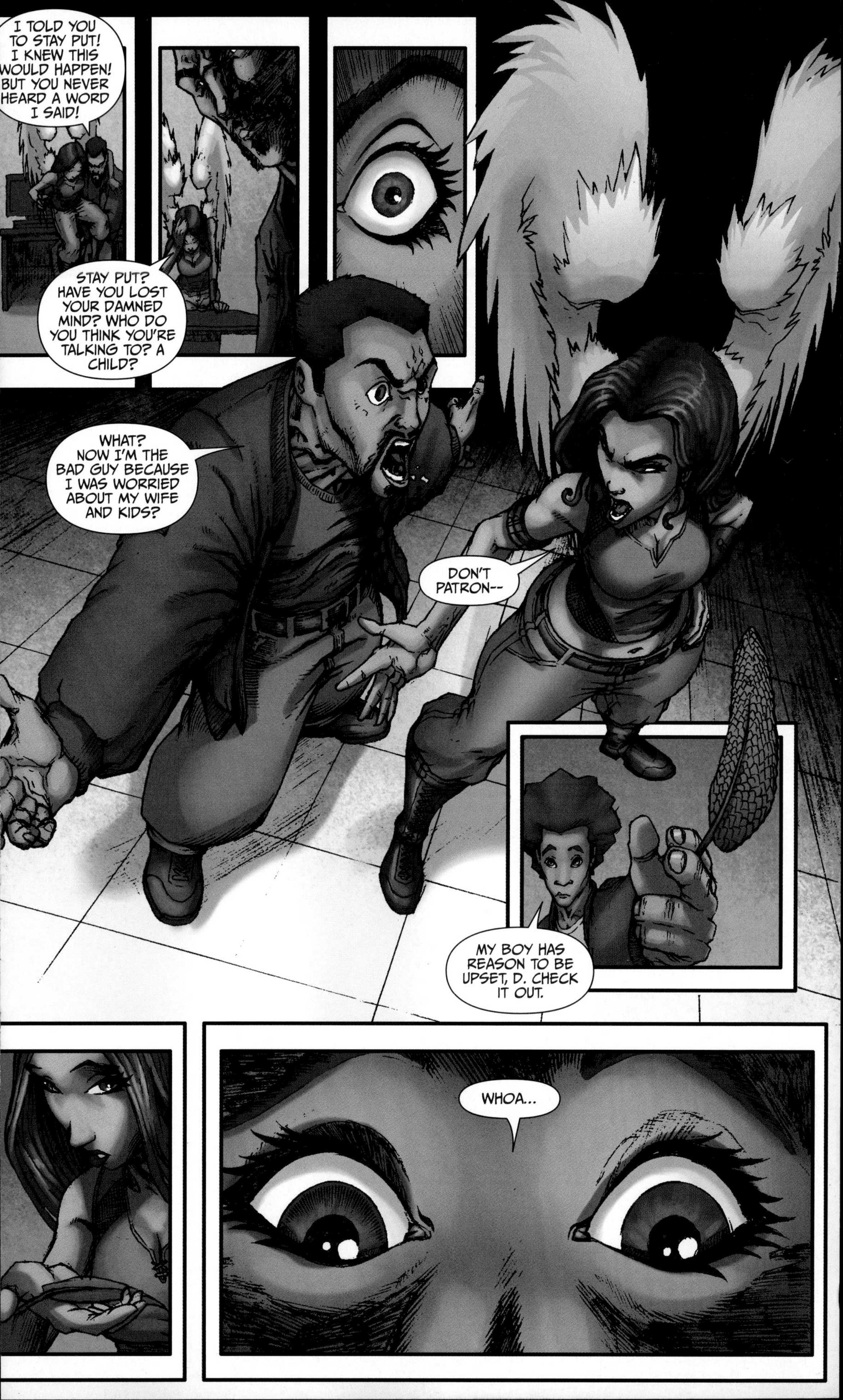
I TOLD YOU TO STAY PUT! I KNEW THIS WOULD HAPPEN! BUT YOU NEVER HEARD A WORD I SAID!
STAY PUT? HAVE YOU LOST YOUR DAMNED MIND? WHO DO YOU THINK YOU'RE TALKING TO? A CHILD?
WHAT? NOW I'M THE BAD GUY BECAUSE I WAS WORRIED ABOUT MY WIFE AND KIDS?
DON'T PATRON--
MY BOY HAS REASON TO BE UPSET, D. CHECK IT OUT.
WHOA...

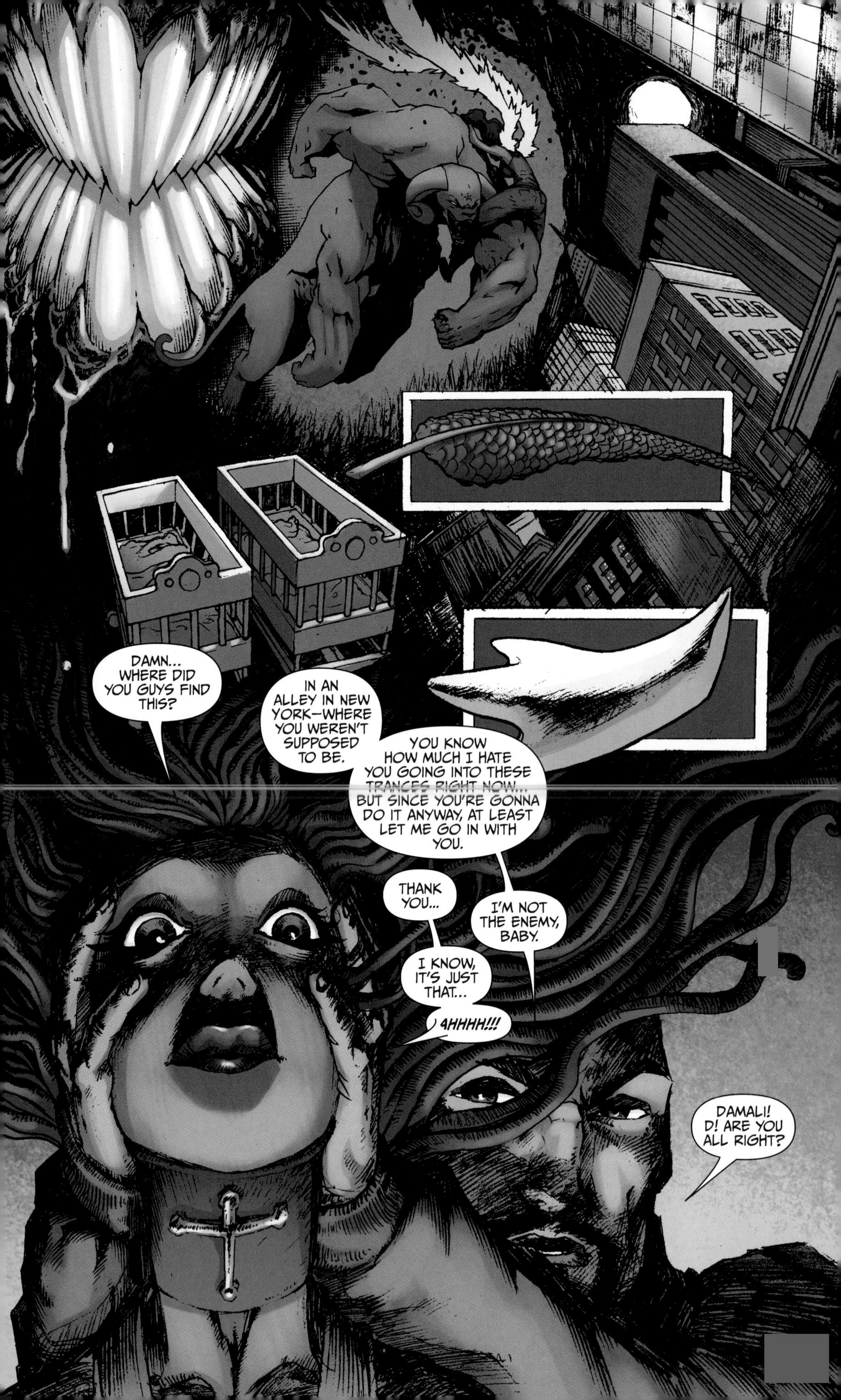
DAMN... WHERE DID YOU GUYS FIND THIS?
IN AN ALLEY IN NEW YORK—WHERE YOU WEREN'T SUPPOSED TO BE.
YOU KNOW HOW MUCH I HATE YOU GOING INTO THESE TRANCES RIGHT NOW... BUT SINCE YOU'RE GONNA DO IT ANYWAY, AT LEAST LET ME GO IN WITH YOU.
THANK YOU...
I'M NOT THE ENEMY, BABY.
I KNOW, IT'S JUST THAT...
AHHHH!!!
DAMALI! D! ARE YOU ALL RIGHT?

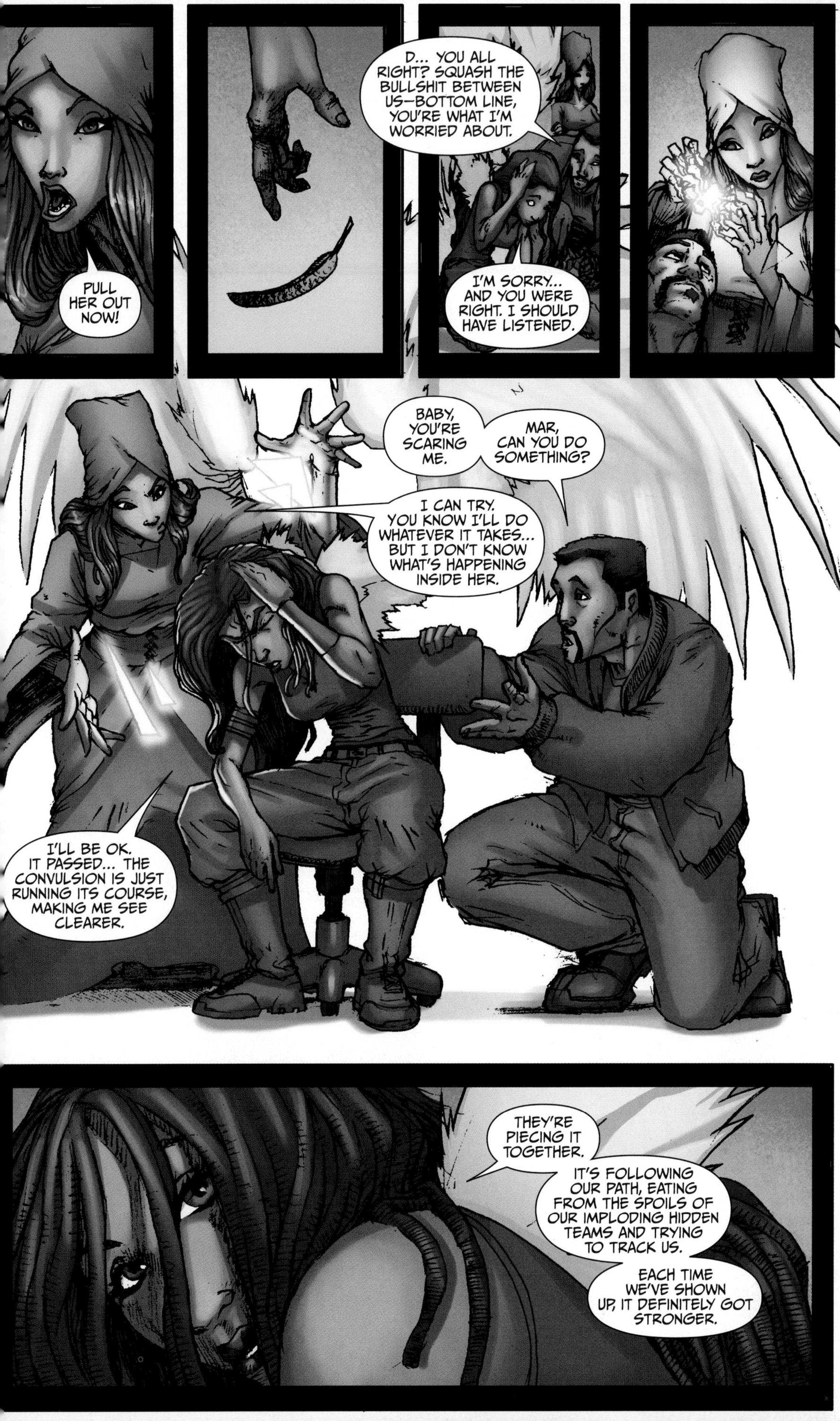

PULL HER OUT NOW!
D... YOU ALL RIGHT? SQUASH THE BULLSHIT BETWEEN US—BOTTOM LINE, YOU'RE WHAT I'M WORRIED ABOUT.
I'M SORRY... AND YOU WERE RIGHT. I SHOULD HAVE LISTENED.
BABY, YOU'RE SCARING ME.
MAR, CAN YOU DO SOMETHING?
I CAN TRY. YOU KNOW I'LL DO WHATEVER IT TAKES... BUT I DON'T KNOW WHAT'S HAPPENING INSIDE HER.
I'LL BE OK. IT PASSED... THE CONVULSION IS JUST RUNNING ITS COURSE, MAKING ME SEE CLEARER.
THEY'RE PIECING IT TOGETHER.
IT'S FOLLOWING OUR PATH, EATING FROM THE SPOILS OF OUR IMPLODING HIDDEN TEAMS AND TRYING TO TRACK US.
EACH TIME WE'VE SHOWN UP, IT DEFINITELY GOT STRONGER.

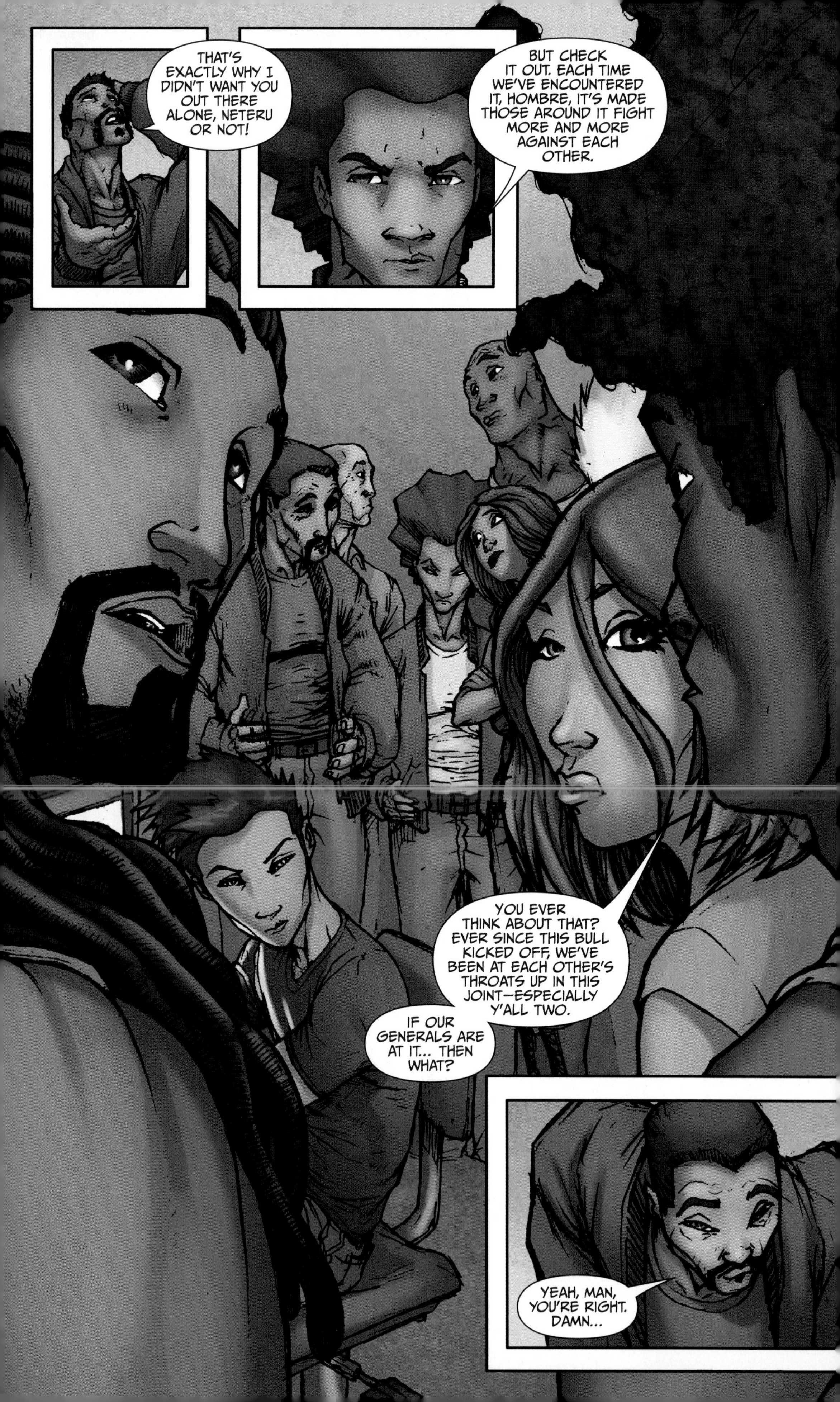
THAT'S EXACTLY WHY I DIDN'T WANT YOU OUT THERE ALONE, NETERU OR NOT!
BUT CHECK IT OUT. EACH TIME WE'VE ENCOUNTERED IT, HOMBRE, IT'S MADE THOSE AROUND IT FIGHT MORE AND MORE AGAINST EACH OTHER.
YOU EVER THINK ABOUT THAT? EVER SINCE THIS BULL KICKED OFF, WE'VE BEEN AT EACH OTHER'S THROATS UP IN THIS JOINT—ESPECIALLY Y'ALL TWO.
IF OUR GENERALS ARE AT IT... THEN WHAT?
YEAH, MAN, YOU'RE RIGHT. DAMN...

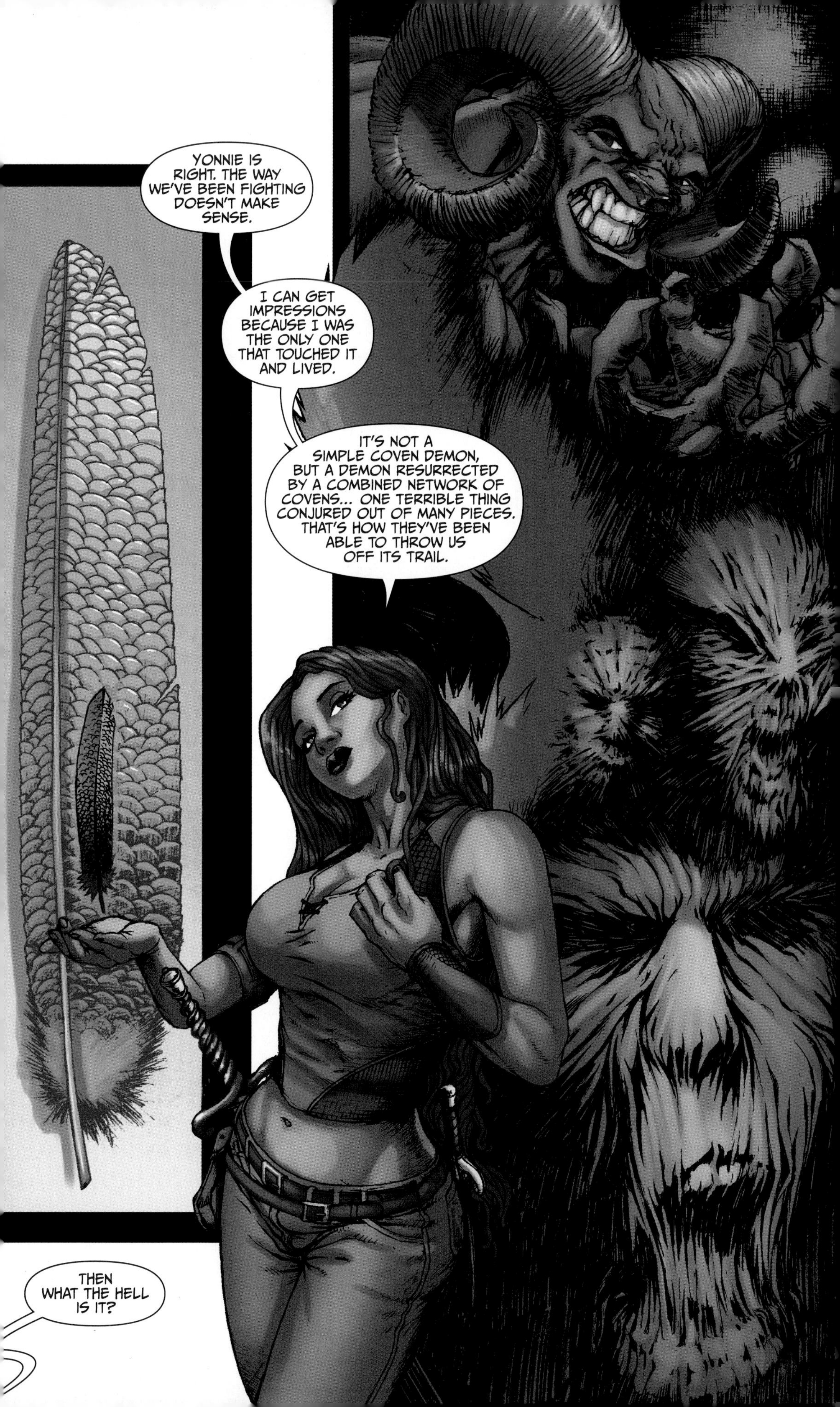
YONNIE IS RIGHT. THE WAY WE'VE BEEN FIGHTING DOESN'T MAKE SENSE.
I CAN GET IMPRESSIONS BECAUSE I WAS THE ONLY ONE THAT TOUCHED IT AND LIVED.
IT'S NOT A SIMPLE COVEN DEMON, BUT A DEMON RESURRECTED BY A COMBINED NETWORK OF COVENS... ONE TERRIBLE THING CONJURED OUT OF MANY PIECES. THAT'S HOW THEY'VE BEEN ABLE TO THROW US OFF ITS TRAIL.
THEN WHAT THE HELL IS IT?

IN HELL – THE LAIR OF THE ANCIENT VAMPIRE COUNCIL

CARLOS RIVERA, YOU USED TO BE ONE OF MY COUNCILMEN—*AND YOU OWE ME.* YOU AND YOUR MATE TOOK MY FIRST BORN SON, THEN MY WIFE, AND INJURED MY NEXT BORN HEIR... AND YOU THINK THERE WILL NOT BE HELL TO PAY FOR THAT, AS WELL AS FOR EXTERMINATING MY ENTIRE VAMPIRE COUNCIL, NETERUS? SO FOOLISH.

NO ONE CHEATS THE ULTIMATE DARKNESS!

BUT OF ALL THE LOSSES... MY DEAR LILITH WAS THE HARDEST TO BEAR. I WILL AVENGE HER.

ALTHOUGH I HAVE WAITED MILLENNIA TO STRIKE, I WILL NOT ENDURE THE TWENTY-ONE YEARS IT WILL TAKE TO REBUILD WHILE MY HEIR HEALS.

THAT SATISFACTION BELONGS TO ME!

I, ALONE, AM BEST QUALIFIED TO EXACT MY REVENGE... AND IT WILL BE BITTERSWEET.

MANY HAVE FAILED ME. DO NOT SUFFER THEIR FATE.

I WANT MORE THAN A POUND OF FLESH TO REPLACE MY LOSSES SUFFERED DURING THE ARMAGEDDON. BRING ME THEIR BABIES, THEIR TEAMMATES, THEIR PEACE OF MIND... UNTIL CARLOS AND DAMALI RANSOM THEIR SOULS.

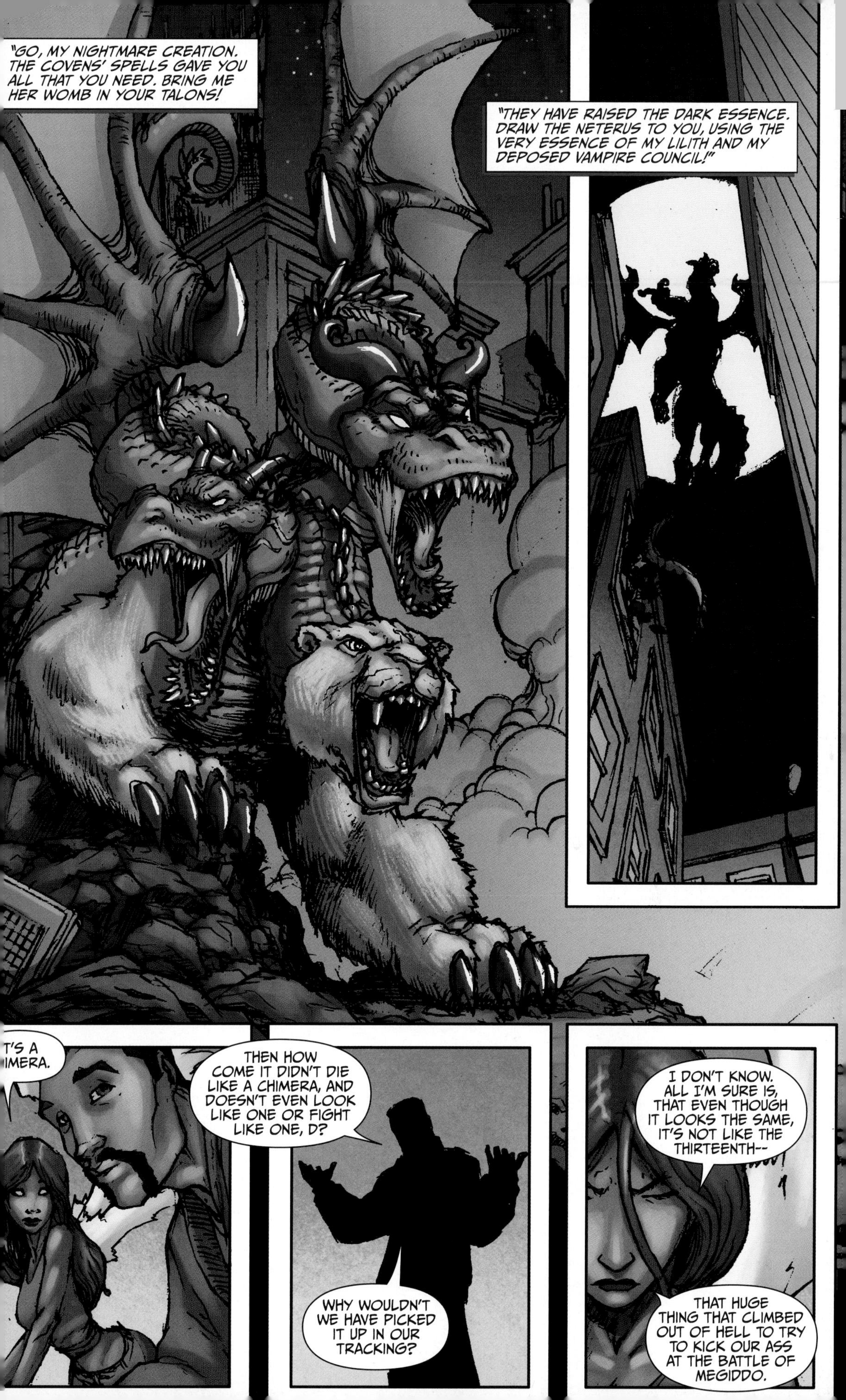
"GO, MY NIGHTMARE CREATION. THE COVENS' SPELLS GAVE YOU ALL THAT YOU NEED. BRING ME HER WOMB IN YOUR TALONS!
"THEY HAVE RAISED THE DARK ESSENCE. DRAW THE NETERUS TO YOU, USING THE VERY ESSENCE OF MY LILITH AND MY DEPOSED VAMPIRE COUNCIL!"
T'S A IMERA.
THEN HOW COME IT DIDN'T DIE LIKE A CHIMERA, AND DOESN'T EVEN LOOK LIKE ONE OR FIGHT LIKE ONE, D?
WHY WOULDN'T WE HAVE PICKED IT UP IN OUR TRACKING?
I DON'T KNOW. ALL I'M SURE IS, THAT EVEN THOUGH IT LOOKS THE SAME, IT'S NOT LIKE THE THIRTEENTH--
THAT HUGE THING THAT CLIMBED OUT OF HELL TO TRY TO KICK OUR ASS AT THE BATTLE OF MEGIDDO.

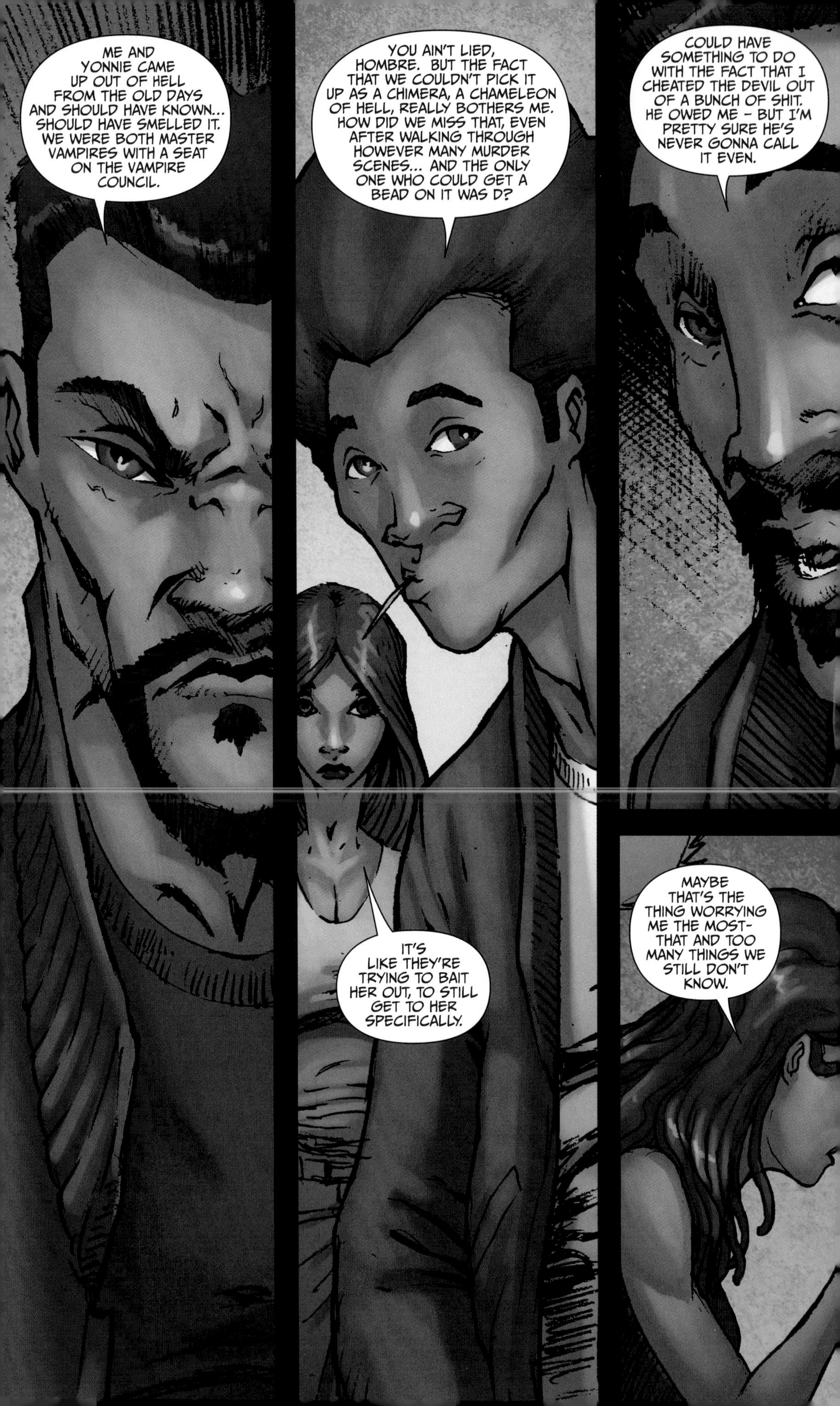

ME AND YONNIE CAME UP OUT OF HELL FROM THE OLD DAYS AND SHOULD HAVE KNOWN... SHOULD HAVE SMELLED IT. WE WERE BOTH MASTER VAMPIRES WITH A SEAT ON THE VAMPIRE COUNCIL.
YOU AIN'T LIED, HOMBRE. BUT THE FACT THAT WE COULDN'T PICK IT UP AS A CHIMERA, A CHAMELEON OF HELL, REALLY BOTHERS ME. HOW DID WE MISS THAT, EVEN AFTER WALKING THROUGH HOWEVER MANY MURDER SCENES... AND THE ONLY ONE WHO COULD GET A BEAD ON IT WAS D?
COULD HAVE SOMETHING TO DO WITH THE FACT THAT I CHEATED THE DEVIL OUT OF A BUNCH OF SHIT. HE OWED ME - BUT I'M PRETTY SURE HE'S NEVER GONNA CALL IT EVEN.
IT'S LIKE THEY'RE TRYING TO BAIT HER OUT, TO STILL GET TO HER SPECIFICALLY.
MAYBE THAT'S THE THING WORRYING ME THE MOST- THAT AND TOO MANY THINGS WE STILL DON'T KNOW.

BOOK FOUR

RIDE or DIE

VAMPIRE HUNTRESS

COVER FOUR ARTWORK BY: BRETT BOOTH

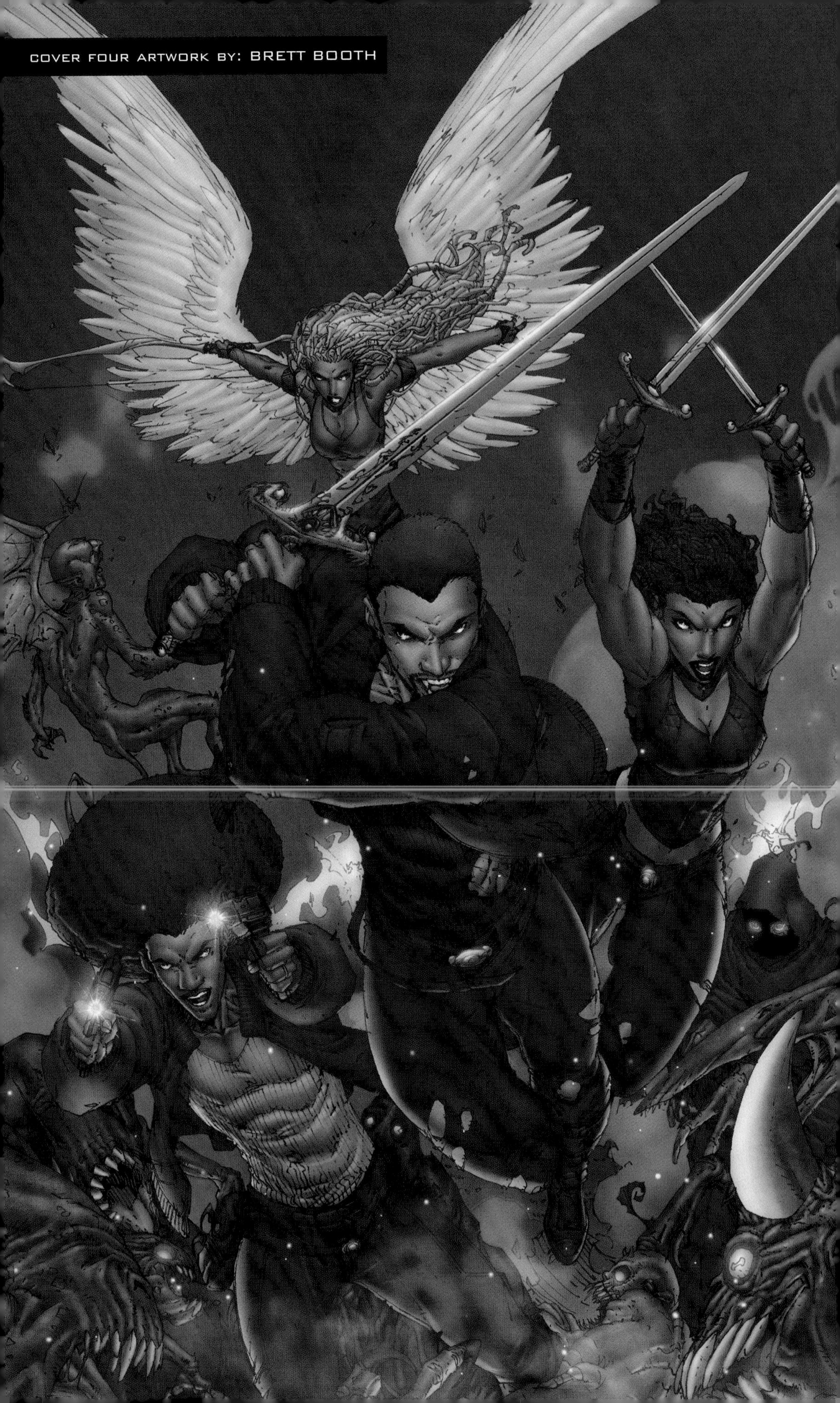

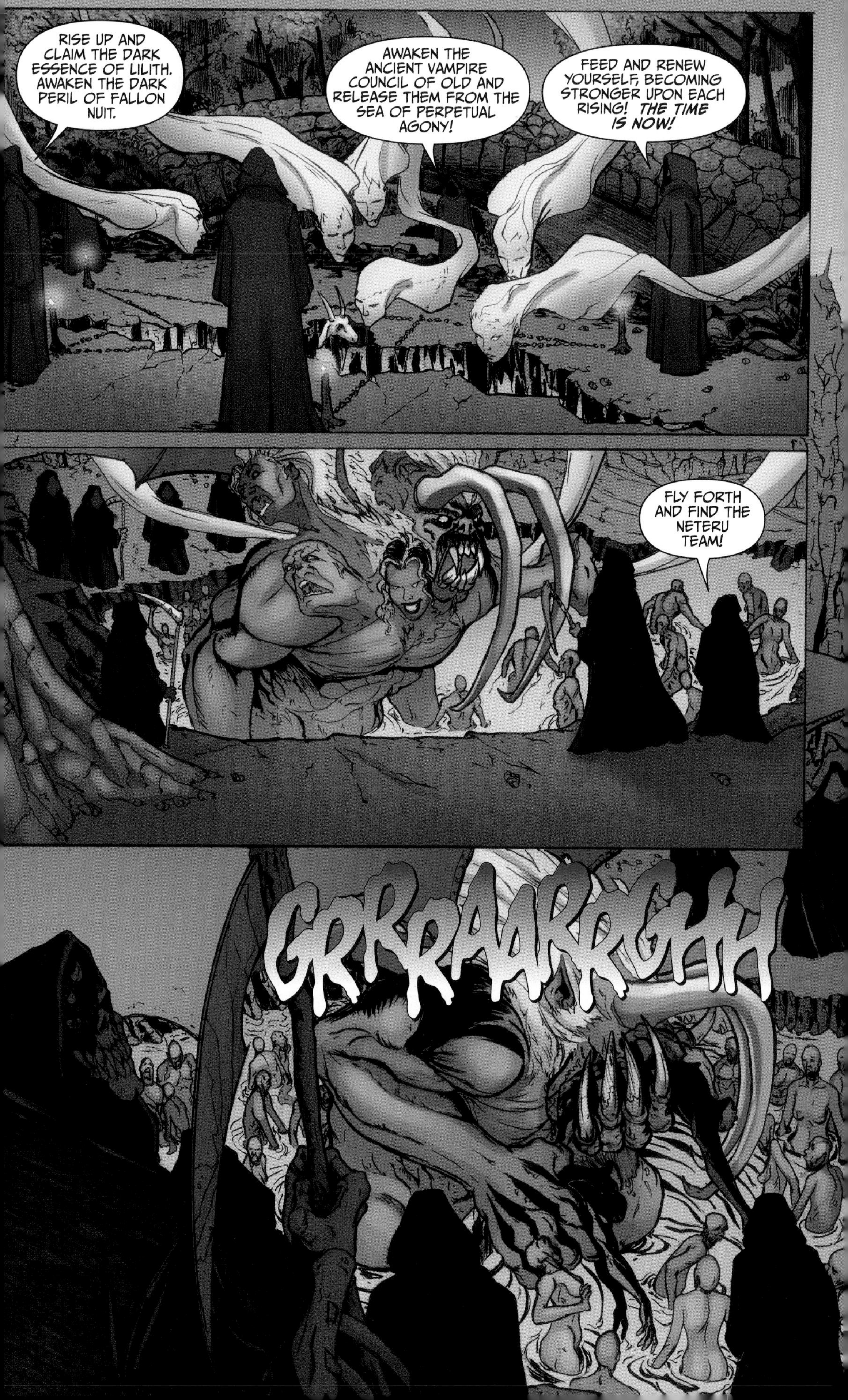
RISE UP AND CLAIM THE DARK ESSENCE OF LILITH. AWAKEN THE DARK PERIL OF FALLON NUIT.
AWAKEN THE ANCIENT VAMPIRE COUNCIL OF OLD AND RELEASE THEM FROM THE SEA OF PERPETUAL AGONY!
FEED AND RENEW YOURSELF, BECOMING STRONGER UPON EACH RISING! *THE TIME IS NOW!*
FLY FORTH AND FIND THE NETERU TEAM!
GRRRAARRGHH

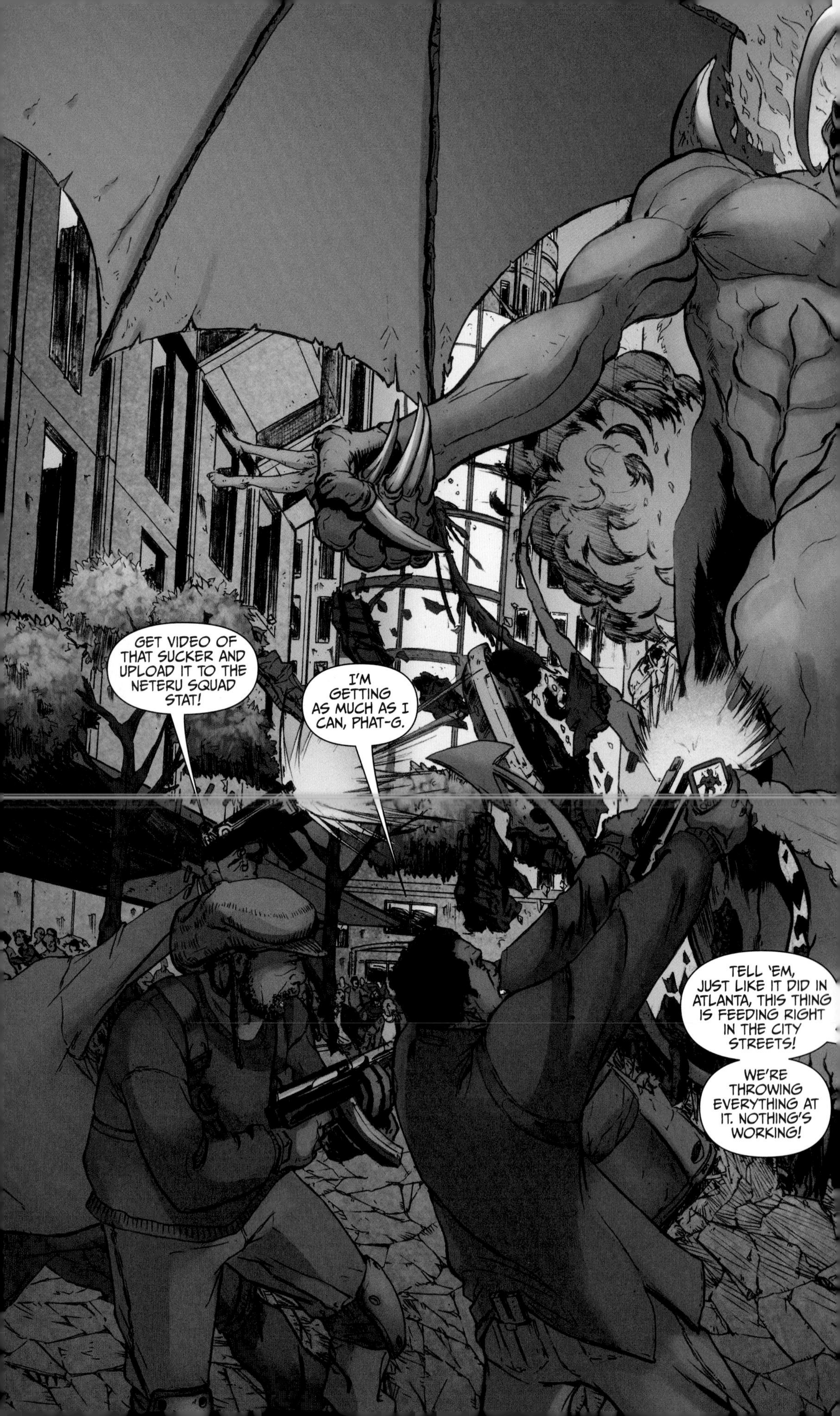
GET VIDEO OF THAT SUCKER AND UPLOAD IT TO THE NETERU SQUAD STAT!
I'M GETTING AS MUCH AS I CAN, PHAT-G.
TELL 'EM, JUST LIKE IT DID IN ATLANTA, THIS THING IS FEEDING RIGHT IN THE CITY STREETS!
WE'RE THROWING EVERYTHING AT IT. NOTHING'S WORKING!

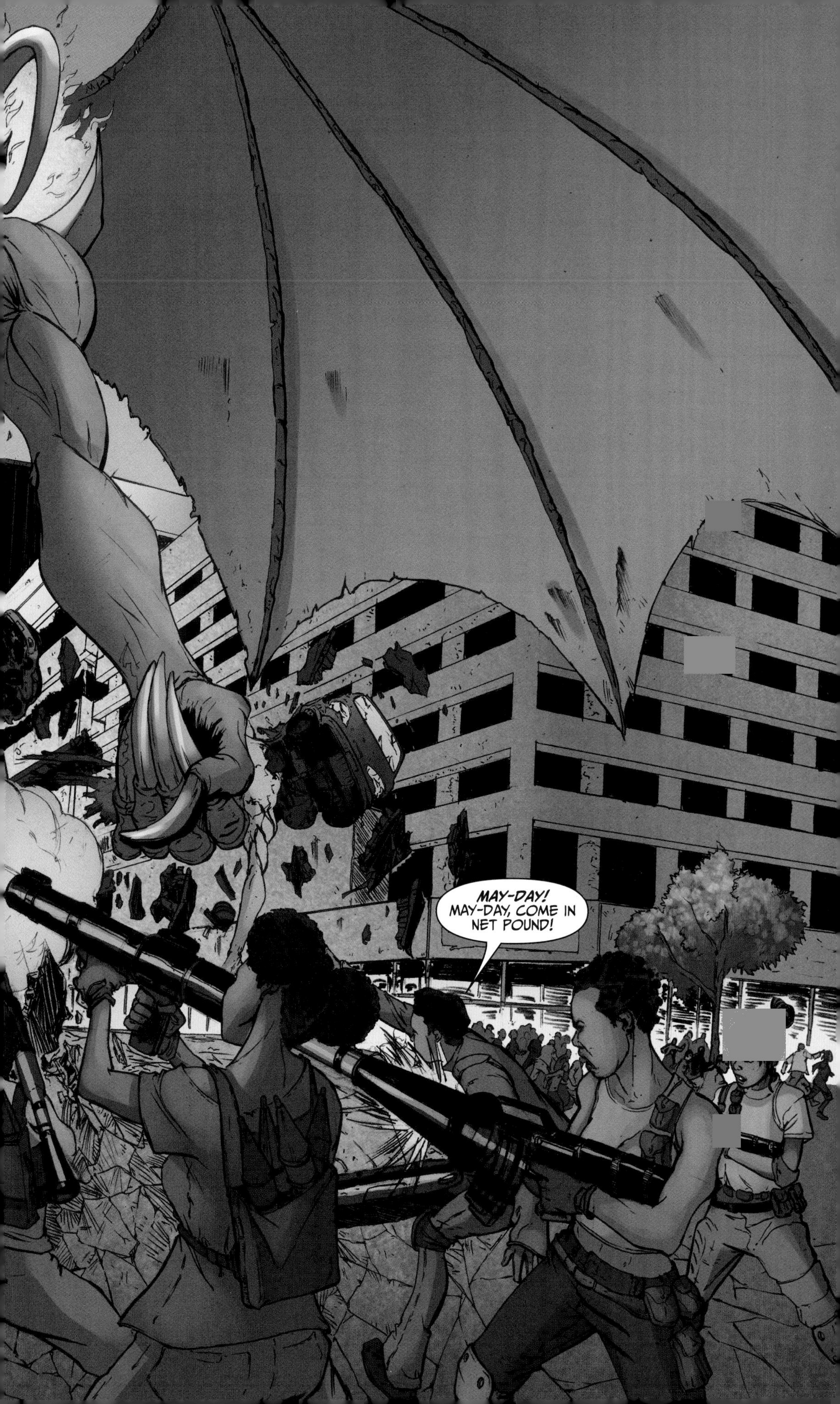
MAY-DAY! MAY-DAY, COME IN NET POUND!

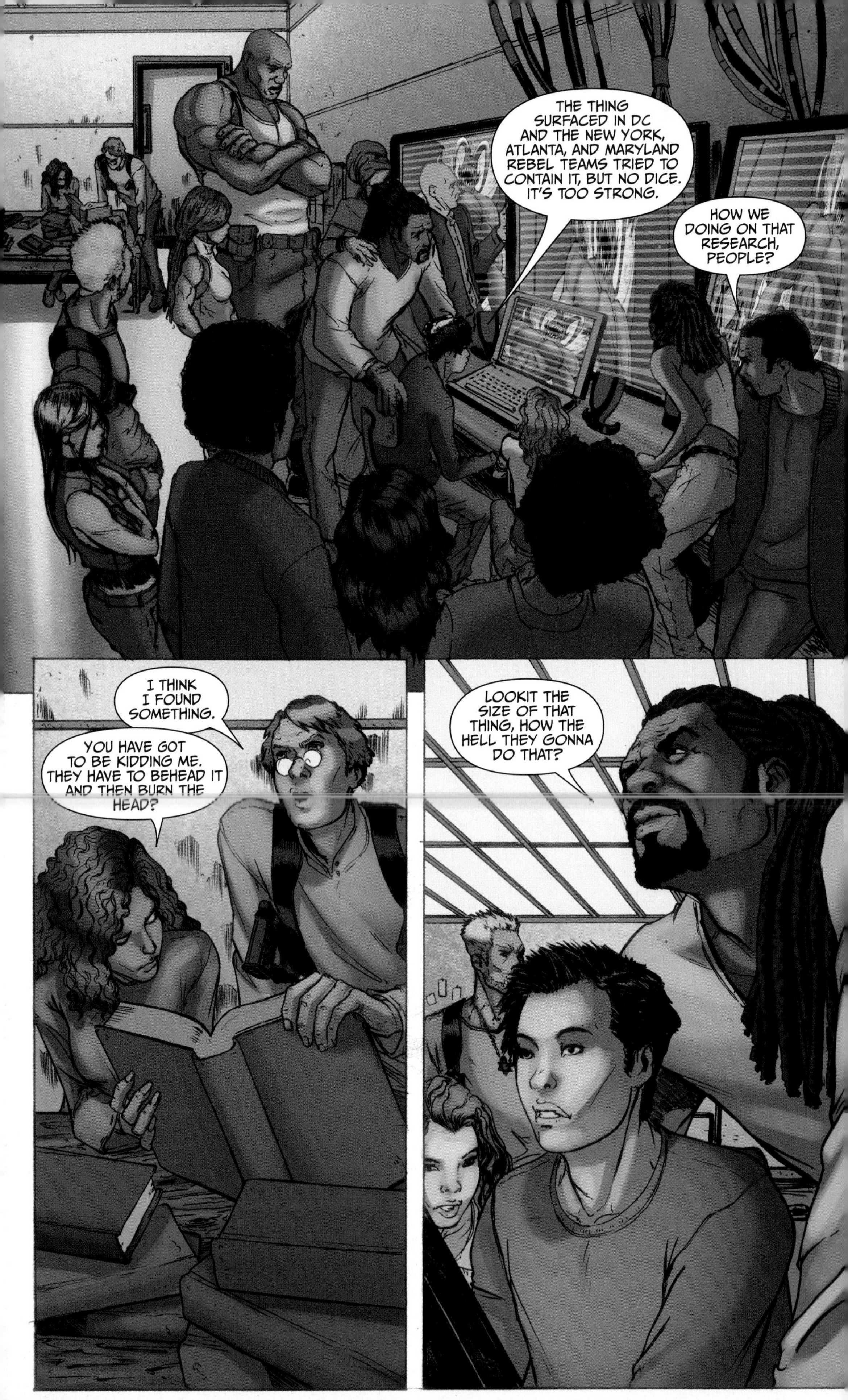
THE THING SURFACED IN DC AND THE NEW YORK, ATLANTA, AND MARYLAND REBEL TEAMS TRIED TO CONTAIN IT, BUT NO DICE. IT'S TOO STRONG.
HOW WE DOING ON THAT RESEARCH, PEOPLE?
I THINK I FOUND SOMETHING.
YOU HAVE GOT TO BE KIDDING ME. THEY HAVE TO BEHEAD IT AND THEN BURN THE HEAD?
LOOKIT THE SIZE OF THAT THING, HOW THE HELL THEY GONNA DO THAT?

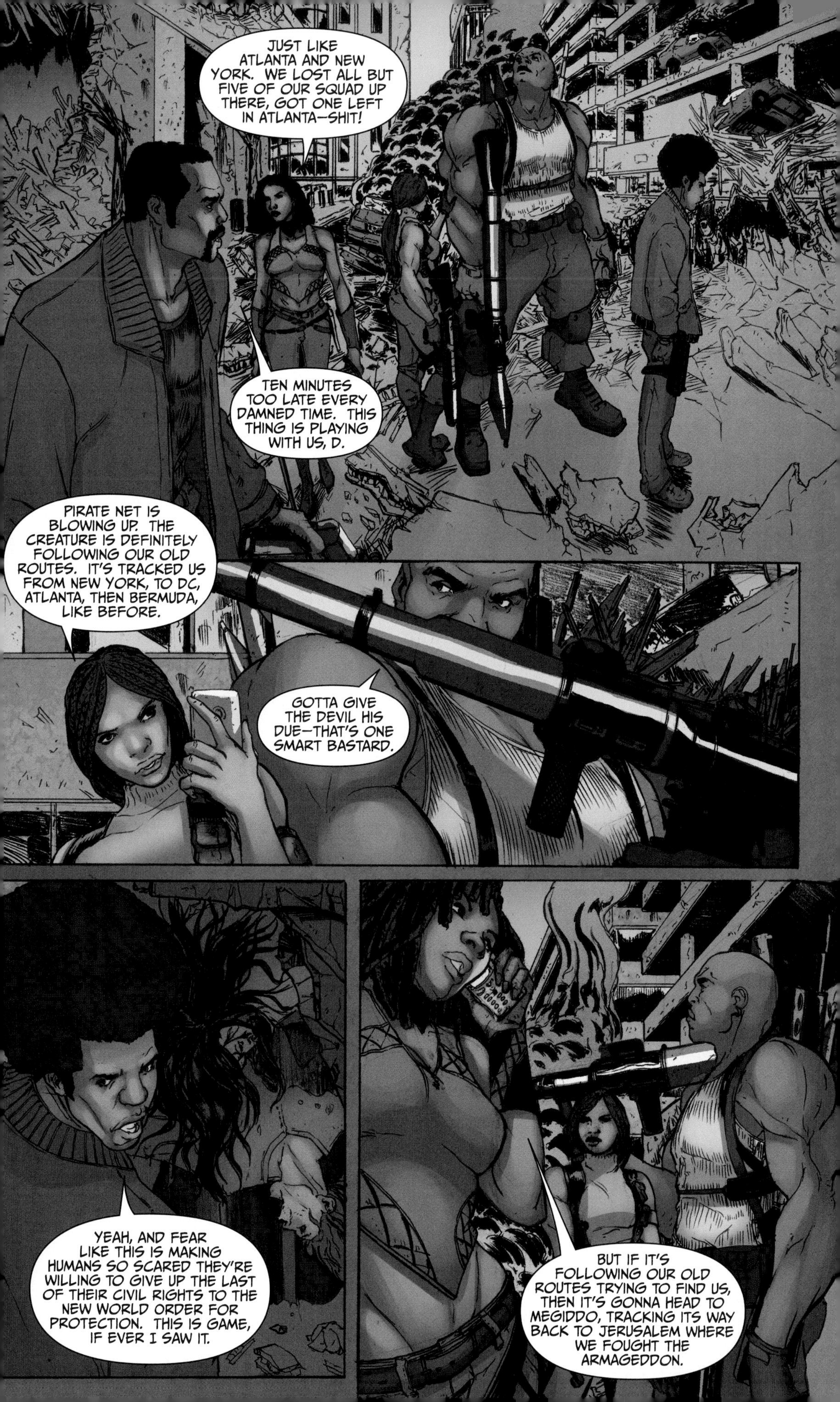

JUST LIKE ATLANTA AND NEW YORK. WE LOST ALL BUT FIVE OF OUR SQUAD UP THERE, GOT ONE LEFT IN ATLANTA—SHIT!
TEN MINUTES TOO LATE EVERY DAMNED TIME. THIS THING IS PLAYING WITH US, D.
PIRATE NET IS BLOWING UP. THE CREATURE IS DEFINITELY FOLLOWING OUR OLD ROUTES. IT'S TRACKED US FROM NEW YORK, TO DC, ATLANTA, THEN BERMUDA, LIKE BEFORE.
GOTTA GIVE THE DEVIL HIS DUE—THAT'S ONE SMART BASTARD.
YEAH, AND FEAR LIKE THIS IS MAKING HUMANS SO SCARED THEY'RE WILLING TO GIVE UP THE LAST OF THEIR CIVIL RIGHTS TO THE NEW WORLD ORDER FOR PROTECTION. THIS IS GAME, IF EVER I SAW IT.
BUT IF IT'S FOLLOWING OUR OLD ROUTES TRYING TO FIND US, THEN IT'S GONNA HEAD TO MEGIDDO, TRACKING ITS WAY BACK TO JERUSALEM WHERE WE FOUGHT THE ARMAGEDDON.

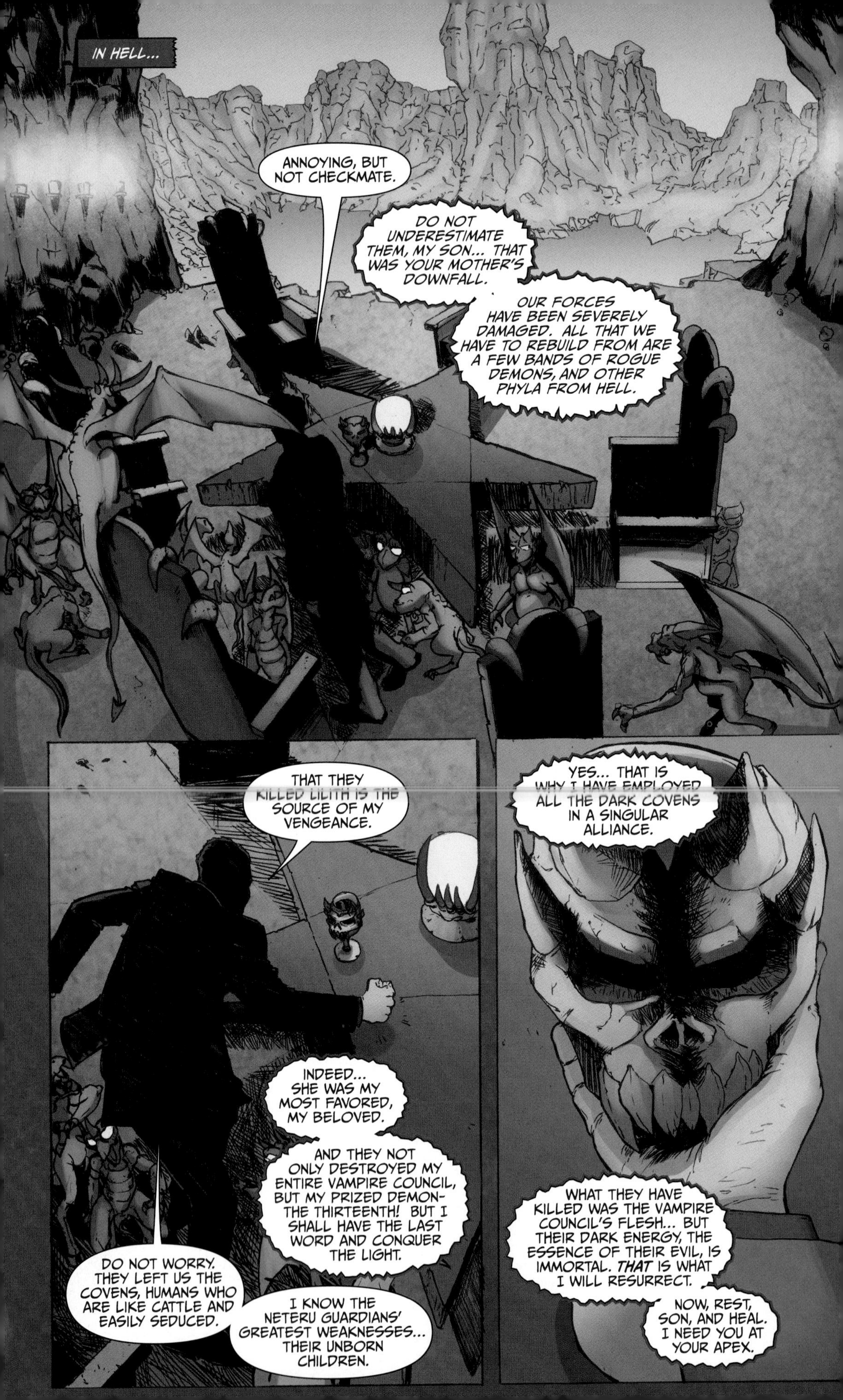
IN HELL...
ANNOYING, BUT NOT CHECKMATE.
DO NOT UNDERESTIMATE THEM, MY SON... THAT WAS YOUR MOTHER'S DOWNFALL.
OUR FORCES HAVE BEEN SEVERELY DAMAGED. ALL THAT WE HAVE TO REBUILD FROM ARE A FEW BANDS OF ROGUE DEMONS, AND OTHER PHYLA FROM HELL.
THAT THEY KILLED LILITH IS THE SOURCE OF MY VENGEANCE.
INDEED... SHE WAS MY MOST FAVORED, MY BELOVED.
AND THEY NOT ONLY DESTROYED MY ENTIRE VAMPIRE COUNCIL, BUT MY PRIZED DEMON-THE THIRTEENTH! BUT I SHALL HAVE THE LAST WORD AND CONQUER THE LIGHT.
DO NOT WORRY. THEY LEFT US THE COVENS, HUMANS WHO ARE LIKE CATTLE AND EASILY SEDUCED.
I KNOW THE NETERU GUARDIANS' GREATEST WEAKNESSES... THEIR UNBORN CHILDREN.
YES... THAT IS WHY I HAVE EMPLOYED ALL THE DARK COVENS IN A SINGULAR ALLIANCE.
WHAT THEY HAVE KILLED WAS THE VAMPIRE COUNCIL'S FLESH... BUT THEIR DARK ENERGY, THE ESSENCE OF THEIR EVIL, IS IMMORTAL. THAT IS WHAT I WILL RESURRECT.
NOW, REST, SON, AND HEAL. I NEED YOU AT YOUR APEX.

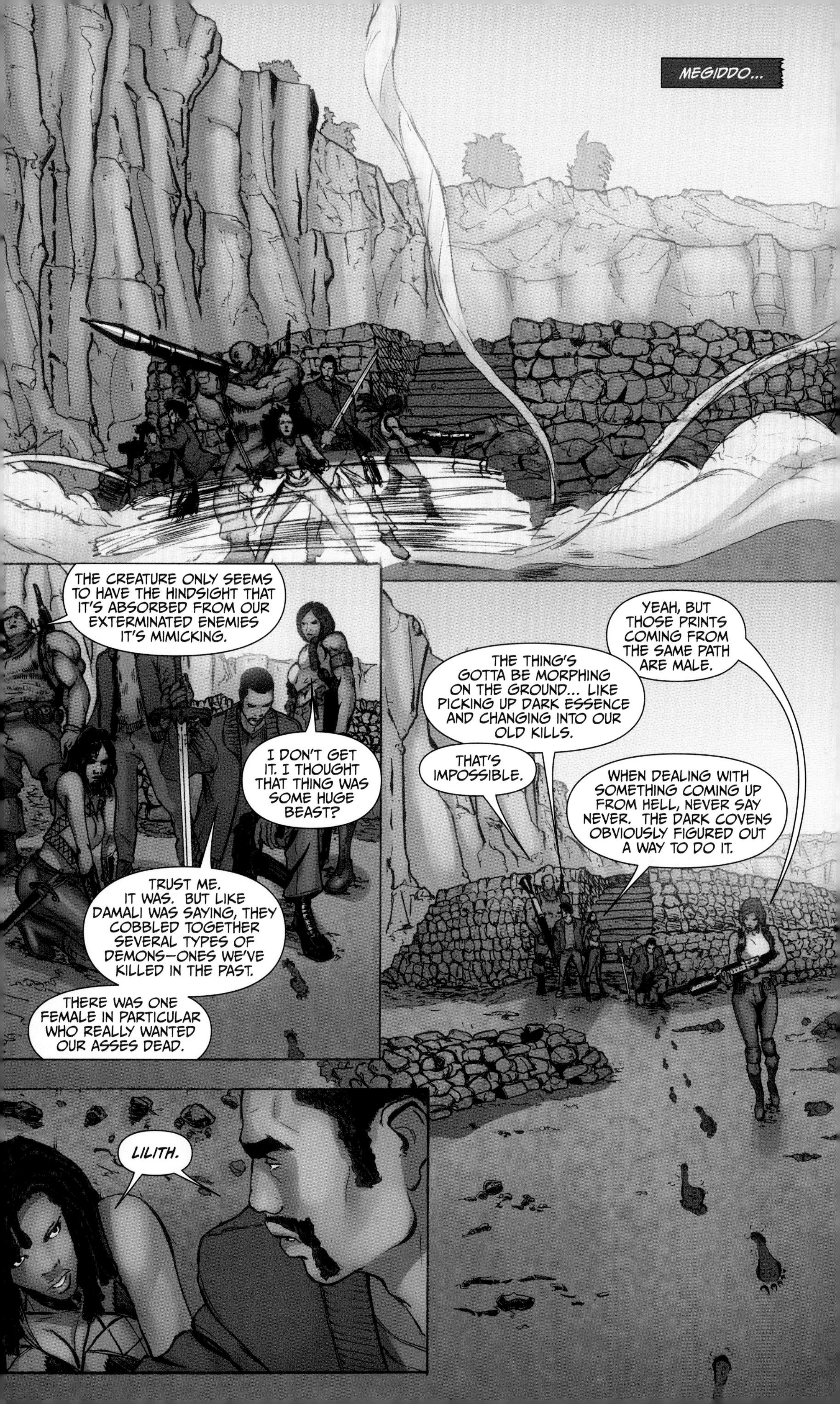
MEGIDDO...
THE CREATURE ONLY SEEMS TO HAVE THE HINDSIGHT THAT IT'S ABSORBED FROM OUR EXTERMINATED ENEMIES IT'S MIMICKING.
I DON'T GET IT. I THOUGHT THAT THING WAS SOME HUGE BEAST?
TRUST ME. IT WAS. BUT LIKE DAMALI WAS SAYING, THEY COBBLED TOGETHER SEVERAL TYPES OF DEMONS—ONES WE'VE KILLED IN THE PAST.
THERE WAS ONE FEMALE IN PARTICULAR WHO REALLY WANTED OUR ASSES DEAD.
YEAH, BUT THOSE PRINTS COMING FROM THE SAME PATH ARE MALE.
THE THING'S GOTTA BE MORPHING ON THE GROUND... LIKE PICKING UP DARK ESSENCE AND CHANGING INTO OUR OLD KILLS.
THAT'S IMPOSSIBLE.
WHEN DEALING WITH SOMETHING COMING UP FROM HELL, NEVER SAY NEVER. THE DARK COVENS OBVIOUSLY FIGURED OUT A WAY TO DO IT.
LILITH.

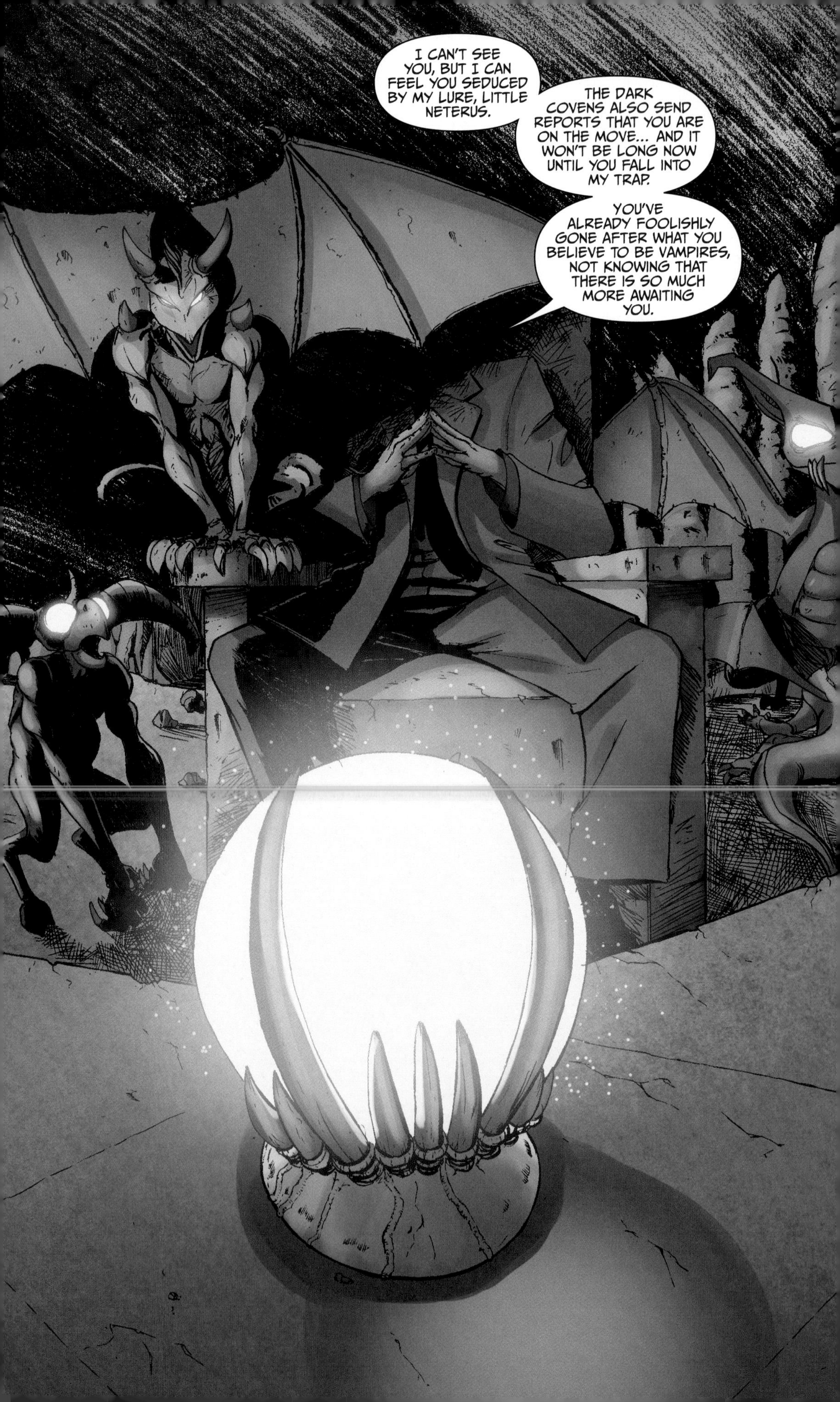
I CAN'T SEE YOU, BUT I CAN FEEL YOU SEDUCED BY MY LURE, LITTLE NETERUS.
THE DARK COVENS ALSO SEND REPORTS THAT YOU ARE ON THE MOVE... AND IT WON'T BE LONG NOW UNTIL YOU FALL INTO MY TRAP.
YOU'VE ALREADY FOOLISHLY GONE AFTER WHAT YOU BELIEVE TO BE VAMPIRES, NOT KNOWING THAT THERE IS SO MUCH MORE AWAITING YOU.

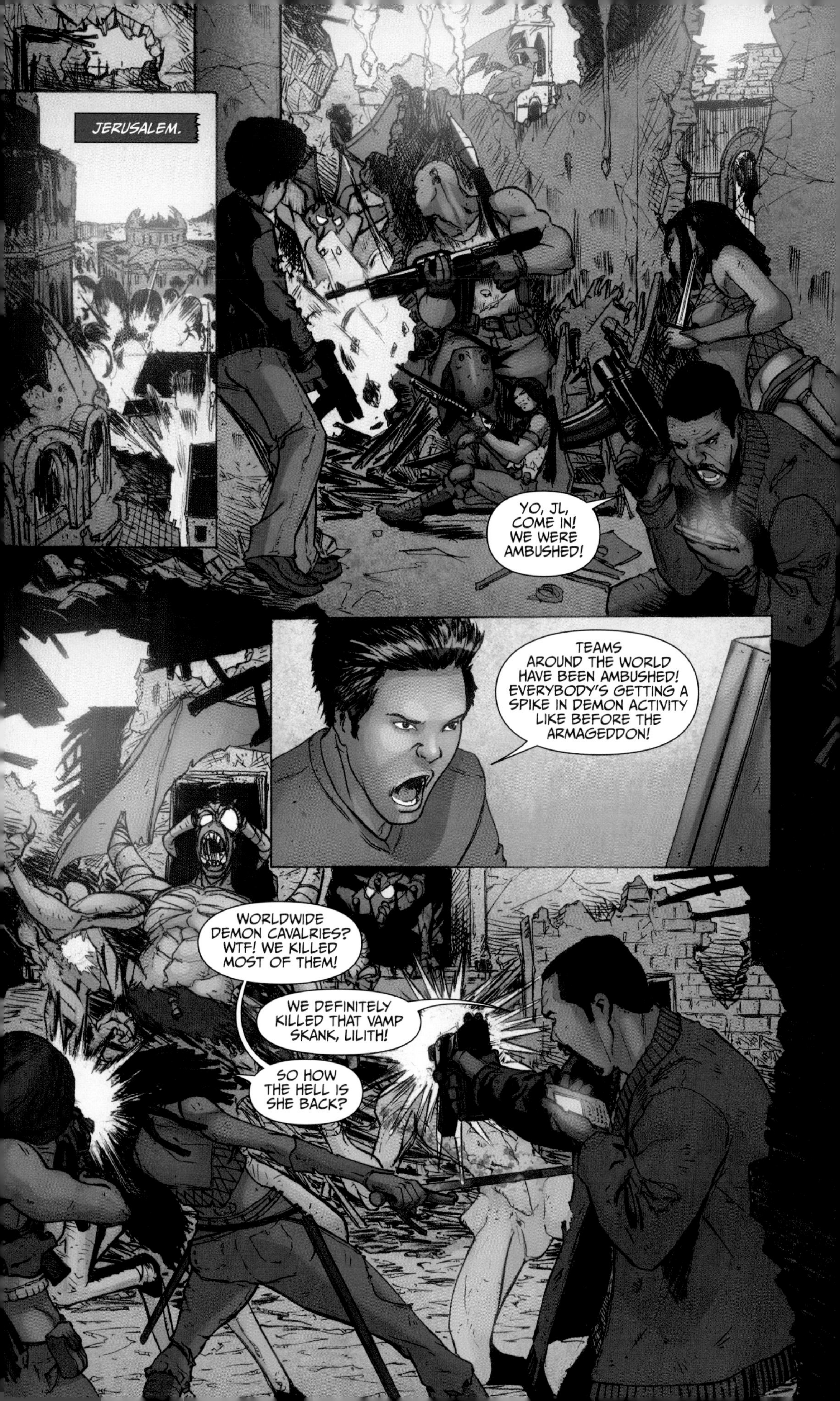
JERUSALEM.
YO, JL, COME IN! WE WERE AMBUSHED!
TEAMS AROUND THE WORLD HAVE BEEN AMBUSHED! EVERYBODY'S GETTING A SPIKE IN DEMON ACTIVITY LIKE BEFORE THE ARMAGEDDON!
WORLDWIDE DEMON CAVALRIES? WTF! WE KILLED MOST OF THEM!
WE DEFINITELY KILLED THAT VAMP SKANK, LILITH!
SO HOW THE HELL IS SHE BACK?

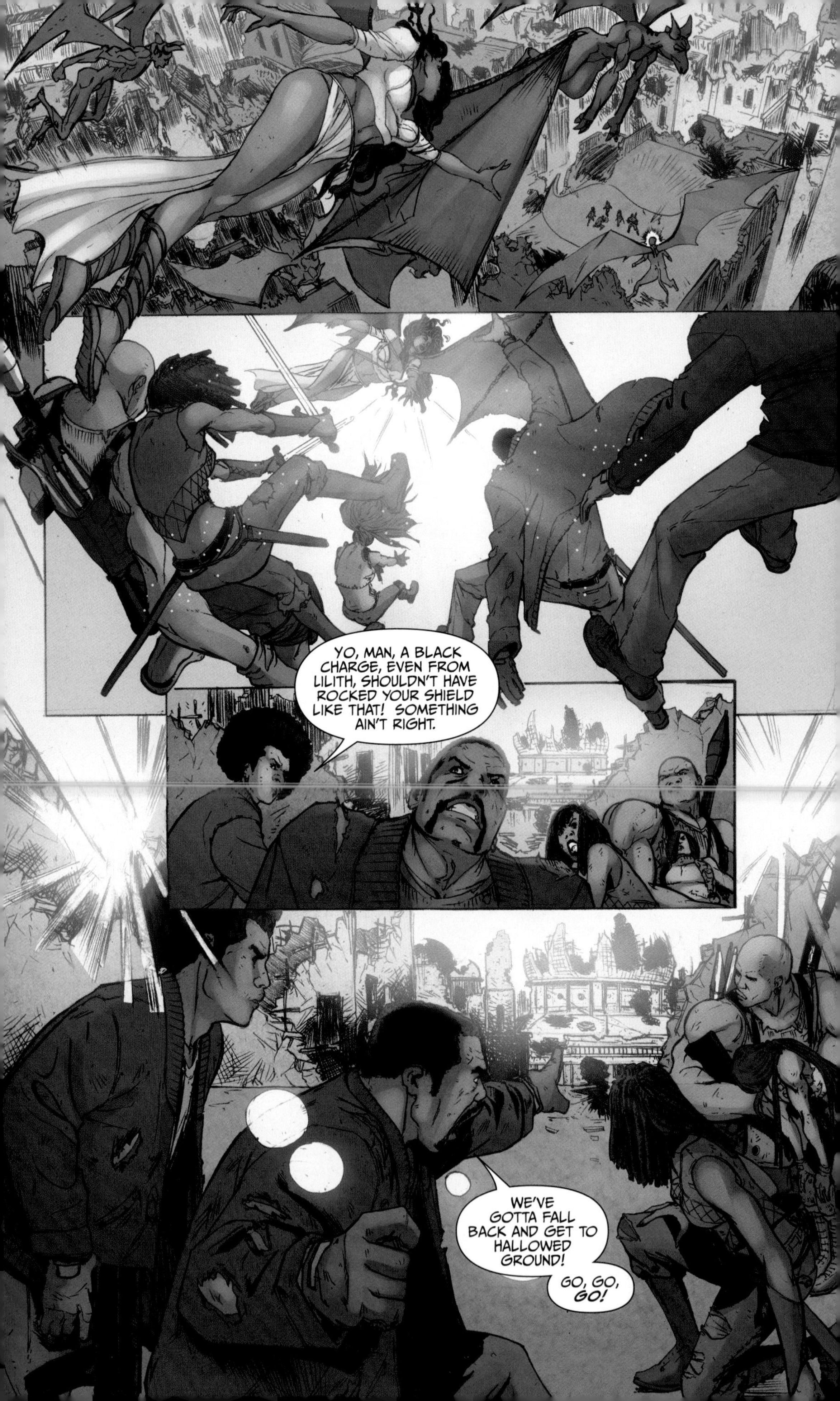
YO, MAN, A BLACK CHARGE, EVEN FROM LILITH, SHOULDN'T HAVE ROCKED YOUR SHIELD LIKE THAT! SOMETHING AIN'T RIGHT.
WE'VE GOTTA FALL BACK AND GET TO HALLOWED GROUND!
GO, GO, GO!

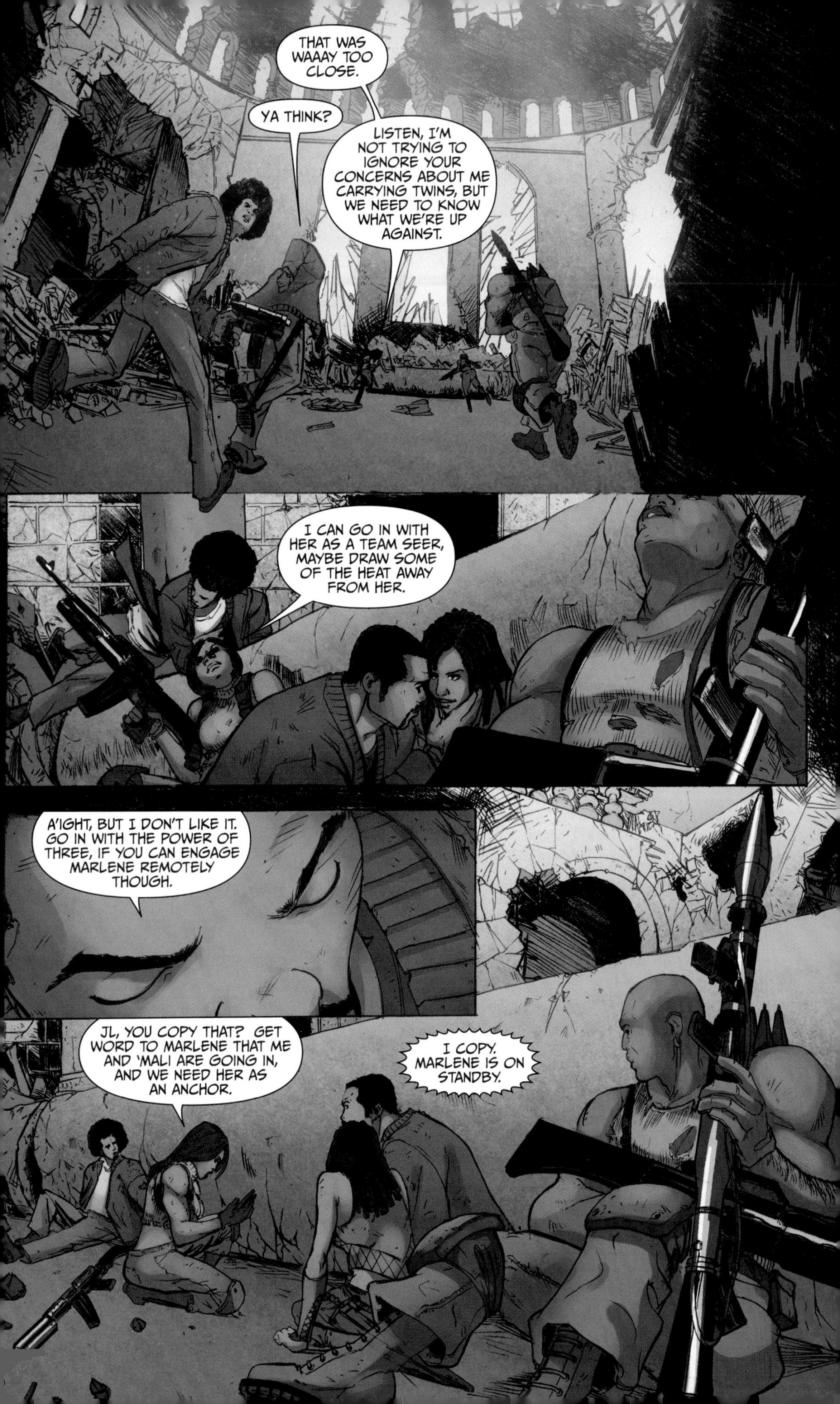
THAT WAS WAAAY TOO CLOSE.
YA THINK?
LISTEN, I'M NOT TRYING TO IGNORE YOUR CONCERNS ABOUT ME CARRYING TWINS, BUT WE NEED TO KNOW WHAT WE'RE UP AGAINST.
I CAN GO IN WITH HER AS A TEAM SEER, MAYBE DRAW SOME OF THE HEAT AWAY FROM HER.
A'IGHT, BUT I DON'T LIKE IT. GO IN WITH THE POWER OF THREE, IF YOU CAN ENGAGE MARLENE REMOTELY THOUGH.
JL, YOU COPY THAT? GET WORD TO MARLENE THAT ME AND 'MALI ARE GOING IN, AND WE NEED HER AS AN ANCHOR.
I COPY. MARLENE IS ON STANDBY.

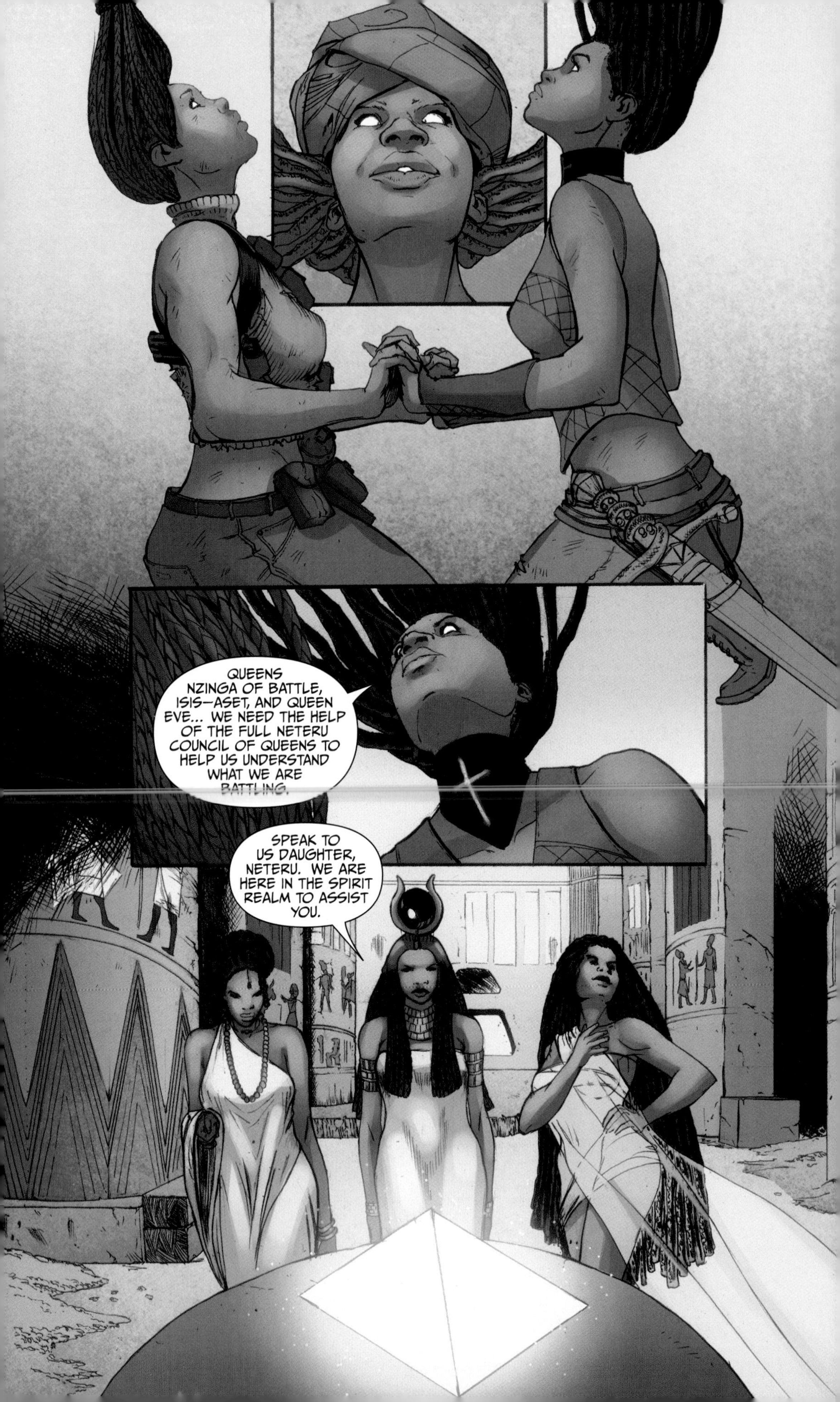
QUEENS NZINGA OF BATTLE, ISIS—ASET, AND QUEEN EVE... WE NEED THE HELP OF THE FULL NETERU COUNCIL OF QUEENS TO HELP US UNDERSTAND WHAT WE ARE BATTLING.
SPEAK TO US DAUGHTER, NETERU. WE ARE HERE IN THE SPIRIT REALM TO ASSIST YOU.

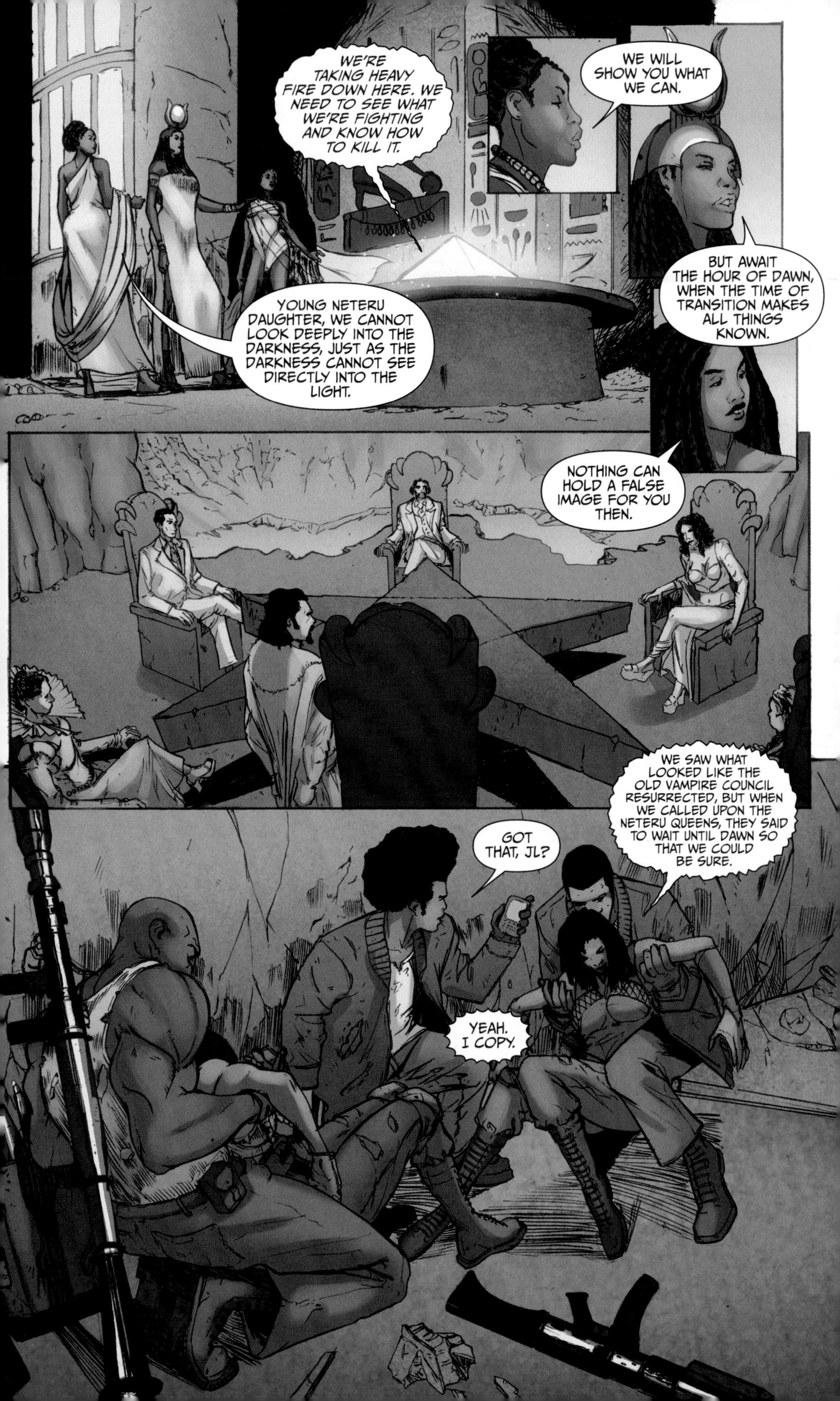
WE'RE TAKING HEAVY FIRE DOWN HERE. WE NEED TO SEE WHAT WE'RE FIGHTING AND KNOW HOW TO KILL IT.
WE WILL SHOW YOU WHAT WE CAN.
YOUNG NETERU DAUGHTER, WE CANNOT LOOK DEEPLY INTO THE DARKNESS, JUST AS THE DARKNESS CANNOT SEE DIRECTLY INTO THE LIGHT.
BUT AWAIT THE HOUR OF DAWN, WHEN THE TIME OF TRANSITION MAKES ALL THINGS KNOWN.
NOTHING CAN HOLD A FALSE IMAGE FOR YOU THEN.
WE SAW WHAT LOOKED LIKE THE OLD VAMPIRE COUNCIL RESURRECTED, BUT WHEN WE CALLED UPON THE NETERU QUEENS, THEY SAID TO WAIT UNTIL DAWN SO THAT WE COULD BE SURE.
GOT THAT, JL?
YEAH. I COPY.

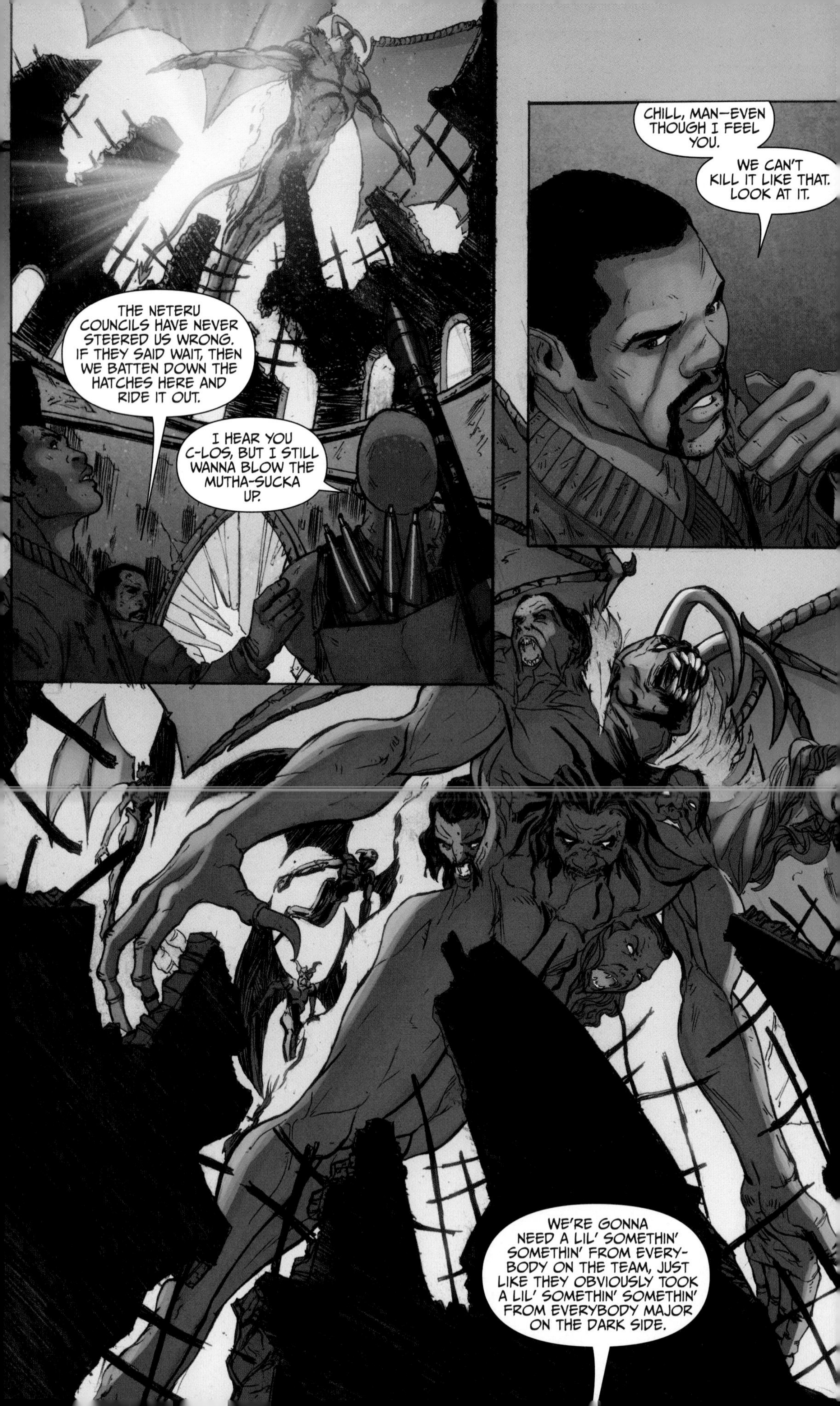
THE NETERU COUNCILS HAVE NEVER STEERED US WRONG. IF THEY SAID WAIT, THEN WE BATTEN DOWN THE HATCHES HERE AND RIDE IT OUT.
I HEAR YOU C-LOS, BUT I STILL WANNA BLOW THE MUTHA-SUCKA UP.
CHILL, MAN—EVEN THOUGH I FEEL YOU.
WE CAN'T KILL IT LIKE THAT. LOOK AT IT.
WE'RE GONNA NEED A LIL' SOMETHIN' SOMETHIN' FROM EVERY-BODY ON THE TEAM, JUST LIKE THEY OBVIOUSLY TOOK A LIL' SOMETHIN' SOMETHIN' FROM EVERYBODY MAJOR ON THE DARK SIDE.

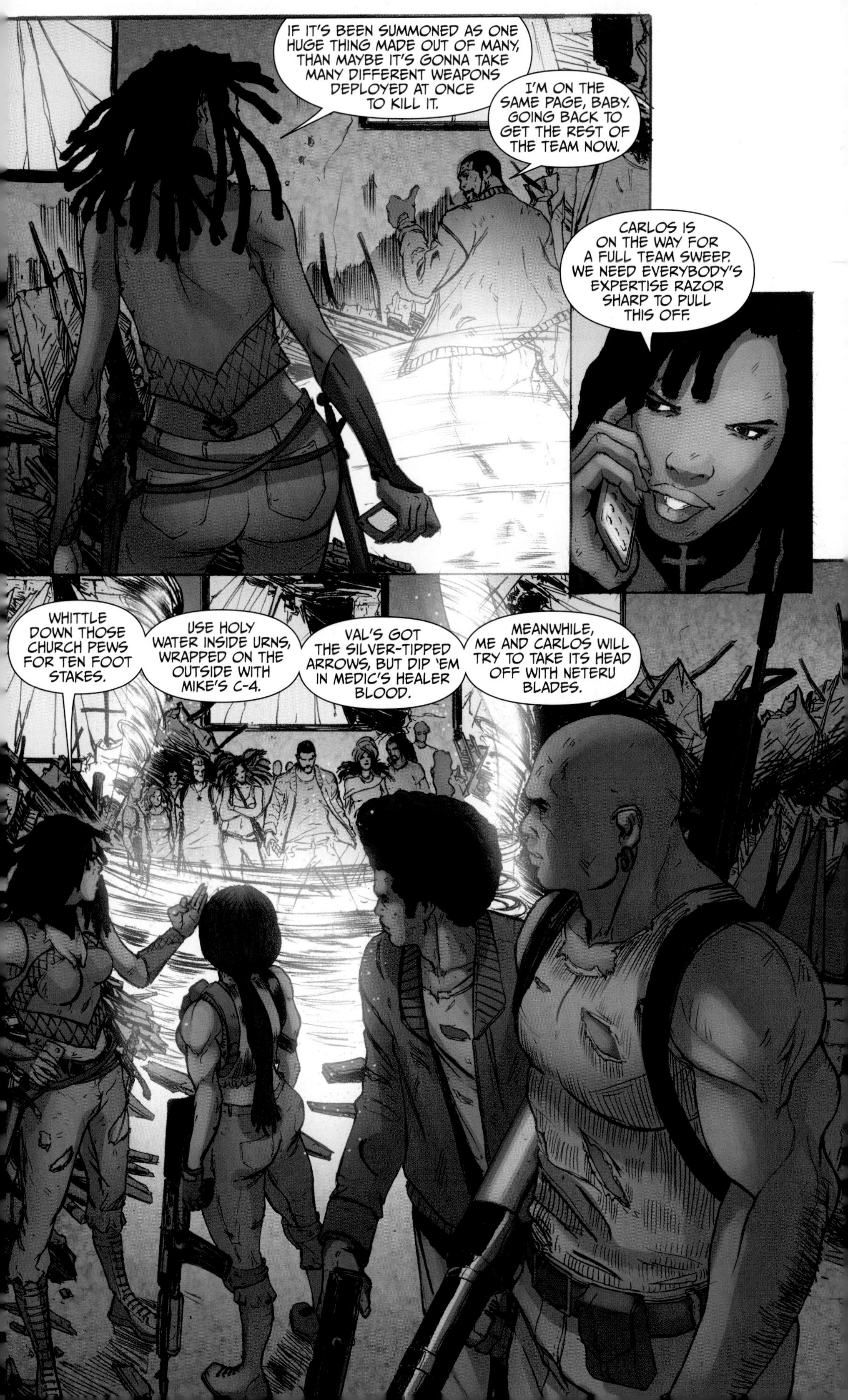
IF IT'S BEEN SUMMONED AS ONE HUGE THING MADE OUT OF MANY, THAN MAYBE IT'S GONNA TAKE MANY DIFFERENT WEAPONS DEPLOYED AT ONCE TO KILL IT.
I'M ON THE SAME PAGE, BABY. GOING BACK TO GET THE REST OF THE TEAM NOW.
CARLOS IS ON THE WAY FOR A FULL TEAM SWEEP. WE NEED EVERYBODY'S EXPERTISE RAZOR SHARP TO PULL THIS OFF.
WHITTLE DOWN THOSE CHURCH PEWS FOR TEN FOOT STAKES.
USE HOLY WATER INSIDE URNS, WRAPPED ON THE OUTSIDE WITH MIKE'S C-4.
VAL'S GOT THE SILVER-TIPPED ARROWS, BUT DIP 'EM IN MEDIC'S HEALER BLOOD.
MEANWHILE, ME AND CARLOS WILL TRY TO TAKE ITS HEAD OFF WITH NETERU BLADES.

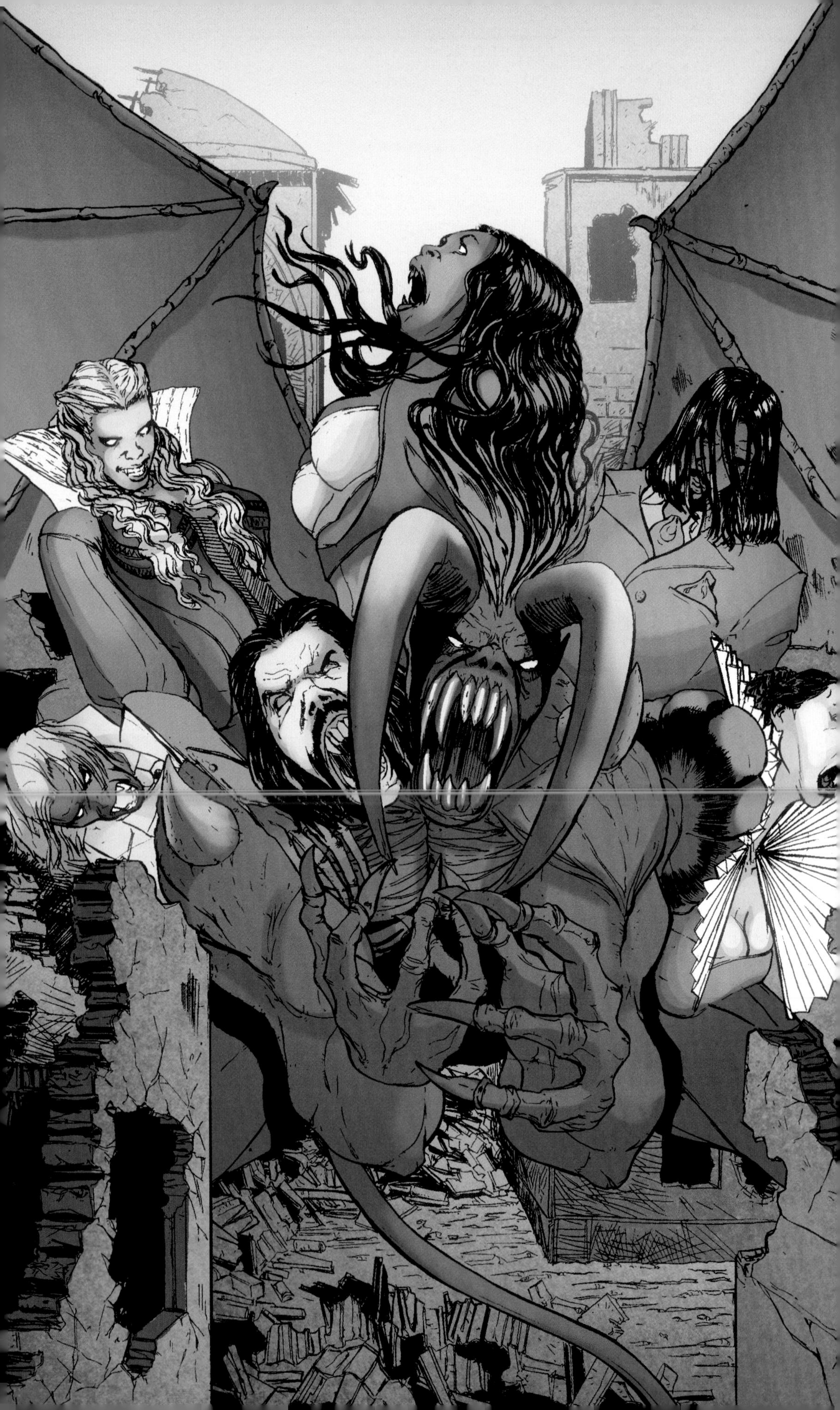

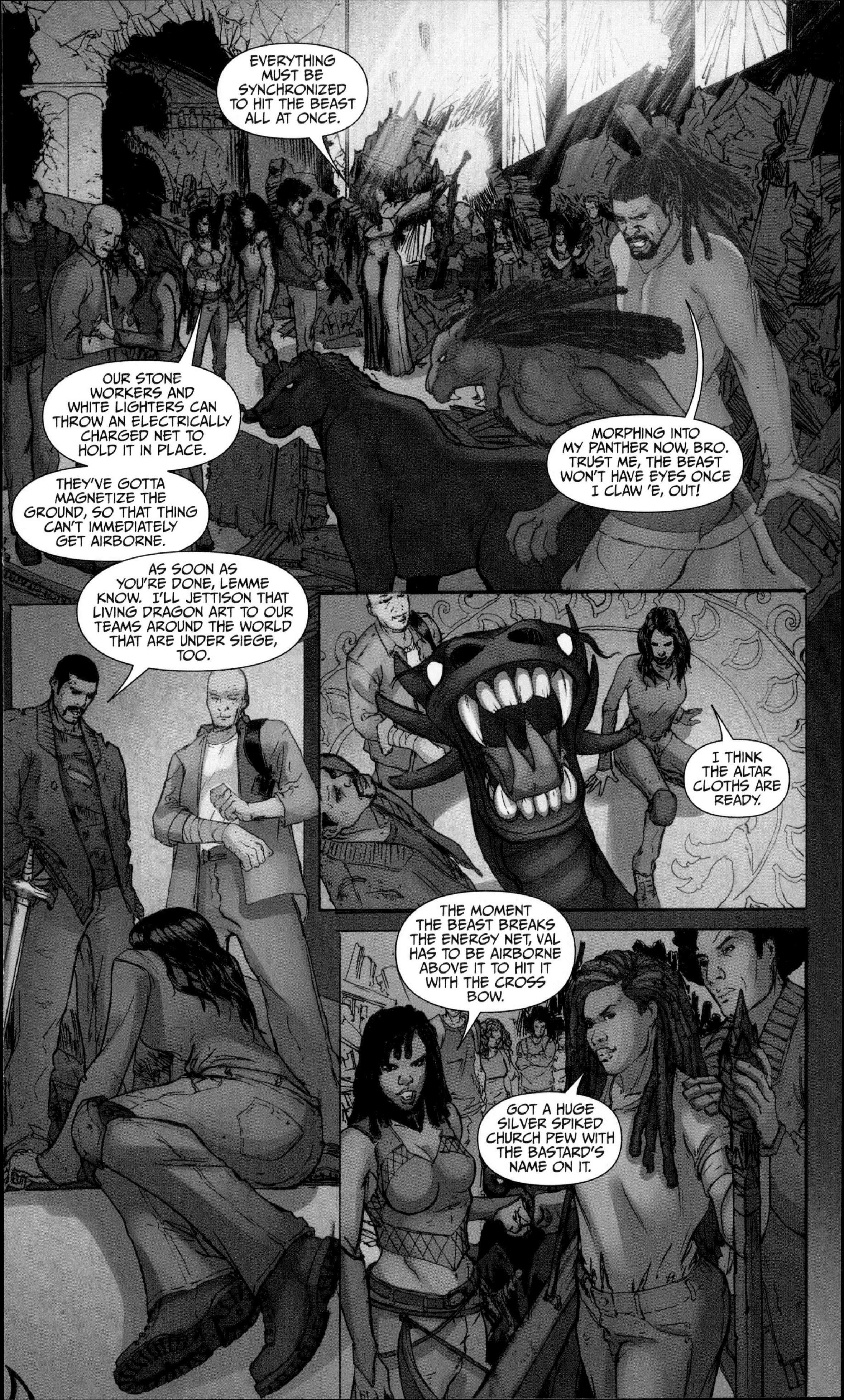
EVERYTHING MUST BE SYNCHRONIZED TO HIT THE BEAST ALL AT ONCE.
OUR STONE WORKERS AND WHITE LIGHTERS CAN THROW AN ELECTRICALLY CHARGED NET TO HOLD IT IN PLACE.
THEY'VE GOTTA MAGNETIZE THE GROUND, SO THAT THING CAN'T IMMEDIATELY GET AIRBORNE.
MORPHING INTO MY PANTHER NOW, BRO. TRUST ME, THE BEAST WON'T HAVE EYES ONCE I CLAW 'E, OUT!
AS SOON AS YOU'RE DONE, LEMME KNOW. I'LL JETTISON THAT LIVING DRAGON ART TO OUR TEAMS AROUND THE WORLD THAT ARE UNDER SIEGE, TOO.
I THINK THE ALTAR CLOTHS ARE READY.
THE MOMENT THE BEAST BREAKS THE ENERGY NET, VAL HAS TO BE AIRBORNE ABOVE IT TO HIT IT WITH THE CROSS BOW.
GOT A HUGE SILVER SPIKED CHURCH PEW WITH THE BASTARD'S NAME ON IT.

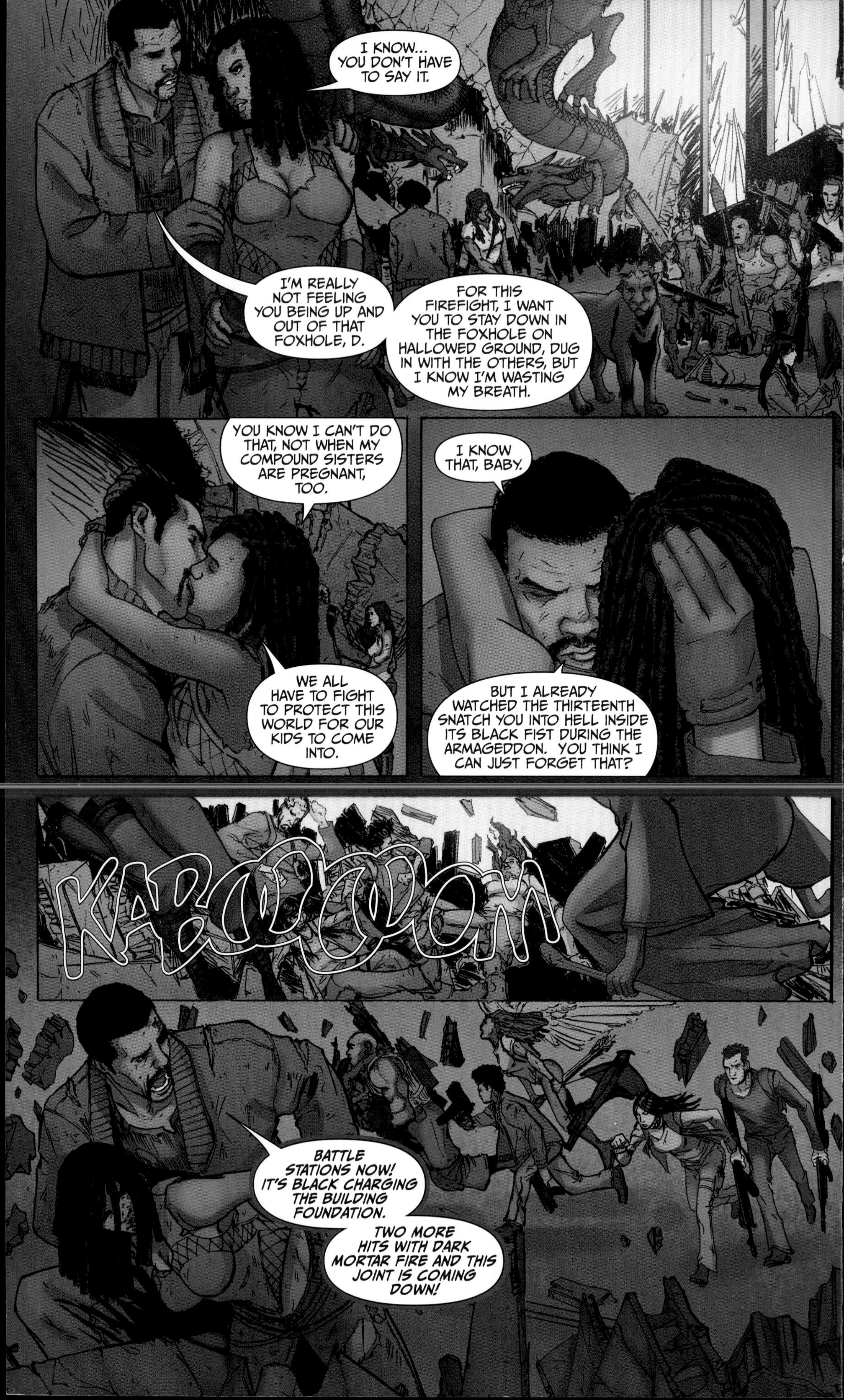

I KNOW... YOU DON'T HAVE TO SAY IT.
I'M REALLY NOT FEELING YOU BEING UP AND OUT OF THAT FOXHOLE, D.
FOR THIS FIREFIGHT, I WANT YOU TO STAY DOWN IN THE FOXHOLE ON HALLOWED GROUND, DUG IN WITH THE OTHERS, BUT I KNOW I'M WASTING MY BREATH.
YOU KNOW I CAN'T DO THAT, NOT WHEN MY COMPOUND SISTERS ARE PREGNANT, TOO.
WE ALL HAVE TO FIGHT TO PROTECT THIS WORLD FOR OUR KIDS TO COME INTO.
I KNOW THAT, BABY.
BUT I ALREADY WATCHED THE THIRTEENTH SNATCH YOU INTO HELL INSIDE ITS BLACK FIST DURING THE ARMAGEDDON. YOU THINK I CAN JUST FORGET THAT?
KABOOOOM
BATTLE STATIONS NOW! IT'S BLACK CHARGING THE BUILDING FOUNDATION.
TWO MORE HITS WITH DARK MORTAR FIRE AND THIS JOINT IS COMING DOWN!

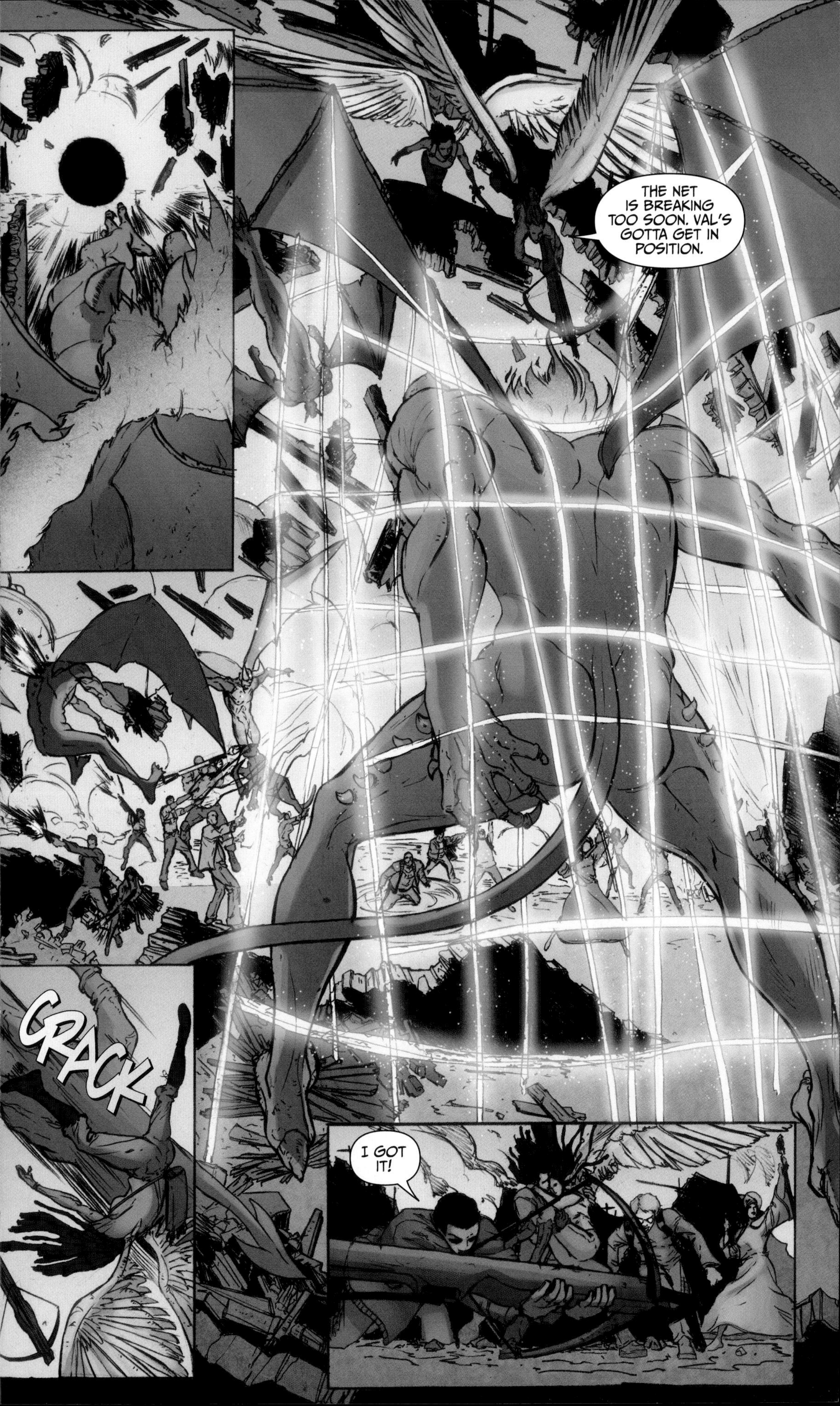
THE NET IS BREAKING TOO SOON. VAL'S GOTTA GET IN POSITION.
CRACK
I GOT IT!

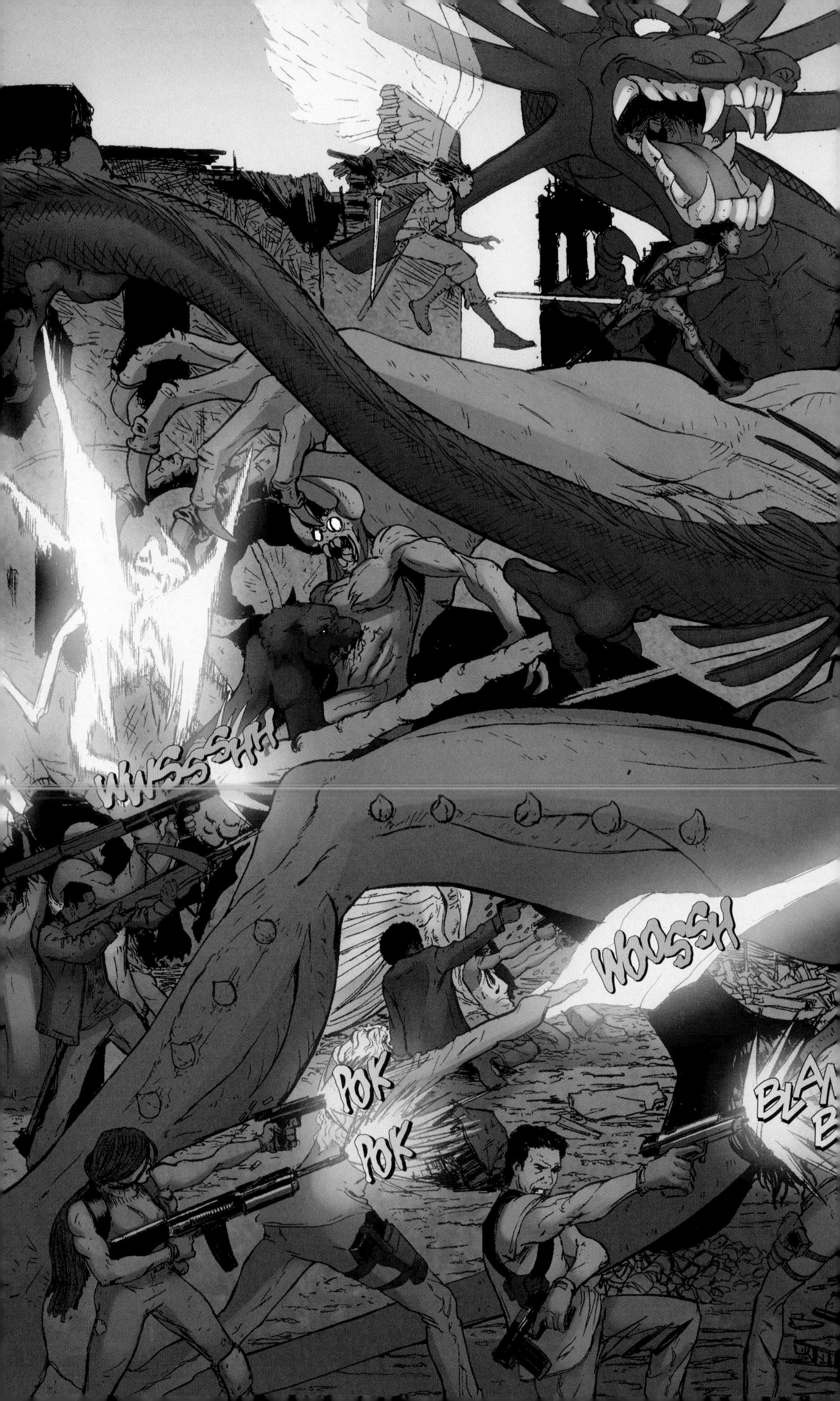
WWSSSHH
WOOSSH
POK
POK

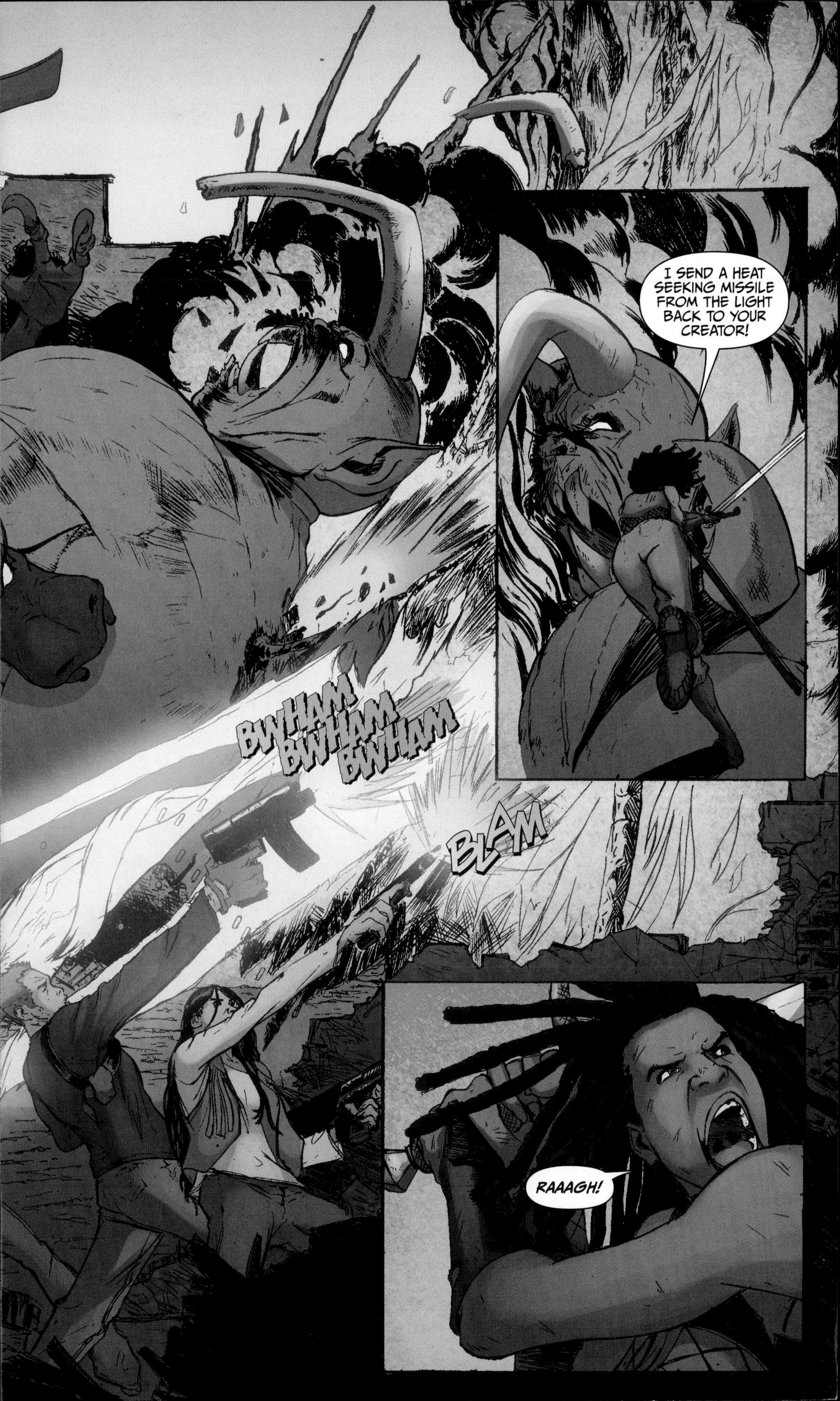
BWHAM BWHAM BWHAM
BLAM
I SEND A HEAT SEEKING MISSILE FROM THE LIGHT BACK TO YOUR CREATOR!
RAAAGH!

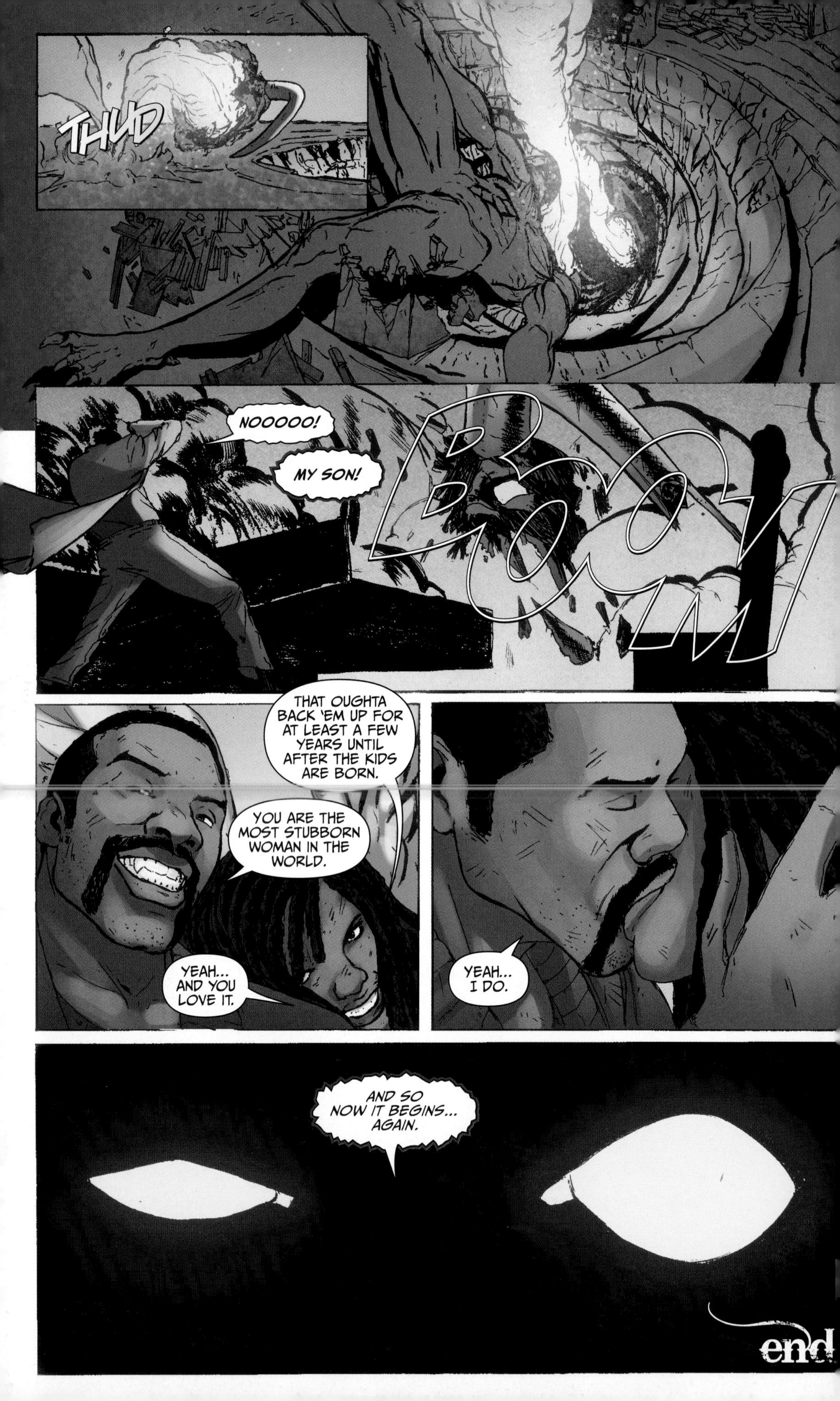
THUD
NOOOOO!
MY SON!
BOOM
THAT OUGHTA BACK 'EM UP FOR AT LEAST A FEW YEARS UNTIL AFTER THE KIDS ARE BORN.
YOU ARE THE MOST STUBBORN WOMAN IN THE WORLD.
YEAH... AND YOU LOVE IT.
YEAH... I DO.
AND SO NOW IT BEGINS... AGAIN.
end

THE VAMPIRE HUNTRESS LEGENDS GRAPHIC NOVEL & COMICS
AN AFTERWORD BY L.A. BANKS

This project can only be described as a true labor of love. After living with the full cadre of characters you see represented in the Vampire Huntress comics and follow on graphic novel through twelve books that spanned approximately 400 manuscript pages each, as a writer you become vested in these fictional (but very real to you) people. Yeah… they live on in your head, and there are days where you're wondering what they might be up to next. Readers also ask you that question and demand that you do "just one more book," but I promised myself unless I had a complete story I would stop… who wants to get to the end of a series they enjoyed only to be disappointed that the last follow on book wasn't as strong as all the others. (Readers I am saving you from yourselves on that one, smile.)

But as a novelist, comics opened up a brand new medium and an awesome new "space in my head." For the first time I could see images of what my beloved characters were doing, and I could think beyond book #12 in the novel series to what types of challenges Damali and Carlos would face as a team after the so-called "big war." Seeing those images made me think outside the box, think about what would happen if half the team of warriors was pregnant… reactions, dangers, threats, all the thrills, chills, and spills. It made me have to conceive of the next day—okay, they won temporarily, you ended the novels on an epic battle… now what?

That's where you start mining for questions like—who would still be after them, how would they come at them, after a catastrophic world event, how would people be living, moving about in a post-apocalyptic environment? Who would be in power, how would they control the masses? What's at stake? And you build from there. But in comics, the story is told 85% in pictures. That was new for me, having had a huge canvas of thousands of words at my disposal in the form of a novel. Not so in comics, I quickly learned (Big Smile!)

Bringing things down to scale is like going from being a muralist to working in the fine art of crafting and minting a limited edition postage stamp. Both are forms of art. Both have their attendant skill sets. Both require mastery. I bow to those comics writers who have set the Olympic bar of excellence and I'm deeply honored that Dynamite Entertainment gave me the opportunity to come out and play in their wonderful sandbox of writers, editors, and artists.

There are absolutely no words to describe what it felt like to see those first pencils, to be in on the art direction, to actually watch the characters take shape on the page and get colored, and then watch the process of the lettering get added in. Even more to the point was being able to be in this highly collaborative industry as a member of a larger team (also a first, because novelists generally work solo, then get edited by one editor, and the project is done.) The added bonus was not only learning a new medium with a fantastic group of people, but also having an outlet for storylines that will not quit banging around in my head. The Vampire Huntress Legends, I suspect, will always haunt me to some degree. It'll always have more to it to tell, and the comics are perfect for that ongoing evolution of the ride or die warrior team. In fact, I was so moved to keep writing about the next generation - those babies the team female warriors were carrying during the comic series - that I couldn't help myself from crafting a new novel about them, entitled, Shadow Walker. How could I resist showing the teenagers of the team that now have to take up their parents battle? But I digress… FUN is the word that comes to mind for all of this. Comics are fun! This project has been a blast. My hat's off to Brett Booth, Greg Titus, and N. Steven Harris, who brought the characters to life with fabulous images. I also have to give a serious nod of respect to Rich Young, who shepherded this baby into manifestation, plus all the staff at Dynamite that midwifed it through edits, lettering, coloring, and got it out of the door. But my biggest thanks go to Nick Barrucci and Juan Collado, who took a chance on a vampire novel franchise by a crazy author. Thank you, gentlemen! All of this was very new and very exciting, and I truly appreciate you and all the readers for your wonderful support along the way!

The Making of: L.A. BANKS' VAMPIRE HUNTRESS

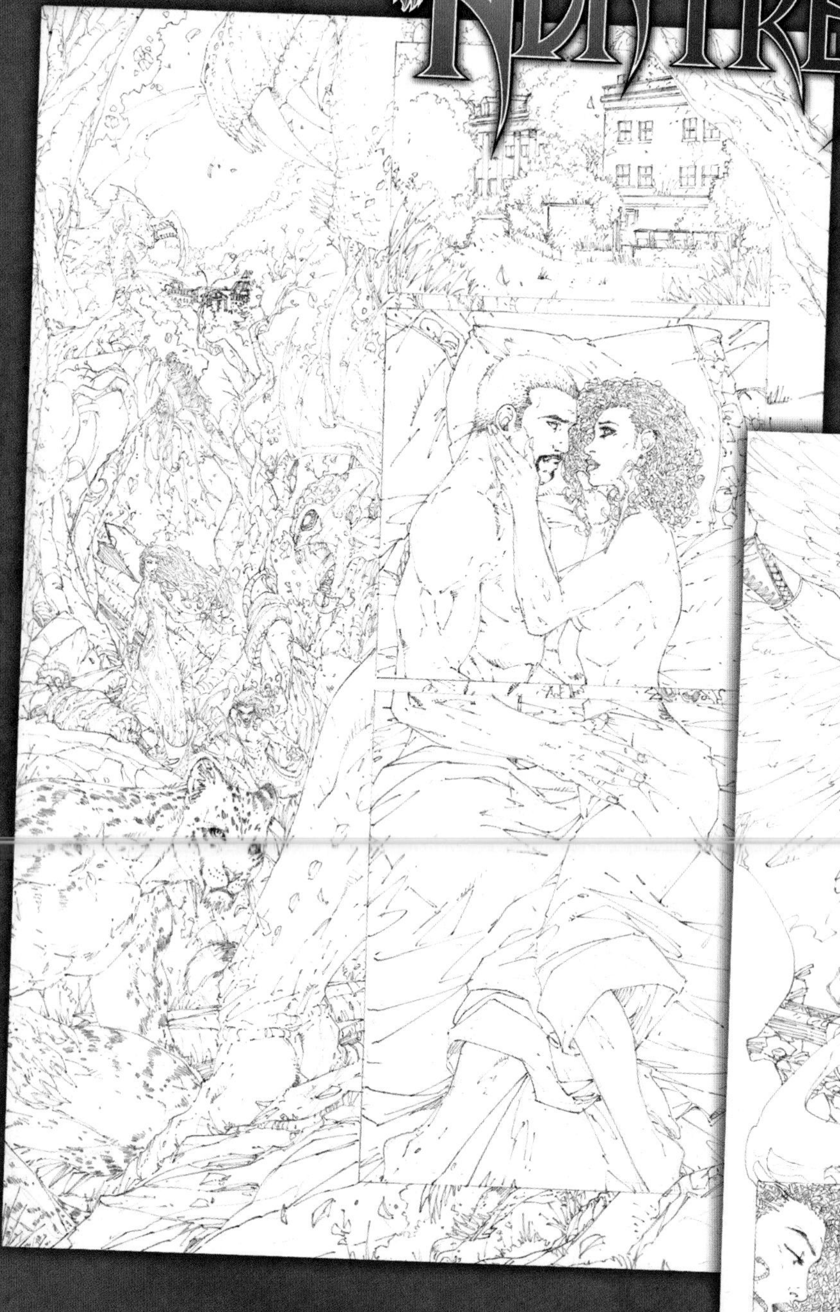

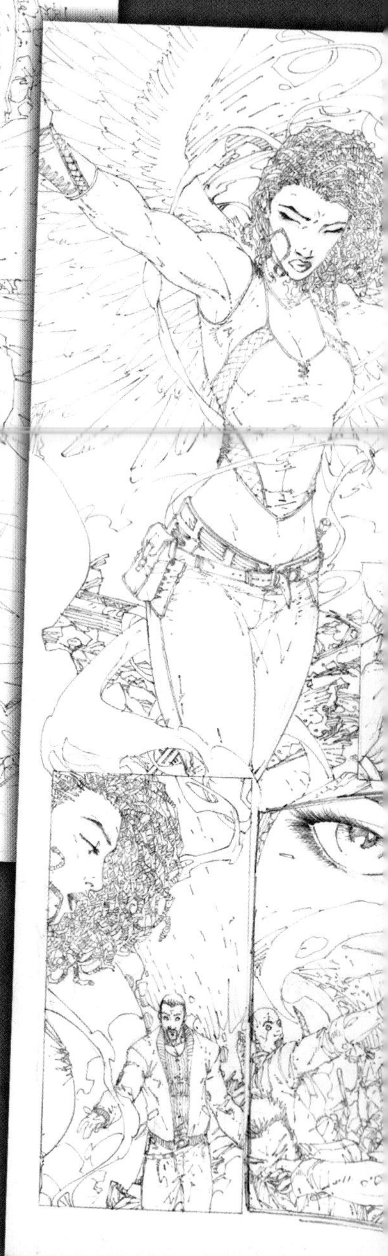

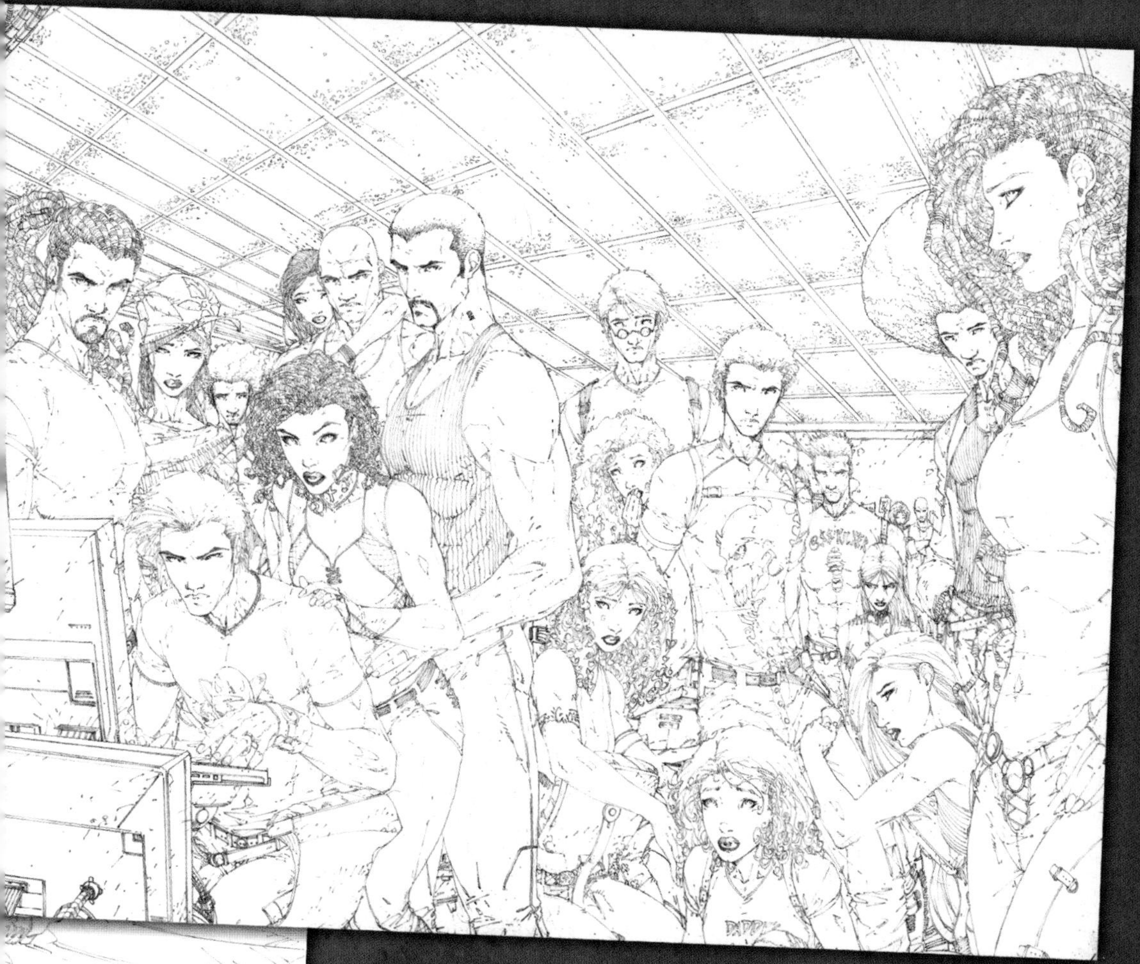

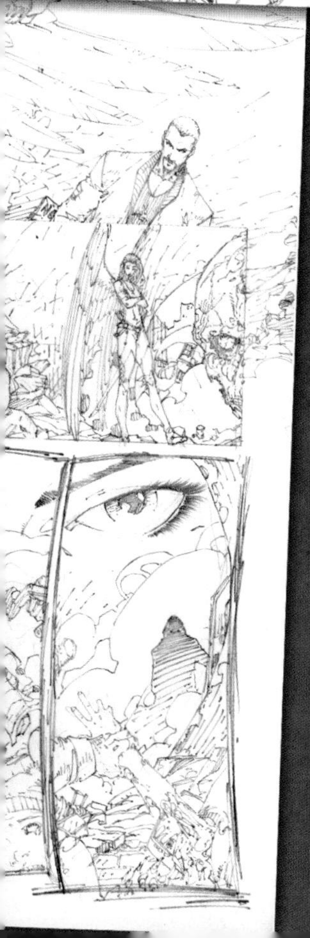

We had to make a decision early on, just when - timing wise in the story - we'd pick up the battle. The consideration would definitely affect the art, since several female characters were pregnant. Being real, fly kicking and demon-battling isn't as sexy with a baby bump, smile... so we opted to go right in during the first trimester. It's amazing how little details like that will make a HUGE difference in the visuals.

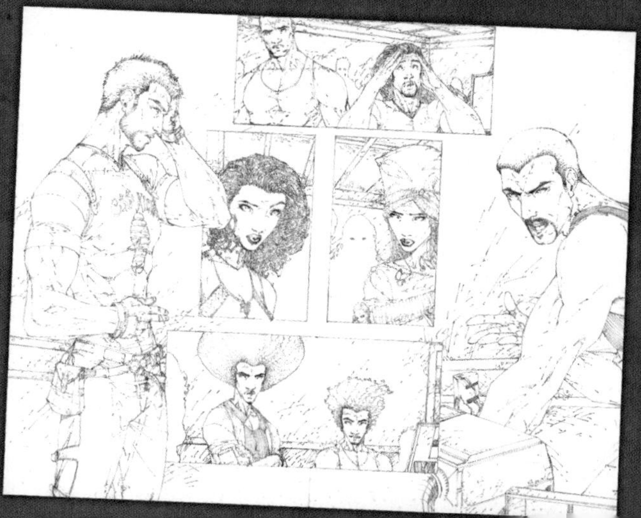

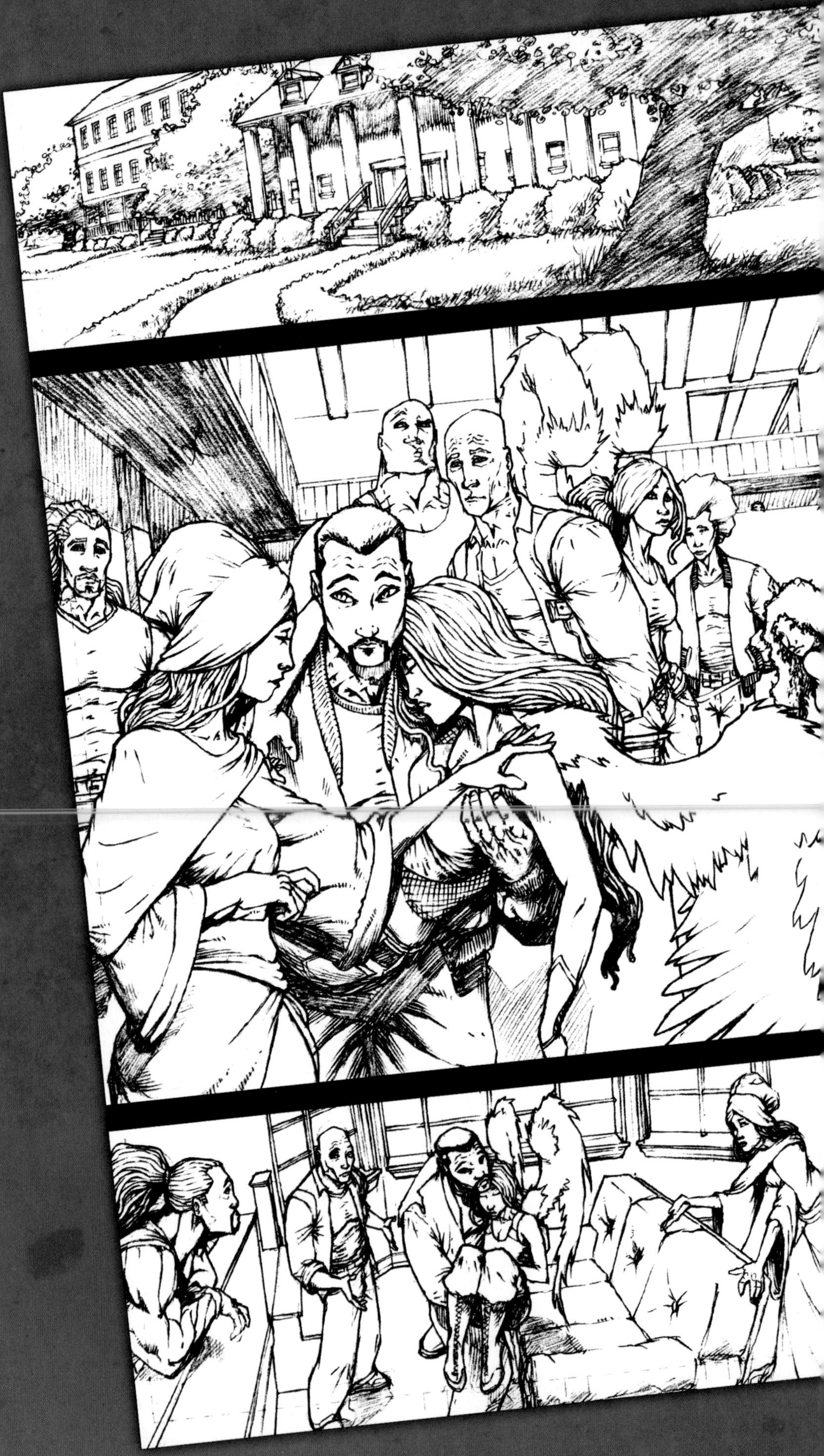

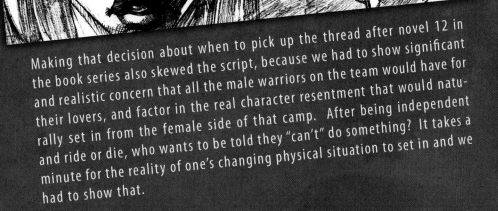

Making that decision about when to pick up the thread after novel 12 in the book series also skewed the script, because we had to show significant and realistic concern that all the male warriors on the team would have for their lovers, and factor in the real character resentment that would naturally set in from the female side of that camp. After being independent and ride or die, who wants to be told they "can't" do something? It takes a minute for the reality of one's changing physical situation to set in and we had to show that.

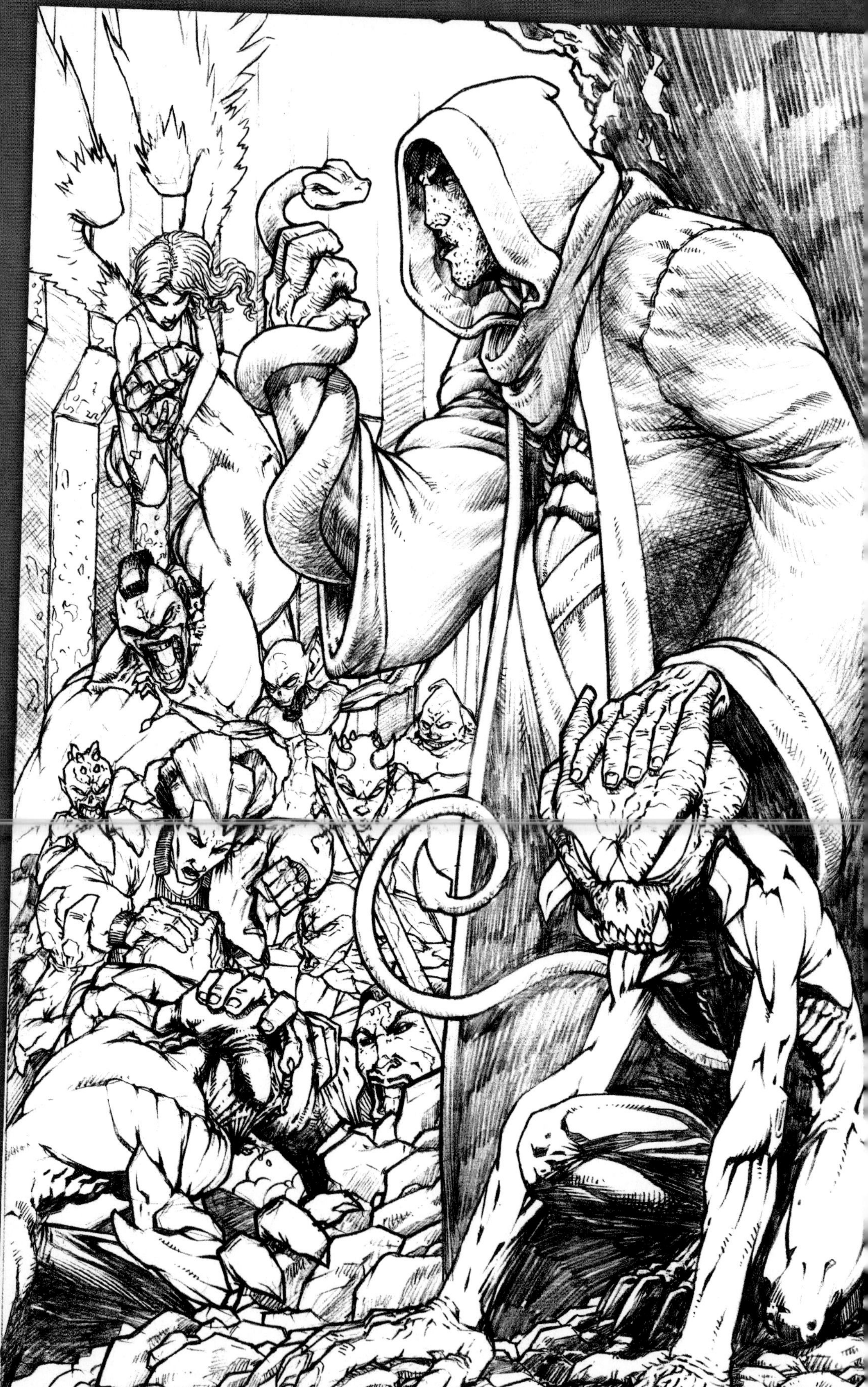

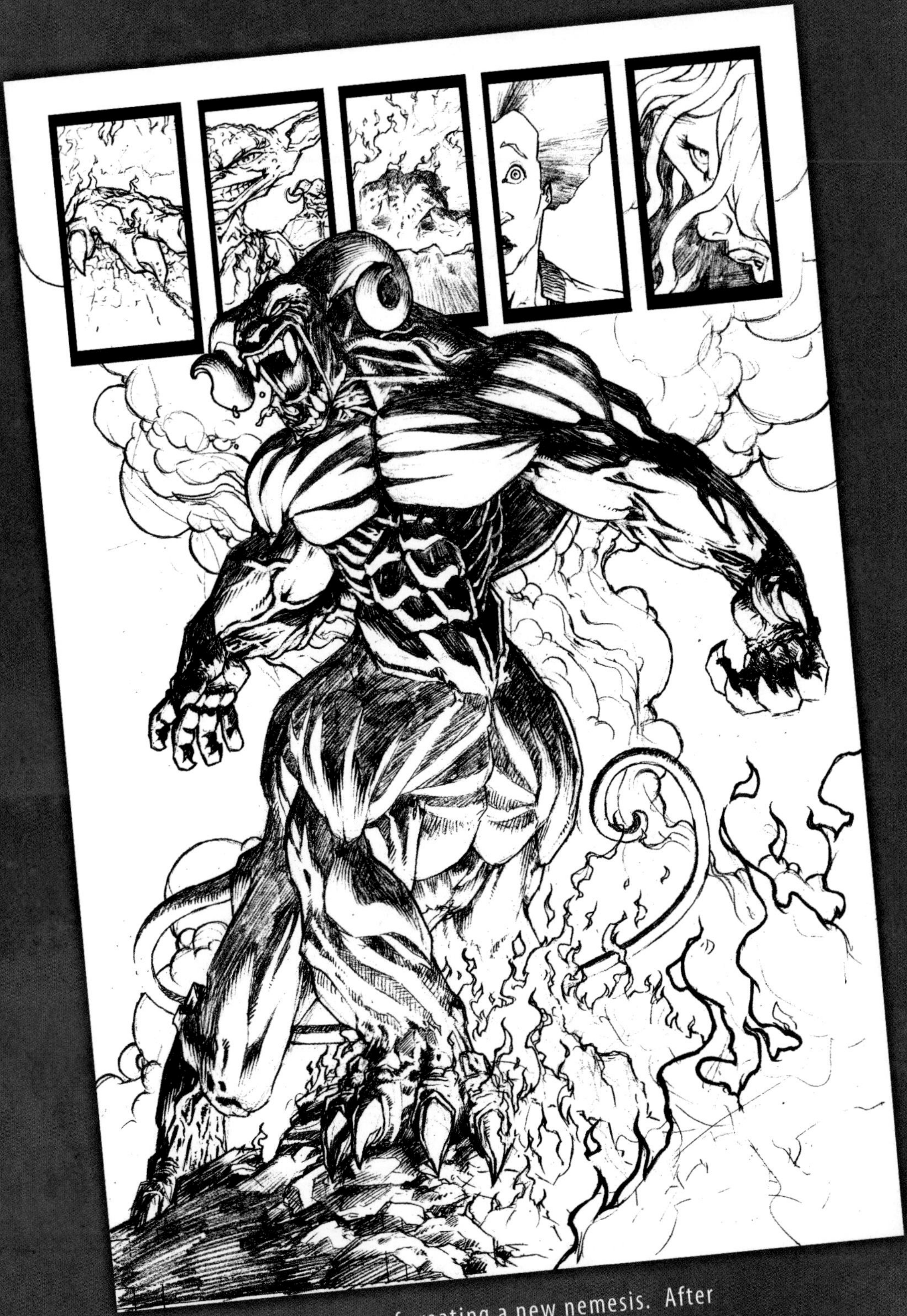

Then there was the issue of creating a new nemesis. After killing off almost every bad guy, we had to brainstorm up something new from Hell. The results were crazy!

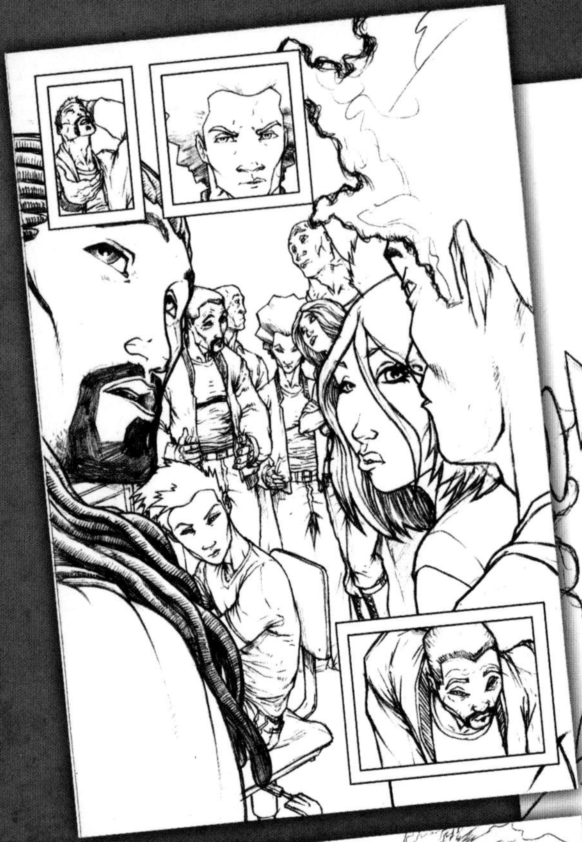

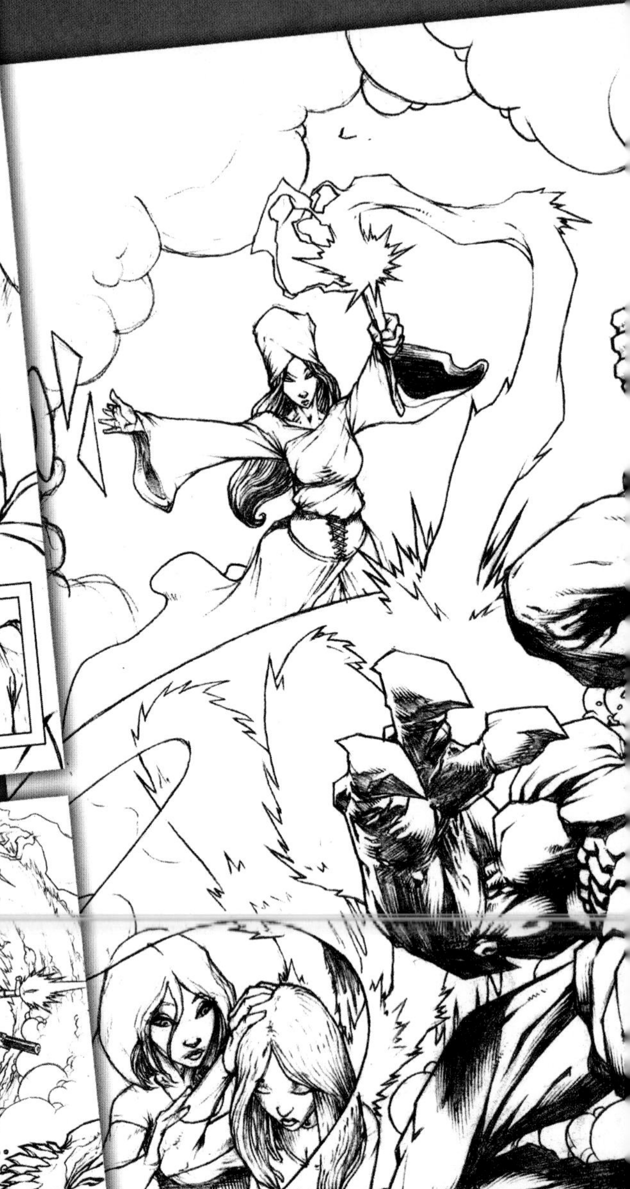

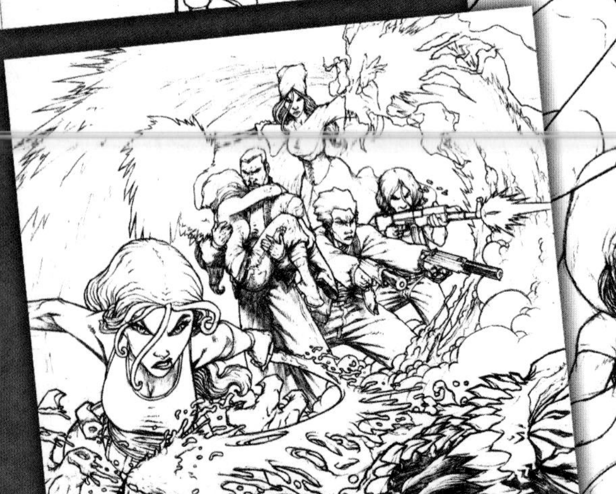

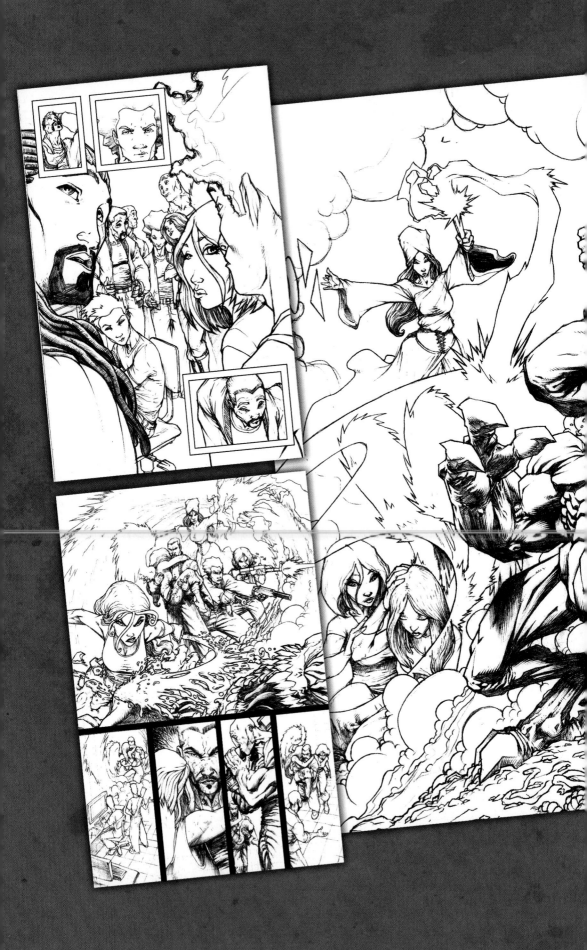

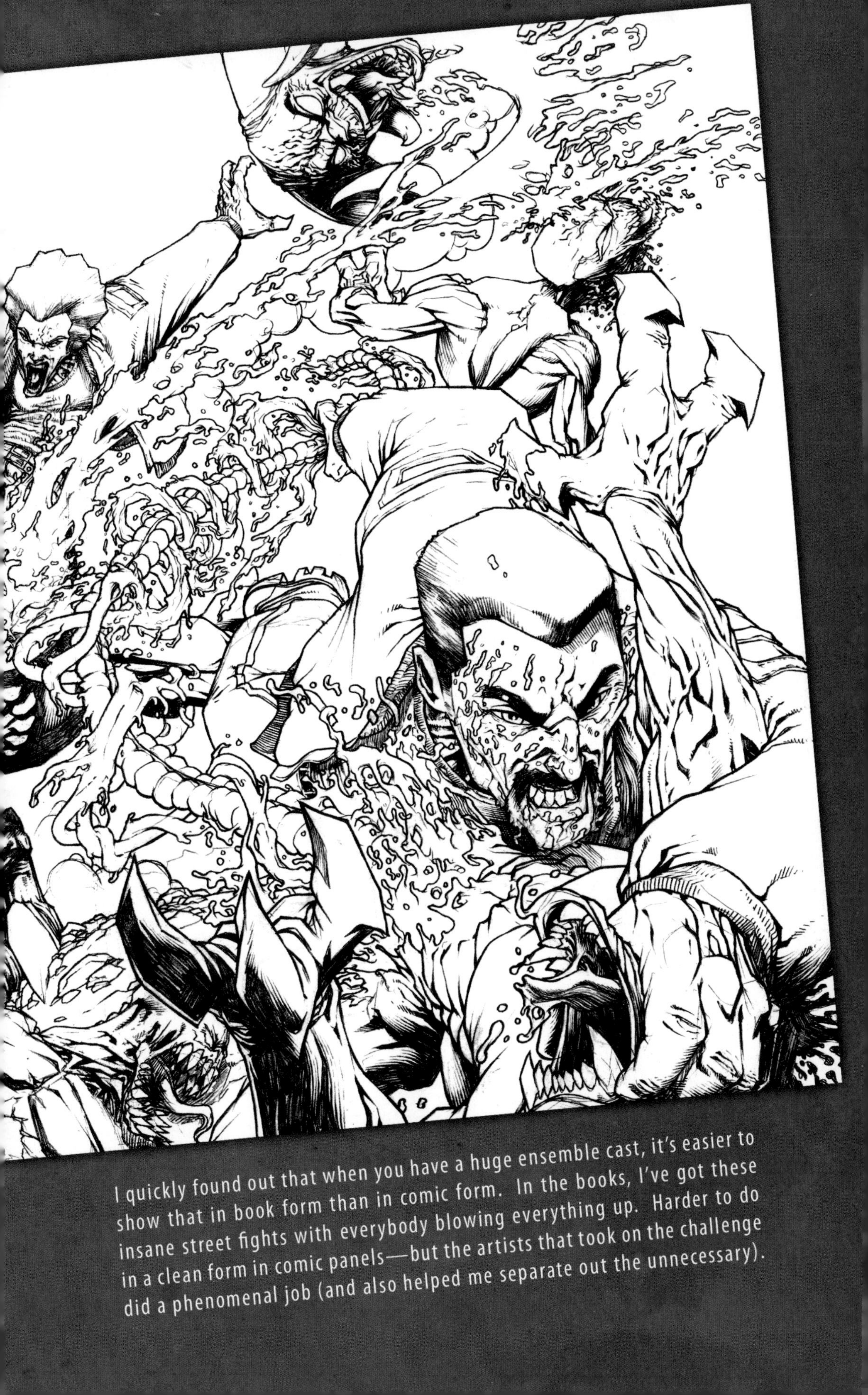

I quickly found out that when you have a huge ensemble cast, it's easier to show that in book form than in comic form. In the books, I've got these insane street fights with everybody blowing everything up. Harder to do in a clean form in comic panels—but the artists that took on the challenge did a phenomenal job (and also helped me separate out the unnecessary).

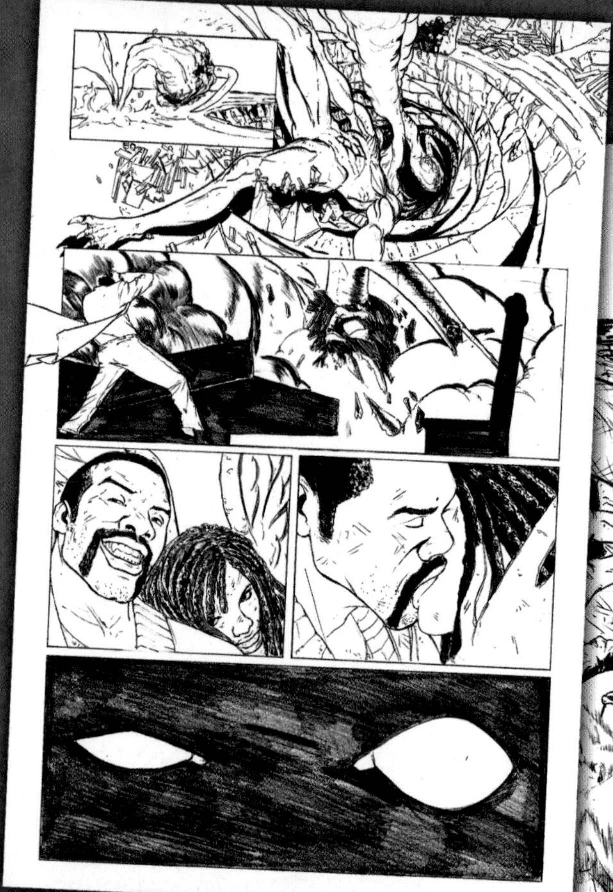

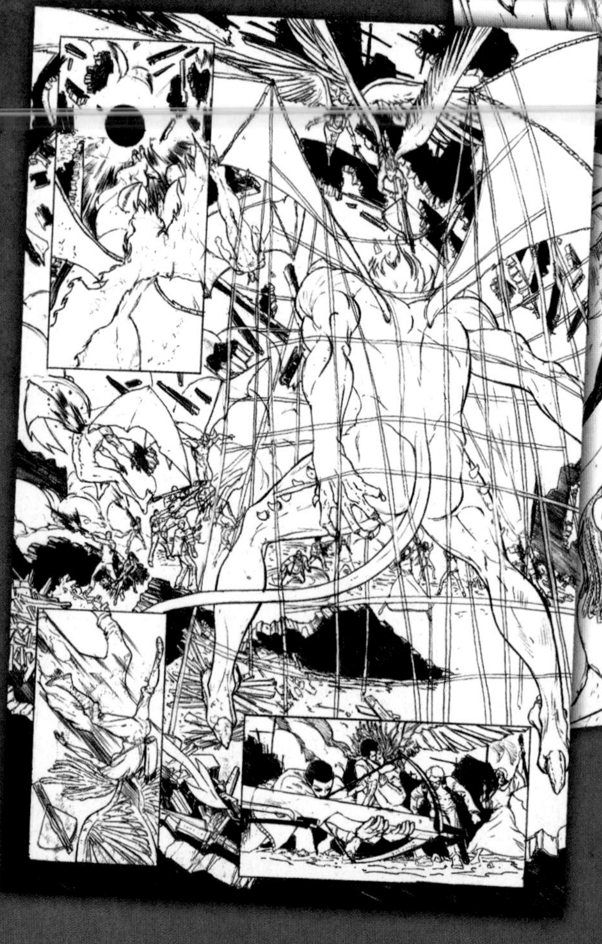

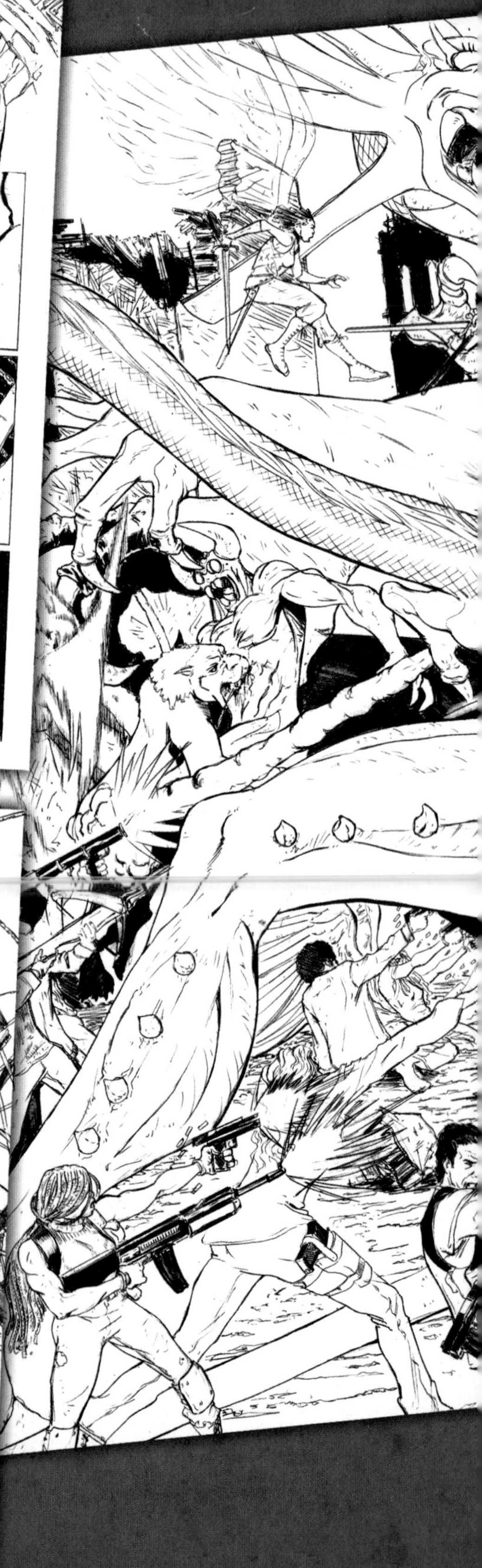

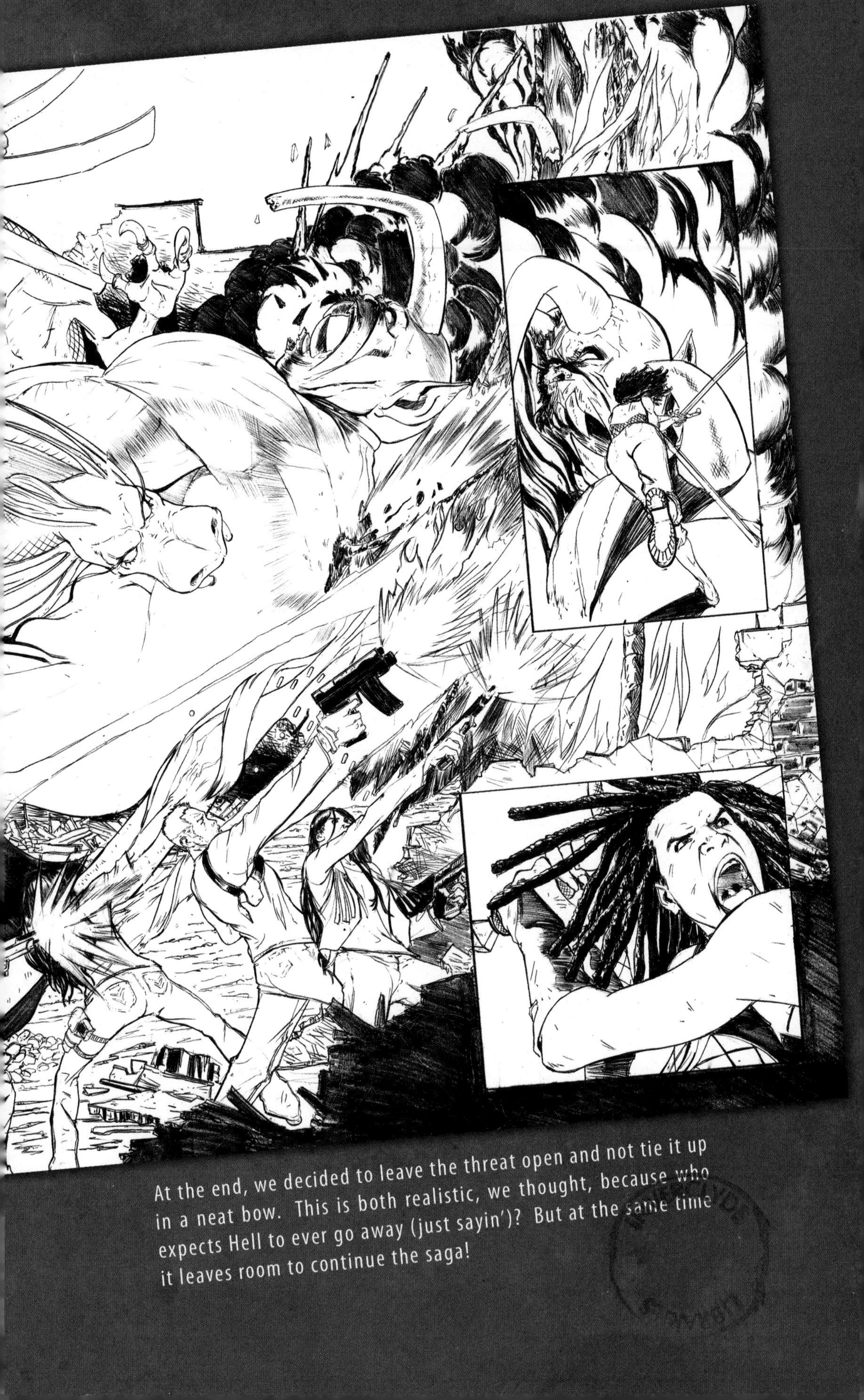

At the end, we decided to leave the threat open and not tie it up in a neat bow. This is both realistic, we thought, because who expects Hell to ever go away (just sayin')? But at the same time it leaves room to continue the saga!

L.A. BANKS'

Vampire Huntress

VOLUME ONE

DAWN AND DARKNESS

RELENTLESS

THE AUTHORITY

WARREN ELLIS
writer

BRYAN HITCH
penciler

PAUL NEARY
inker

LAURA DEPUY
colorist

David Baron - Chris Garcia - Michael Garcia - Eric Guerrero
color assists

Bill O'Neil - Ali Fuchs - Robbie Robbins
letterers

Cover Illustration and Gallery Art by
Bryan Hitch, Paul Neary and Laura DePuy

Collected Edition Design by
Darren Nylec

The Authority Created by
Warren Ellis and Bryan Hitch

THE AUTHORITY: RELENTLESS Published by WildStorm Productions. Editorial offices: 888 Prospect St. Suite #240, La Jolla, CA 92037.
Cover and compilation copyright © 2000 WildStorm Productions, an imprint of DC Comics. All Rights Reserved. Originally published in
single magazine f   as THE AUTHORITY 1-8. Copyright © 1999 WildStorm Productio   AUTHORITY, all characters, the distinctive
likenesses the   d related indicia are trademarks of DC Comics. The stories, char   and incidents featured in this publication
are entirely fictional. WildStorm does not read or accept unsolicited subm   of ideas, stories or artwork.

Printed in Canada. Fourth Printing. ISBN: 1-56389-661-3
DC Comics. A division of Warner Bros. - An AOL Time Warner Company

THE AUTHORITY is the first great superhero team book of the 21st century. Beside it everything else seems pale and stale and repetitive. Be honest.

These words are like thoughts which ran through my mind when I read THE AUTHORITY number one back in early 1999: Warren peaking on pure intravenous Warren, self-generating. Hitch and Neary downloading and reprocessing epic DVDs to reimagine the way superheroes might look one more time for the hell of it, reaching higher again. Laura DePuy with God's own Paintshop splashing beauty across these pages. How could it fail to define the way everything felt? Warren knows what he's playing around with, and it's your head. Don't forget that. He harbors many a grudge, and a number of those are political.

Because traditional superhero teams always put the flag back on top of the White House, don't they? They always dust down the statues and repair the highways and everything ends up just the way it was before...

But what "IF"? What if the superheroes really decided to make a few changes according to a "higher moral authority"? What if they started to act the way WE might act faced with impossible problems? What if every problem was a solution in disguise? What if WE began to think like superhumans, on a scale we never imagined before?

THE AUTHORITY dares to imagine a world beyond the post-modern ironic hopelessness of endless recycled TV quotes and retro-nostalgic feedback. Welcome to a superteam with an agenda, on a scale beyond the billion dollar budgets. A superteam whose headquarters looks like a dog's nose and still kicks ass.

At a stroke THE AUTHORITY has endowed the tired superhero archetypes with vigorous new meaning, pumping the volume until noses bleed and bass patterns register deep on the Richter scale in Norway.

Welcome to the first volume of continuing mind-battering adventures in a landmark series, ye lucky bastards....

Tell your jealous brats: the storm broke here...

-Grant Morrison
LA 2000

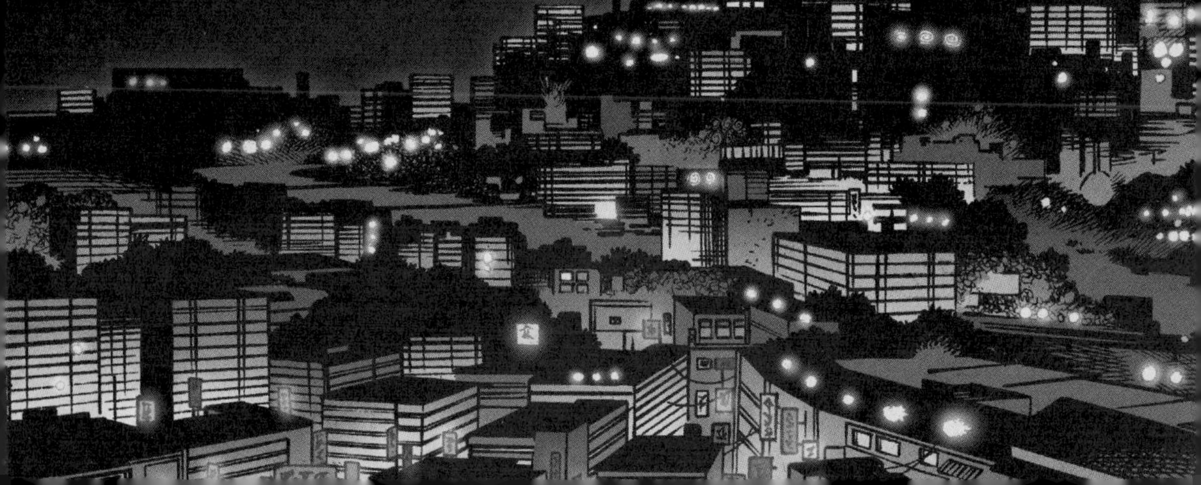

"THE CIRCLE"

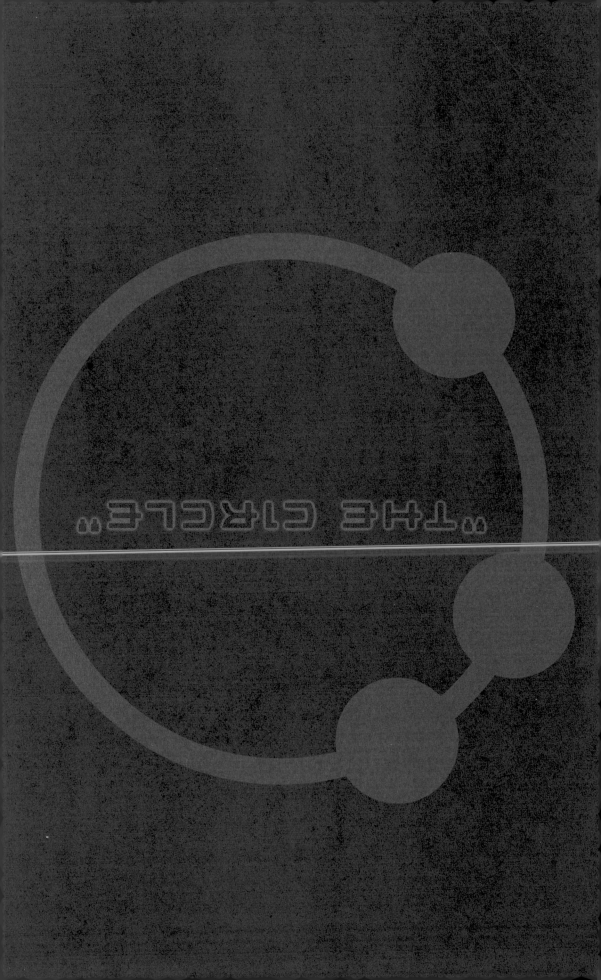

They think there's
no one left to
save the world.

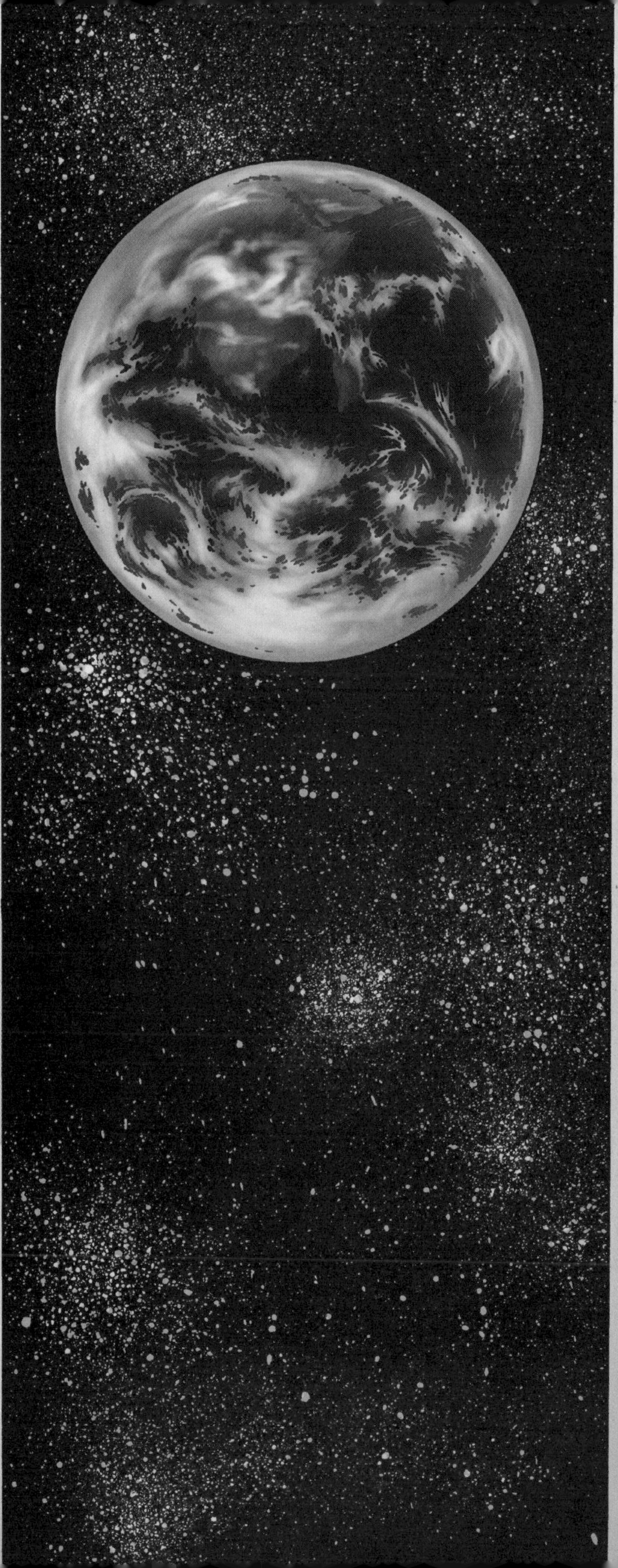

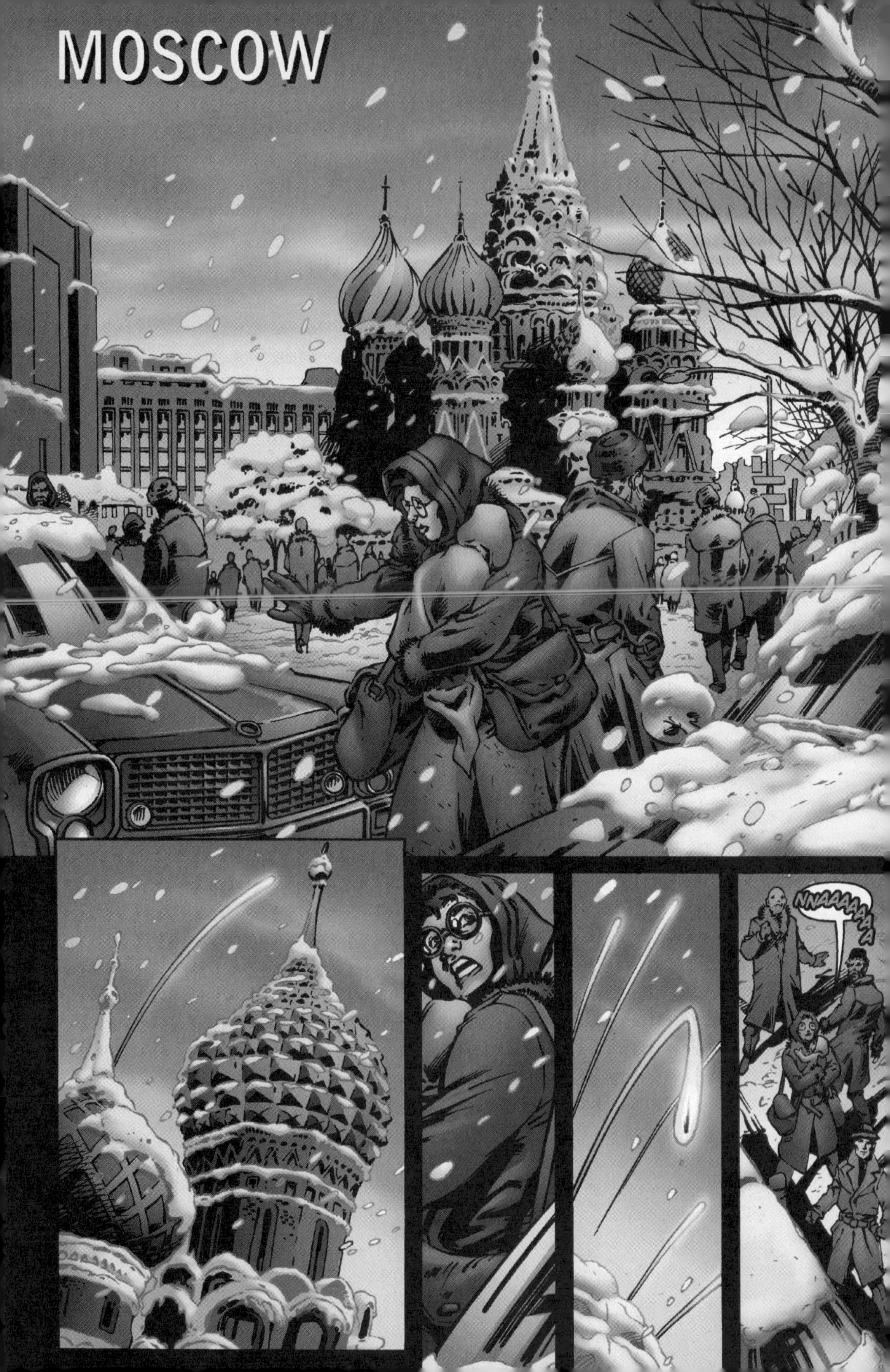
MOSCOW
NNAAAAAAAA

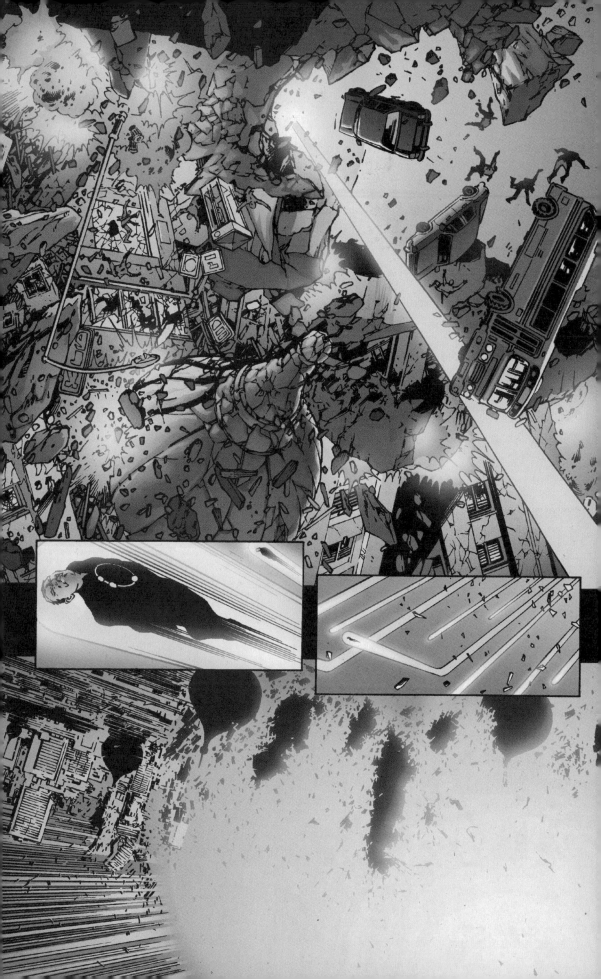

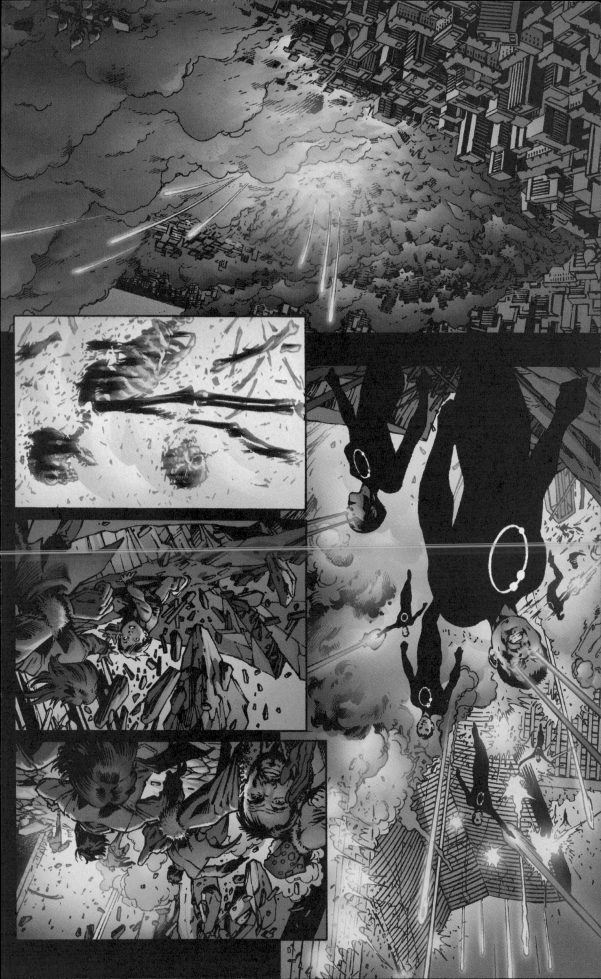

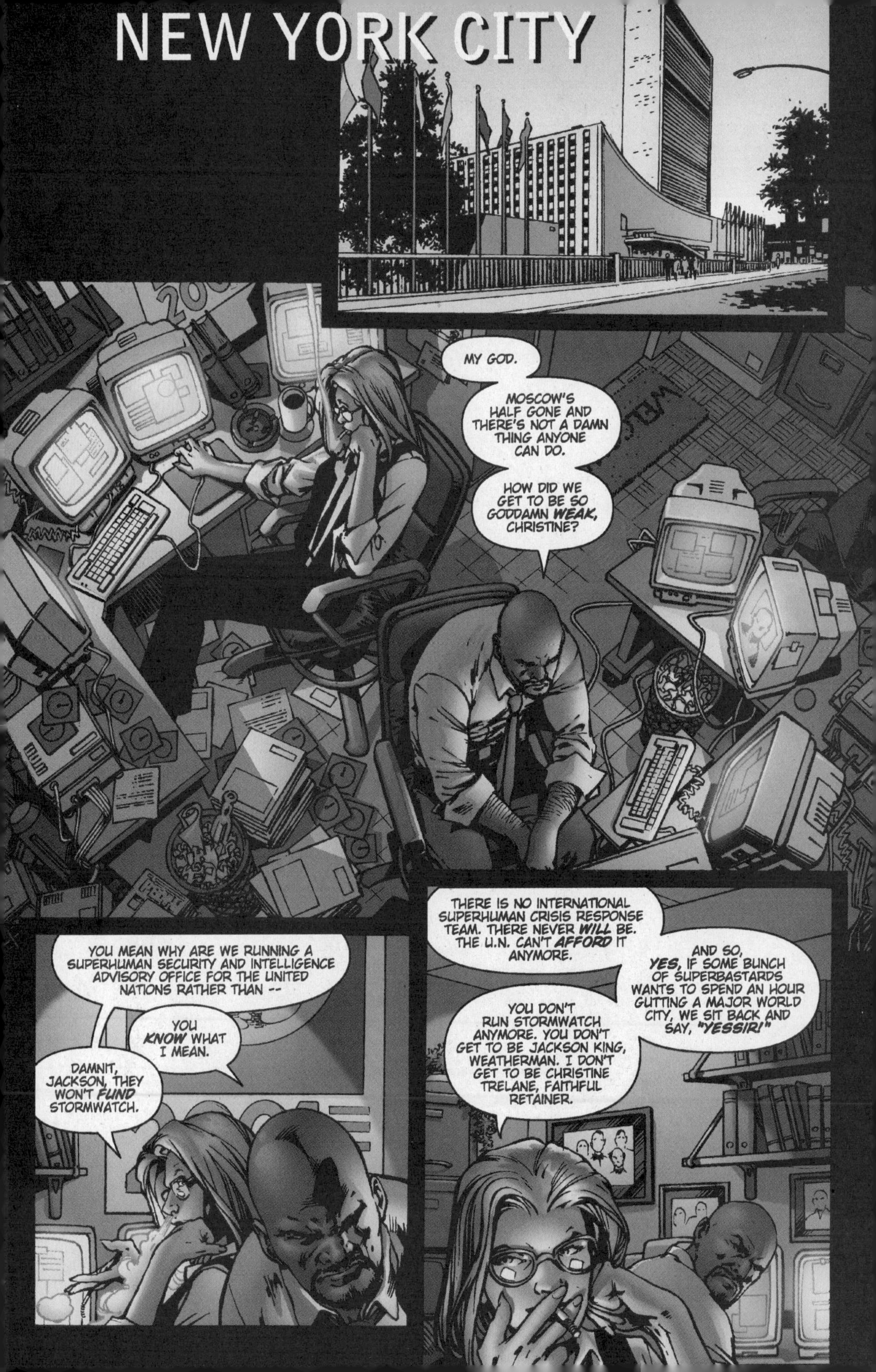
NEW YORK CITY
MY GOD.
MOSCOW'S HALF GONE AND THERE'S NOT A DAMN THING ANYONE CAN DO.
HOW DID WE GET TO BE SO GODDAMN WEAK, CHRISTINE?
YOU MEAN WHY ARE WE RUNNING A SUPERHUMAN SECURITY AND INTELLIGENCE ADVISORY OFFICE FOR THE UNITED NATIONS RATHER THAN --
YOU KNOW WHAT I MEAN.
DAMNIT, JACKSON, THEY WON'T FUND STORMWATCH.
THERE IS NO INTERNATIONAL SUPERHUMAN CRISIS RESPONSE TEAM. THERE NEVER WILL BE. THE U.N. CAN'T AFFORD IT ANYMORE.
AND SO, YES, IF SOME BUNCH OF SUPERBASTARDS WANTS TO SPEND AN HOUR GUTTING A MAJOR WORLD CITY, WE SIT BACK AND SAY, "YESSIR!"
YOU DON'T RUN STORMWATCH ANYMORE. YOU DON'T GET TO BE JACKSON KING, WEATHERMAN. I DON'T GET TO BE CHRISTINE TRELANE, FAITHFUL RETAINER.

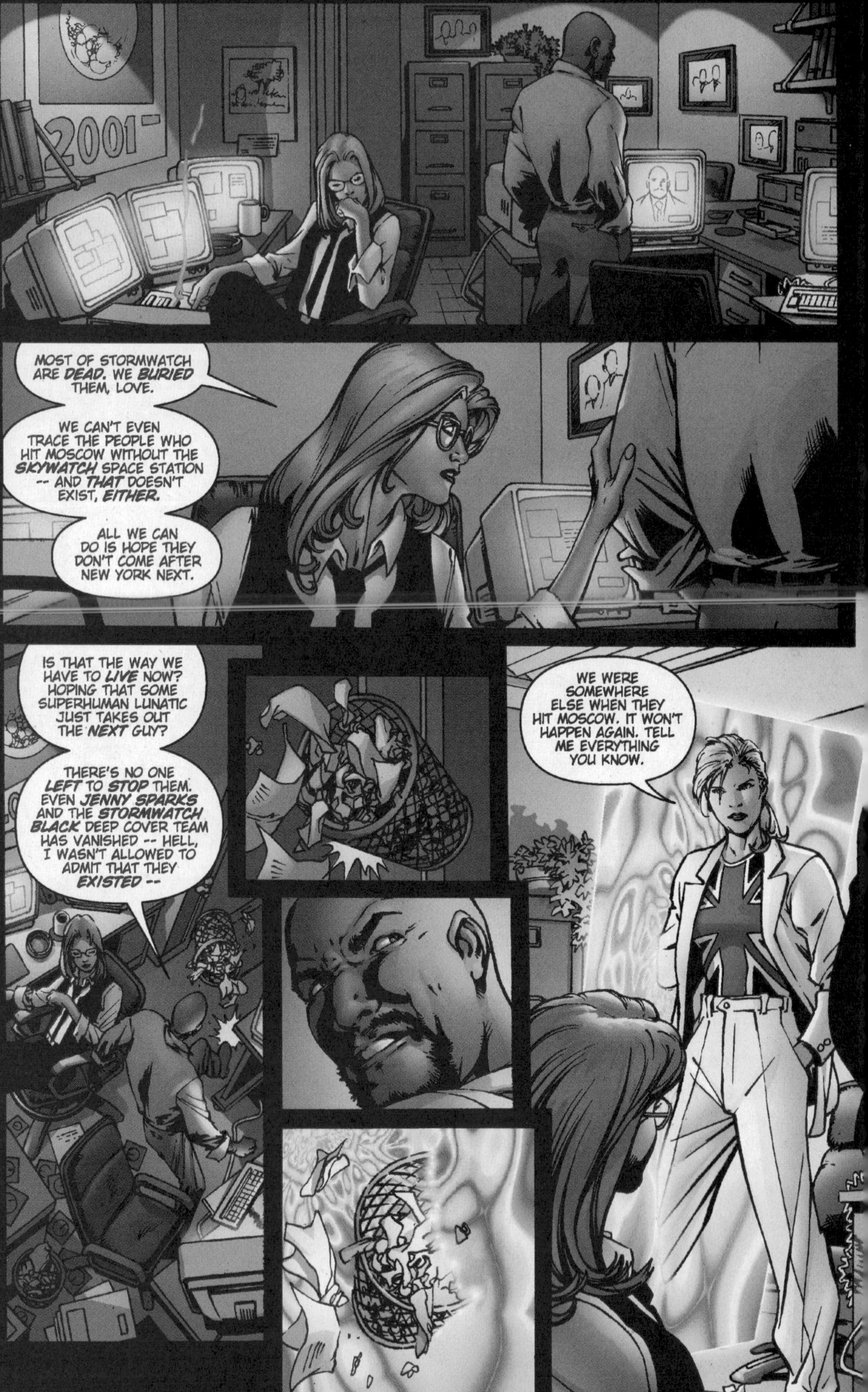
2001
MOST OF STORMWATCH ARE **DEAD**. WE **BURIED** THEM, LOVE.
WE CAN'T EVEN TRACE THE PEOPLE WHO HIT MOSCOW WITHOUT THE **SKYWATCH** SPACE STATION -- AND **THAT** DOESN'T EXIST, **EITHER**.
ALL WE CAN DO IS HOPE THEY DON'T COME AFTER NEW YORK NEXT.
IS THAT THE WAY WE HAVE TO **LIVE** NOW? HOPING THAT SOME SUPERHUMAN LUNATIC JUST TAKES OUT THE **NEXT** GUY?
THERE'S NO ONE **LEFT** TO **STOP** THEM. EVEN **JENNY SPARKS** AND THE **STORMWATCH BLACK** DEEP COVER TEAM HAS VANISHED -- HELL, I WASN'T ALLOWED TO ADMIT THAT THEY **EXISTED** --
WE WERE SOMEWHERE ELSE WHEN THEY HIT MOSCOW. IT WON'T HAPPEN AGAIN. TELL ME EVERYTHING YOU KNOW.

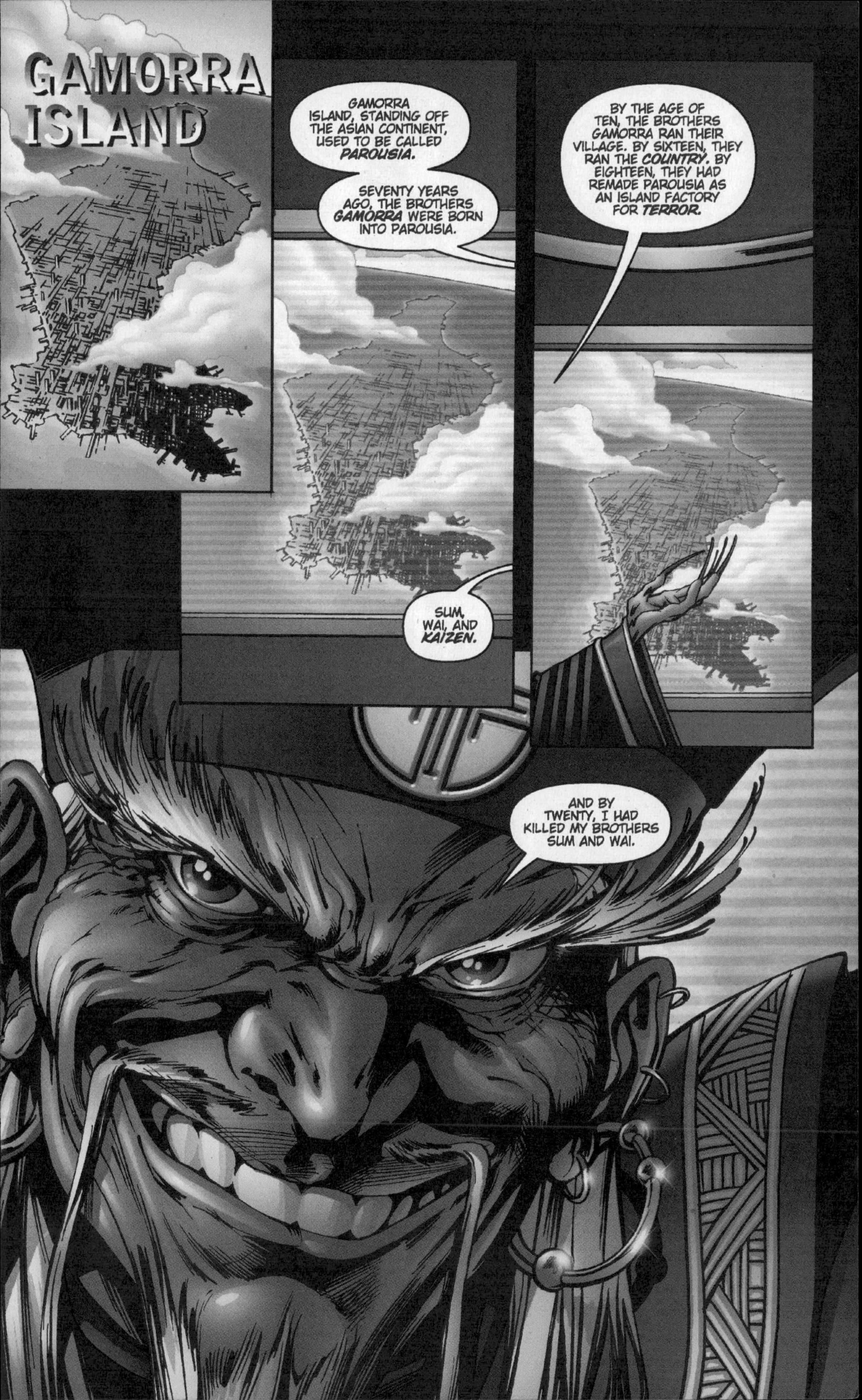
GAMORRA ISLAND
GAMORRA ISLAND, STANDING OFF THE ASIAN CONTINENT, USED TO BE CALLED *PAROUSIA*.
SEVENTY YEARS AGO, THE BROTHERS *GAMORRA* WERE BORN INTO PAROUSIA.
SUM, WAI, AND *KAIZEN*.
BY THE AGE OF TEN, THE BROTHERS GAMORRA RAN THEIR VILLAGE. BY SIXTEEN, THEY RAN THE *COUNTRY*. BY EIGHTEEN, THEY HAD REMADE PAROUSIA AS AN ISLAND FACTORY FOR *TERROR*.
AND BY TWENTY, I HAD KILLED MY BROTHERS SUM AND WAI.

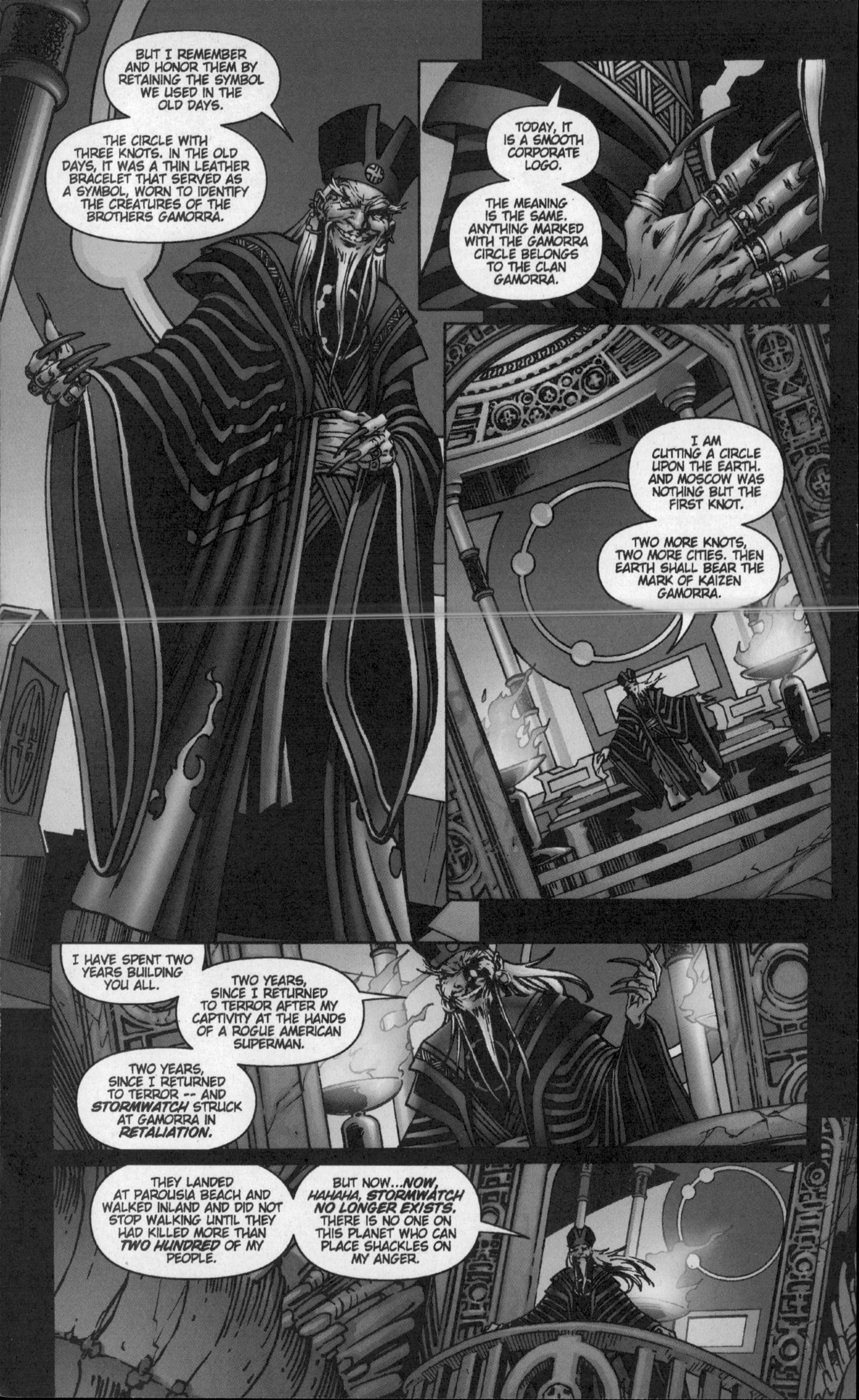
BUT I REMEMBER AND HONOR THEM BY RETAINING THE SYMBOL WE USED IN THE OLD DAYS.
THE CIRCLE WITH THREE KNOTS. IN THE OLD DAYS, IT WAS A THIN LEATHER BRACELET THAT SERVED AS A SYMBOL, WORN TO IDENTIFY THE CREATURES OF THE BROTHERS GAMORRA.
TODAY, IT IS A SMOOTH CORPORATE LOGO.
THE MEANING IS THE SAME. ANYTHING MARKED WITH THE GAMORRA CIRCLE BELONGS TO THE CLAN GAMORRA.
I AM CUTTING A CIRCLE UPON THE EARTH. AND MOSCOW WAS NOTHING BUT THE FIRST KNOT.
TWO MORE KNOTS, TWO MORE CITIES. THEN EARTH SHALL BEAR THE MARK OF KAIZEN GAMORRA.
I HAVE SPENT TWO YEARS BUILDING YOU ALL.
TWO YEARS, SINCE I RETURNED TO TERROR AFTER MY CAPTIVITY AT THE HANDS OF A ROGUE AMERICAN SUPERMAN.
TWO YEARS, SINCE I RETURNED TO TERROR -- AND ***STORMWATCH*** STRUCK AT GAMORRA IN ***RETALIATION.***
THEY LANDED AT PAROUSIA BEACH AND WALKED INLAND AND DID NOT STOP WALKING UNTIL THEY HAD KILLED MORE THAN ***TWO HUNDRED*** OF MY PEOPLE.
BUT NOW...***NOW, HAHAHA, STORMWATCH NO LONGER EXISTS.*** THERE IS NO ONE ON THIS PLANET WHO CAN PLACE SHACKLES ON MY ANGER.

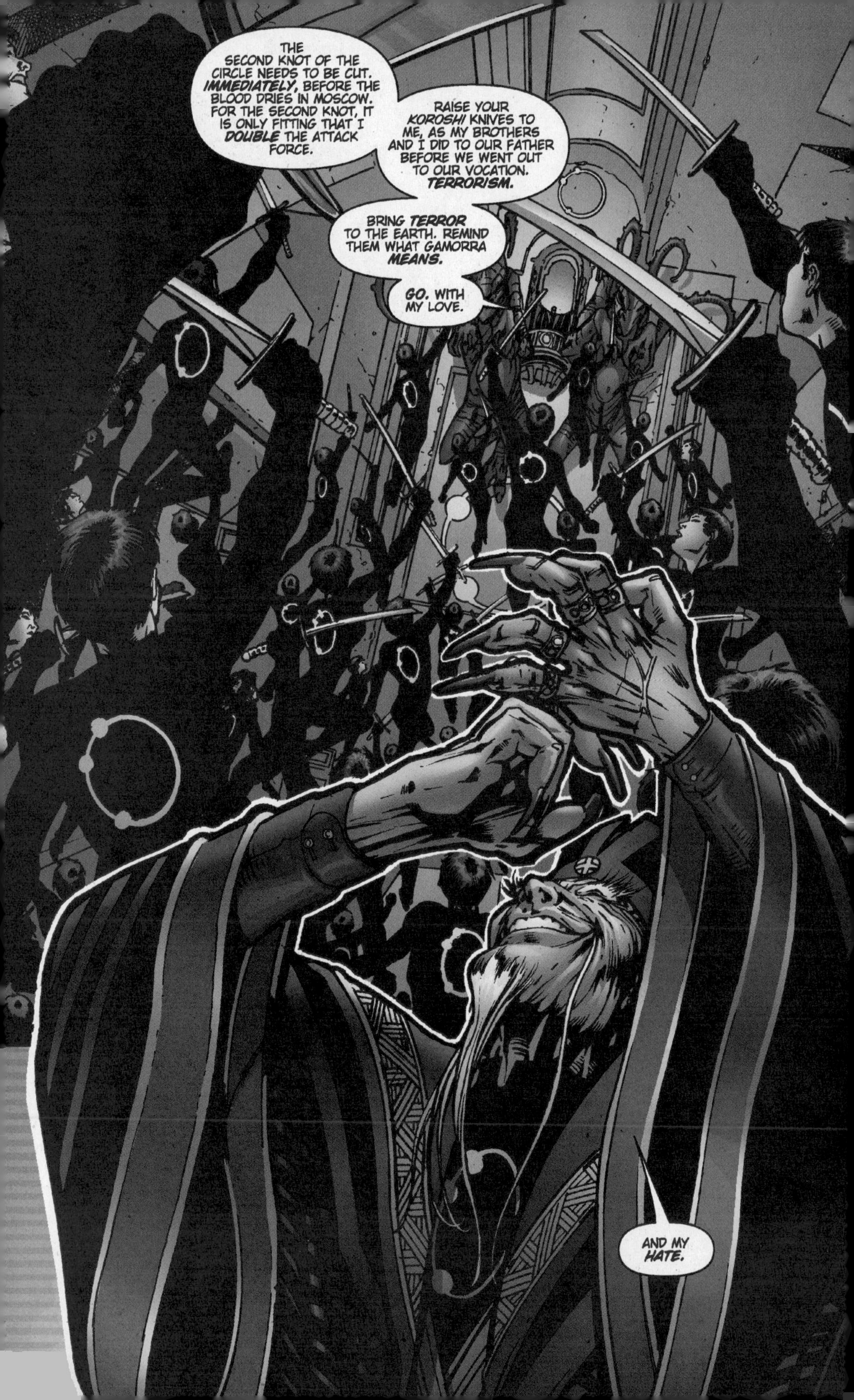
THE SECOND KNOT OF THE CIRCLE NEEDS TO BE CUT. **IMMEDIATELY**, BEFORE THE BLOOD DRIES IN MOSCOW. FOR THE SECOND KNOT, IT IS ONLY FITTING THAT I **DOUBLE** THE ATTACK FORCE.
RAISE YOUR *KOROSHI* KNIVES TO ME, AS MY BROTHERS AND I DID TO OUR FATHER BEFORE WE WENT OUT TO OUR VOCATION. **TERRORISM.**
BRING **TERROR** TO THE EARTH. REMIND THEM WHAT GAMORRA **MEANS.**
GO. WITH MY LOVE.
AND MY **HATE.**

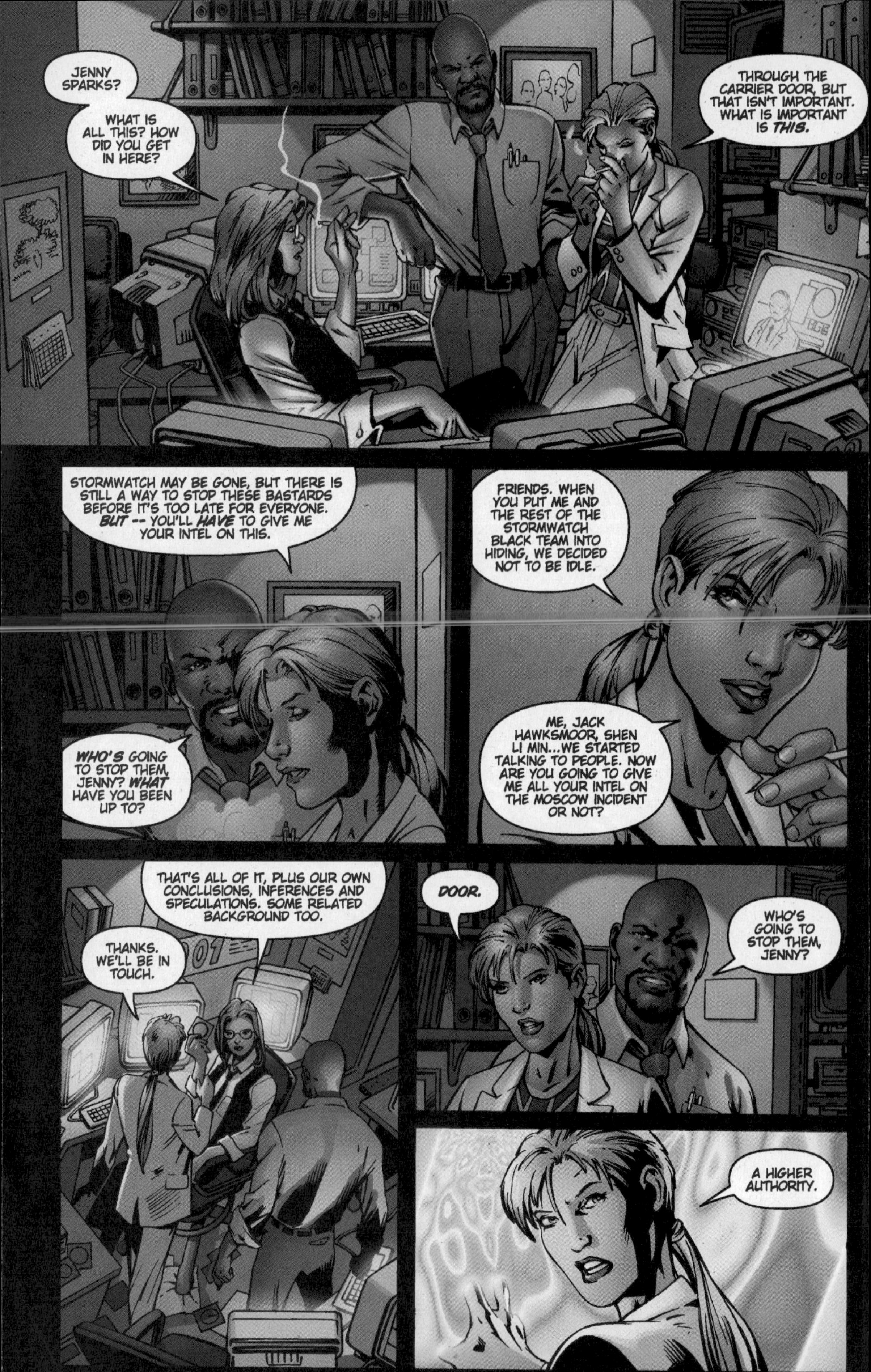
JENNY SPARKS?
WHAT IS ALL THIS? HOW DID YOU GET IN HERE?
THROUGH THE CARRIER DOOR, BUT THAT ISN'T IMPORTANT. WHAT IS IMPORTANT IS *THIS.*
STORMWATCH MAY BE GONE, BUT THERE IS STILL A WAY TO STOP THESE BASTARDS BEFORE IT'S TOO LATE FOR EVERYONE. *BUT* -- YOU'LL *HAVE* TO GIVE ME YOUR INTEL ON THIS.
WHO'S GOING TO STOP THEM, JENNY? *WHAT* HAVE YOU BEEN UP TO?
FRIENDS. WHEN YOU PUT ME AND THE REST OF THE STORMWATCH BLACK TEAM INTO HIDING, WE DECIDED NOT TO BE IDLE.
ME, JACK HAWKSMOOR, SHEN LI MIN...WE STARTED TALKING TO PEOPLE. NOW ARE YOU GOING TO GIVE ME ALL YOUR INTEL ON THE MOSCOW INCIDENT OR NOT?
THAT'S ALL OF IT, PLUS OUR OWN CONCLUSIONS, INFERENCES AND SPECULATIONS. SOME RELATED BACKGROUND TOO.
THANKS. WE'LL BE IN TOUCH.
DOOR.
WHO'S GOING TO STOP THEM, JENNY?
A HIGHER AUTHORITY.

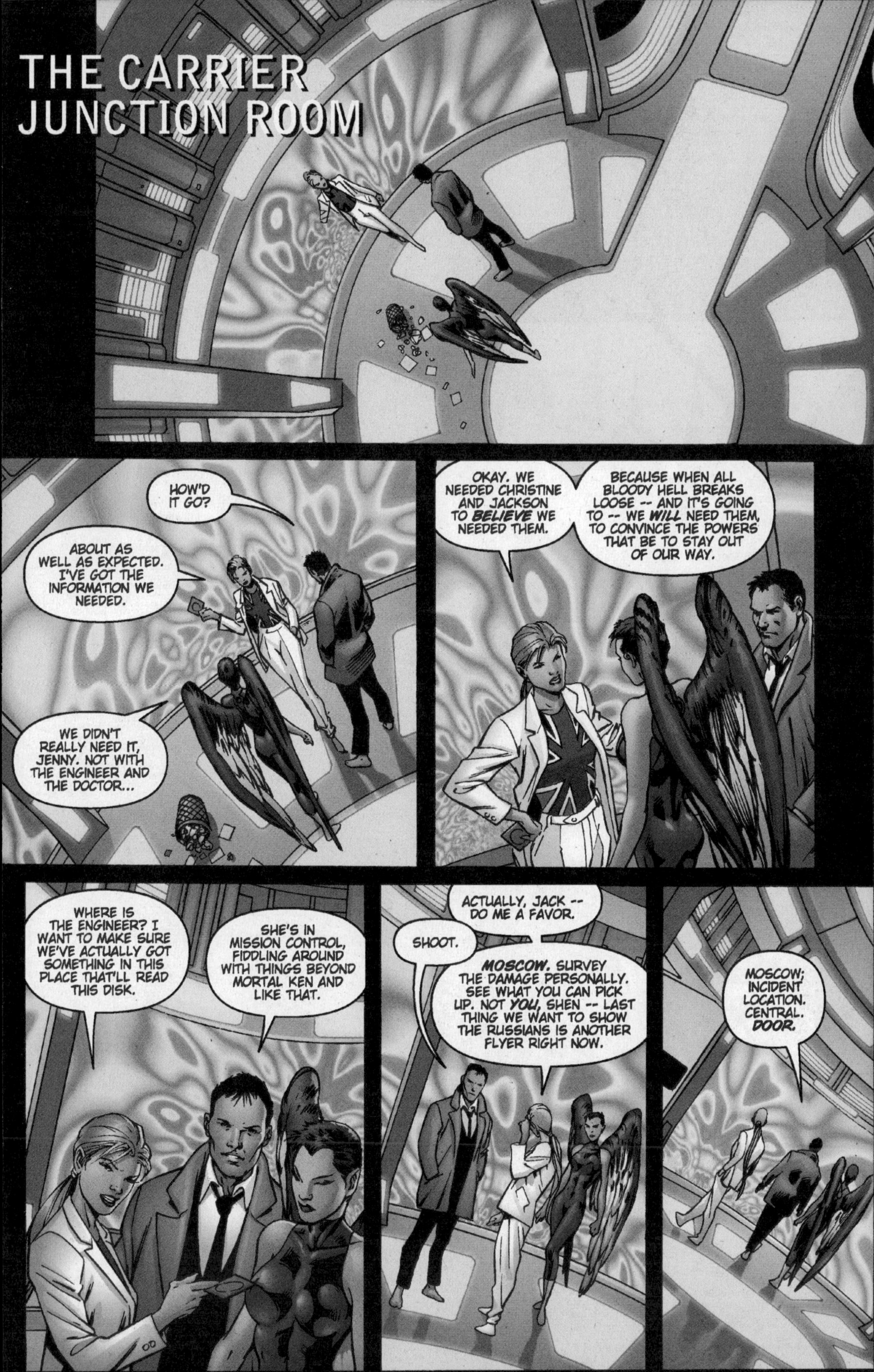
THE CARRIER JUNCTION ROOM
HOW'D IT GO?
ABOUT AS WELL AS EXPECTED. I'VE GOT THE INFORMATION WE NEEDED.
WE DIDN'T REALLY NEED IT, JENNY. NOT WITH THE ENGINEER AND THE DOCTOR...
OKAY. WE NEEDED CHRISTINE AND JACKSON TO *BELIEVE* WE NEEDED THEM.
BECAUSE WHEN ALL BLOODY HELL BREAKS LOOSE -- AND IT'S GOING TO -- WE *WILL* NEED THEM, TO CONVINCE THE POWERS THAT BE TO STAY OUT OF OUR WAY.
WHERE IS THE ENGINEER? I WANT TO MAKE SURE WE'VE ACTUALLY GOT SOMETHING IN THIS PLACE THAT'LL READ THIS DISK.
SHE'S IN MISSION CONTROL, FIDDLING AROUND WITH THINGS BEYOND MORTAL KEN AND LIKE THAT.
ACTUALLY, JACK -- DO ME A FAVOR.
SHOOT.
MOSCOW. SURVEY THE DAMAGE PERSONALLY. SEE WHAT YOU CAN PICK UP. NOT *YOU,* SHEN -- LAST THING WE WANT TO SHOW THE RUSSIANS IS ANOTHER FLYER RIGHT NOW.
MOSCOW; INCIDENT LOCATION. CENTRAL. *DOOR.*

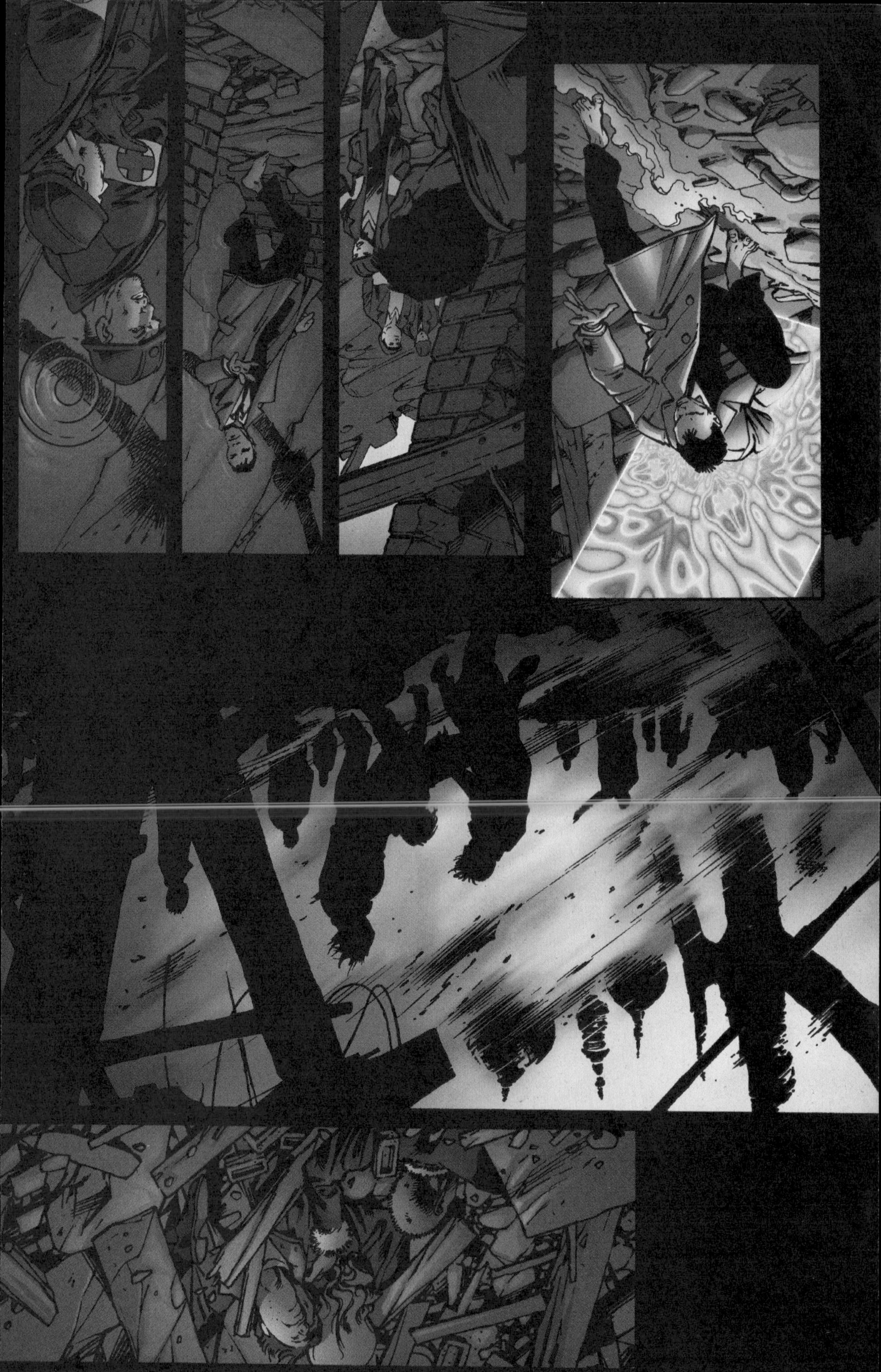

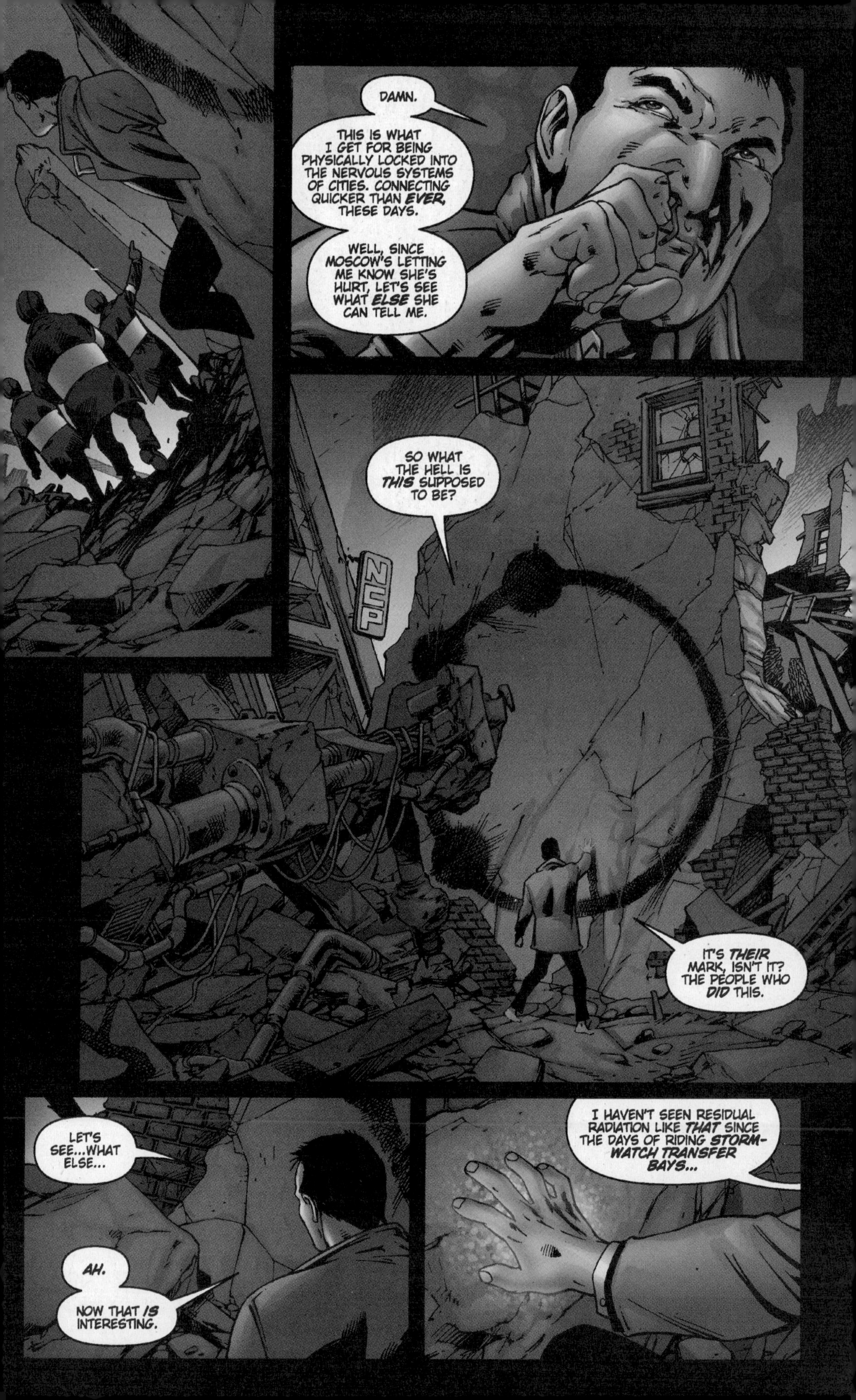
DAMN.
THIS IS WHAT I GET FOR BEING PHYSICALLY LOCKED INTO THE NERVOUS SYSTEMS OF CITIES. CONNECTING QUICKER THAN *EVER*, THESE DAYS.
WELL, SINCE MOSCOW'S LETTING ME KNOW SHE'S HURT, LET'S SEE WHAT *ELSE* SHE CAN TELL ME.
SO WHAT THE HELL IS *THIS* SUPPOSED TO BE?
NCP
IT'S *THEIR* MARK, ISN'T IT? THE PEOPLE WHO *DID* THIS.
LET'S SEE...WHAT ELSE...
AH.
NOW THAT *IS* INTERESTING.
I HAVEN'T SEEN RESIDUAL RADIATION LIKE *THAT* SINCE THE DAYS OF RIDING *STORM-WATCH TRANSFER BAYS...*

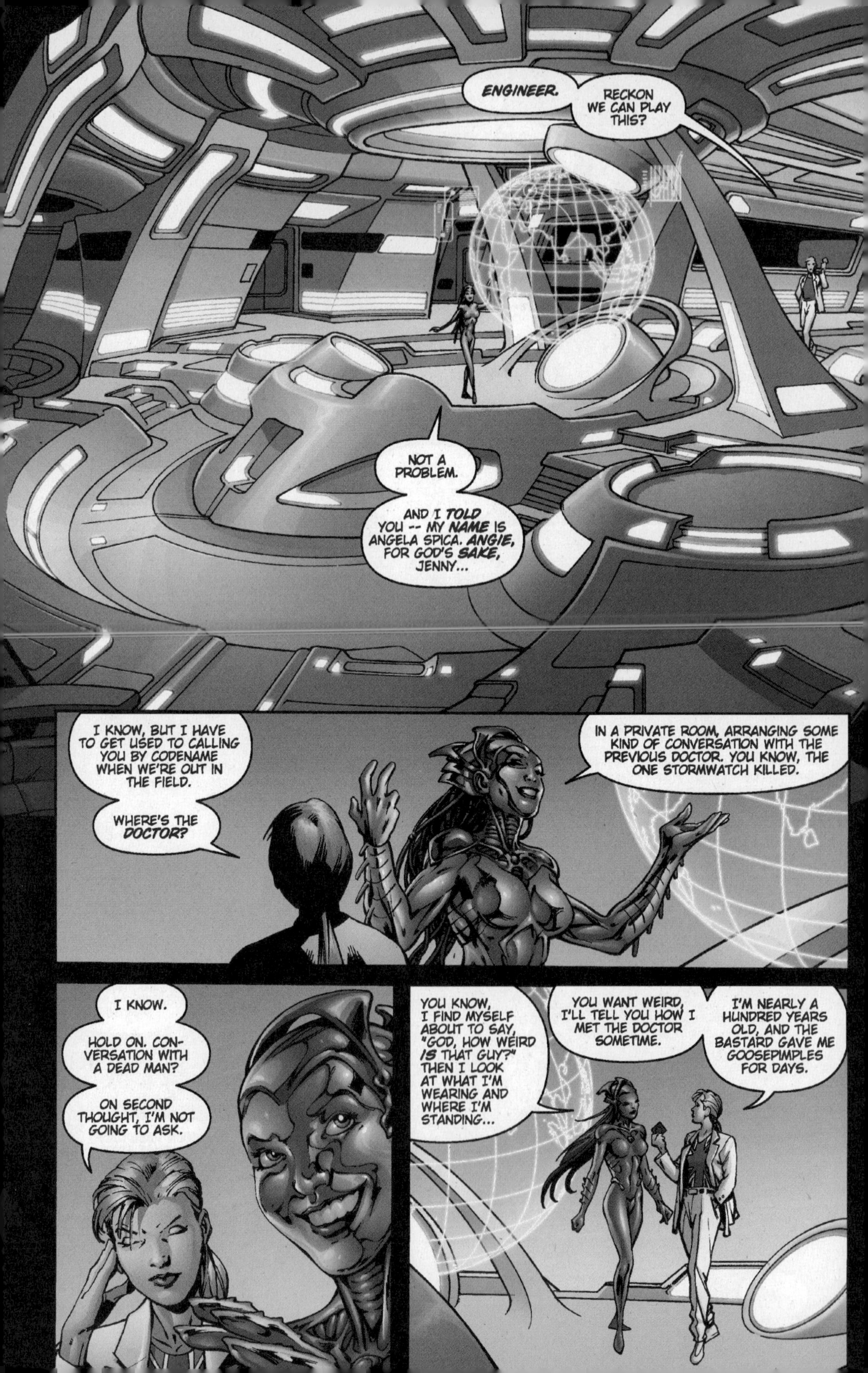
ENGINEER.
RECKON WE CAN PLAY THIS?
NOT A PROBLEM.
AND I TOLD YOU -- MY NAME IS ANGELA SPICA. ANGIE, FOR GOD'S SAKE, JENNY...
I KNOW, BUT I HAVE TO GET USED TO CALLING YOU BY CODENAME WHEN WE'RE OUT IN THE FIELD.
WHERE'S THE DOCTOR?
IN A PRIVATE ROOM, ARRANGING SOME KIND OF CONVERSATION WITH THE PREVIOUS DOCTOR. YOU KNOW, THE ONE STORMWATCH KILLED.
I KNOW.
HOLD ON. CONVERSATION WITH A DEAD MAN?
ON SECOND THOUGHT, I'M NOT GOING TO ASK.
YOU KNOW, I FIND MYSELF ABOUT TO SAY, "GOD, HOW WEIRD IS THAT GUY?" THEN I LOOK AT WHAT I'M WEARING AND WHERE I'M STANDING...
YOU WANT WEIRD, I'LL TELL YOU HOW I MET THE DOCTOR SOMETIME.
I'M NEARLY A HUNDRED YEARS OLD, AND THE BASTARD GAVE ME GOOSEPIMPLES FOR DAYS.

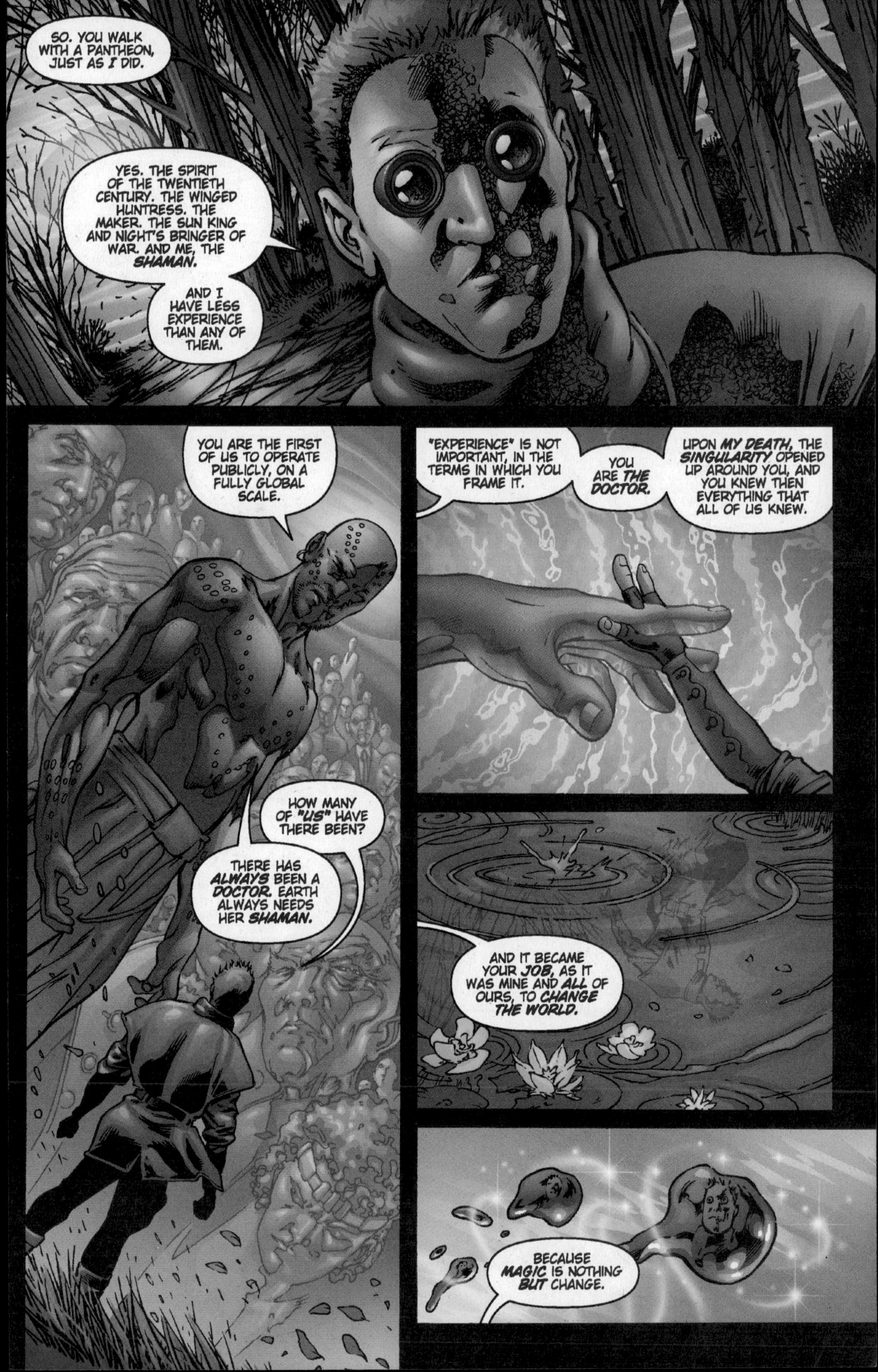
SO. YOU WALK WITH A PANTHEON, JUST AS I DID.
YES. THE SPIRIT OF THE TWENTIETH CENTURY. THE WINGED HUNTRESS. THE MAKER. THE SUN KING AND NIGHT'S BRINGER OF WAR. AND ME, THE SHAMAN.
AND I HAVE LESS EXPERIENCE THAN ANY OF THEM.
YOU ARE THE FIRST OF US TO OPERATE PUBLICLY, ON A FULLY GLOBAL SCALE.
HOW MANY OF "US" HAVE THERE BEEN?
THERE HAS ALWAYS BEEN A DOCTOR. EARTH ALWAYS NEEDS HER SHAMAN.
"EXPERIENCE" IS NOT IMPORTANT, IN THE TERMS IN WHICH YOU FRAME IT.
YOU ARE THE DOCTOR.
UPON MY DEATH, THE SINGULARITY OPENED UP AROUND YOU, AND YOU KNEW THEN EVERYTHING THAT ALL OF US KNEW.
AND IT BECAME YOUR JOB, AS IT WAS MINE AND ALL OF OURS, TO CHANGE THE WORLD.
BECAUSE MAGIC IS NOTHING BUT CHANGE.

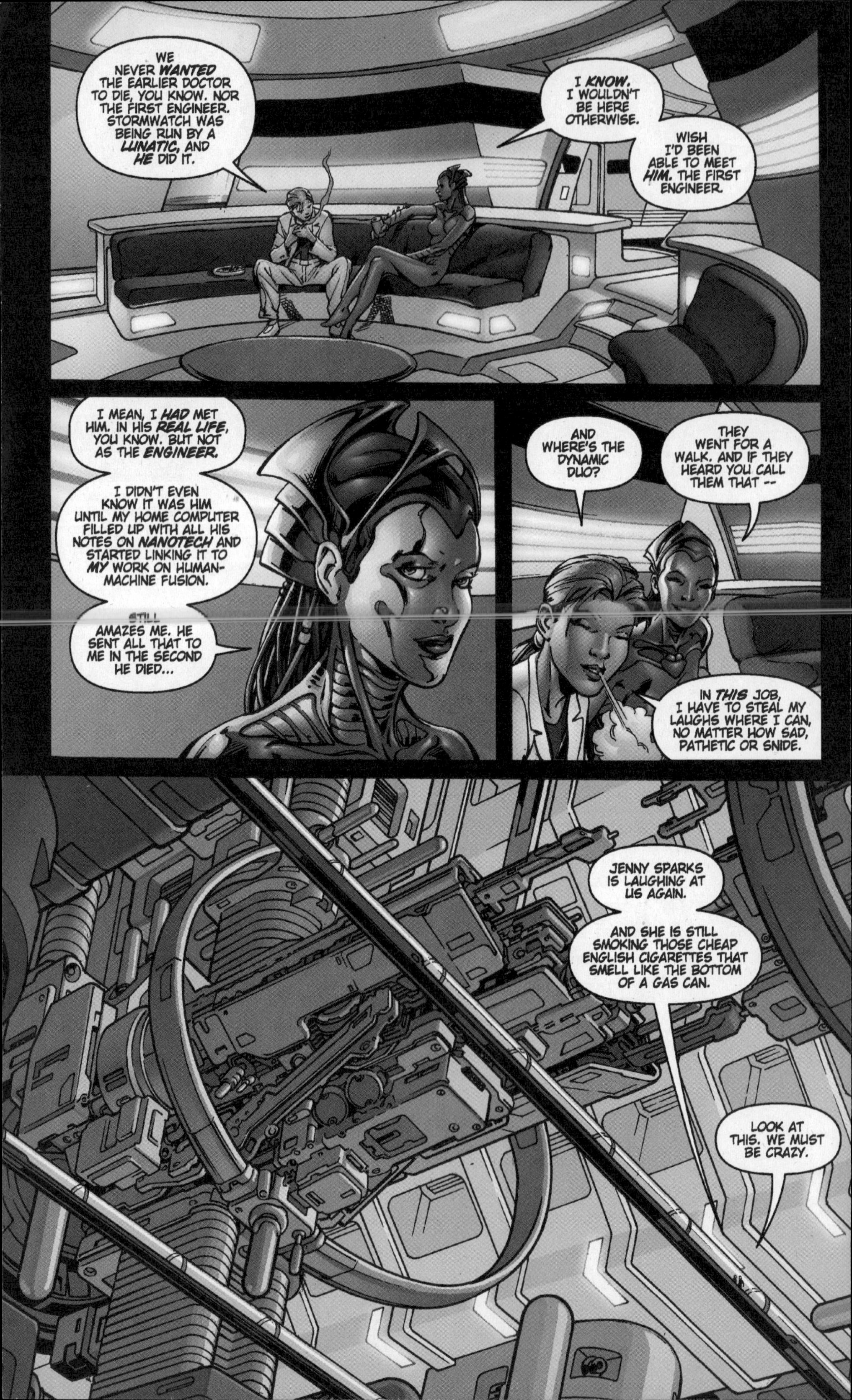
WE NEVER WANTED THE EARLIER DOCTOR TO DIE, YOU KNOW. NOR THE FIRST ENGINEER. STORMWATCH WAS BEING RUN BY A LUNATIC, AND HE DID IT.
I KNOW. I WOULDN'T BE HERE OTHERWISE.
WISH I'D BEEN ABLE TO MEET HIM. THE FIRST ENGINEER.
I MEAN, I HAD MET HIM. IN HIS REAL LIFE, YOU KNOW. BUT NOT AS THE ENGINEER.
I DIDN'T EVEN KNOW IT WAS HIM UNTIL MY HOME COMPUTER FILLED UP WITH ALL HIS NOTES ON NANOTECH AND STARTED LINKING IT TO MY WORK ON HUMAN-MACHINE FUSION.
STILL AMAZES ME. HE SENT ALL THAT TO ME IN THE SECOND HE DIED...
AND WHERE'S THE DYNAMIC DUO?
THEY WENT FOR A WALK. AND IF THEY HEARD YOU CALL THEM THAT --
IN THIS JOB, I HAVE TO STEAL MY LAUGHS WHERE I CAN, NO MATTER HOW SAD, PATHETIC OR SNIDE.
JENNY SPARKS IS LAUGHING AT US AGAIN.
AND SHE IS STILL SMOKING THOSE CHEAP ENGLISH CIGARETTES THAT SMELL LIKE THE BOTTOM OF A GAS CAN.
LOOK AT THIS. WE MUST BE CRAZY.

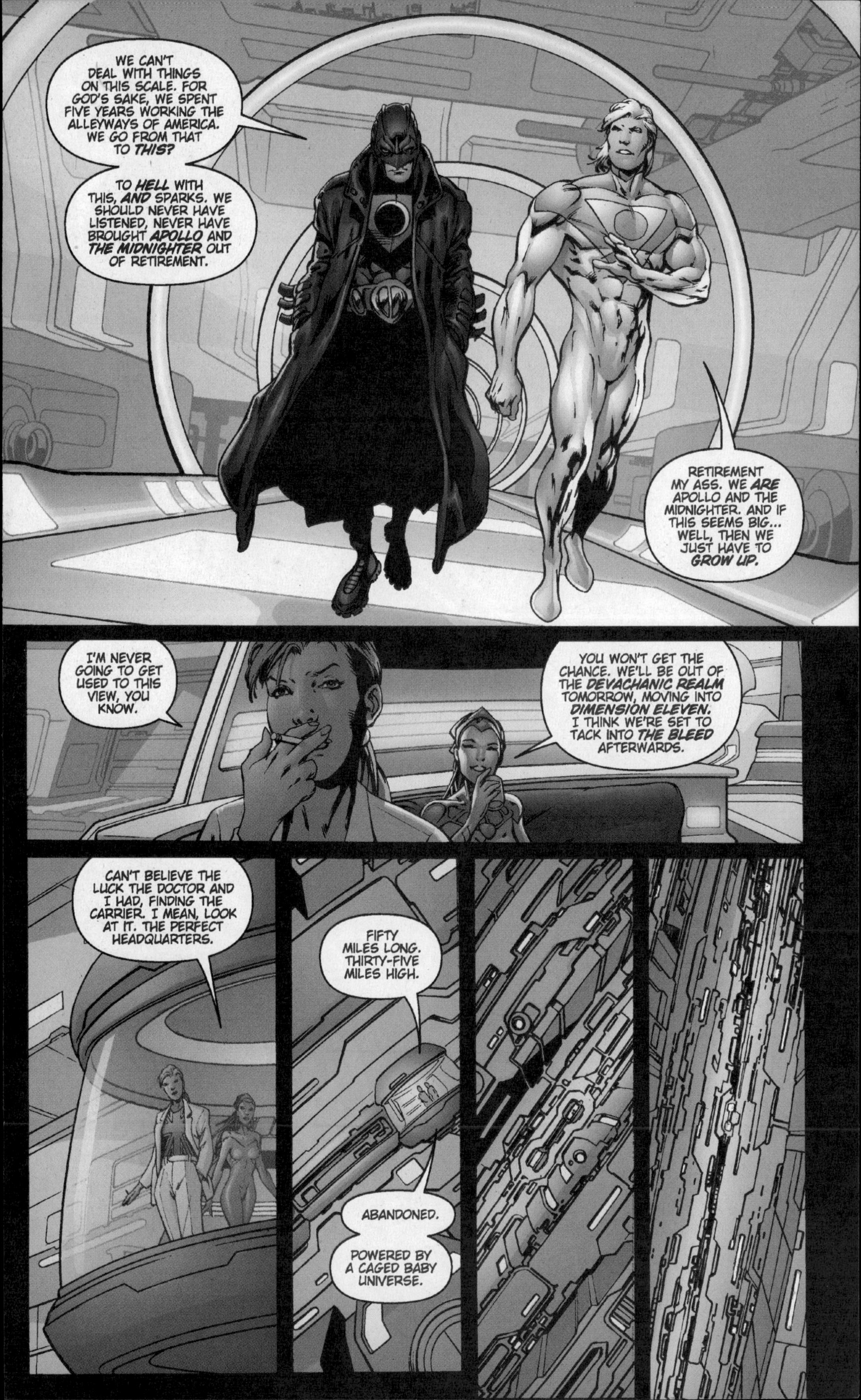
WE CAN'T DEAL WITH THINGS ON THIS SCALE. FOR GOD'S SAKE, WE SPENT FIVE YEARS WORKING THE ALLEYWAYS OF AMERICA. WE GO FROM THAT TO *THIS?*
TO ***HELL*** WITH THIS, ***AND*** SPARKS. WE SHOULD NEVER HAVE LISTENED, NEVER HAVE BROUGHT ***APOLLO*** AND ***THE MIDNIGHTER*** OUT OF RETIREMENT.
RETIREMENT MY ASS. WE ***ARE*** APOLLO AND THE MIDNIGHTER. AND IF THIS SEEMS BIG... WELL, THEN WE JUST HAVE TO ***GROW UP.***
I'M NEVER GOING TO GET USED TO THIS VIEW, YOU KNOW.
YOU WON'T GET THE CHANCE. WE'LL BE OUT OF THE ***DEVACHANIC REALM*** TOMORROW, MOVING INTO ***DIMENSION ELEVEN.*** I THINK WE'RE SET TO TACK INTO ***THE BLEED*** AFTERWARDS.
CAN'T BELIEVE THE LUCK THE DOCTOR AND I HAD, FINDING THE CARRIER. I MEAN, LOOK AT IT. THE PERFECT HEADQUARTERS.
FIFTY MILES LONG. THIRTY-FIVE MILES HIGH.
ABANDONED.
POWERED BY A CAGED BABY UNIVERSE.

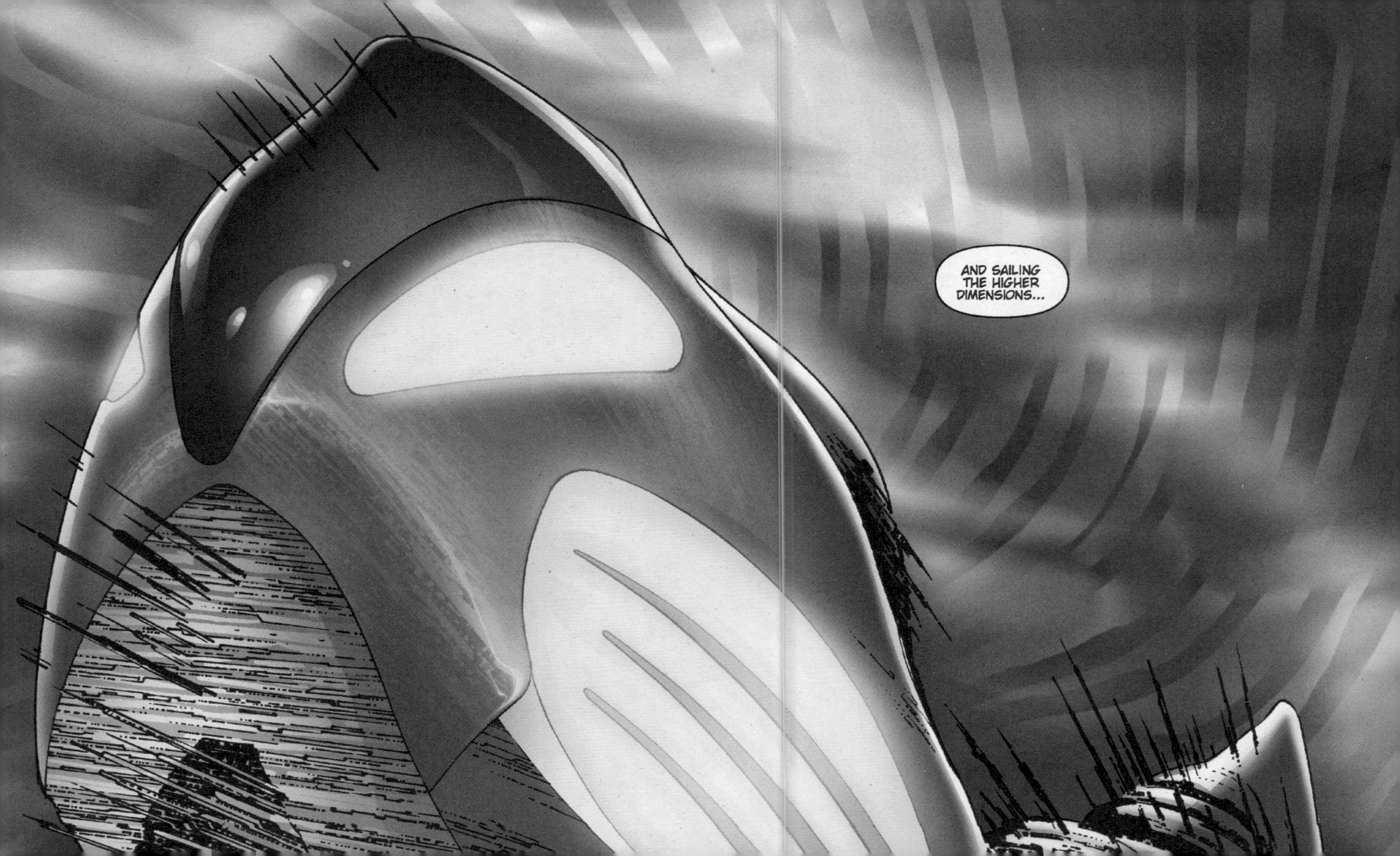
AND SAILING THE HIGHER DIMENSIONS...

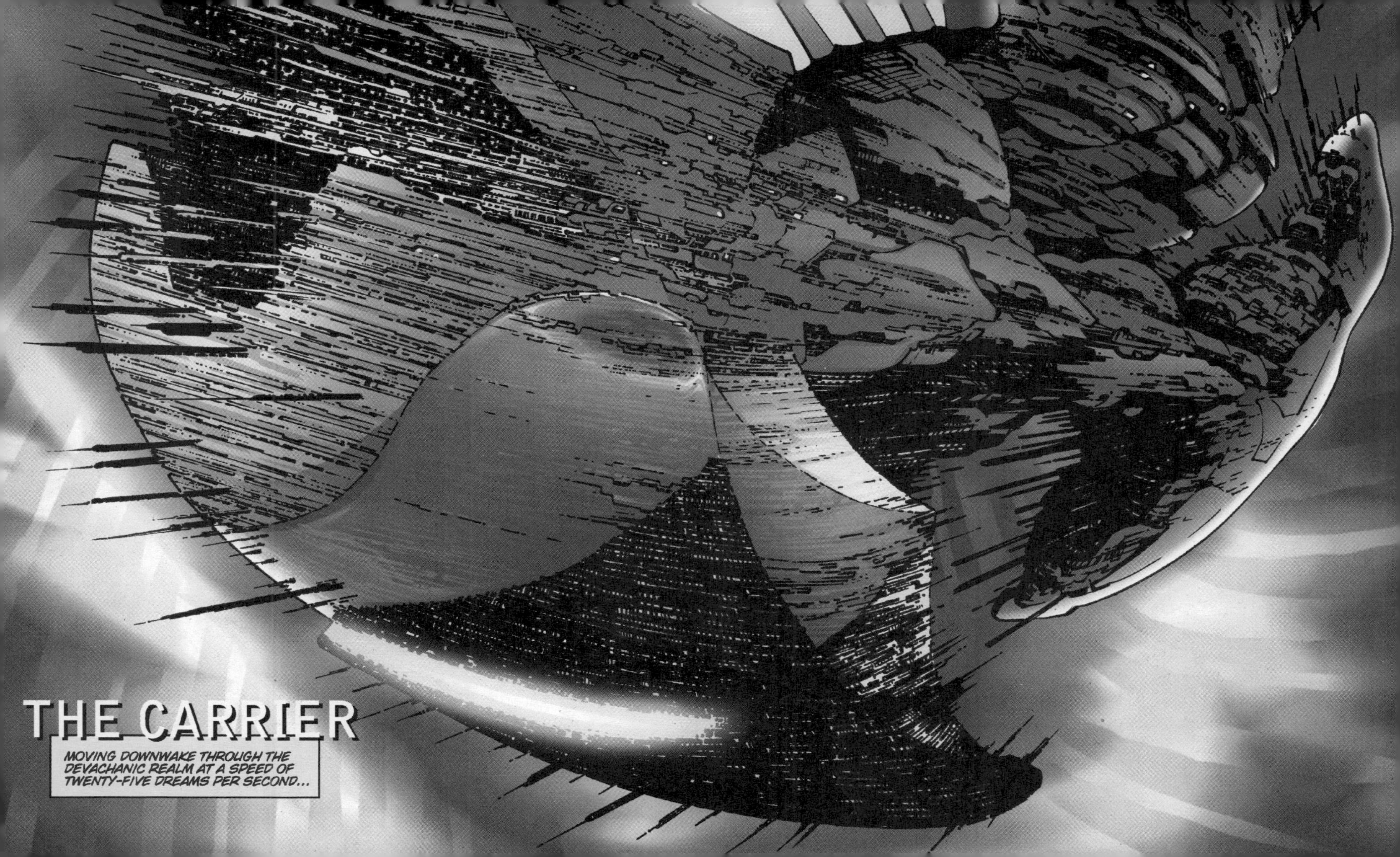
THE CARRIER
MOVING DOWNWAKE THROUGH THE DEVACHANIC REALM AT A SPEED OF TWENTY-FIVE DREAMS PER SECOND...

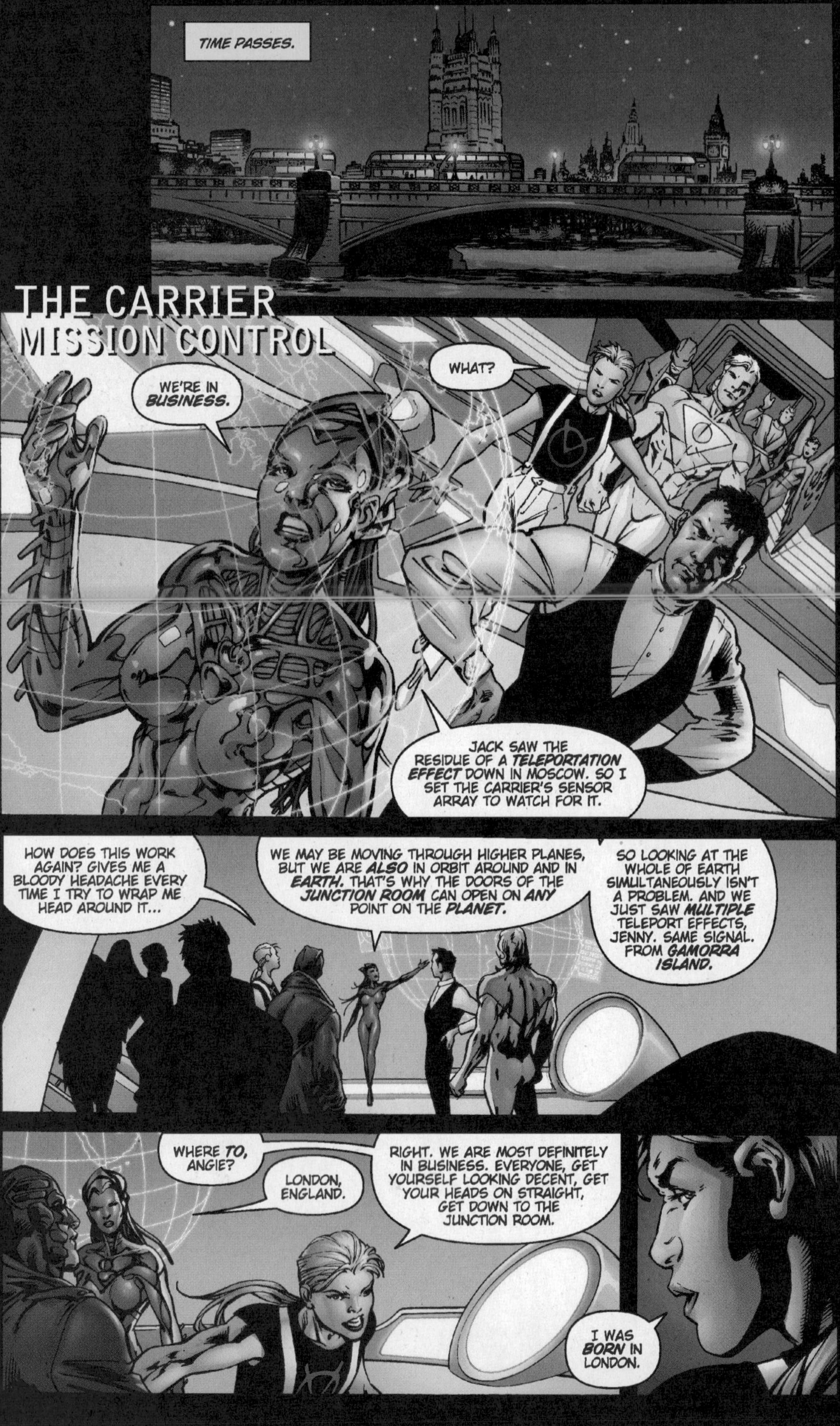
TIME PASSES.
THE CARRIER MISSION CONTROL
WE'RE IN ***BUSINESS.***
WHAT?
JACK SAW THE RESIDUE OF A ***TELEPORTATION EFFECT*** DOWN IN MOSCOW. SO I SET THE CARRIER'S SENSOR ARRAY TO WATCH FOR IT.
HOW DOES THIS WORK AGAIN? GIVES ME A BLOODY HEADACHE EVERY TIME I TRY TO WRAP ME HEAD AROUND IT...
WE MAY BE MOVING THROUGH HIGHER PLANES, BUT WE ARE ***ALSO*** IN ORBIT AROUND AND IN ***EARTH.*** THAT'S WHY THE DOORS OF THE ***JUNCTION ROOM*** CAN OPEN ON ***ANY*** POINT ON THE ***PLANET.***
SO LOOKING AT THE WHOLE OF EARTH SIMULTANEOUSLY ISN'T A PROBLEM. AND WE JUST SAW ***MULTIPLE*** TELEPORT EFFECTS, JENNY. SAME SIGNAL. FROM ***GAMORRA ISLAND.***
WHERE ***TO,*** ANGIE?
LONDON, ENGLAND.
RIGHT. WE ARE MOST DEFINITELY IN BUSINESS. EVERYONE, GET YOURSELF LOOKING DECENT, GET YOUR HEADS ON STRAIGHT, GET DOWN TO THE JUNCTION ROOM.
I WAS ***BORN*** IN LONDON.

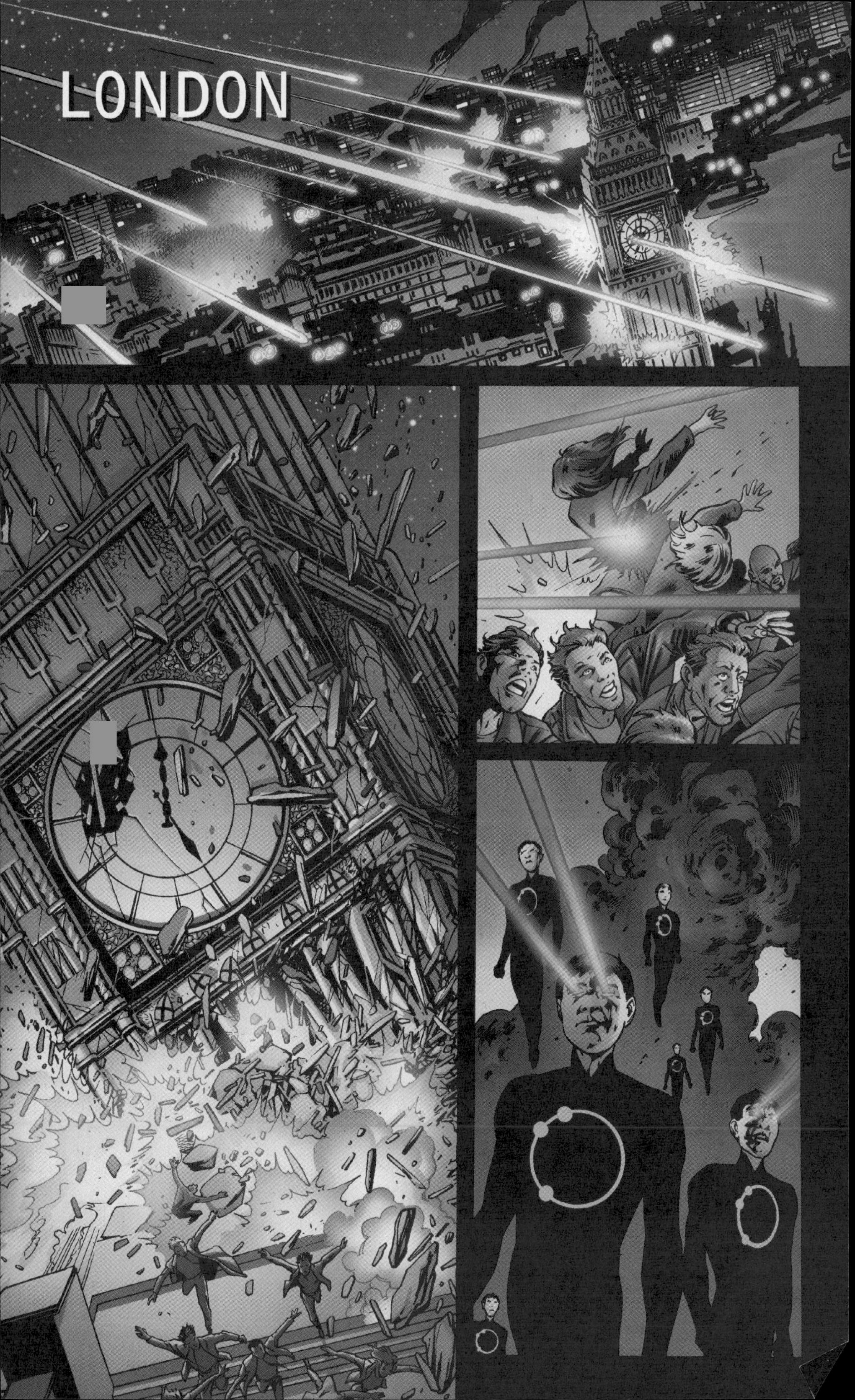
LONDON

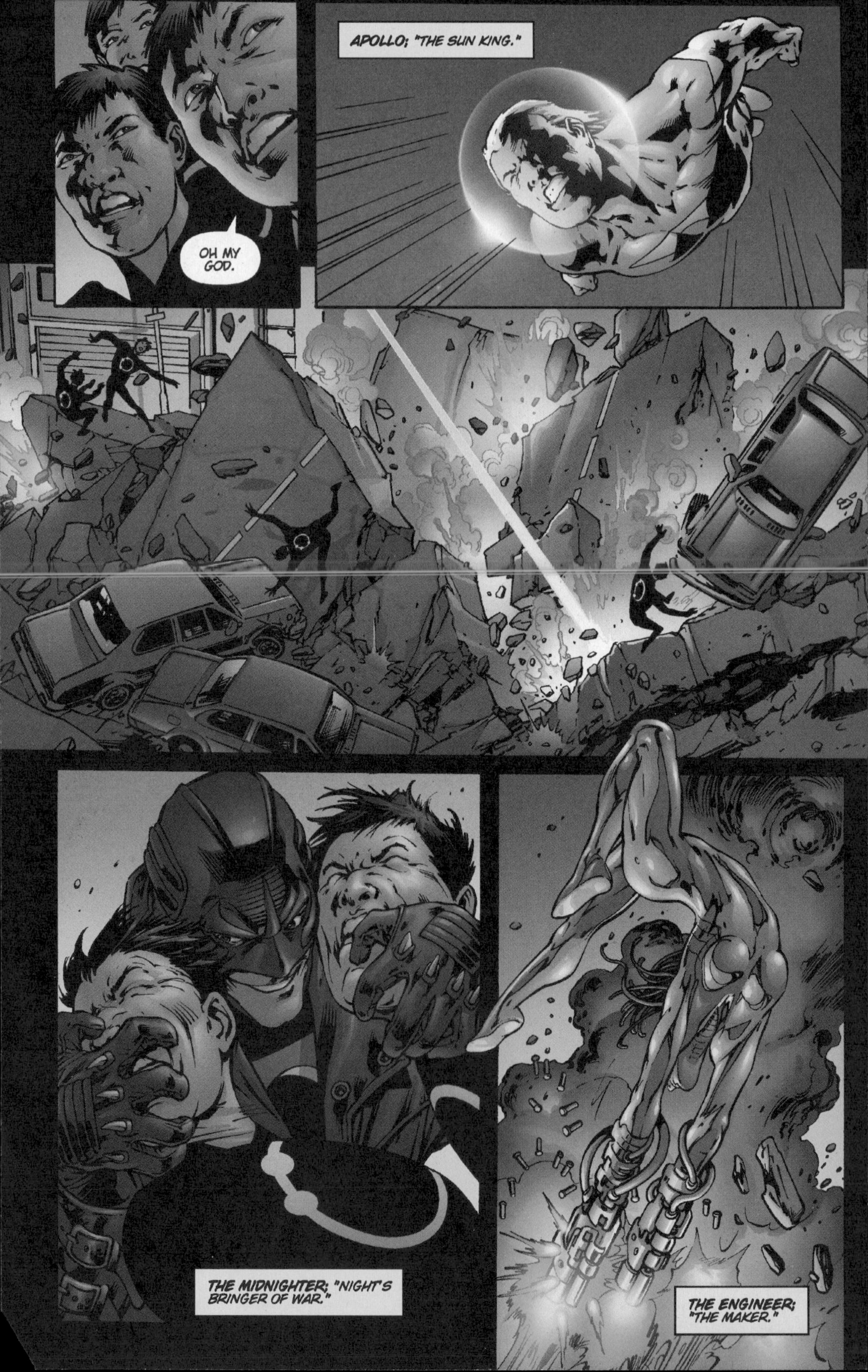
OH MY GOD.
APOLLO; "THE SUN KING."
THE MIDNIGHTER; "NIGHT'S BRINGER OF WAR."
THE ENGINEER; "THE MAKER."

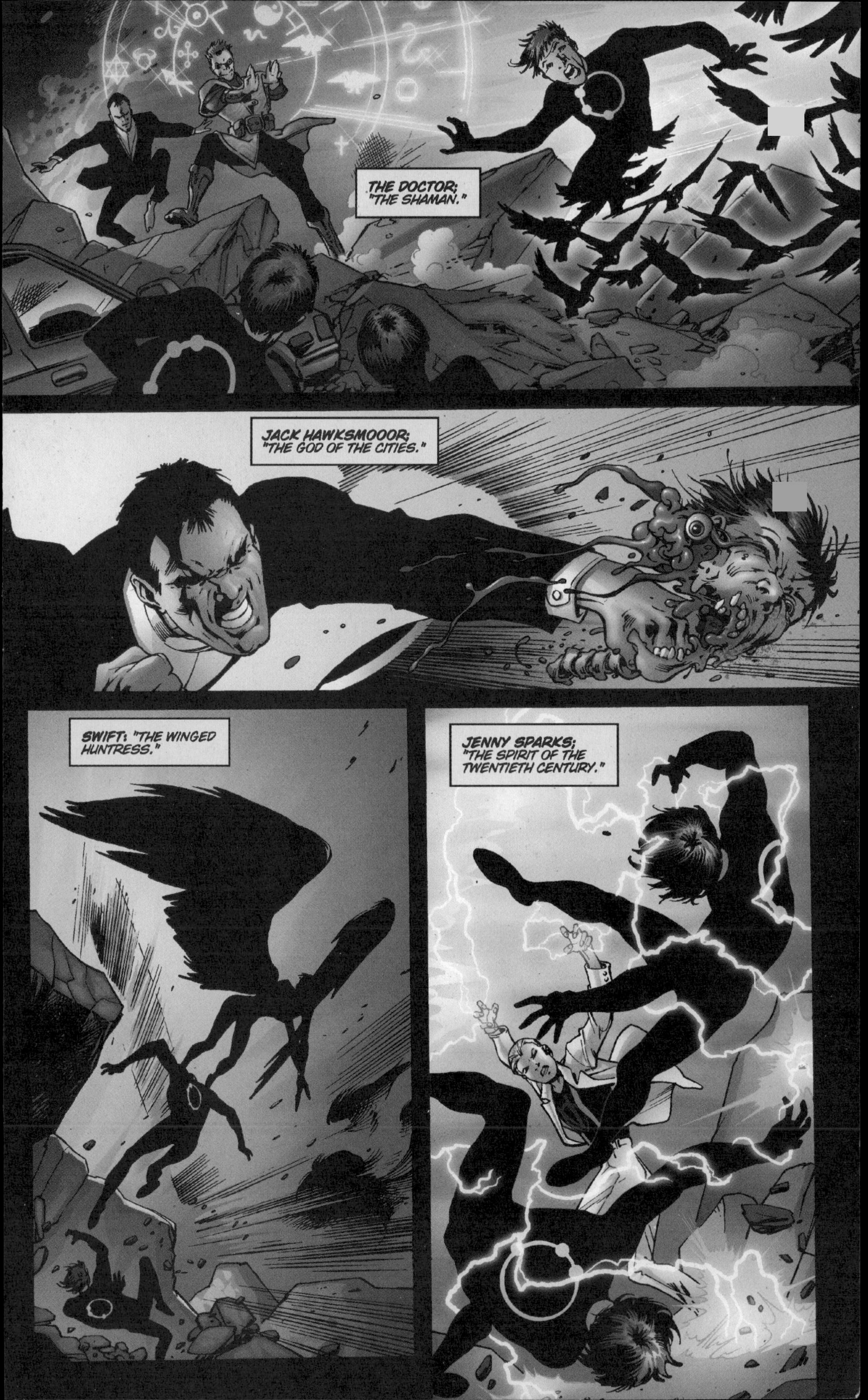
THE DOCTOR; "THE SHAMAN."
JACK HAWKSMOOOR; "THE GOD OF THE CITIES."
SWIFT: "THE WINGED HUNTRESS."
JENNY SPARKS; "THE SPIRIT OF THE TWENTIETH CENTURY."

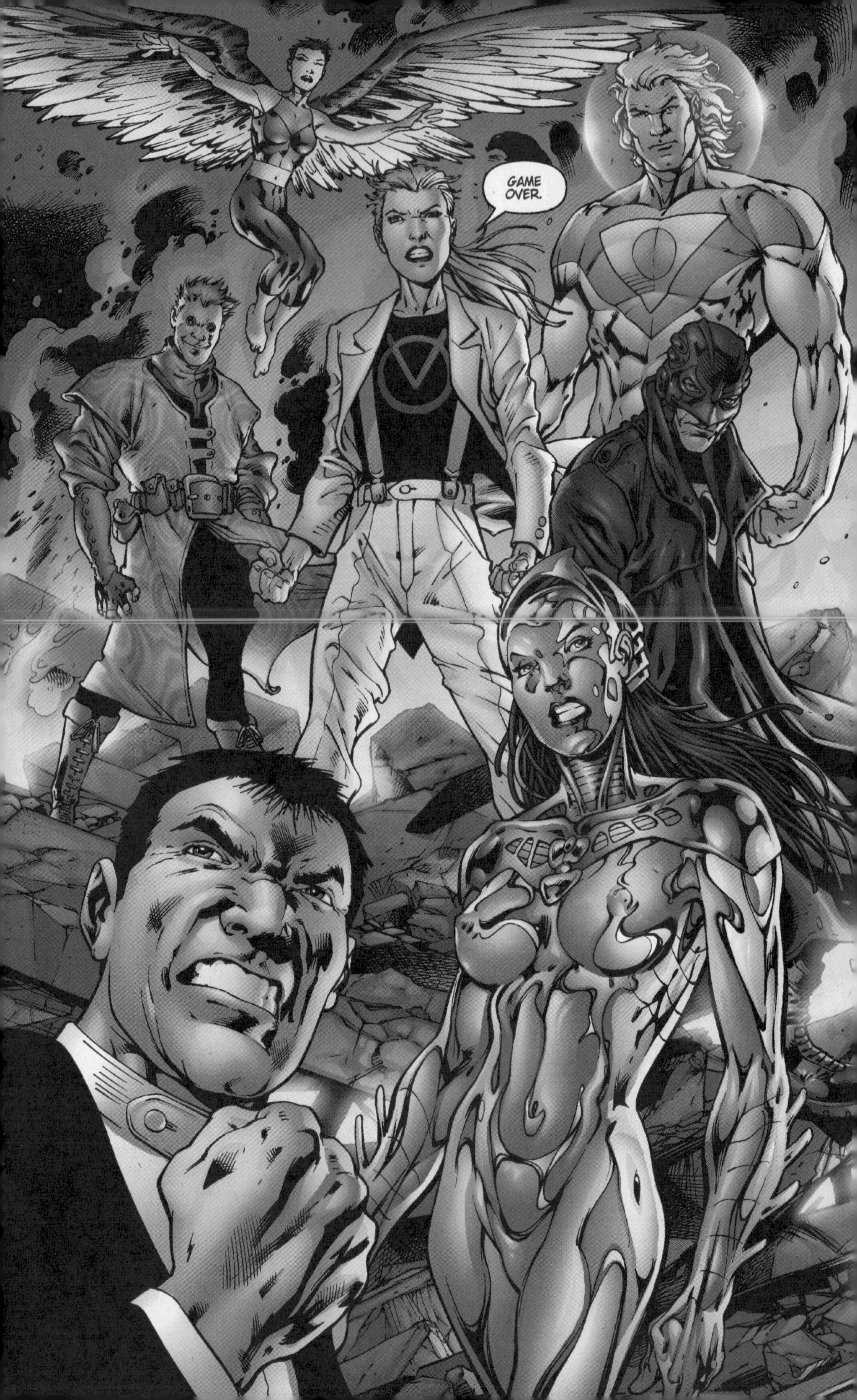
GAME OVER.

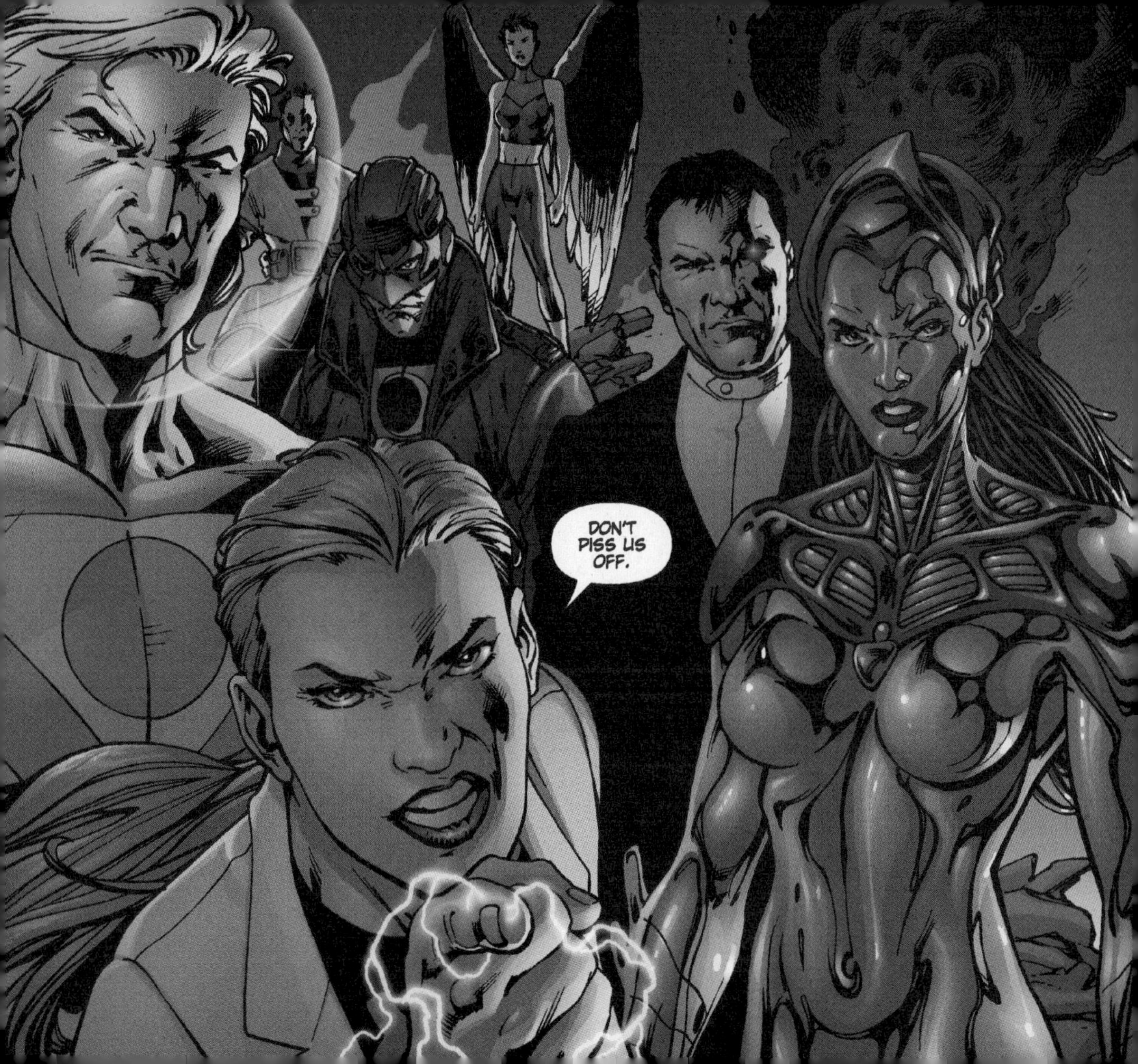
DON'T PISS US OFF.

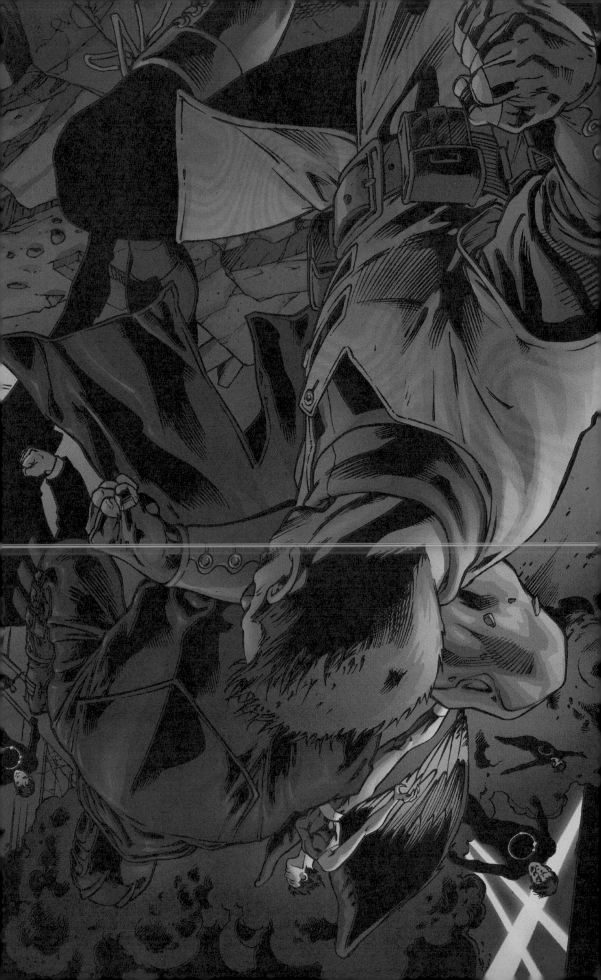

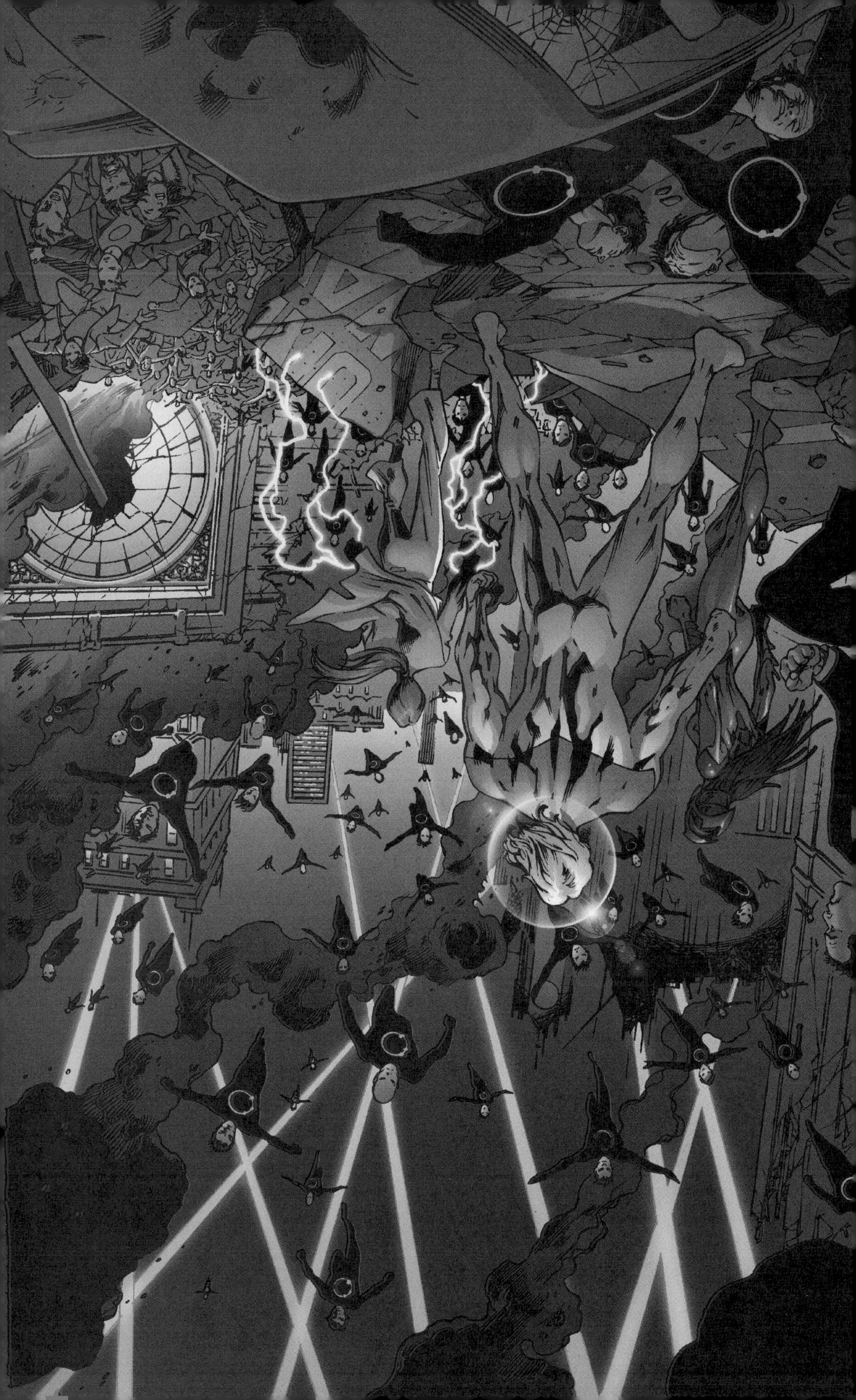

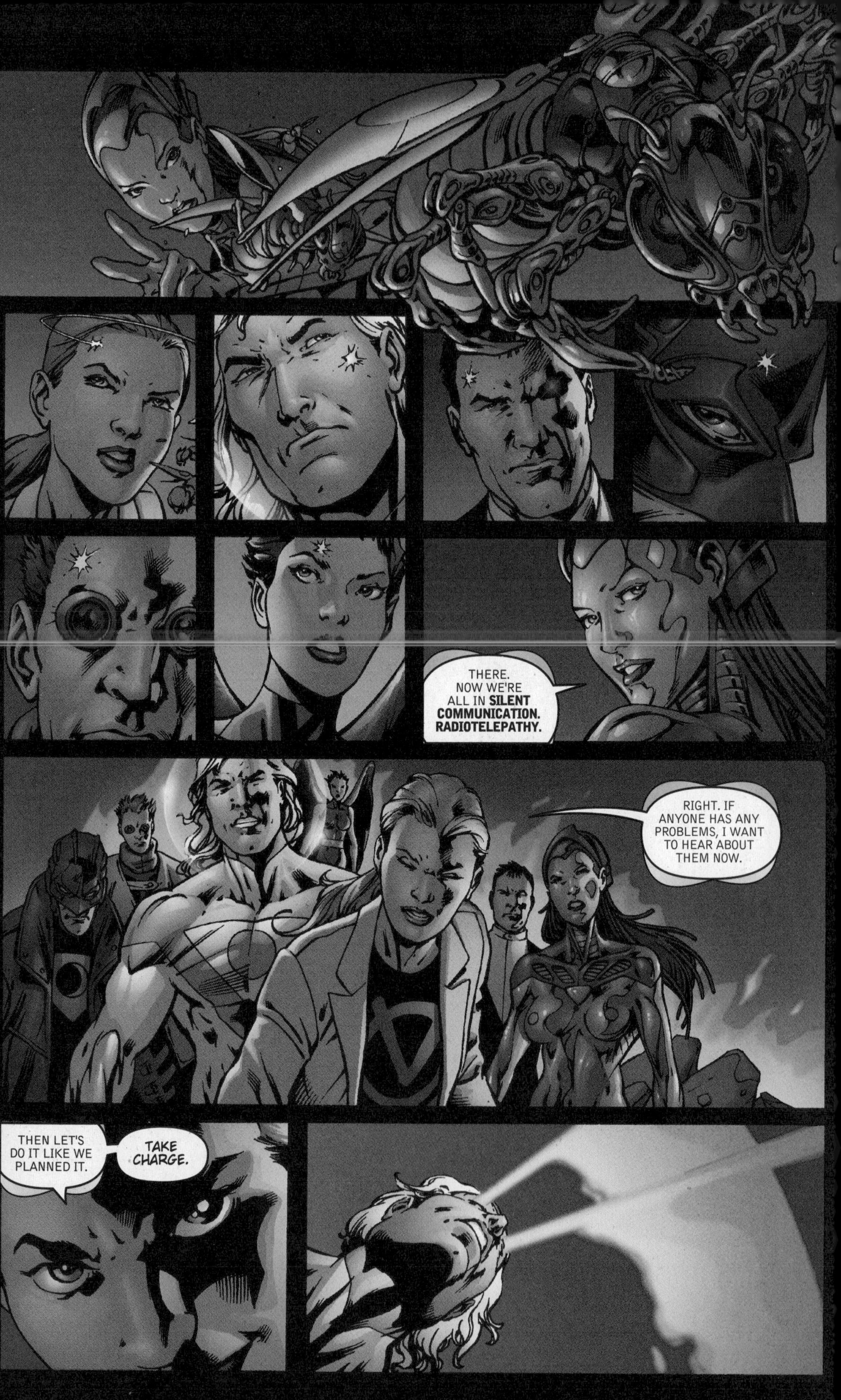
THERE. NOW WE'RE ALL IN **SILENT COMMUNICATION. RADIOTELEPATHY.**
RIGHT. IF ANYONE HAS ANY PROBLEMS, I WANT TO HEAR ABOUT THEM NOW.
THEN LET'S DO IT LIKE WE PLANNED IT.
TAKE CHARGE.

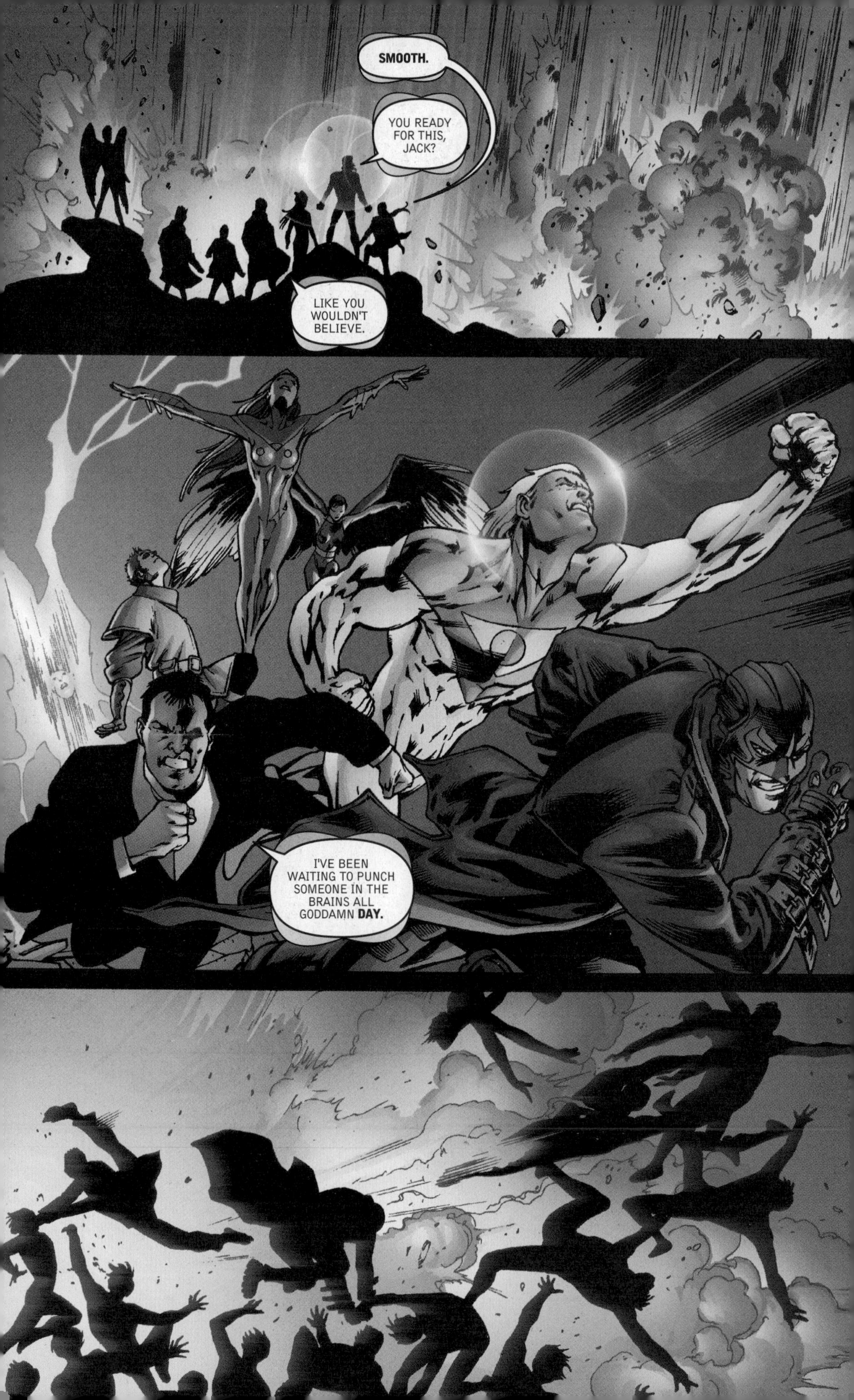
YOU READY FOR THIS, JACK?
SMOOTH.
LIKE YOU WOULDN'T BELIEVE.
I'VE BEEN WAITING TO PUNCH SOMEONE IN THE BRAINS ALL GODDAMN **DAY.**

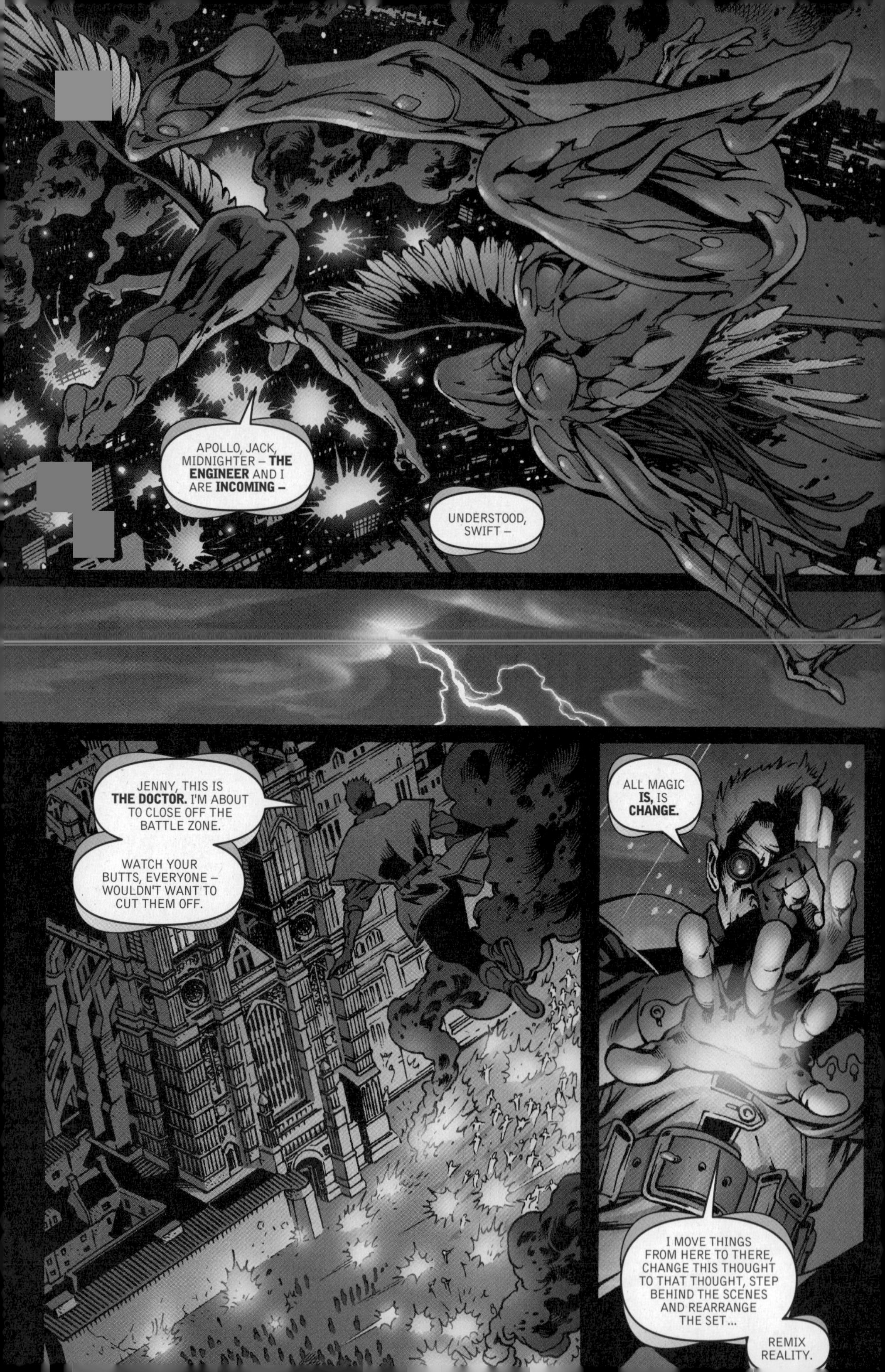
APOLLO, JACK, MIDNIGHTER – **THE ENGINEER** AND I ARE **INCOMING** –
UNDERSTOOD, SWIFT –
JENNY, THIS IS **THE DOCTOR.** I'M ABOUT TO CLOSE OFF THE BATTLE ZONE.
WATCH YOUR BUTTS, EVERYONE – WOULDN'T WANT TO CUT THEM OFF.
ALL MAGIC **IS,** IS **CHANGE.**
I MOVE THINGS FROM HERE TO THERE, CHANGE THIS THOUGHT TO THAT THOUGHT, STEP BEHIND THE SCENES AND REARRANGE THE SET...
REMIX REALITY.

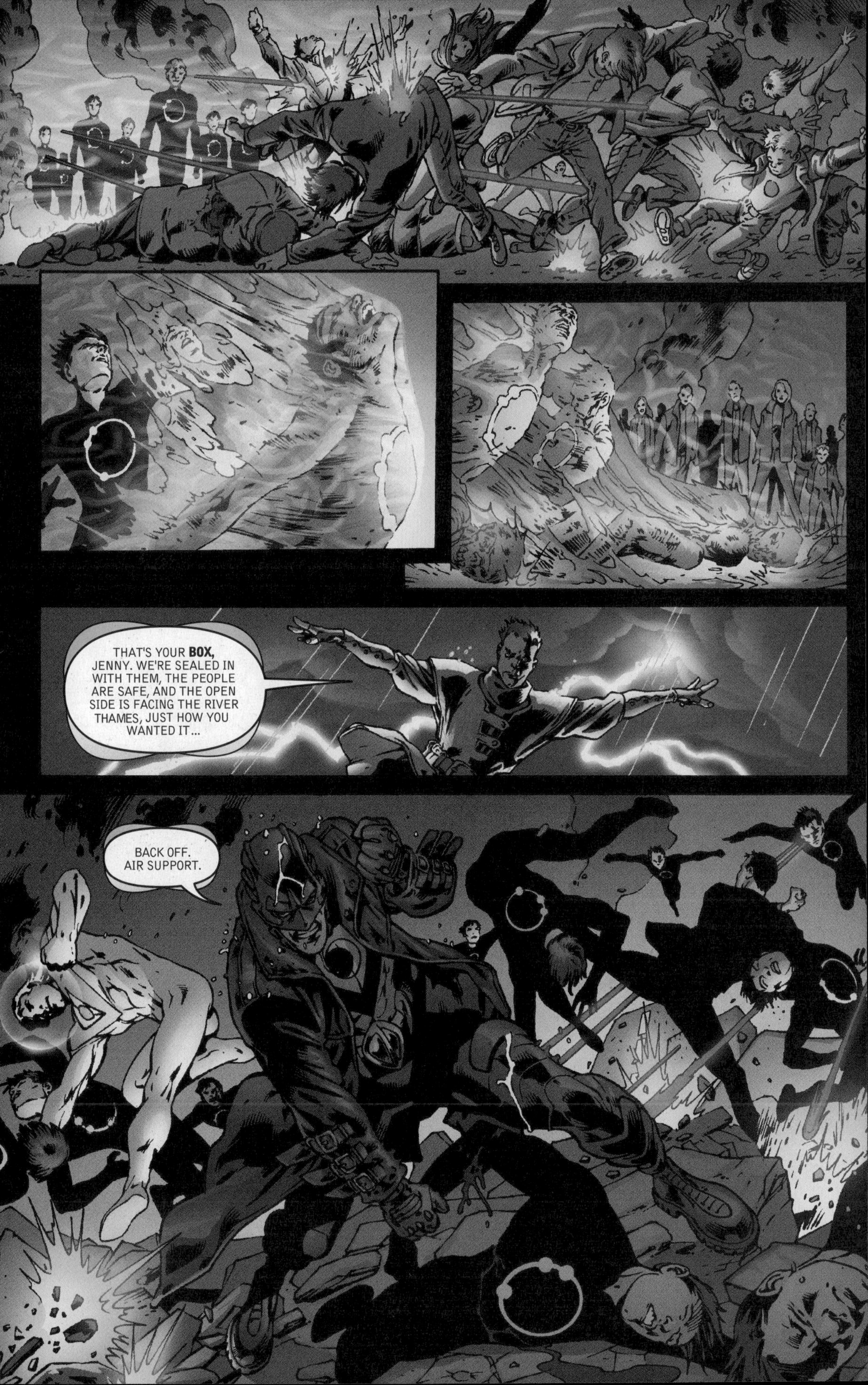
THAT'S YOUR **BOX,** JENNY. WE'RE SEALED IN WITH THEM, THE PEOPLE ARE SAFE, AND THE OPEN SIDE IS FACING THE RIVER THAMES, JUST HOW YOU WANTED IT...
BACK OFF. AIR SUPPORT.

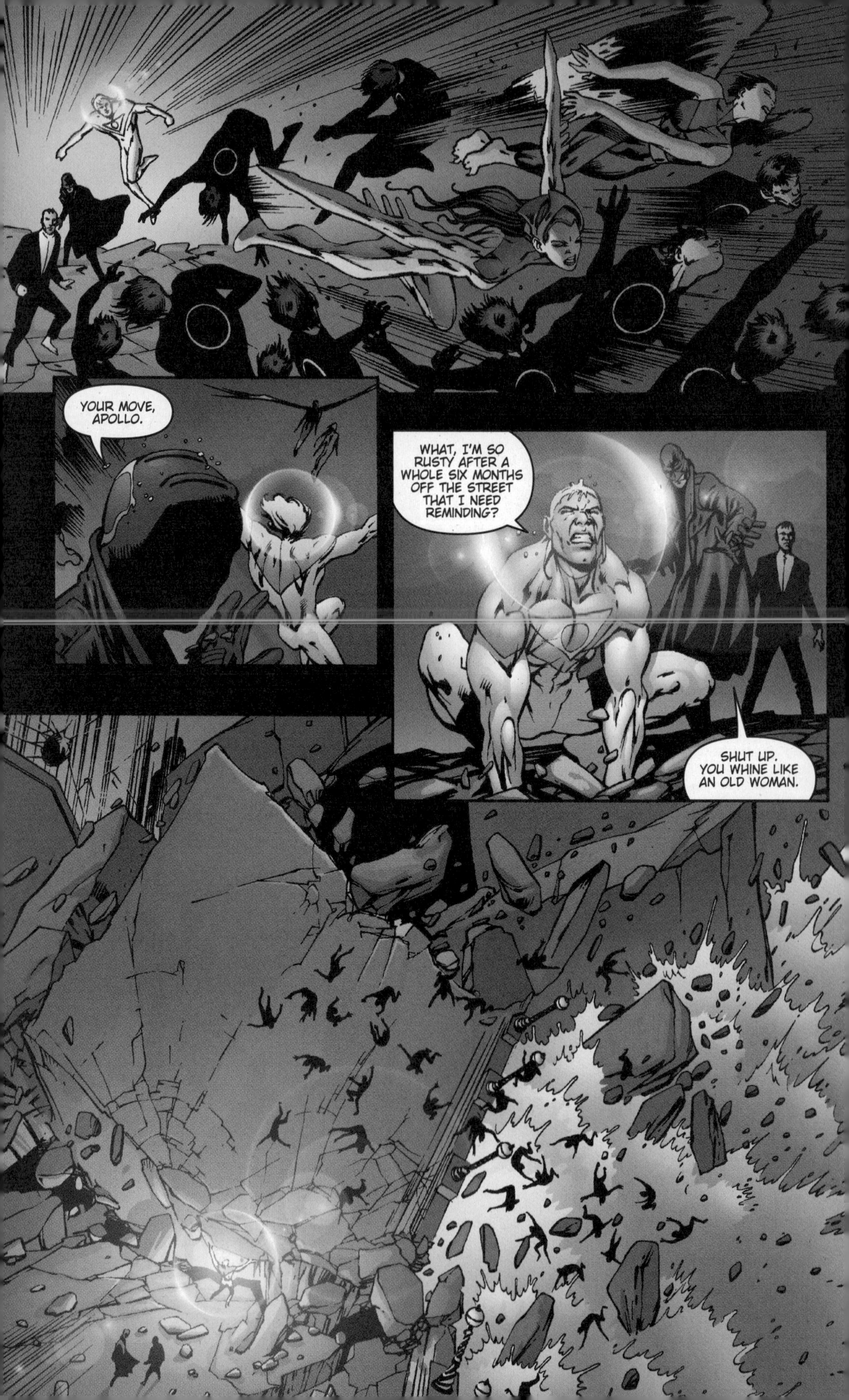
YOUR MOVE, APOLLO.
WHAT, I'M SO RUSTY AFTER A WHOLE SIX MONTHS OFF THE STREET THAT I NEED REMINDING?
SHUT UP. YOU WHINE LIKE AN OLD WOMAN.

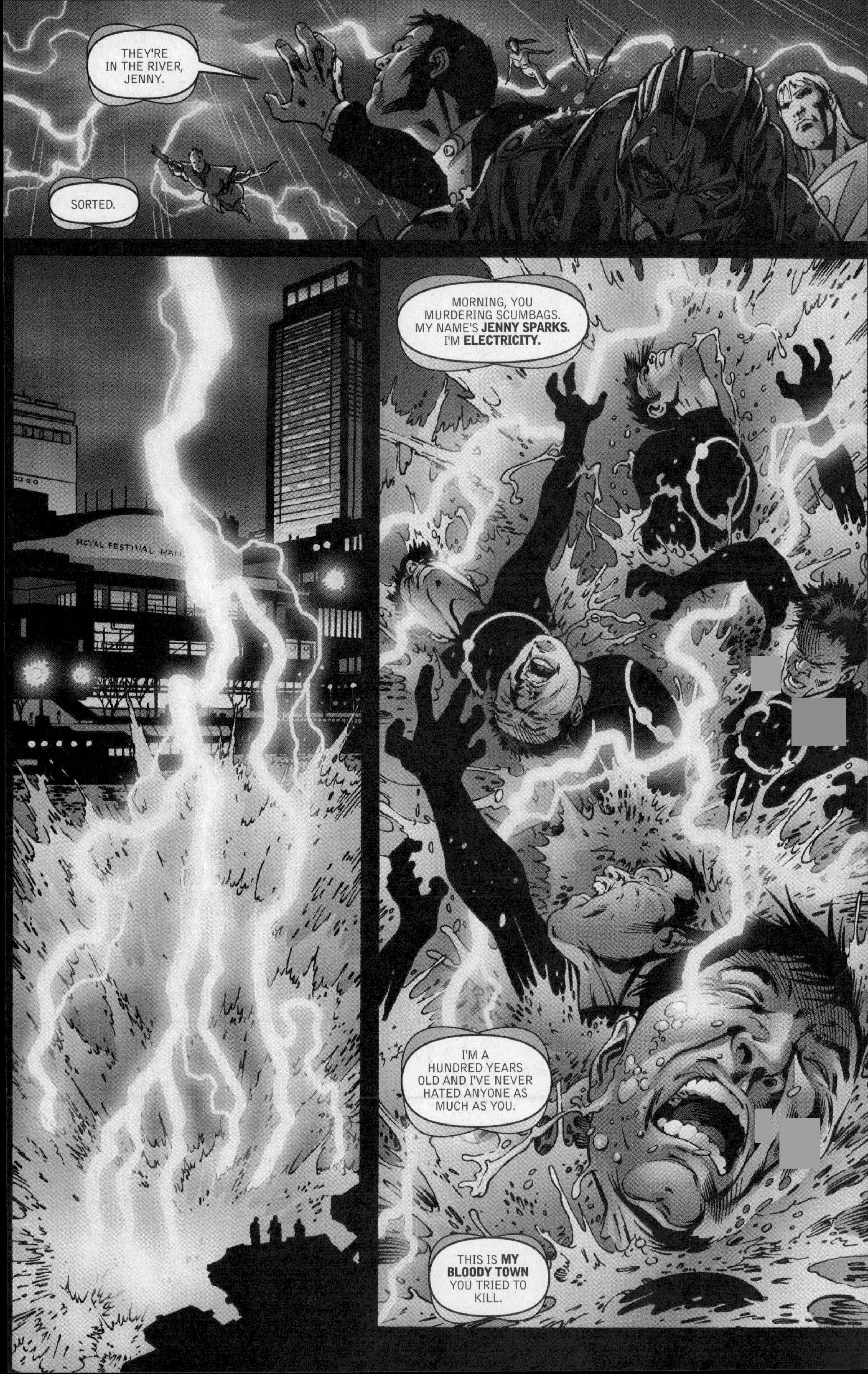
THEY'RE IN THE RIVER, JENNY.
SORTED.
ROYAL FESTIVAL HALL
MORNING, YOU MURDERING SCUMBAGS. MY NAME'S **JENNY SPARKS.** I'M **ELECTRICITY.**
I'M A HUNDRED YEARS OLD AND I'VE NEVER HATED ANYONE AS MUCH AS YOU.
THIS IS **MY BLOODY TOWN** YOU TRIED TO KILL.

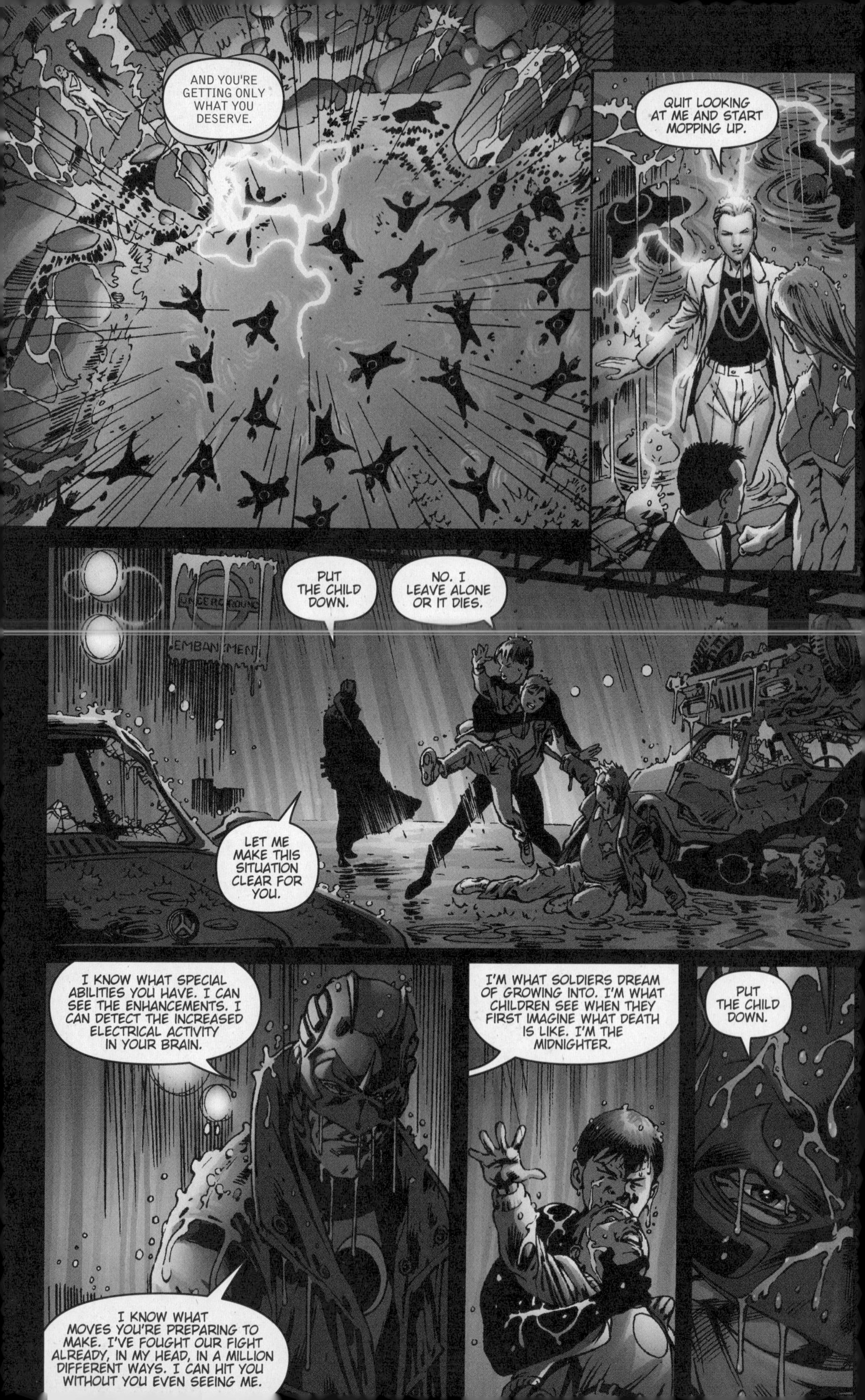
AND YOU'RE GETTING ONLY WHAT YOU DESERVE.
QUIT LOOKING AT ME AND START MOPPING UP.
PUT THE CHILD DOWN.
NO. I LEAVE ALONE OR IT DIES.
LET ME MAKE THIS SITUATION CLEAR FOR YOU.
I KNOW WHAT SPECIAL ABILITIES YOU HAVE. I CAN SEE THE ENHANCEMENTS. I CAN DETECT THE INCREASED ELECTRICAL ACTIVITY IN YOUR BRAIN.
I KNOW WHAT MOVES YOU'RE PREPARING TO MAKE. I'VE FOUGHT OUR FIGHT ALREADY, IN MY HEAD, IN A MILLION DIFFERENT WAYS. I CAN HIT YOU WITHOUT YOU EVEN SEEING ME.
I'M WHAT SOLDIERS DREAM OF GROWING INTO. I'M WHAT CHILDREN SEE WHEN THEY FIRST IMAGINE WHAT DEATH IS LIKE. I'M THE MIDNIGHTER.
PUT THE CHILD DOWN.

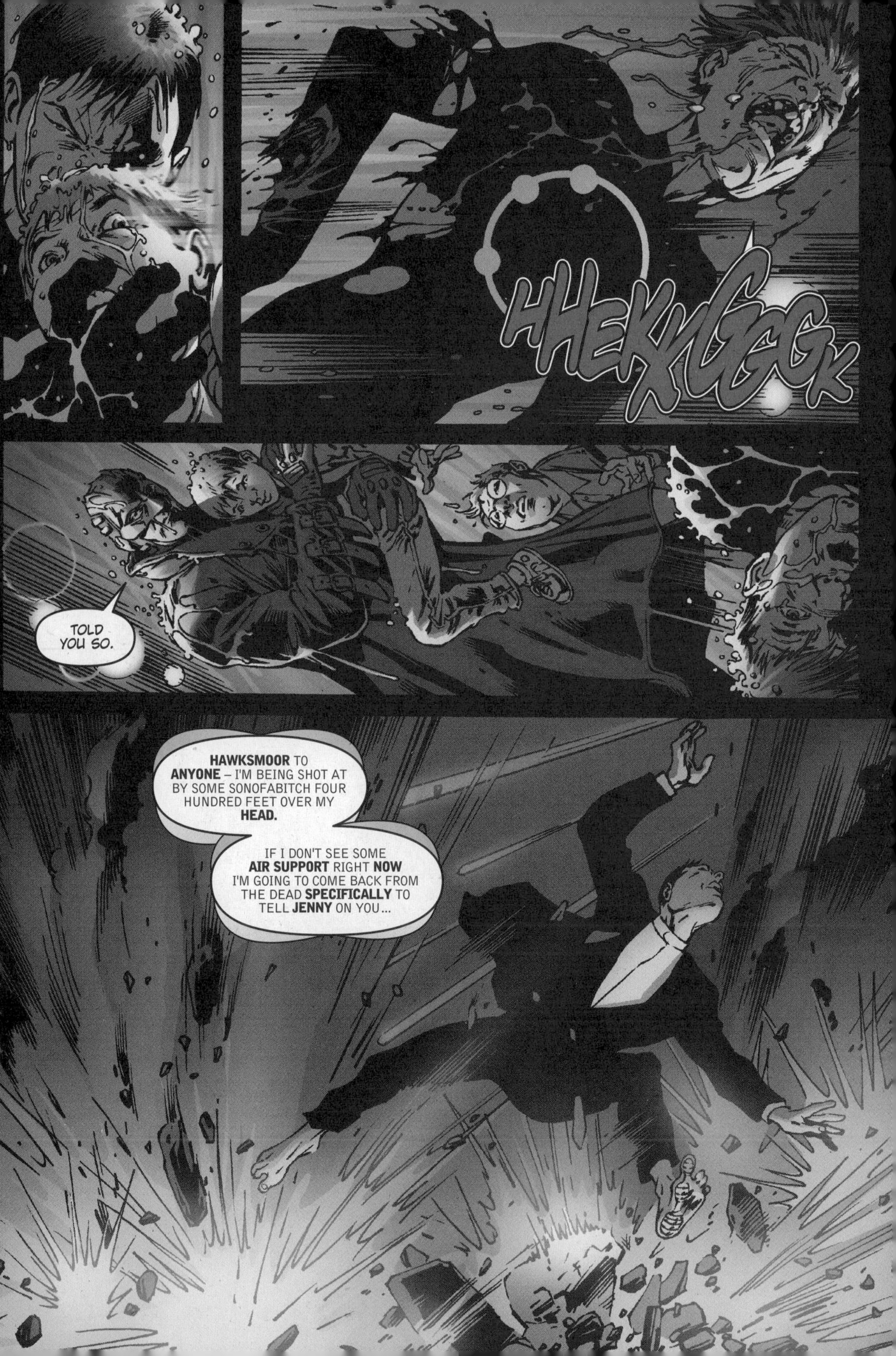
HHEKKGGGK
TOLD YOU SO.
HAWKSMOOR TO ANYONE – I'M BEING SHOT AT BY SOME SONOFABITCH FOUR HUNDRED FEET OVER MY HEAD.
IF I DON'T SEE SOME AIR SUPPORT RIGHT NOW I'M GOING TO COME BACK FROM THE DEAD SPECIFICALLY TO TELL JENNY ON YOU...

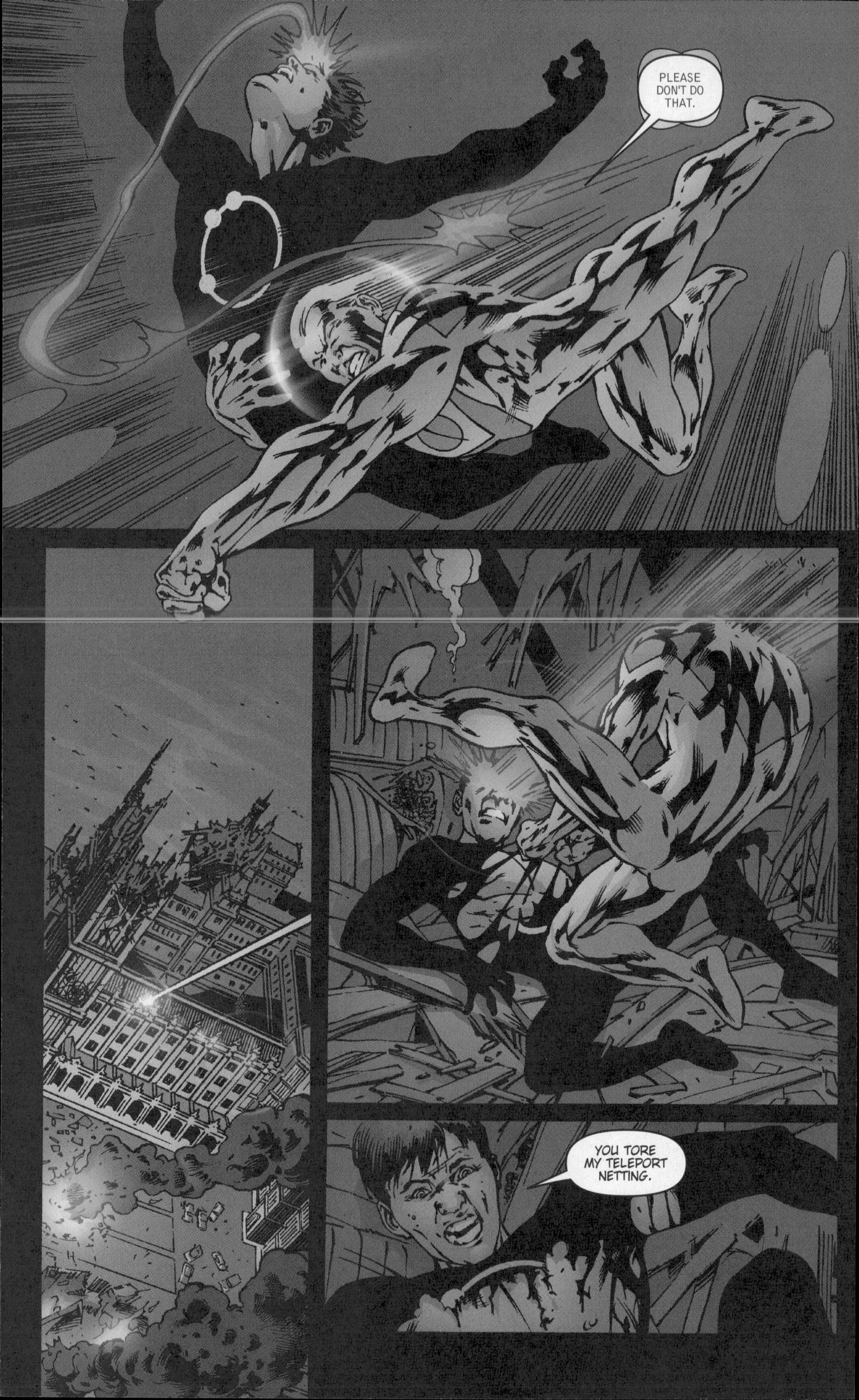
PLEASE DON'T DO THAT.
YOU TORE MY TELEPORT NETTING.

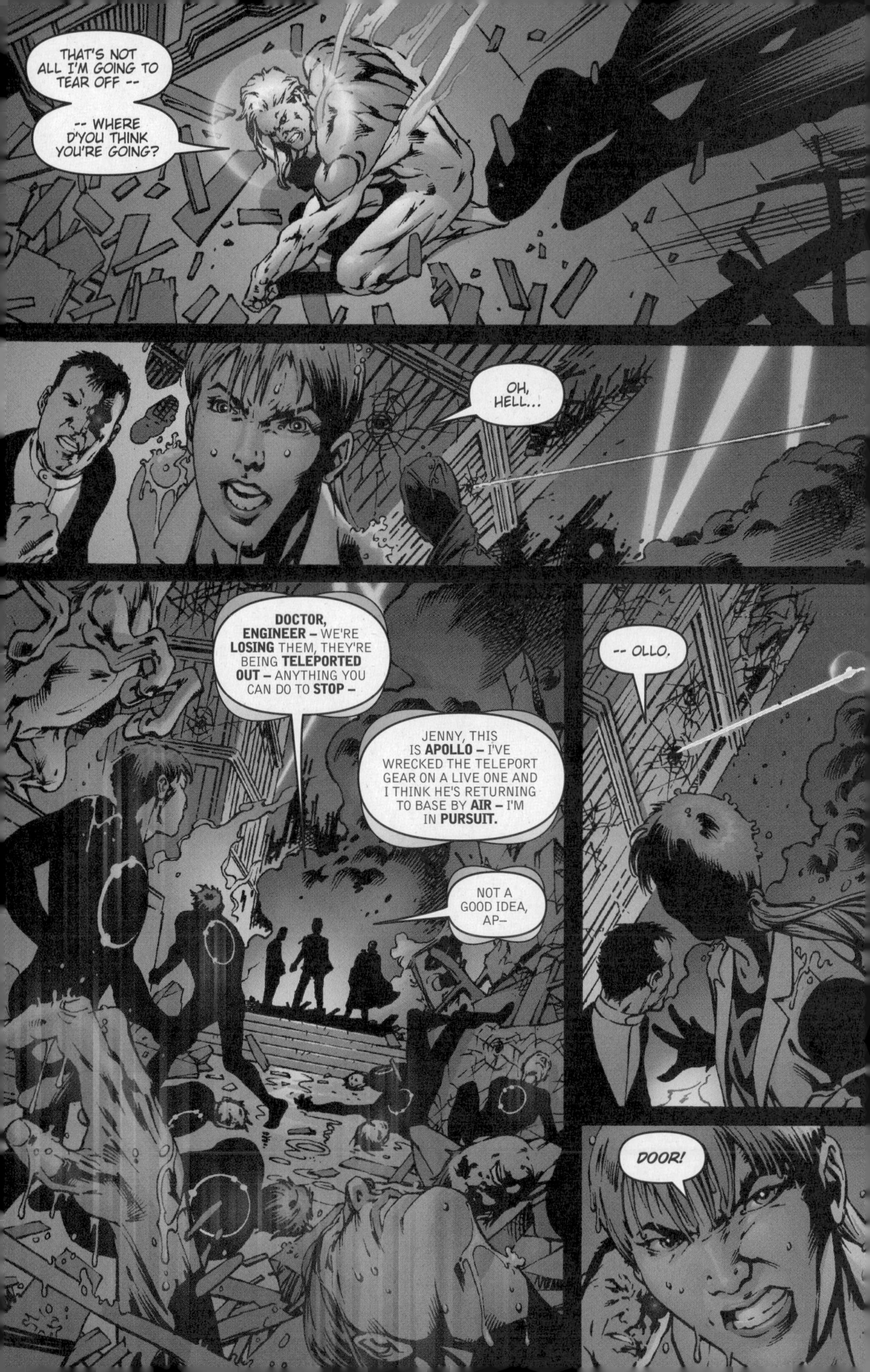
THAT'S NOT ALL I'M GOING TO TEAR OFF --
-- WHERE D'YOU THINK YOU'RE GOING?
OH, HELL...
DOCTOR, ENGINEER – WE'RE **LOSING** THEM, THEY'RE BEING **TELEPORTED OUT** – ANYTHING YOU CAN DO TO **STOP** –
JENNY, THIS IS **APOLLO** – I'VE WRECKED THE TELEPORT GEAR ON A LIVE ONE AND I THINK HE'S RETURNING TO BASE BY **AIR** – I'M IN **PURSUIT.**
NOT A GOOD IDEA, AP–
-- OLLO.
DOOR!

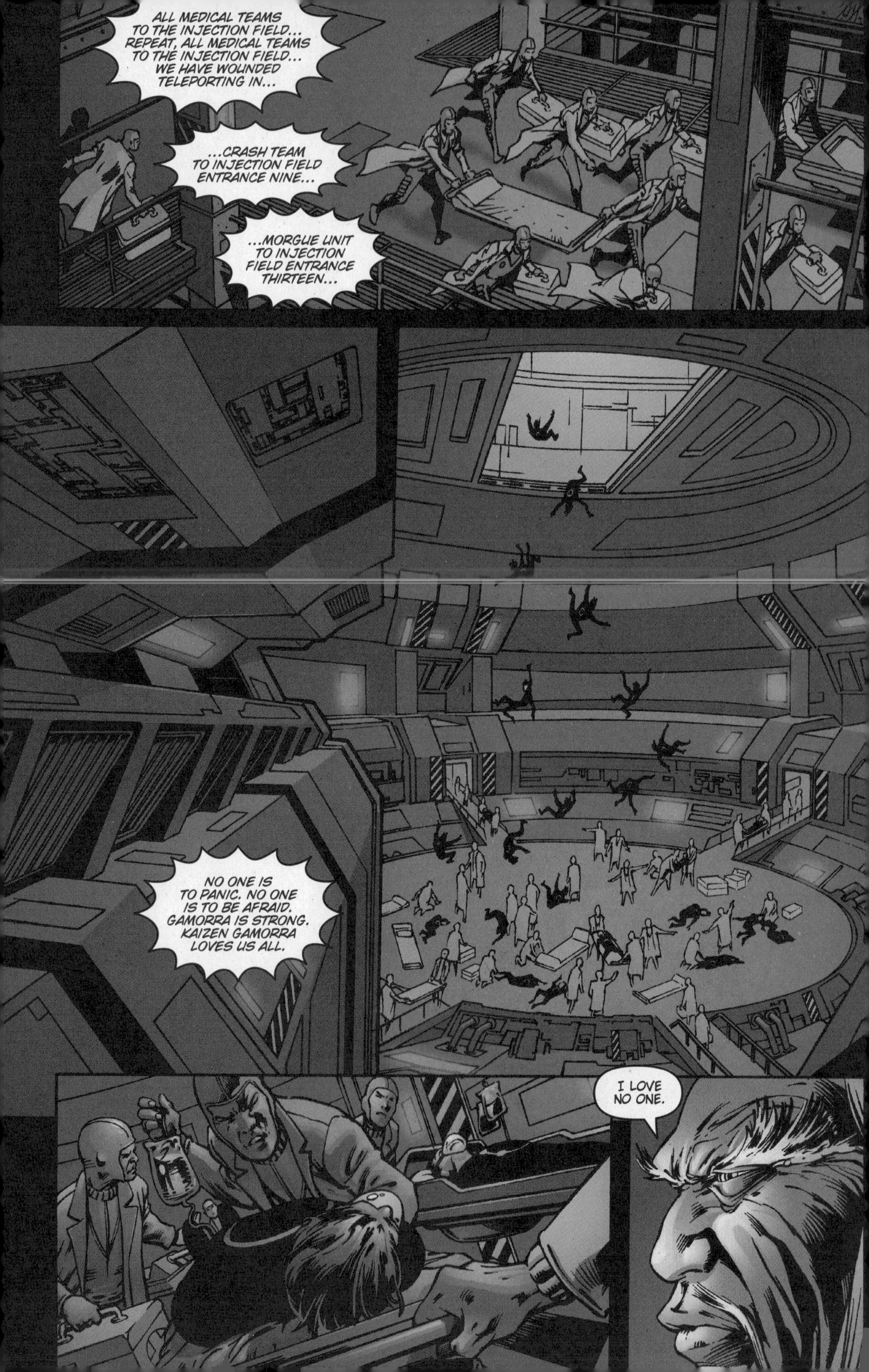
ALL MEDICAL TEAMS TO THE INJECTION FIELD... REPEAT, ALL MEDICAL TEAMS TO THE INJECTION FIELD... WE HAVE WOUNDED TELEPORTING IN...
...CRASH TEAM TO INJECTION FIELD ENTRANCE NINE...
...MORGUE UNIT TO INJECTION FIELD ENTRANCE THIRTEEN...
NO ONE IS TO PANIC. NO ONE IS TO BE AFRAID. GAMORRA IS STRONG. KAIZEN GAMORRA LOVES US ALL.
I LOVE NO ONE.

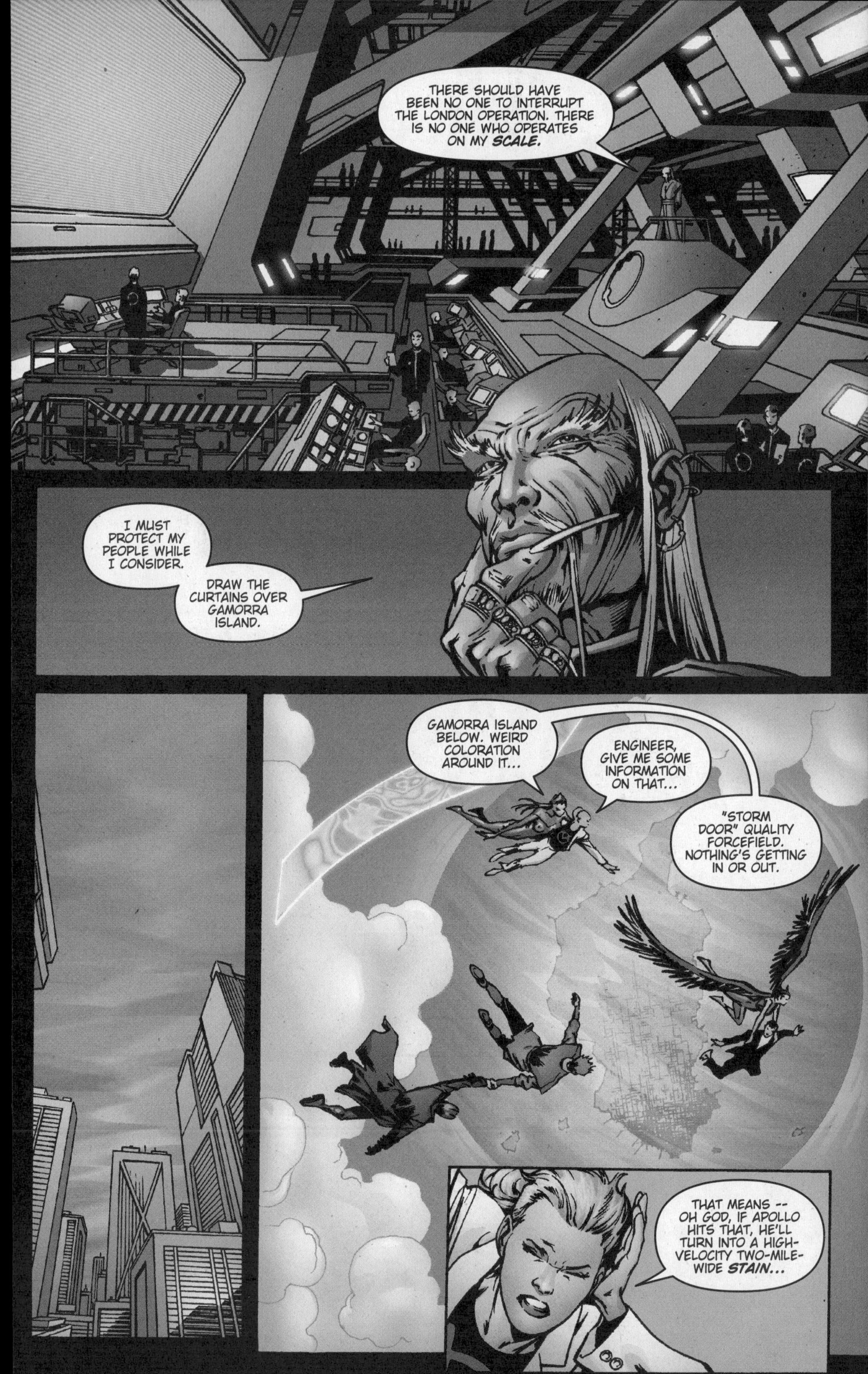
THERE SHOULD HAVE BEEN NO ONE TO INTERRUPT THE LONDON OPERATION. THERE IS NO ONE WHO OPERATES ON MY *SCALE.*
I MUST PROTECT MY PEOPLE WHILE I CONSIDER.
DRAW THE CURTAINS OVER GAMORRA ISLAND.
GAMORRA ISLAND BELOW. WEIRD COLORATION AROUND IT...
ENGINEER, GIVE ME SOME INFORMATION ON THAT...
"STORM DOOR" QUALITY FORCEFIELD. NOTHING'S GETTING IN OR OUT.
THAT MEANS -- OH GOD, IF APOLLO HITS THAT, HE'LL TURN INTO A HIGH-VELOCITY TWO-MILE-WIDE *STAIN...*

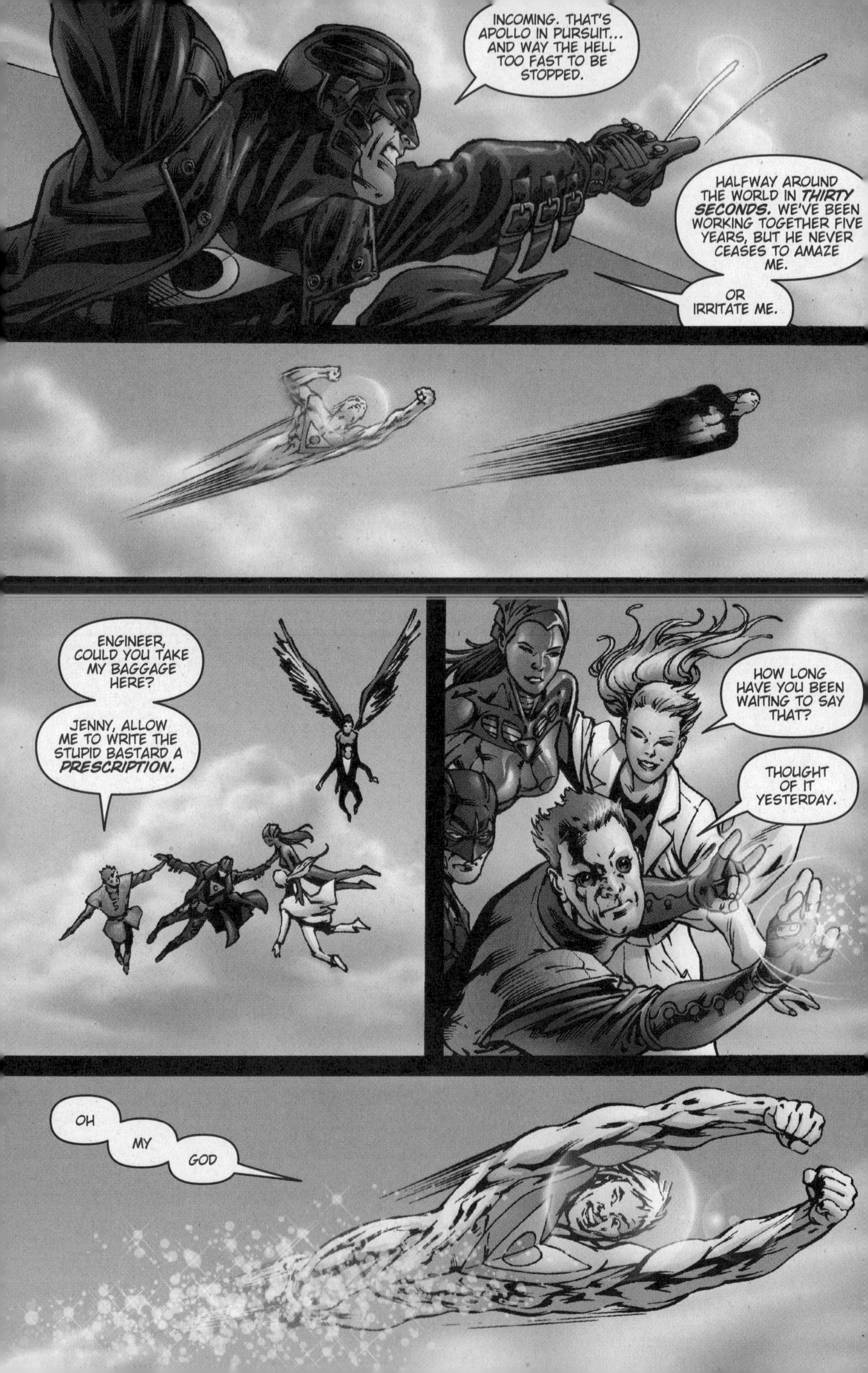
INCOMING. THAT'S APOLLO IN PURSUIT... AND WAY THE HELL TOO FAST TO BE STOPPED.
HALFWAY AROUND THE WORLD IN ***THIRTY SECONDS.*** WE'VE BEEN WORKING TOGETHER FIVE YEARS, BUT HE NEVER CEASES TO AMAZE ME.
OR IRRITATE ME.
ENGINEER, COULD YOU TAKE MY BAGGAGE HERE?
JENNY, ALLOW ME TO WRITE THE STUPID BASTARD A ***PRESCRIPTION.***
HOW LONG HAVE YOU BEEN WAITING TO SAY THAT?
THOUGHT OF IT YESTERDAY.
OH
MY
GOD

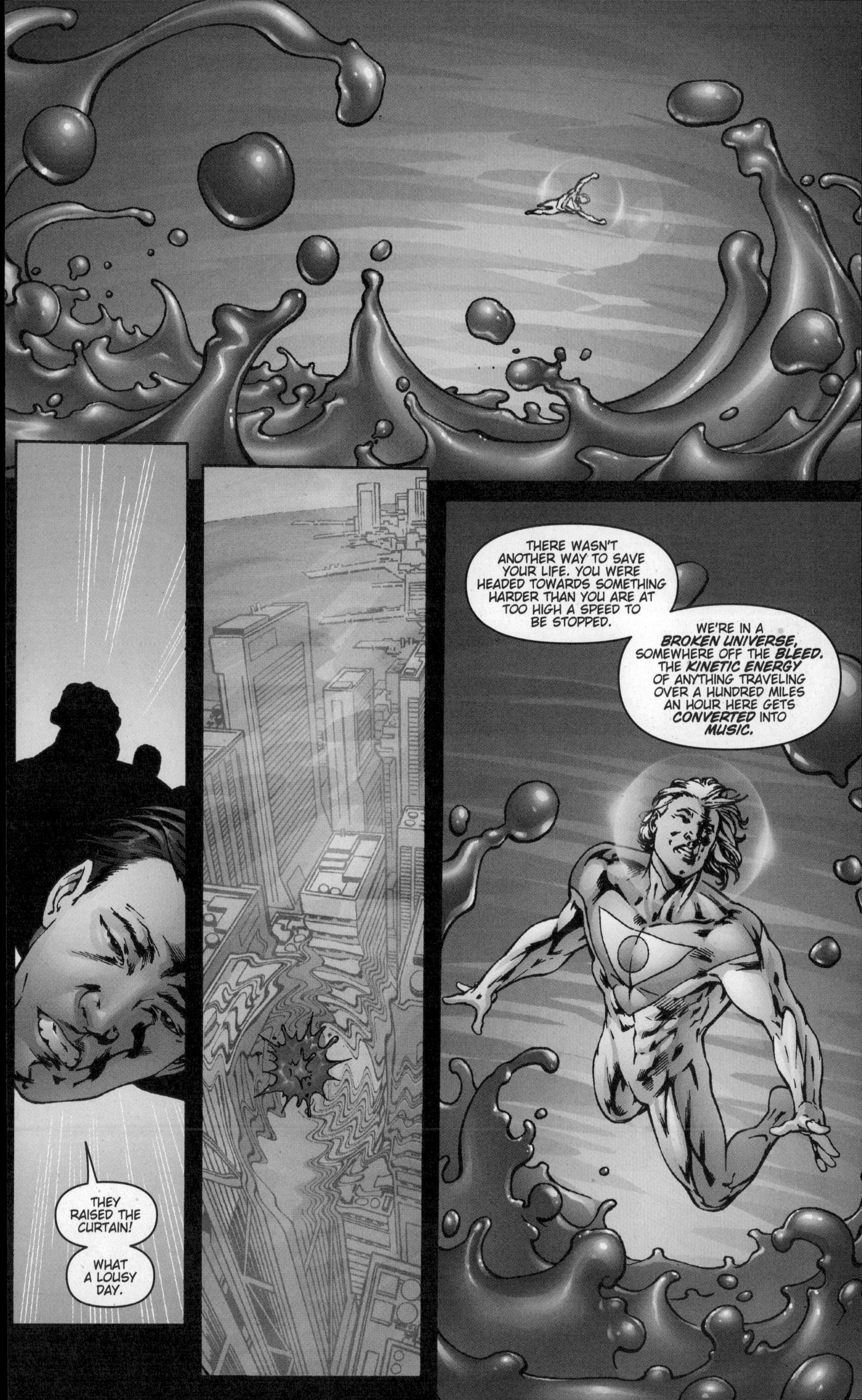
THEY RAISED THE CURTAIN!
WHAT A LOUSY DAY.
THERE WASN'T ANOTHER WAY TO SAVE YOUR LIFE. YOU WERE HEADED TOWARDS SOMETHING HARDER THAN YOU ARE AT TOO HIGH A SPEED TO BE STOPPED.
WE'RE IN A **BROKEN UNIVERSE**, SOMEWHERE OFF THE **BLEED**. THE **KINETIC ENERGY** OF ANYTHING TRAVELING OVER A HUNDRED MILES AN HOUR HERE GETS **CONVERTED** INTO **MUSIC**.

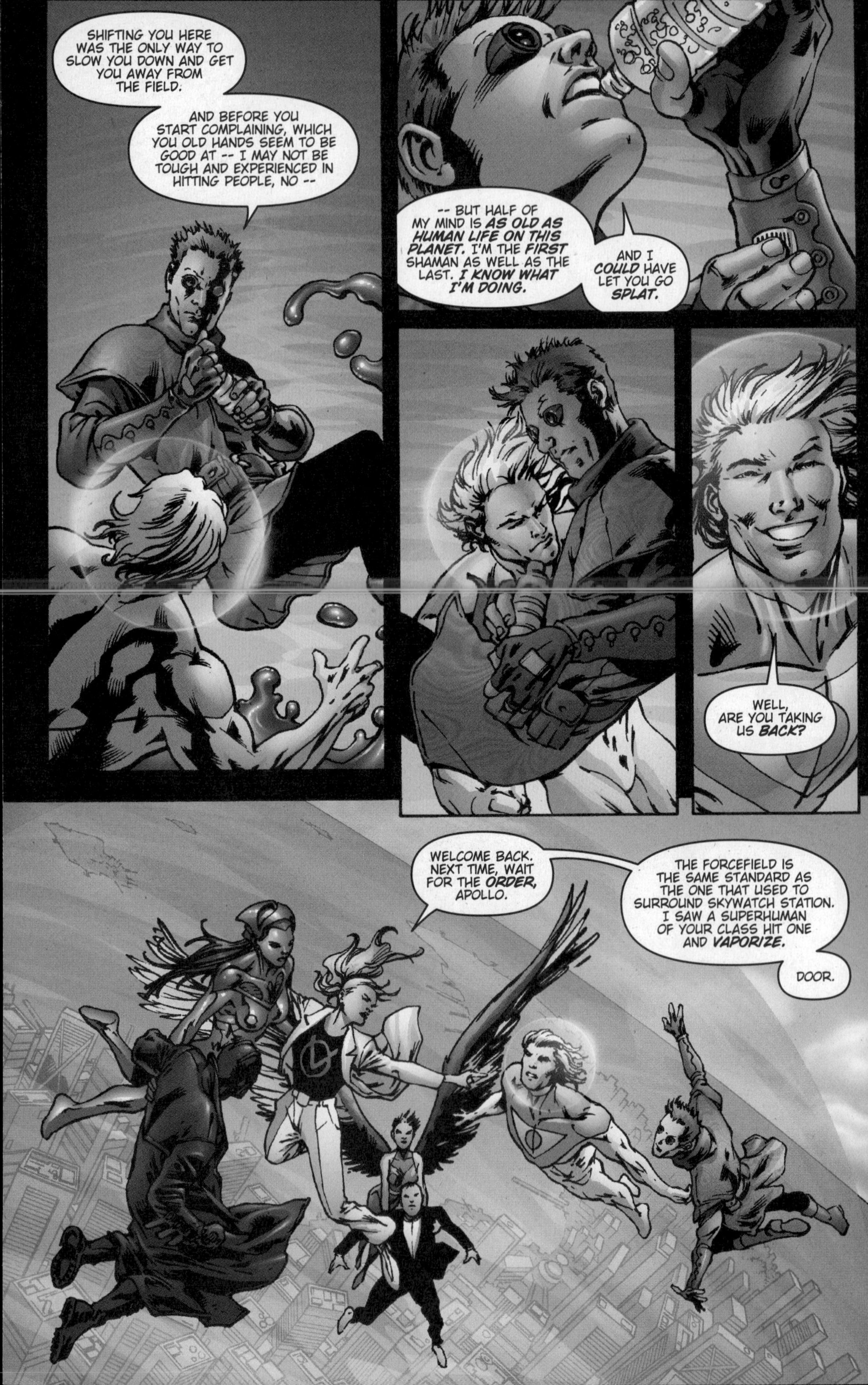
SHIFTING YOU HERE WAS THE ONLY WAY TO SLOW YOU DOWN AND GET YOU AWAY FROM THE FIELD.
AND BEFORE YOU START COMPLAINING, WHICH YOU OLD HANDS SEEM TO BE GOOD AT -- I MAY NOT BE TOUGH AND EXPERIENCED IN HITTING PEOPLE, NO --
-- BUT HALF OF MY MIND IS **AS OLD AS HUMAN LIFE ON THIS PLANET.** I'M THE **FIRST** SHAMAN AS WELL AS THE LAST. **I KNOW WHAT I'M DOING.**
AND I **COULD** HAVE LET YOU GO **SPLAT.**
WELL, ARE YOU TAKING US **BACK?**
WELCOME BACK. NEXT TIME, WAIT FOR THE **ORDER,** APOLLO.
THE FORCEFIELD IS THE SAME STANDARD AS THE ONE THAT USED TO SURROUND SKYWATCH STATION. I SAW A SUPERHUMAN OF YOUR CLASS HIT ONE AND **VAPORIZE.**
DOOR.

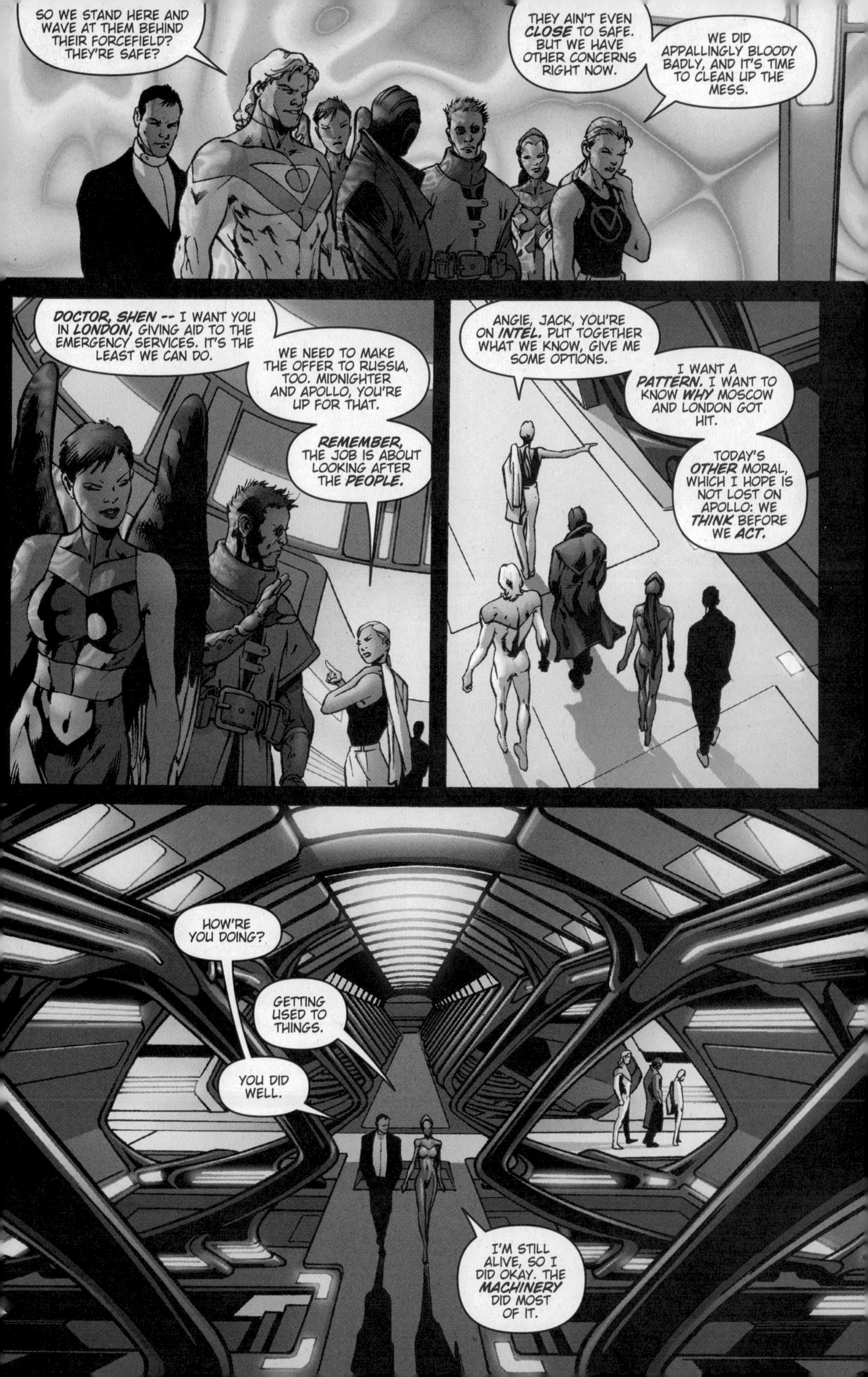
SO WE STAND HERE AND WAVE AT THEM BEHIND THEIR FORCEFIELD? THEY'RE SAFE?
THEY AIN'T EVEN **CLOSE** TO SAFE. BUT WE HAVE OTHER CONCERNS RIGHT NOW.
WE DID APPALLINGLY BLOODY BADLY, AND IT'S TIME TO CLEAN UP THE MESS.
DOCTOR, SHEN -- I WANT YOU IN **LONDON,** GIVING AID TO THE EMERGENCY SERVICES. IT'S THE LEAST WE CAN DO.
WE NEED TO MAKE THE OFFER TO RUSSIA, TOO. MIDNIGHTER AND APOLLO, YOU'RE UP FOR THAT.
REMEMBER, THE JOB IS ABOUT LOOKING AFTER THE **PEOPLE.**
ANGIE, JACK, YOU'RE ON **INTEL.** PUT TOGETHER WHAT WE KNOW, GIVE ME SOME OPTIONS.
I WANT A **PATTERN.** I WANT TO KNOW **WHY** MOSCOW AND LONDON GOT HIT.
TODAY'S **OTHER** MORAL, WHICH I HOPE IS NOT LOST ON APOLLO: WE **THINK** BEFORE WE **ACT.**
HOW'RE YOU DOING?
GETTING USED TO THINGS.
YOU DID WELL.
I'M STILL ALIVE, SO I DID OKAY. THE **MACHINERY** DID MOST OF IT.

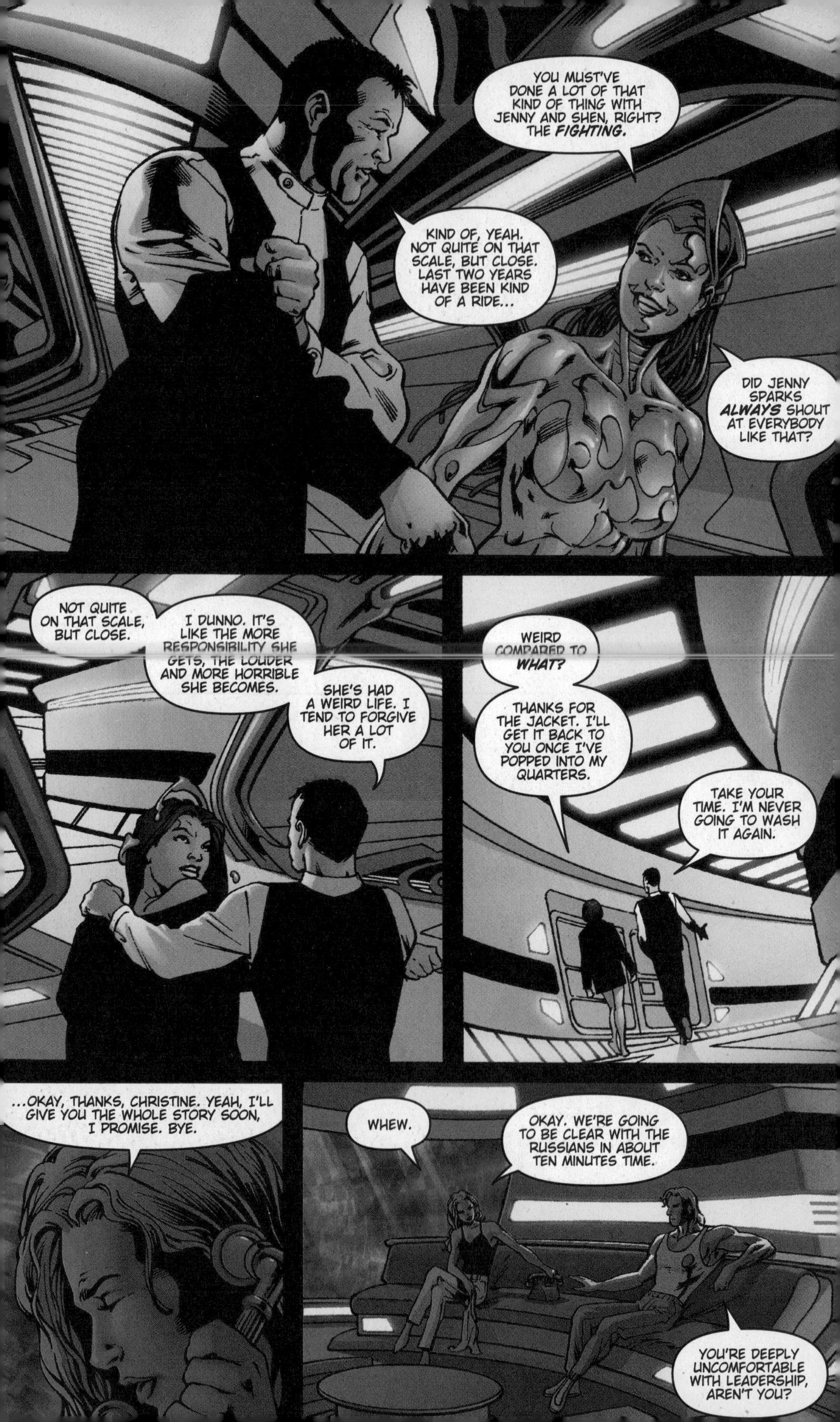
YOU MUST'VE DONE A LOT OF THAT KIND OF THING WITH JENNY AND SHEN, RIGHT? THE ***FIGHTING.***
KIND OF, YEAH. NOT QUITE ON THAT SCALE, BUT CLOSE. LAST TWO YEARS HAVE BEEN KIND OF A RIDE...
DID JENNY SPARKS ***ALWAYS*** SHOUT AT EVERYBODY LIKE THAT?
NOT QUITE ON THAT SCALE, BUT CLOSE.
I DUNNO. IT'S LIKE THE MORE RESPONSIBILITY SHE GETS, THE LOUDER AND MORE HORRIBLE SHE BECOMES.
SHE'S HAD A WEIRD LIFE. I TEND TO FORGIVE HER A LOT OF IT.
WEIRD COMPARED TO ***WHAT?***
THANKS FOR THE JACKET. I'LL GET IT BACK TO YOU ONCE I'VE POPPED INTO MY QUARTERS.
TAKE YOUR TIME. I'M NEVER GOING TO WASH IT AGAIN.
...OKAY, THANKS, CHRISTINE. YEAH, I'LL GIVE YOU THE WHOLE STORY SOON, I PROMISE. BYE.
WHEW.
OKAY. WE'RE GOING TO BE CLEAR WITH THE RUSSIANS IN ABOUT TEN MINUTES TIME.
YOU'RE DEEPLY UNCOMFORTABLE WITH LEADERSHIP, AREN'T YOU?

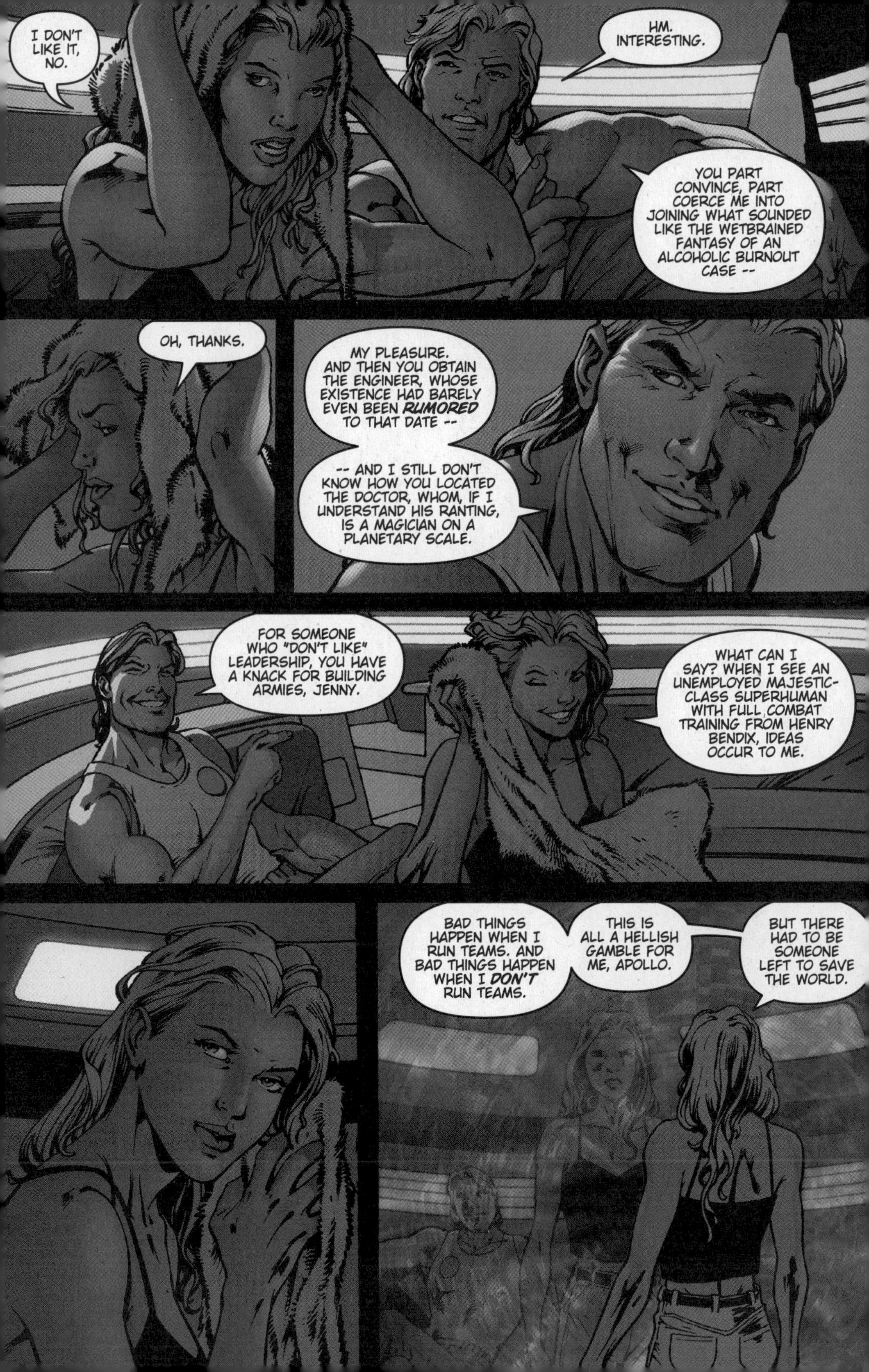
I DON'T LIKE IT, NO.
HM. INTERESTING.
YOU PART CONVINCE, PART COERCE ME INTO JOINING WHAT SOUNDED LIKE THE WETBRAINED FANTASY OF AN ALCOHOLIC BURNOUT CASE --
OH, THANKS.
MY PLEASURE. AND THEN YOU OBTAIN THE ENGINEER, WHOSE EXISTENCE HAD BARELY EVEN BEEN ***RUMORED*** TO THAT DATE --
-- AND I STILL DON'T KNOW HOW YOU LOCATED THE DOCTOR, WHOM, IF I UNDERSTAND HIS RANTING, IS A MAGICIAN ON A PLANETARY SCALE.
FOR SOMEONE WHO "DON'T LIKE" LEADERSHIP, YOU HAVE A KNACK FOR BUILDING ARMIES, JENNY.
WHAT CAN I SAY? WHEN I SEE AN UNEMPLOYED MAJESTIC-CLASS SUPERHUMAN WITH FULL COMBAT TRAINING FROM HENRY BENDIX, IDEAS OCCUR TO ME.
BAD THINGS HAPPEN WHEN I RUN TEAMS. AND BAD THINGS HAPPEN WHEN I ***DON'T*** RUN TEAMS.
THIS IS ALL A HELLISH GAMBLE FOR ME, APOLLO.
BUT THERE HAD TO BE SOMEONE LEFT TO SAVE THE WORLD.

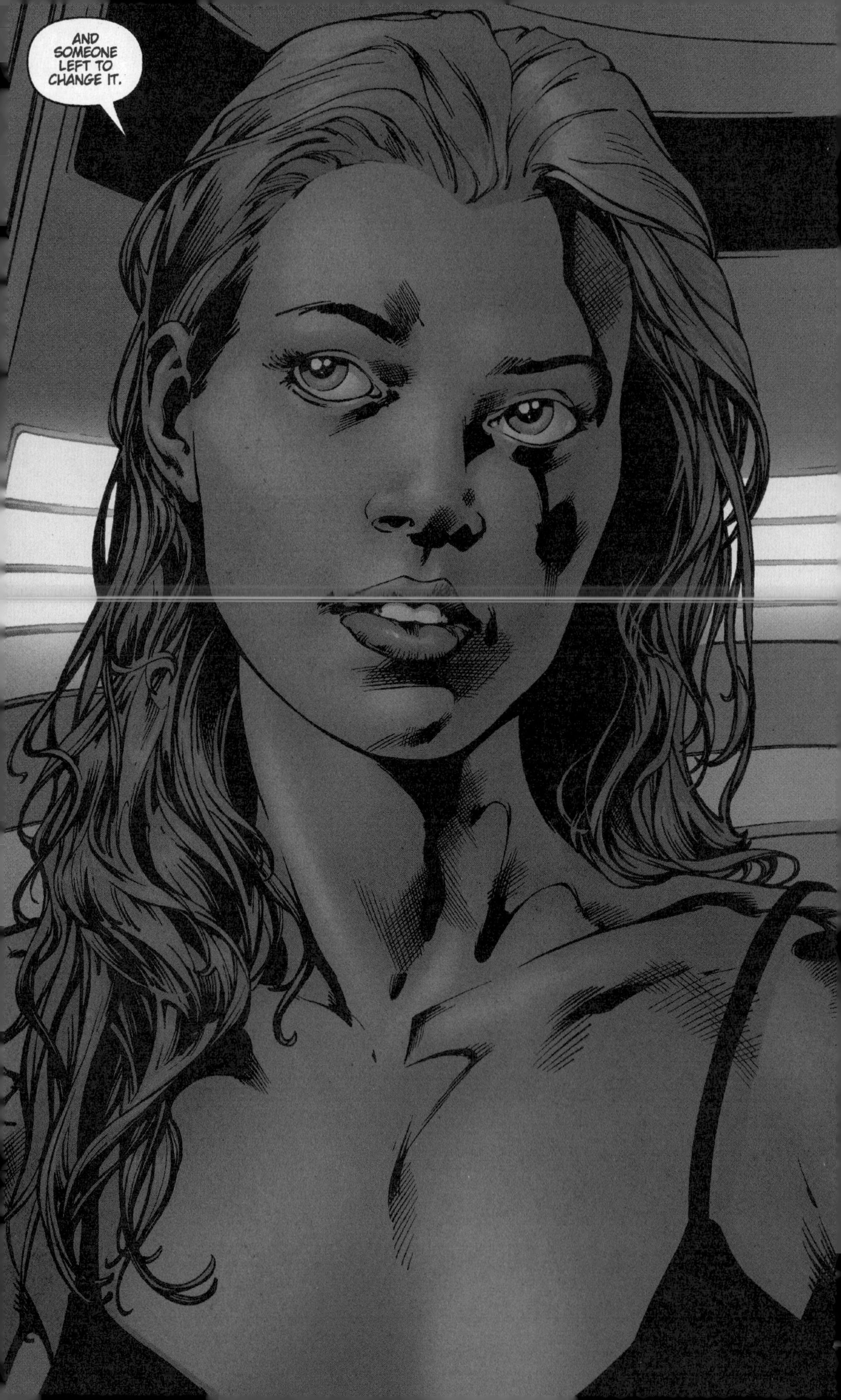
AND SOMEONE LEFT TO CHANGE IT.

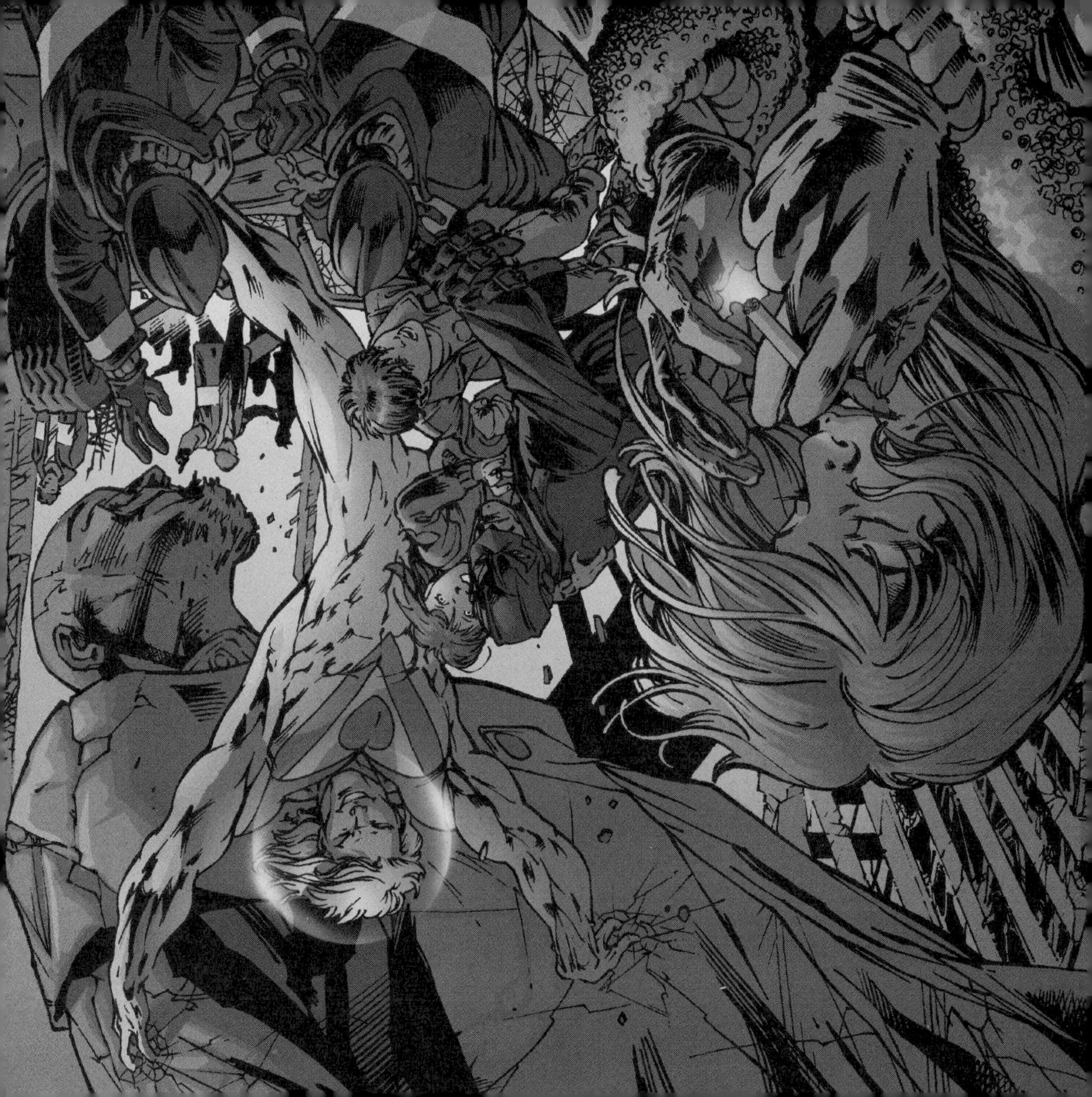

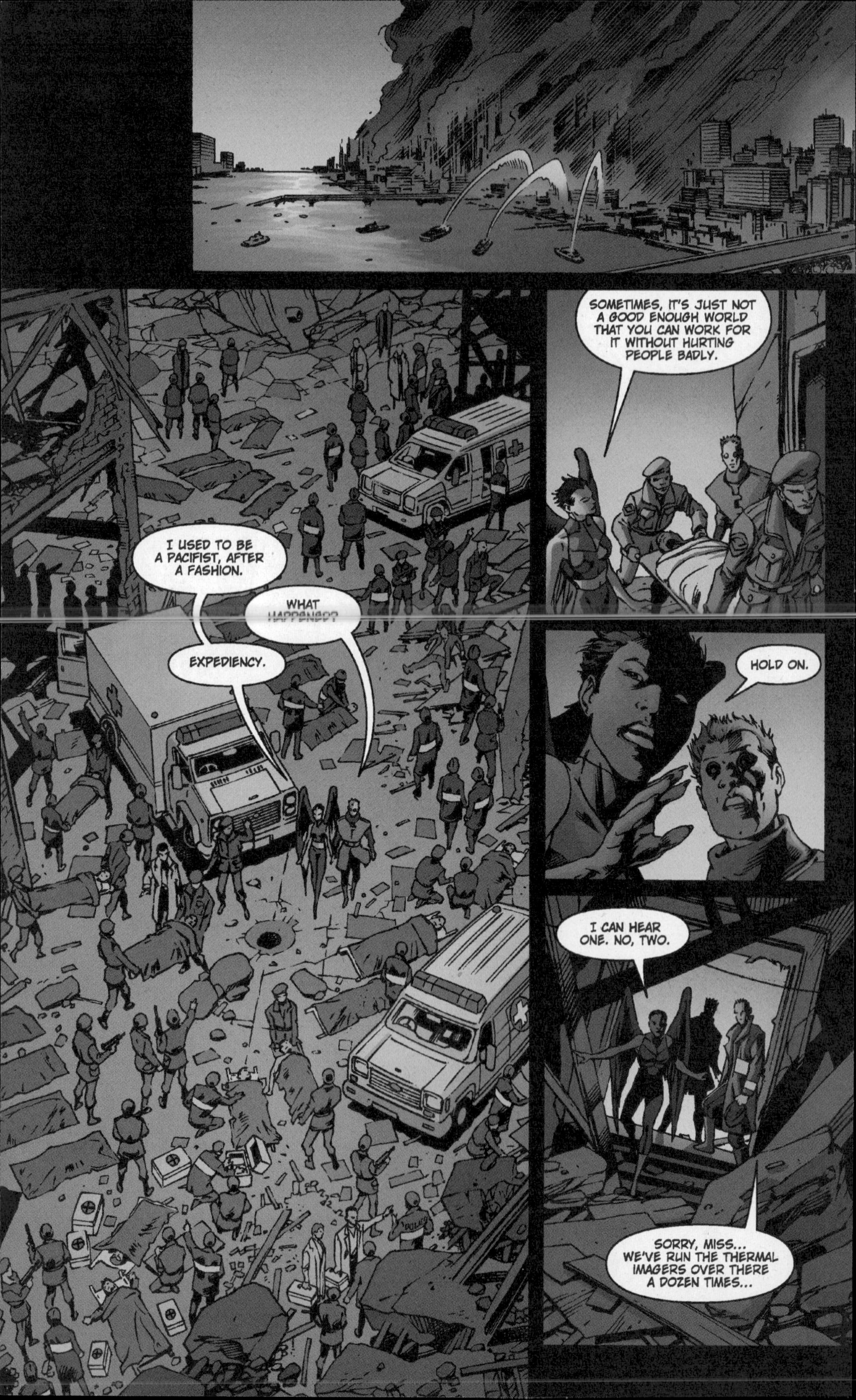
I USED TO BE A PACIFIST, AFTER A FASHION.
WHAT HAPPENED?
EXPEDIENCY.
SOMETIMES, IT'S JUST NOT A GOOD ENOUGH WORLD THAT YOU CAN WORK FOR IT WITHOUT HURTING PEOPLE BADLY.
HOLD ON.
I CAN HEAR ONE. NO, TWO.
SORRY, MISS... WE'VE RUN THE THERMAL IMAGERS OVER THERE A DOZEN TIMES...

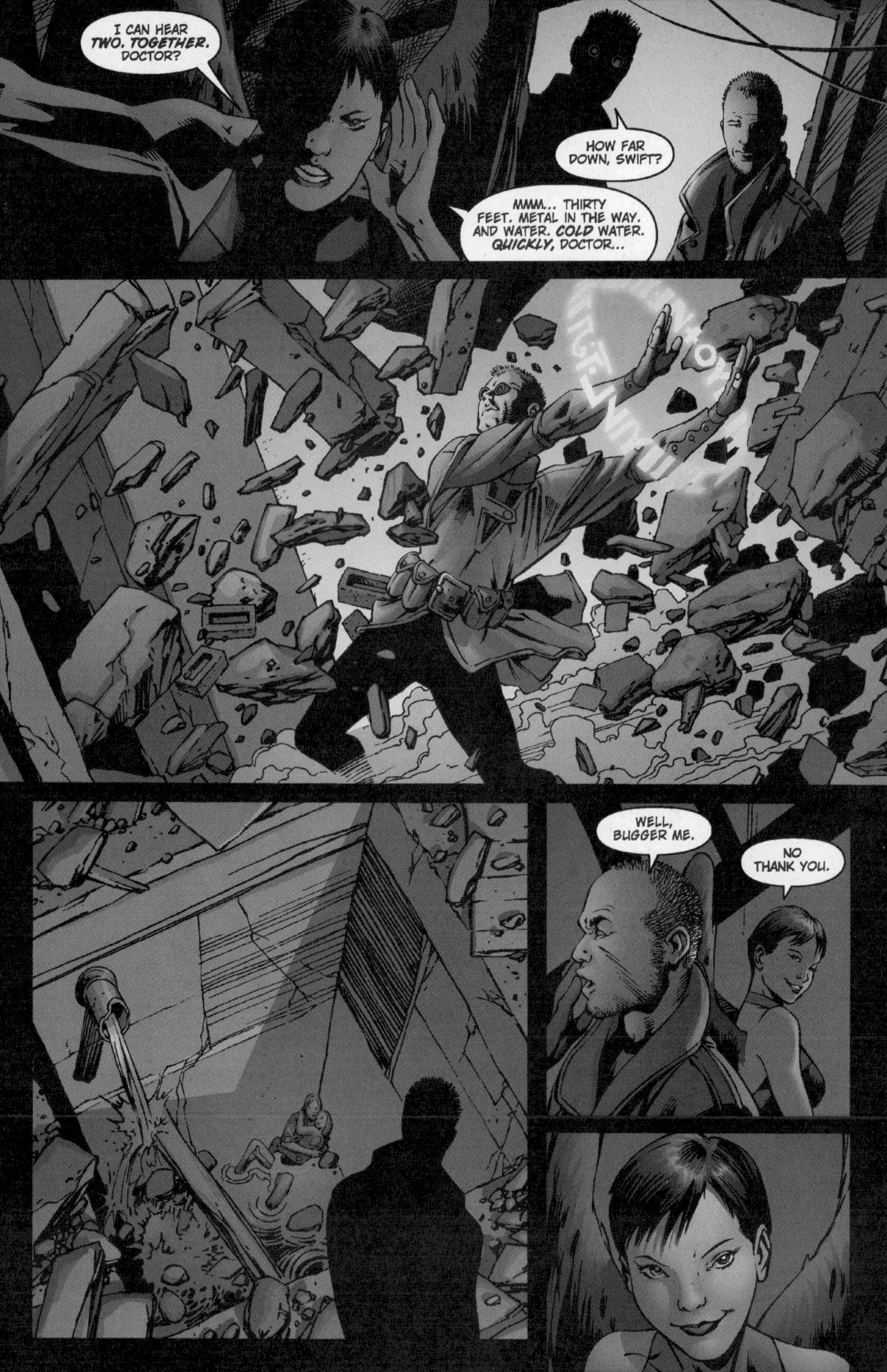
I CAN HEAR **TWO. TOGETHER.** DOCTOR?
HOW FAR DOWN, SWIFT?
MMM... THIRTY FEET. METAL IN THE WAY. AND WATER. **COLD** WATER. **QUICKLY**, DOCTOR...
WELL, BUGGER ME.
NO THANK YOU.

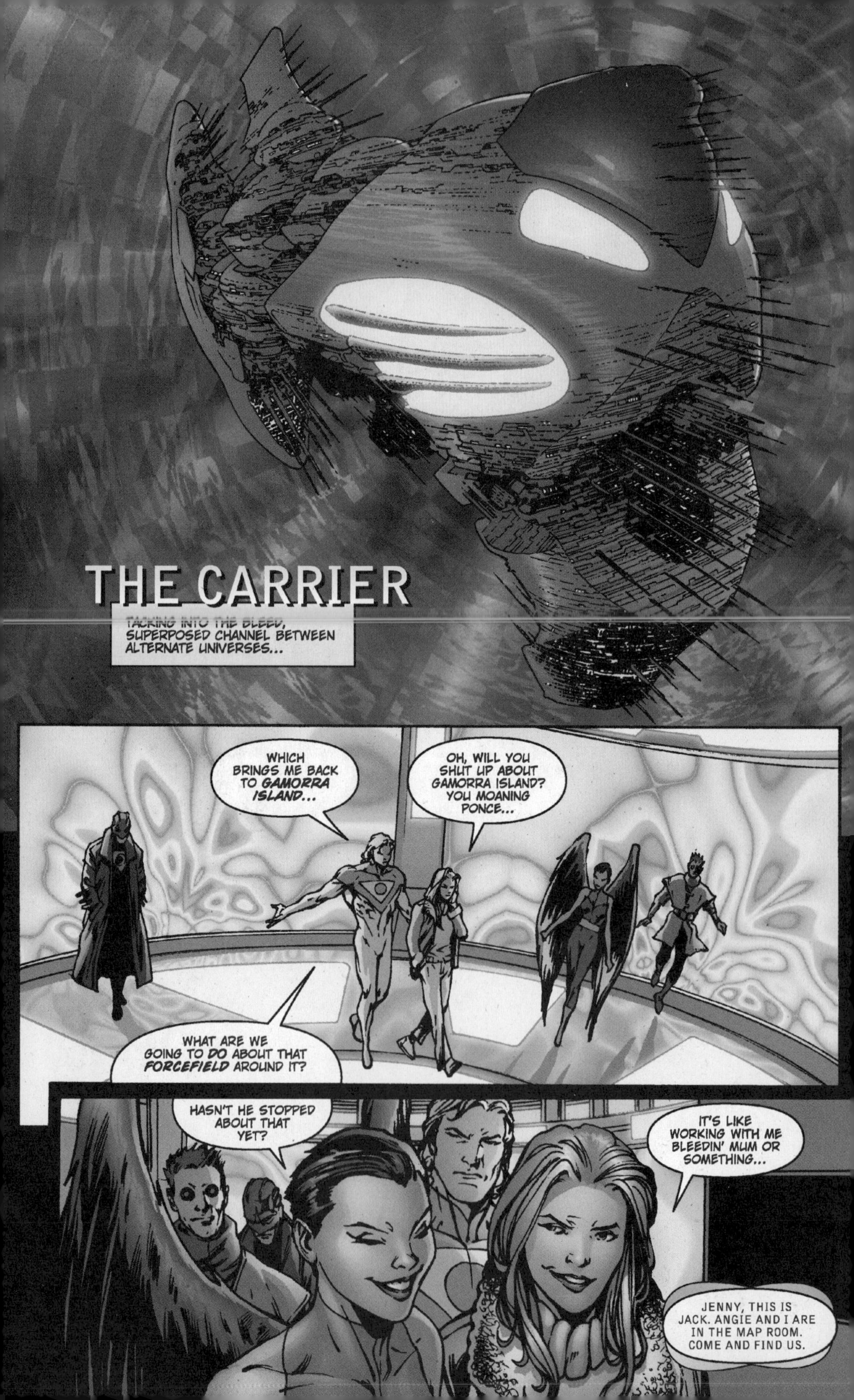
THE CARRIER
TACKING INTO THE BLEED, SUPERPOSED CHANNEL BETWEEN ALTERNATE UNIVERSES...
WHICH BRINGS ME BACK TO GAMORRA ISLAND...
OH, WILL YOU SHUT UP ABOUT GAMORRA ISLAND? YOU MOANING PONCE...
WHAT ARE WE GOING TO DO ABOUT THAT FORCEFIELD AROUND IT?
HASN'T HE STOPPED ABOUT THAT YET?
IT'S LIKE WORKING WITH ME BLEEDIN' MUM OR SOMETHING...
JENNY, THIS IS JACK. ANGIE AND I ARE IN THE MAP ROOM. COME AND FIND US.

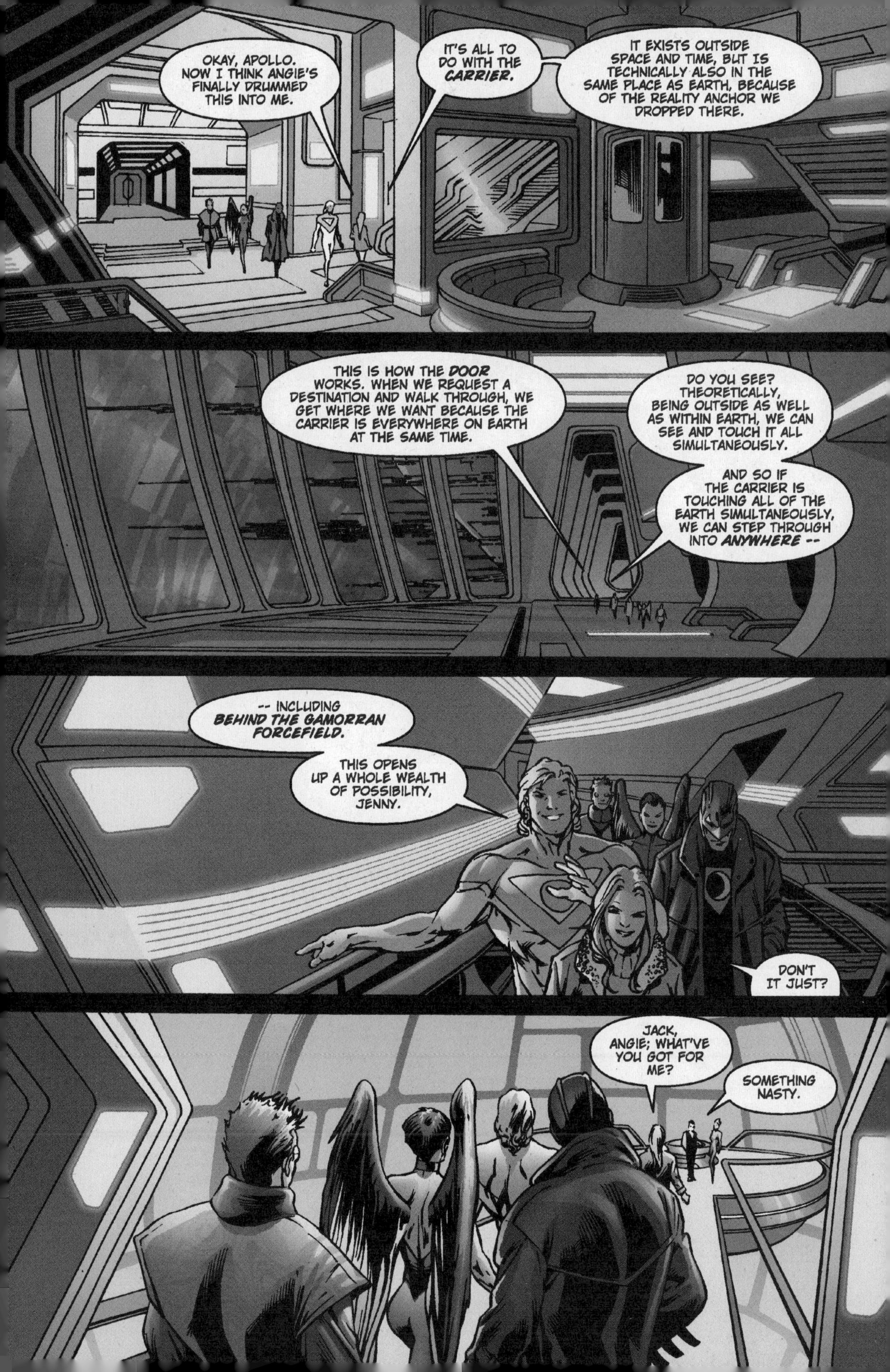
OKAY, APOLLO. NOW I THINK ANGIE'S FINALLY DRUMMED THIS INTO ME.
IT'S ALL TO DO WITH THE *CARRIER.*
IT EXISTS OUTSIDE SPACE AND TIME, BUT IS TECHNICALLY ALSO IN THE SAME PLACE AS EARTH, BECAUSE OF THE REALITY ANCHOR WE DROPPED THERE.
THIS IS HOW THE *DOOR* WORKS. WHEN WE REQUEST A DESTINATION AND WALK THROUGH, WE GET WHERE WE WANT BECAUSE THE CARRIER IS EVERYWHERE ON EARTH AT THE SAME TIME.
DO YOU SEE? THEORETICALLY, BEING OUTSIDE AS WELL AS WITHIN EARTH, WE CAN SEE AND TOUCH IT ALL SIMULTANEOUSLY.
AND SO IF THE CARRIER IS TOUCHING ALL OF THE EARTH SIMULTANEOUSLY, WE CAN STEP THROUGH INTO *ANYWHERE* --
-- INCLUDING *BEHIND THE GAMORRAN FORCEFIELD.*
THIS OPENS UP A WHOLE WEALTH OF POSSIBILITY, JENNY.
DON'T IT JUST?
JACK, ANGIE; WHAT'VE YOU GOT FOR ME?
SOMETHING NASTY.

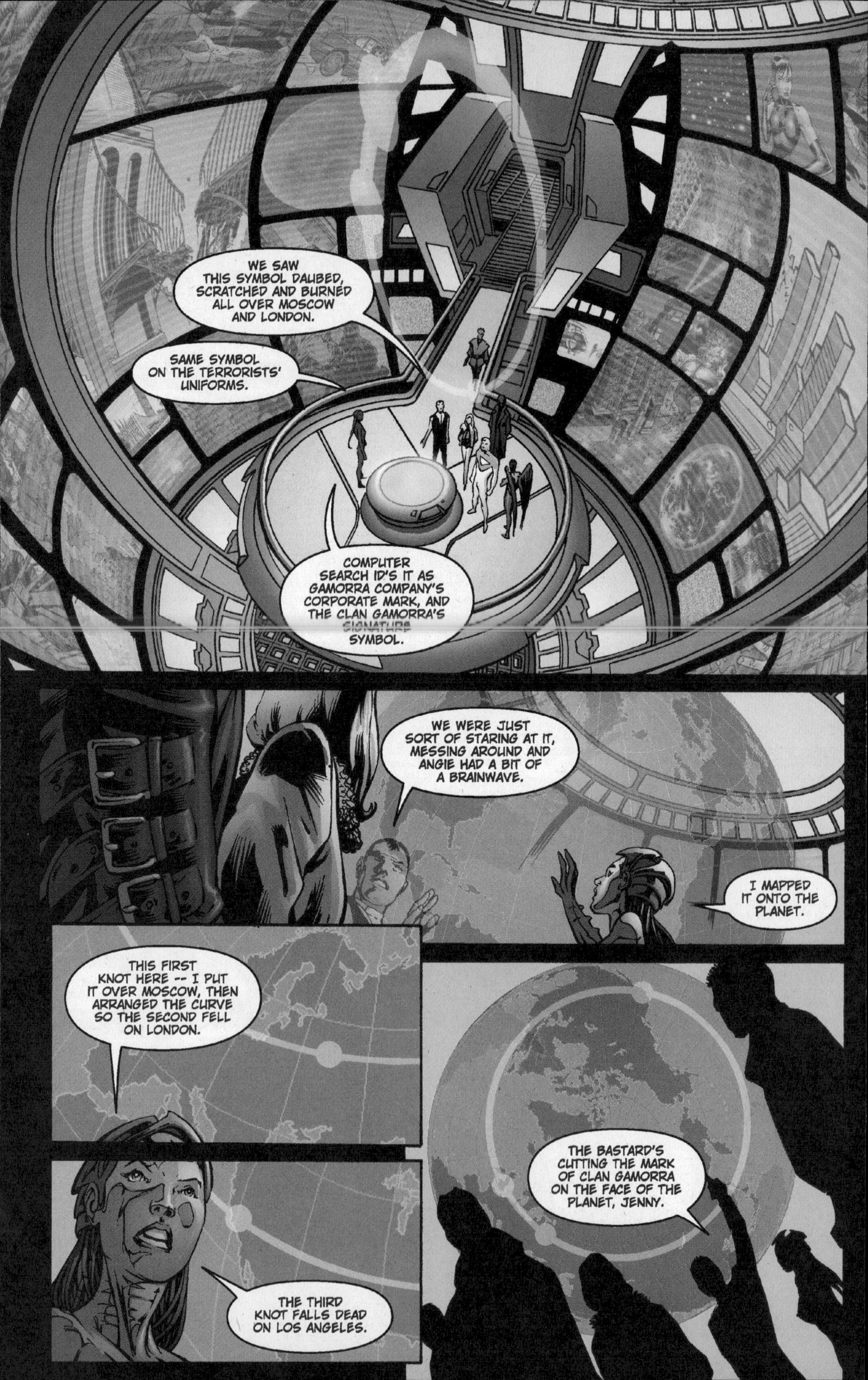
WE SAW THIS SYMBOL DAUBED, SCRATCHED AND BURNED ALL OVER MOSCOW AND LONDON.
SAME SYMBOL ON THE TERRORISTS' UNIFORMS.
COMPUTER SEARCH ID'S IT AS GAMORRA COMPANY'S CORPORATE MARK, AND THE CLAN GAMORRA'S SIGNATURE SYMBOL.
WE WERE JUST SORT OF STARING AT IT, MESSING AROUND AND ANGIE HAD A BIT OF A BRAINWAVE.
I MAPPED IT ONTO THE PLANET.
THIS FIRST KNOT HERE -- I PUT IT OVER MOSCOW, THEN ARRANGED THE CURVE SO THE SECOND FELL ON LONDON.
THE THIRD KNOT FALLS DEAD ON LOS ANGELES.
THE BASTARD'S CUTTING THE MARK OF CLAN GAMORRA ON THE FACE OF THE PLANET, JENNY.

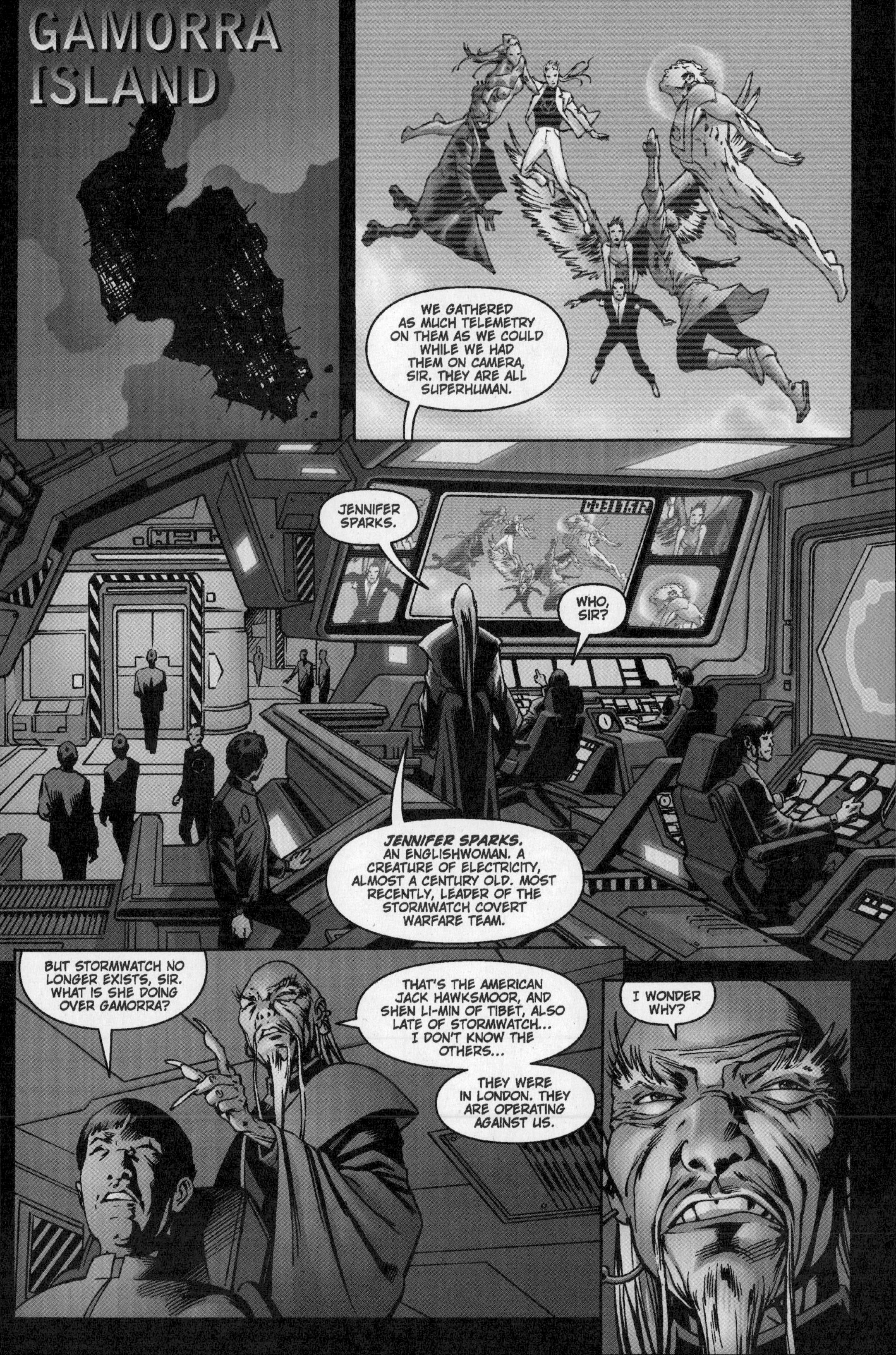
GAMORRA ISLAND
WE GATHERED AS MUCH TELEMETRY ON THEM AS WE COULD WHILE WE HAD THEM ON CAMERA, SIR. THEY ARE ALL SUPERHUMAN.
JENNIFER SPARKS.
WHO, SIR?
JENNIFER SPARKS. AN ENGLISHWOMAN. A CREATURE OF ELECTRICITY, ALMOST A CENTURY OLD. MOST RECENTLY, LEADER OF THE STORMWATCH COVERT WARFARE TEAM.
BUT STORMWATCH NO LONGER EXISTS, SIR. WHAT IS SHE DOING OVER GAMORRA?
THAT'S THE AMERICAN JACK HAWKSMOOR, AND SHEN LI-MIN OF TIBET, ALSO LATE OF STORMWATCH... I DON'T KNOW THE OTHERS...
THEY WERE IN LONDON. THEY ARE OPERATING AGAINST US.
I WONDER WHY?

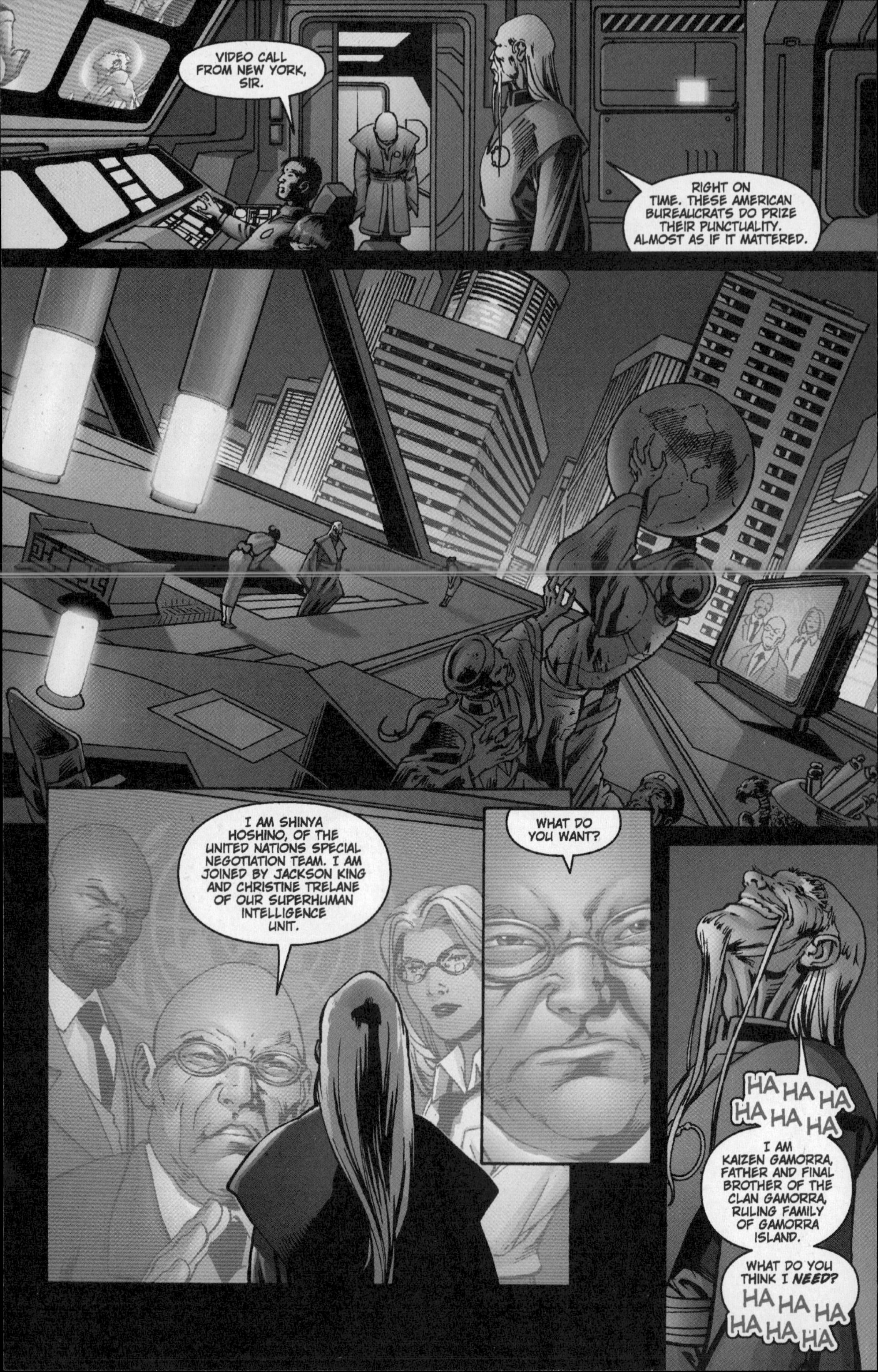
VIDEO CALL FROM NEW YORK, SIR.
RIGHT ON TIME. THESE AMERICAN BUREAUCRATS DO PRIZE THEIR PUNCTUALITY. ALMOST AS IF IT MATTERED.
I AM SHINYA HOSHINO, OF THE UNITED NATIONS SPECIAL NEGOTIATION TEAM. I AM JOINED BY JACKSON KING AND CHRISTINE TRELANE OF OUR SUPERHUMAN INTELLIGENCE UNIT.
WHAT DO YOU WANT?
HA HA HA HA HA HA
I AM KAIZEN GAMORRA, FATHER AND FINAL BROTHER OF THE CLAN GAMORRA, RULING FAMILY OF GAMORRA ISLAND.
WHAT DO YOU THINK I *NEED?*
HA HA HA HA HA HA HA

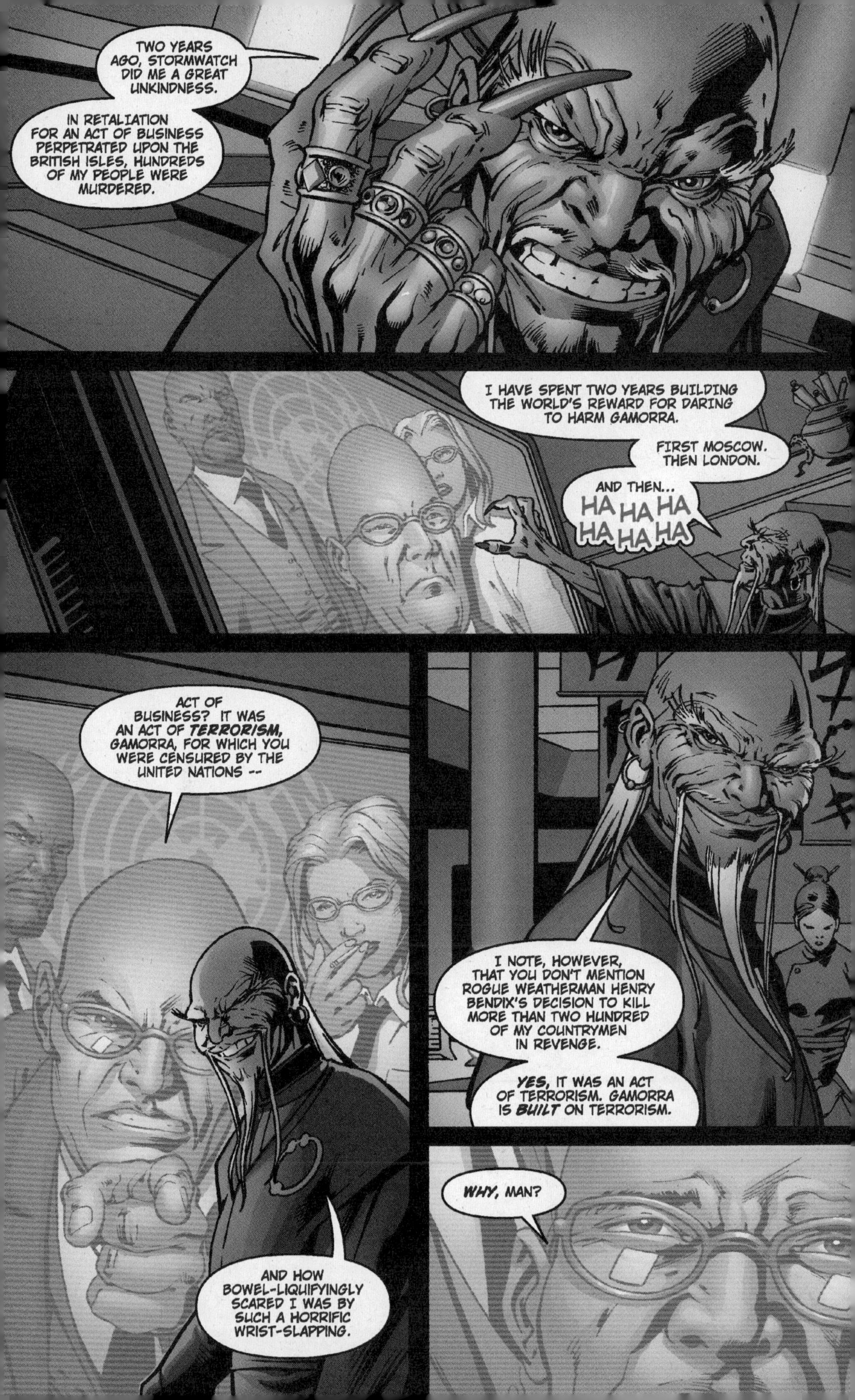
TWO YEARS AGO, STORMWATCH DID ME A GREAT UNKINDNESS.
IN RETALIATION FOR AN ACT OF BUSINESS PERPETRATED UPON THE BRITISH ISLES, HUNDREDS OF MY PEOPLE WERE MURDERED.
I HAVE SPENT TWO YEARS BUILDING THE WORLD'S REWARD FOR DARING TO HARM GAMORRA.
FIRST MOSCOW. THEN LONDON.
AND THEN... HA HA HA HA HA HA
ACT OF BUSINESS? IT WAS AN ACT OF *TERRORISM*, GAMORRA, FOR WHICH YOU WERE CENSURED BY THE UNITED NATIONS --
AND HOW BOWEL-LIQUIFYINGLY SCARED I WAS BY SUCH A HORRIFIC WRIST-SLAPPING.
I NOTE, HOWEVER, THAT YOU DON'T MENTION ROGUE WEATHERMAN HENRY BENDIX'S DECISION TO KILL MORE THAN TWO HUNDRED OF MY COUNTRYMEN IN REVENGE.
YES, IT WAS AN ACT OF TERRORISM. GAMORRA IS *BUILT* ON TERRORISM.
WHY, MAN?

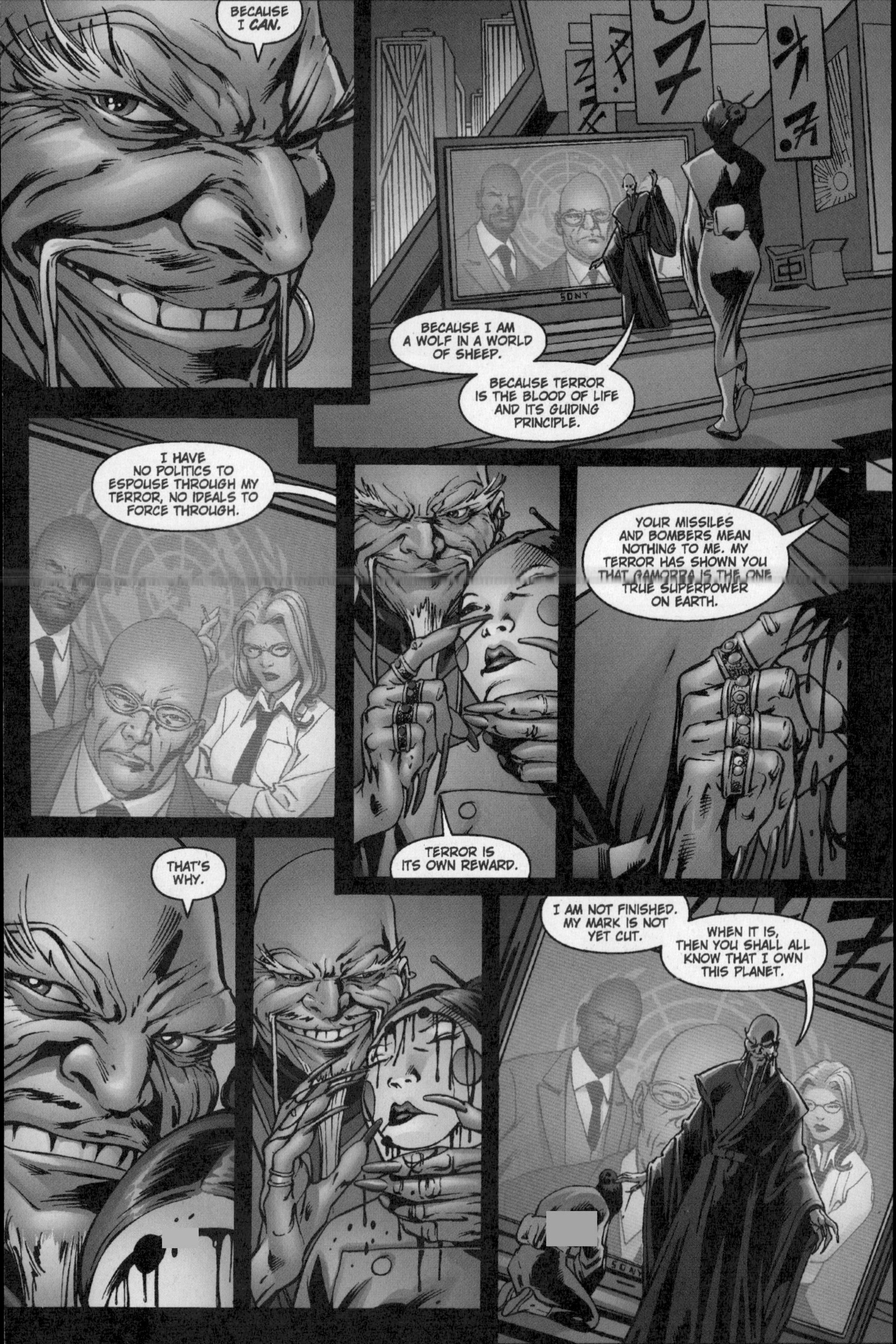
BECAUSE I CAN.
BECAUSE I AM A WOLF IN A WORLD OF SHEEP.
BECAUSE TERROR IS THE BLOOD OF LIFE AND ITS GUIDING PRINCIPLE.
I HAVE NO POLITICS TO ESPOUSE THROUGH MY TERROR, NO IDEALS TO FORCE THROUGH.
TERROR IS ITS OWN REWARD.
YOUR MISSILES AND BOMBERS MEAN NOTHING TO ME. MY TERROR HAS SHOWN YOU THAT GAMORRA IS THE ONE TRUE SUPERPOWER ON EARTH.
THAT'S WHY.
I AM NOT FINISHED. MY MARK IS NOT YET CUT.
WHEN IT IS, THEN YOU SHALL ALL KNOW THAT I OWN THIS PLANET.

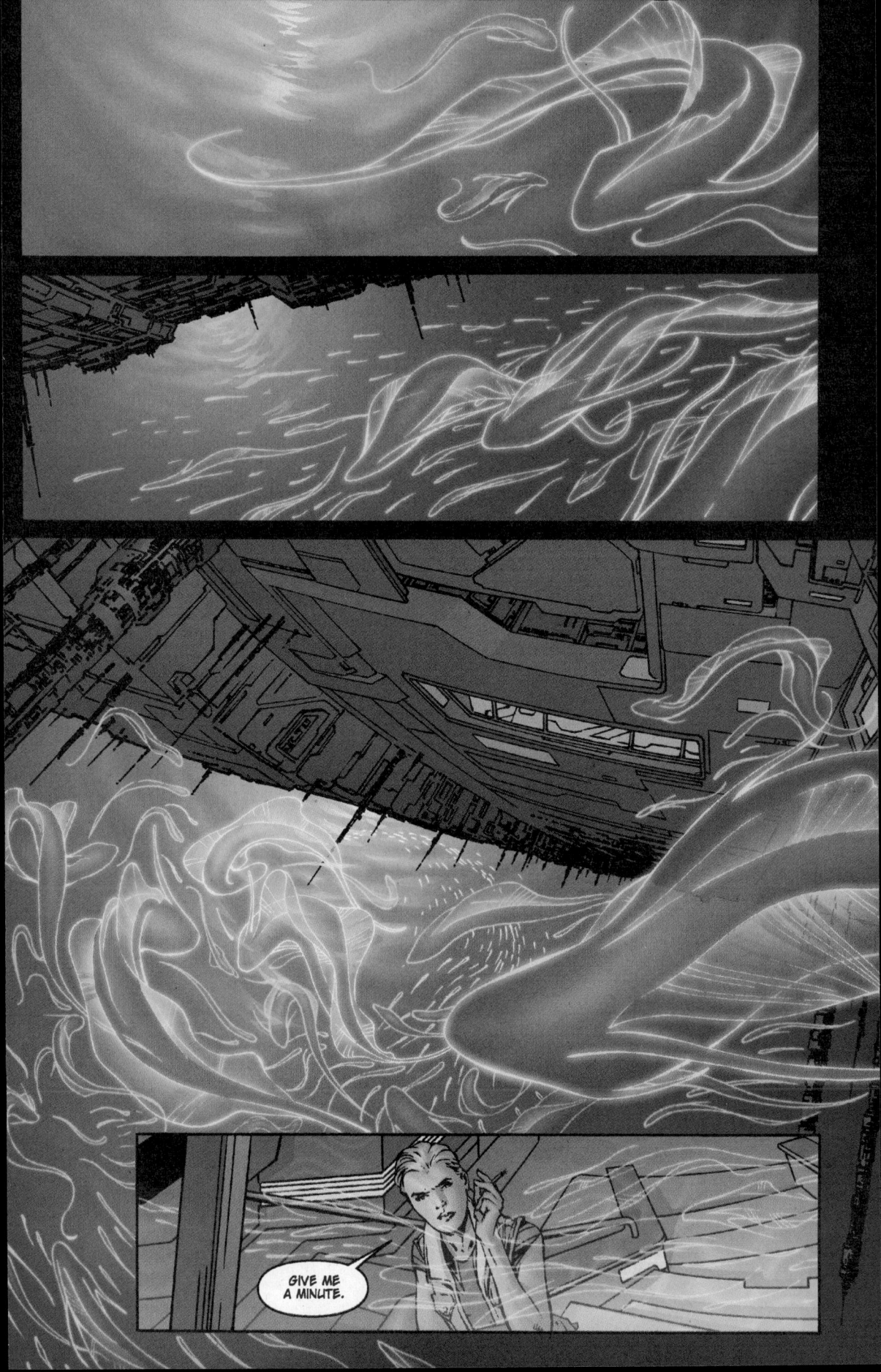

GIVE ME
A MINUTE.

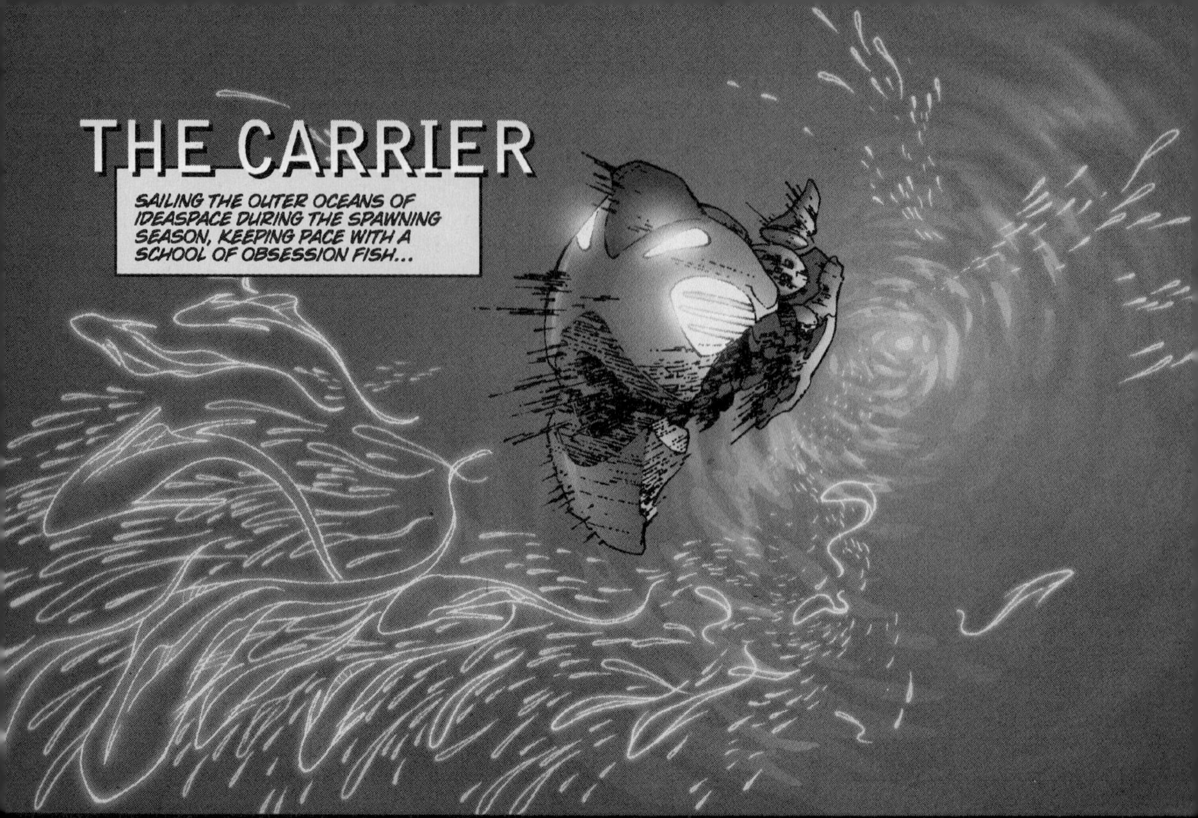
THE CARRIER
SAILING THE OUTER OCEANS OF IDEASPACE DURING THE SPAWNING SEASON, KEEPING PACE WITH A SCHOOL OF OBSESSION FISH...

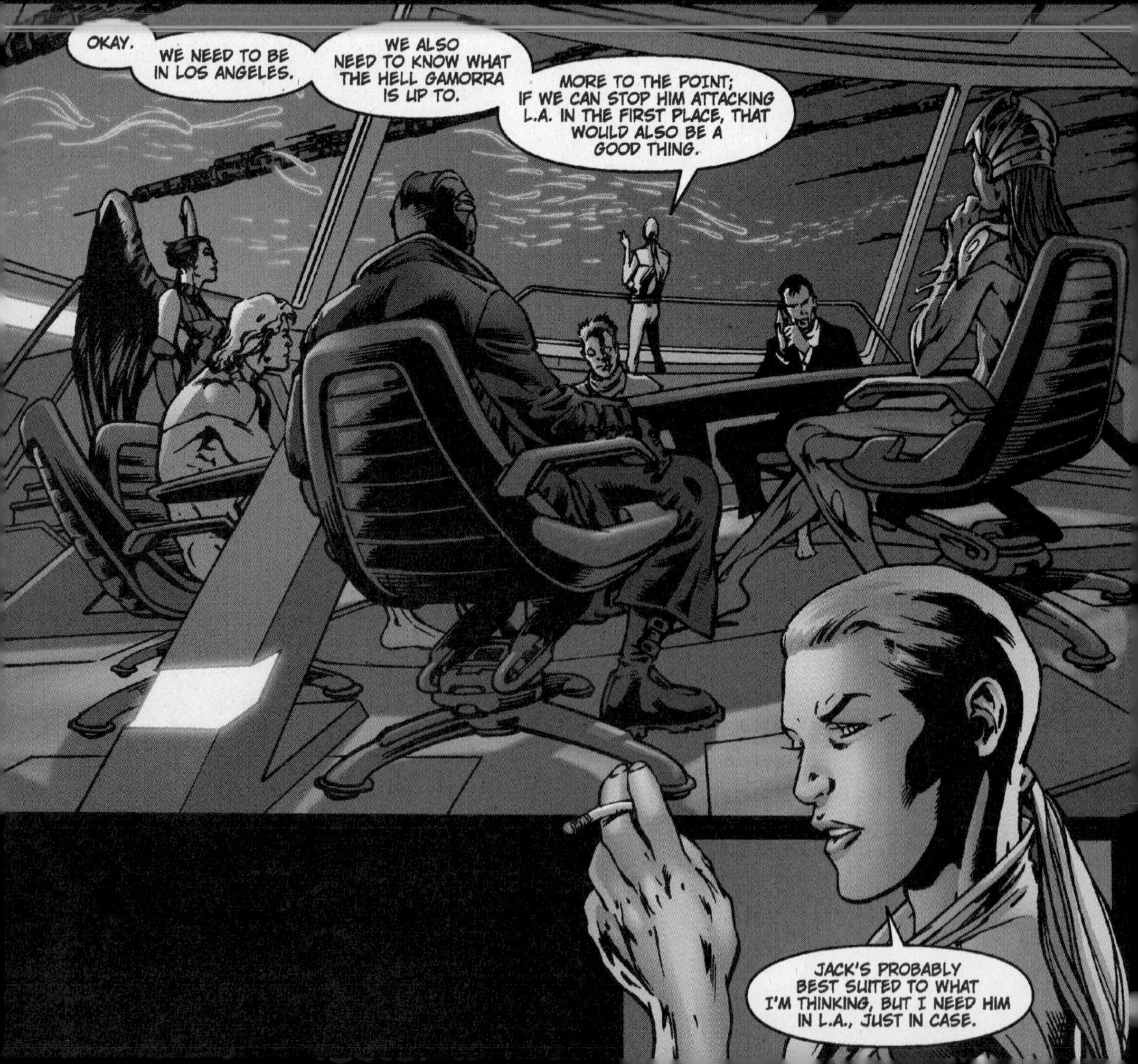
OKAY.
WE NEED TO BE IN LOS ANGELES.
WE ALSO NEED TO KNOW WHAT THE HELL GAMORRA IS UP TO.
MORE TO THE POINT; IF WE CAN STOP HIM ATTACKING L.A. IN THE FIRST PLACE, THAT WOULD ALSO BE A GOOD THING.
JACK'S PROBABLY BEST SUITED TO WHAT I'M THINKING, BUT I NEED HIM IN L.A., JUST IN CASE.

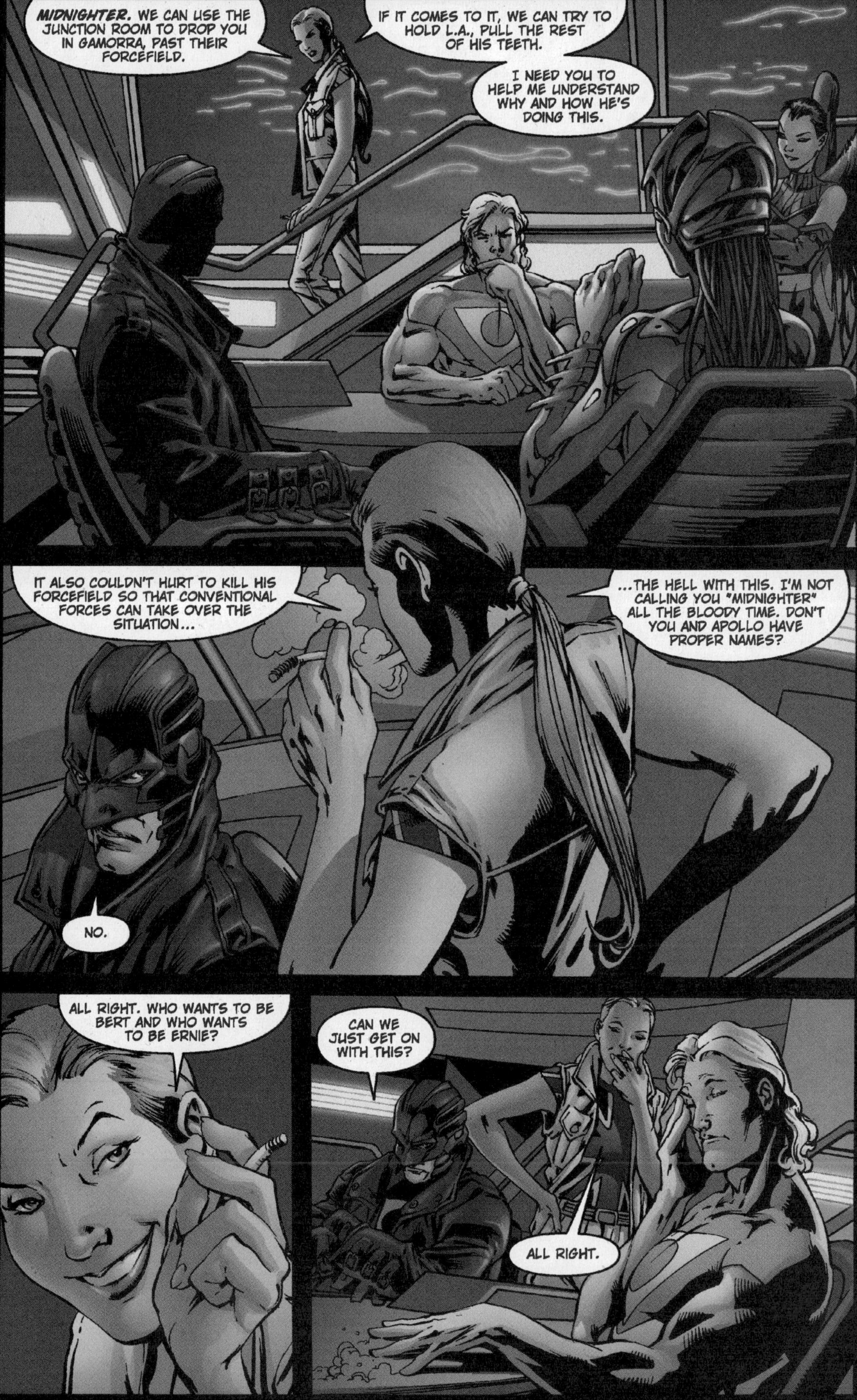

MIDNIGHTER. WE CAN USE THE JUNCTION ROOM TO DROP YOU IN GAMORRA, PAST THEIR FORCEFIELD.
IF IT COMES TO IT, WE CAN TRY TO HOLD L.A., PULL THE REST OF HIS TEETH.
I NEED YOU TO HELP ME UNDERSTAND WHY AND HOW HE'S DOING THIS.
IT ALSO COULDN'T HURT TO KILL HIS FORCEFIELD SO THAT CONVENTIONAL FORCES CAN TAKE OVER THE SITUATION...
...THE HELL WITH THIS. I'M NOT CALLING YOU "MIDNIGHTER" ALL THE BLOODY TIME. DON'T YOU AND APOLLO HAVE PROPER NAMES?
NO.
ALL RIGHT. WHO WANTS TO BE BERT AND WHO WANTS TO BE ERNIE?
CAN WE JUST GET ON WITH THIS?
ALL RIGHT.

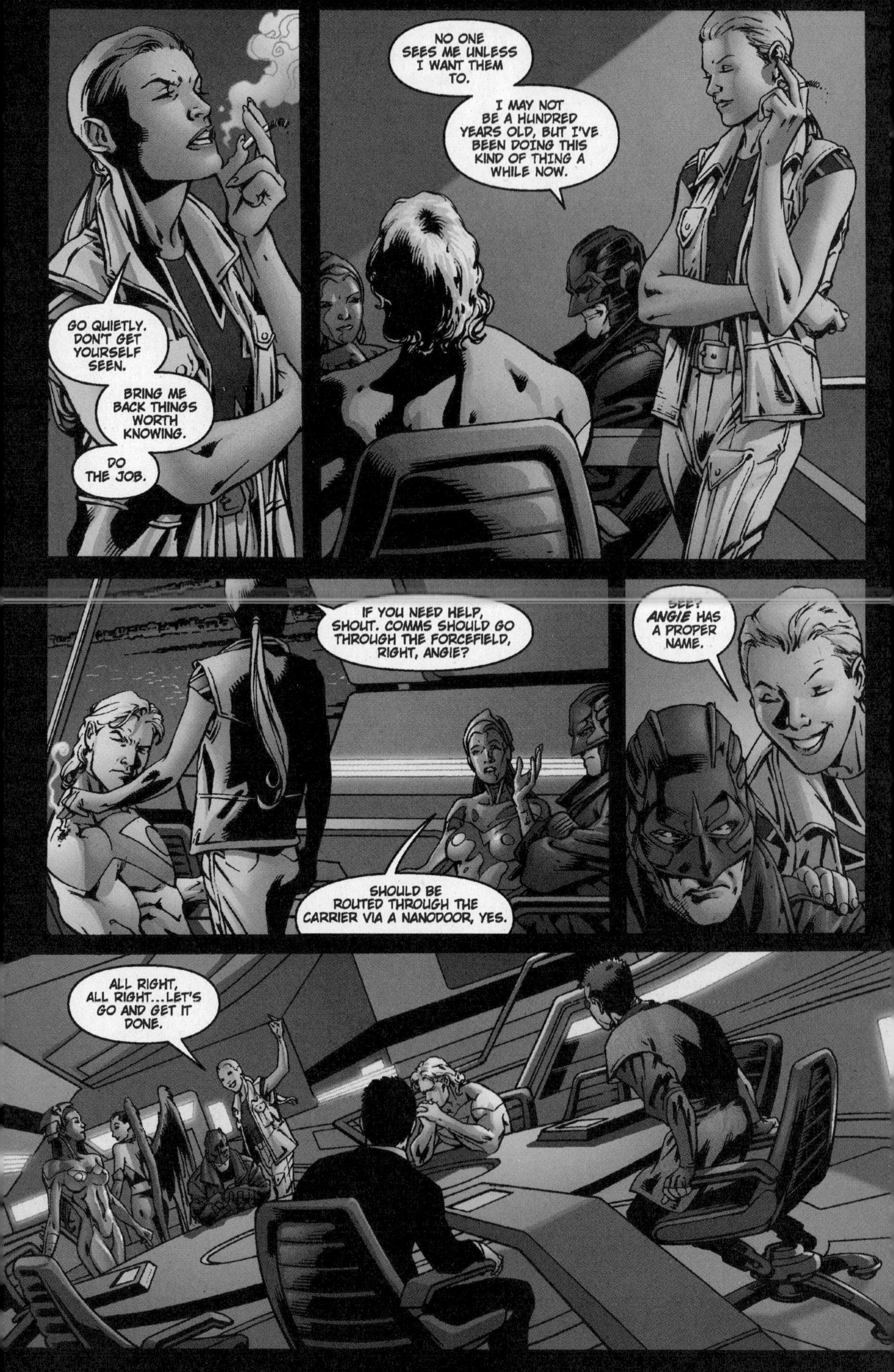
GO QUIETLY. DON'T GET YOURSELF SEEN.
BRING ME BACK THINGS WORTH KNOWING.
DO THE JOB.
NO ONE SEES ME UNLESS I WANT THEM TO.
I MAY NOT BE A HUNDRED YEARS OLD, BUT I'VE BEEN DOING THIS KIND OF THING A WHILE NOW.
IF YOU NEED HELP, SHOUT. COMMS SHOULD GO THROUGH THE FORCEFIELD, RIGHT, ANGIE?
SHOULD BE ROUTED THROUGH THE CARRIER VIA A NANODOOR, YES.
SEE? *ANGIE* HAS A PROPER NAME.
ALL RIGHT, ALL RIGHT...LET'S GO AND GET IT DONE.

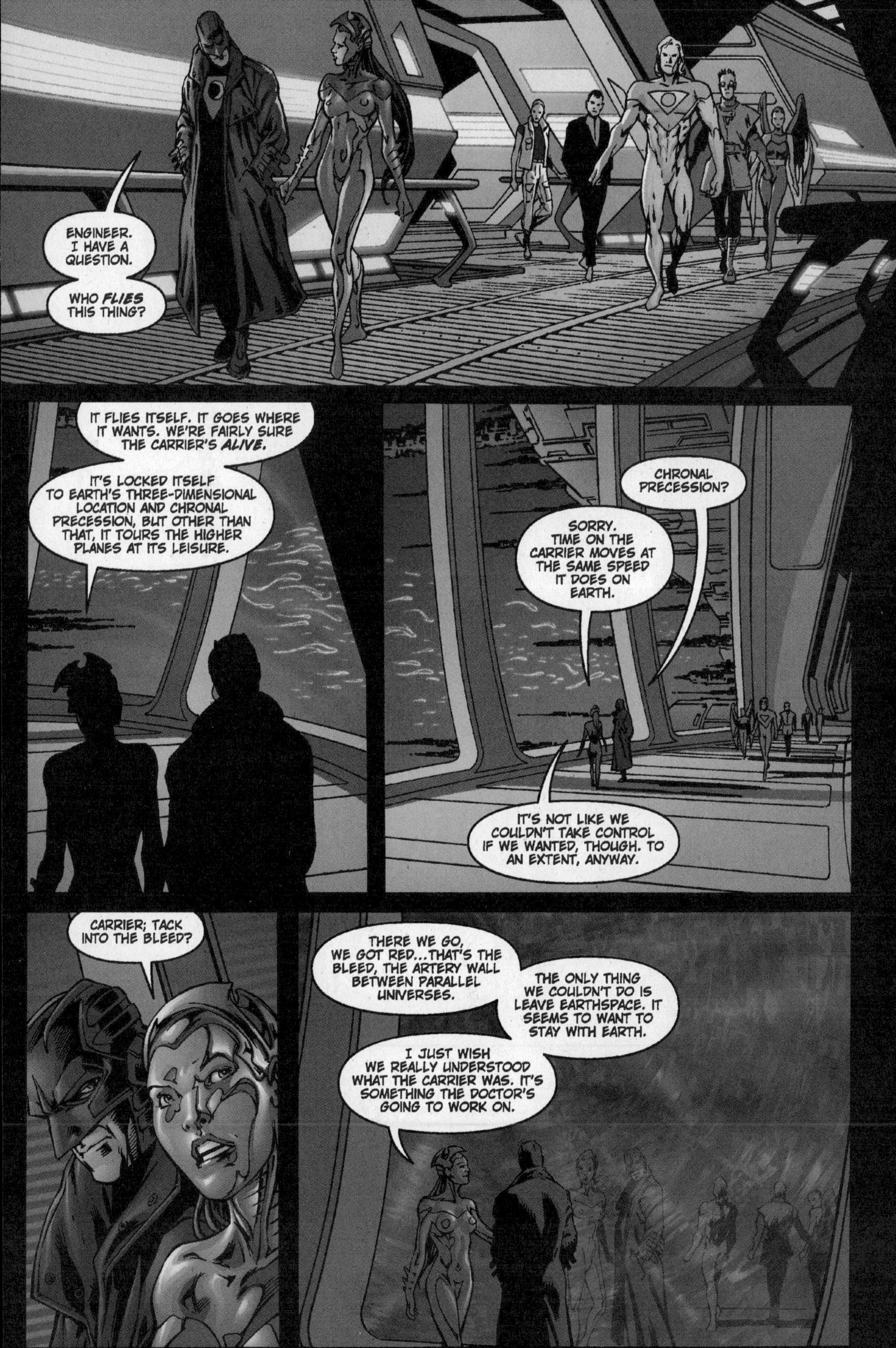
ENGINEER. I HAVE A QUESTION.
WHO *FLIES* THIS THING?
IT FLIES ITSELF. IT GOES WHERE IT WANTS. WE'RE FAIRLY SURE THE CARRIER'S *ALIVE.*
IT'S LOCKED ITSELF TO EARTH'S THREE-DIMENSIONAL LOCATION AND CHRONAL PRECESSION, BUT OTHER THAN THAT, IT TOURS THE HIGHER PLANES AT ITS LEISURE.
CHRONAL PRECESSION?
SORRY. TIME ON THE CARRIER MOVES AT THE SAME SPEED IT DOES ON EARTH.
IT'S NOT LIKE WE COULDN'T TAKE CONTROL IF WE WANTED, THOUGH. TO AN EXTENT, ANYWAY.
CARRIER; TACK INTO THE BLEED?
THERE WE GO, WE GOT RED...THAT'S THE BLEED, THE ARTERY WALL BETWEEN PARALLEL UNIVERSES.
THE ONLY THING WE COULDN'T DO IS LEAVE EARTHSPACE. IT SEEMS TO WANT TO STAY WITH EARTH.
I JUST WISH WE REALLY UNDERSTOOD WHAT THE CARRIER WAS. IT'S SOMETHING THE DOCTOR'S GOING TO WORK ON.

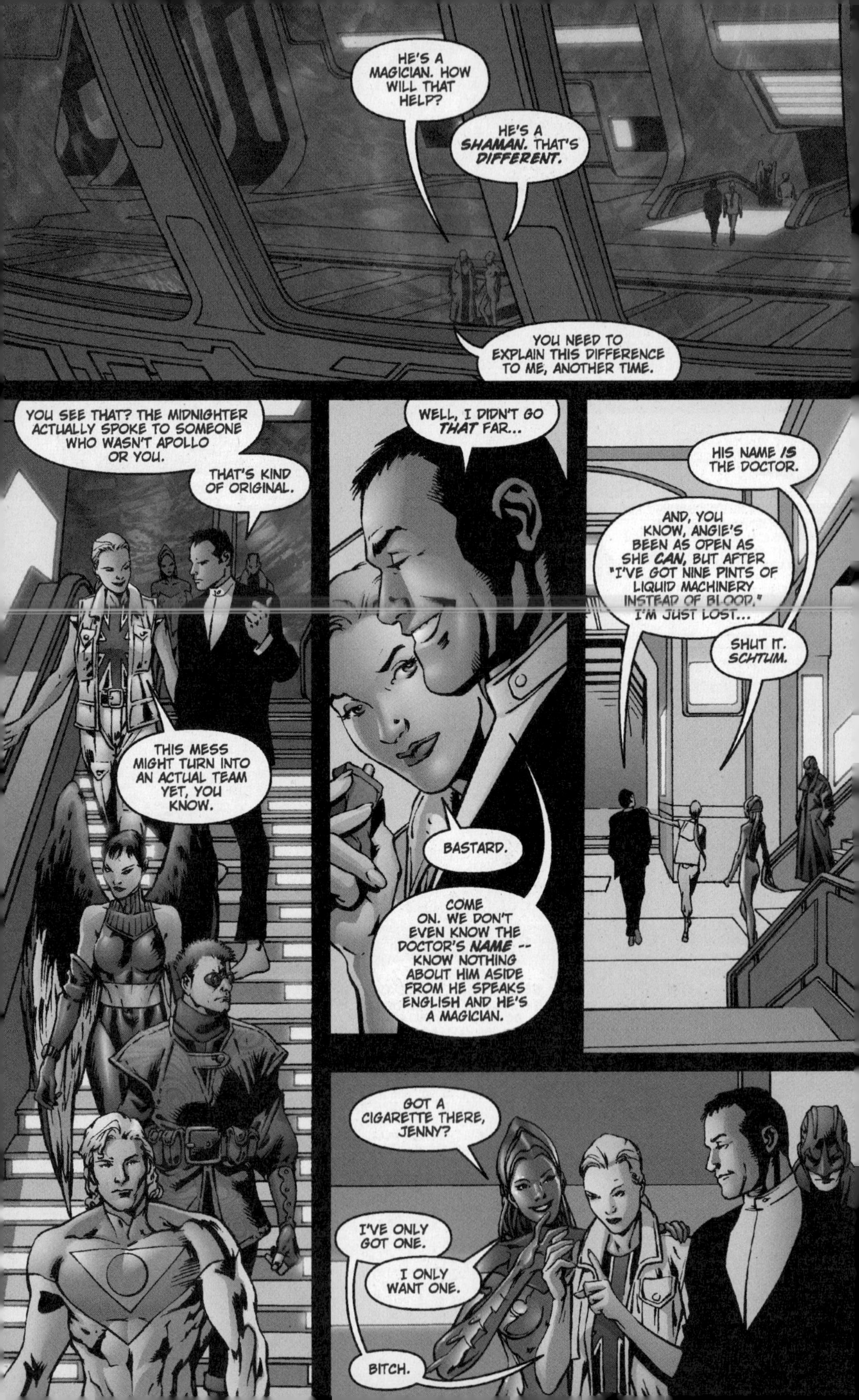
HE'S A MAGICIAN. HOW WILL THAT HELP?
HE'S A *SHAMAN.* THAT'S *DIFFERENT.*
YOU NEED TO EXPLAIN THIS DIFFERENCE TO ME, ANOTHER TIME.
YOU SEE THAT? THE MIDNIGHTER ACTUALLY SPOKE TO SOMEONE WHO WASN'T APOLLO OR YOU.
THAT'S KIND OF ORIGINAL.
THIS MESS MIGHT TURN INTO AN ACTUAL TEAM YET, YOU KNOW.
WELL, I DIDN'T GO *THAT* FAR...
BASTARD.
COME ON. WE DON'T EVEN KNOW THE DOCTOR'S *NAME* -- KNOW NOTHING ABOUT HIM ASIDE FROM HE SPEAKS ENGLISH AND HE'S A MAGICIAN.
HIS NAME *IS* THE DOCTOR.
AND, YOU KNOW, ANGIE'S BEEN AS OPEN AS SHE *CAN,* BUT AFTER "I'VE GOT NINE PINTS OF LIQUID MACHINERY INSTEAD OF BLOOD," I'M JUST LOST...
SHUT IT. *SCHTUM.*
GOT A CIGARETTE THERE, JENNY?
I'VE ONLY GOT ONE.
I ONLY WANT ONE.
BITCH.

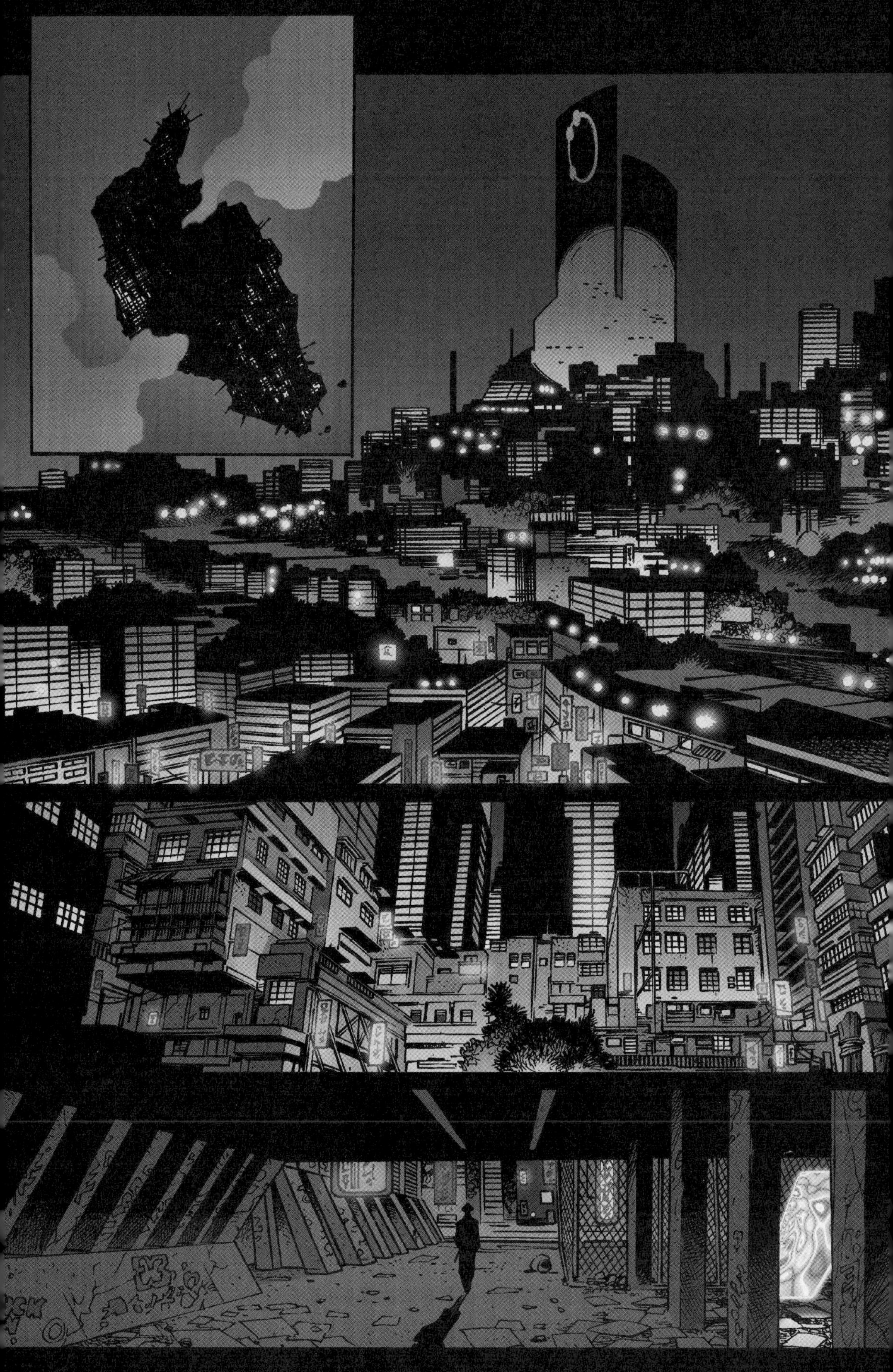

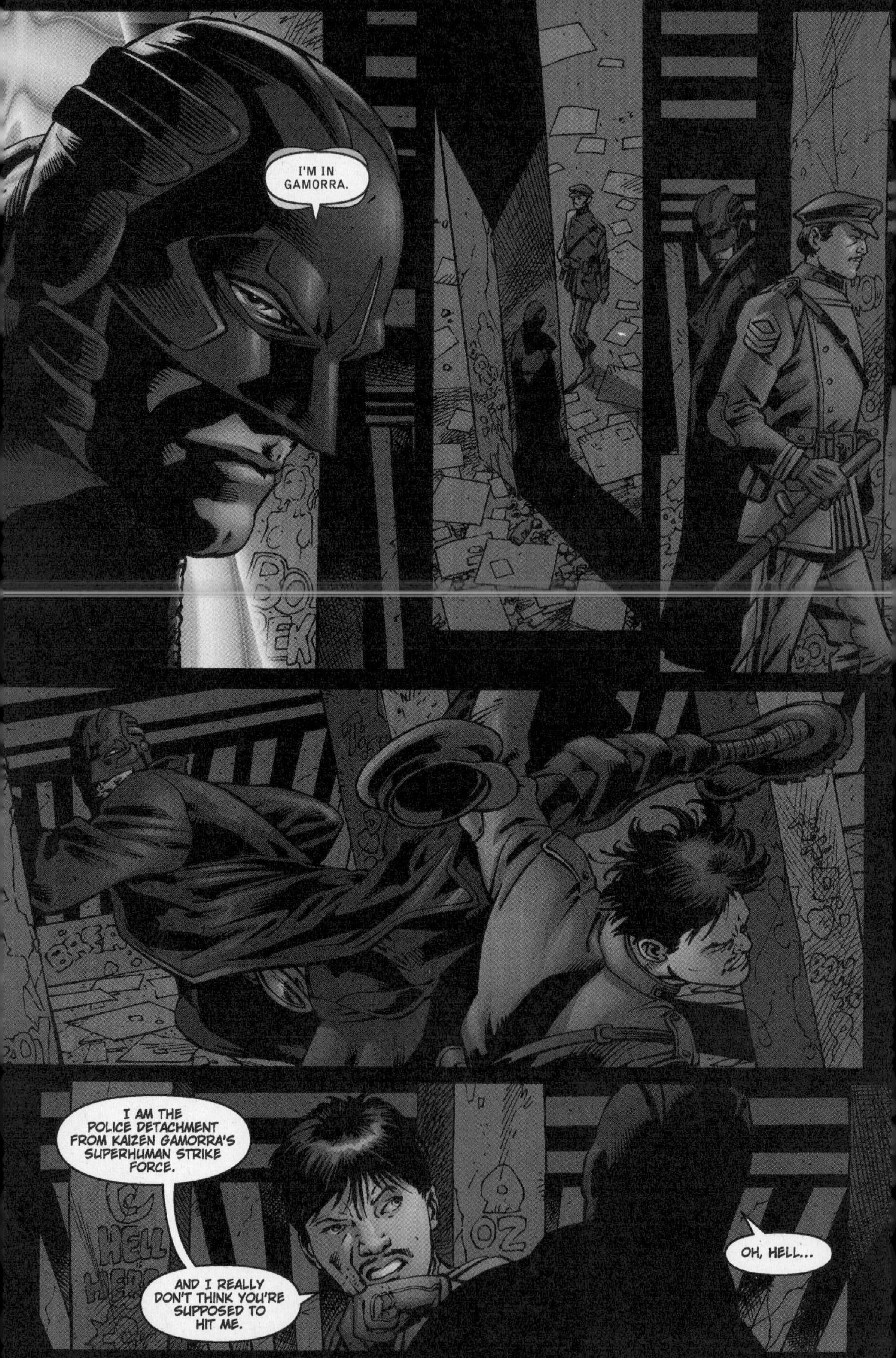
I'M IN GAMORRA.
I AM THE POLICE DETACHMENT FROM KAIZEN GAMORRA'S SUPERHUMAN STRIKE FORCE.
AND I REALLY DON'T THINK YOU'RE SUPPOSED TO HIT ME.
OH, HELL...

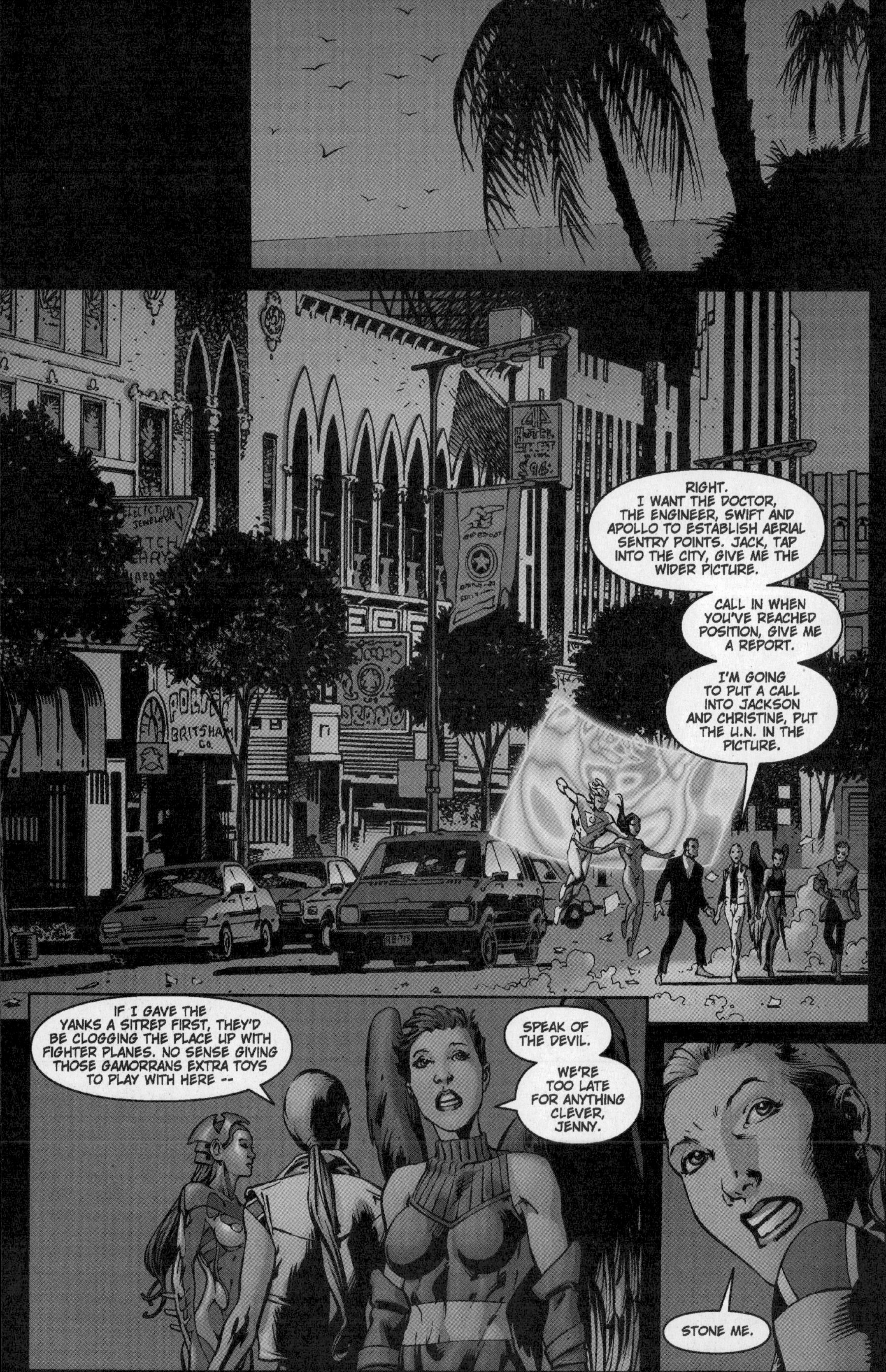
RIGHT. I WANT THE DOCTOR, THE ENGINEER, SWIFT AND APOLLO TO ESTABLISH AERIAL SENTRY POINTS. JACK, TAP INTO THE CITY, GIVE ME THE WIDER PICTURE.
CALL IN WHEN YOU'VE REACHED POSITION, GIVE ME A REPORT.
I'M GOING TO PUT A CALL INTO JACKSON AND CHRISTINE, PUT THE U.N. IN THE PICTURE.
IF I GAVE THE YANKS A SITREP FIRST, THEY'D BE CLOGGING THE PLACE UP WITH FIGHTER PLANES. NO SENSE GIVING THOSE GAMORRANS EXTRA TOYS TO PLAY WITH HERE --
SPEAK OF THE DEVIL.
WE'RE TOO LATE FOR ANYTHING CLEVER, JENNY.
STONE ME.

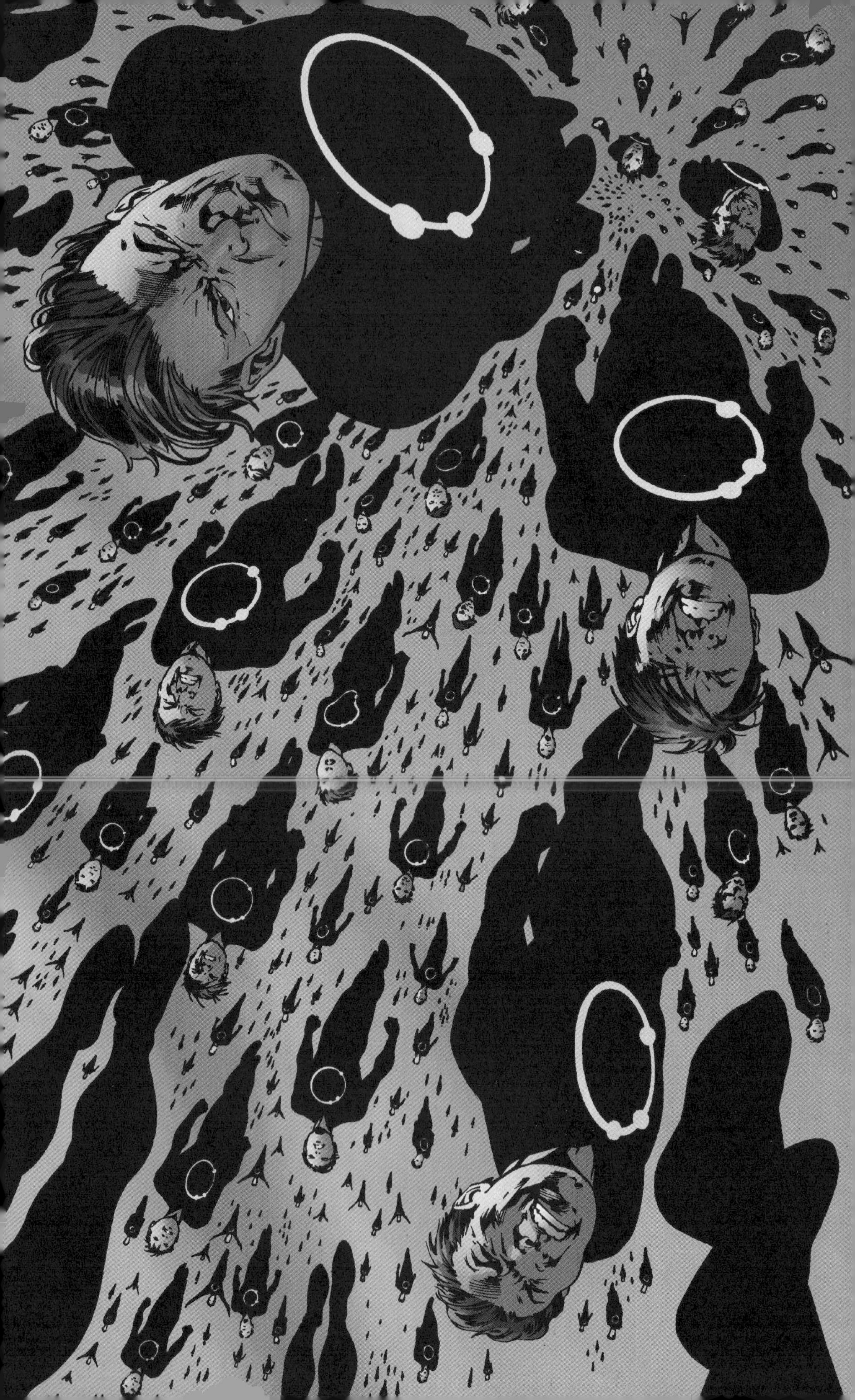

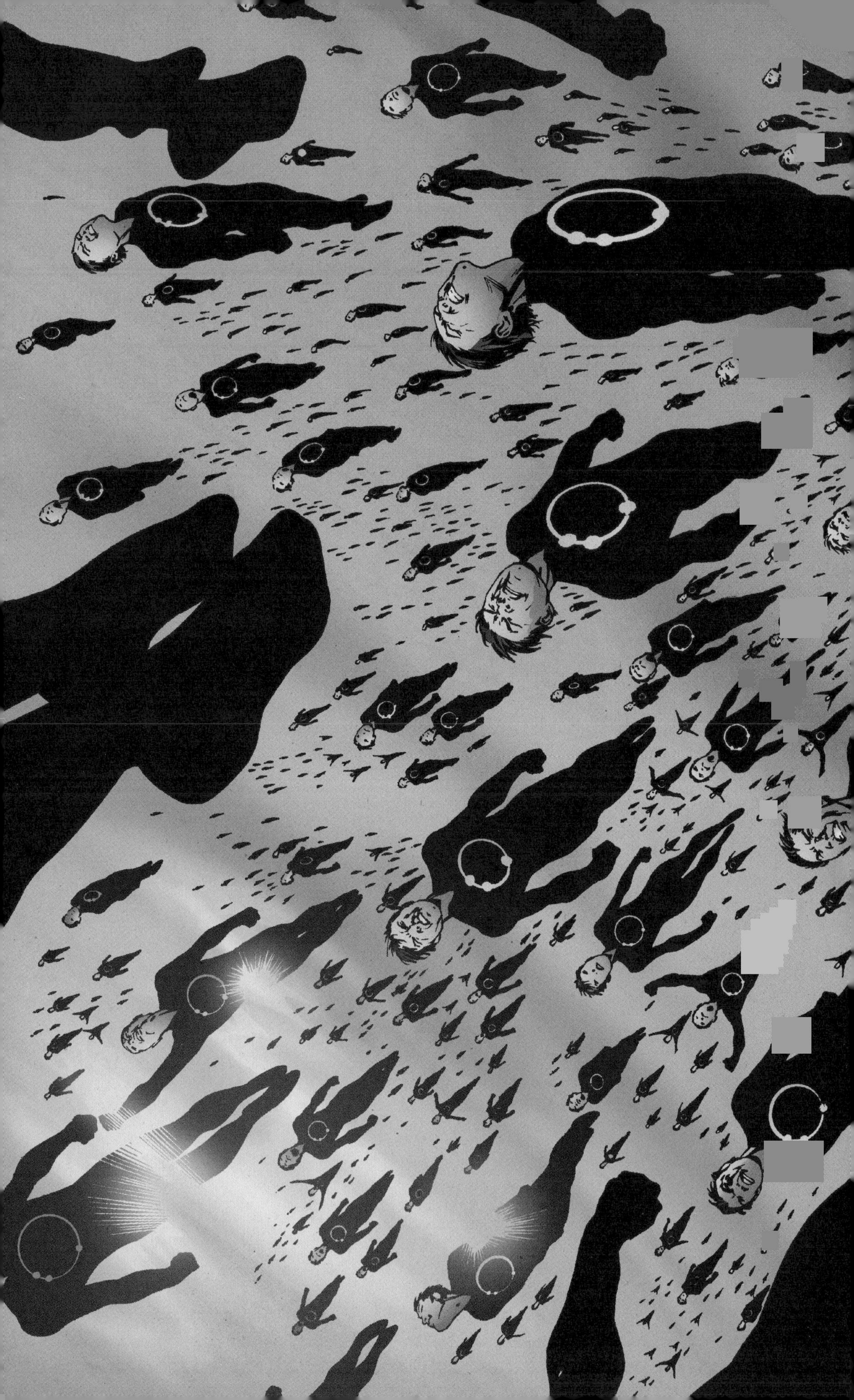

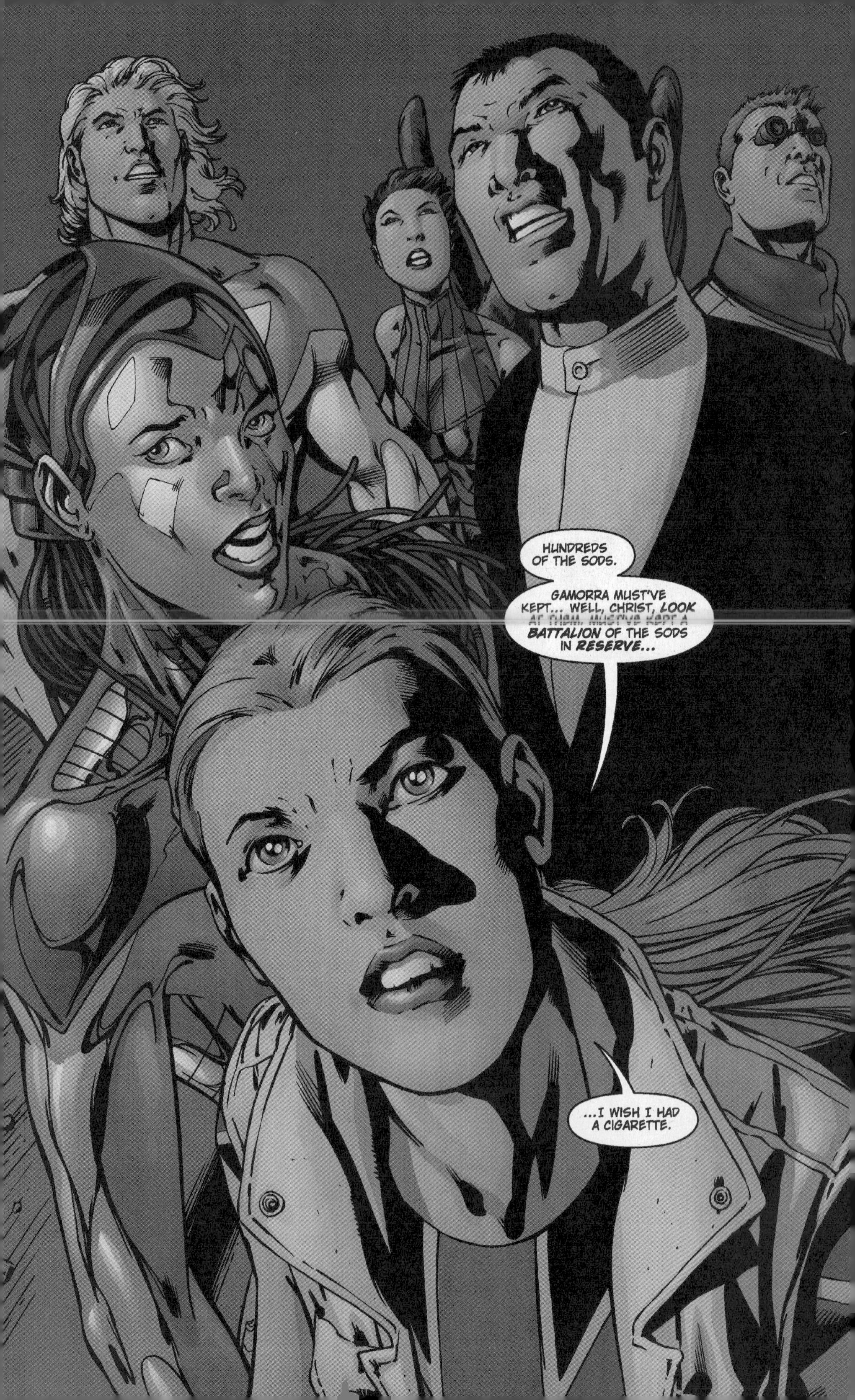
HUNDREDS OF THE SODS.
GAMORRA MUST'VE KEPT... WELL, CHRIST, LOOK AT THEM. MUST'VE KEPT A BATTALION OF THE SODS IN RESERVE...
...I WISH I HAD A CIGARETTE.

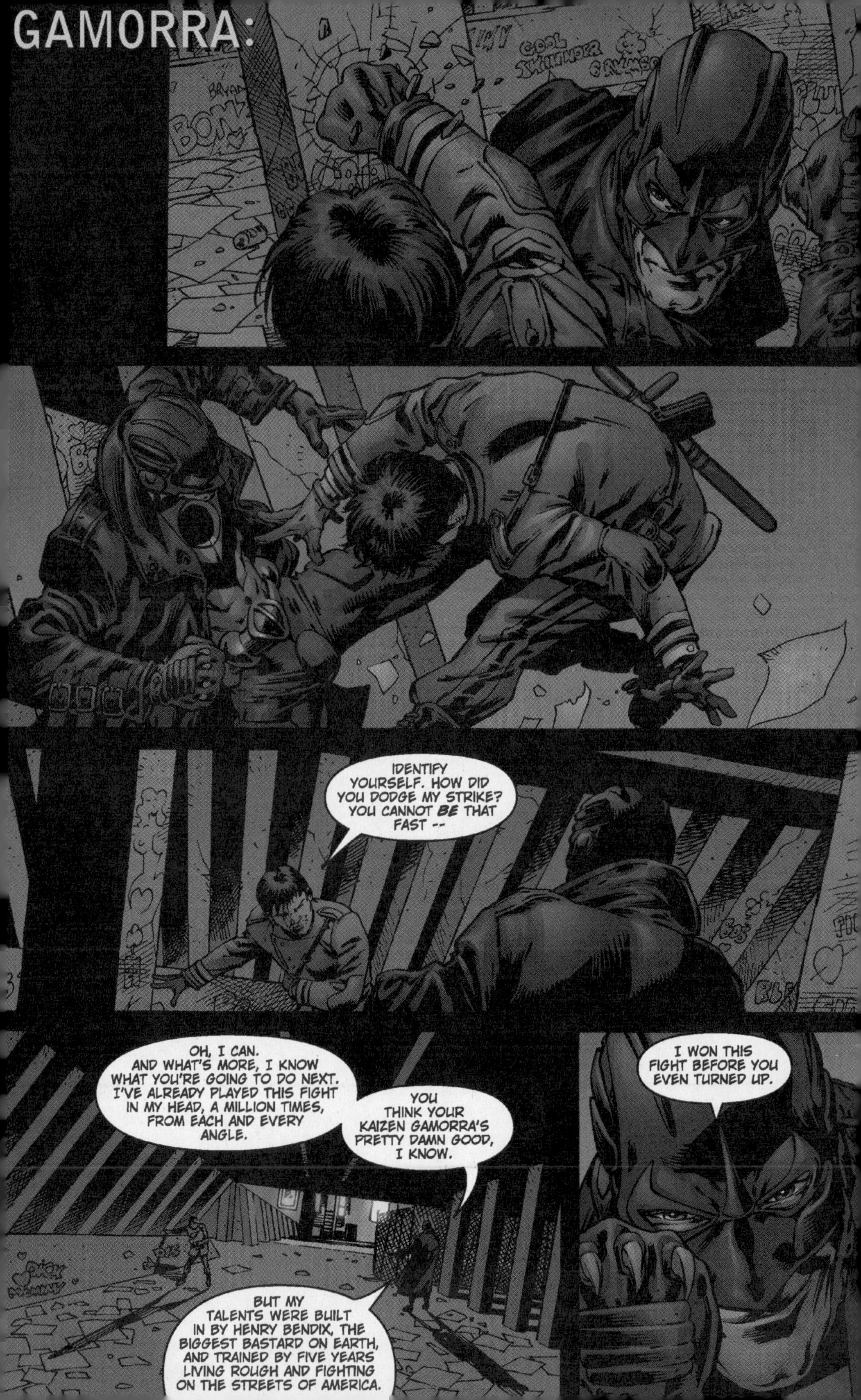
GAMORRA:
IDENTIFY YOURSELF. HOW DID YOU DODGE MY STRIKE? YOU CANNOT *BE* THAT FAST --
OH, I CAN. AND WHAT'S MORE, I KNOW WHAT YOU'RE GOING TO DO NEXT. I'VE ALREADY PLAYED THIS FIGHT IN MY HEAD, A MILLION TIMES, FROM EACH AND EVERY ANGLE.
YOU THINK YOUR KAIZEN GAMORRA'S PRETTY DAMN GOOD, I KNOW.
BUT MY TALENTS WERE BUILT IN BY HENRY BENDIX, THE BIGGEST BASTARD ON EARTH, AND TRAINED BY FIVE YEARS LIVING ROUGH AND FIGHTING ON THE STREETS OF AMERICA.
I WON THIS FIGHT BEFORE YOU EVEN TURNED UP.

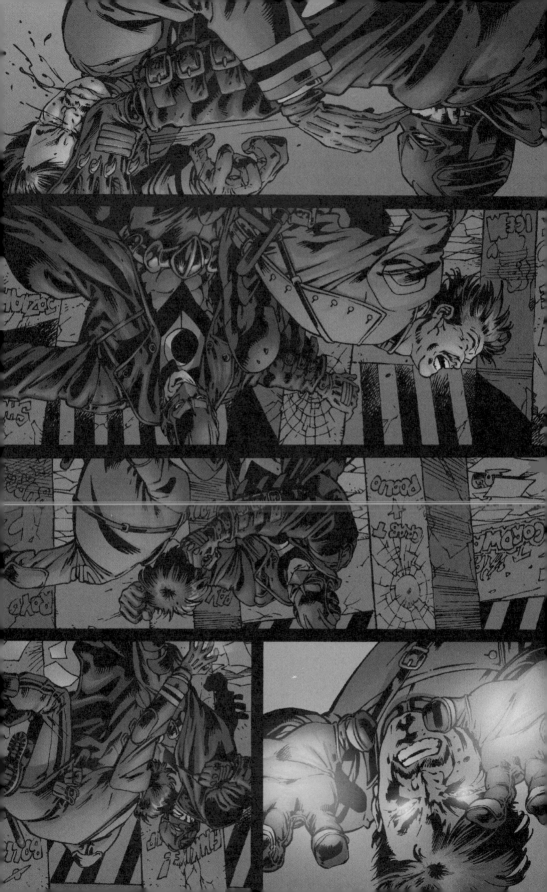

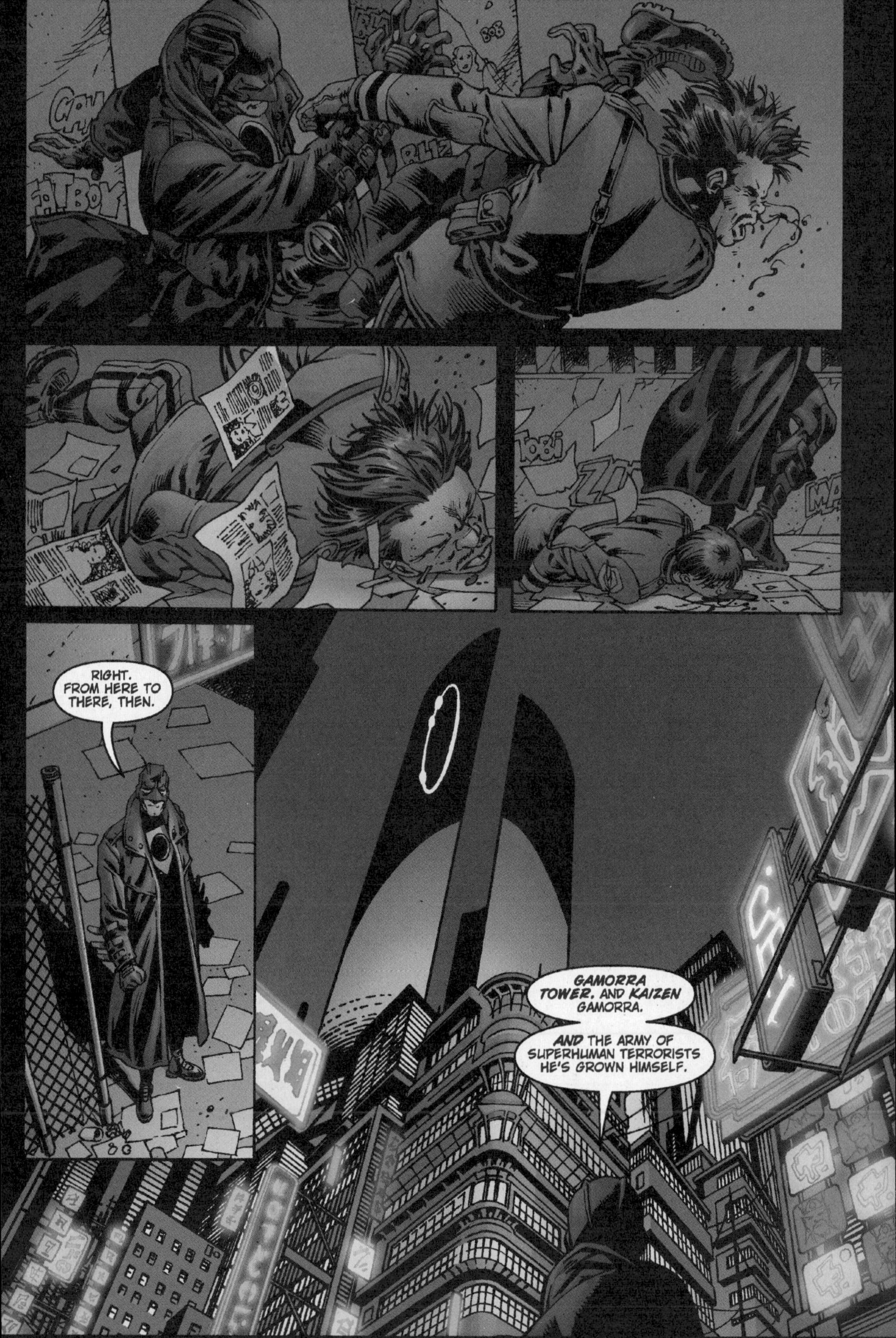
FATBOY
RIGHT. FROM HERE TO THERE, THEN.
GAMORRA TOWER. AND ***KAIZEN*** GAMORRA.
AND THE ARMY OF SUPERHUMAN TERRORISTS HE'S GROWN HIMSELF.

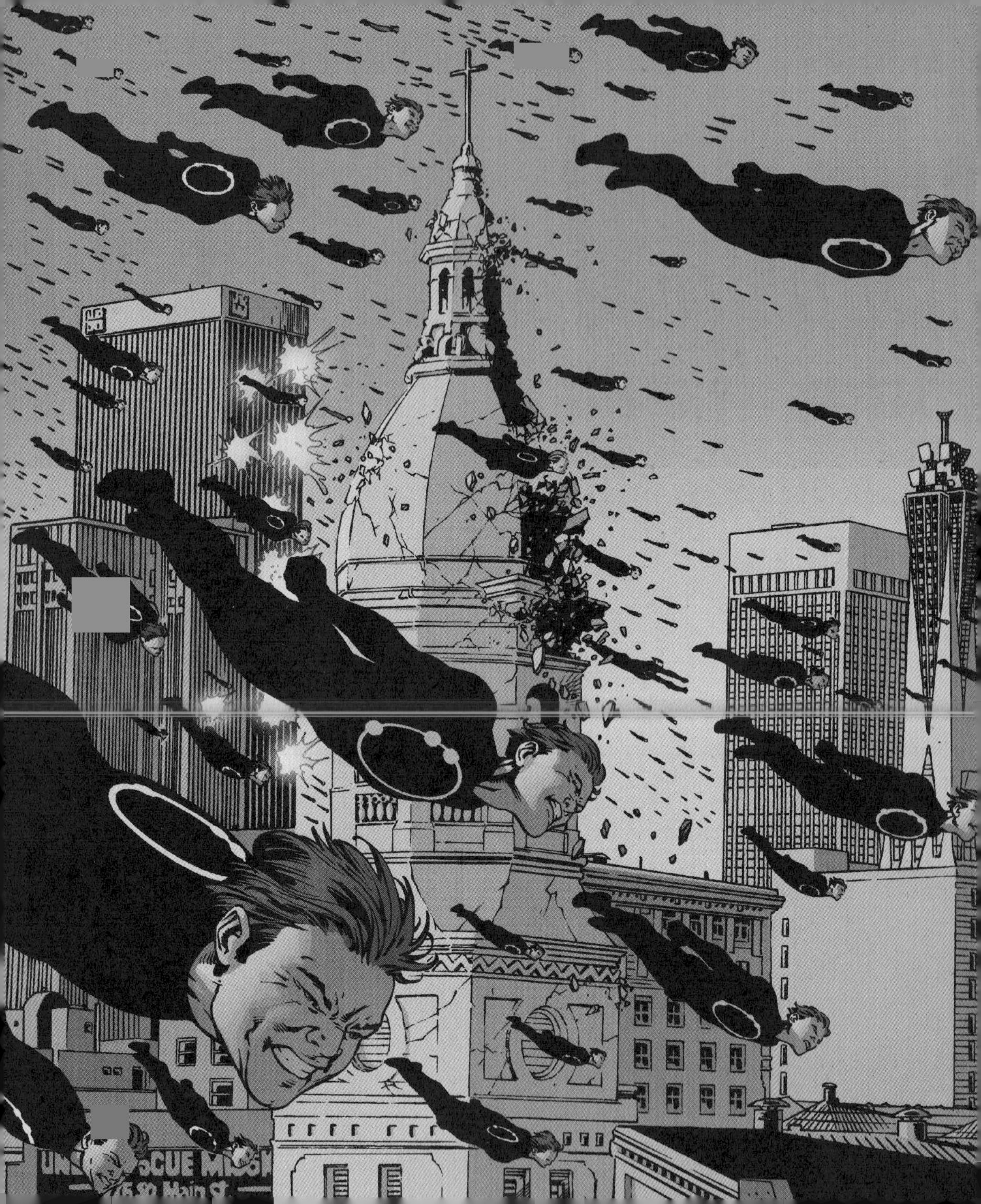

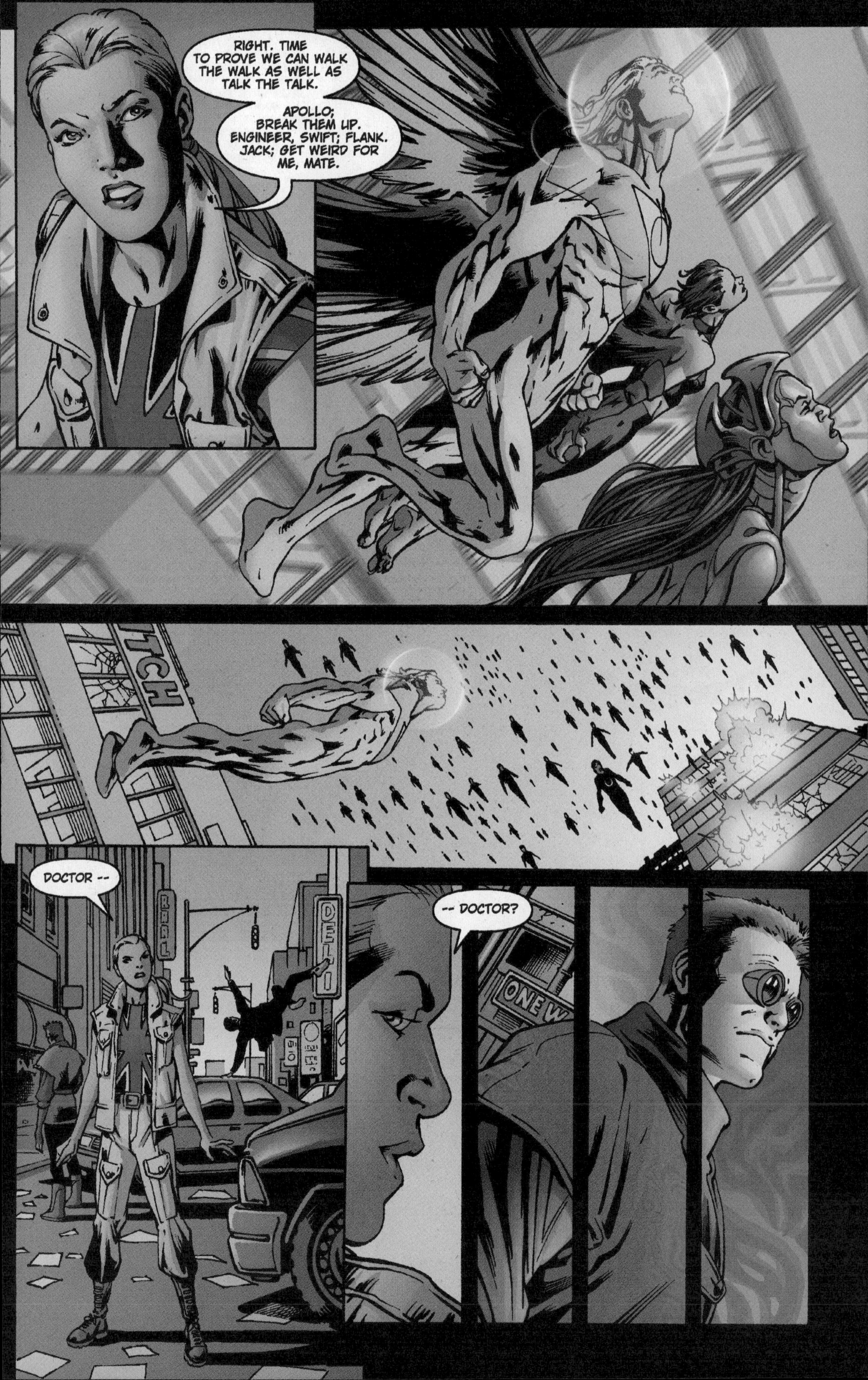
RIGHT. TIME TO PROVE WE CAN WALK THE WALK AS WELL AS TALK THE TALK.
APOLLO; BREAK THEM UP. ENGINEER, SWIFT; FLANK. JACK; GET WEIRD FOR ME, MATE.
DOCTOR --
-- DOCTOR?

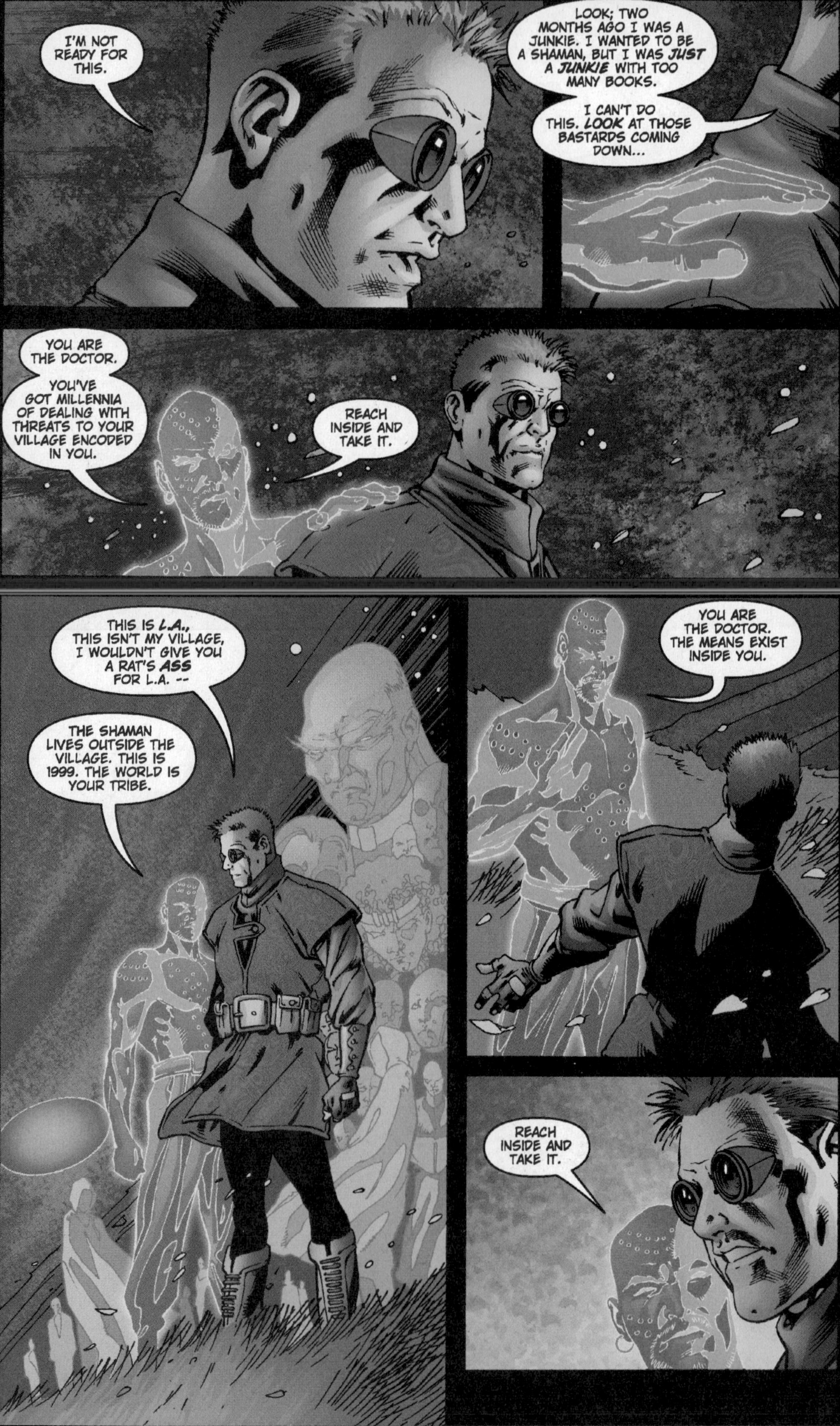
I'M NOT READY FOR THIS.
LOOK; TWO MONTHS AGO I WAS A JUNKIE. I WANTED TO BE A SHAMAN, BUT I WAS **JUST** A **JUNKIE** WITH TOO MANY BOOKS.
I CAN'T DO THIS. **LOOK** AT THOSE BASTARDS COMING DOWN...
YOU ARE THE DOCTOR.
YOU'VE GOT MILLENNIA OF DEALING WITH THREATS TO YOUR VILLAGE ENCODED IN YOU.
REACH INSIDE AND TAKE IT.
THIS IS **L.A.**, THIS ISN'T MY VILLAGE, I WOULDN'T GIVE YOU A RAT'S **ASS** FOR L.A. --
THE SHAMAN LIVES OUTSIDE THE VILLAGE. THIS IS 1999. THE WORLD IS YOUR TRIBE.
YOU ARE THE DOCTOR. THE MEANS EXIST INSIDE YOU.
REACH INSIDE AND TAKE IT.

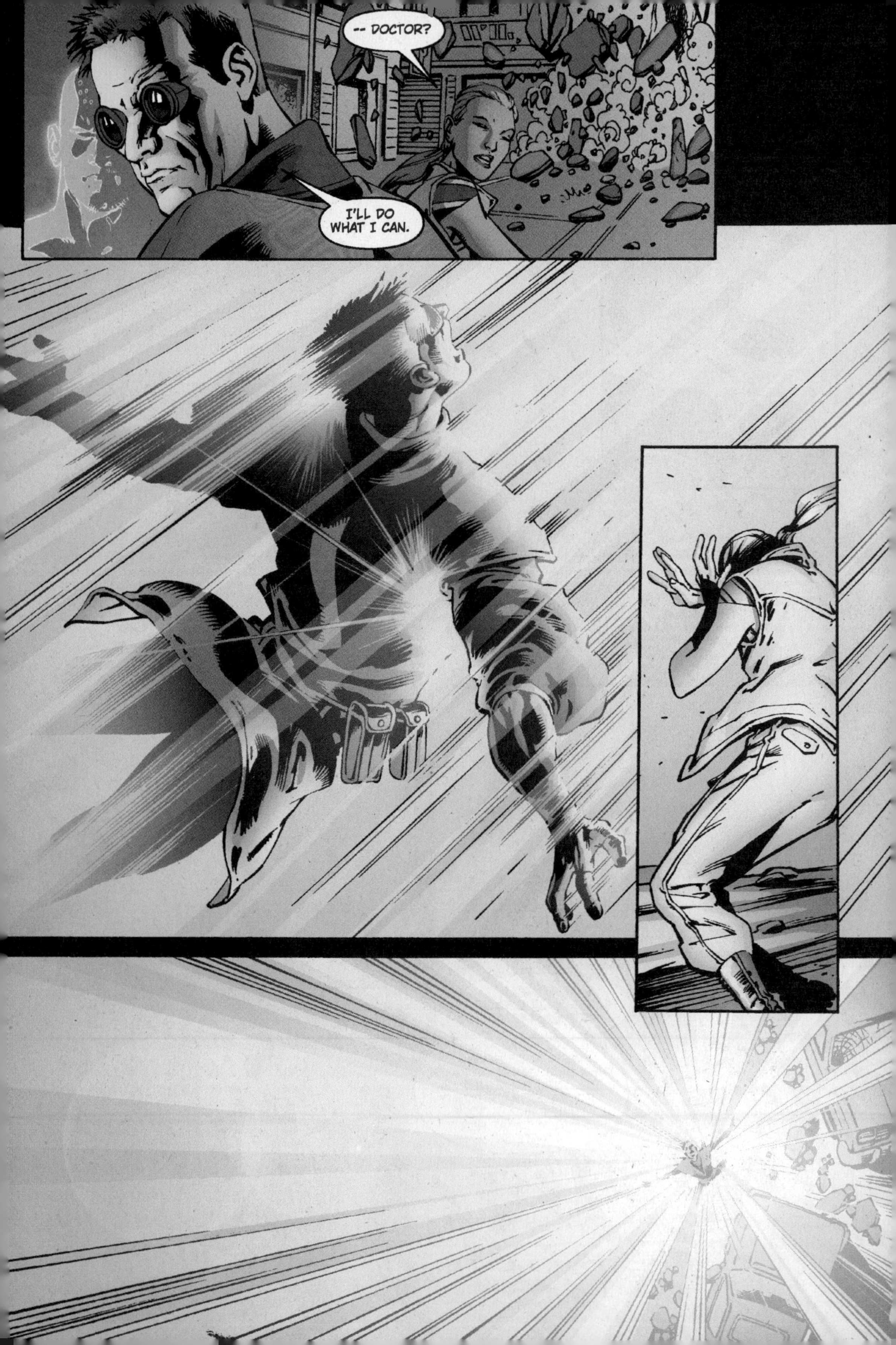
-- DOCTOR?
I'LL DO WHAT I CAN.

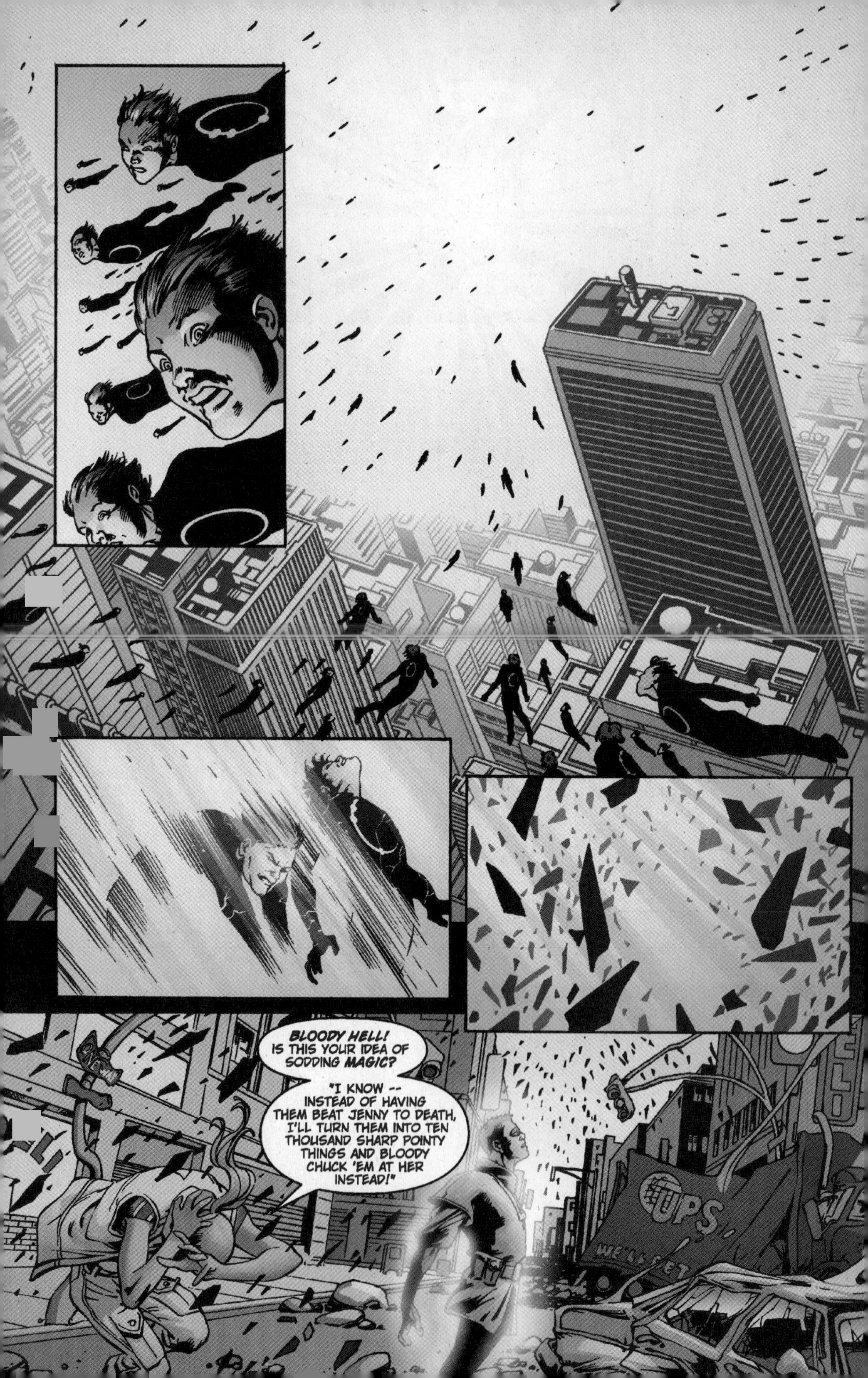
BLOODY HELL! IS THIS YOUR IDEA OF SODDING MAGIC?
"I KNOW -- INSTEAD OF HAVING THEM BEAT JENNY TO DEATH, I'LL TURN THEM INTO TEN THOUSAND SHARP POINTY THINGS AND BLOODY CHUCK 'EM AT HER INSTEAD!"
UPS
WE'LL GET

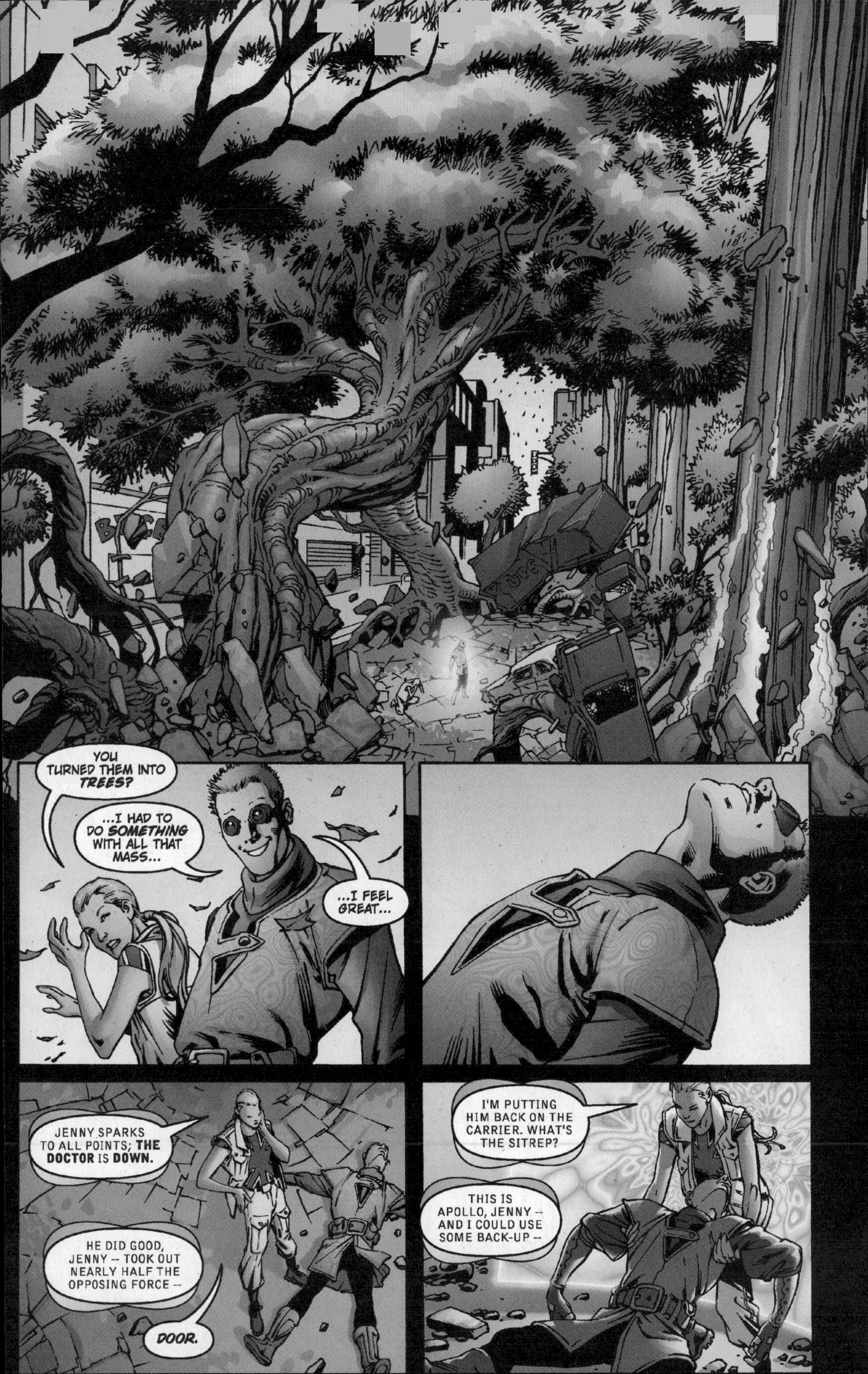
YOU TURNED THEM INTO *TREES?*
...I HAD TO DO ***SOMETHING*** WITH ALL THAT MASS...
...I FEEL GREAT...
JENNY SPARKS TO ALL POINTS; **THE DOCTOR** IS **DOWN.**
HE DID GOOD, JENNY -- TOOK OUT NEARLY HALF THE OPPOSING FORCE --
DOOR.
I'M PUTTING HIM BACK ON THE CARRIER. WHAT'S THE SITREP?
THIS IS APOLLO, JENNY -- AND I COULD USE SOME BACK-UP --

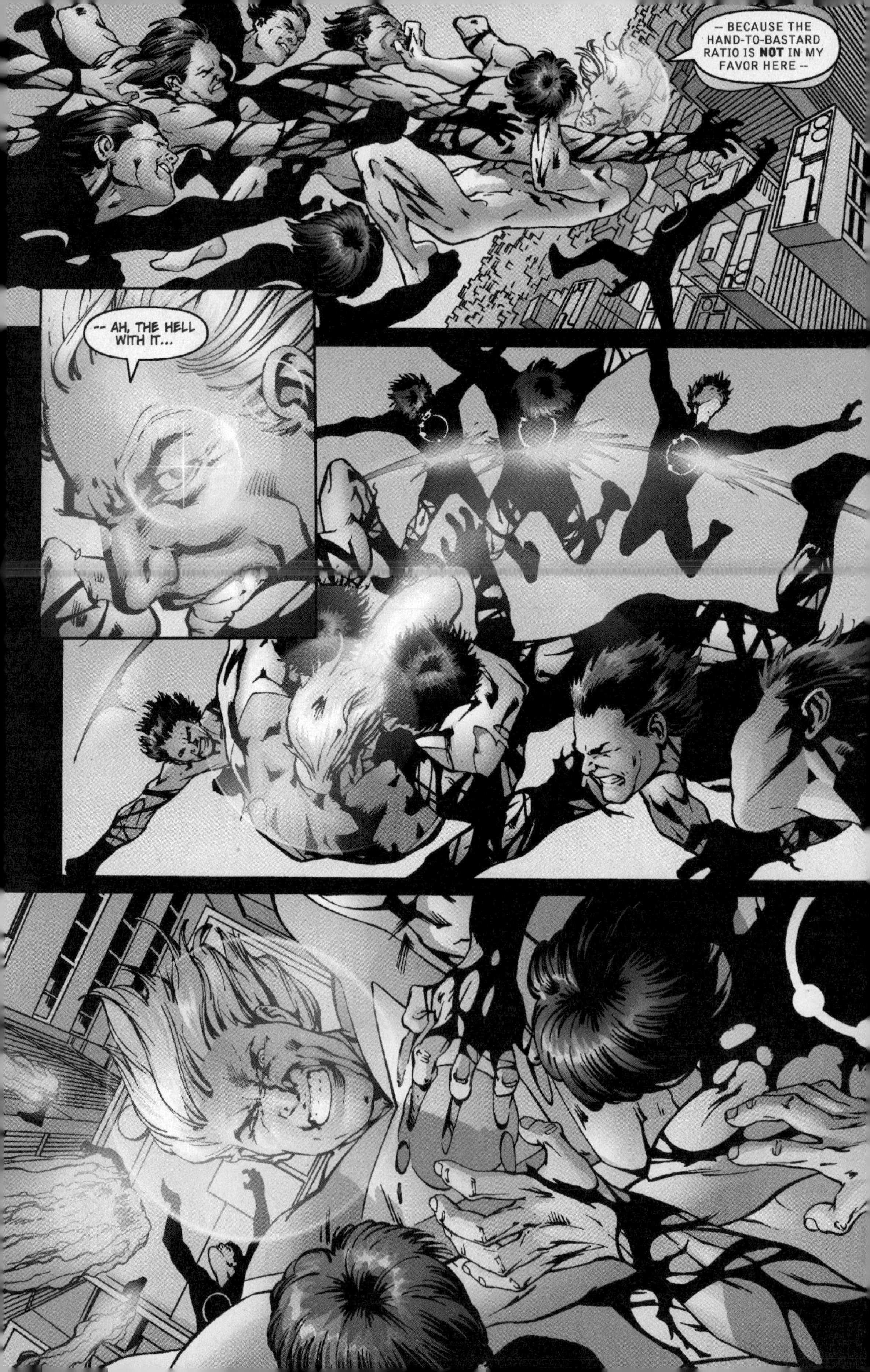
-- BECAUSE THE HAND-TO-BASTARD RATIO IS **NOT** IN MY FAVOR HERE --
-- AH, THE HELL WITH IT...

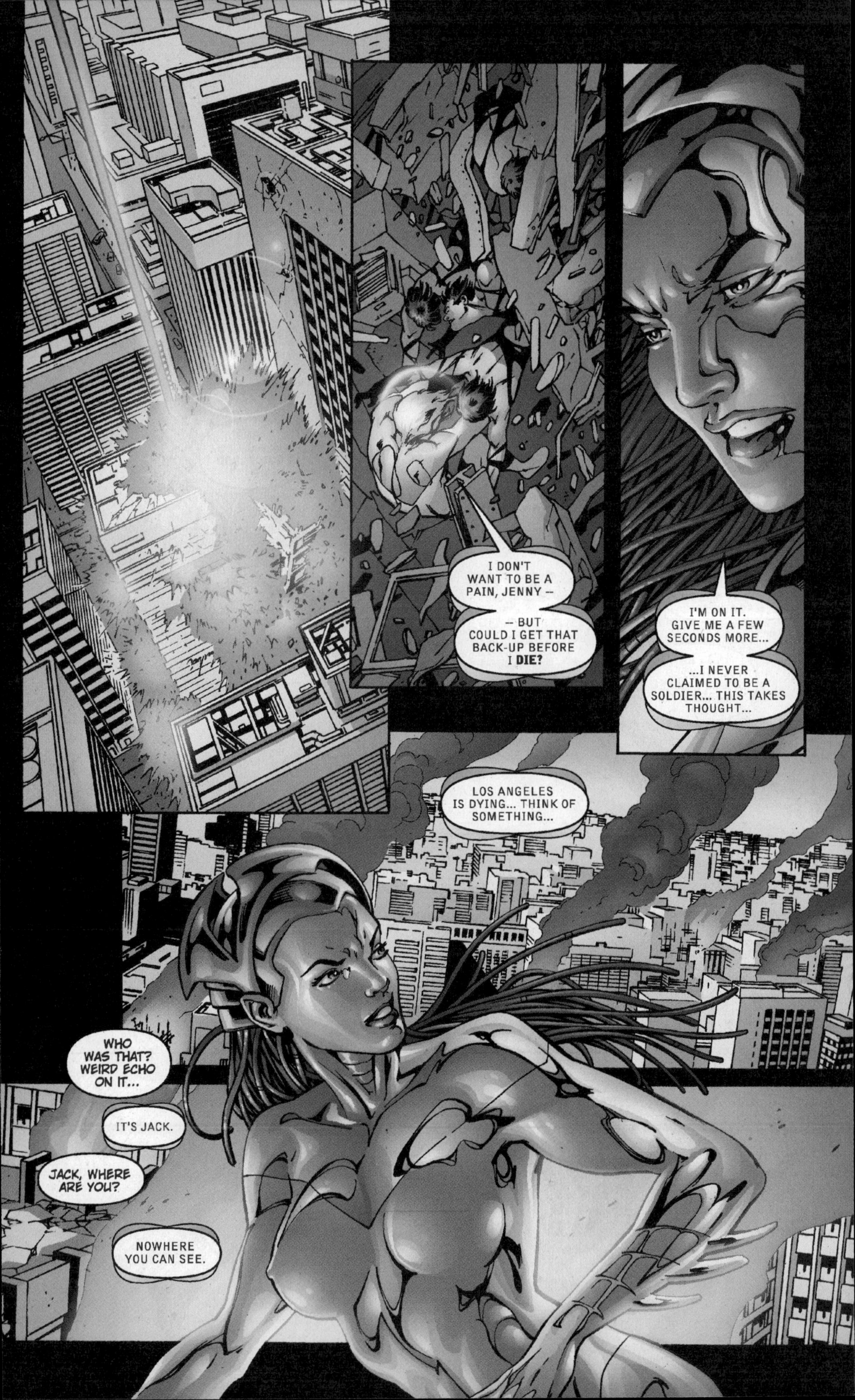
I DON'T WANT TO BE A PAIN, JENNY --
-- BUT COULD I GET THAT BACK-UP BEFORE I **DIE?**
I'M ON IT. GIVE ME A FEW SECONDS MORE...
...I NEVER CLAIMED TO BE A SOLDIER... THIS TAKES THOUGHT...
LOS ANGELES IS DYING... THINK OF SOMETHING...
WHO WAS THAT? WEIRD ECHO ON IT...
IT'S JACK.
JACK, WHERE ARE YOU?
NOWHERE YOU CAN SEE.

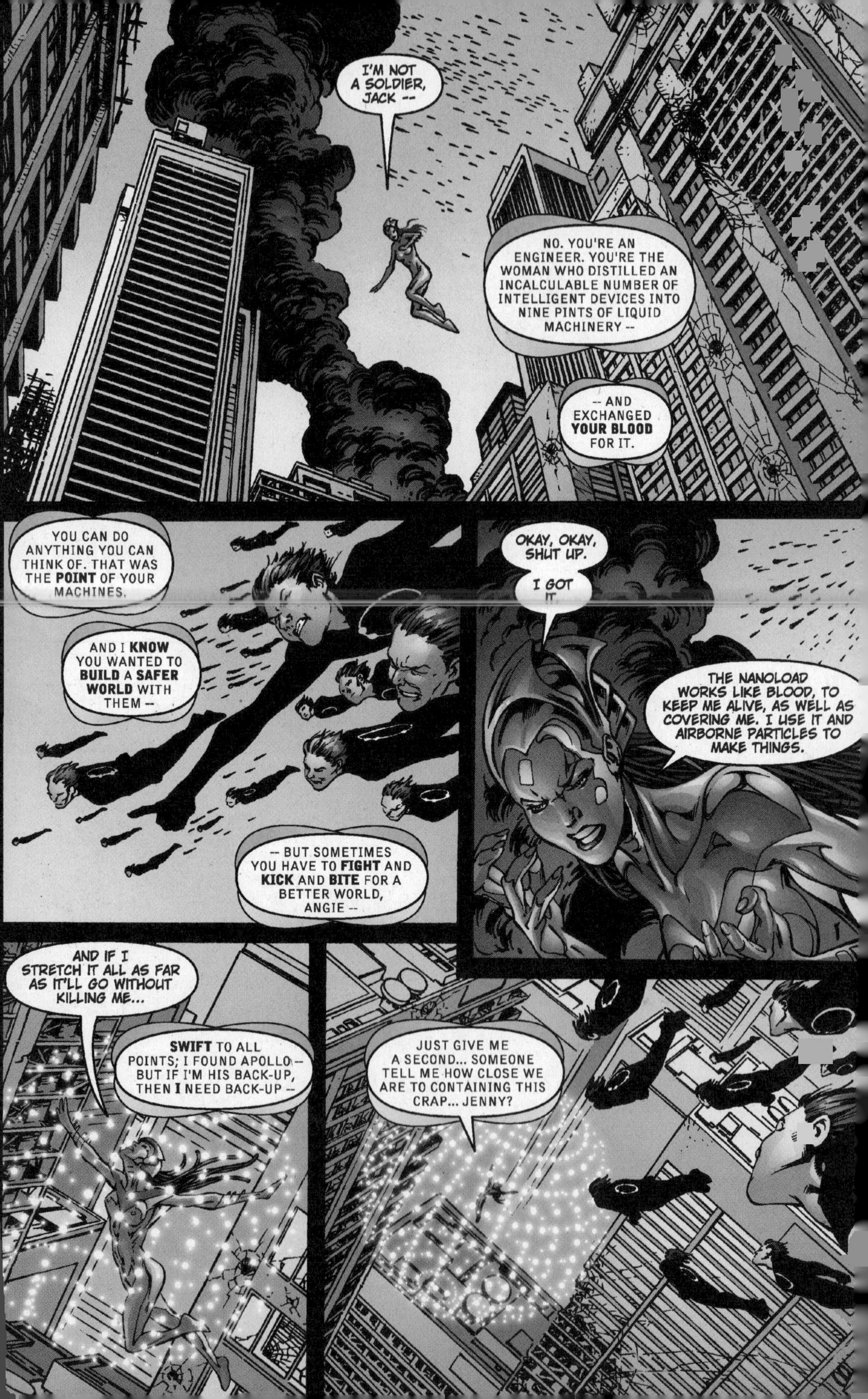
I'M NOT A SOLDIER, JACK --
NO. YOU'RE AN ENGINEER. YOU'RE THE WOMAN WHO DISTILLED AN INCALCULABLE NUMBER OF INTELLIGENT DEVICES INTO NINE PINTS OF LIQUID MACHINERY --
-- AND EXCHANGED **YOUR BLOOD** FOR IT.
YOU CAN DO ANYTHING YOU CAN THINK OF. THAT WAS THE **POINT** OF YOUR MACHINES.
AND I **KNOW** YOU WANTED TO **BUILD** A **SAFER WORLD** WITH THEM --
-- BUT SOMETIMES YOU HAVE TO **FIGHT** AND **KICK** AND **BITE** FOR A BETTER WORLD, ANGIE --
OKAY, OKAY, SHUT UP.
I GOT IT
THE NANOLOAD WORKS LIKE BLOOD, TO KEEP ME ALIVE, AS WELL AS COVERING ME. I USE IT AND AIRBORNE PARTICLES TO MAKE THINGS.
AND IF I STRETCH IT ALL AS FAR AS IT'LL GO WITHOUT KILLING ME...
SWIFT TO ALL POINTS; I FOUND APOLLO -- BUT IF I'M HIS BACK-UP, THEN **I** NEED BACK-UP --
JUST GIVE ME A SECOND... SOMEONE TELL ME HOW CLOSE WE ARE TO CONTAINING THIS CRAP... JENNY?

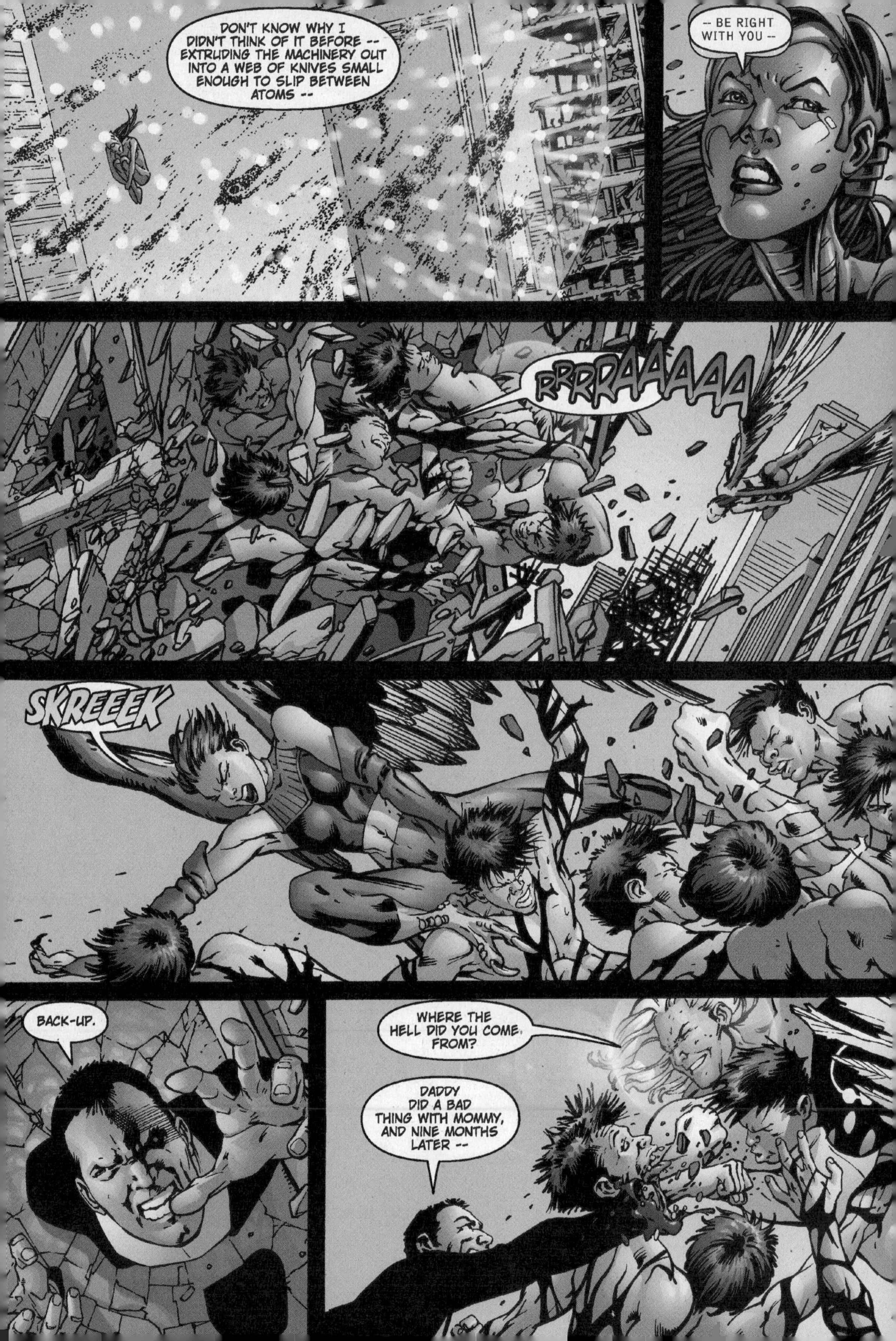

DON'T KNOW WHY I DIDN'T THINK OF IT BEFORE -- EXTRUDING THE MACHINERY OUT INTO A WEB OF KNIVES SMALL ENOUGH TO SLIP BETWEEN ATOMS --
-- BE RIGHT WITH YOU --
RRRRAAAAAA
SKREEEK
BACK-UP.
WHERE THE HELL DID YOU COME FROM?
DADDY DID A BAD THING WITH MOMMY, AND NINE MONTHS LATER --

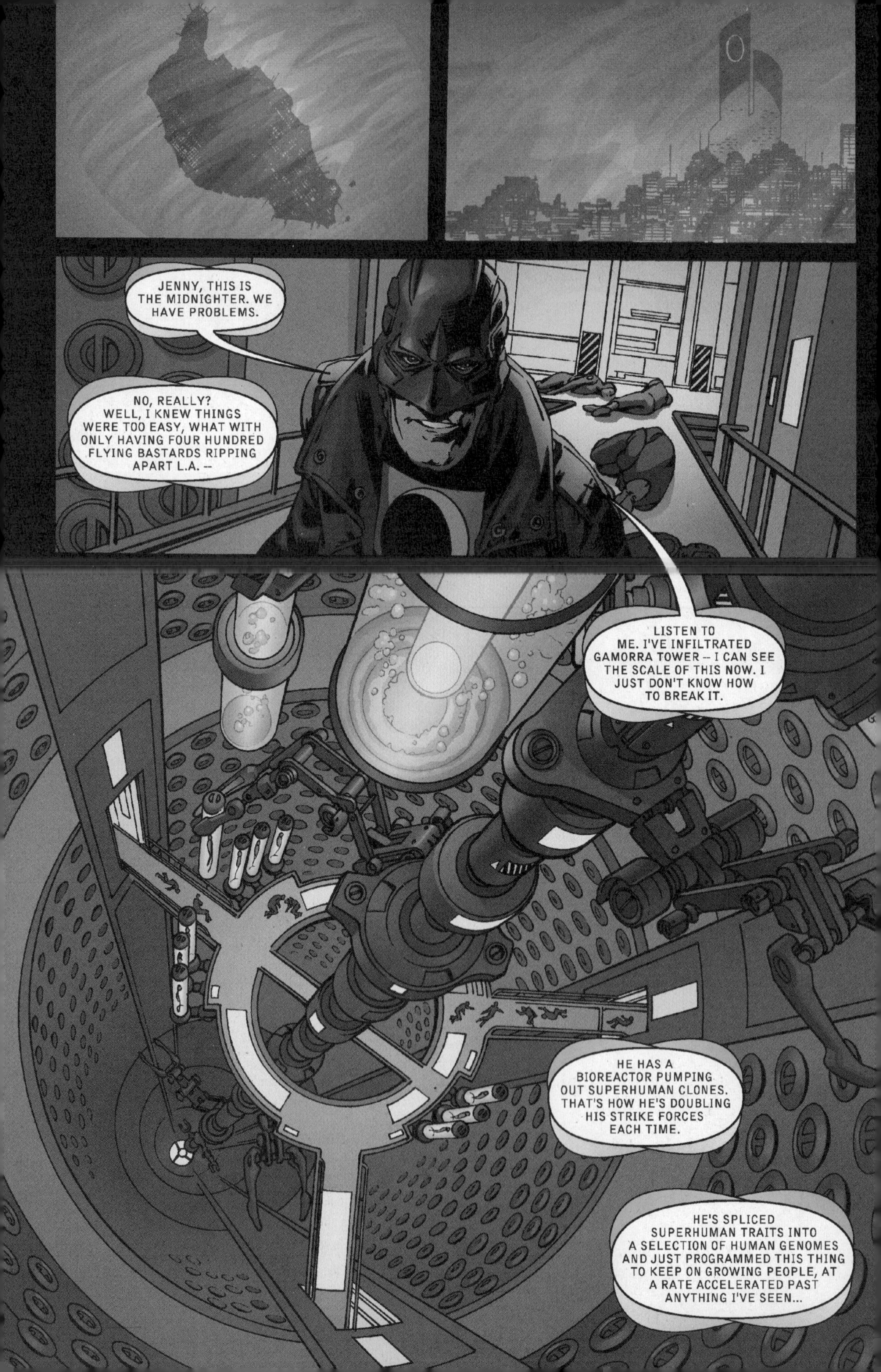
JENNY, THIS IS THE MIDNIGHTER. WE HAVE PROBLEMS.
NO, REALLY? WELL, I KNEW THINGS WERE TOO EASY, WHAT WITH ONLY HAVING FOUR HUNDRED FLYING BASTARDS RIPPING APART L.A. --
LISTEN TO ME. I'VE INFILTRATED GAMORRA TOWER -- I CAN SEE THE SCALE OF THIS NOW. I JUST DON'T KNOW HOW TO BREAK IT.
HE HAS A BIOREACTOR PUMPING OUT SUPERHUMAN CLONES. THAT'S HOW HE'S DOUBLING HIS STRIKE FORCES EACH TIME.
HE'S SPLICED SUPERHUMAN TRAITS INTO A SELECTION OF HUMAN GENOMES AND JUST PROGRAMMED THIS THING TO KEEP ON GROWING PEOPLE, AT A RATE ACCELERATED PAST ANYTHING I'VE SEEN...

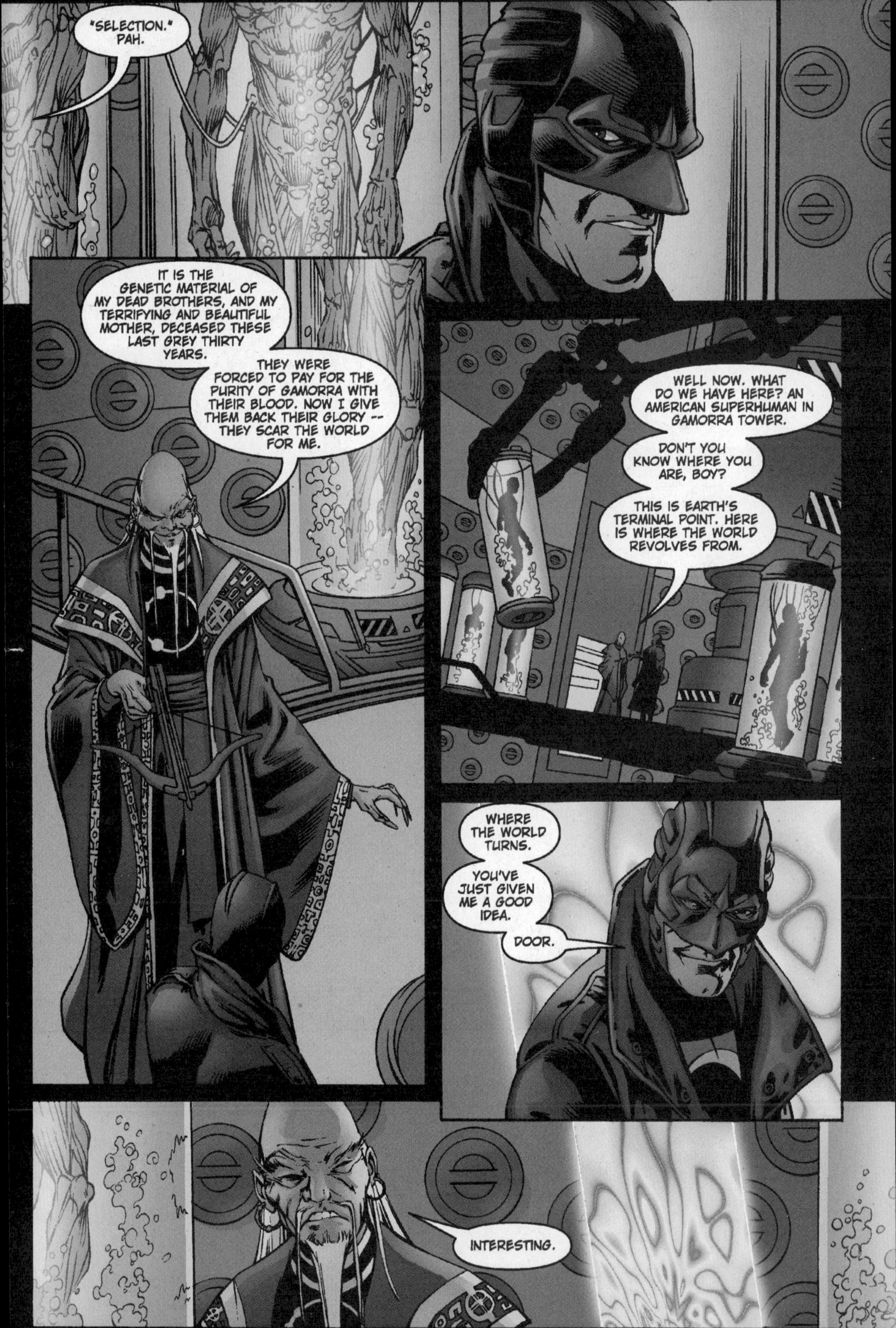
"SELECTION." PAH.
IT IS THE GENETIC MATERIAL OF MY DEAD BROTHERS, AND MY TERRIFYING AND BEAUTIFUL MOTHER, DECEASED THESE LAST GREY THIRTY YEARS.
THEY WERE FORCED TO PAY FOR THE PURITY OF GAMORRA WITH THEIR BLOOD. NOW I GIVE THEM BACK THEIR GLORY -- THEY SCAR THE WORLD FOR ME.
WELL NOW. WHAT DO WE HAVE HERE? AN AMERICAN SUPERHUMAN IN GAMORRA TOWER.
DON'T YOU KNOW WHERE YOU ARE, BOY?
THIS IS EARTH'S TERMINAL POINT. HERE IS WHERE THE WORLD REVOLVES FROM.
WHERE THE WORLD TURNS.
YOU'VE JUST GIVEN ME A GOOD IDEA.
DOOR.
INTERESTING.

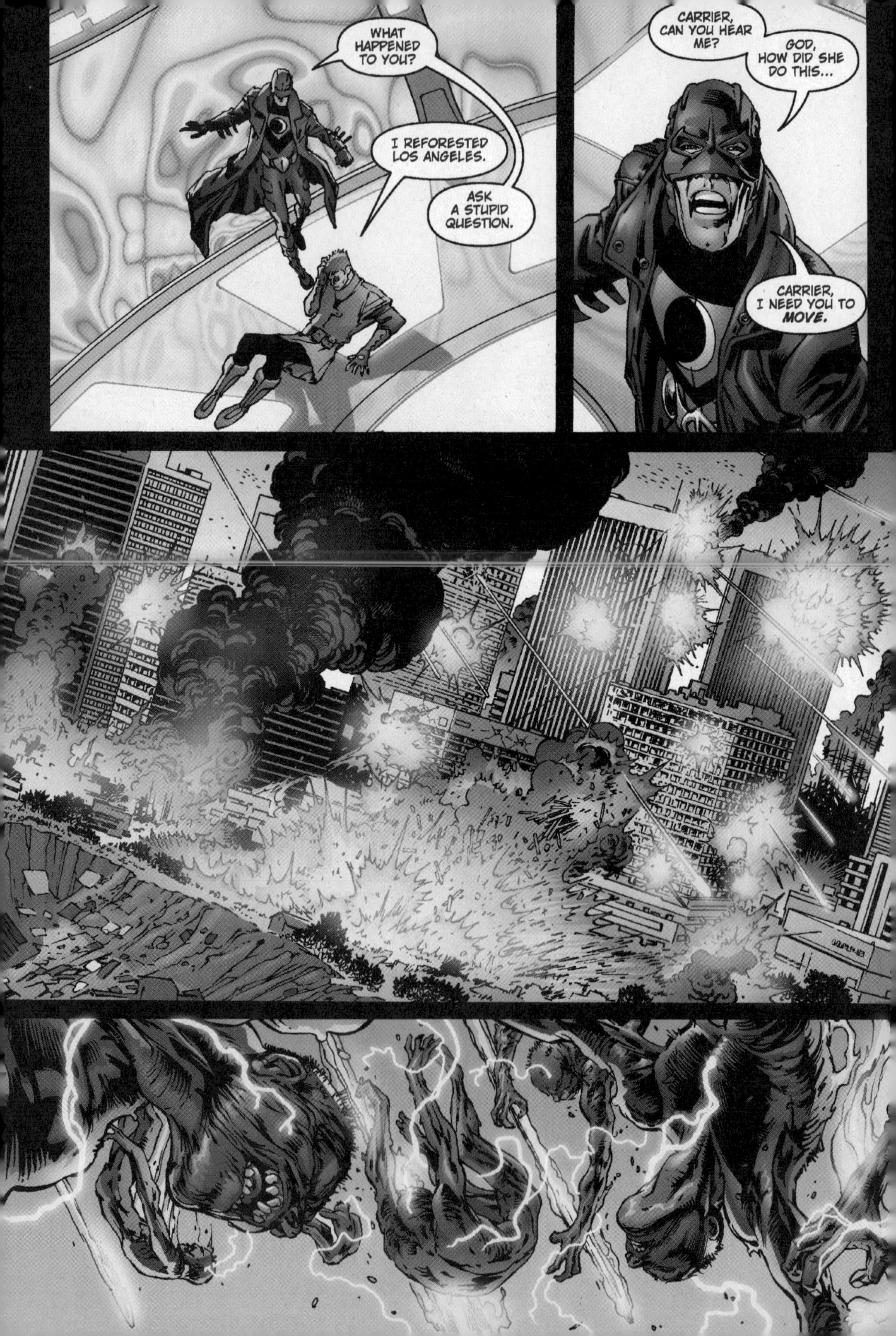
WHAT HAPPENED TO YOU?
I REFORESTED LOS ANGELES.
ASK A STUPID QUESTION.
CARRIER, CAN YOU HEAR ME?
GOD, HOW DID SHE DO THIS...
CARRIER, I NEED YOU TO MOVE.

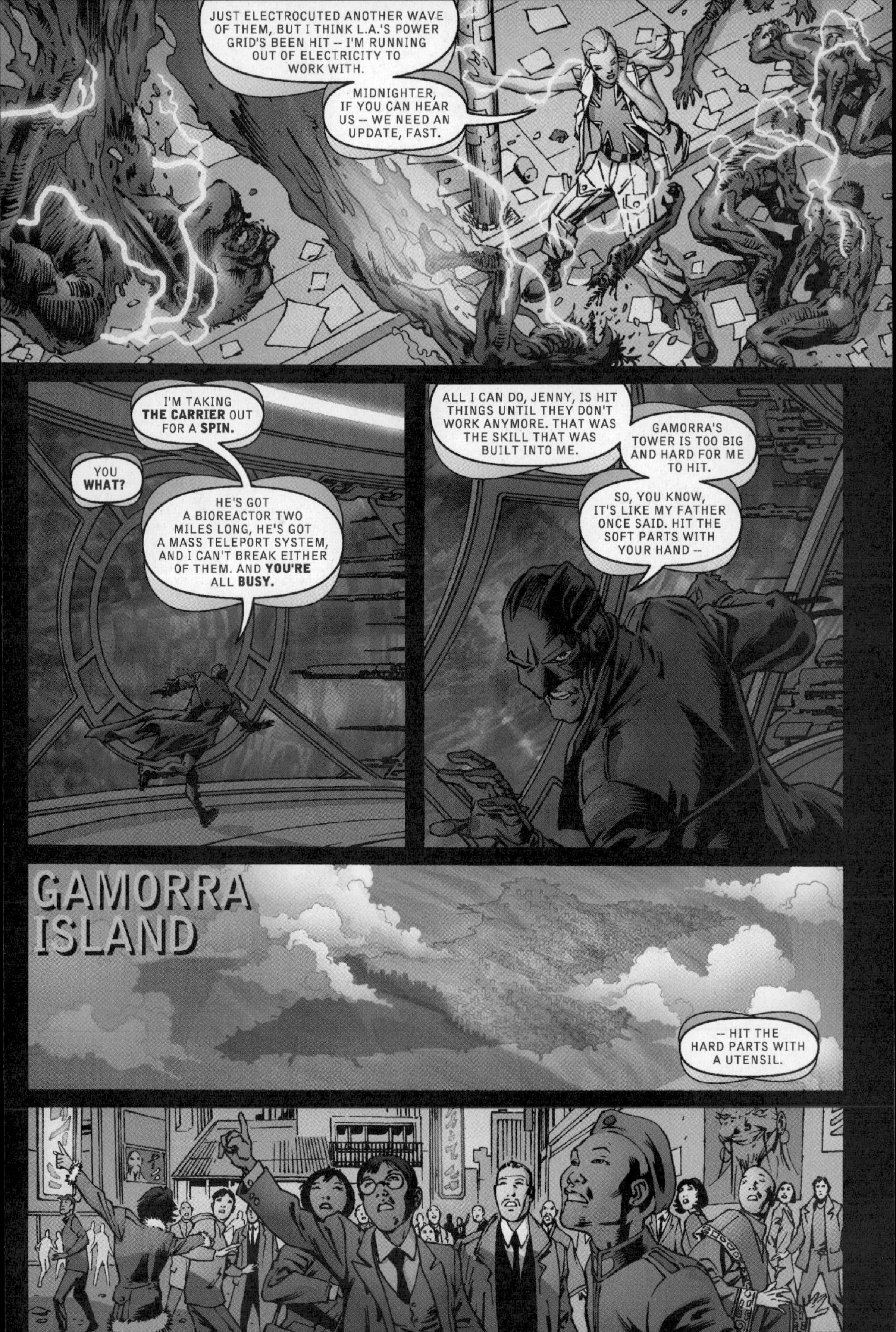

JUST ELECTROCUTED ANOTHER WAVE OF THEM, BUT I THINK L.A.'S POWER GRID'S BEEN HIT -- I'M RUNNING OUT OF ELECTRICITY TO WORK WITH.
MIDNIGHTER, IF YOU CAN HEAR US -- WE NEED AN UPDATE, FAST.
I'M TAKING **THE CARRIER** OUT FOR A **SPIN.**
YOU **WHAT?**
HE'S GOT A BIOREACTOR TWO MILES LONG, HE'S GOT A MASS TELEPORT SYSTEM, AND I CAN'T BREAK EITHER OF THEM. AND **YOU'RE** ALL **BUSY.**
ALL I CAN DO, JENNY, IS HIT THINGS UNTIL THEY DON'T WORK ANYMORE. THAT WAS THE SKILL THAT WAS BUILT INTO ME.
GAMORRA'S TOWER IS TOO BIG AND HARD FOR ME TO HIT.
SO, YOU KNOW, IT'S LIKE MY FATHER ONCE SAID. HIT THE SOFT PARTS WITH YOUR HAND --
GAMORRA ISLAND
-- HIT THE HARD PARTS WITH A UTENSIL.

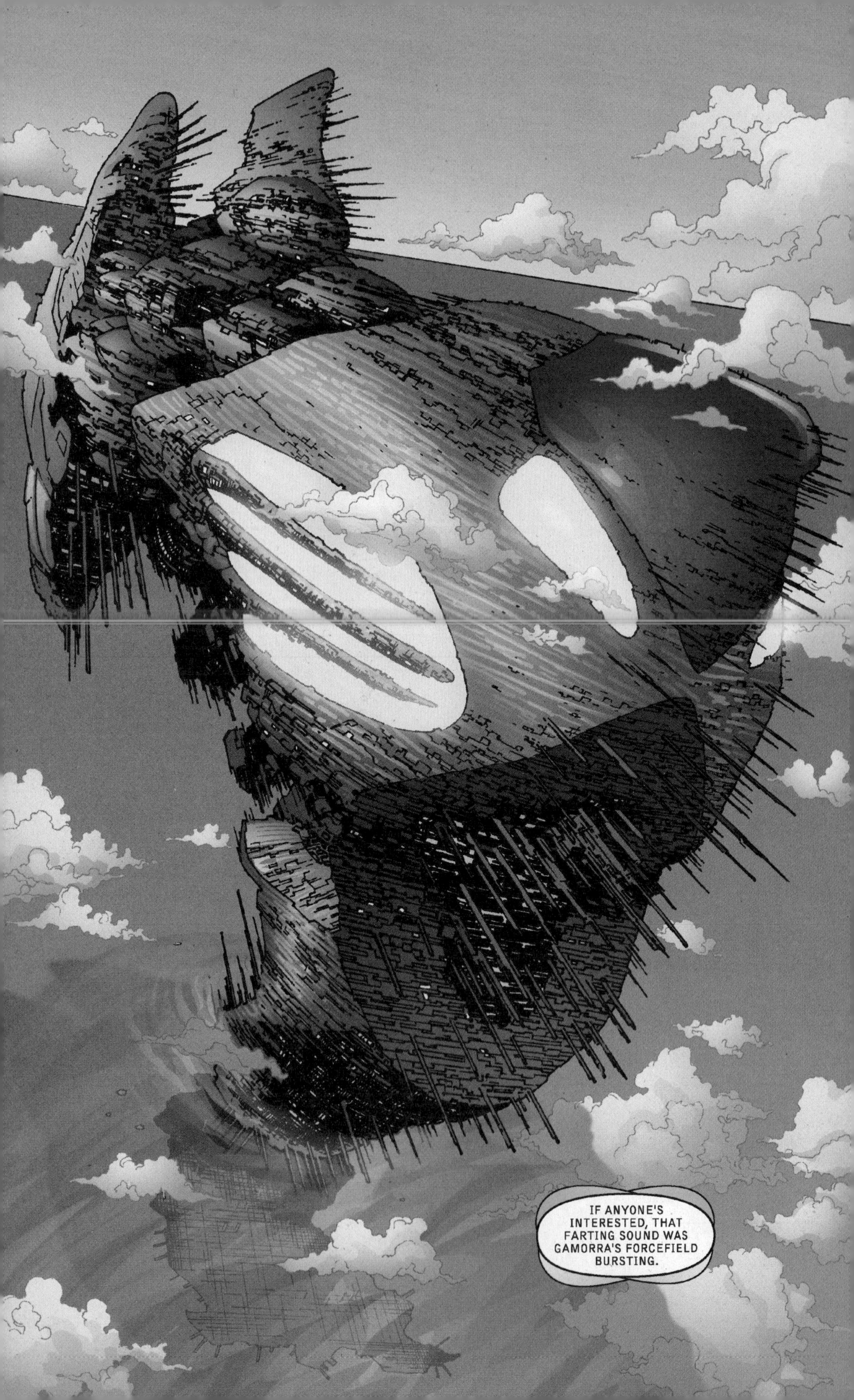
IF ANYONE'S INTERESTED, THAT FARTING SOUND WAS GAMORRA'S FORCEFIELD BURSTING.

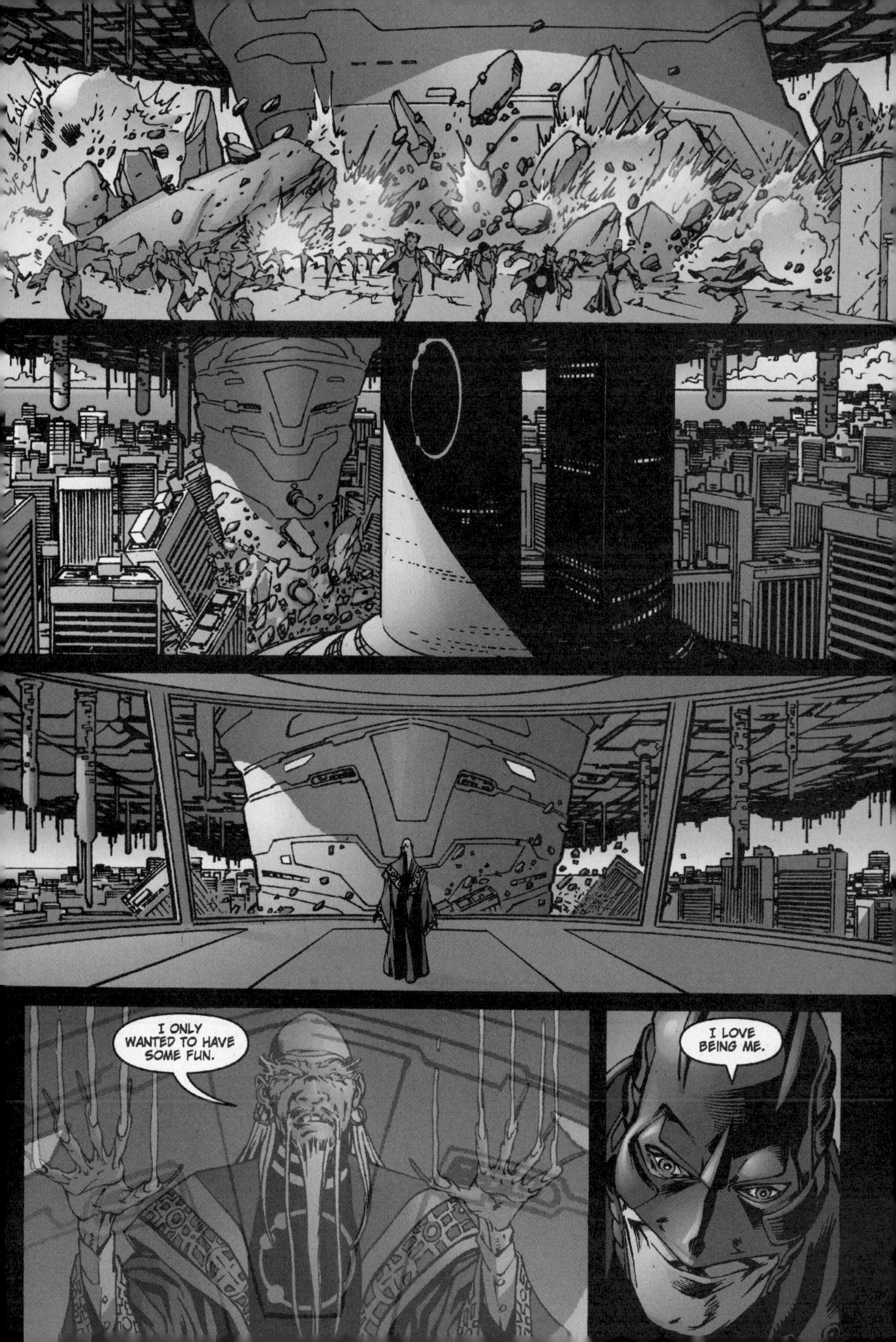
I ONLY WANTED TO HAVE SOME FUN.
I LOVE BEING ME.

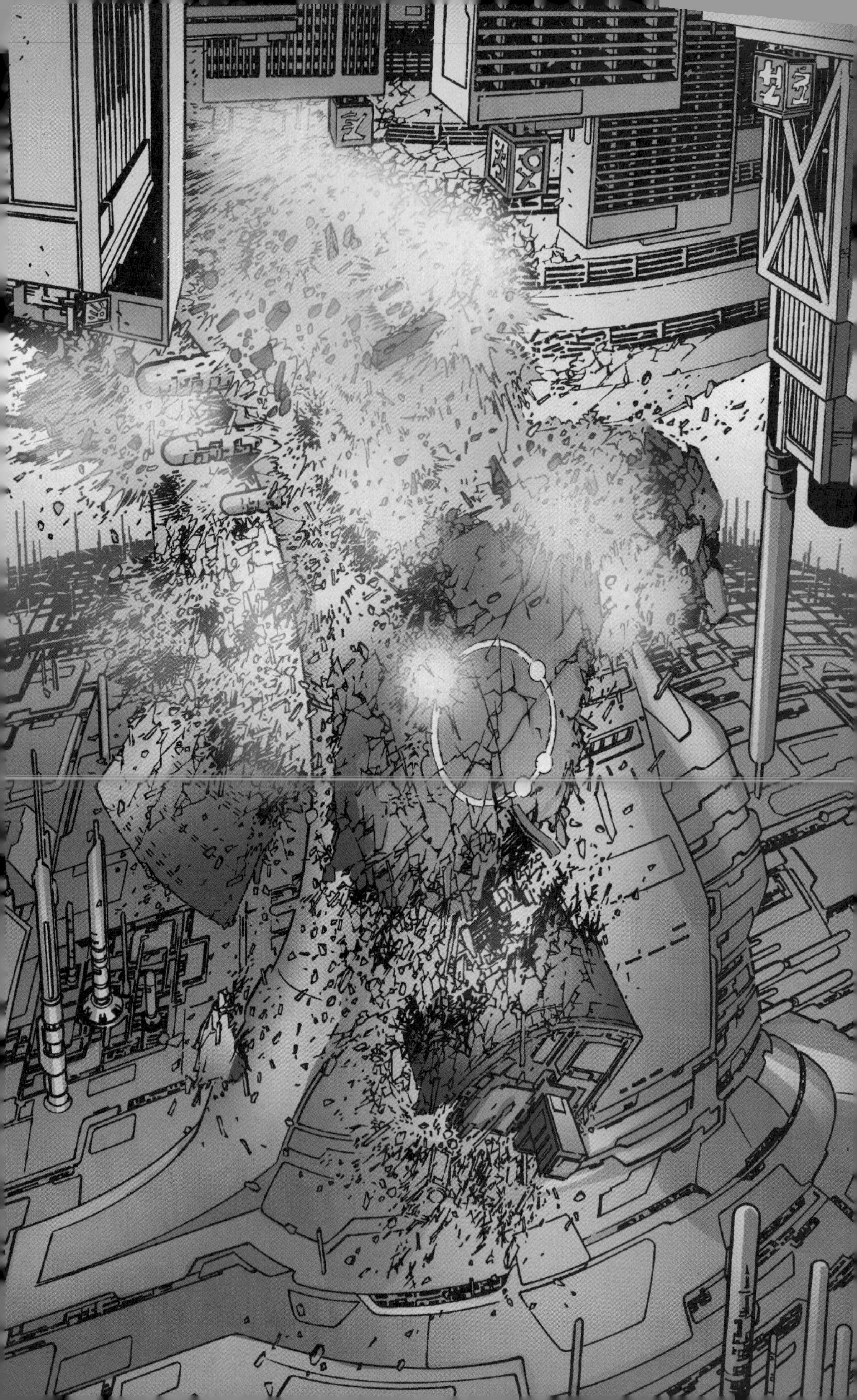

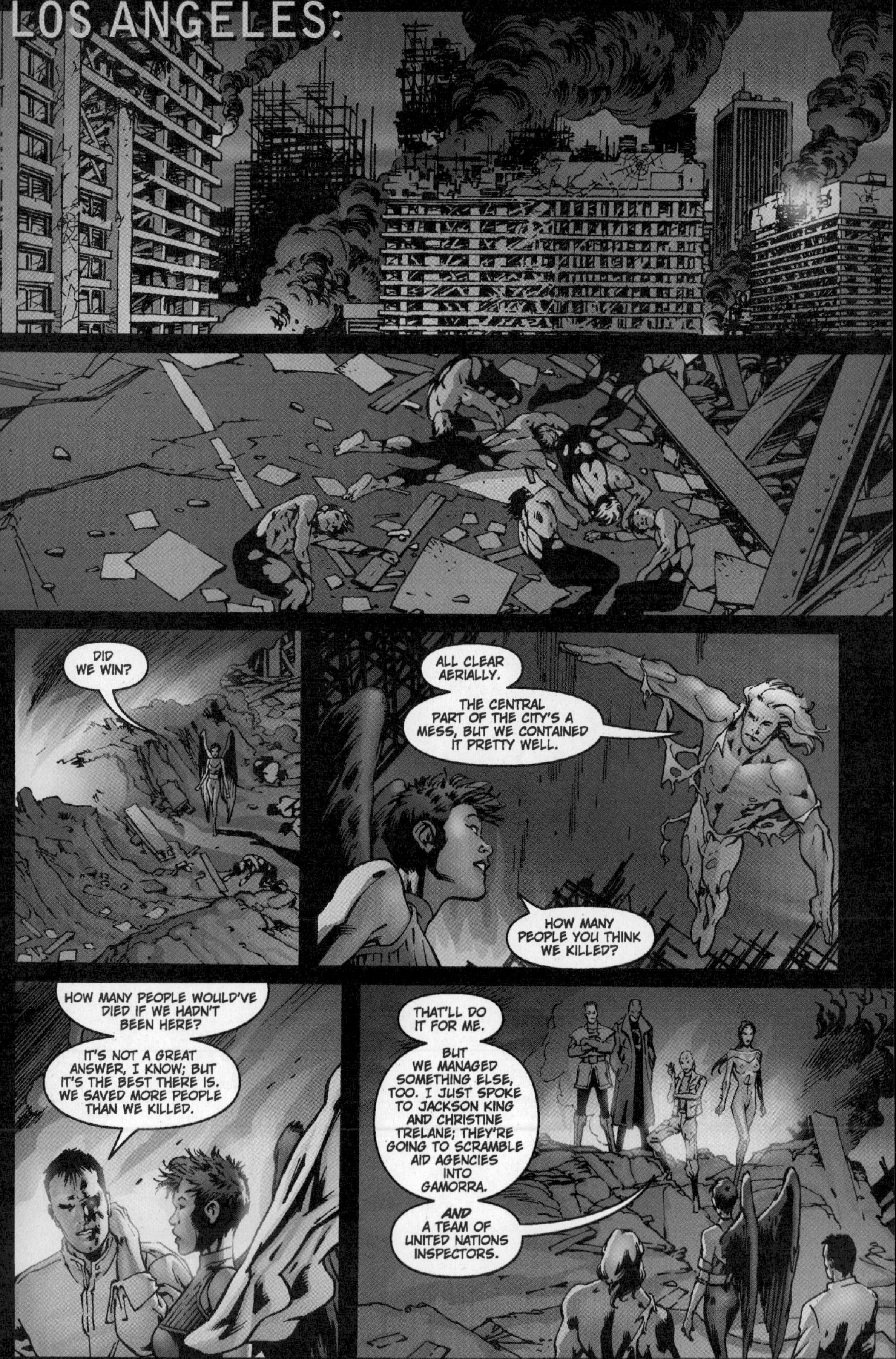
LOS ANGELES:
DID WE WIN?
ALL CLEAR AERIALLY.
THE CENTRAL PART OF THE CITY'S A MESS, BUT WE CONTAINED IT PRETTY WELL.
HOW MANY PEOPLE YOU THINK WE KILLED?
HOW MANY PEOPLE WOULD'VE DIED IF WE HADN'T BEEN HERE?
IT'S NOT A GREAT ANSWER, I KNOW; BUT IT'S THE BEST THERE IS. WE SAVED MORE PEOPLE THAN WE KILLED.
THAT'LL DO IT FOR ME.
BUT WE MANAGED SOMETHING ELSE, TOO. I JUST SPOKE TO JACKSON KING AND CHRISTINE TRELANE; THEY'RE GOING TO SCRAMBLE AID AGENCIES INTO GAMORRA.
AND A TEAM OF UNITED NATIONS INSPECTORS.

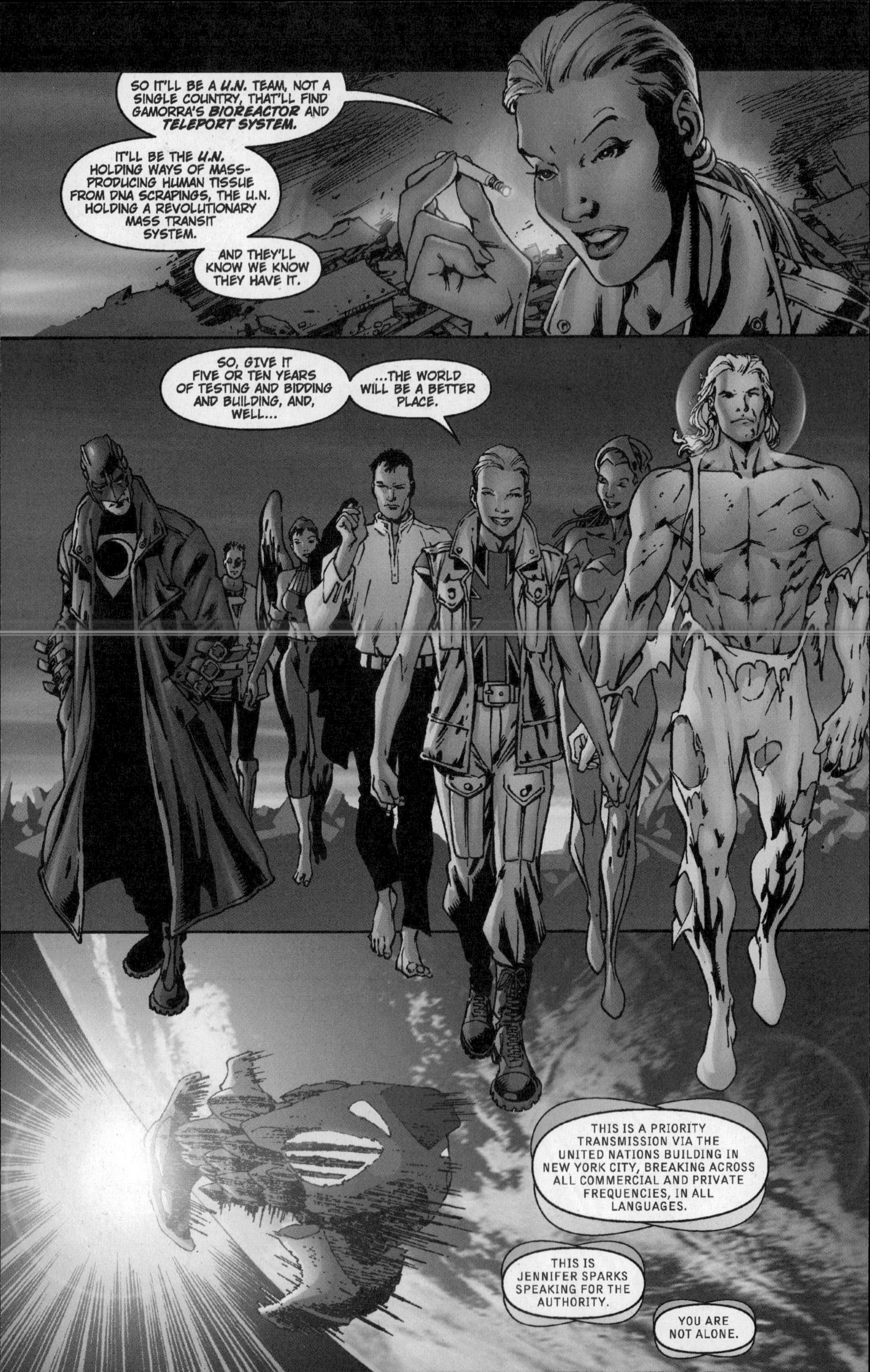
SO IT'LL BE A *U.N.* TEAM, NOT A SINGLE COUNTRY, THAT'LL FIND GAMORRA'S *BIOREACTOR* AND *TELEPORT SYSTEM.*
IT'LL BE THE *U.N.* HOLDING WAYS OF MASS-PRODUCING HUMAN TISSUE FROM DNA SCRAPINGS, THE U.N. HOLDING A REVOLUTIONARY MASS TRANSIT SYSTEM.
AND THEY'LL KNOW WE KNOW THEY HAVE IT.
SO, GIVE IT FIVE OR TEN YEARS OF TESTING AND BIDDING AND BUILDING, AND, WELL...
...THE WORLD WILL BE A BETTER PLACE.
THIS IS A PRIORITY TRANSMISSION VIA THE UNITED NATIONS BUILDING IN NEW YORK CITY, BREAKING ACROSS ALL COMMERCIAL AND PRIVATE FREQUENCIES, IN ALL LANGUAGES.
THIS IS JENNIFER SPARKS SPEAKING FOR THE AUTHORITY.
YOU ARE NOT ALONE.

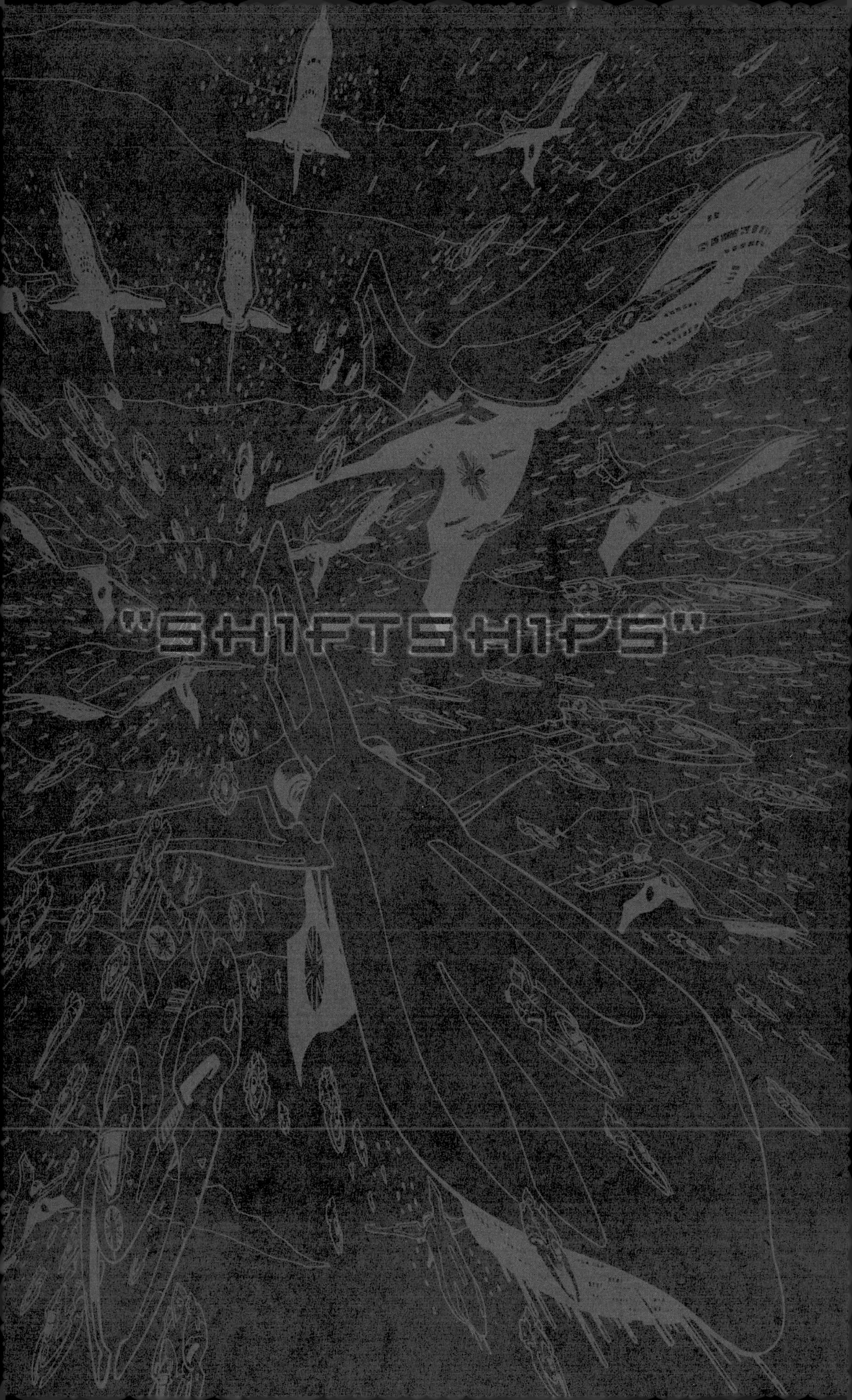
"SHIFTSHIPS"

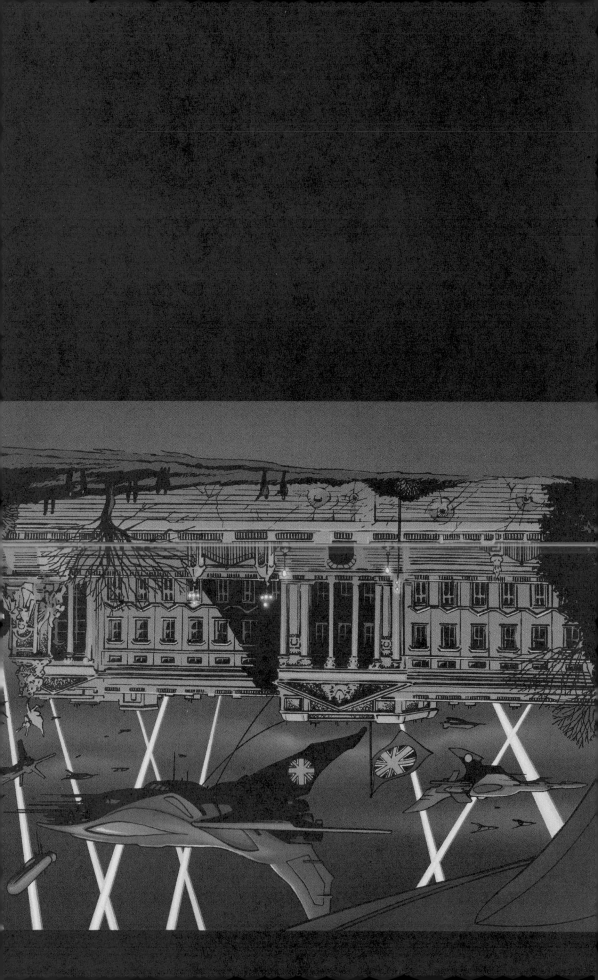

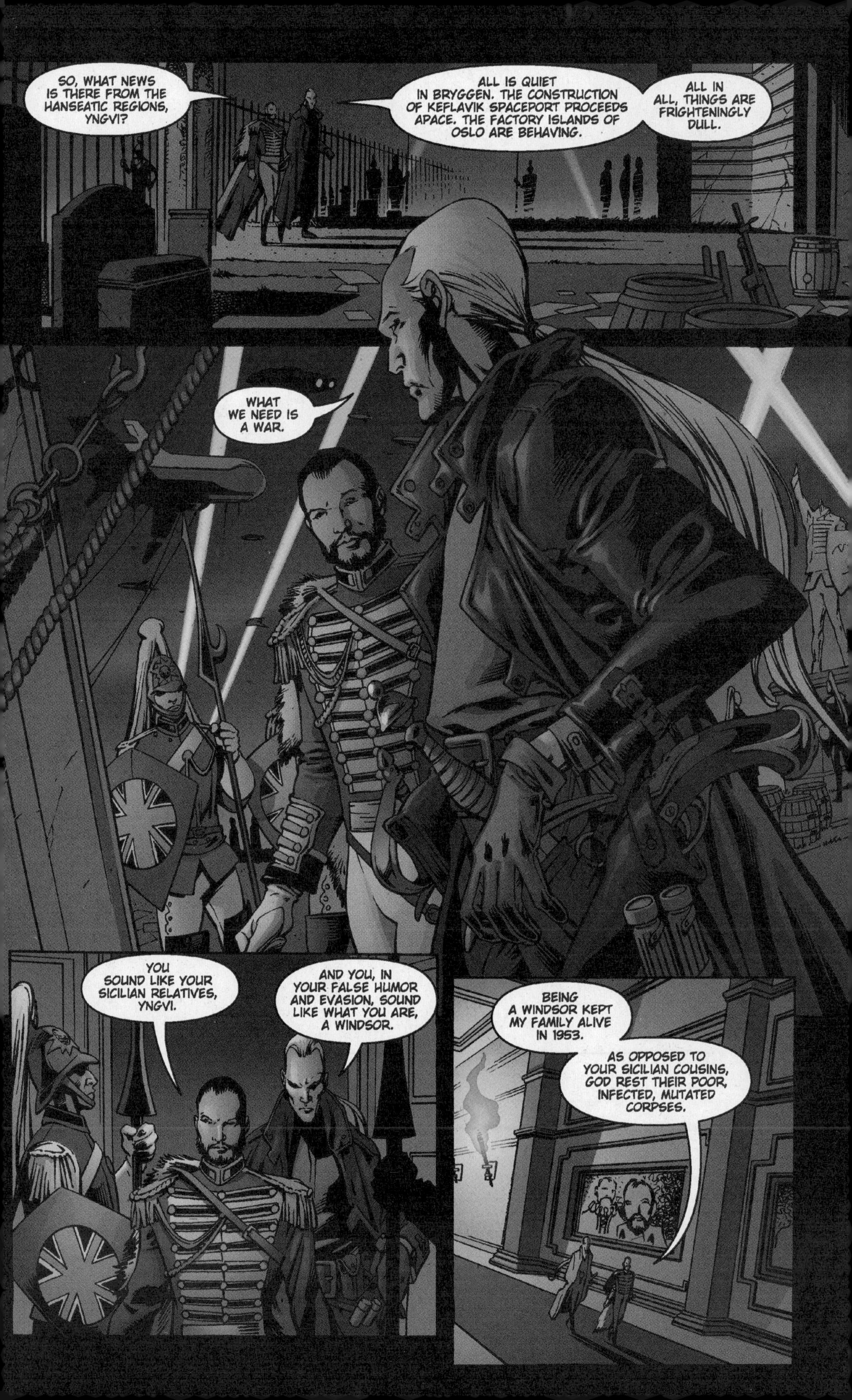
SO, WHAT NEWS IS THERE FROM THE HANSEATIC REGIONS, YNGVI?
ALL IS QUIET IN BRYGGEN. THE CONSTRUCTION OF KEFLAVIK SPACEPORT PROCEEDS APACE. THE FACTORY ISLANDS OF OSLO ARE BEHAVING.
ALL IN ALL, THINGS ARE FRIGHTENINGLY DULL.
WHAT WE NEED IS A WAR.
YOU SOUND LIKE YOUR SICILIAN RELATIVES, YNGVI.
AND YOU, IN YOUR FALSE HUMOR AND EVASION, SOUND LIKE WHAT YOU ARE, A WINDSOR.
BEING A WINDSOR KEPT MY FAMILY ALIVE IN 1953.
AS OPPOSED TO YOUR SICILIAN COUSINS, GOD REST THEIR POOR, INFECTED, MUTATED CORPSES.

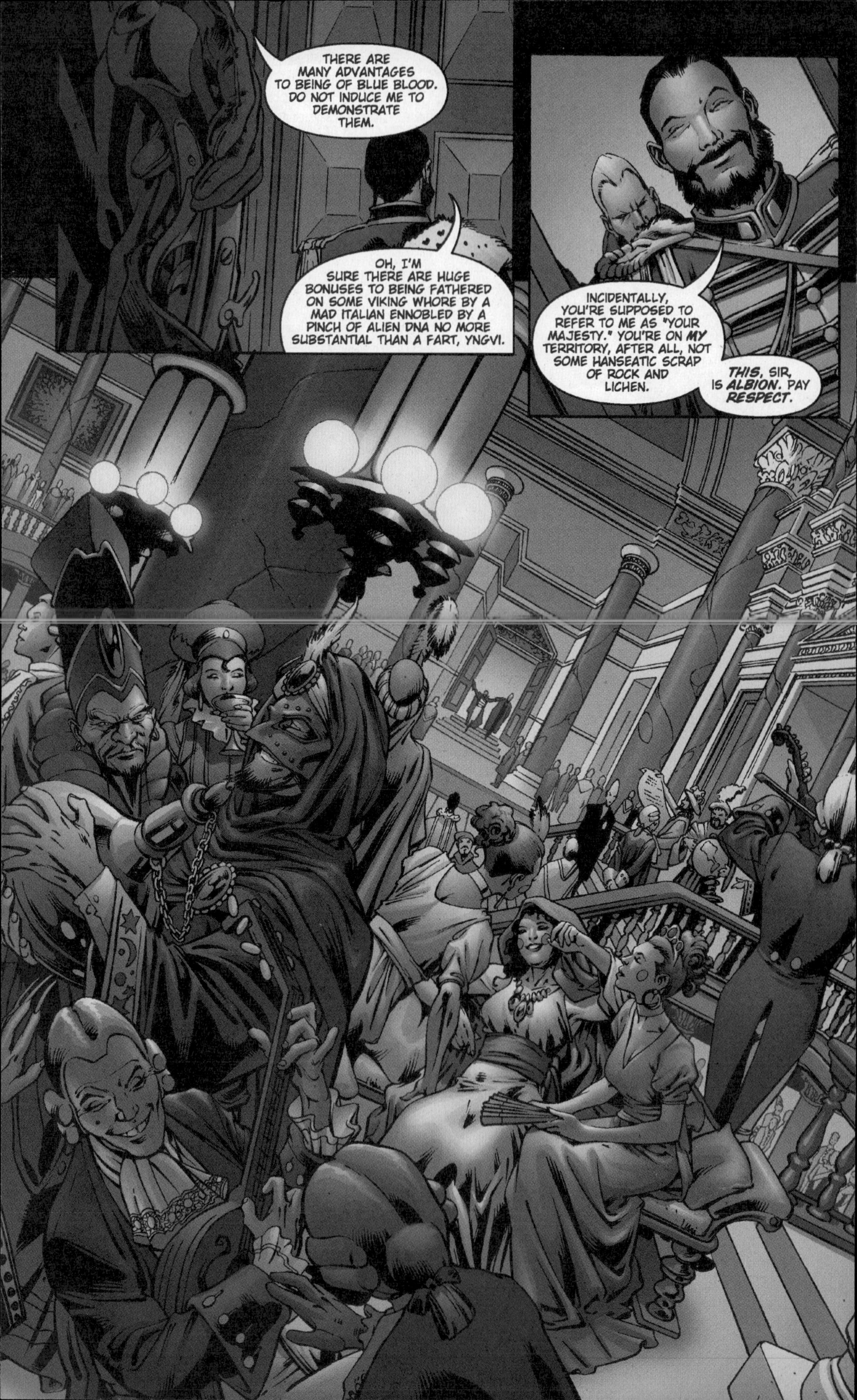
THERE ARE MANY ADVANTAGES TO BEING OF BLUE BLOOD. DO NOT INDUCE ME TO DEMONSTRATE THEM.
OH, I'M SURE THERE ARE HUGE BONUSES TO BEING FATHERED ON SOME VIKING WHORE BY A MAD ITALIAN ENNOBLED BY A PINCH OF ALIEN DNA NO MORE SUBSTANTIAL THAN A FART, YNGVI.
INCIDENTALLY, YOU'RE SUPPOSED TO REFER TO ME AS "YOUR MAJESTY." YOU'RE ON MY TERRITORY, AFTER ALL, NOT SOME HANSEATIC SCRAP OF ROCK AND LICHEN.
THIS, SIR, IS ALBION. PAY RESPECT.

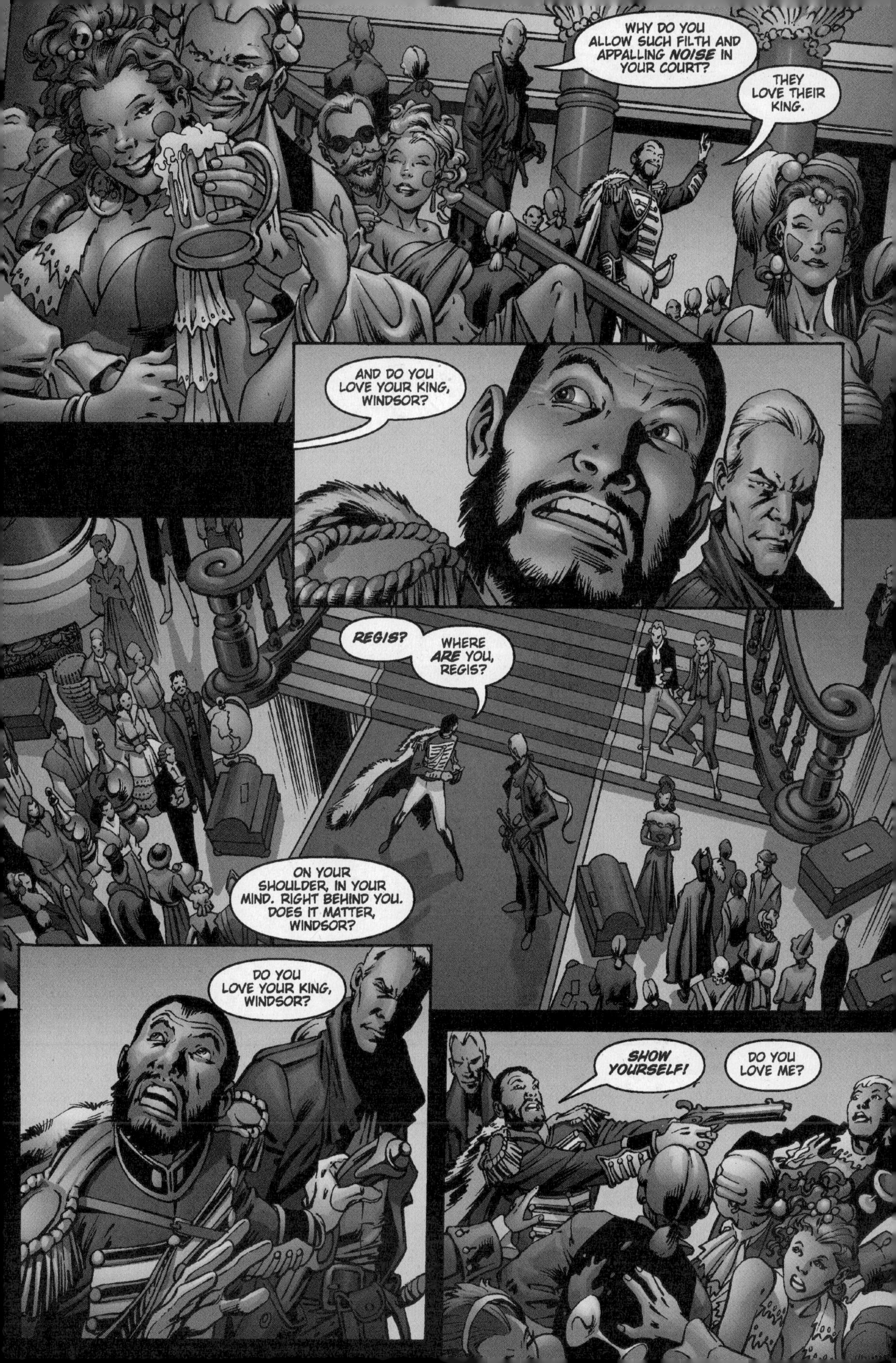
WHY DO YOU ALLOW SUCH FILTH AND APPALLING *NOISE* IN YOUR COURT?
THEY LOVE THEIR KING.
AND DO YOU LOVE YOUR KING, WINDSOR?
REGIS?
WHERE *ARE* YOU, REGIS?
ON YOUR SHOULDER, IN YOUR MIND. RIGHT BEHIND YOU. DOES IT MATTER, WINDSOR?
DO YOU LOVE YOUR KING, WINDSOR?
SHOW YOURSELF!
DO YOU LOVE ME?

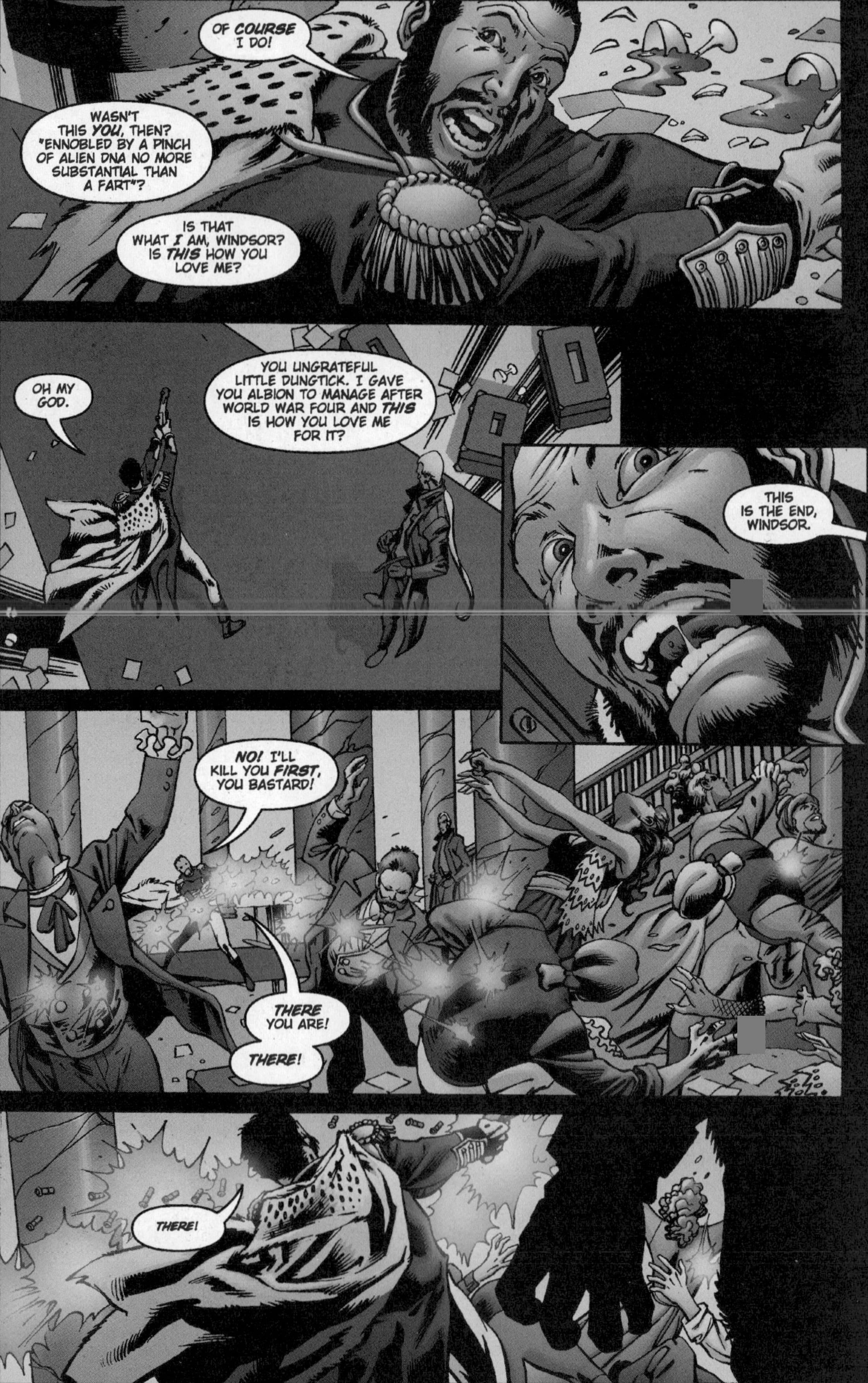
OF **COURSE** I DO!
WASN'T THIS **YOU**, THEN? "ENNOBLED BY A PINCH OF ALIEN DNA NO MORE SUBSTANTIAL THAN A FART"?
IS THAT WHAT **I** AM, WINDSOR? IS **THIS** HOW YOU LOVE ME?
OH MY GOD.
YOU UNGRATEFUL LITTLE DUNGTICK. I GAVE YOU ALBION TO MANAGE AFTER WORLD WAR FOUR AND **THIS** IS HOW YOU LOVE ME FOR IT?
THIS IS THE END, WINDSOR.
NO! I'LL KILL YOU **FIRST**, YOU BASTARD!
THERE YOU ARE!
THERE!
THERE!

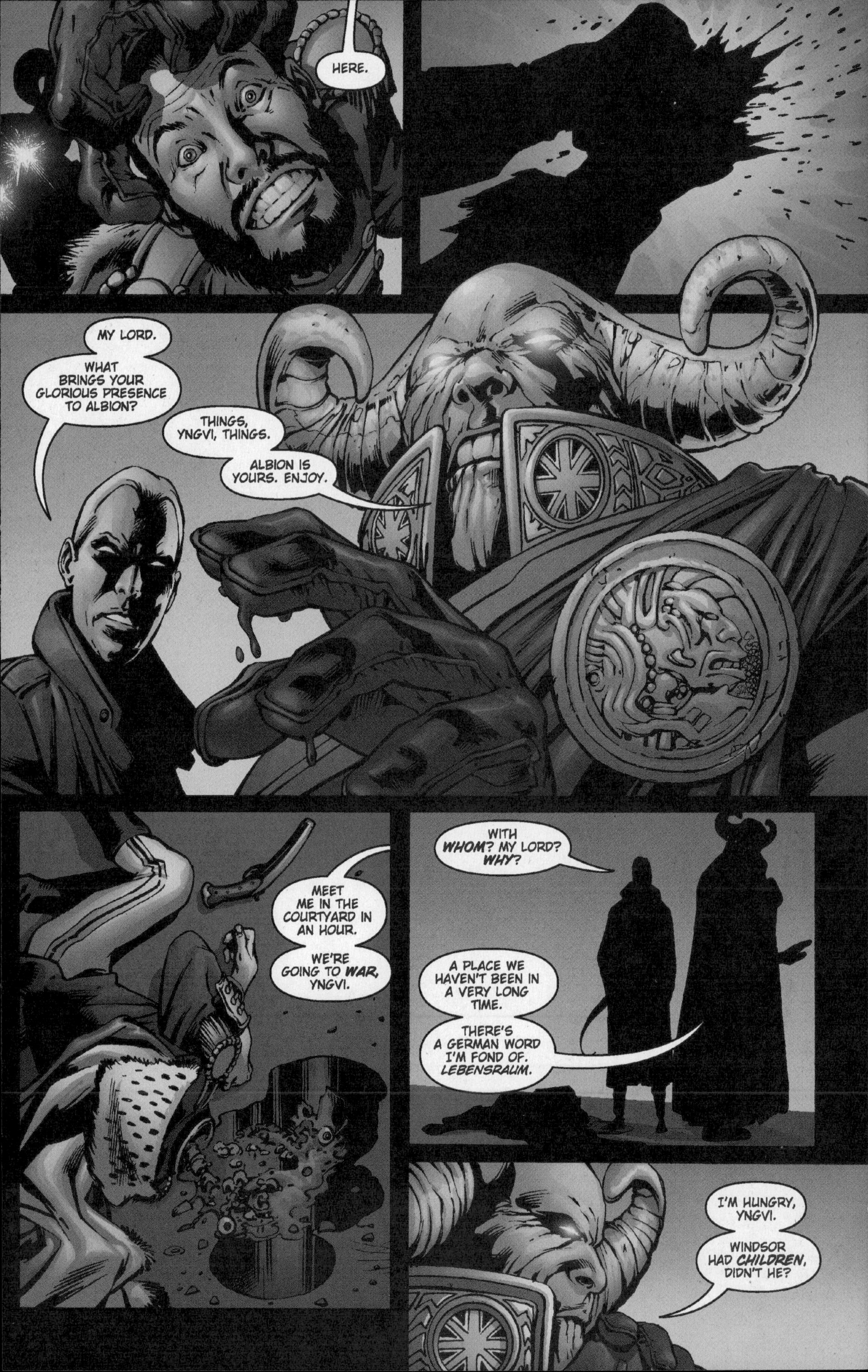

HERE.
MY LORD.
WHAT BRINGS YOUR GLORIOUS PRESENCE TO ALBION?
THINGS, YNGVI, THINGS.
ALBION IS YOURS. ENJOY.
MEET ME IN THE COURTYARD IN AN HOUR.
WE'RE GOING TO **WAR**, YNGVI.
WITH **WHOM**? MY LORD? **WHY**?
A PLACE WE HAVEN'T BEEN IN A VERY LONG TIME.
THERE'S A GERMAN WORD I'M FOND OF. *LEBENSRAUM*.
I'M HUNGRY, YNGVI.
WINDSOR HAD **CHILDREN**, DIDN'T HE?

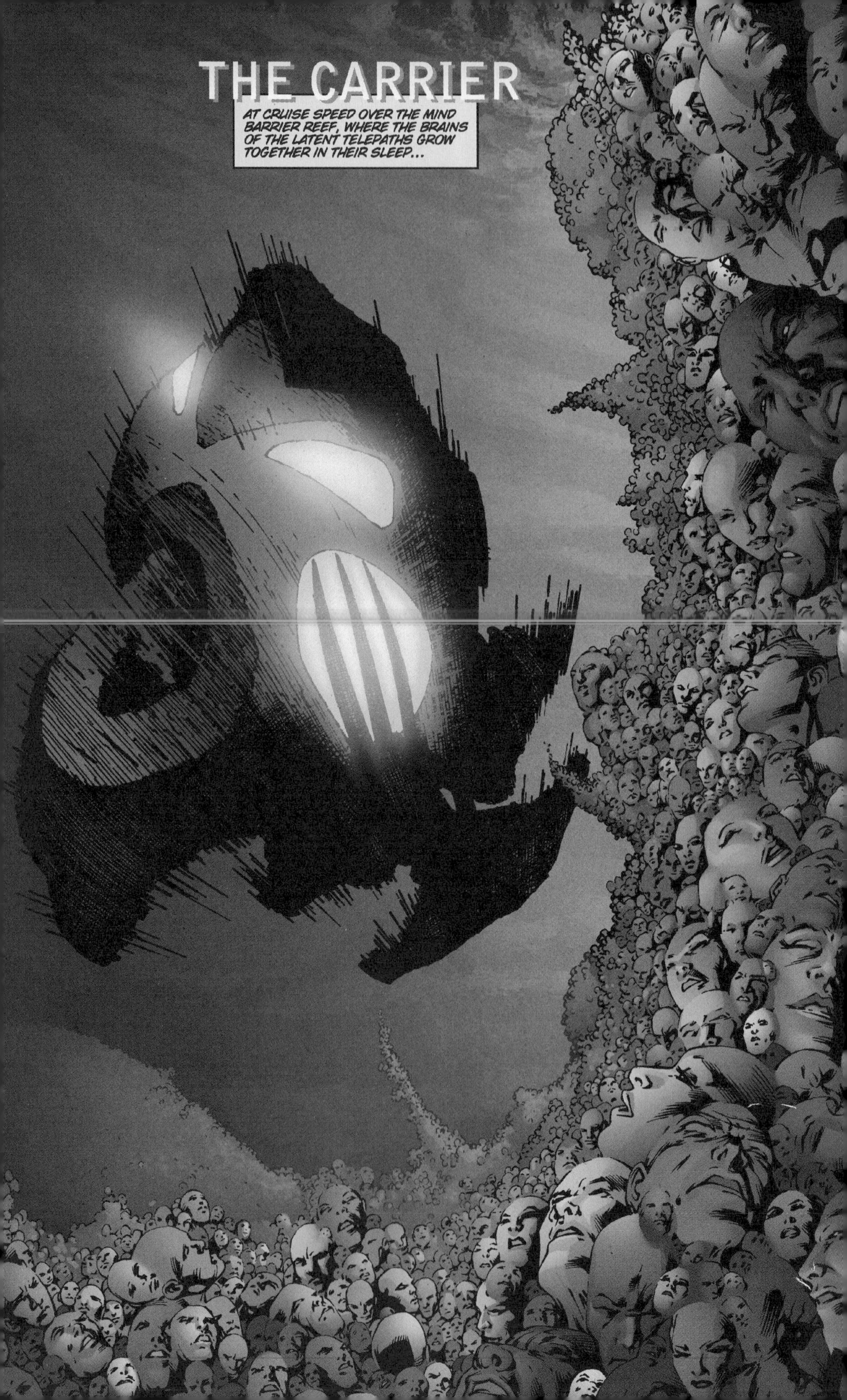
THE CARRIER
AT CRUISE SPEED OVER THE MIND BARRIER REEF, WHERE THE BRAINS OF THE LATENT TELEPATHS GROW TOGETHER IN THEIR SLEEP...

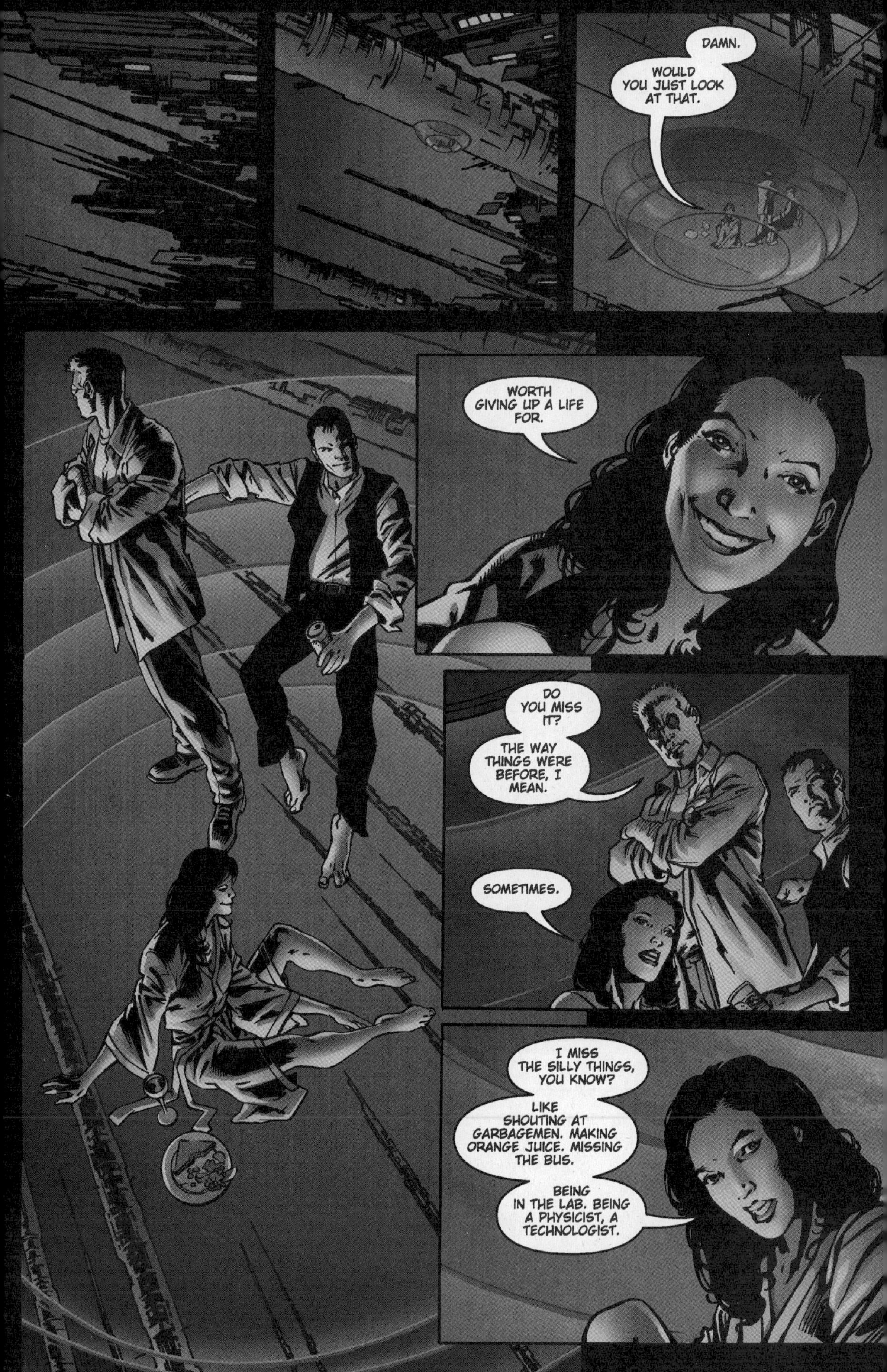
DAMN.
WOULD YOU JUST LOOK AT THAT.
WORTH GIVING UP A LIFE FOR.
DO YOU MISS IT?
THE WAY THINGS WERE BEFORE, I MEAN.
SOMETIMES.
I MISS THE SILLY THINGS, YOU KNOW?
LIKE SHOUTING AT GARBAGEMEN. MAKING ORANGE JUICE. MISSING THE BUS.
BEING IN THE LAB. BEING A PHYSICIST, A TECHNOLOGIST.

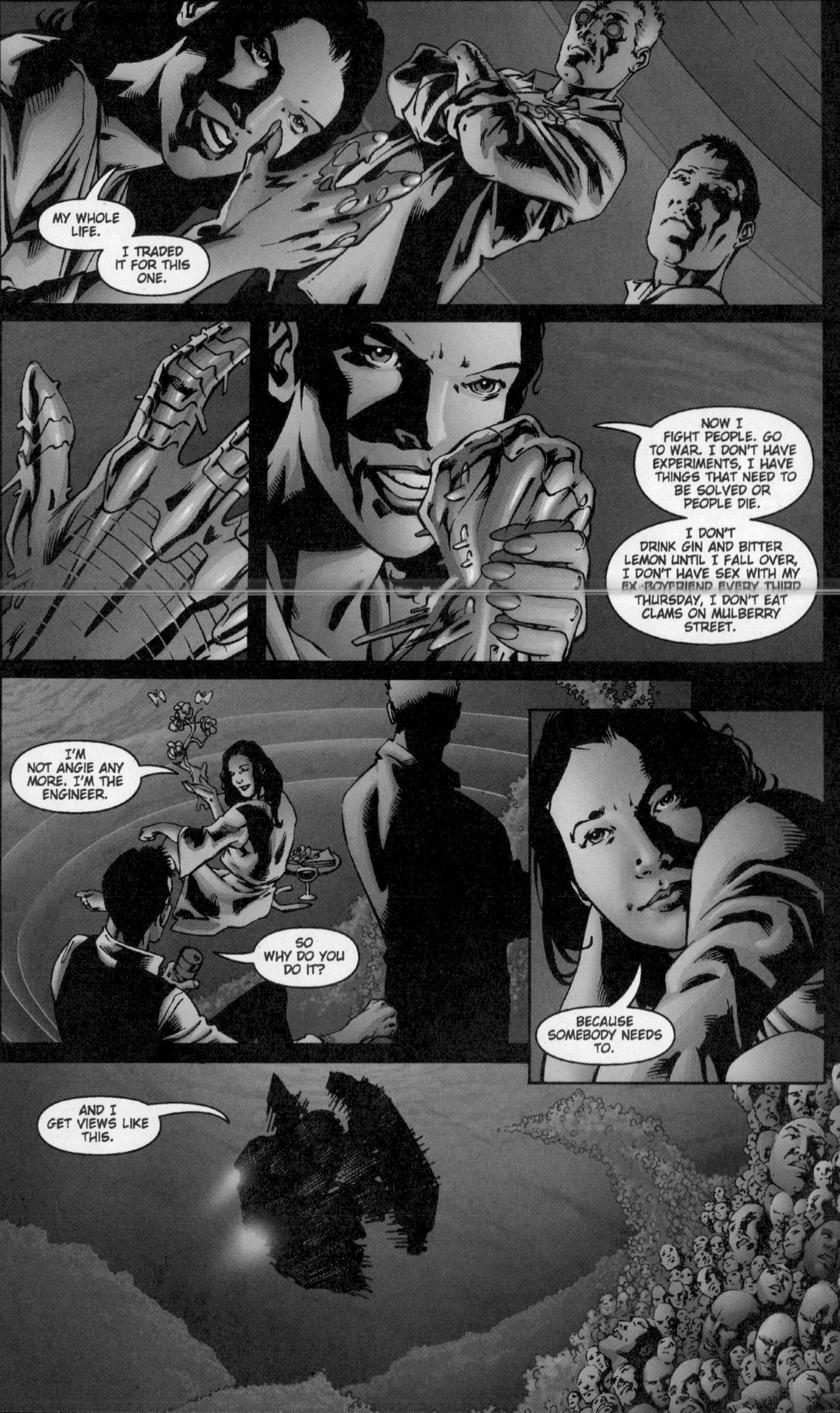
MY WHOLE LIFE.
I TRADED IT FOR THIS ONE.
NOW I FIGHT PEOPLE. GO TO WAR. I DON'T HAVE EXPERIMENTS, I HAVE THINGS THAT NEED TO BE SOLVED OR PEOPLE DIE.
I DON'T DRINK GIN AND BITTER LEMON UNTIL I FALL OVER, I DON'T HAVE SEX WITH MY EX-BOYFRIEND EVERY THIRD THURSDAY, I DON'T EAT CLAMS ON MULBERRY STREET.
I'M NOT ANGIE ANY MORE. I'M THE ENGINEER.
SO WHY DO YOU DO IT?
BECAUSE SOMEBODY NEEDS TO.
AND I GET VIEWS LIKE THIS.

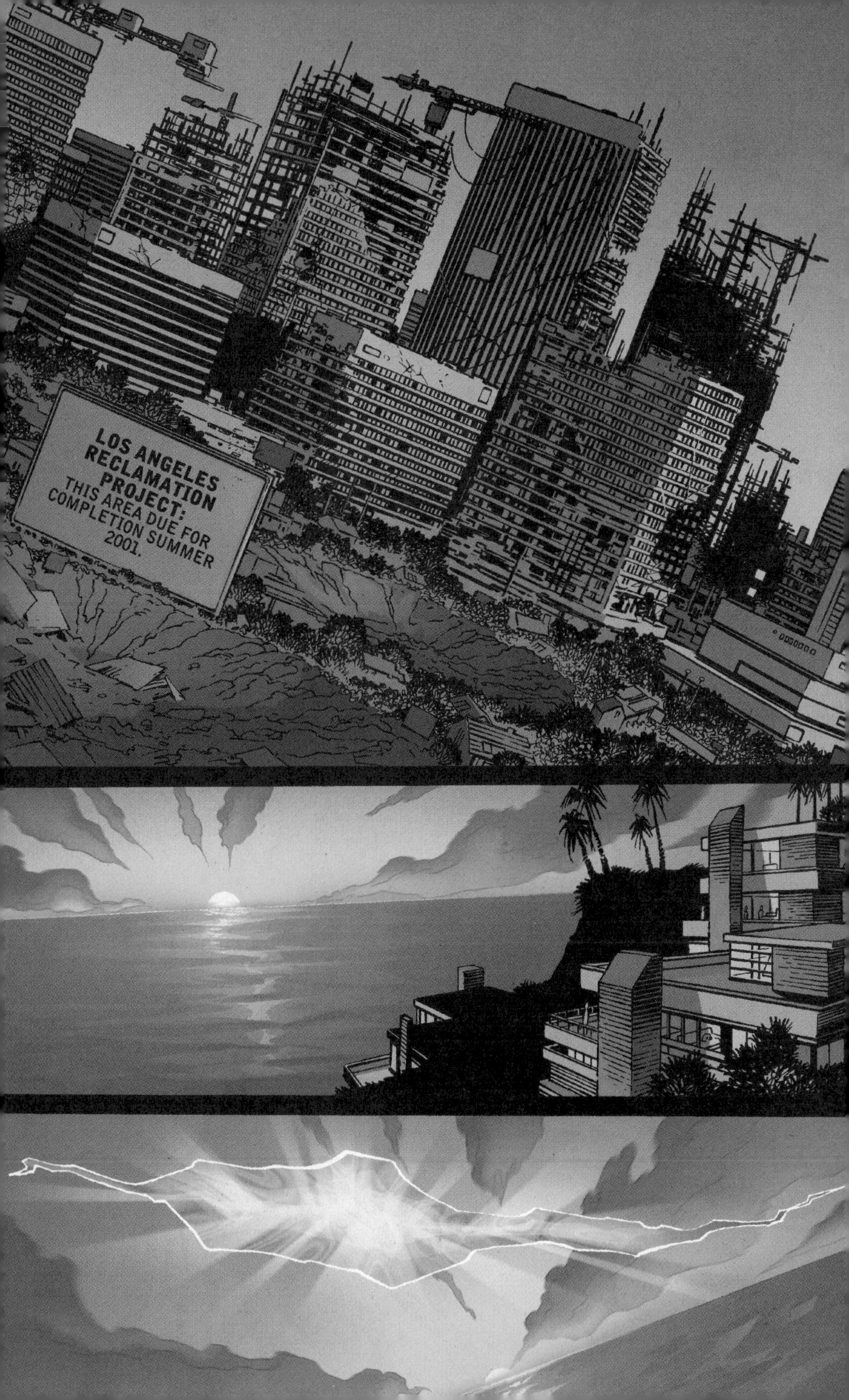
LOS ANGELES RECLAMATION PROJECT:
THIS AREA DUE FOR COMPLETION SUMMER 2001.

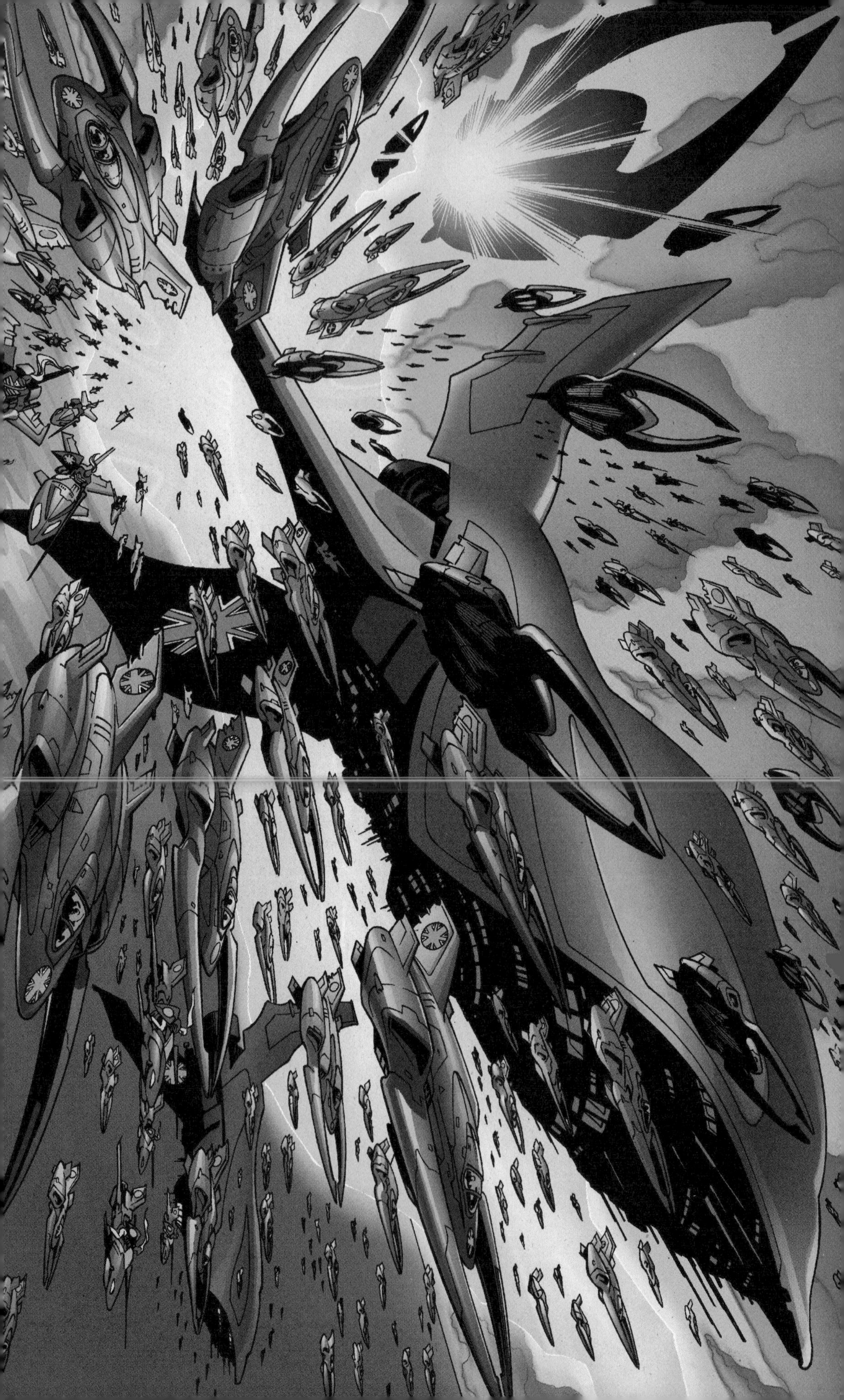

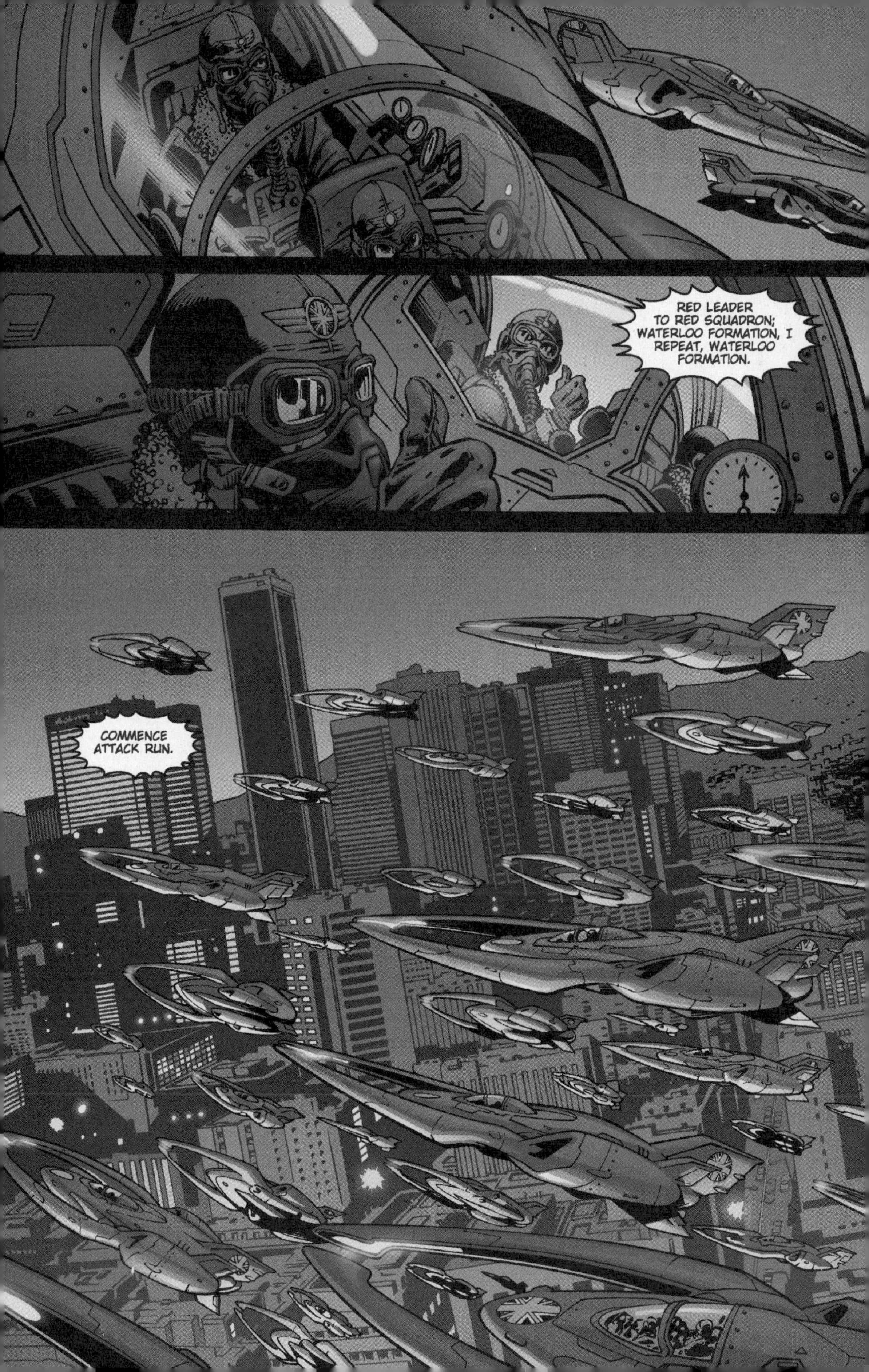
RED LEADER TO RED SQUADRON; WATERLOO FORMATION, I REPEAT, WATERLOO FORMATION.
COMMENCE ATTACK RUN.

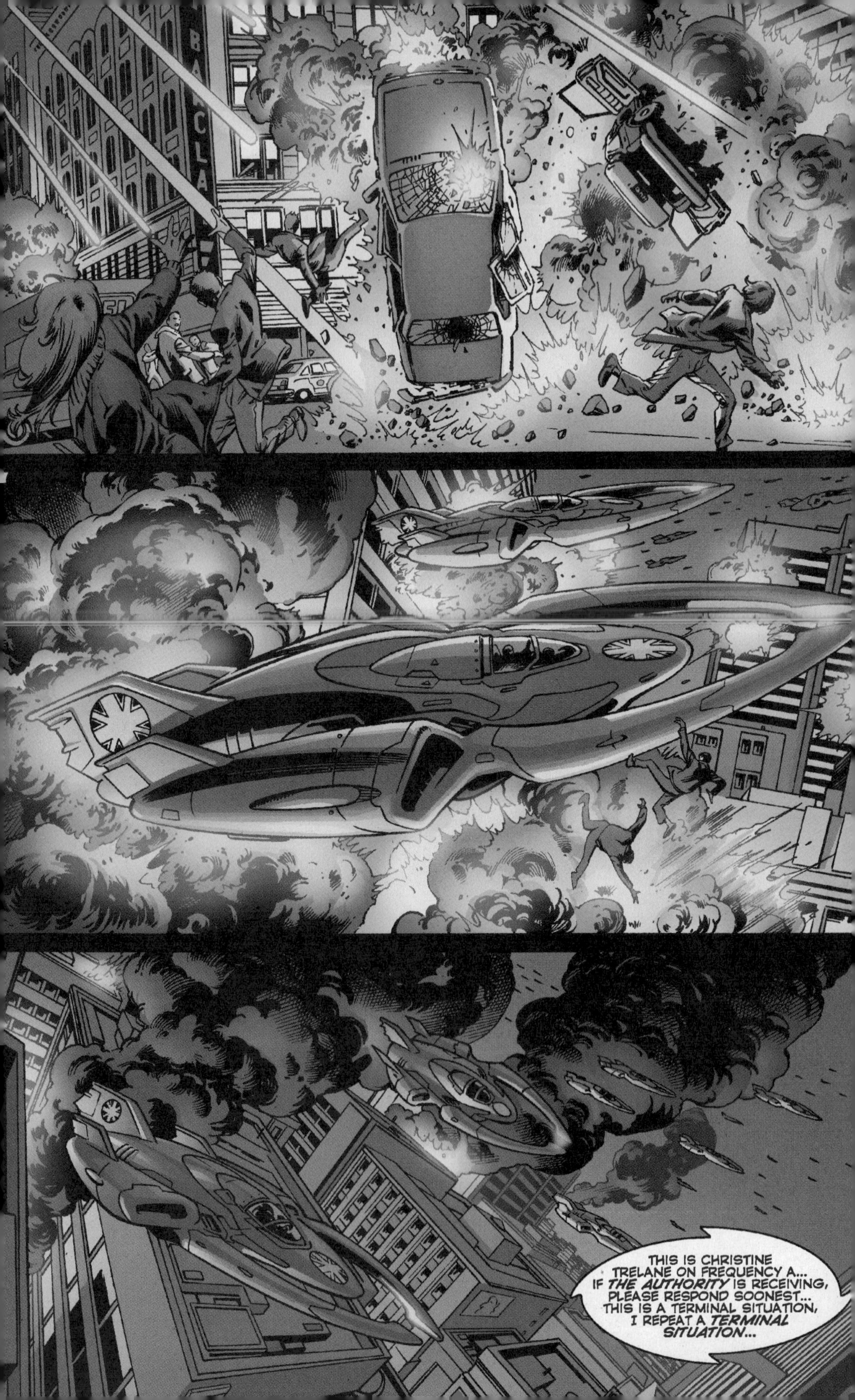
THIS IS CHRISTINE TRELANE ON FREQUENCY A... IF *THE AUTHORITY* IS RECEIVING, PLEASE RESPOND SOONEST... THIS IS A TERMINAL SITUATION, I REPEAT A *TERMINAL SITUATION*...

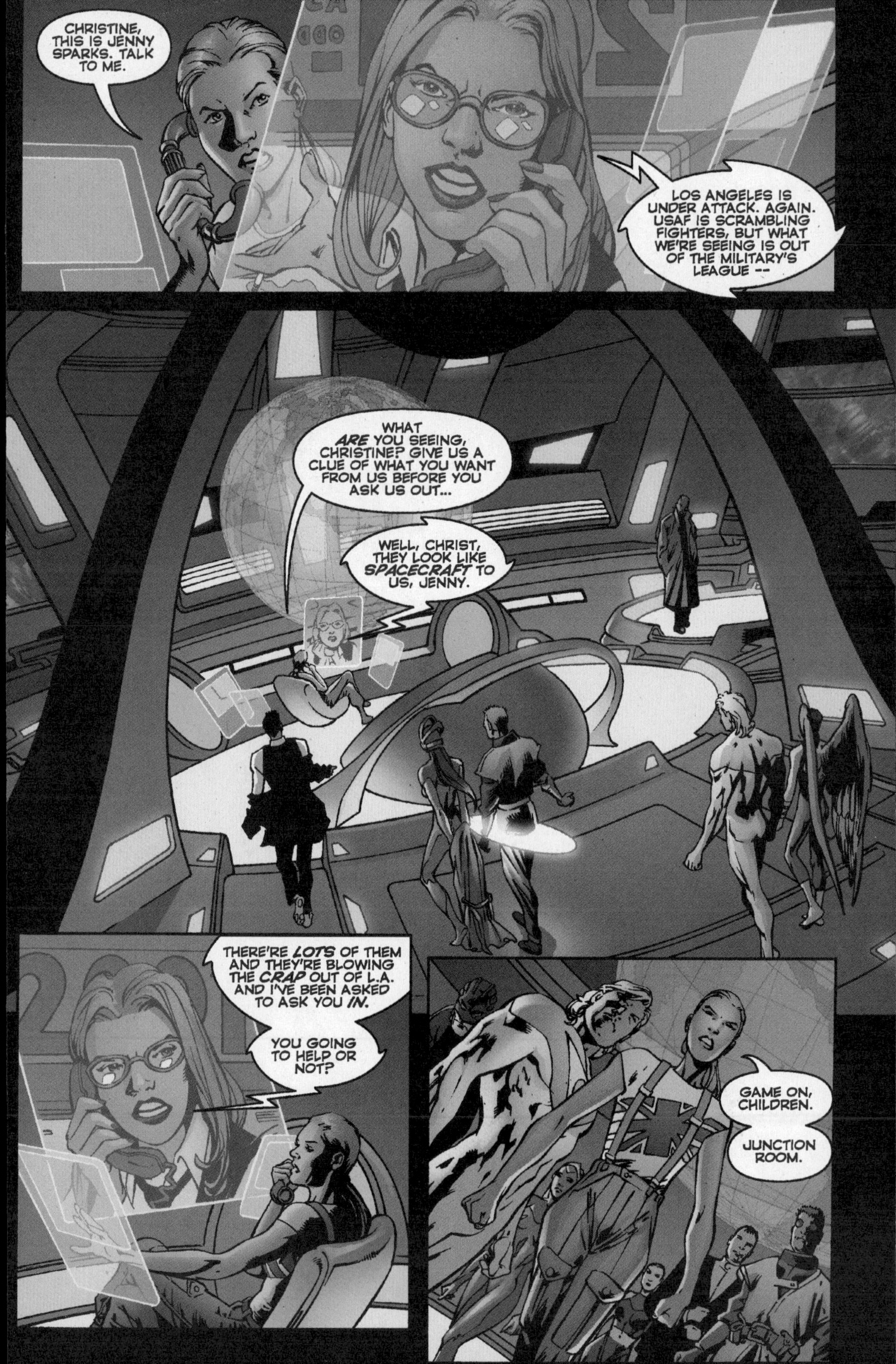
CHRISTINE, THIS IS JENNY SPARKS. TALK TO ME.
LOS ANGELES IS UNDER ATTACK. AGAIN. USAF IS SCRAMBLING FIGHTERS, BUT WHAT WE'RE SEEING IS OUT OF THE MILITARY'S LEAGUE --
WHAT *ARE* YOU SEEING, CHRISTINE? GIVE US A CLUE OF WHAT YOU WANT FROM US BEFORE YOU ASK US OUT...
WELL, CHRIST, THEY LOOK LIKE *SPACECRAFT* TO US, JENNY.
THERE'RE *LOTS* OF THEM AND THEY'RE BLOWING THE *CRAP* OUT OF L.A. AND I'VE BEEN ASKED TO ASK YOU *IN*.
YOU GOING TO HELP OR NOT?
GAME ON, CHILDREN.
JUNCTION ROOM.

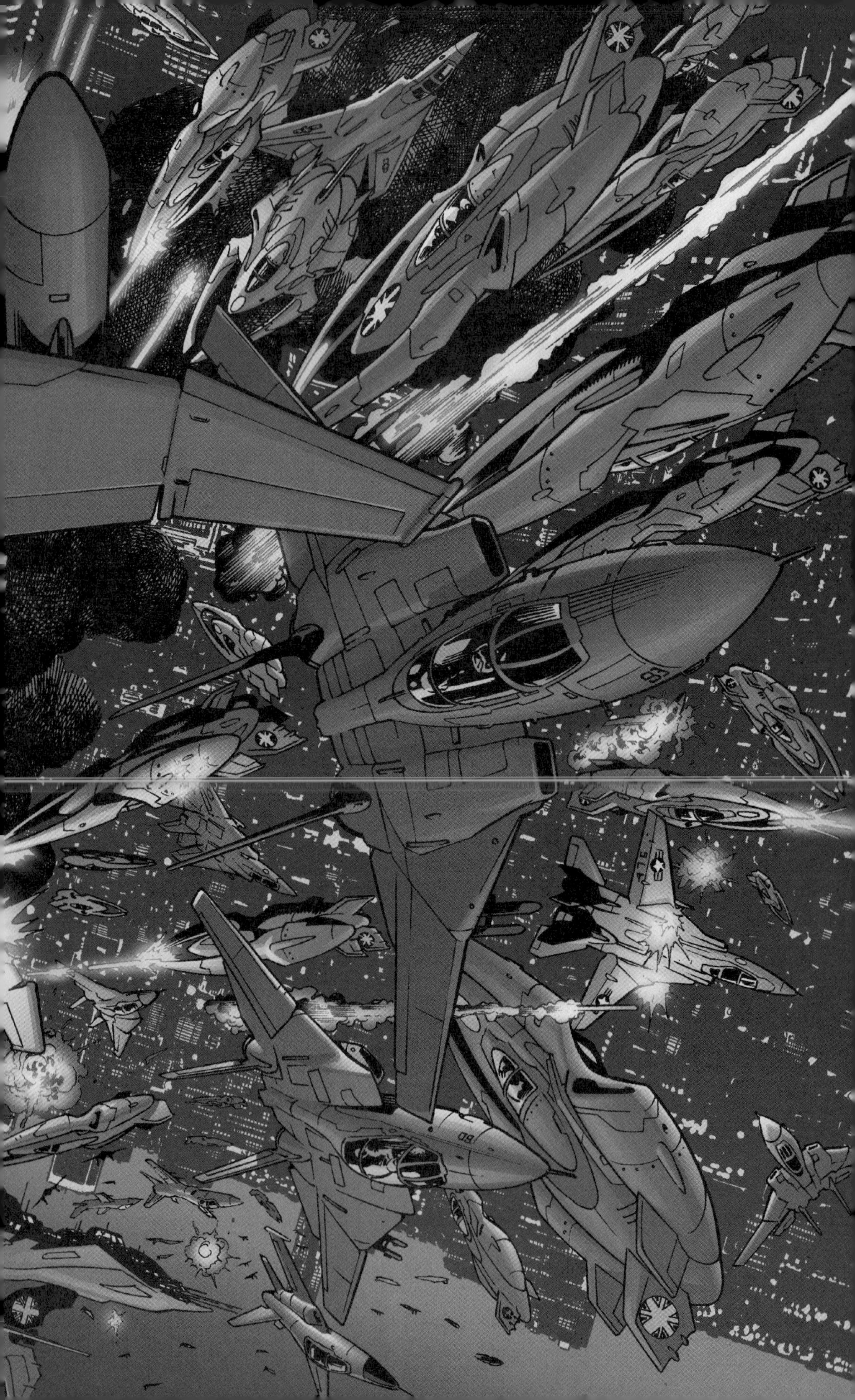

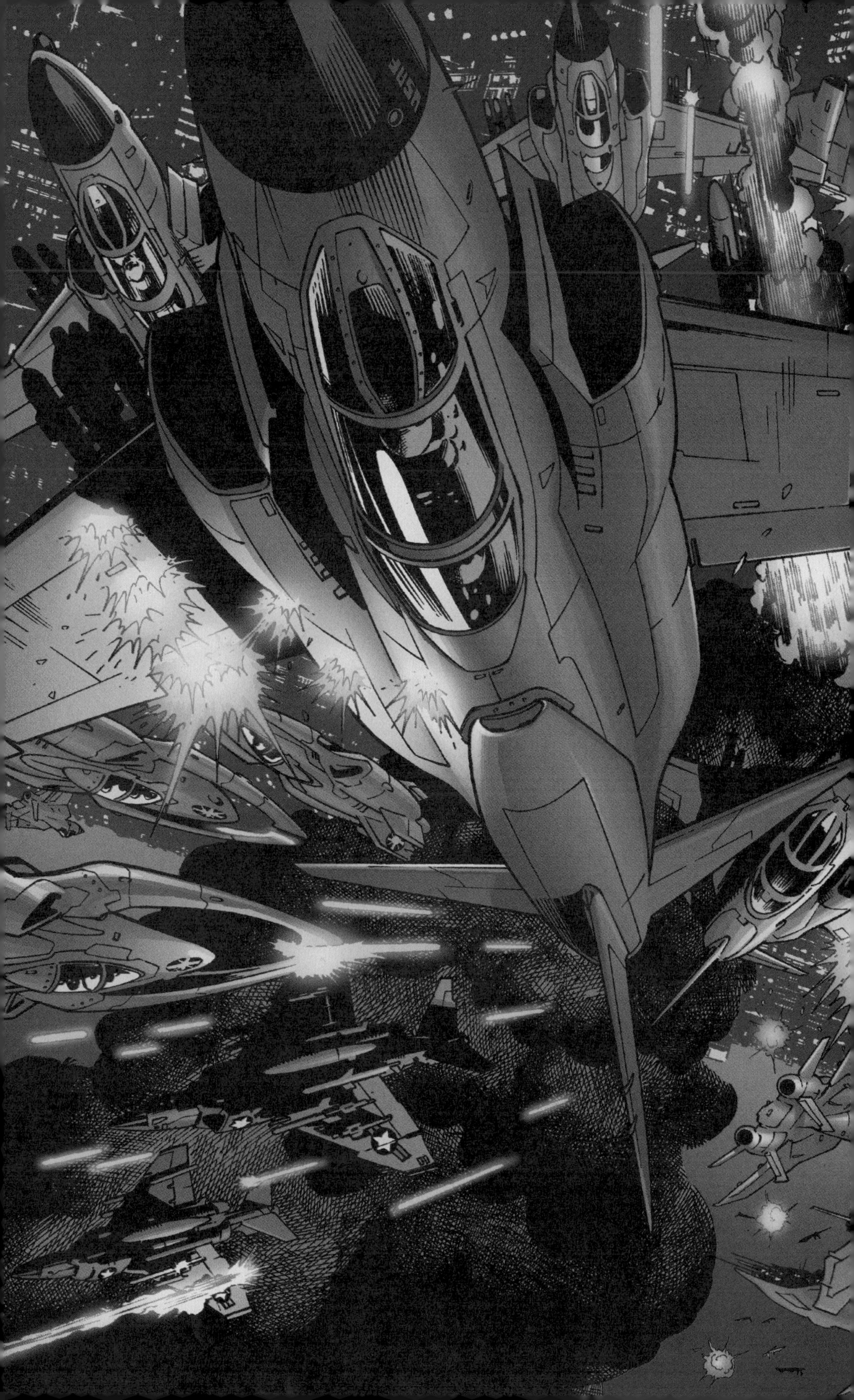

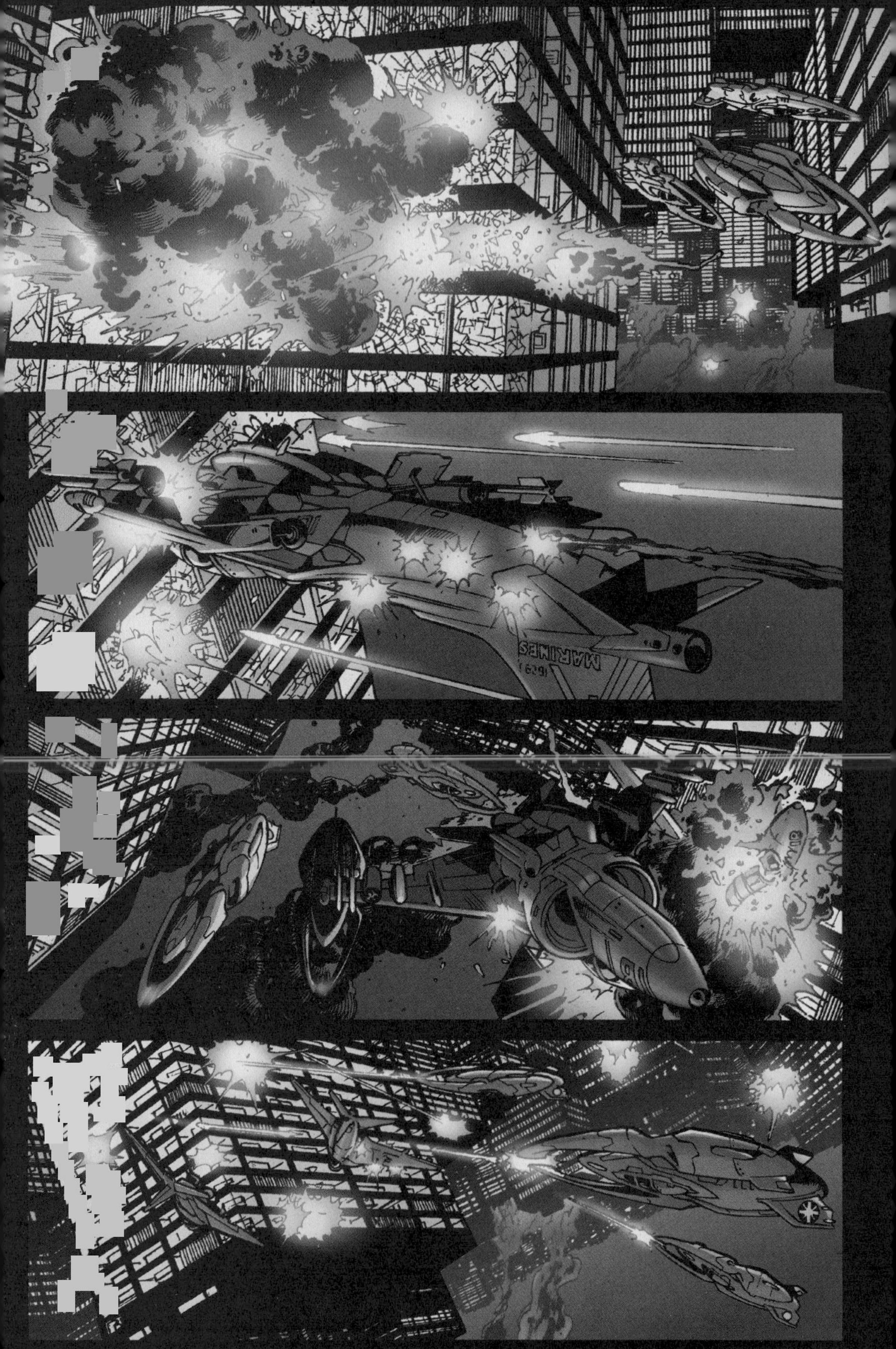
MARINES

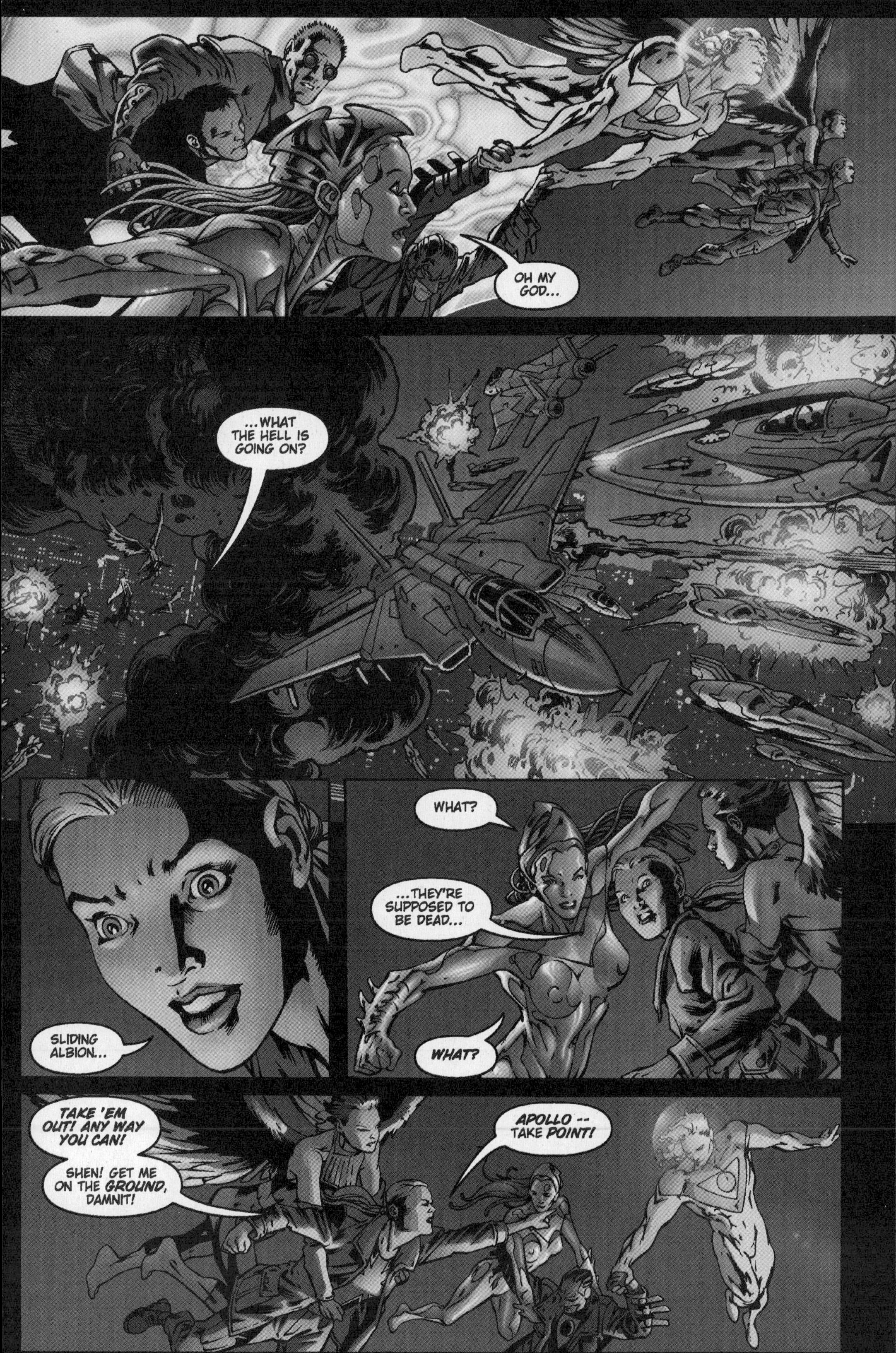
OH MY GOD...
...WHAT THE HELL IS GOING ON?
SLIDING ALBION...
WHAT?
...THEY'RE SUPPOSED TO BE DEAD...
WHAT?
TAKE 'EM OUT! ANY WAY YOU CAN!
SHEN! GET ME ON THE GROUND, DAMNIT!
APOLLO -- TAKE POINT!

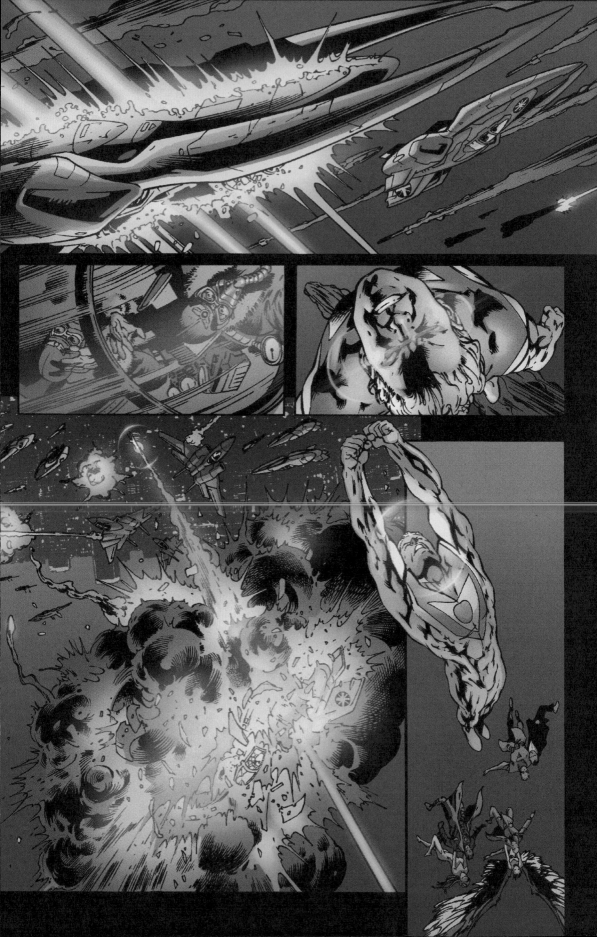

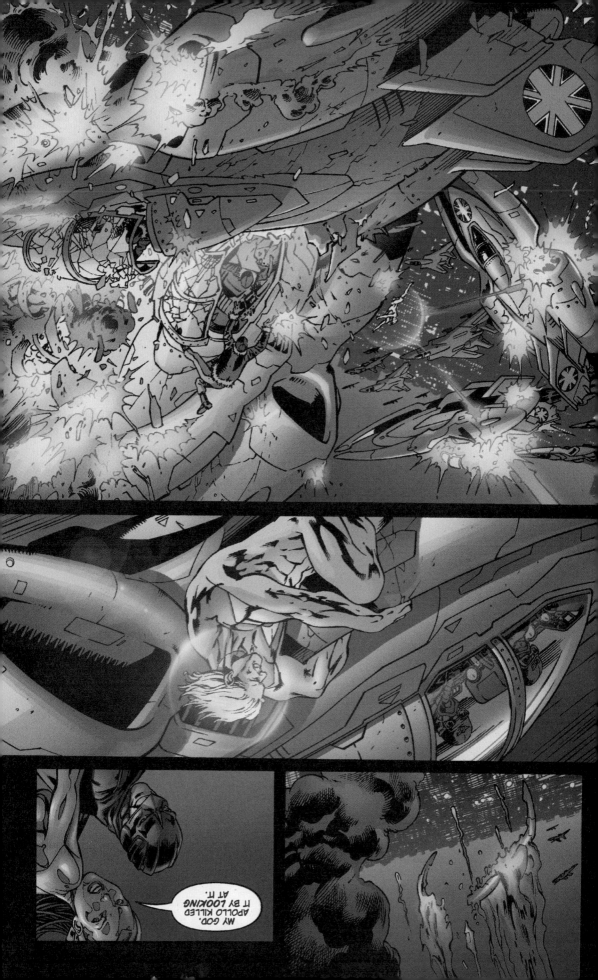

MY GOD. APOLLO KILLED IT BY LOOKING AT IT.

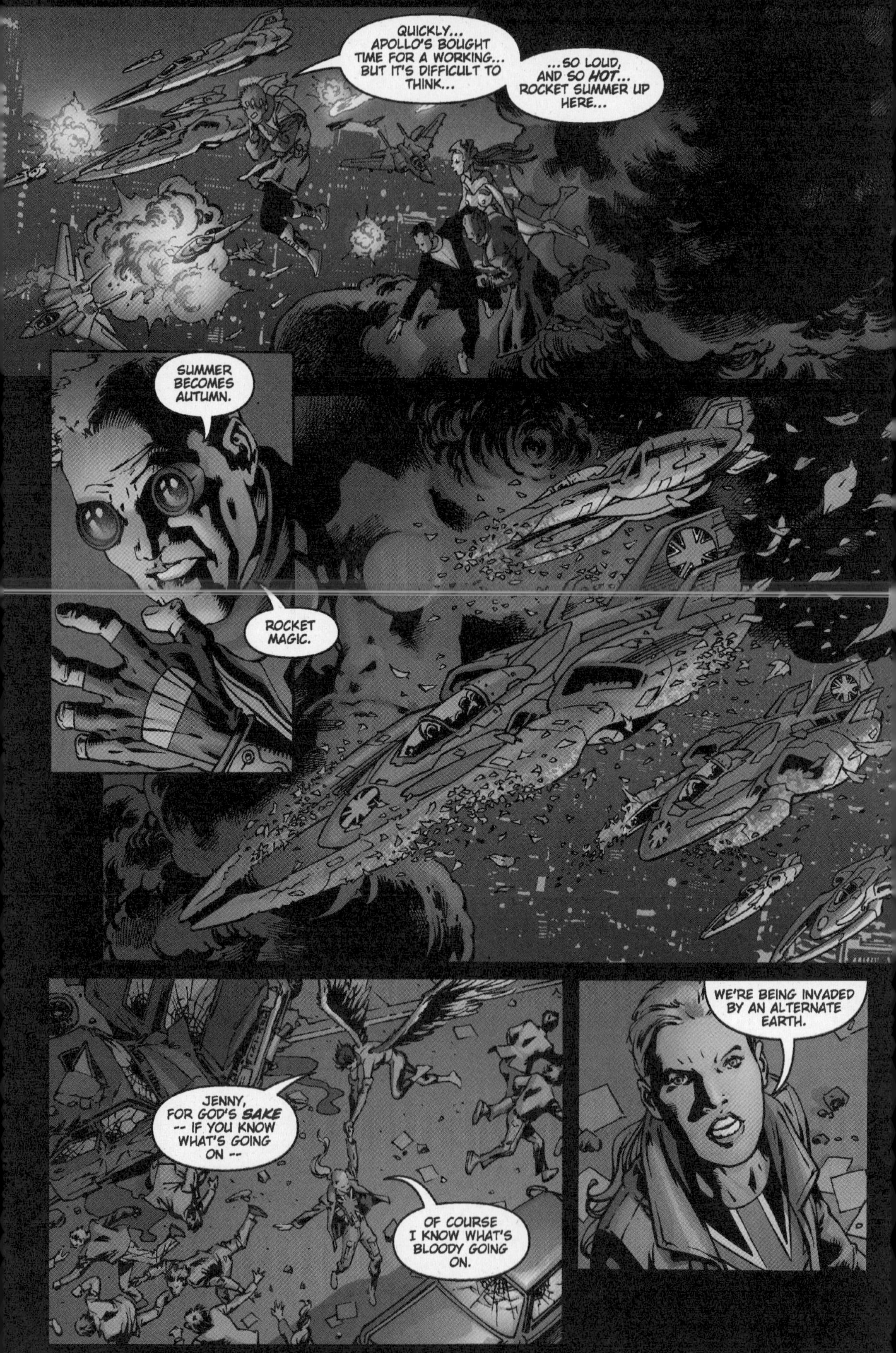
QUICKLY... APOLLO'S BOUGHT TIME FOR A WORKING... BUT IT'S DIFFICULT TO THINK...
...SO LOUD, AND SO *HOT*... ROCKET SUMMER UP HERE...
SUMMER BECOMES AUTUMN.
ROCKET MAGIC.
JENNY, FOR GOD'S *SAKE* -- IF YOU KNOW WHAT'S GOING ON --
OF COURSE I KNOW WHAT'S BLOODY GOING ON.
WE'RE BEING INVADED BY AN ALTERNATE EARTH.

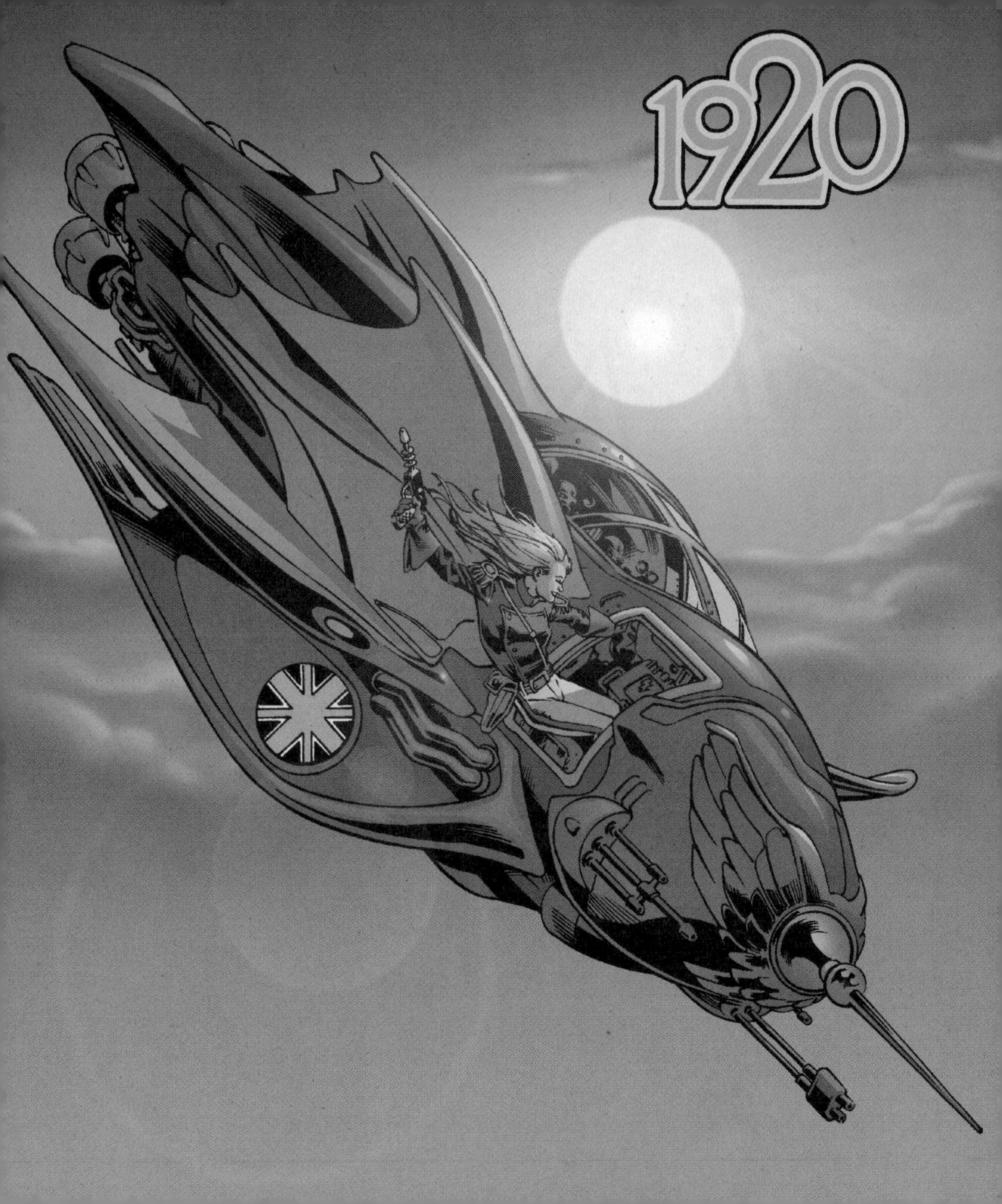
1920

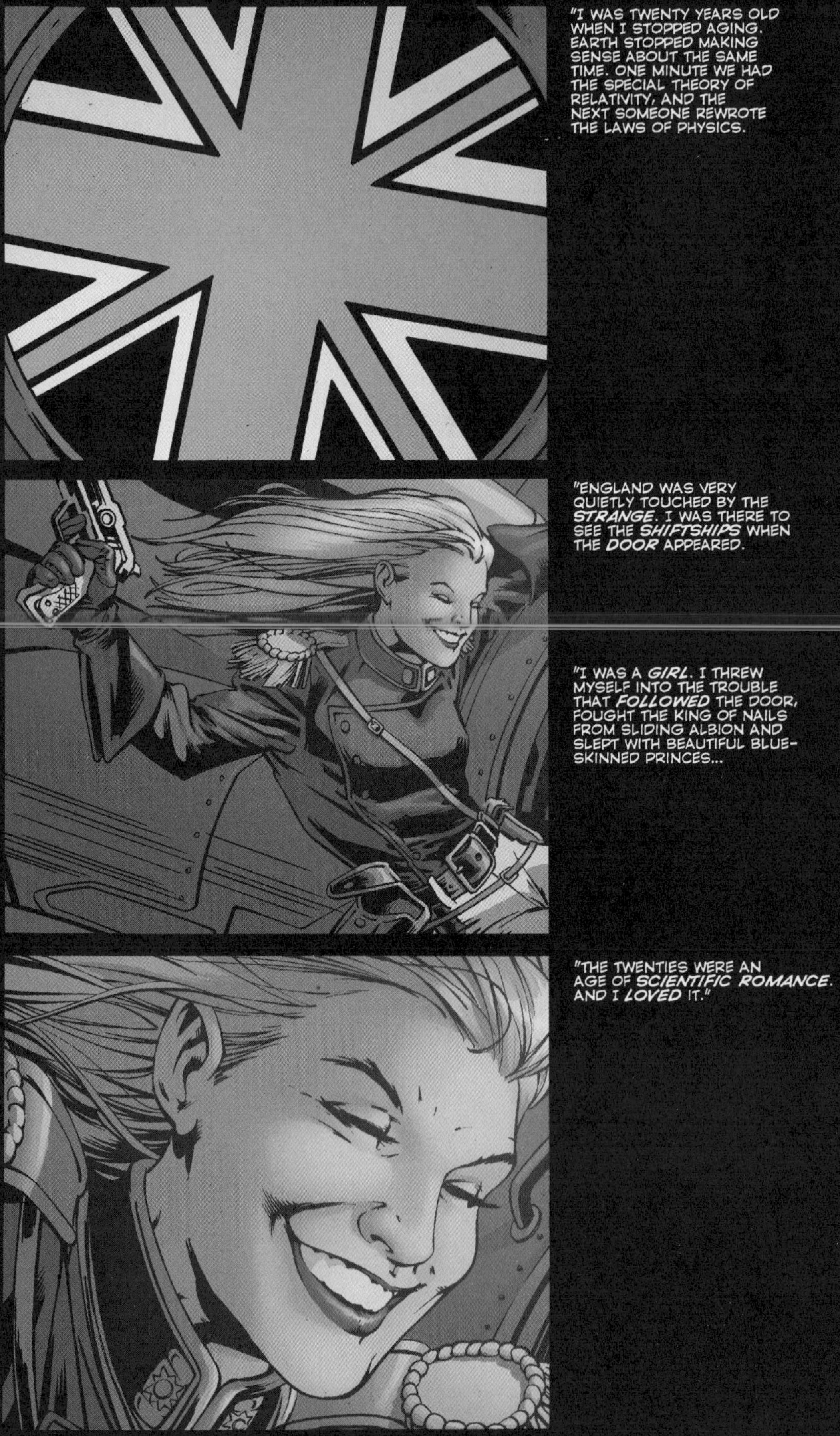
"I WAS TWENTY YEARS OLD WHEN I STOPPED AGING. EARTH STOPPED MAKING SENSE ABOUT THE SAME TIME. ONE MINUTE WE HAD THE SPECIAL THEORY OF RELATIVITY, AND THE NEXT SOMEONE REWROTE THE LAWS OF PHYSICS.
"ENGLAND WAS VERY QUIETLY TOUCHED BY THE *STRANGE*. I WAS THERE TO SEE THE *SHIFTSHIPS* WHEN THE *DOOR* APPEARED.
"I WAS A *GIRL*. I THREW MYSELF INTO THE TROUBLE THAT *FOLLOWED* THE DOOR, FOUGHT THE KING OF NAILS FROM SLIDING ALBION AND SLEPT WITH BEAUTIFUL BLUE-SKINNED PRINCES...
"THE TWENTIES WERE AN AGE OF *SCIENTIFIC ROMANCE*. AND I *LOVED* IT."

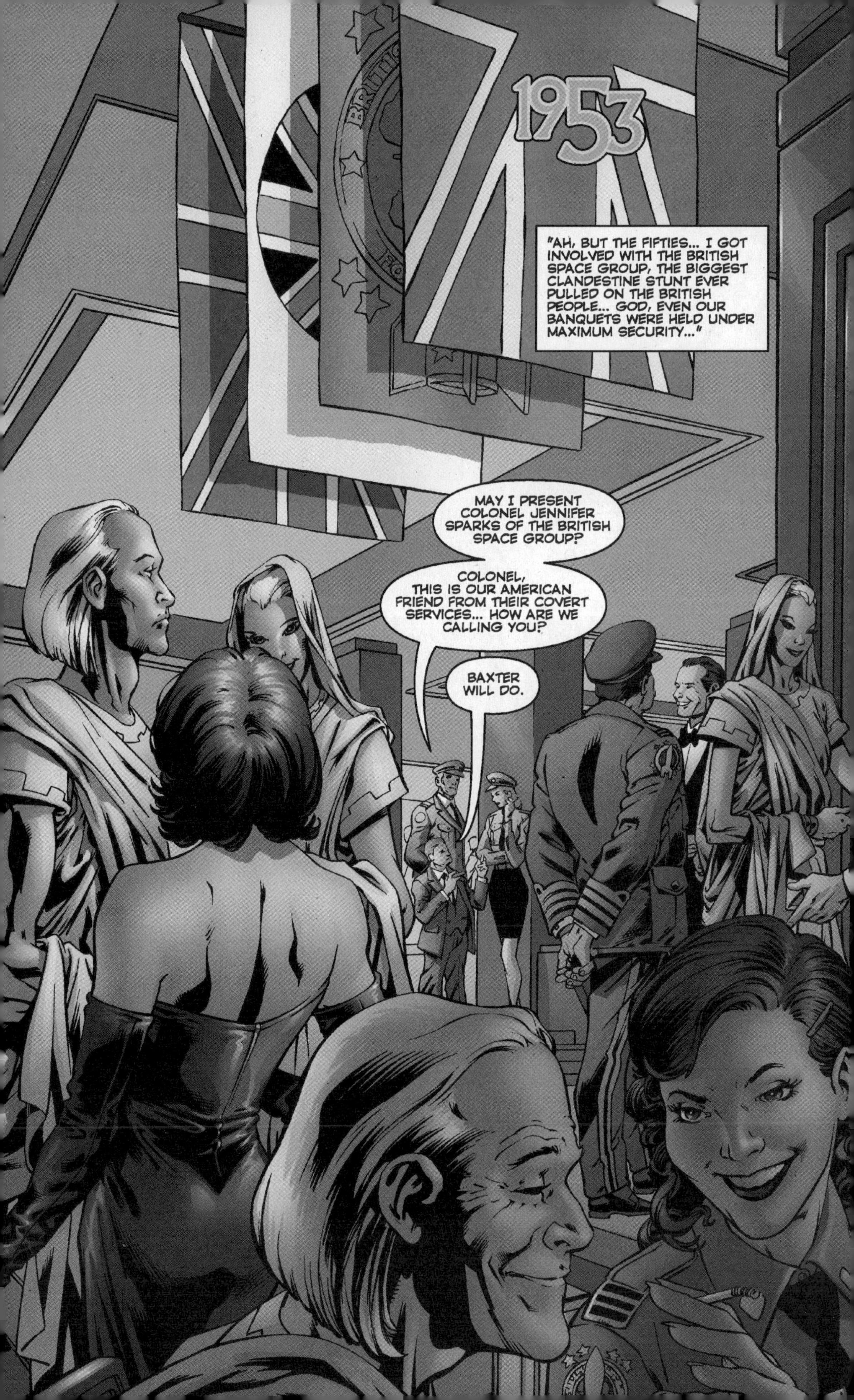
1953
"AH, BUT THE FIFTIES... I GOT INVOLVED WITH THE BRITISH SPACE GROUP, THE BIGGEST CLANDESTINE STUNT EVER PULLED ON THE BRITISH PEOPLE... GOD, EVEN OUR BANQUETS WERE HELD UNDER MAXIMUM SECURITY..."
MAY I PRESENT COLONEL JENNIFER SPARKS OF THE BRITISH SPACE GROUP?
COLONEL, THIS IS OUR AMERICAN FRIEND FROM THEIR COVERT SERVICES... HOW ARE WE CALLING YOU?
BAXTER WILL DO.

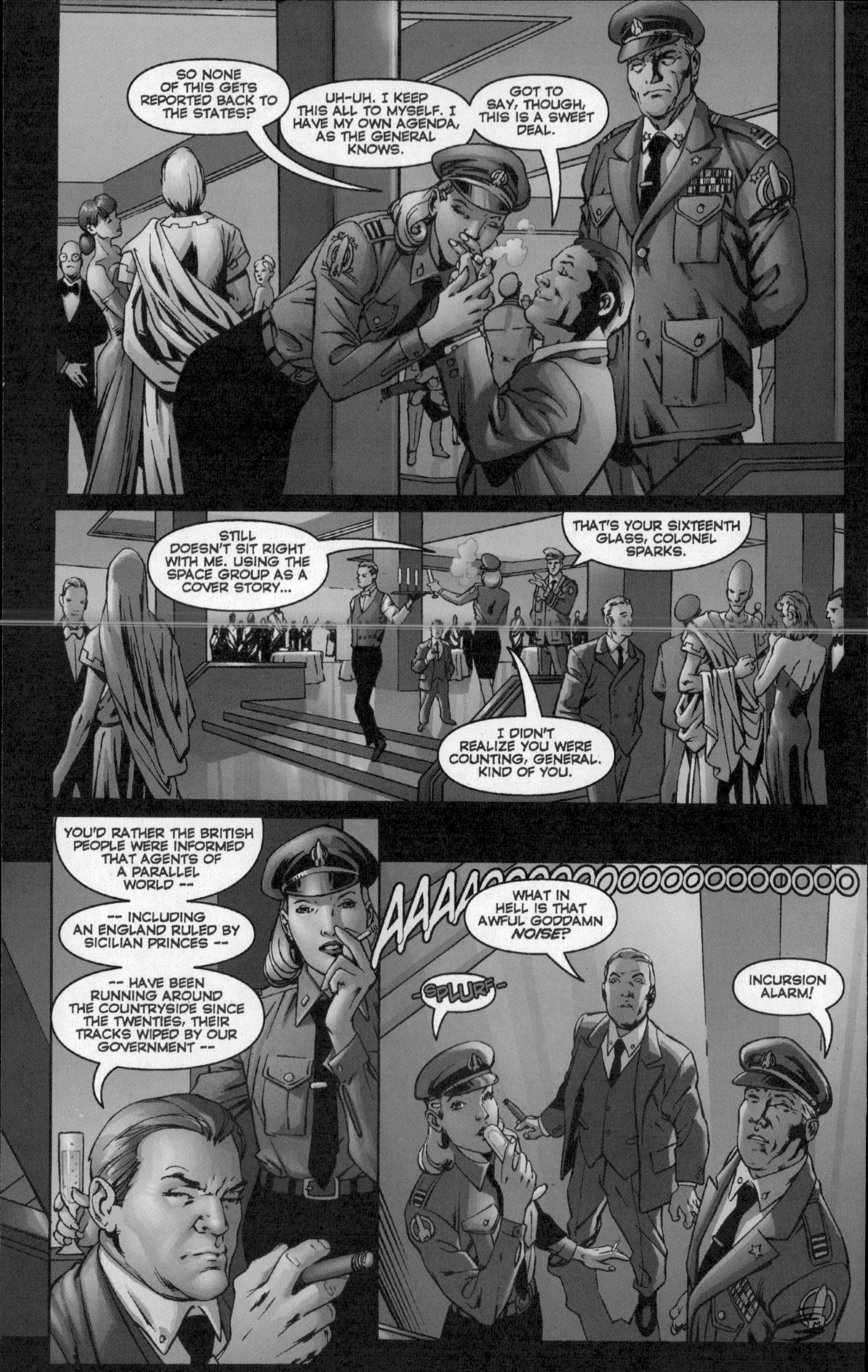
SO NONE OF THIS GETS REPORTED BACK TO THE STATES?
UH-UH. I KEEP THIS ALL TO MYSELF. I HAVE MY OWN AGENDA, AS THE GENERAL KNOWS.
GOT TO SAY, THOUGH, THIS IS A SWEET DEAL.
STILL DOESN'T SIT RIGHT WITH ME. USING THE SPACE GROUP AS A COVER STORY...
THAT'S YOUR SIXTEENTH GLASS, COLONEL SPARKS.
I DIDN'T REALIZE YOU WERE COUNTING, GENERAL. KIND OF YOU.
YOU'D RATHER THE BRITISH PEOPLE WERE INFORMED THAT AGENTS OF A PARALLEL WORLD --
-- INCLUDING AN ENGLAND RULED BY SICILIAN PRINCES --
-- HAVE BEEN RUNNING AROUND THE COUNTRYSIDE SINCE THE TWENTIES, THEIR TRACKS WIPED BY OUR GOVERNMENT --
AAAAOOOOOOOOOOOOOOOOOO
WHAT IN HELL IS THAT AWFUL GODDAMN *NOISE?*
-SPLURF-
INCURSION ALARM!

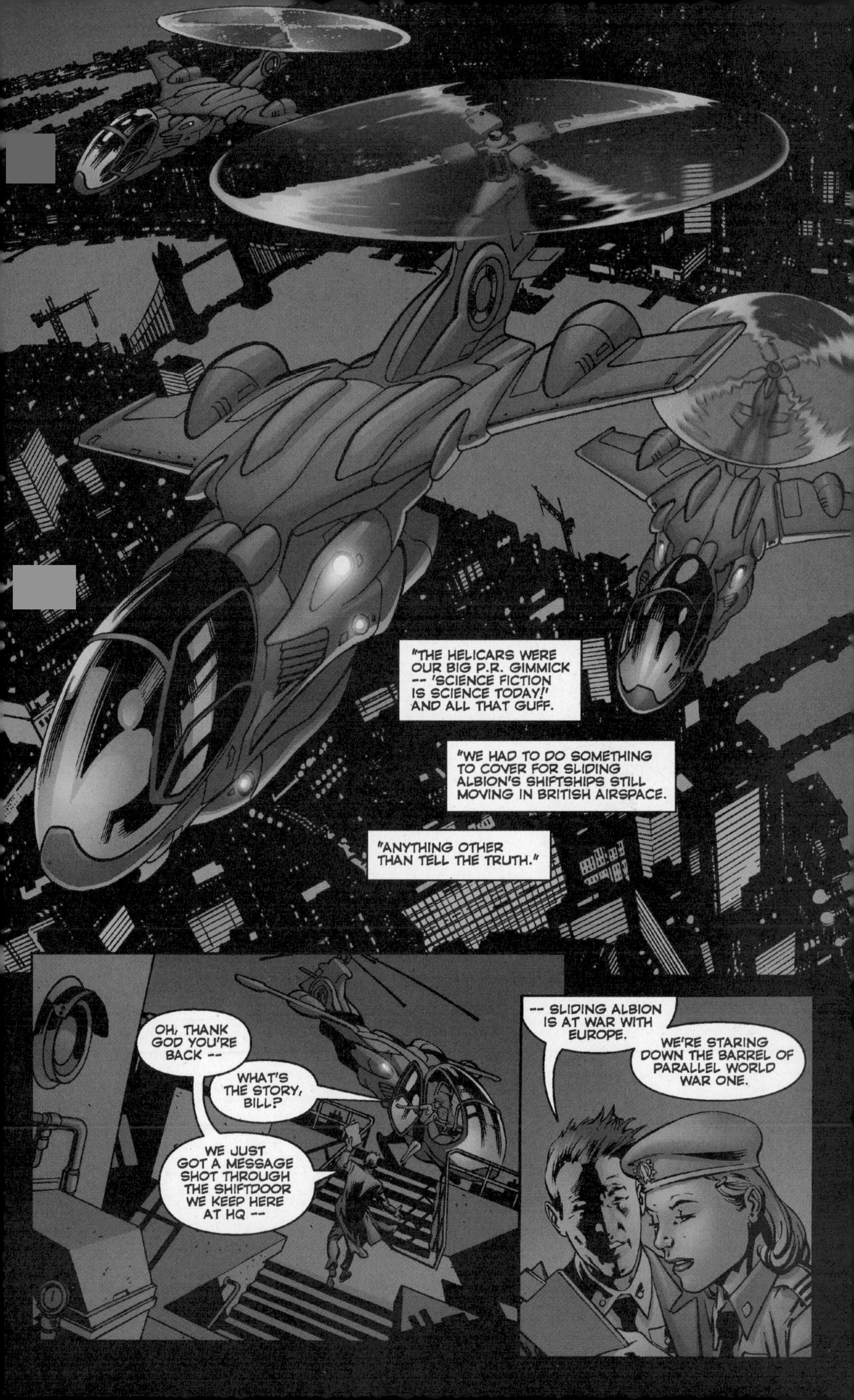
"THE HELICARS WERE OUR BIG P.R. GIMMICK -- 'SCIENCE FICTION IS SCIENCE TODAY!' AND ALL THAT GUFF.
"WE HAD TO DO SOMETHING TO COVER FOR SLIDING ALBION'S SHIFTSHIPS STILL MOVING IN BRITISH AIRSPACE.
"ANYTHING OTHER THAN TELL THE TRUTH."
OH, THANK GOD YOU'RE BACK --
WHAT'S THE STORY, BILL?
WE JUST GOT A MESSAGE SHOT THROUGH THE SHIFTDOOR WE KEEP HERE AT HQ --
-- SLIDING ALBION IS AT WAR WITH EUROPE.
WE'RE STARING DOWN THE BARREL OF PARALLEL WORLD WAR ONE.

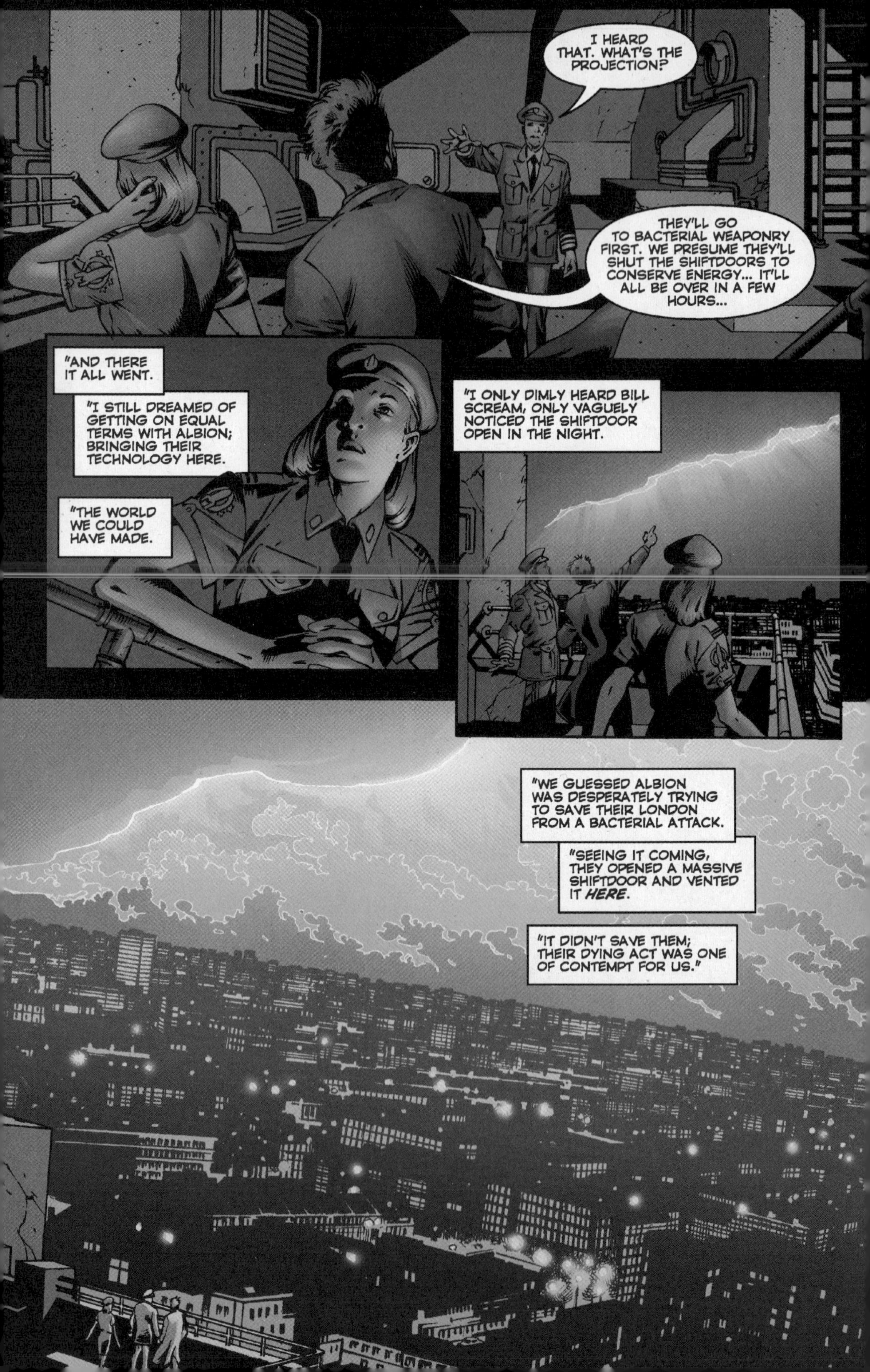
I HEARD THAT. WHAT'S THE PROJECTION?
THEY'LL GO TO BACTERIAL WEAPONRY FIRST. WE PRESUME THEY'LL SHUT THE SHIFTDOORS TO CONSERVE ENERGY... IT'LL ALL BE OVER IN A FEW HOURS...
"AND THERE IT ALL WENT.
"I STILL DREAMED OF GETTING ON EQUAL TERMS WITH ALBION; BRINGING THEIR TECHNOLOGY HERE.
"THE WORLD WE COULD HAVE MADE.
"I ONLY DIMLY HEARD BILL SCREAM, ONLY VAGUELY NOTICED THE SHIFTDOOR OPEN IN THE NIGHT.
"WE GUESSED ALBION WAS DESPERATELY TRYING TO SAVE THEIR LONDON FROM A BACTERIAL ATTACK.
"SEEING IT COMING, THEY OPENED A MASSIVE SHIFTDOOR AND VENTED IT *HERE*.
"IT DIDN'T SAVE THEM; THEIR DYING ACT WAS ONE OF CONTEMPT FOR US."

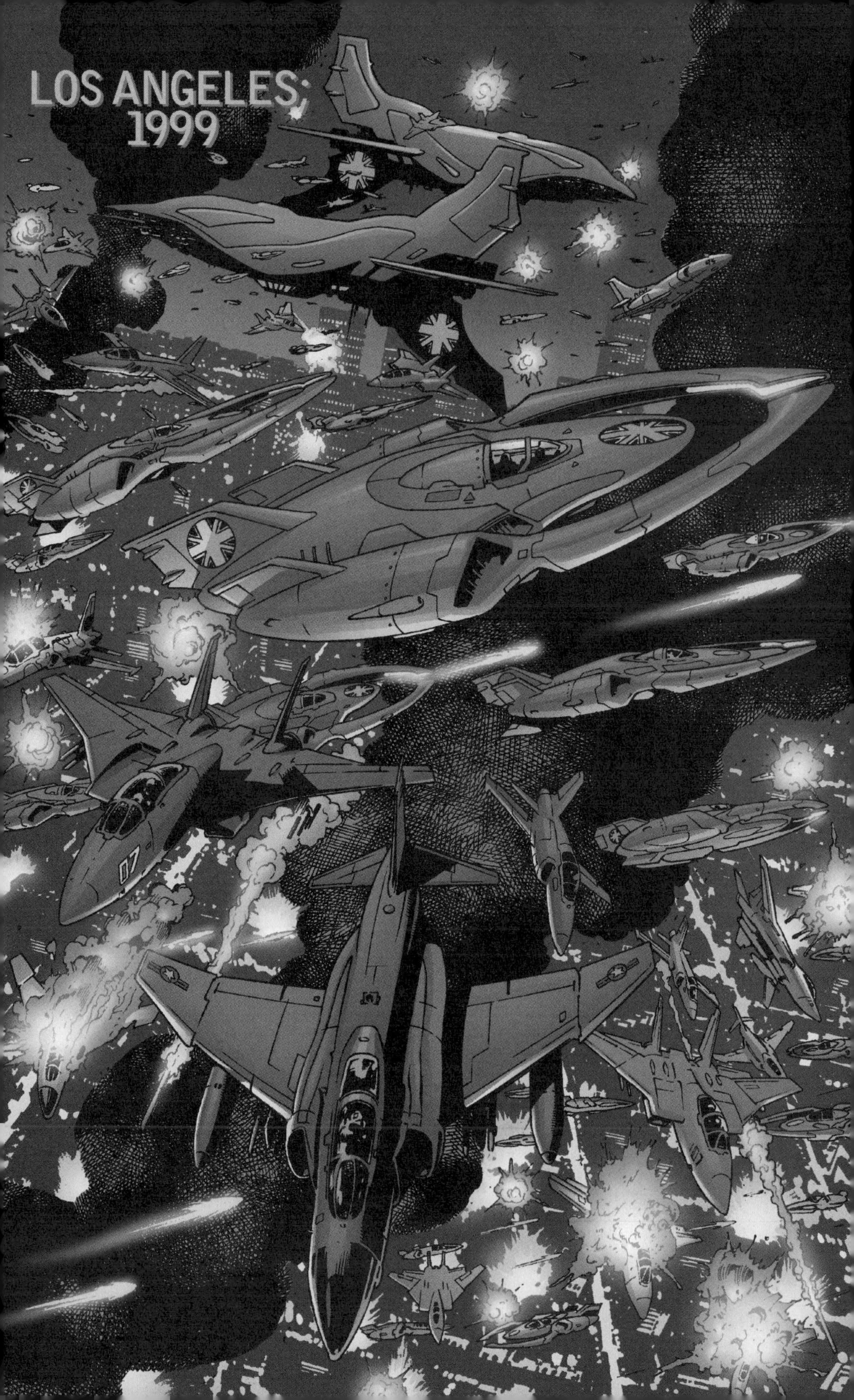
LOS ANGELES;
1999

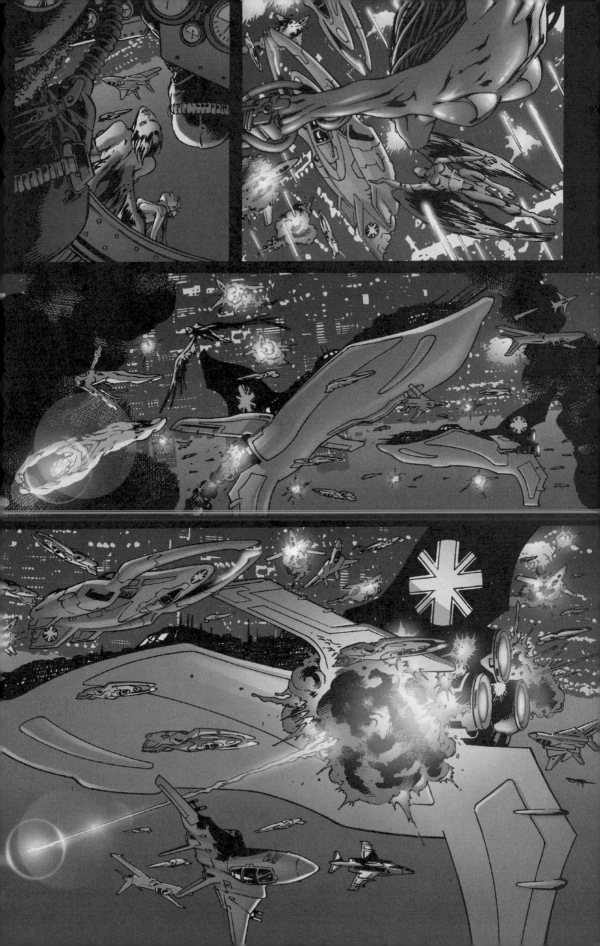

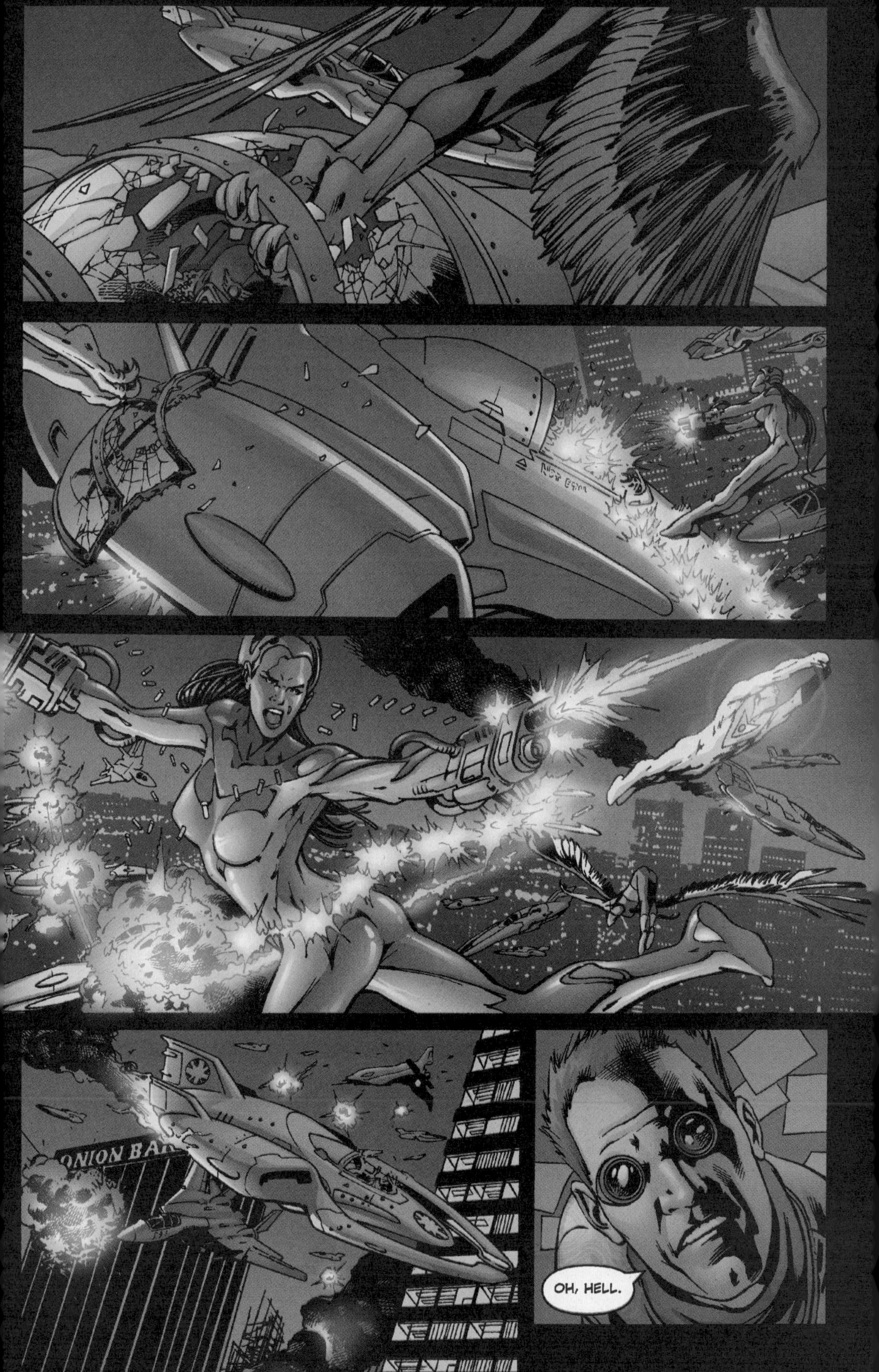
ONION BA
OH, HELL.

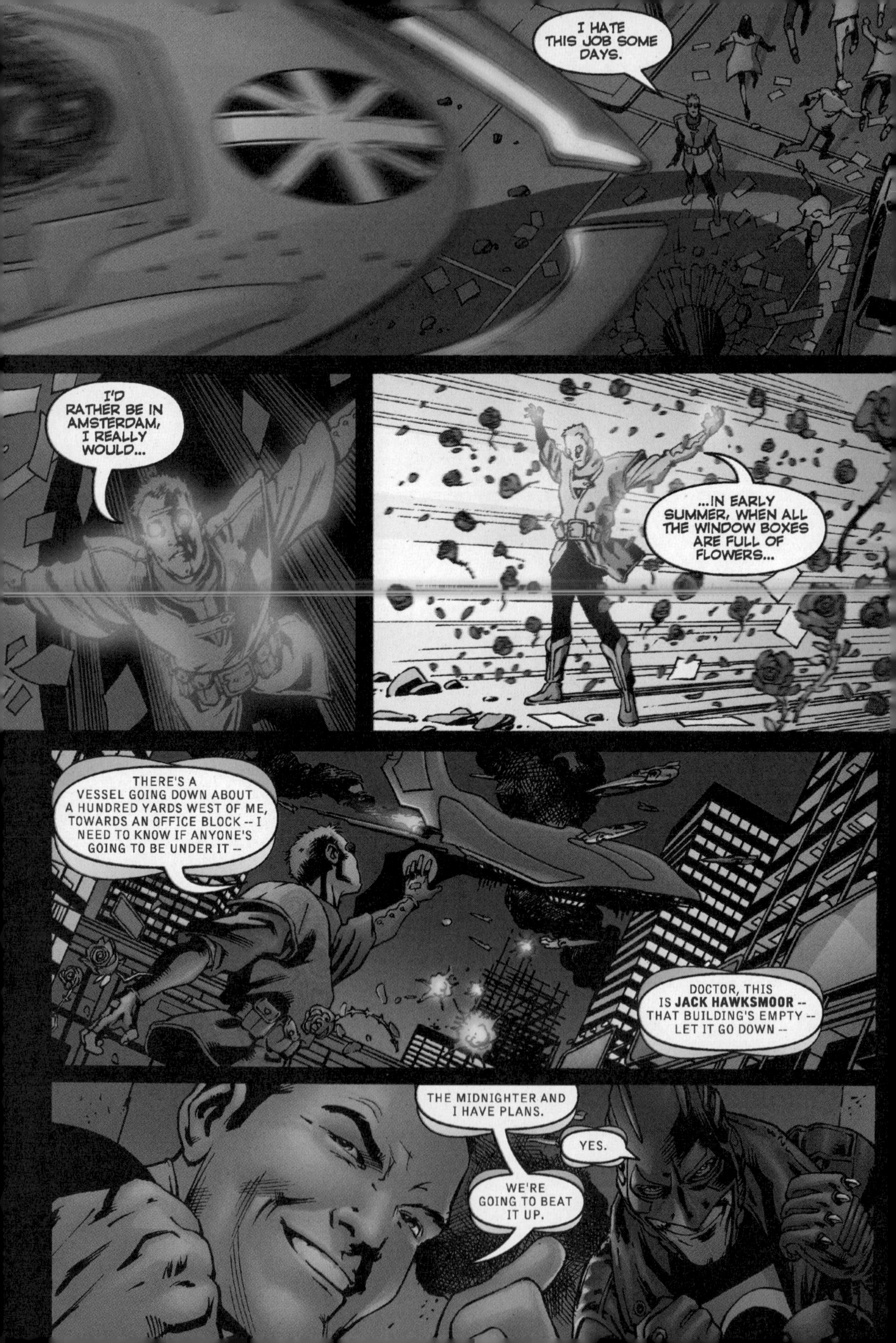
I HATE THIS JOB SOME DAYS.
I'D RATHER BE IN AMSTERDAM, I REALLY WOULD...
...IN EARLY SUMMER, WHEN ALL THE WINDOW BOXES ARE FULL OF FLOWERS...
THERE'S A VESSEL GOING DOWN ABOUT A HUNDRED YARDS WEST OF ME, TOWARDS AN OFFICE BLOCK -- I NEED TO KNOW IF ANYONE'S GOING TO BE UNDER IT --
DOCTOR, THIS IS **JACK HAWKSMOOR** -- THAT BUILDING'S EMPTY -- LET IT GO DOWN --
THE MIDNIGHTER AND I HAVE PLANS.
YES.
WE'RE GOING TO BEAT IT UP.

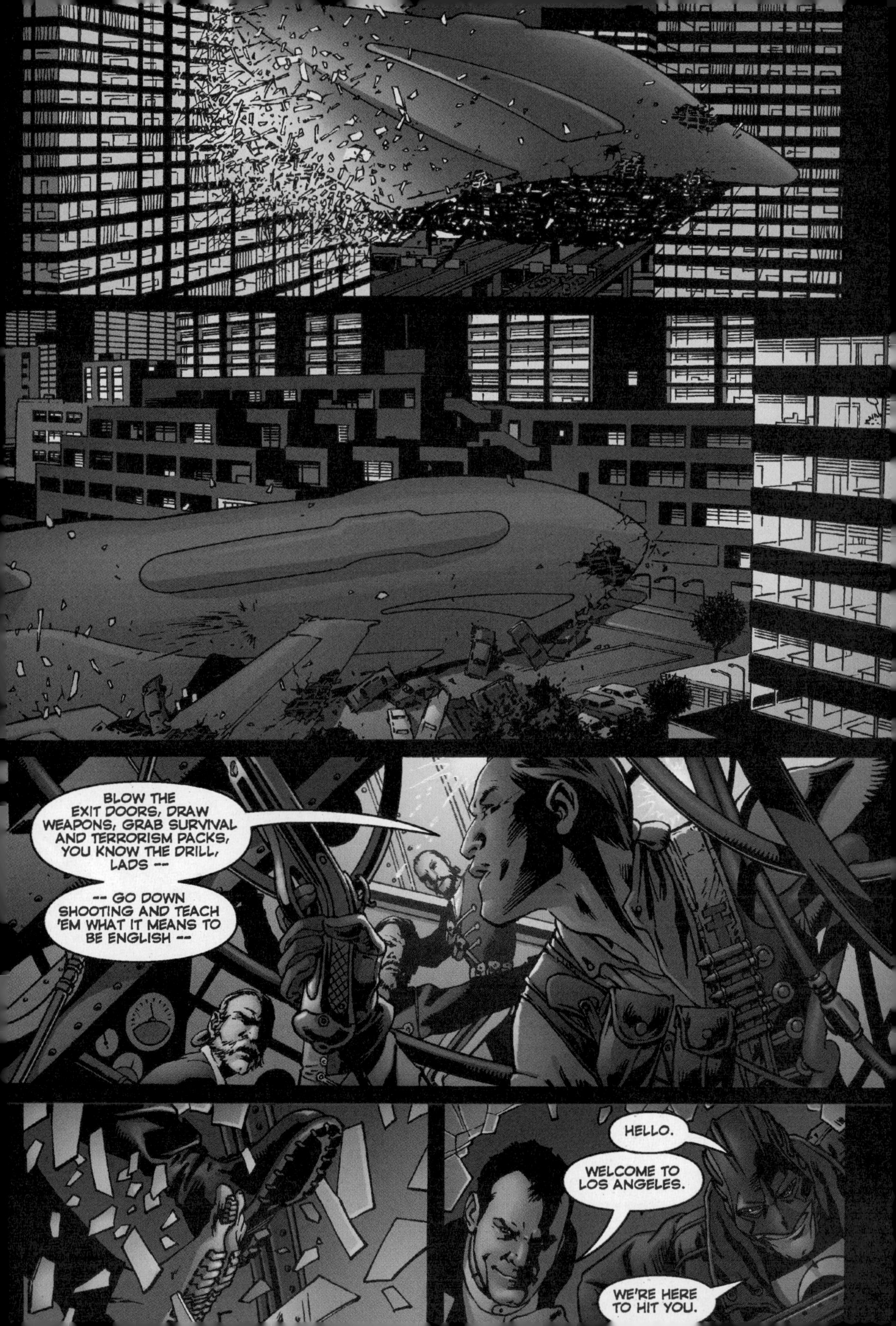
BLOW THE EXIT DOORS, DRAW WEAPONS, GRAB SURVIVAL AND TERRORISM PACKS, YOU KNOW THE DRILL, LADS --
-- GO DOWN SHOOTING AND TEACH 'EM WHAT IT MEANS TO BE ENGLISH --
HELLO.
WELCOME TO LOS ANGELES.
WE'RE HERE TO HIT YOU.

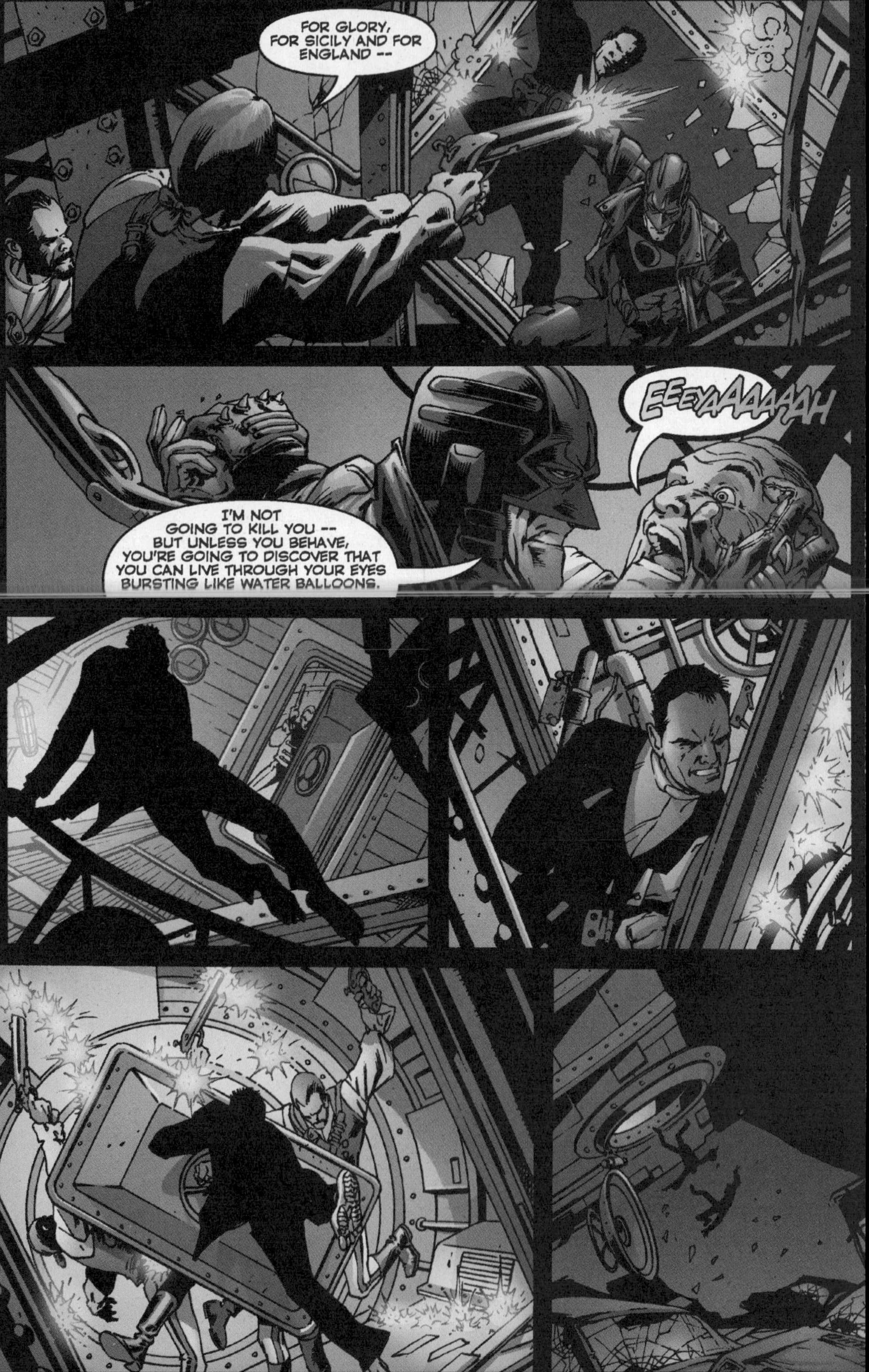
FOR GLORY, FOR SICILY AND FOR ENGLAND --
EEEYAAAAAAH
I'M NOT GOING TO KILL YOU -- BUT UNLESS YOU BEHAVE, YOU'RE GOING TO DISCOVER THAT YOU CAN LIVE THROUGH YOUR EYES BURSTING LIKE WATER BALLOONS.

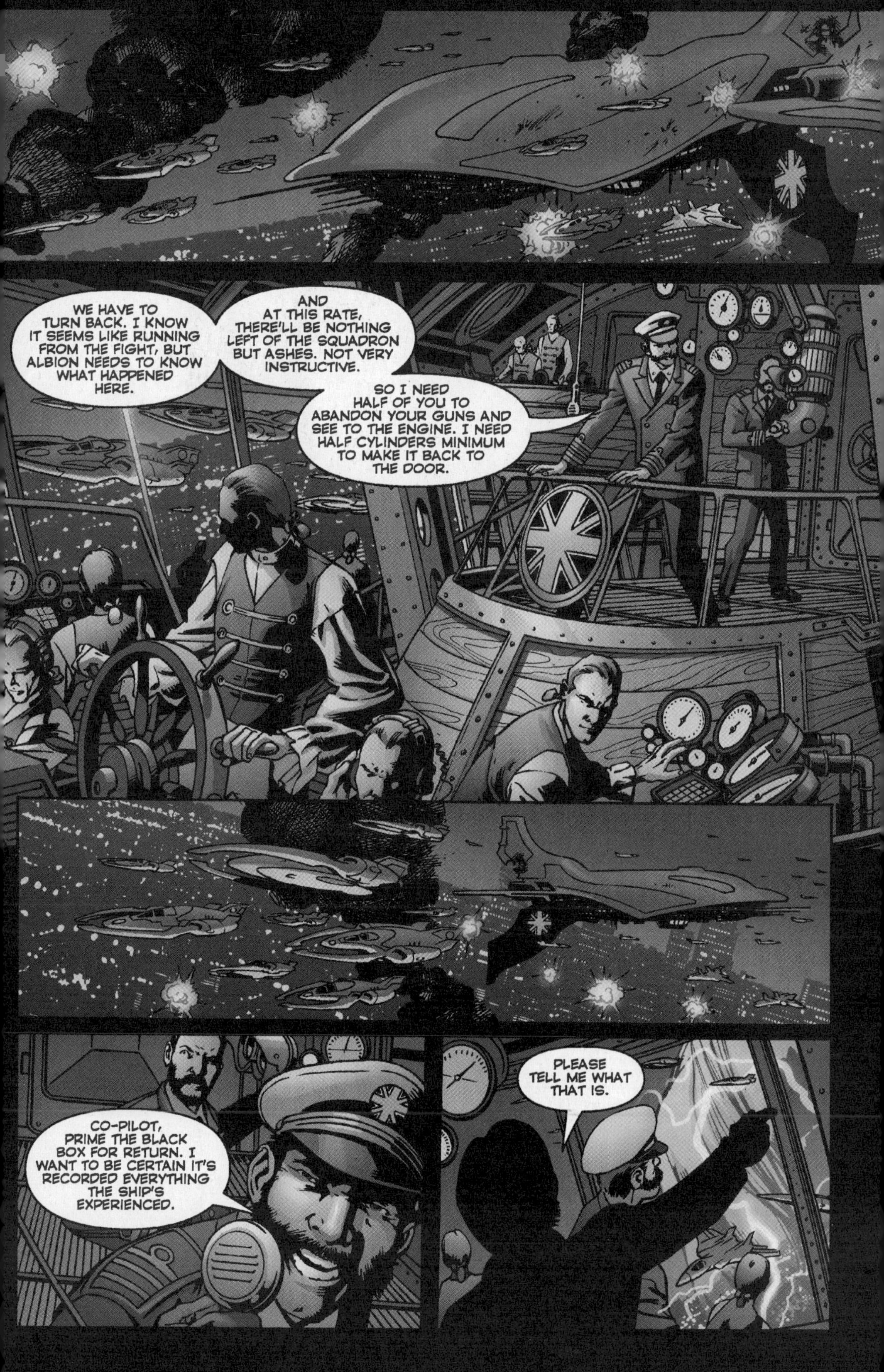
WE HAVE TO TURN BACK. I KNOW IT SEEMS LIKE RUNNING FROM THE FIGHT, BUT ALBION NEEDS TO KNOW WHAT HAPPENED HERE.
AND AT THIS RATE, THERE'LL BE NOTHING LEFT OF THE SQUADRON BUT ASHES. NOT VERY INSTRUCTIVE.
SO I NEED HALF OF YOU TO ABANDON YOUR GUNS AND SEE TO THE ENGINE. I NEED HALF CYLINDERS MINIMUM TO MAKE IT BACK TO THE DOOR.
CO-PILOT, PRIME THE BLACK BOX FOR RETURN. I WANT TO BE CERTAIN IT'S RECORDED EVERYTHING THE SHIP'S EXPERIENCED.
PLEASE TELL ME WHAT THAT IS.

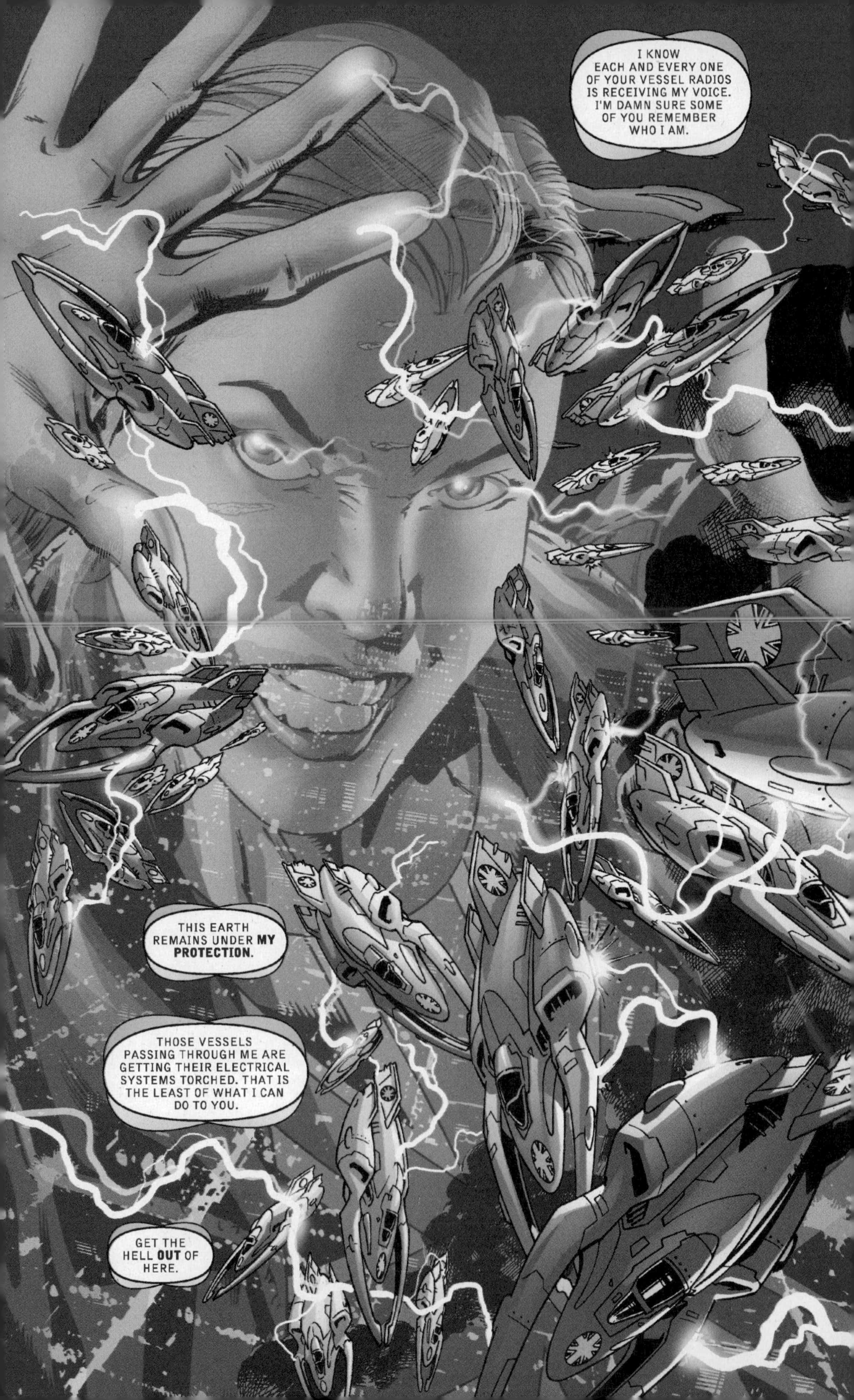

I KNOW EACH AND EVERY ONE OF YOUR VESSEL RADIOS IS RECEIVING MY VOICE. I'M DAMN SURE SOME OF YOU REMEMBER WHO I AM.
THIS EARTH REMAINS UNDER **MY PROTECTION**.
THOSE VESSELS PASSING THROUGH ME ARE GETTING THEIR ELECTRICAL SYSTEMS TORCHED. THAT IS THE LEAST OF WHAT I CAN DO TO YOU.
GET THE HELL **OUT** OF HERE.

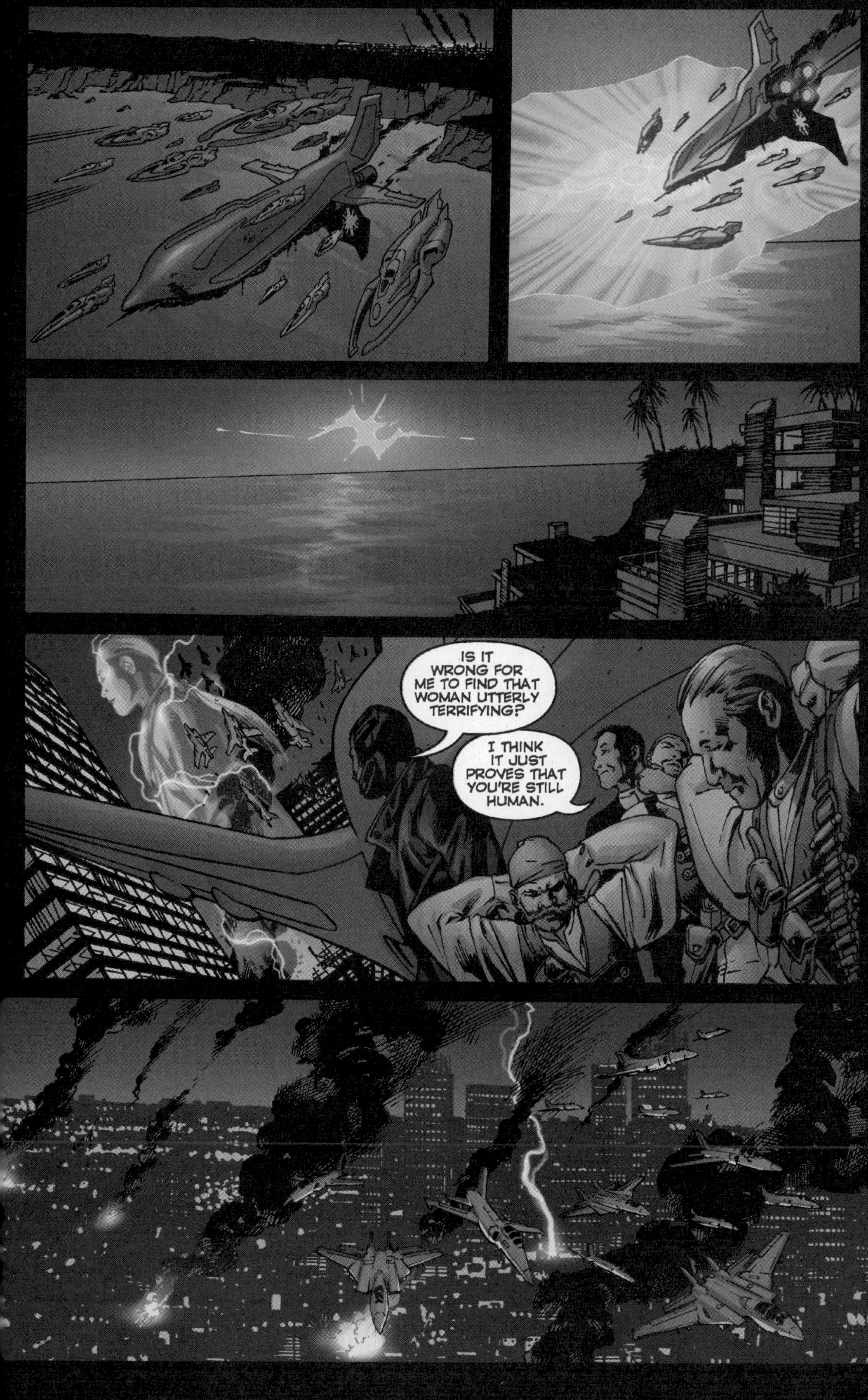
IS IT WRONG FOR ME TO FIND THAT WOMAN UTTERLY TERRIFYING?
I THINK IT JUST PROVES THAT YOU'RE STILL HUMAN.

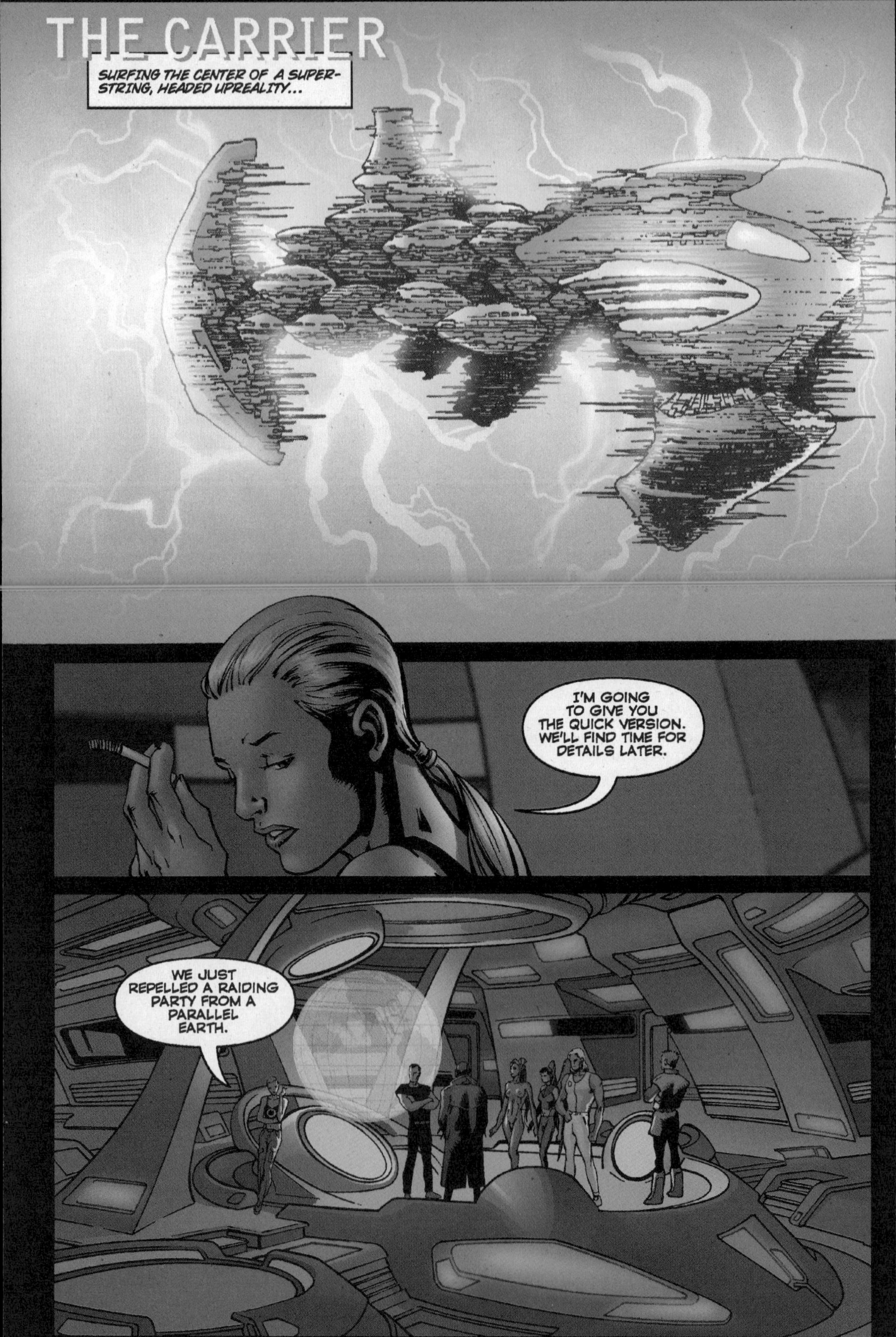
THE CARRIER
SURFING THE CENTER OF A SUPER-STRING, HEADED UPREALITY...
I'M GOING TO GIVE YOU THE QUICK VERSION. WE'LL FIND TIME FOR DETAILS LATER.
WE JUST REPELLED A RAIDING PARTY FROM A PARALLEL EARTH.

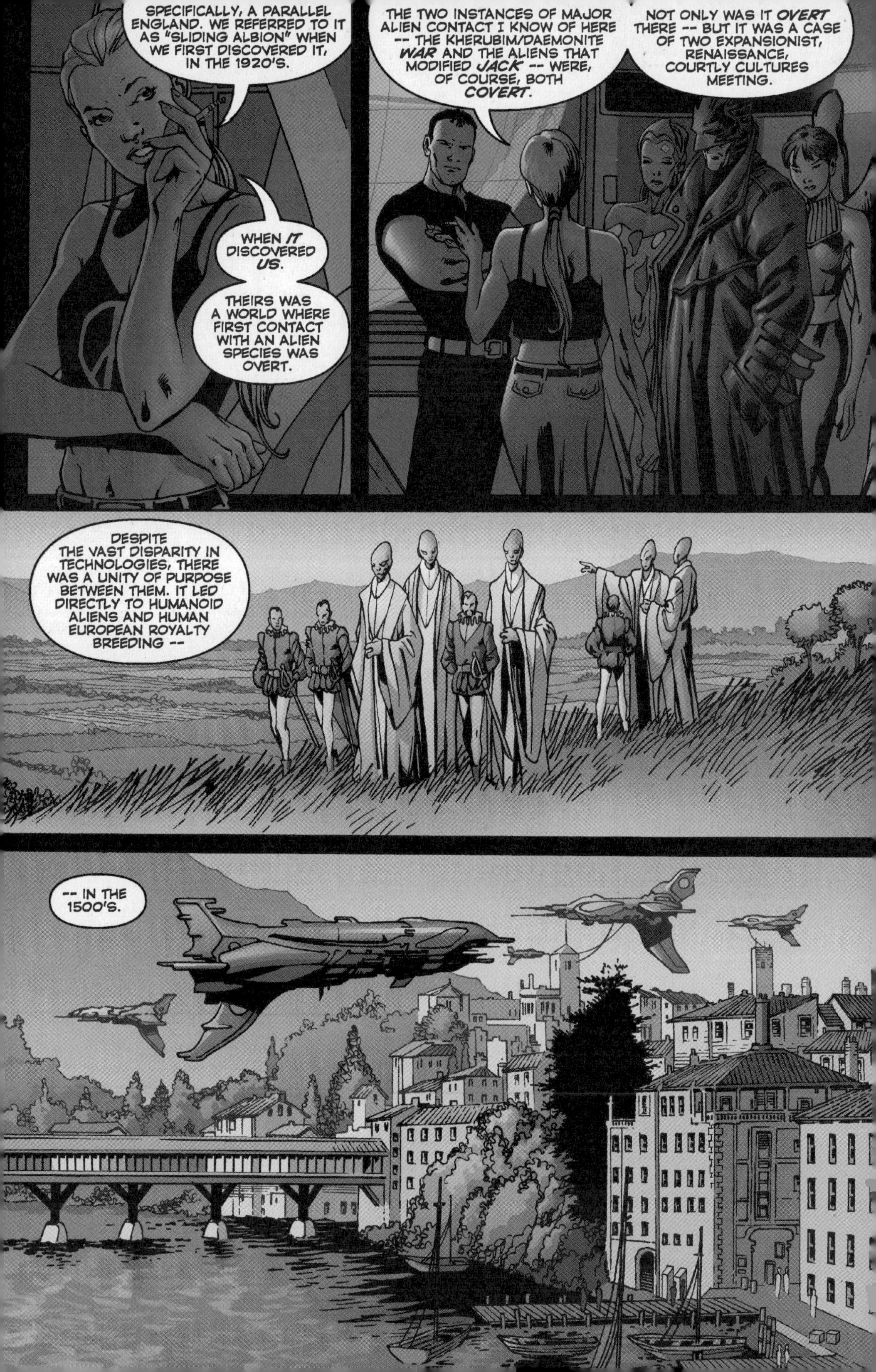
SPECIFICALLY, A PARALLEL ENGLAND. WE REFERRED TO IT AS "SLIDING ALBION" WHEN WE FIRST DISCOVERED IT, IN THE 1920'S.
WHEN *IT* DISCOVERED *US*.
THEIRS WAS A WORLD WHERE FIRST CONTACT WITH AN ALIEN SPECIES WAS OVERT.
THE TWO INSTANCES OF MAJOR ALIEN CONTACT I KNOW OF HERE -- THE KHERUBIM/DAEMONITE *WAR* AND THE ALIENS THAT MODIFIED *JACK* -- WERE, OF COURSE, BOTH *COVERT*.
NOT ONLY WAS IT *OVERT* THERE -- BUT IT WAS A CASE OF TWO EXPANSIONIST, RENAISSANCE, COURTLY CULTURES MEETING.
DESPITE THE VAST DISPARITY IN TECHNOLOGIES, THERE WAS A UNITY OF PURPOSE BETWEEN THEM. IT LED DIRECTLY TO HUMANOID ALIENS AND HUMAN EUROPEAN ROYALTY BREEDING --
-- IN THE 1500'S.

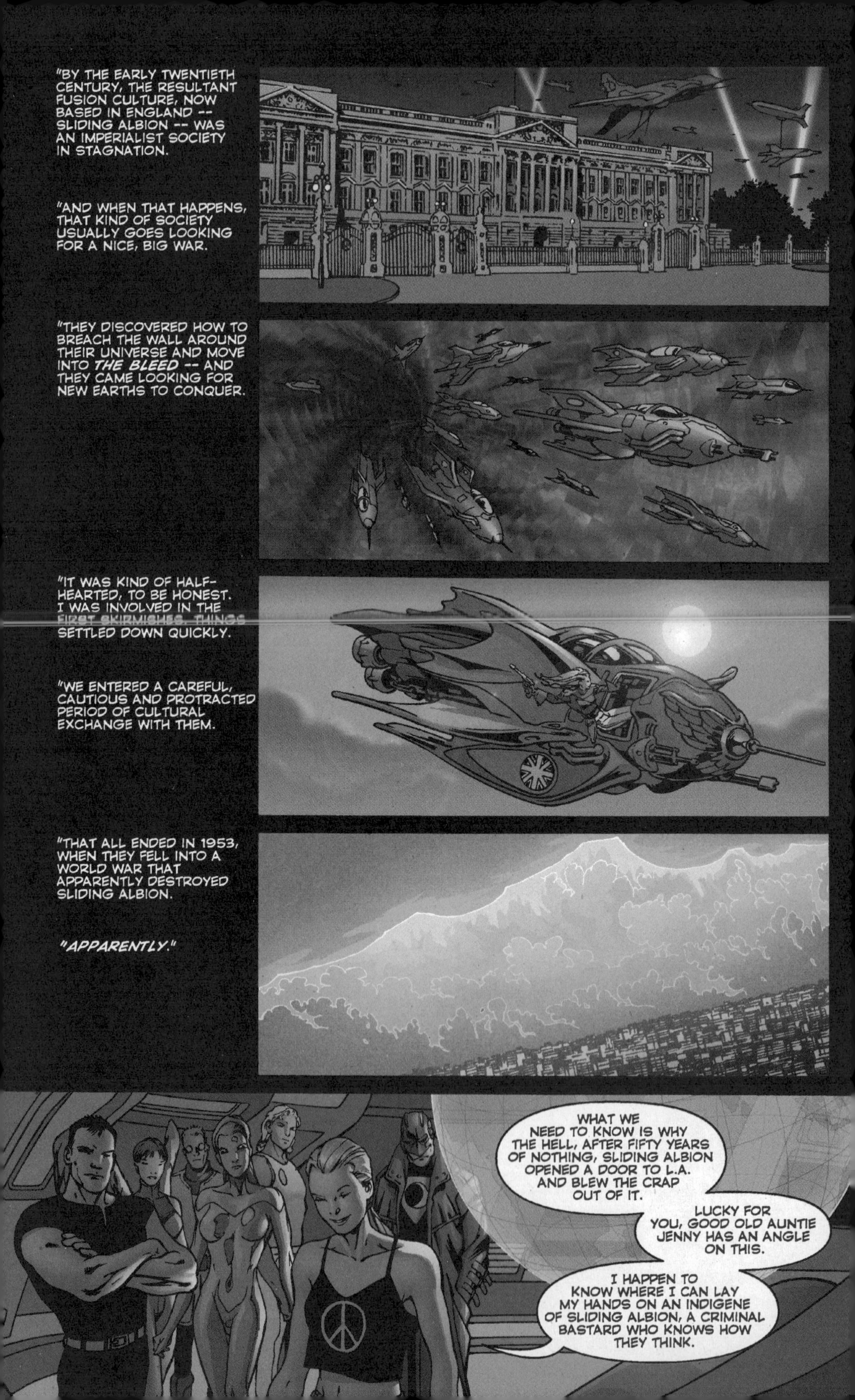
"BY THE EARLY TWENTIETH CENTURY, THE RESULTANT FUSION CULTURE, NOW BASED IN ENGLAND -- SLIDING ALBION -- WAS AN IMPERIALIST SOCIETY IN STAGNATION.
"AND WHEN THAT HAPPENS, THAT KIND OF SOCIETY USUALLY GOES LOOKING FOR A NICE, BIG WAR.
"THEY DISCOVERED HOW TO BREACH THE WALL AROUND THEIR UNIVERSE AND MOVE INTO *THE BLEED* -- AND THEY CAME LOOKING FOR NEW EARTHS TO CONQUER.
"IT WAS KIND OF HALF-HEARTED, TO BE HONEST. I WAS INVOLVED IN THE FIRST SKIRMISHES. THINGS SETTLED DOWN QUICKLY.
"WE ENTERED A CAREFUL, CAUTIOUS AND PROTRACTED PERIOD OF CULTURAL EXCHANGE WITH THEM.
"THAT ALL ENDED IN 1953, WHEN THEY FELL INTO A WORLD WAR THAT APPARENTLY DESTROYED SLIDING ALBION.
"APPARENTLY."
WHAT WE NEED TO KNOW IS WHY THE HELL, AFTER FIFTY YEARS OF NOTHING, SLIDING ALBION OPENED A DOOR TO L.A. AND BLEW THE CRAP OUT OF IT.
LUCKY FOR YOU, GOOD OLD AUNTIE JENNY HAS AN ANGLE ON THIS.
I HAPPEN TO KNOW WHERE I CAN LAY MY HANDS ON AN INDIGENE OF SLIDING ALBION, A CRIMINAL BASTARD WHO KNOWS HOW THEY THINK.

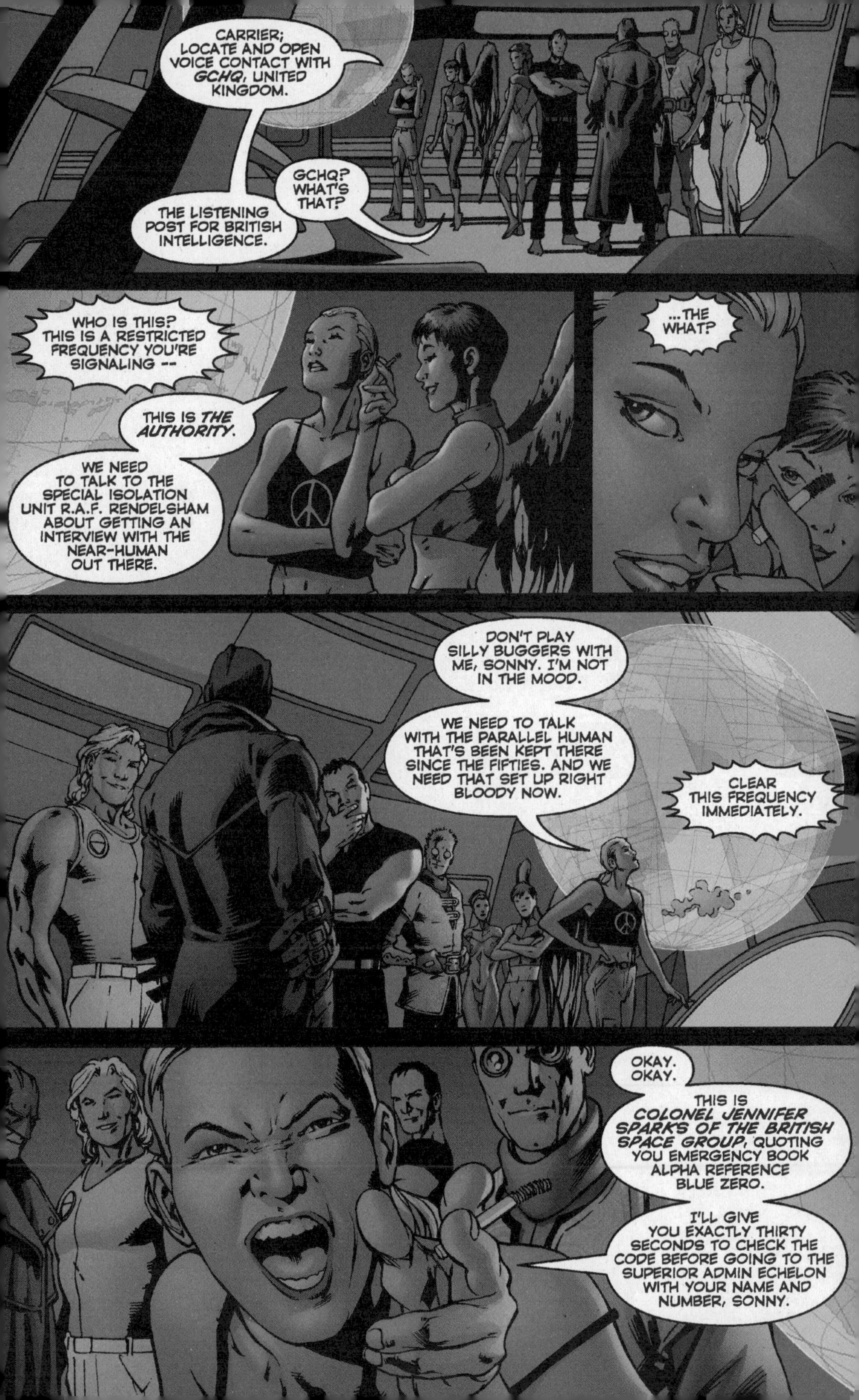
CARRIER; LOCATE AND OPEN VOICE CONTACT WITH *GCHQ*, UNITED KINGDOM.
GCHQ? WHAT'S THAT?
THE LISTENING POST FOR BRITISH INTELLIGENCE.
WHO IS THIS? THIS IS A RESTRICTED FREQUENCY YOU'RE SIGNALING --
THIS IS *THE AUTHORITY*.
WE NEED TO TALK TO THE SPECIAL ISOLATION UNIT R.A.F. RENDELSHAM ABOUT GETTING AN INTERVIEW WITH THE NEAR-HUMAN OUT THERE.
...THE WHAT?
DON'T PLAY SILLY BUGGERS WITH ME, SONNY. I'M NOT IN THE MOOD.
WE NEED TO TALK WITH THE PARALLEL HUMAN THAT'S BEEN KEPT THERE SINCE THE FIFTIES. AND WE NEED THAT SET UP RIGHT BLOODY NOW.
CLEAR THIS FREQUENCY IMMEDIATELY.
OKAY. OKAY.
THIS IS *COLONEL JENNIFER SPARKS OF THE BRITISH SPACE GROUP*, QUOTING YOU EMERGENCY BOOK ALPHA REFERENCE BLUE ZERO.
I'LL GIVE YOU EXACTLY THIRTY SECONDS TO CHECK THE CODE BEFORE GOING TO THE SUPERIOR ADMIN ECHELON WITH YOUR NAME AND NUMBER, SONNY.

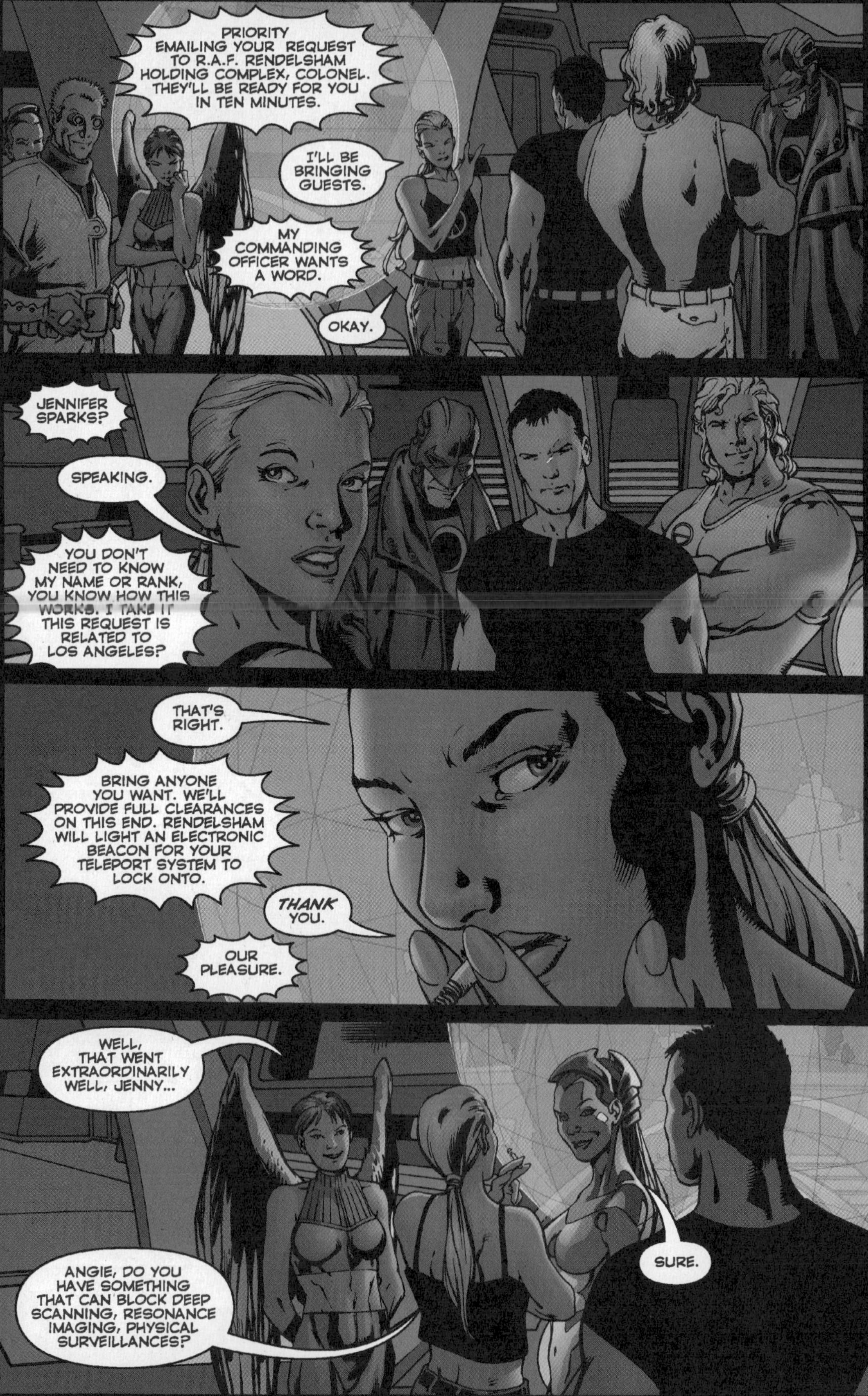
PRIORITY EMAILING YOUR REQUEST TO R.A.F. RENDELSHAM HOLDING COMPLEX, COLONEL. THEY'LL BE READY FOR YOU IN TEN MINUTES.
I'LL BE BRINGING GUESTS.
MY COMMANDING OFFICER WANTS A WORD.
OKAY.
JENNIFER SPARKS?
SPEAKING.
YOU DON'T NEED TO KNOW MY NAME OR RANK, YOU KNOW HOW THIS WORKS. I TAKE IT THIS REQUEST IS RELATED TO LOS ANGELES?
THAT'S RIGHT.
BRING ANYONE YOU WANT. WE'LL PROVIDE FULL CLEARANCES ON THIS END. RENDELSHAM WILL LIGHT AN ELECTRONIC BEACON FOR YOUR TELEPORT SYSTEM TO LOCK ONTO.
THANK YOU.
OUR PLEASURE.
WELL, THAT WENT EXTRAORDINARILY WELL, JENNY...
ANGIE, DO YOU HAVE SOMETHING THAT CAN BLOCK DEEP SCANNING, RESONANCE IMAGING, PHYSICAL SURVEILLANCES?
SURE.

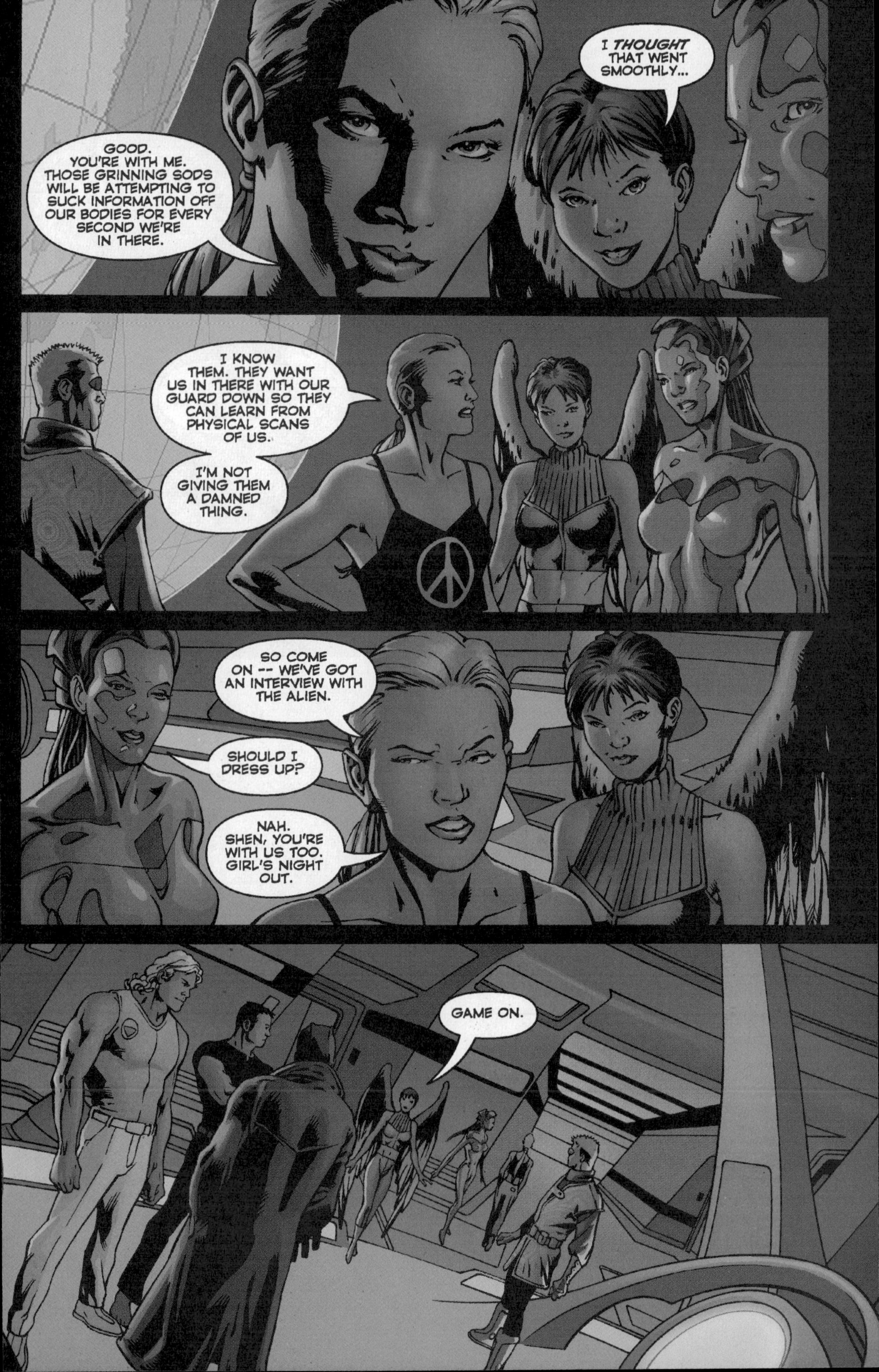
I *THOUGHT* THAT WENT SMOOTHLY...
GOOD. YOU'RE WITH ME. THOSE GRINNING SODS WILL BE ATTEMPTING TO SUCK INFORMATION OFF OUR BODIES FOR EVERY SECOND WE'RE IN THERE.
I KNOW THEM. THEY WANT US IN THERE WITH OUR GUARD DOWN SO THEY CAN LEARN FROM PHYSICAL SCANS OF US.
I'M NOT GIVING THEM A DAMNED THING.
SO COME ON -- WE'VE GOT AN INTERVIEW WITH THE ALIEN.
SHOULD I DRESS UP?
NAH. SHEN, YOU'RE WITH US TOO. GIRL'S NIGHT OUT.
GAME ON.

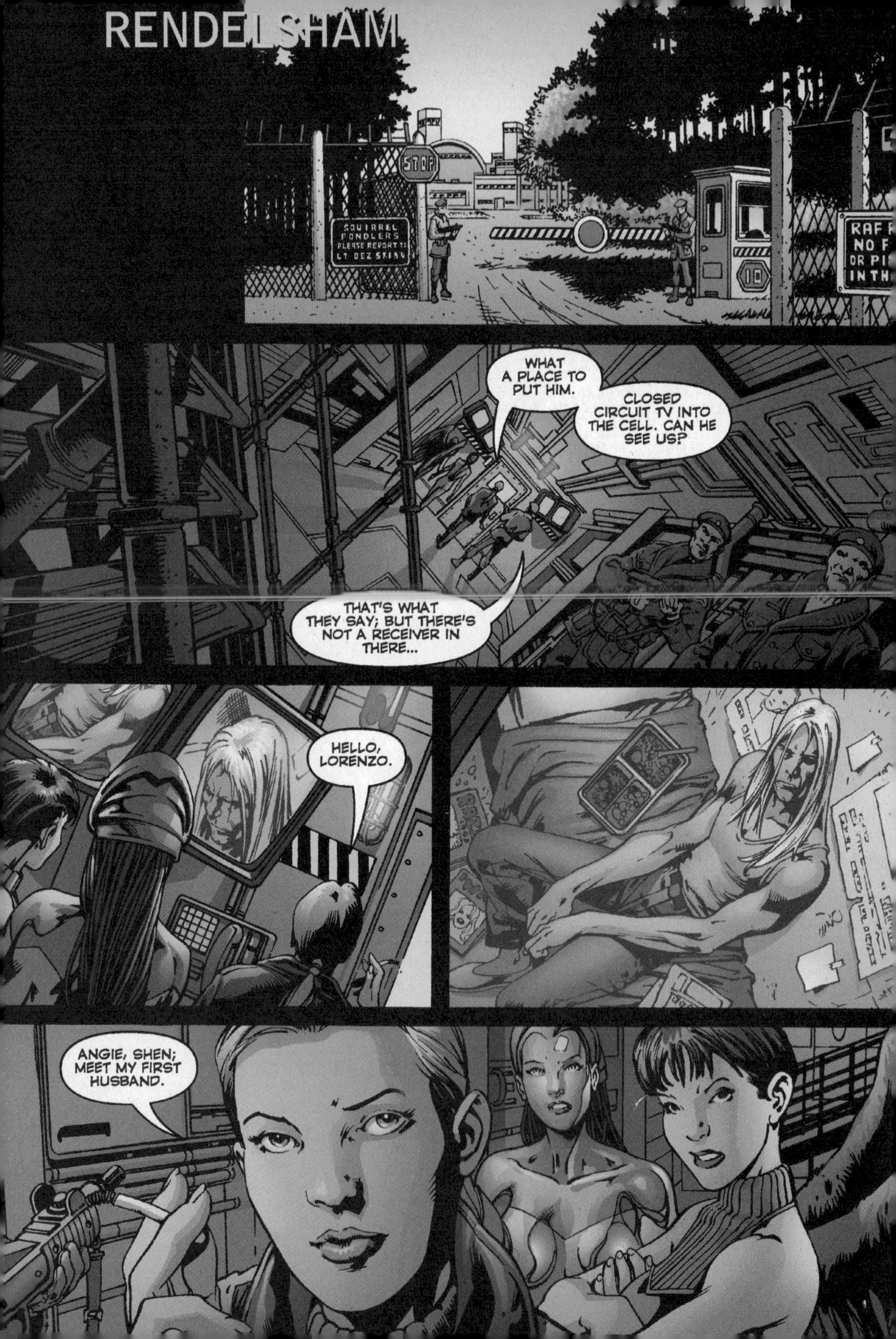
RENDELSHAM
SQUIRREL FONDLERS PLEASE REPORT TO LT DEZ STIRY
STOP
WHAT A PLACE TO PUT HIM.
CLOSED CIRCUIT TV INTO THE CELL. CAN HE SEE US?
THAT'S WHAT THEY SAY; BUT THERE'S NOT A RECEIVER IN THERE...
HELLO, LORENZO.
ANGIE, SHEN; MEET MY FIRST HUSBAND.

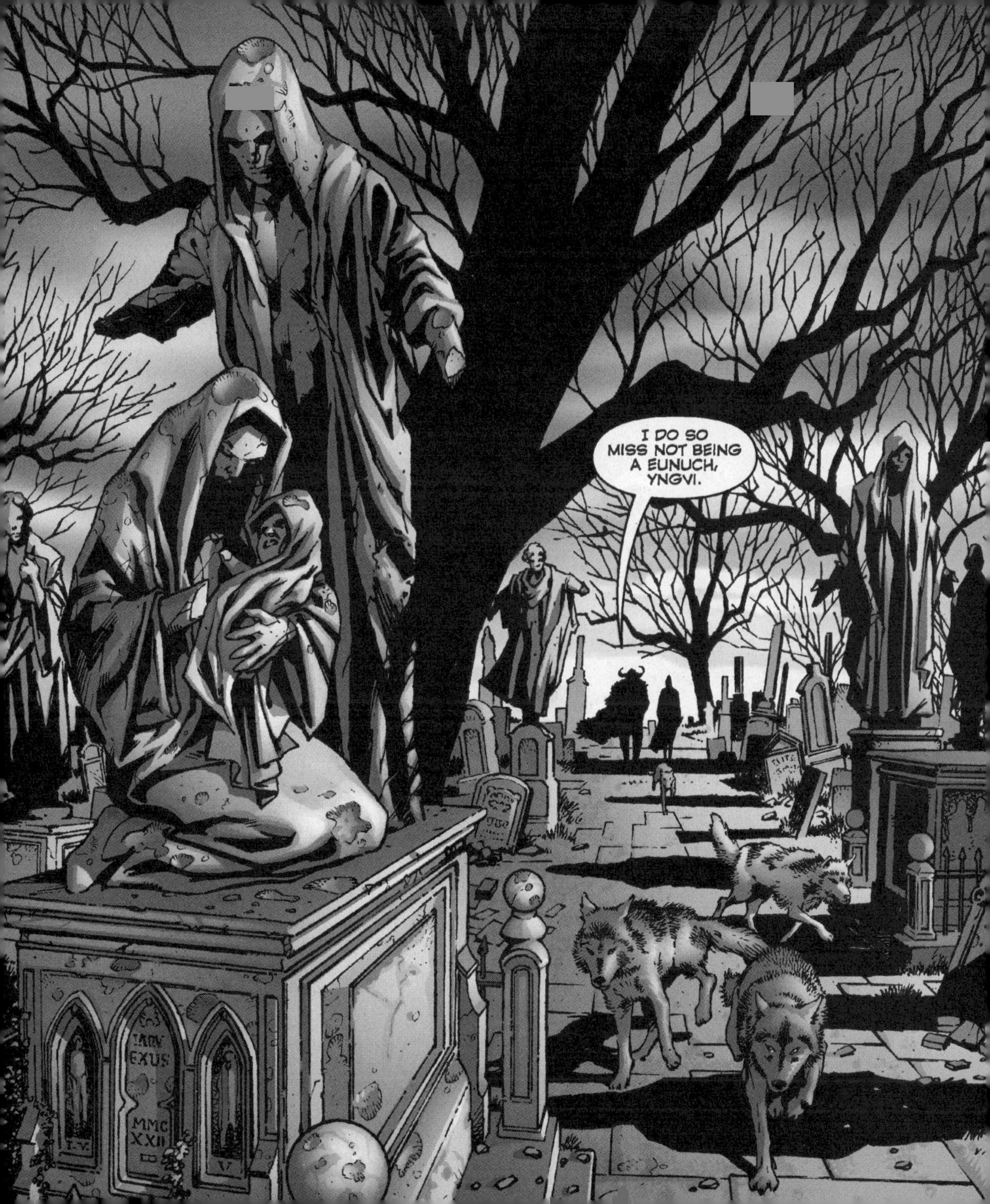
I DO SO MISS NOT BEING A EUNUCH, YNGVI.

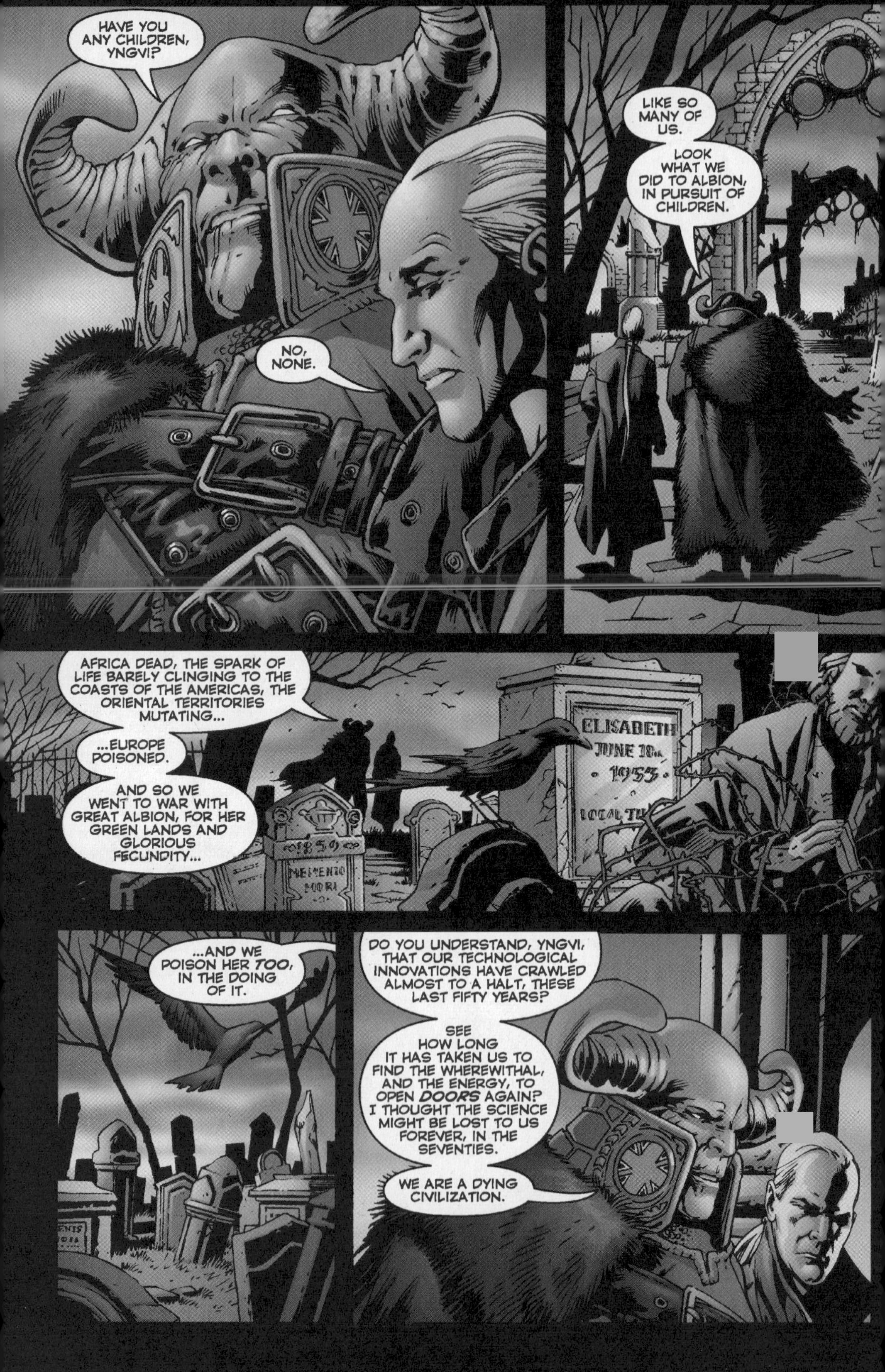
HAVE YOU ANY CHILDREN, YNGVI?
NO, NONE.
LIKE SO MANY OF US.
LOOK WHAT WE DID TO ALBION, IN PURSUIT OF CHILDREN.
AFRICA DEAD, THE SPARK OF LIFE BARELY CLINGING TO THE COASTS OF THE AMERICAS, THE ORIENTAL TERRITORIES MUTATING...
...EUROPE POISONED.
AND SO WE WENT TO WAR WITH GREAT ALBION, FOR HER GREEN LANDS AND GLORIOUS FECUNDITY...
ELISABETH
JUNE 18th
1953
MEMENTO MORI
...AND WE POISON HER *TOO*, IN THE DOING OF IT.
DO YOU UNDERSTAND, YNGVI, THAT OUR TECHNOLOGICAL INNOVATIONS HAVE CRAWLED ALMOST TO A HALT, THESE LAST FIFTY YEARS?
SEE HOW LONG IT HAS TAKEN US TO FIND THE WHEREWITHAL, AND THE ENERGY, TO OPEN *DOORS* AGAIN? I THOUGHT THE SCIENCE MIGHT BE LOST TO US FOREVER, IN THE SEVENTIES.
WE ARE A DYING CIVILIZATION.

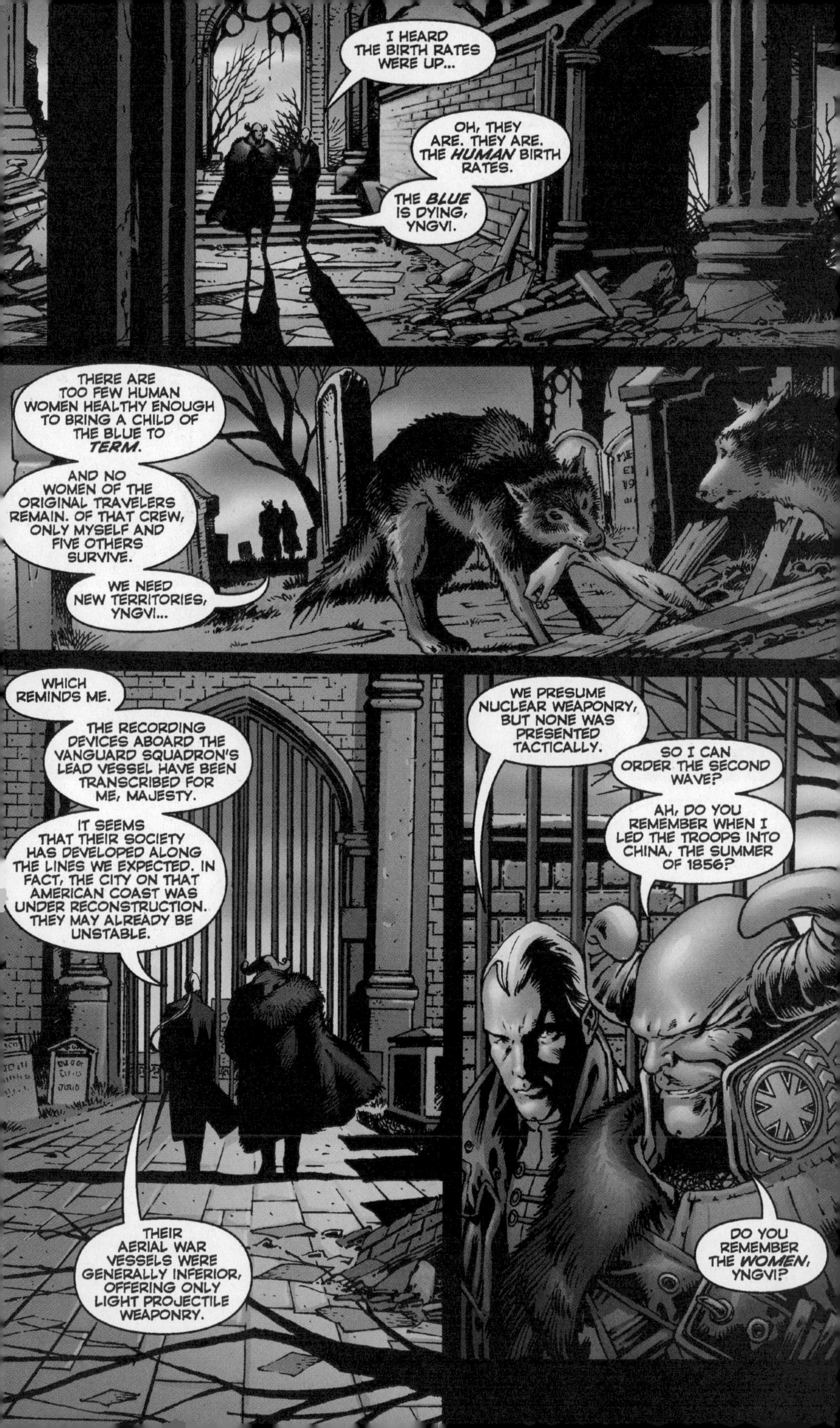
I HEARD THE BIRTH RATES WERE UP...
OH, THEY ARE. THEY ARE. THE *HUMAN* BIRTH RATES.
THE *BLUE* IS DYING, YNGVI.
THERE ARE TOO FEW HUMAN WOMEN HEALTHY ENOUGH TO BRING A CHILD OF THE BLUE TO *TERM*.
AND NO WOMEN OF THE ORIGINAL TRAVELERS REMAIN. OF THAT CREW, ONLY MYSELF AND FIVE OTHERS SURVIVE.
WE NEED NEW TERRITORIES, YNGVI...
WHICH REMINDS ME.
THE RECORDING DEVICES ABOARD THE VANGUARD SQUADRON'S LEAD VESSEL HAVE BEEN TRANSCRIBED FOR ME, MAJESTY.
IT SEEMS THAT THEIR SOCIETY HAS DEVELOPED ALONG THE LINES WE EXPECTED. IN FACT, THE CITY ON THAT AMERICAN COAST WAS UNDER RECONSTRUCTION. THEY MAY ALREADY BE UNSTABLE.
THEIR AERIAL WAR VESSELS WERE GENERALLY INFERIOR, OFFERING ONLY LIGHT PROJECTILE WEAPONRY.
WE PRESUME NUCLEAR WEAPONRY, BUT NONE WAS PRESENTED TACTICALLY.
SO I CAN ORDER THE SECOND WAVE?
AH, DO YOU REMEMBER WHEN I LED THE TROOPS INTO CHINA, THE SUMMER OF 1856?
DO YOU REMEMBER THE *WOMEN*, YNGVI?

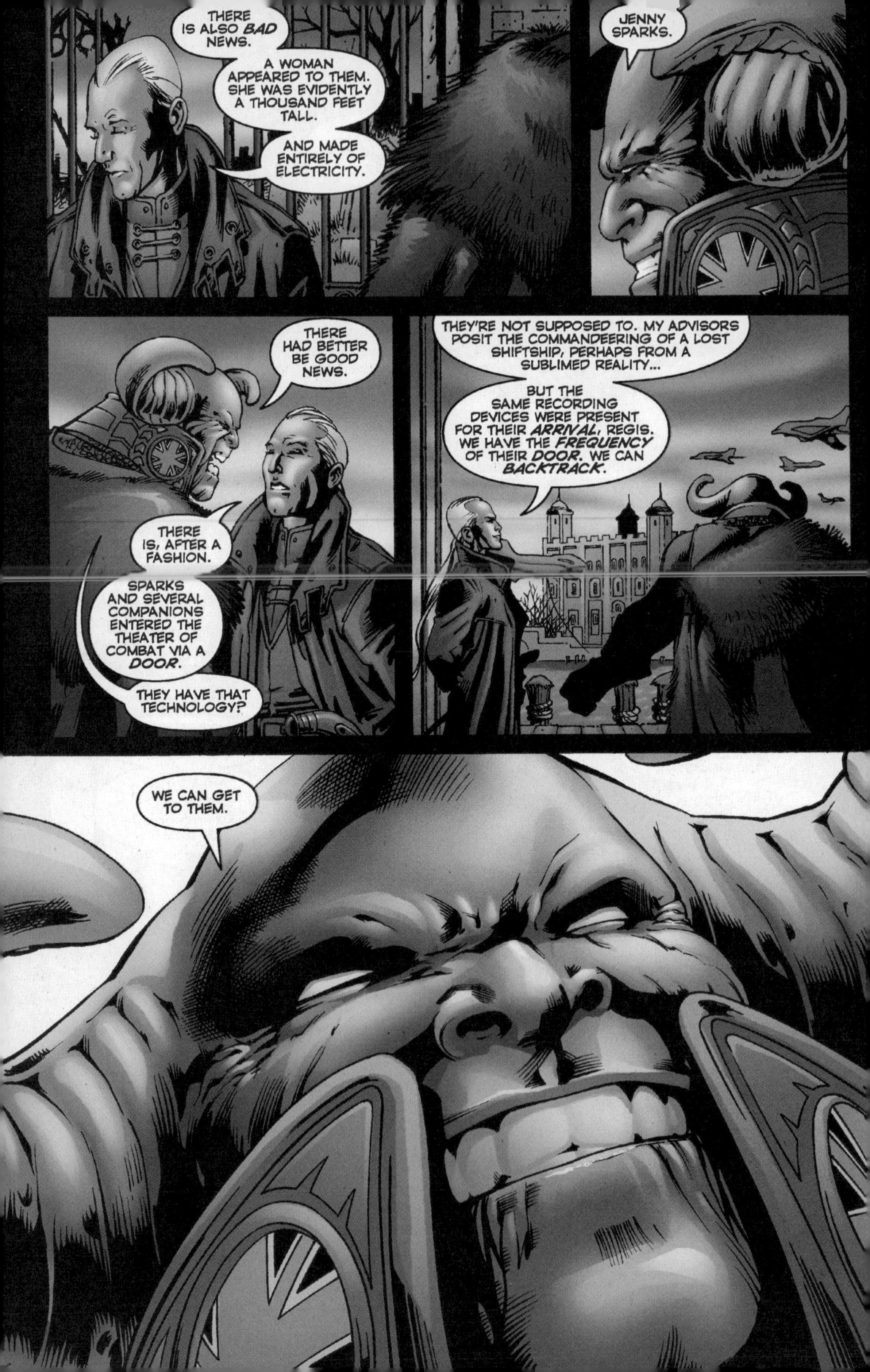
THERE IS ALSO *BAD* NEWS.
A WOMAN APPEARED TO THEM. SHE WAS EVIDENTLY A THOUSAND FEET TALL.
AND MADE ENTIRELY OF ELECTRICITY.
JENNY SPARKS.
THERE HAD BETTER BE GOOD NEWS.
THERE IS, AFTER A FASHION.
SPARKS AND SEVERAL COMPANIONS ENTERED THE THEATER OF COMBAT VIA A *DOOR*.
THEY HAVE THAT TECHNOLOGY?
THEY'RE NOT SUPPOSED TO. MY ADVISORS POSIT THE COMMANDEERING OF A LOST SHIFTSHIP, PERHAPS FROM A SUBLIMED REALITY...
BUT THE SAME RECORDING DEVICES WERE PRESENT FOR THEIR *ARRIVAL*, REGIS. WE HAVE THE *FREQUENCY* OF THEIR *DOOR*. WE CAN *BACKTRACK*.
WE CAN GET TO THEM.

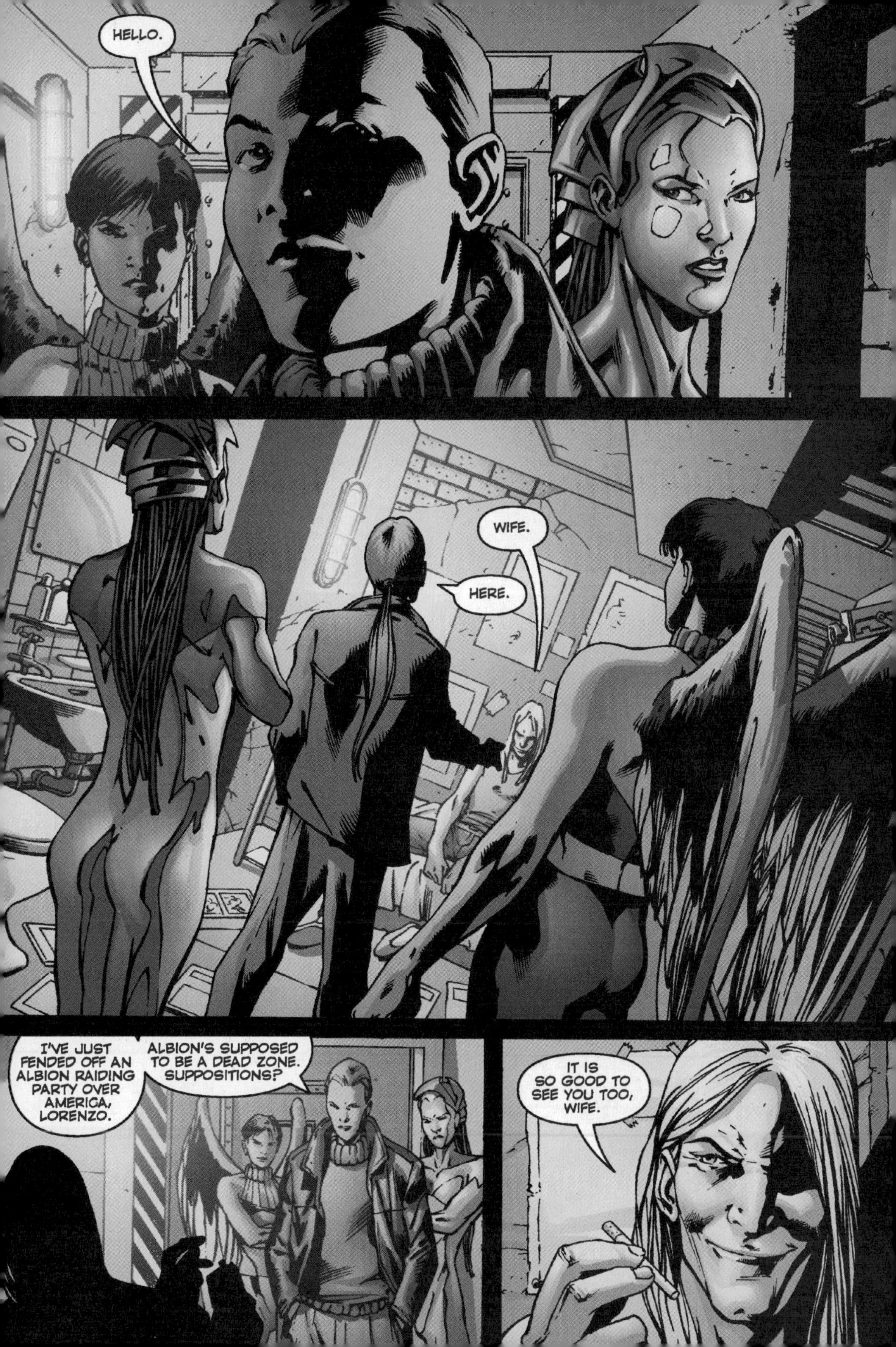
HELLO.
HERE.
WIFE.
I'VE JUST FENDED OFF AN ALBION RAIDING PARTY OVER AMERICA, LORENZO.
ALBION'S SUPPOSED TO BE A DEAD ZONE. SUPPOSITIONS?
IT IS SO GOOD TO SEE YOU TOO, WIFE.

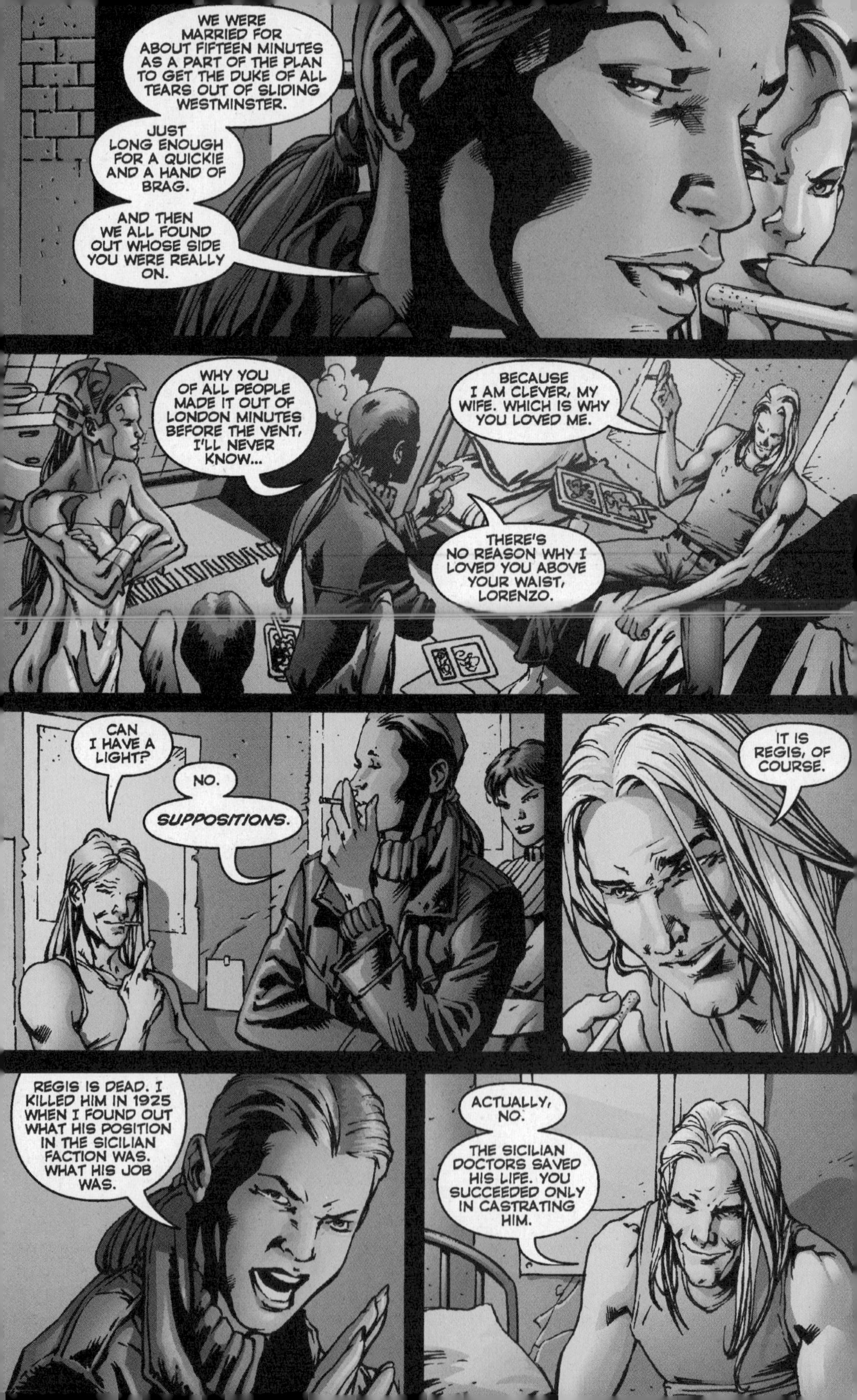
WE WERE MARRIED FOR ABOUT FIFTEEN MINUTES AS A PART OF THE PLAN TO GET THE DUKE OF ALL TEARS OUT OF SLIDING WESTMINSTER.
JUST LONG ENOUGH FOR A QUICKIE AND A HAND OF BRAG.
AND THEN WE ALL FOUND OUT WHOSE SIDE YOU WERE REALLY ON.
WHY YOU OF ALL PEOPLE MADE IT OUT OF LONDON MINUTES BEFORE THE VENT, I'LL NEVER KNOW...
BECAUSE I AM CLEVER, MY WIFE. WHICH IS WHY YOU LOVED ME.
THERE'S NO REASON WHY I LOVED YOU ABOVE YOUR WAIST, LORENZO.
CAN I HAVE A LIGHT?
NO.
SUPPOSITIONS.
IT IS REGIS, OF COURSE.
REGIS IS DEAD. I KILLED HIM IN 1925 WHEN I FOUND OUT WHAT HIS POSITION IN THE SICILIAN FACTION WAS. WHAT HIS JOB WAS.
ACTUALLY, NO.
THE SICILIAN DOCTORS SAVED HIS LIFE. YOU SUCCEEDED ONLY IN CASTRATING HIM.

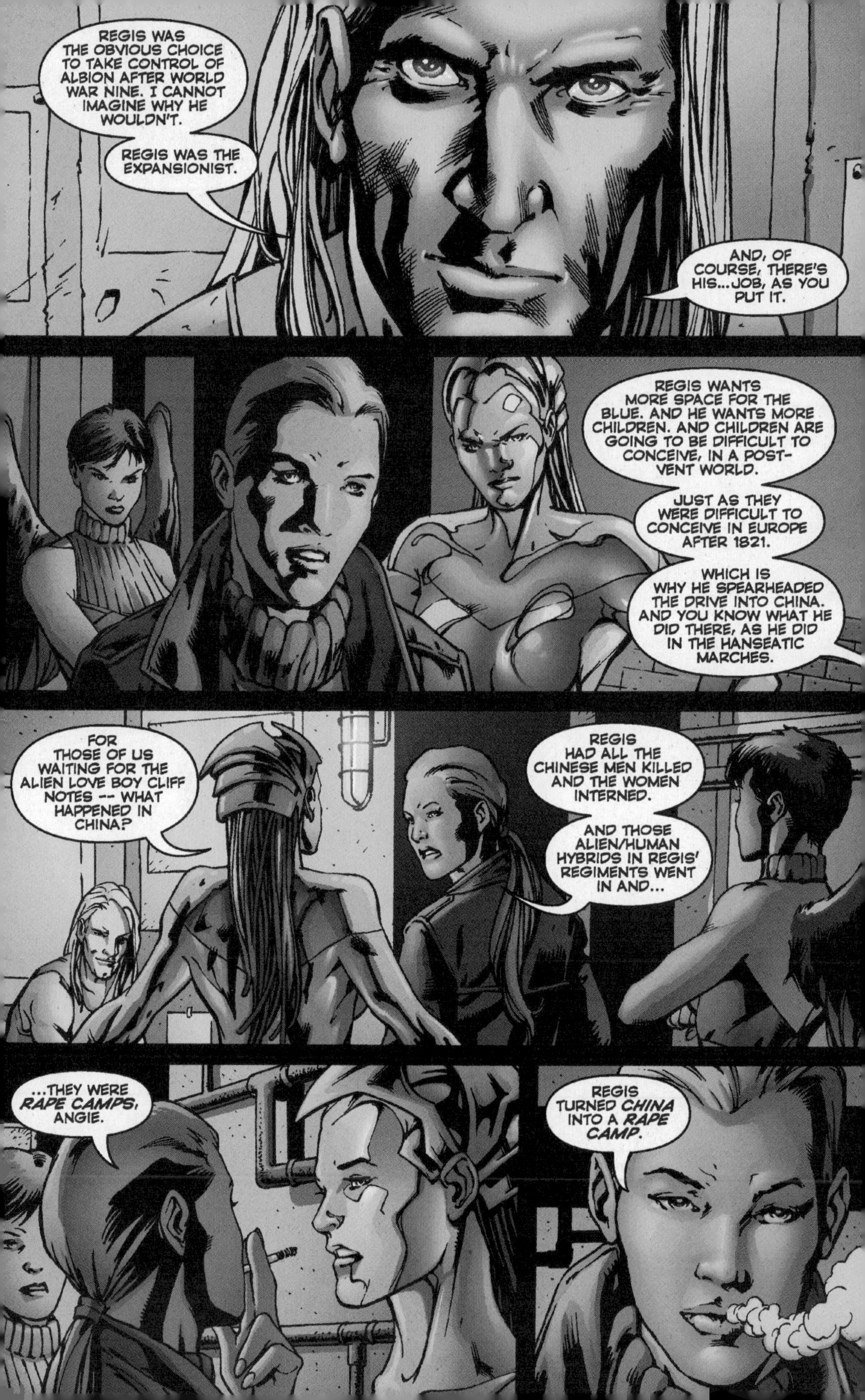
REGIS WAS THE OBVIOUS CHOICE TO TAKE CONTROL OF ALBION AFTER WORLD WAR NINE. I CANNOT IMAGINE WHY HE WOULDN'T.
REGIS WAS THE EXPANSIONIST.
AND, OF COURSE, THERE'S HIS...JOB, AS YOU PUT IT.
REGIS WANTS MORE SPACE FOR THE BLUE. AND HE WANTS MORE CHILDREN. AND CHILDREN ARE GOING TO BE DIFFICULT TO CONCEIVE, IN A POST-VENT WORLD.
JUST AS THEY WERE DIFFICULT TO CONCEIVE IN EUROPE AFTER 1821.
WHICH IS WHY HE SPEARHEADED THE DRIVE INTO CHINA. AND YOU KNOW WHAT HE DID THERE, AS HE DID IN THE HANSEATIC MARCHES.
FOR THOSE OF US WAITING FOR THE ALIEN LOVE BOY CLIFF NOTES -- WHAT HAPPENED IN CHINA?
REGIS HAD ALL THE CHINESE MEN KILLED AND THE WOMEN INTERNED.
AND THOSE ALIEN/HUMAN HYBRIDS IN REGIS' REGIMENTS WENT IN AND...
...THEY WERE *RAPE CAMPS*, ANGIE.
REGIS TURNED *CHINA* INTO A *RAPE CAMP*.

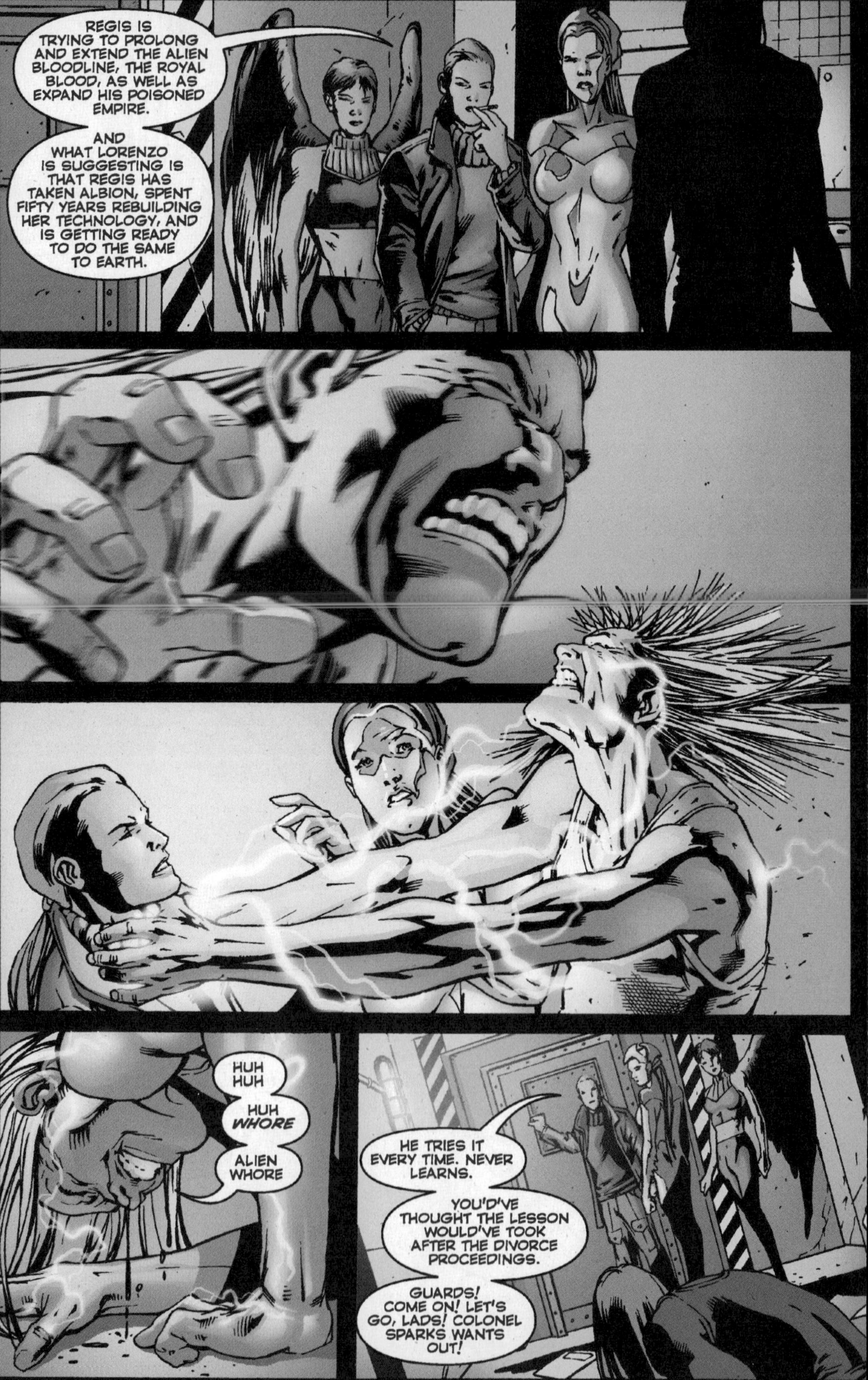
REGIS IS TRYING TO PROLONG AND EXTEND THE ALIEN BLOODLINE, THE ROYAL BLOOD, AS WELL AS EXPAND HIS POISONED EMPIRE.
AND WHAT LORENZO IS SUGGESTING IS THAT REGIS HAS TAKEN ALBION, SPENT FIFTY YEARS REBUILDING HER TECHNOLOGY, AND IS GETTING READY TO DO THE SAME TO EARTH.
HUH HUH
HUH *WHORE*
ALIEN WHORE
HE TRIES IT EVERY TIME. NEVER LEARNS.
YOU'D'VE THOUGHT THE LESSON WOULD'VE TOOK AFTER THE DIVORCE PROCEEDINGS.
GUARDS! COME ON! LET'S GO, LADS! COLONEL SPARKS WANTS OUT!

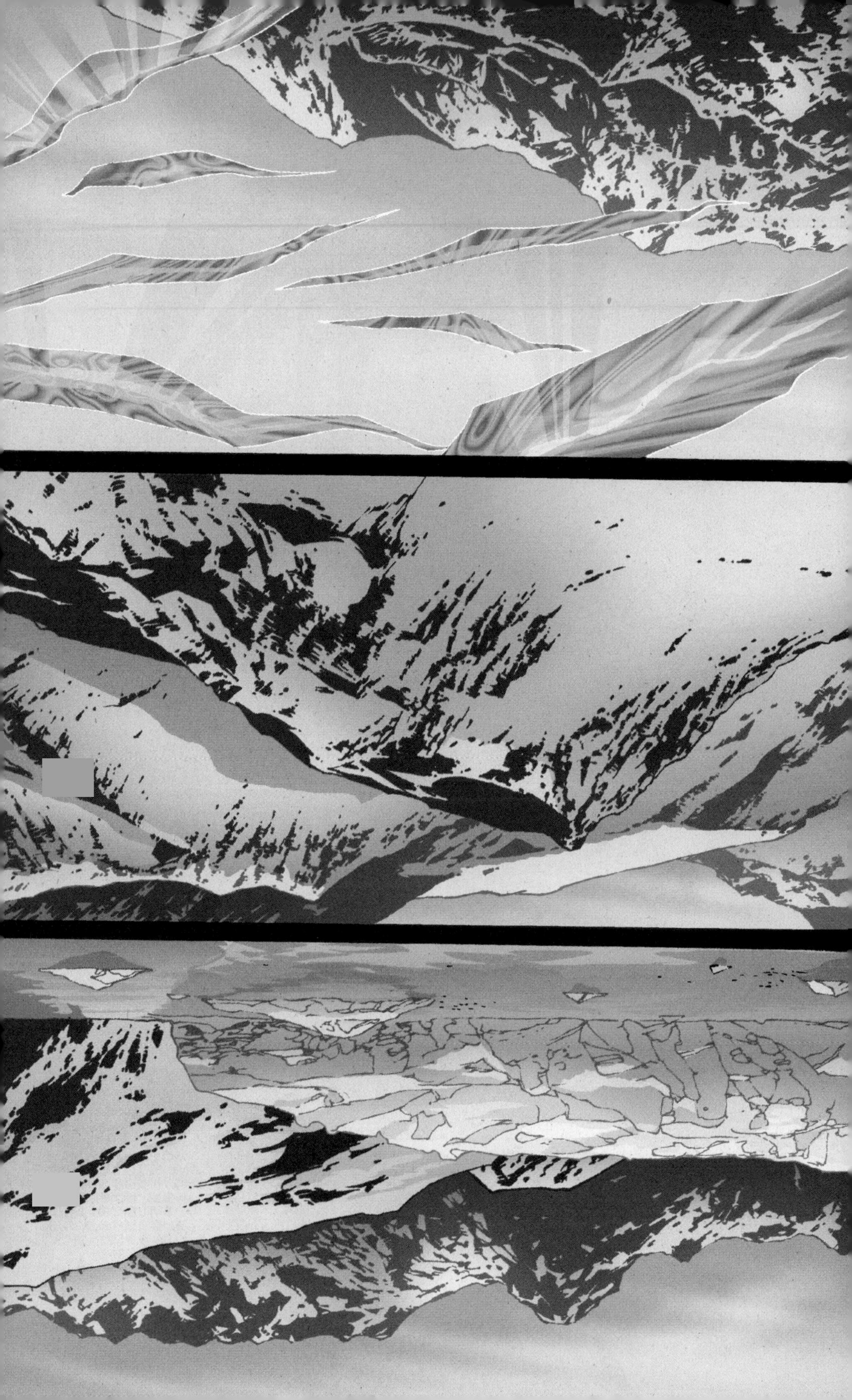

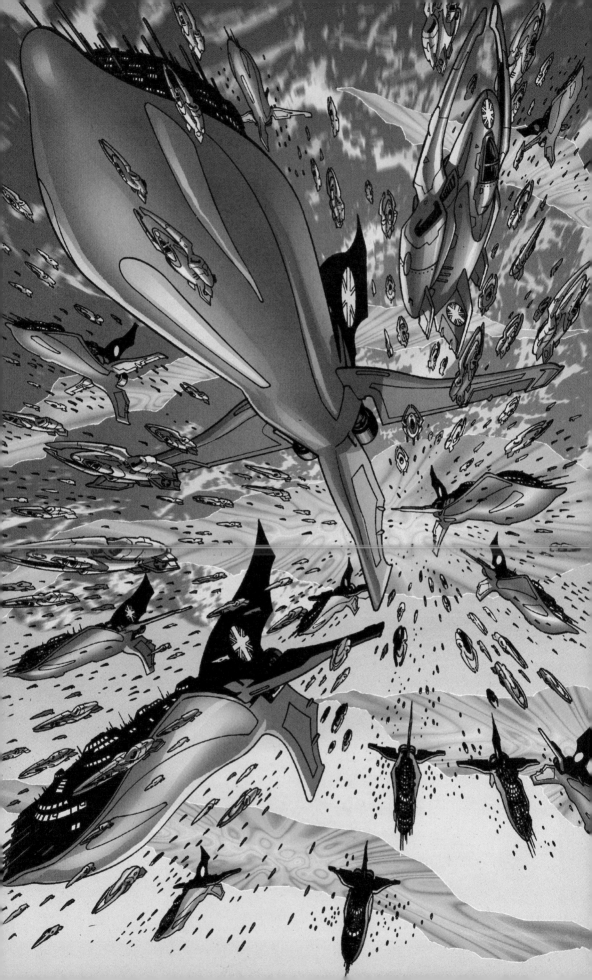

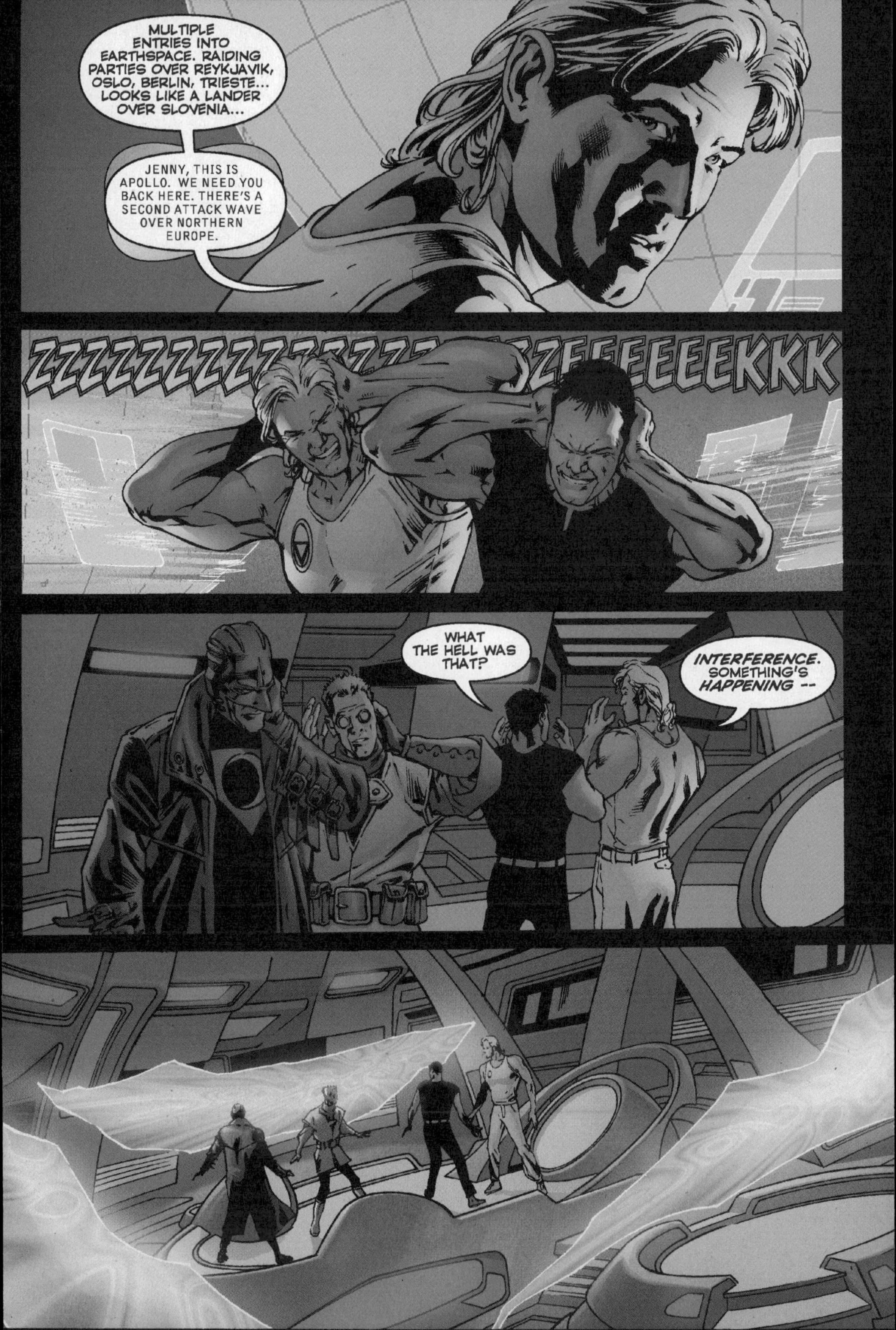
MULTIPLE ENTRIES INTO EARTHSPACE. RAIDING PARTIES OVER REYKJAVIK, OSLO, BERLIN, TRIESTE... LOOKS LIKE A LANDER OVER SLOVENIA...
JENNY, THIS IS APOLLO. WE NEED YOU BACK HERE. THERE'S A SECOND ATTACK WAVE OVER NORTHERN EUROPE.
ZZZZZZZZZZZZZZZZZZZZEEEEEEKKK
WHAT THE HELL WAS THAT?
INTERFERENCE. SOMETHING'S HAPPENING --

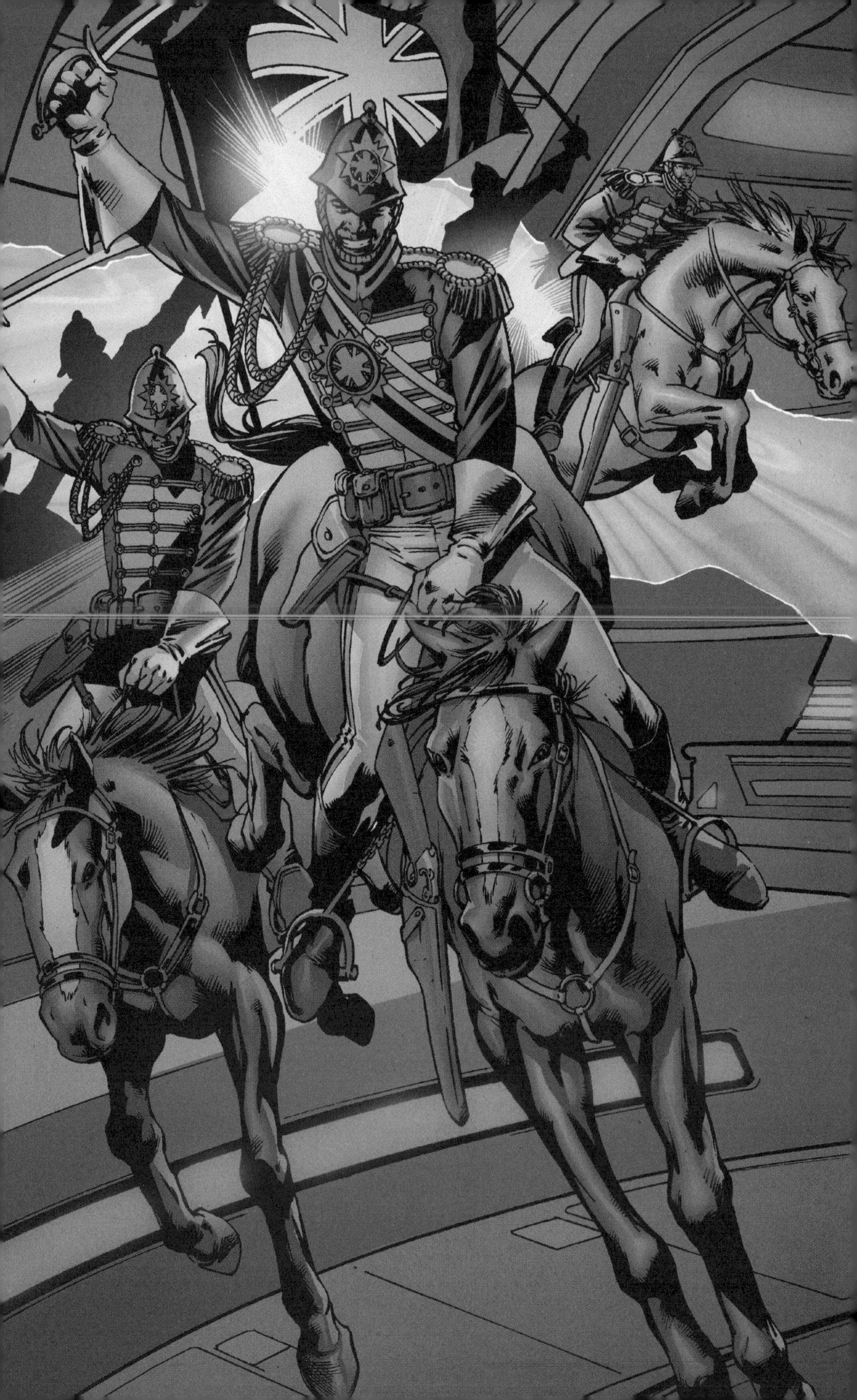

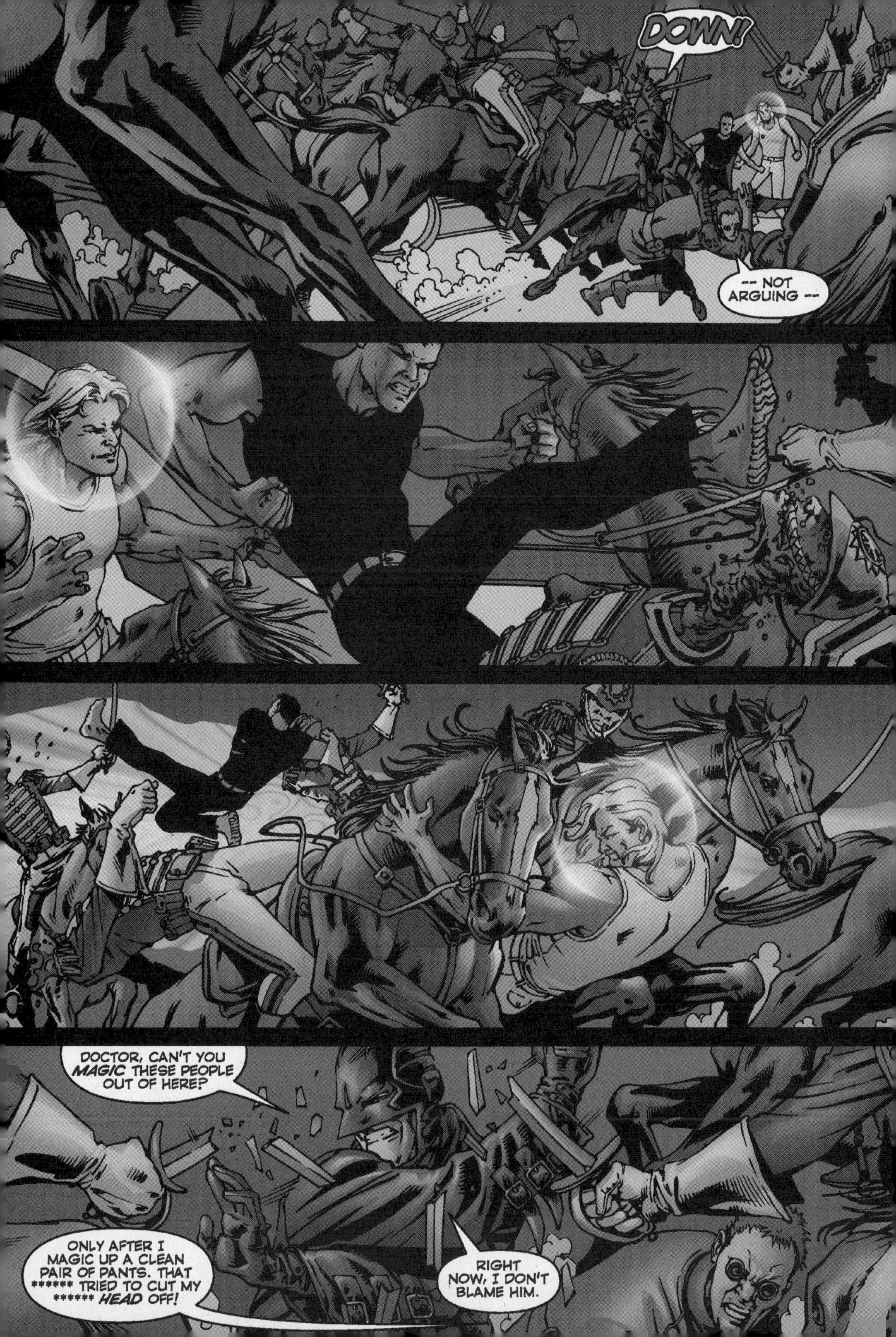
DOWN!
-- NOT ARGUING --
DOCTOR, CAN'T YOU *MAGIC* THESE PEOPLE OUT OF HERE?
ONLY AFTER I MAGIC UP A CLEAN PAIR OF PANTS. THAT ****** TRIED TO CUT MY ****** *HEAD* OFF!
RIGHT NOW, I DON'T BLAME HIM.

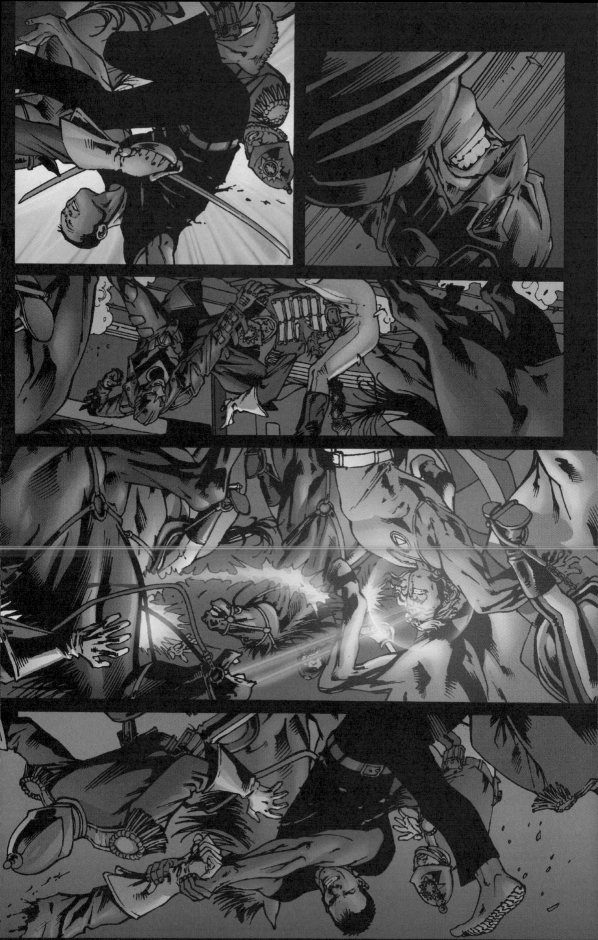

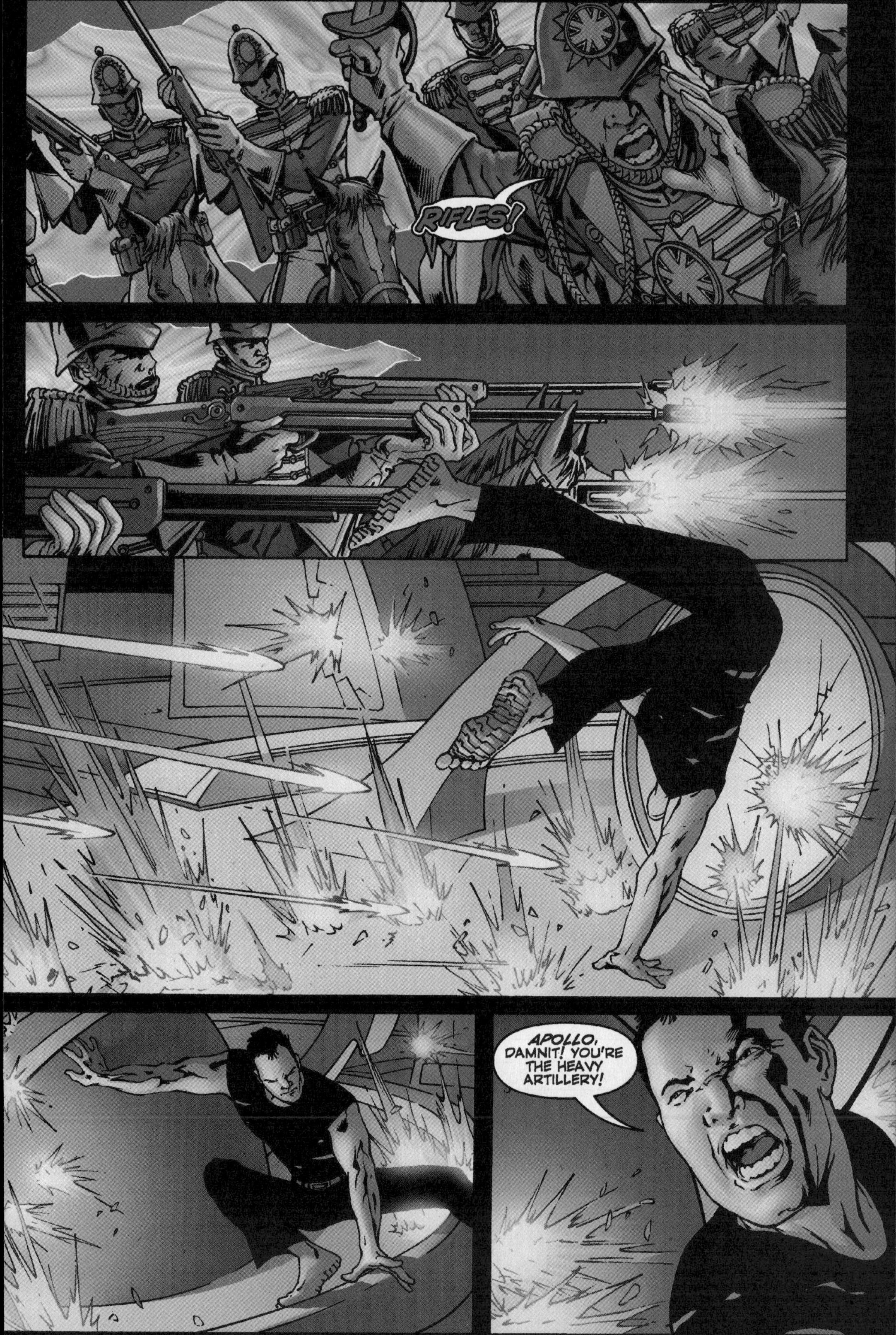
RIFLES!
APOLLO, DAMNIT! YOU'RE THE HEAVY ARTILLERY!

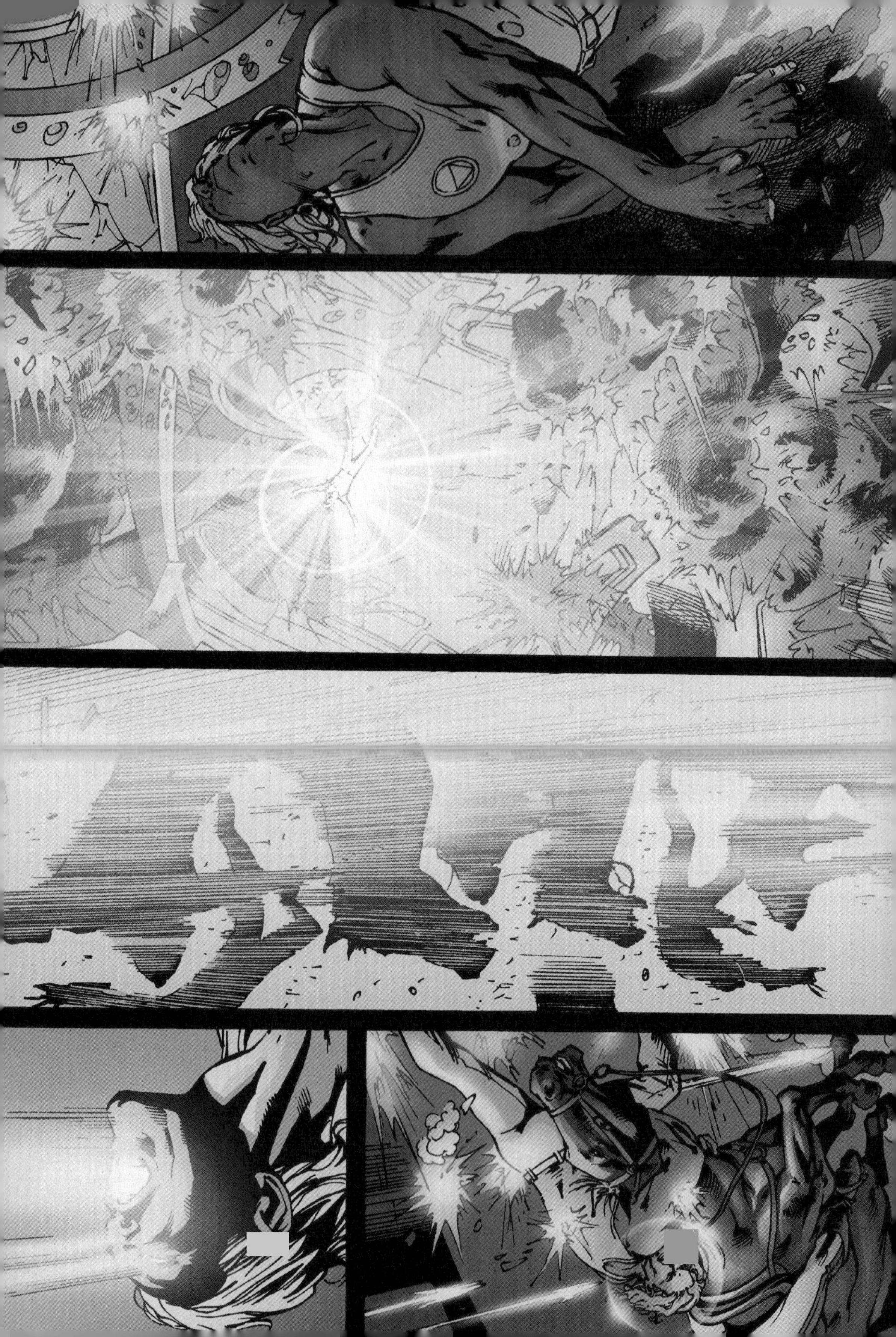

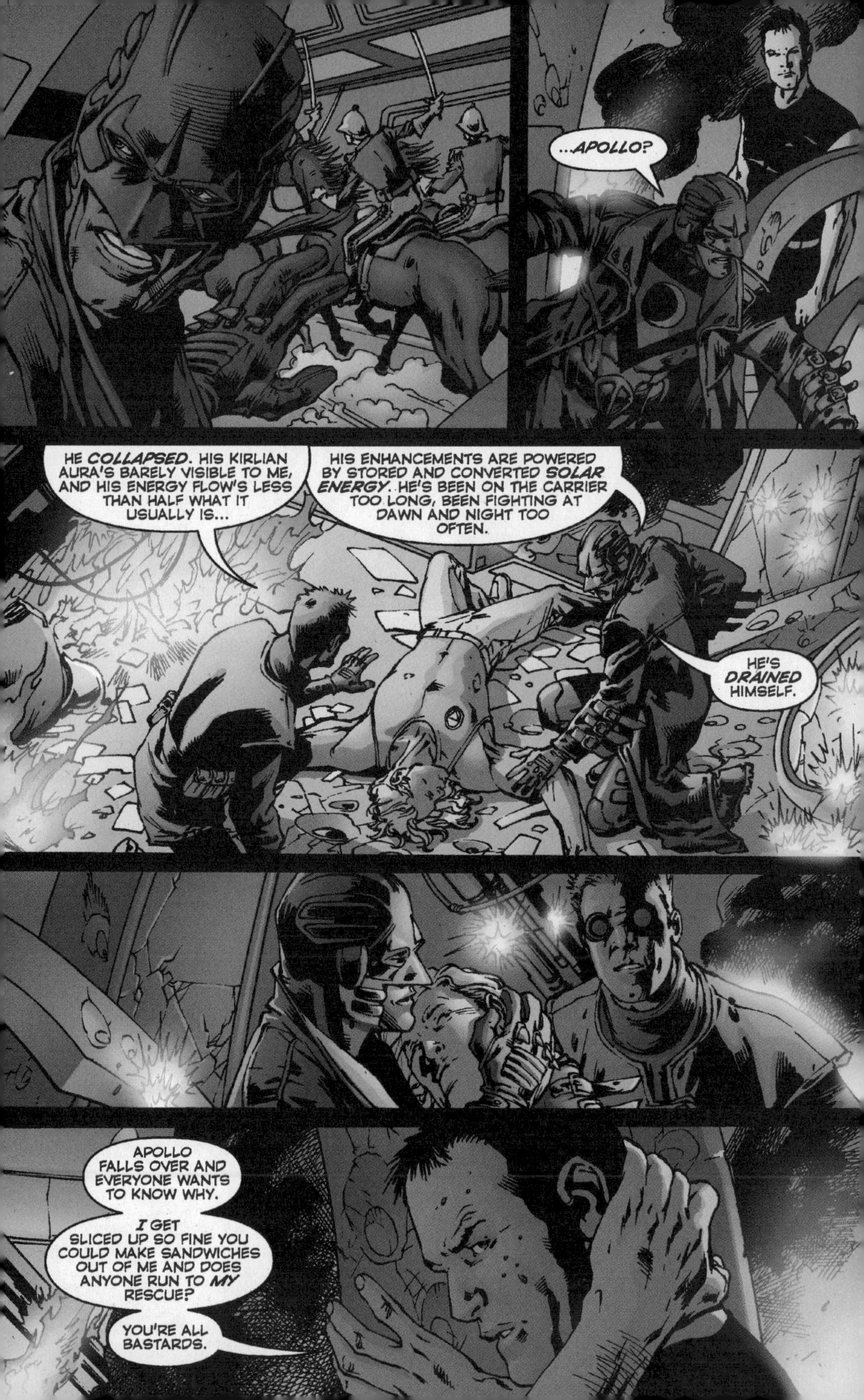
...APOLLO?
HE COLLAPSED. HIS KIRLIAN AURA'S BARELY VISIBLE TO ME, AND HIS ENERGY FLOW'S LESS THAN HALF WHAT IT USUALLY IS...
HIS ENHANCEMENTS ARE POWERED BY STORED AND CONVERTED SOLAR ENERGY. HE'S BEEN ON THE CARRIER TOO LONG, BEEN FIGHTING AT DAWN AND NIGHT TOO OFTEN.
HE'S DRAINED HIMSELF.
APOLLO FALLS OVER AND EVERYONE WANTS TO KNOW WHY.
I GET SLICED UP SO FINE YOU COULD MAKE SANDWICHES OUT OF ME AND DOES ANYONE RUN TO MY RESCUE?
YOU'RE ALL BASTARDS.

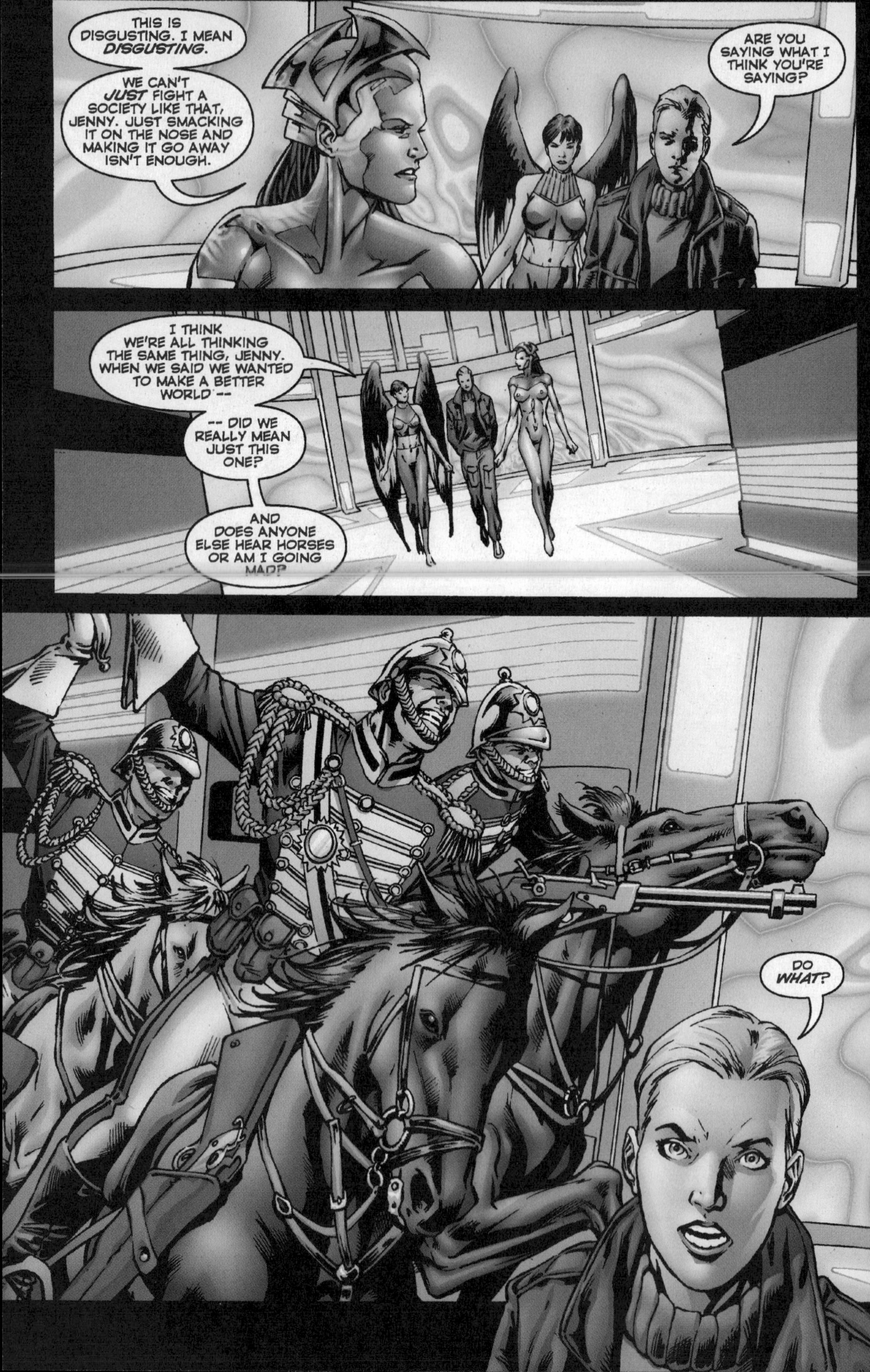
THIS IS DISGUSTING. I MEAN *DISGUSTING*.
WE CAN'T *JUST* FIGHT A SOCIETY LIKE THAT, JENNY. JUST SMACKING IT ON THE NOSE AND MAKING IT GO AWAY ISN'T ENOUGH.
ARE YOU SAYING WHAT I THINK YOU'RE SAYING?
I THINK WE'RE ALL THINKING THE SAME THING, JENNY. WHEN WE SAID WE WANTED TO MAKE A BETTER WORLD --
-- DID WE REALLY MEAN JUST THIS ONE?
AND DOES ANYONE ELSE HEAR HORSES OR AM I GOING MAD?
DO *WHAT?*

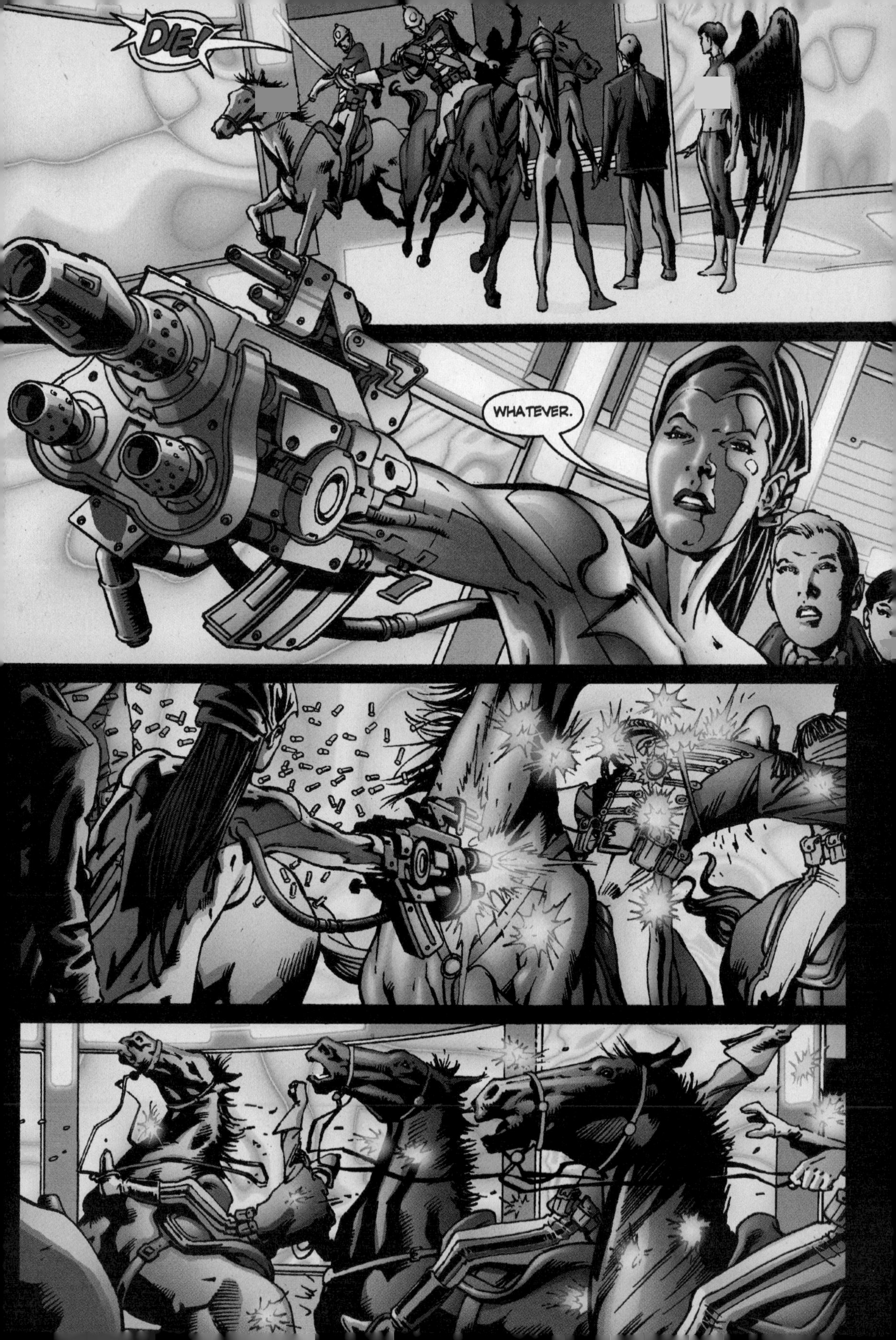
DIE!
WHATEVER.

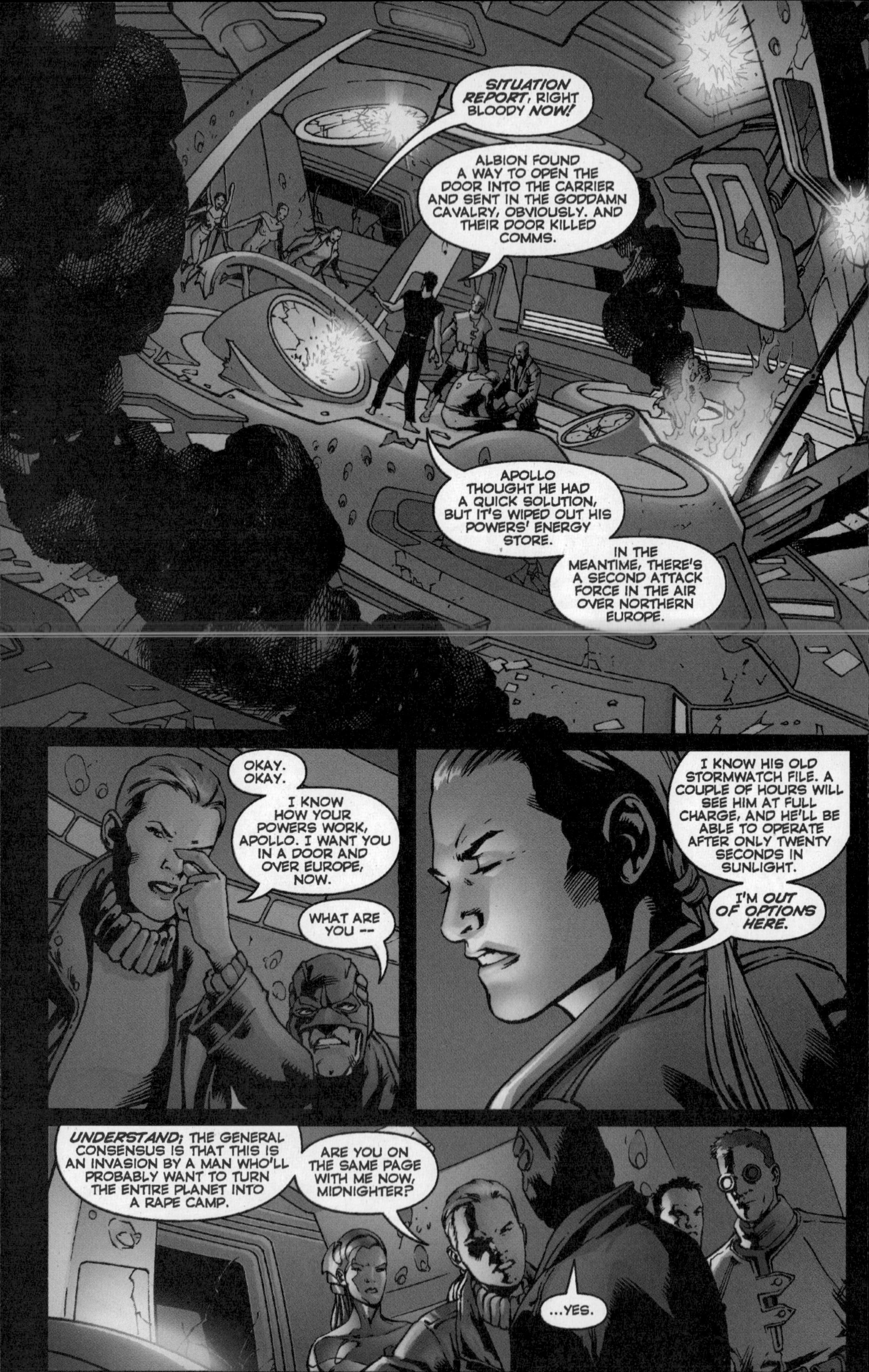
SITUATION REPORT, RIGHT BLOODY NOW!
ALBION FOUND A WAY TO OPEN THE DOOR INTO THE CARRIER AND SENT IN THE GODDAMN CAVALRY, OBVIOUSLY. AND THEIR DOOR KILLED COMMS.
APOLLO THOUGHT HE HAD A QUICK SOLUTION, BUT IT'S WIPED OUT HIS POWERS' ENERGY STORE.
IN THE MEANTIME, THERE'S A SECOND ATTACK FORCE IN THE AIR OVER NORTHERN EUROPE.
OKAY. OKAY.
I KNOW HOW YOUR POWERS WORK, APOLLO. I WANT YOU IN A DOOR AND OVER EUROPE, NOW.
WHAT ARE YOU --
I KNOW HIS OLD STORMWATCH FILE. A COUPLE OF HOURS WILL SEE HIM AT FULL CHARGE, AND HE'LL BE ABLE TO OPERATE AFTER ONLY TWENTY SECONDS IN SUNLIGHT.
I'M OUT OF OPTIONS HERE.
UNDERSTAND; THE GENERAL CONSENSUS IS THAT THIS IS AN INVASION BY A MAN WHO'LL PROBABLY WANT TO TURN THE ENTIRE PLANET INTO A RAPE CAMP.
ARE YOU ON THE SAME PAGE WITH ME NOW, MIDNIGHTER?
...YES.

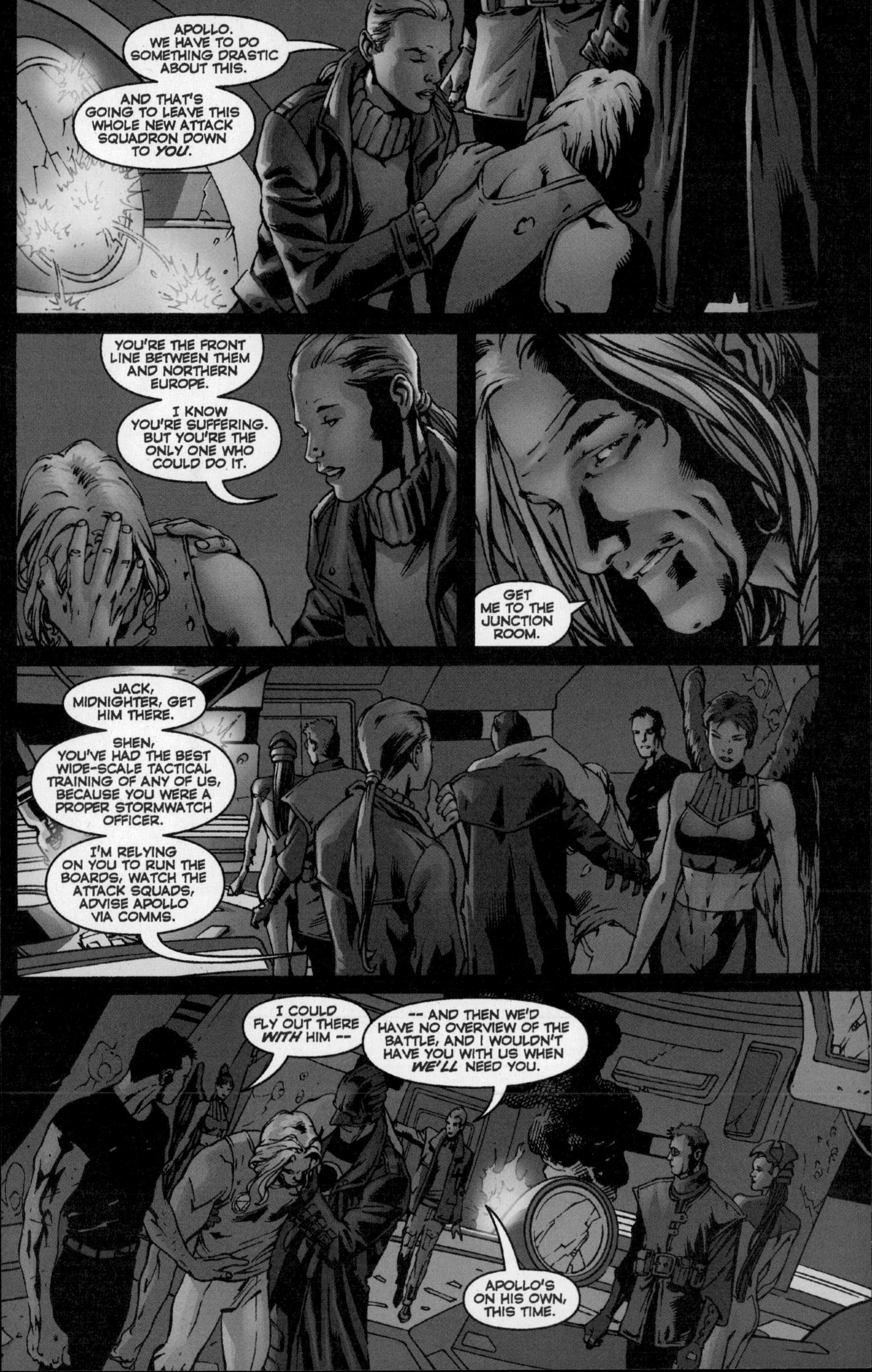
APOLLO. WE HAVE TO DO SOMETHING DRASTIC ABOUT THIS.
AND THAT'S GOING TO LEAVE THIS WHOLE NEW ATTACK SQUADRON DOWN TO *YOU*.
YOU'RE THE FRONT LINE BETWEEN THEM AND NORTHERN EUROPE.
I KNOW YOU'RE SUFFERING. BUT YOU'RE THE ONLY ONE WHO COULD DO IT.
GET ME TO THE JUNCTION ROOM.
JACK, MIDNIGHTER, GET HIM THERE.
SHEN, YOU'VE HAD THE BEST WIDE-SCALE TACTICAL TRAINING OF ANY OF US, BECAUSE YOU WERE A PROPER STORMWATCH OFFICER.
I'M RELYING ON YOU TO RUN THE BOARDS, WATCH THE ATTACK SQUADS, ADVISE APOLLO VIA COMMS.
I COULD FLY OUT THERE *WITH* HIM --
-- AND THEN WE'D HAVE NO OVERVIEW OF THE BATTLE, AND I WOULDN'T HAVE YOU WITH US WHEN *WE'LL* NEED YOU.
APOLLO'S ON HIS OWN, THIS TIME.

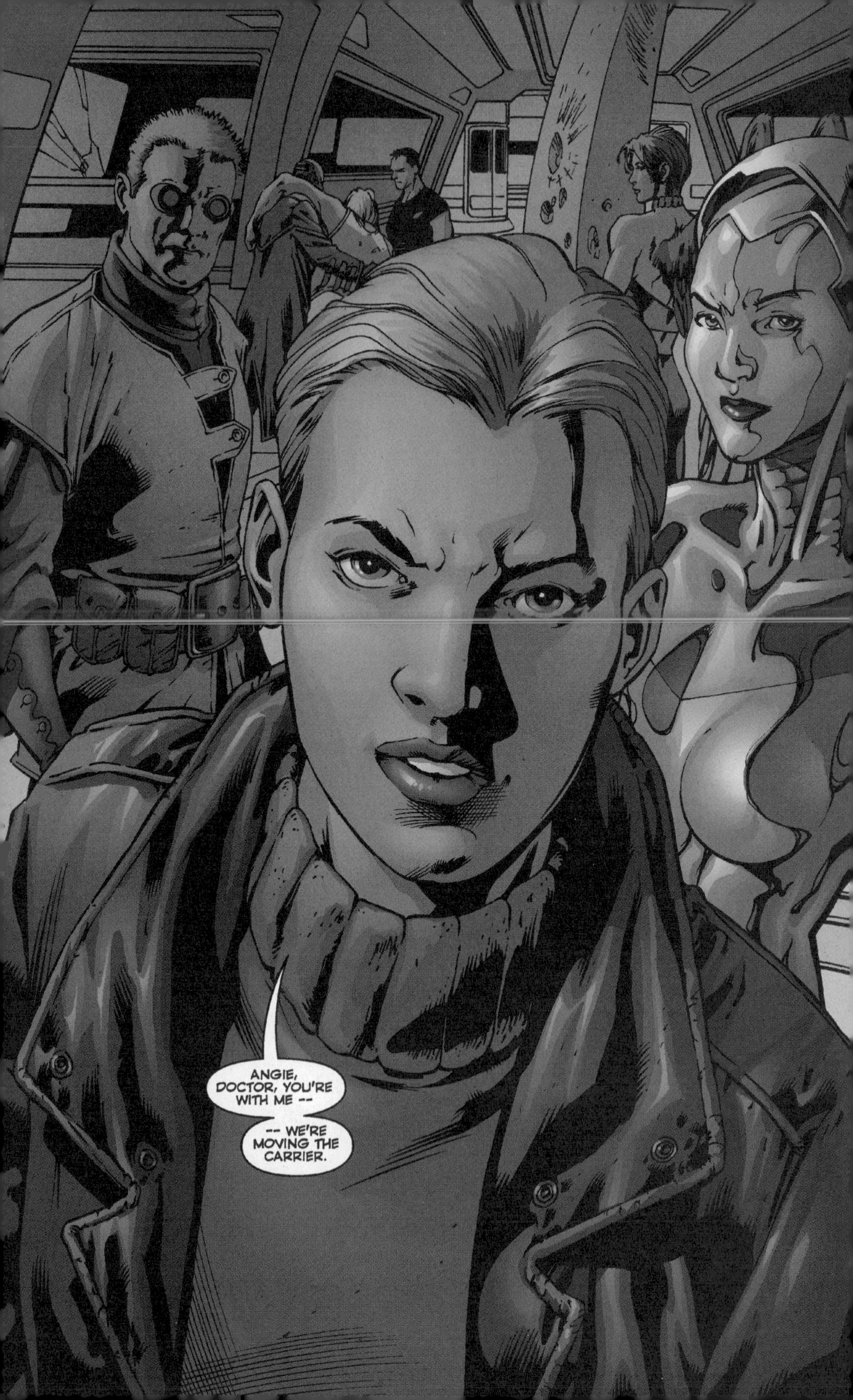
ANGIE, DOCTOR, YOU'RE WITH ME --
-- WE'RE MOVING THE CARRIER.

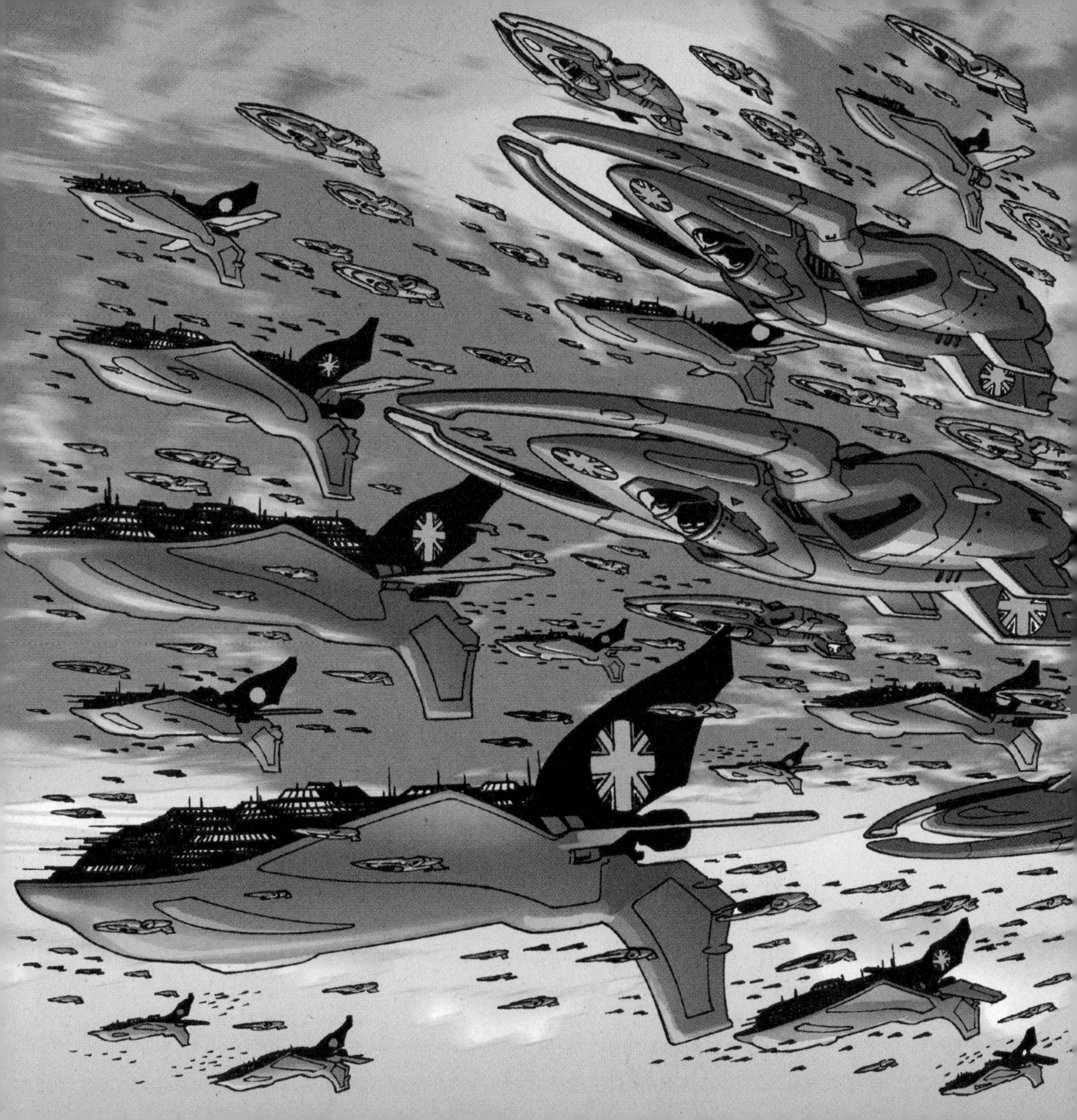

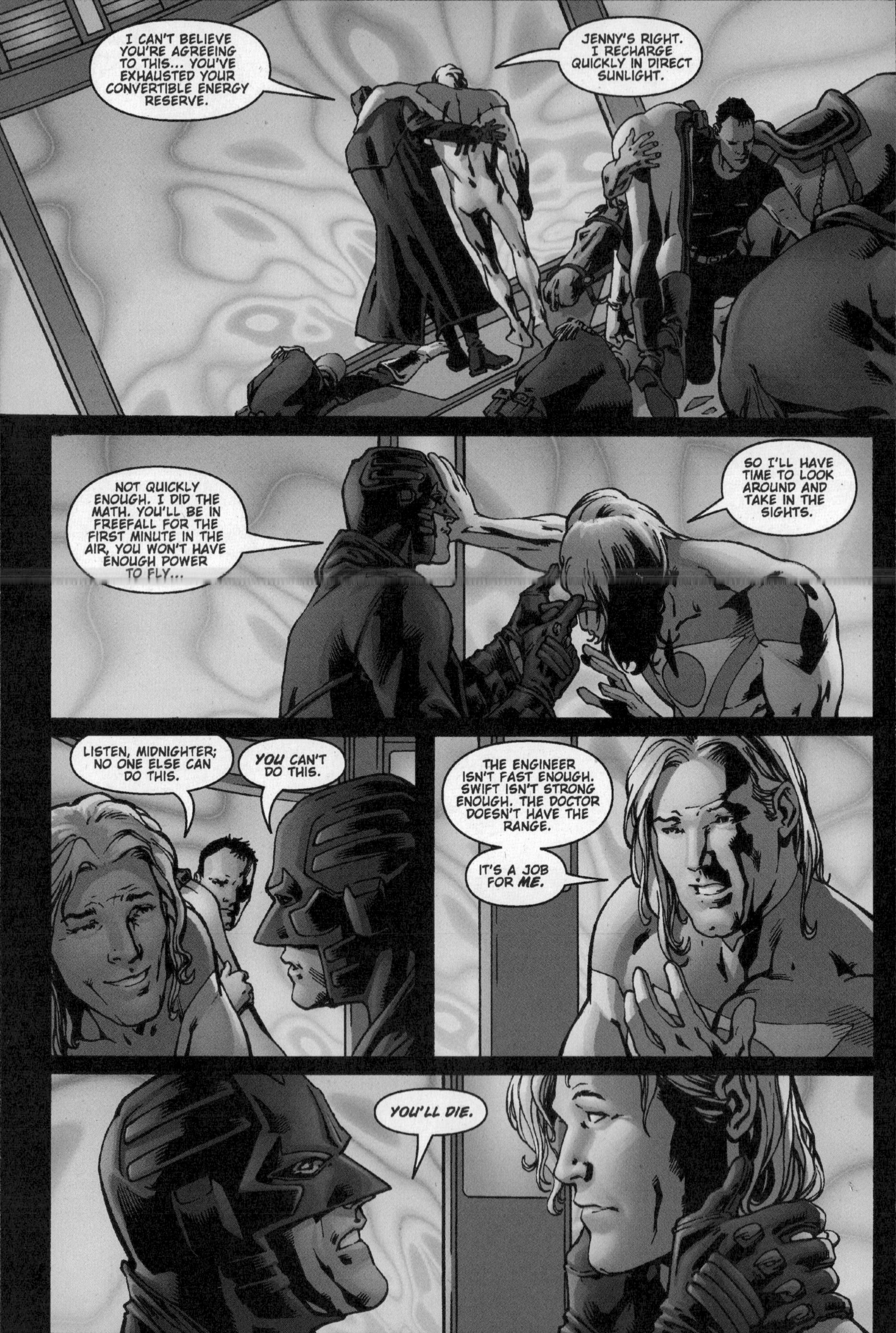
I CAN'T BELIEVE YOU'RE AGREEING TO THIS... YOU'VE EXHAUSTED YOUR CONVERTIBLE ENERGY RESERVE.
JENNY'S RIGHT. I RECHARGE QUICKLY IN DIRECT SUNLIGHT.
NOT QUICKLY ENOUGH. I DID THE MATH. YOU'LL BE IN FREEFALL FOR THE FIRST MINUTE IN THE AIR, YOU WON'T HAVE ENOUGH POWER TO FLY...
SO I'LL HAVE TIME TO LOOK AROUND AND TAKE IN THE SIGHTS.
LISTEN, MIDNIGHTER; NO ONE ELSE CAN DO THIS.
YOU CAN'T DO THIS.
THE ENGINEER ISN'T FAST ENOUGH. SWIFT ISN'T STRONG ENOUGH. THE DOCTOR DOESN'T HAVE THE RANGE.
IT'S A JOB FOR *ME*.
YOU'LL DIE.

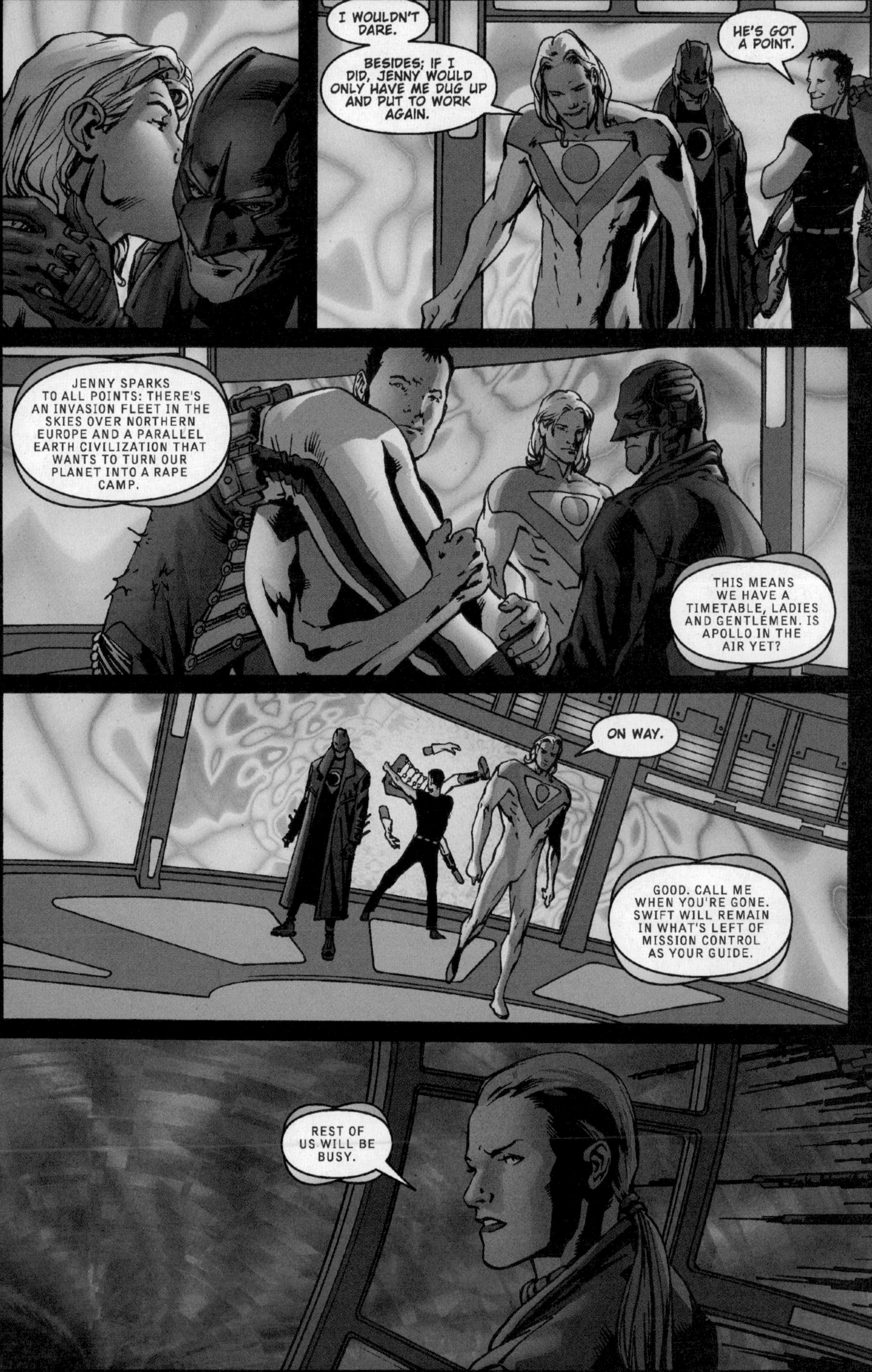
I WOULDN'T DARE.
BESIDES; IF I DID, JENNY WOULD ONLY HAVE ME DUG UP AND PUT TO WORK AGAIN.
HE'S GOT A POINT.
JENNY SPARKS TO ALL POINTS: THERE'S AN INVASION FLEET IN THE SKIES OVER NORTHERN EUROPE AND A PARALLEL EARTH CIVILIZATION THAT WANTS TO TURN OUR PLANET INTO A RAPE CAMP.
THIS MEANS WE HAVE A TIMETABLE, LADIES AND GENTLEMEN. IS APOLLO IN THE AIR YET?
ON WAY.
GOOD. CALL ME WHEN YOU'RE GONE. SWIFT WILL REMAIN IN WHAT'S LEFT OF MISSION CONTROL AS YOUR GUIDE.
REST OF US WILL BE BUSY.

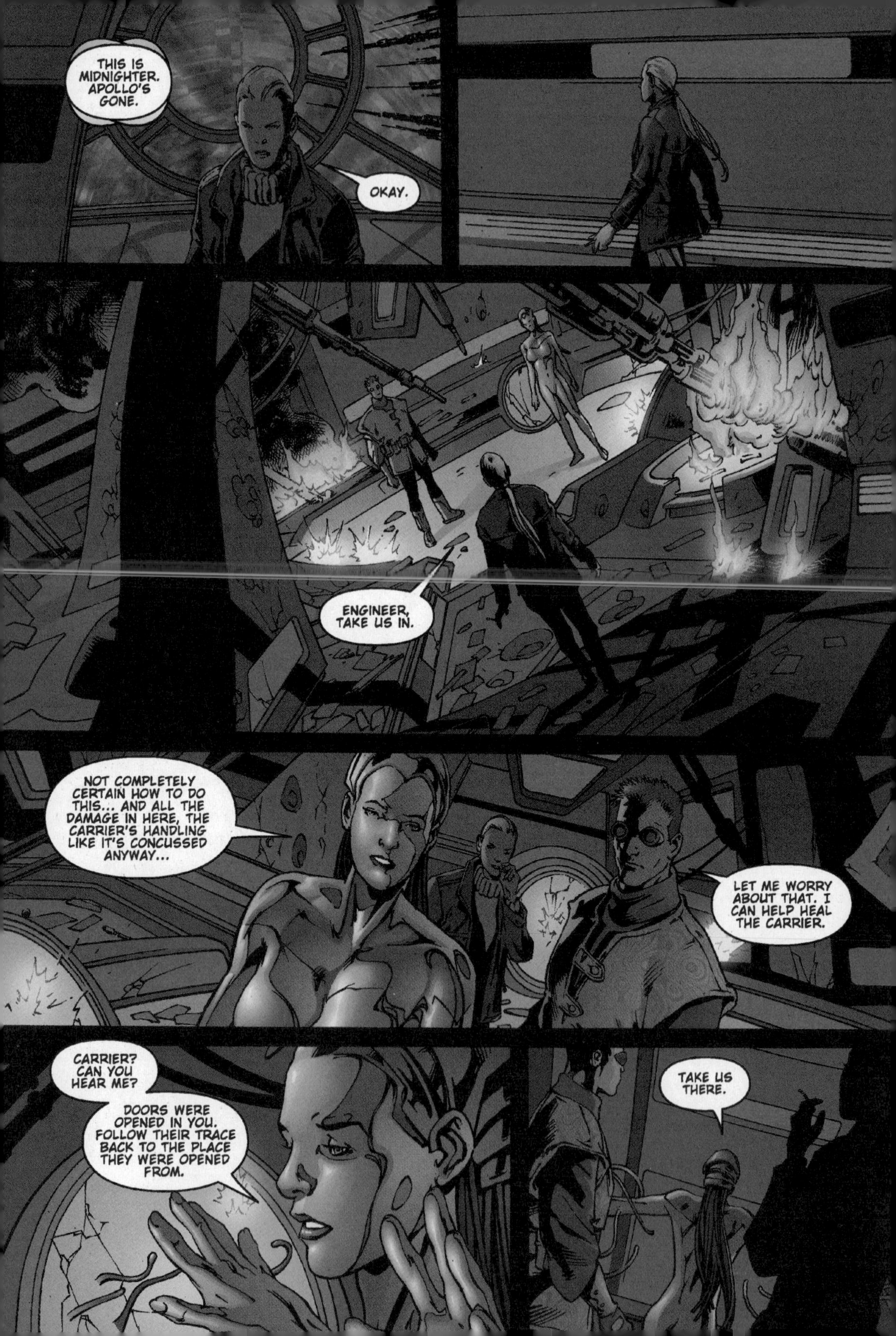
THIS IS MIDNIGHTER. APOLLO'S GONE.
OKAY.
ENGINEER, TAKE US IN.
NOT COMPLETELY CERTAIN HOW TO DO THIS... AND ALL THE DAMAGE IN HERE, THE CARRIER'S HANDLING LIKE IT'S CONCUSSED ANYWAY...
LET ME WORRY ABOUT THAT. I CAN HELP HEAL THE CARRIER.
CARRIER? CAN YOU HEAR ME?
DOORS WERE OPENED IN YOU. FOLLOW THEIR TRACE BACK TO THE PLACE THEY WERE OPENED FROM.
TAKE US THERE.

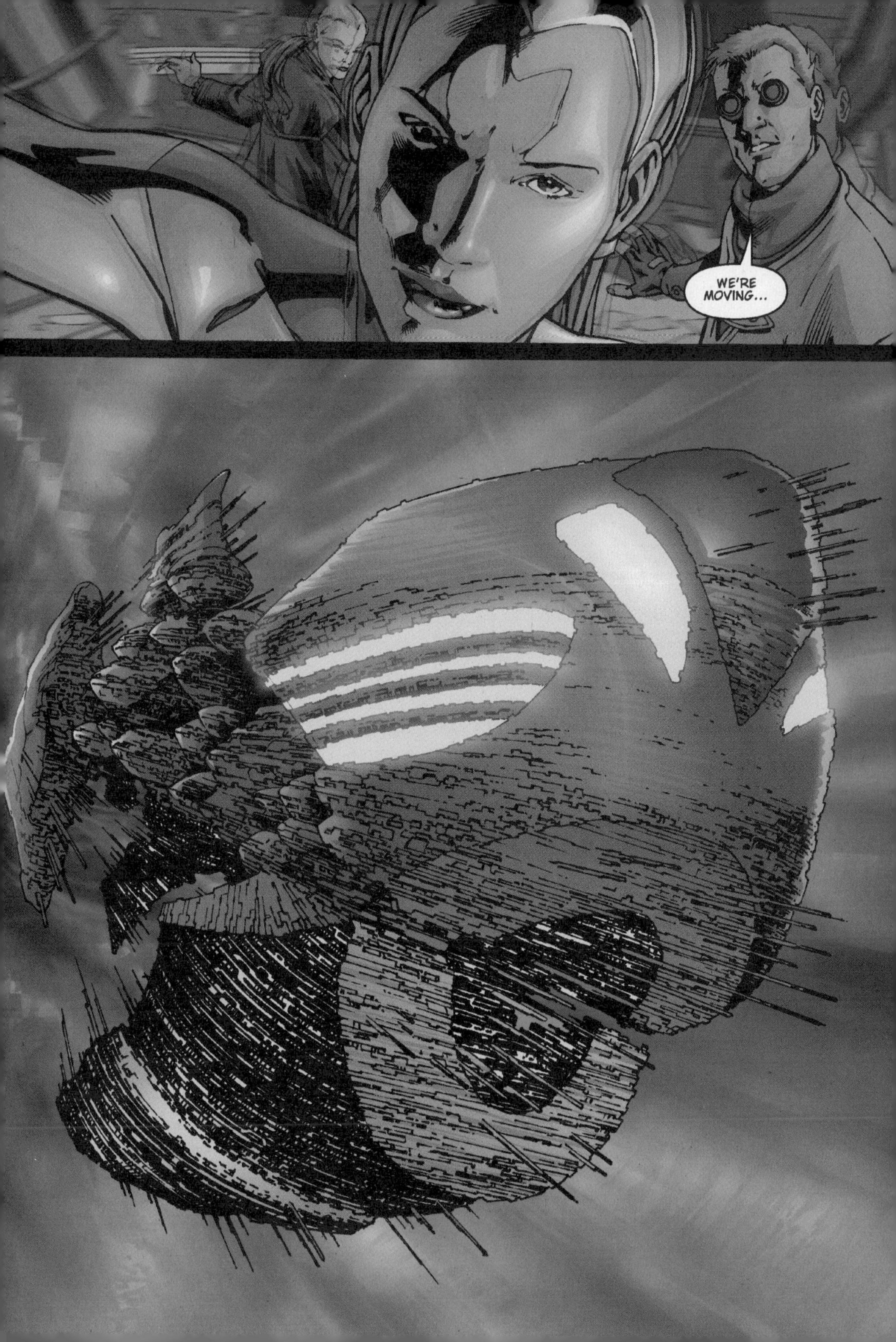
WE'RE MOVING…

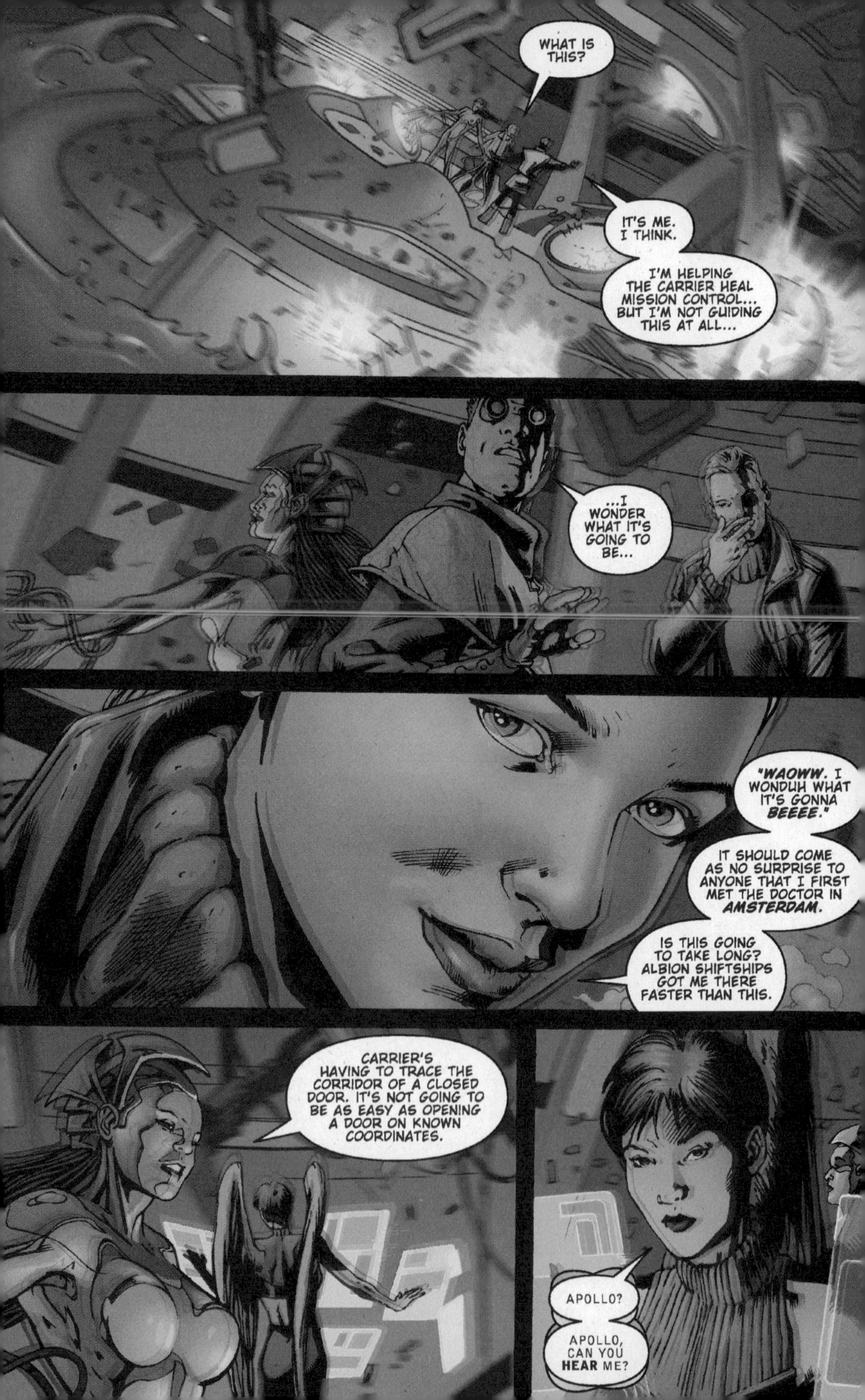
WHAT IS THIS?
IT'S ME. I THINK.
I'M HELPING THE CARRIER HEAL MISSION CONTROL... BUT I'M NOT GUIDING THIS AT ALL...
...I WONDER WHAT IT'S GOING TO BE...
"WAOWW. I WONDUH WHAT IT'S GONNA BEEEE."
IT SHOULD COME AS NO SURPRISE TO ANYONE THAT I FIRST MET THE DOCTOR IN AMSTERDAM.
IS THIS GOING TO TAKE LONG? ALBION SHIFTSHIPS GOT ME THERE FASTER THAN THIS.
CARRIER'S HAVING TO TRACE THE CORRIDOR OF A CLOSED DOOR. IT'S NOT GOING TO BE AS EASY AS OPENING A DOOR ON KNOWN COORDINATES.
APOLLO?
APOLLO, CAN YOU HEAR ME?

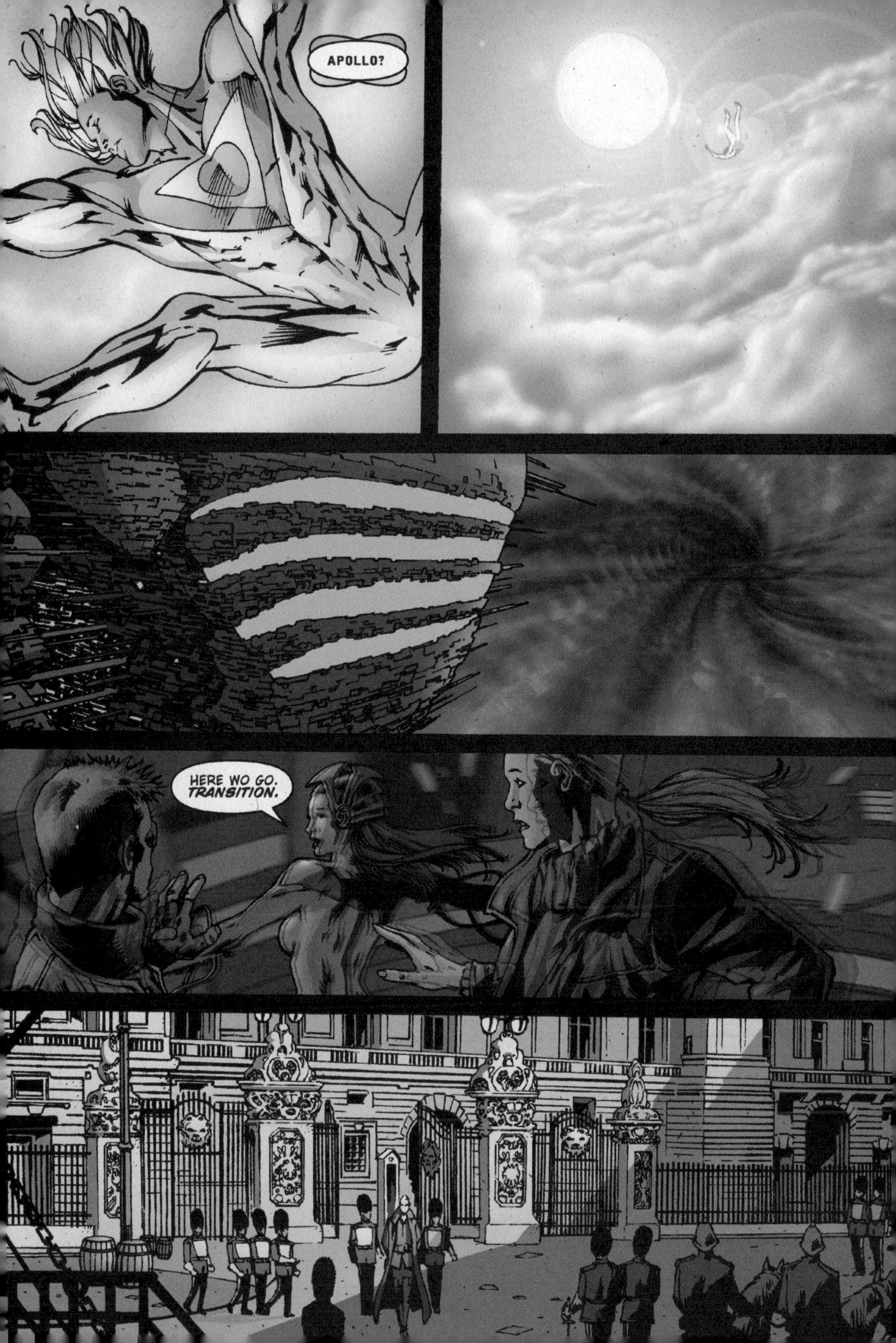
APOLLO?
HERE WO GO. TRANSITION.

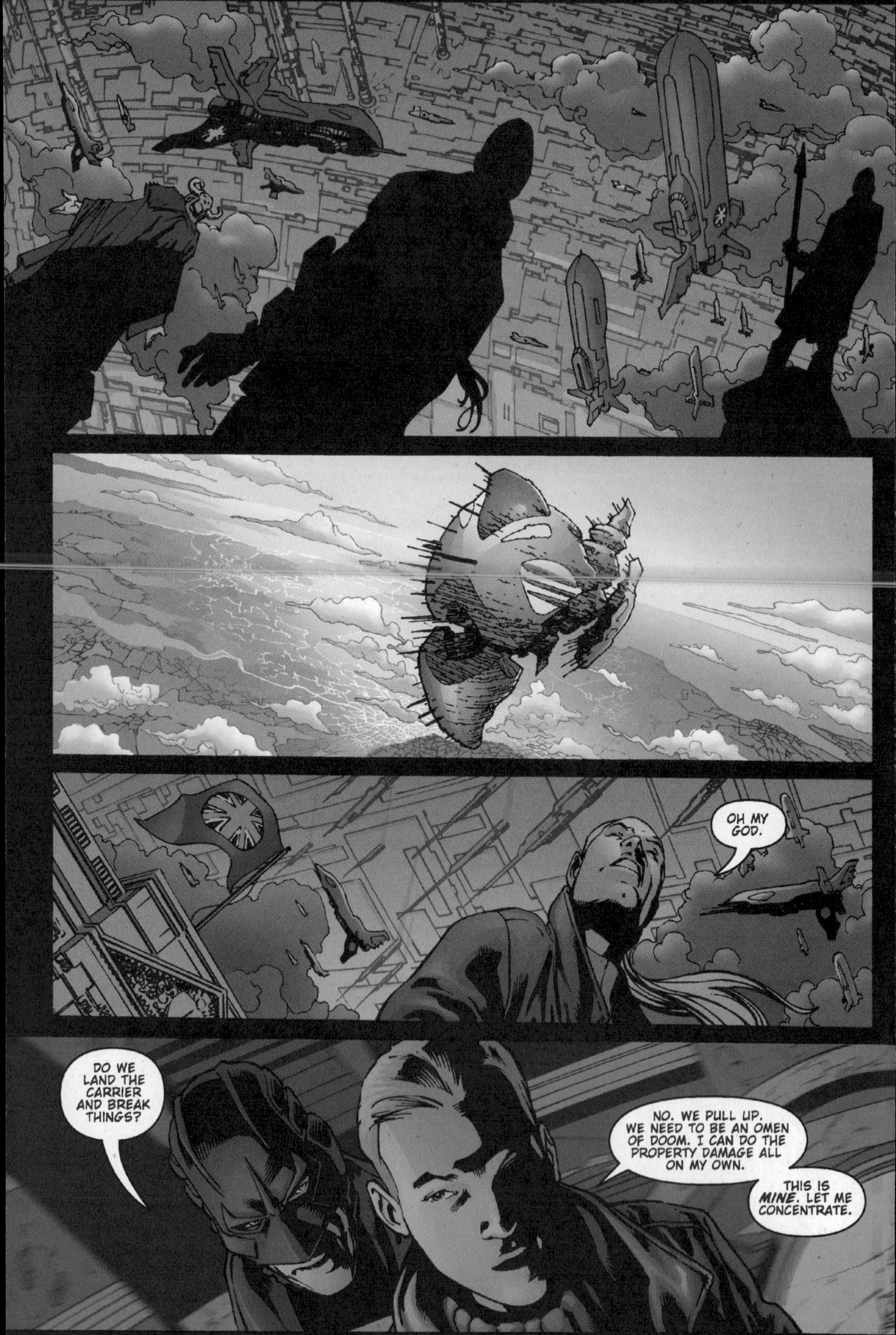
OH MY GOD.
DO WE LAND THE CARRIER AND BREAK THINGS?
NO. WE PULL UP. WE NEED TO BE AN OMEN OF DOOM. I CAN DO THE PROPERTY DAMAGE ALL ON MY OWN.
THIS IS *MINE*. LET ME CONCENTRATE.

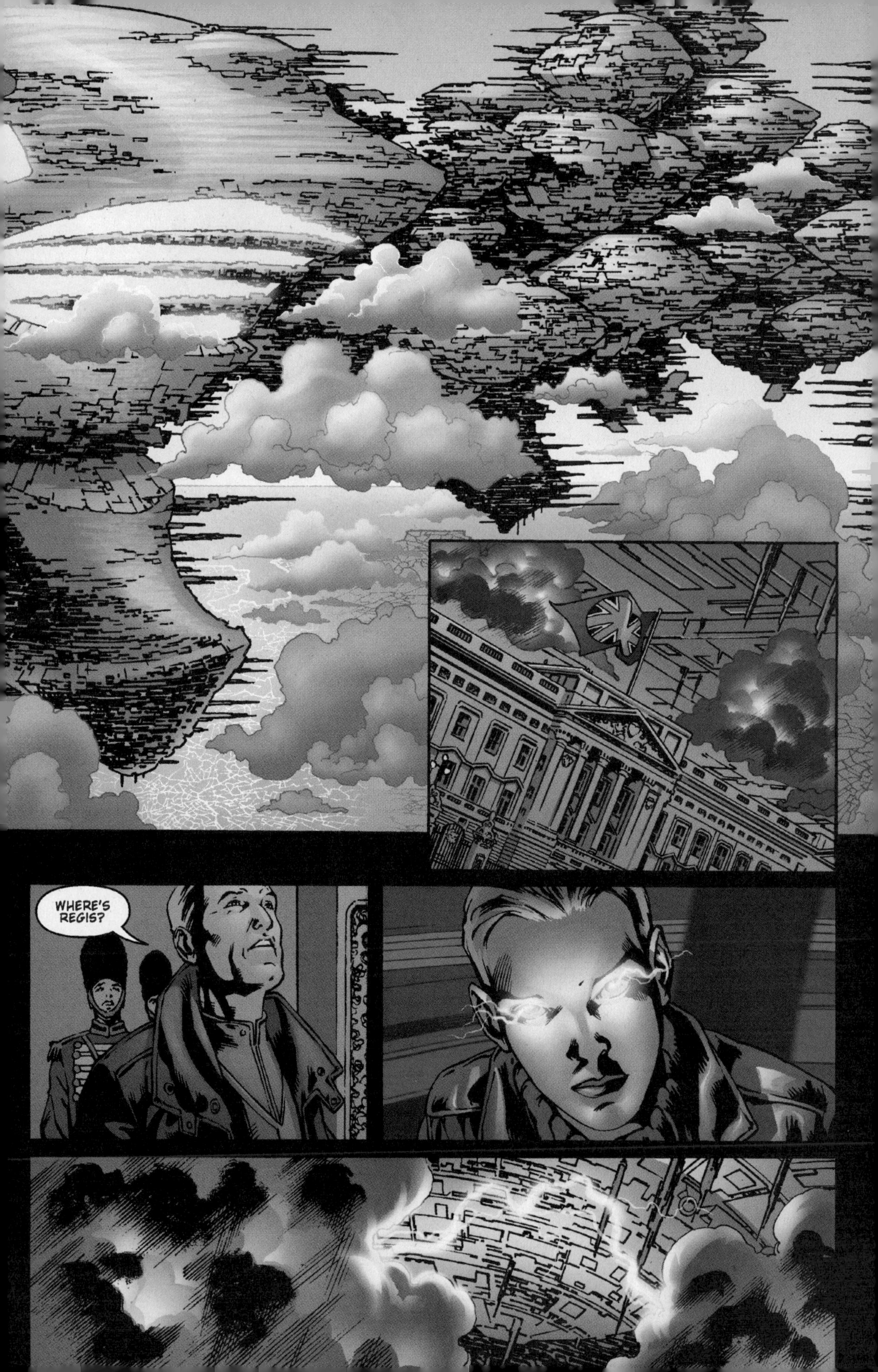
WHERE'S REGIS?

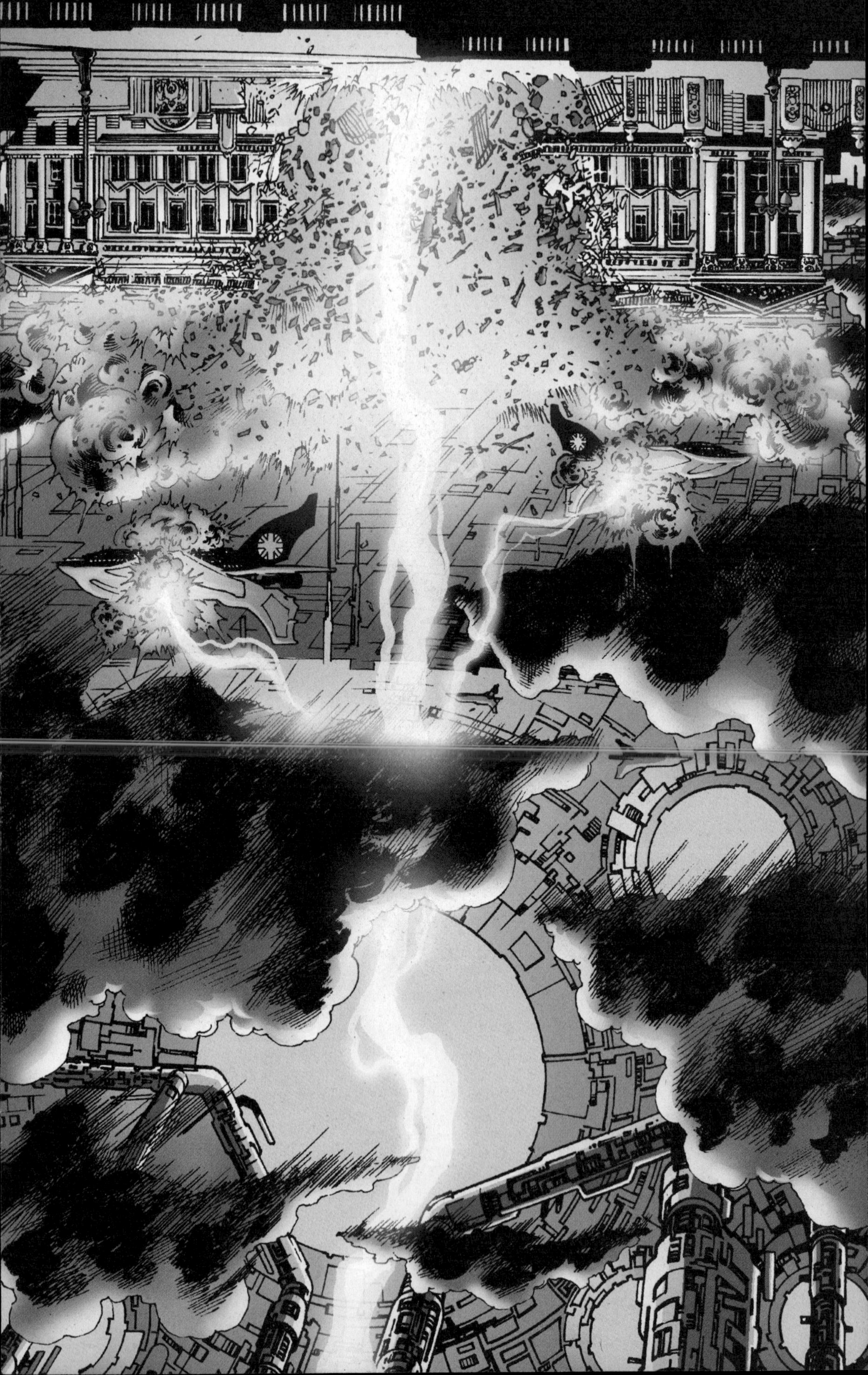

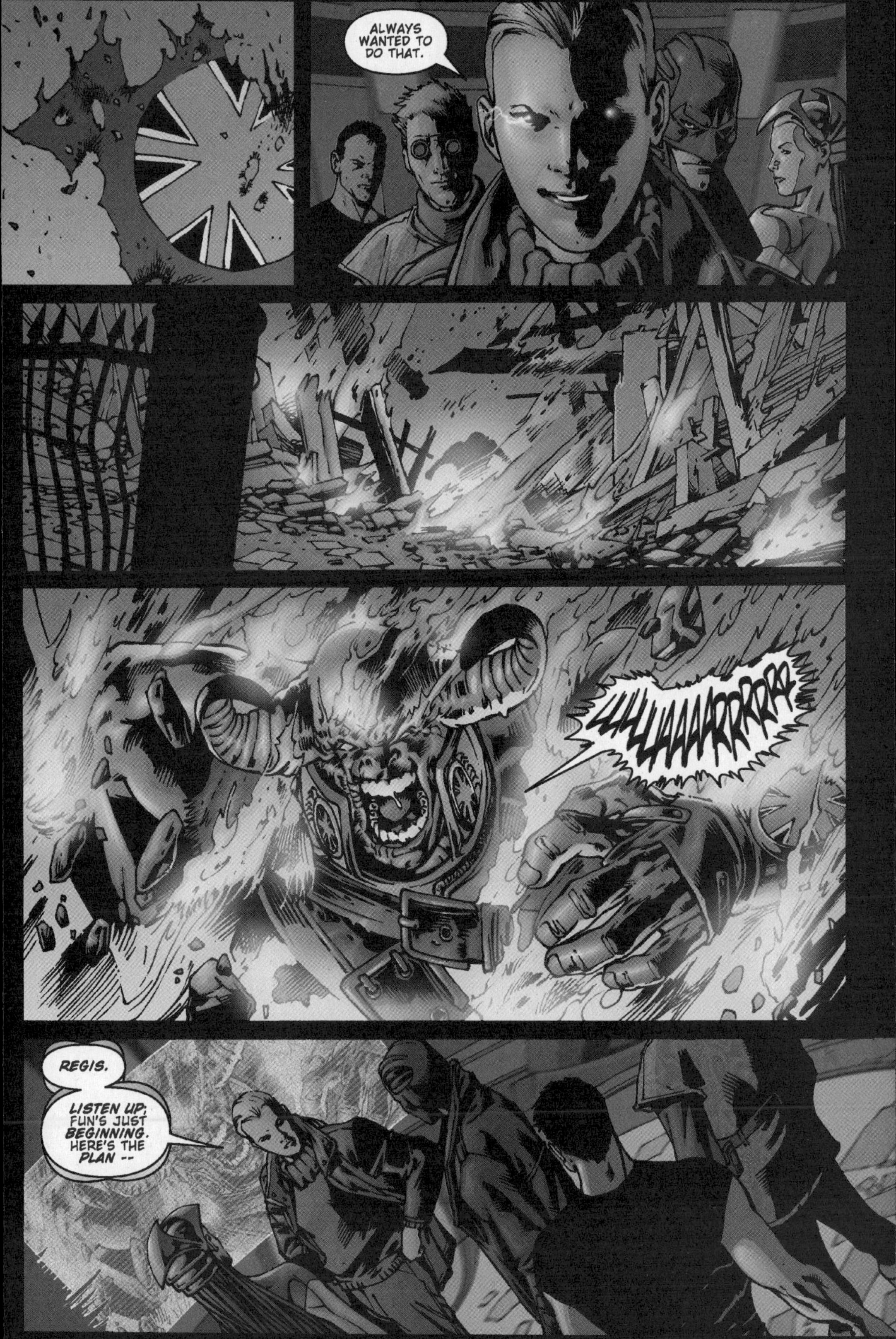
ALWAYS WANTED TO DO THAT.
LLLLLAAAAARRRRRRR
REGIS.
LISTEN UP: FUN'S JUST BEGINNING. HERE'S THE PLAN --

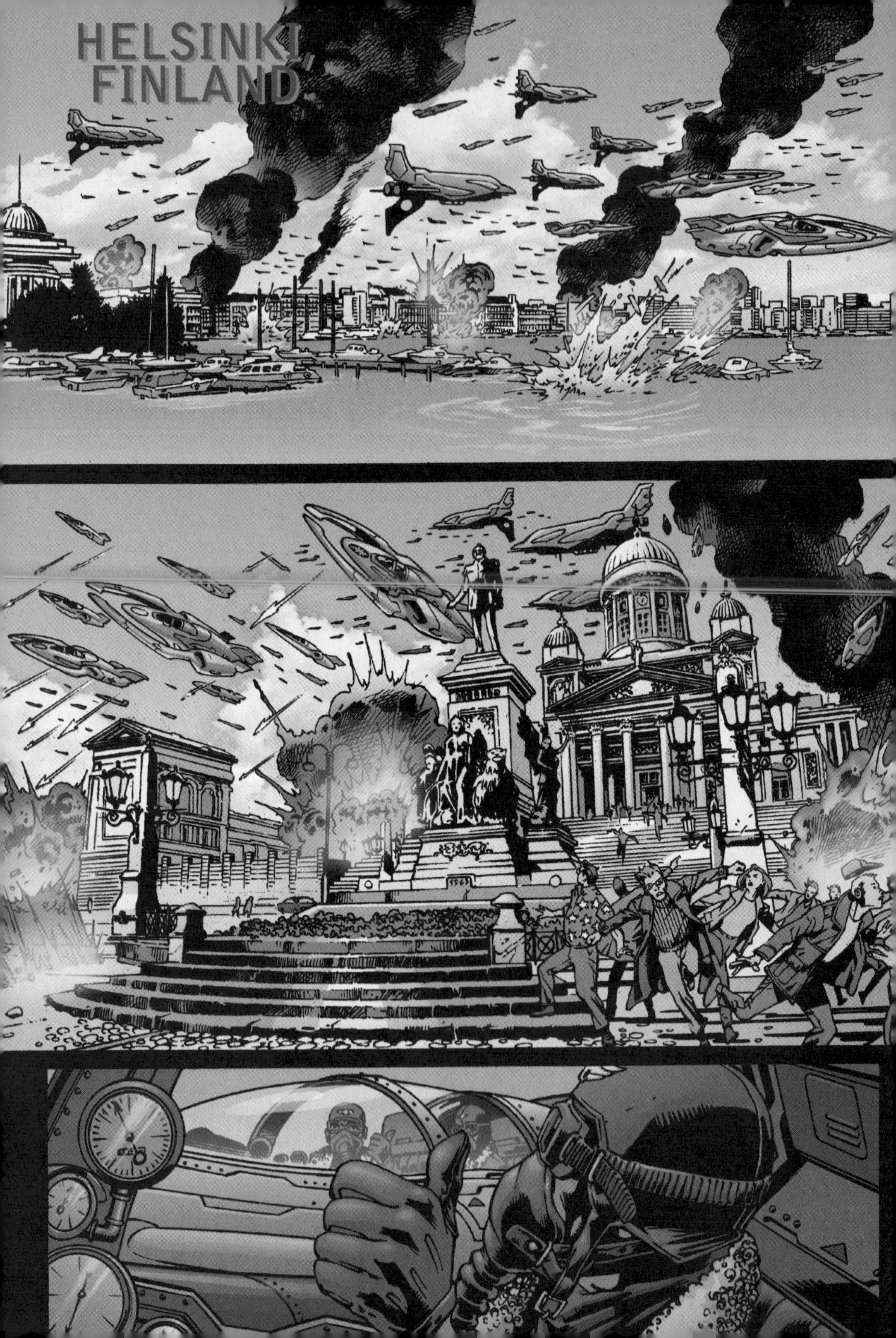
HELSINKI, FINLAND

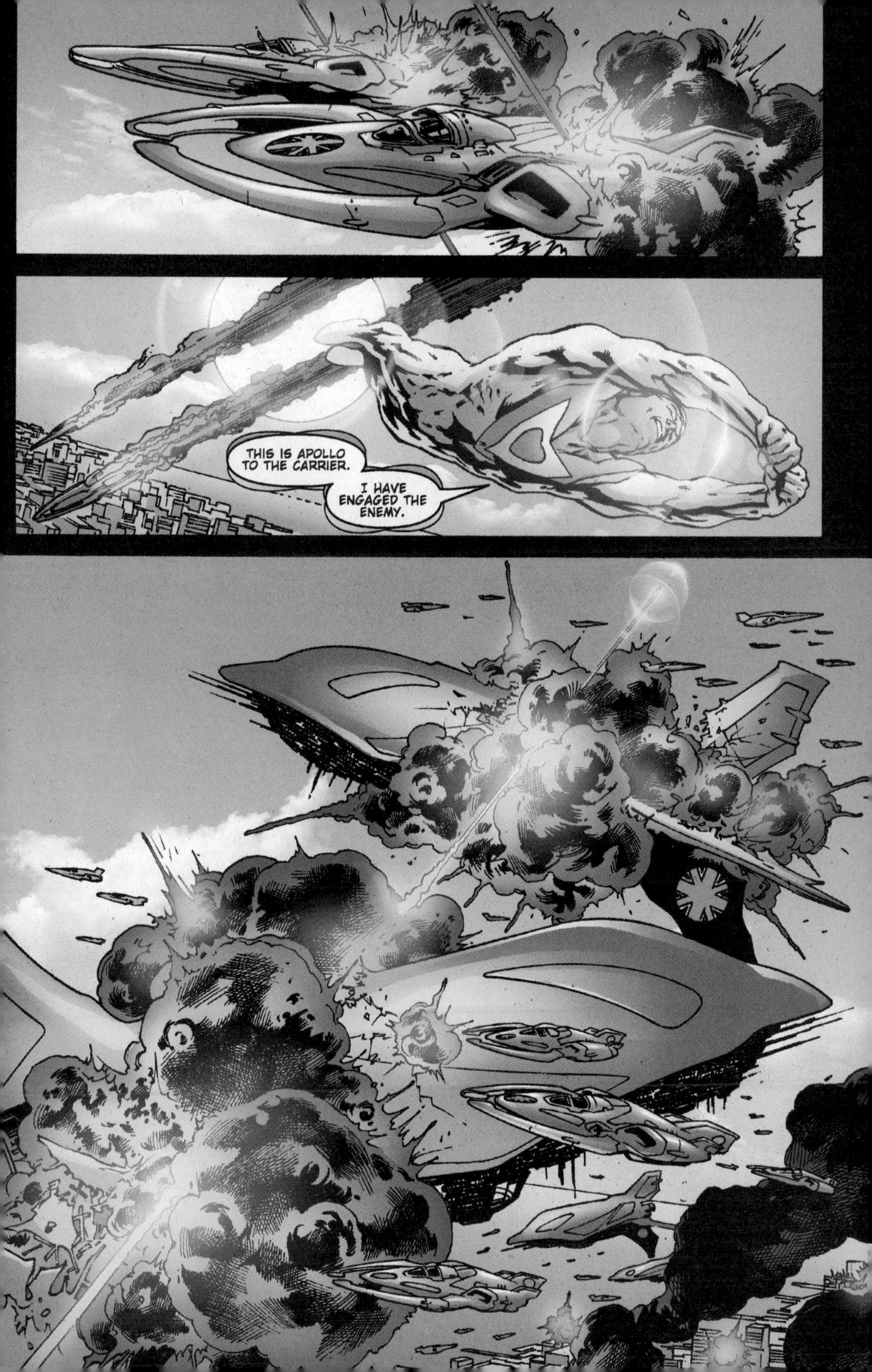
THIS IS APOLLO TO THE CARRIER.
I HAVE ENGAGED THE ENEMY.

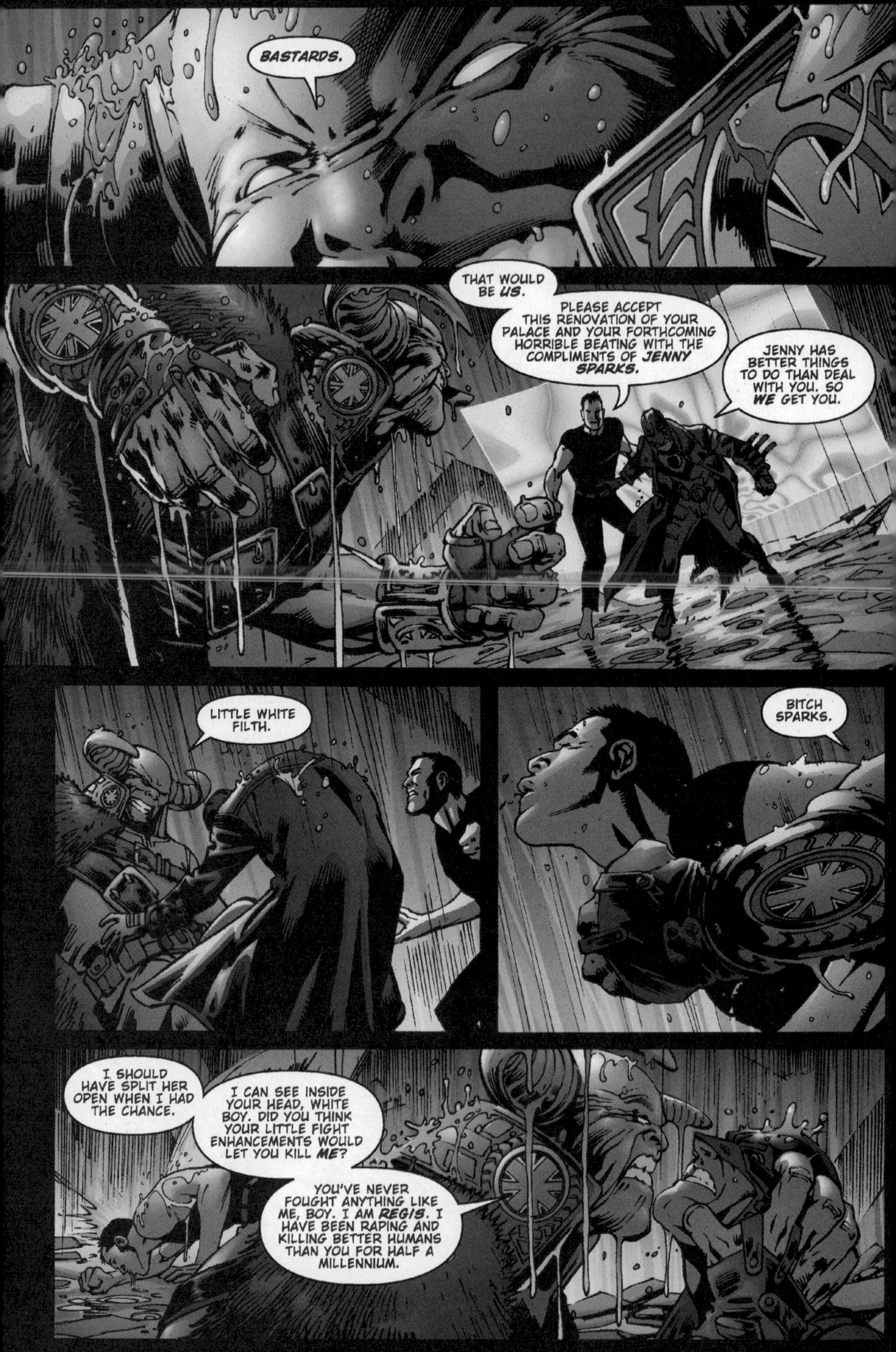
BASTARDS.
THAT WOULD BE US.
PLEASE ACCEPT THIS RENOVATION OF YOUR PALACE AND YOUR FORTHCOMING HORRIBLE BEATING WITH THE COMPLIMENTS OF JENNY SPARKS.
JENNY HAS BETTER THINGS TO DO THAN DEAL WITH YOU. SO WE GET YOU.
LITTLE WHITE FILTH.
BITCH SPARKS.
I SHOULD HAVE SPLIT HER OPEN WHEN I HAD THE CHANCE.
I CAN SEE INSIDE YOUR HEAD, WHITE BOY. DID YOU THINK YOUR LITTLE FIGHT ENHANCEMENTS WOULD LET YOU KILL ME?
YOU'VE NEVER FOUGHT ANYTHING LIKE ME, BOY. I AM REGIS. I HAVE BEEN RAPING AND KILLING BETTER HUMANS THAN YOU FOR HALF A MILLENNIUM.

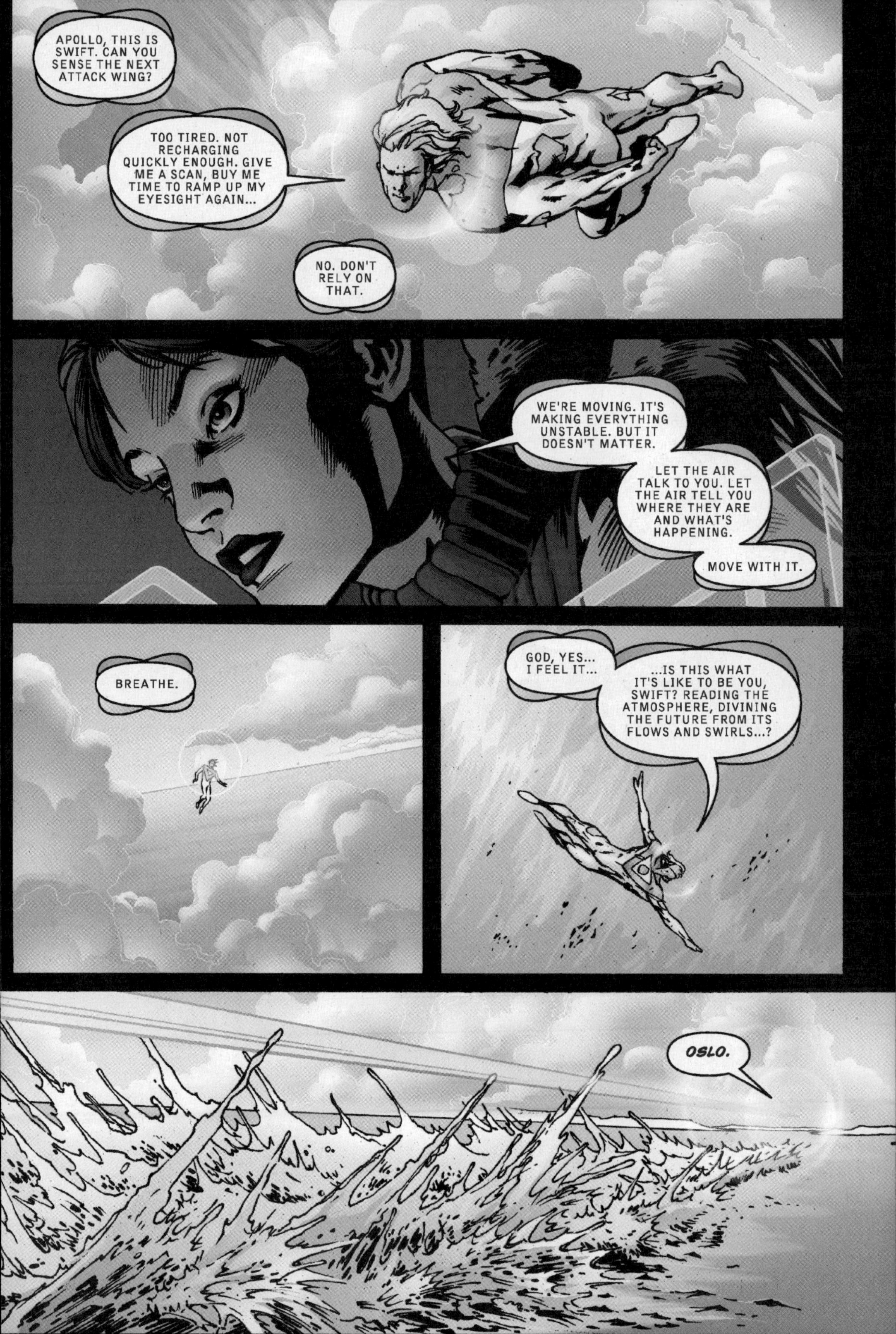
APOLLO, THIS IS SWIFT. CAN YOU SENSE THE NEXT ATTACK WING?
TOO TIRED. NOT RECHARGING QUICKLY ENOUGH. GIVE ME A SCAN, BUY ME TIME TO RAMP UP MY EYESIGHT AGAIN...
NO. DON'T RELY ON THAT.
WE'RE MOVING. IT'S MAKING EVERYTHING UNSTABLE. BUT IT DOESN'T MATTER.
LET THE AIR TALK TO YOU. LET THE AIR TELL YOU WHERE THEY ARE AND WHAT'S HAPPENING.
MOVE WITH IT.
BREATHE.
GOD, YES... I FEEL IT...
...IS THIS WHAT IT'S LIKE TO BE YOU, SWIFT? READING THE ATMOSPHERE, DIVINING THE FUTURE FROM ITS FLOWS AND SWIRLS...?
OSLO.

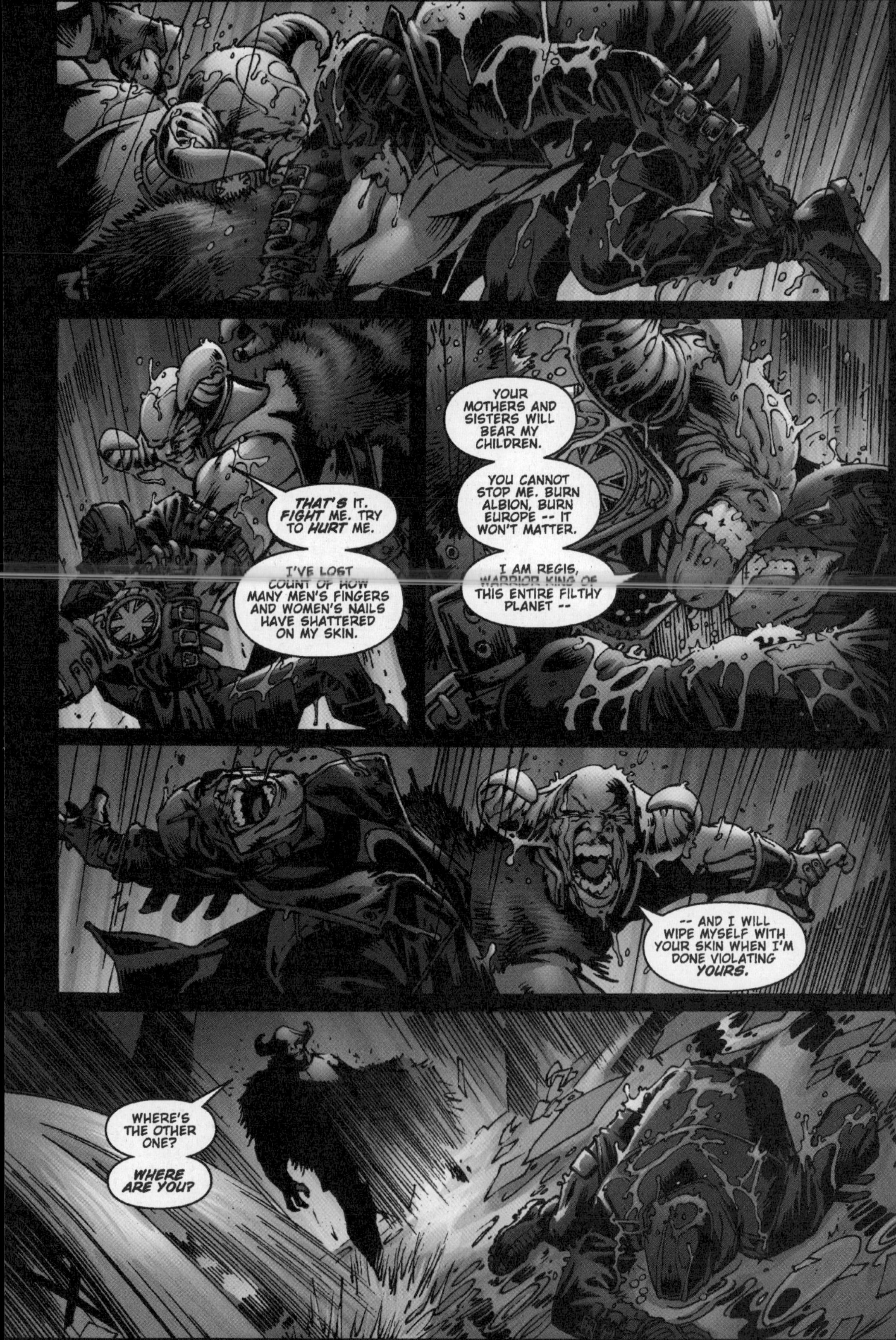
THAT'S IT. FIGHT ME. TRY TO HURT ME.
I'VE LOST COUNT OF HOW MANY MEN'S FINGERS AND WOMEN'S NAILS HAVE SHATTERED ON MY SKIN.
YOUR MOTHERS AND SISTERS WILL BEAR MY CHILDREN.
YOU CANNOT STOP ME. BURN ALBION, BURN EUROPE -- IT WON'T MATTER.
I AM REGIS, WARRIOR KING OF THIS ENTIRE FILTHY PLANET --
-- AND I WILL WIPE MYSELF WITH YOUR SKIN WHEN I'M DONE VIOLATING YOURS.
WHERE'S THE OTHER ONE?
WHERE ARE YOU?

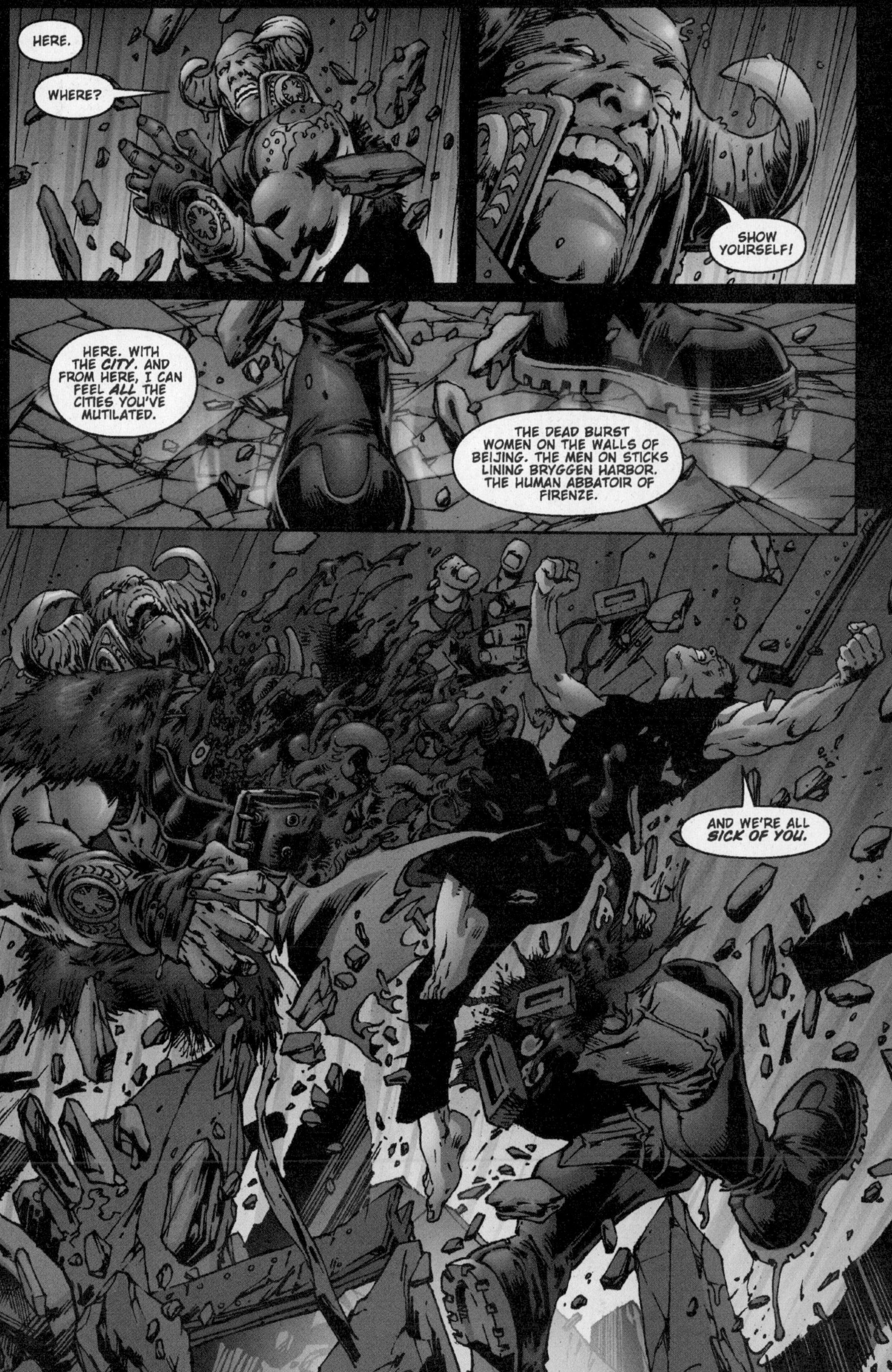
HERE.
WHERE?
SHOW YOURSELF!
HERE. WITH THE *CITY*. AND FROM HERE, I CAN FEEL *ALL* THE CITIES YOU'VE MUTILATED.
THE DEAD BURST WOMEN ON THE WALLS OF BEIJING. THE MEN ON STICKS LINING BRYGGEN HARBOR. THE HUMAN ABBATOIR OF FIRENZE.
AND WE'RE ALL *SICK OF YOU.*

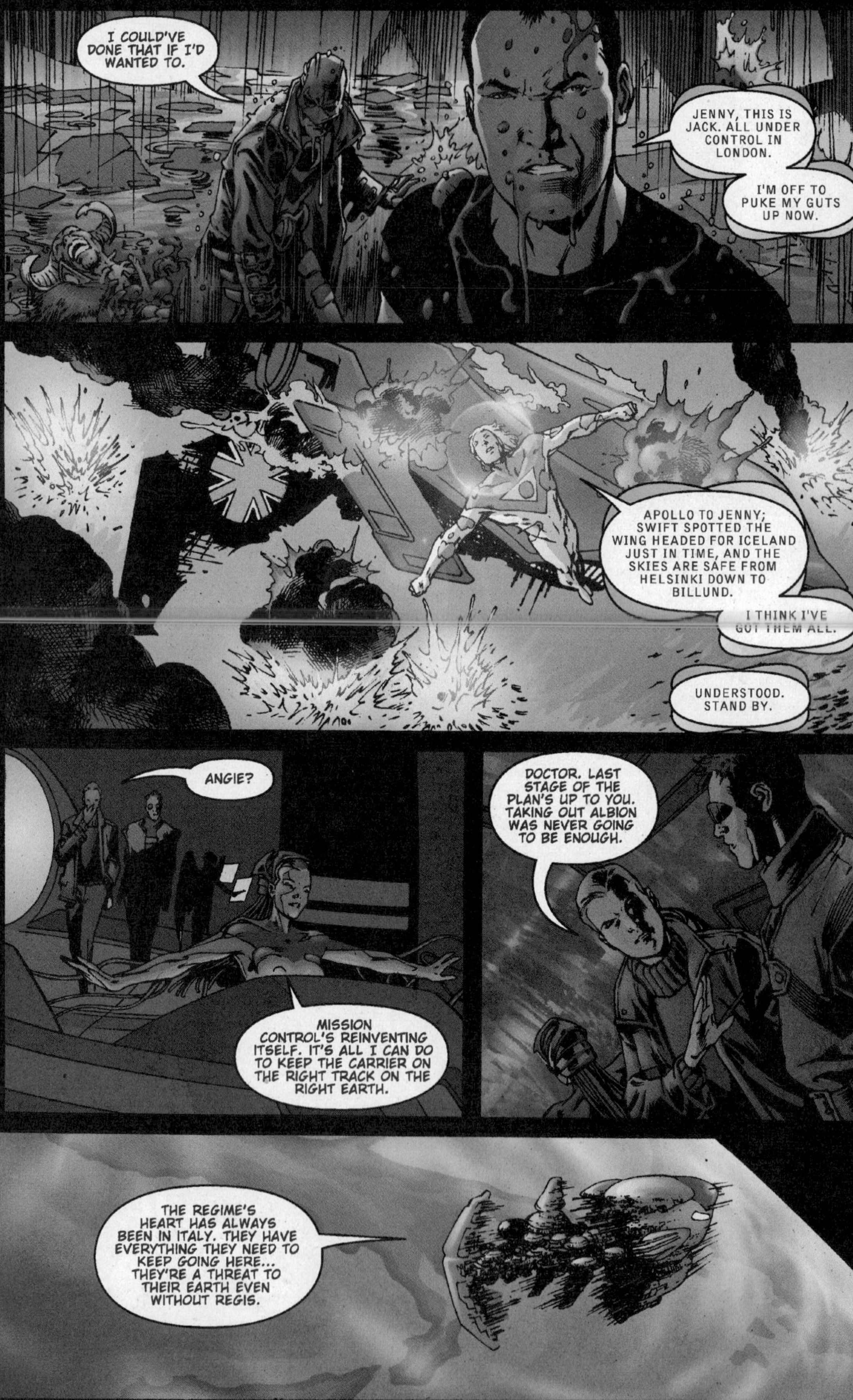
I COULD'VE DONE THAT IF I'D WANTED TO.
JENNY, THIS IS JACK. ALL UNDER CONTROL IN LONDON.
I'M OFF TO PUKE MY GUTS UP NOW.
APOLLO TO JENNY; SWIFT SPOTTED THE WING HEADED FOR ICELAND JUST IN TIME, AND THE SKIES ARE SAFE FROM HELSINKI DOWN TO BILLUND.
I THINK I'VE GOT THEM ALL.
UNDERSTOOD. STAND BY.
ANGIE?
MISSION CONTROL'S REINVENTING ITSELF. IT'S ALL I CAN DO TO KEEP THE CARRIER ON THE RIGHT TRACK ON THE RIGHT EARTH.
DOCTOR. LAST STAGE OF THE PLAN'S UP TO YOU. TAKING OUT ALBION WAS NEVER GOING TO BE ENOUGH.
THE REGIME'S HEART HAS ALWAYS BEEN IN ITALY. THEY HAVE EVERYTHING THEY NEED TO KEEP GOING HERE... THEY'RE A THREAT TO THEIR EARTH EVEN WITHOUT REGIS.

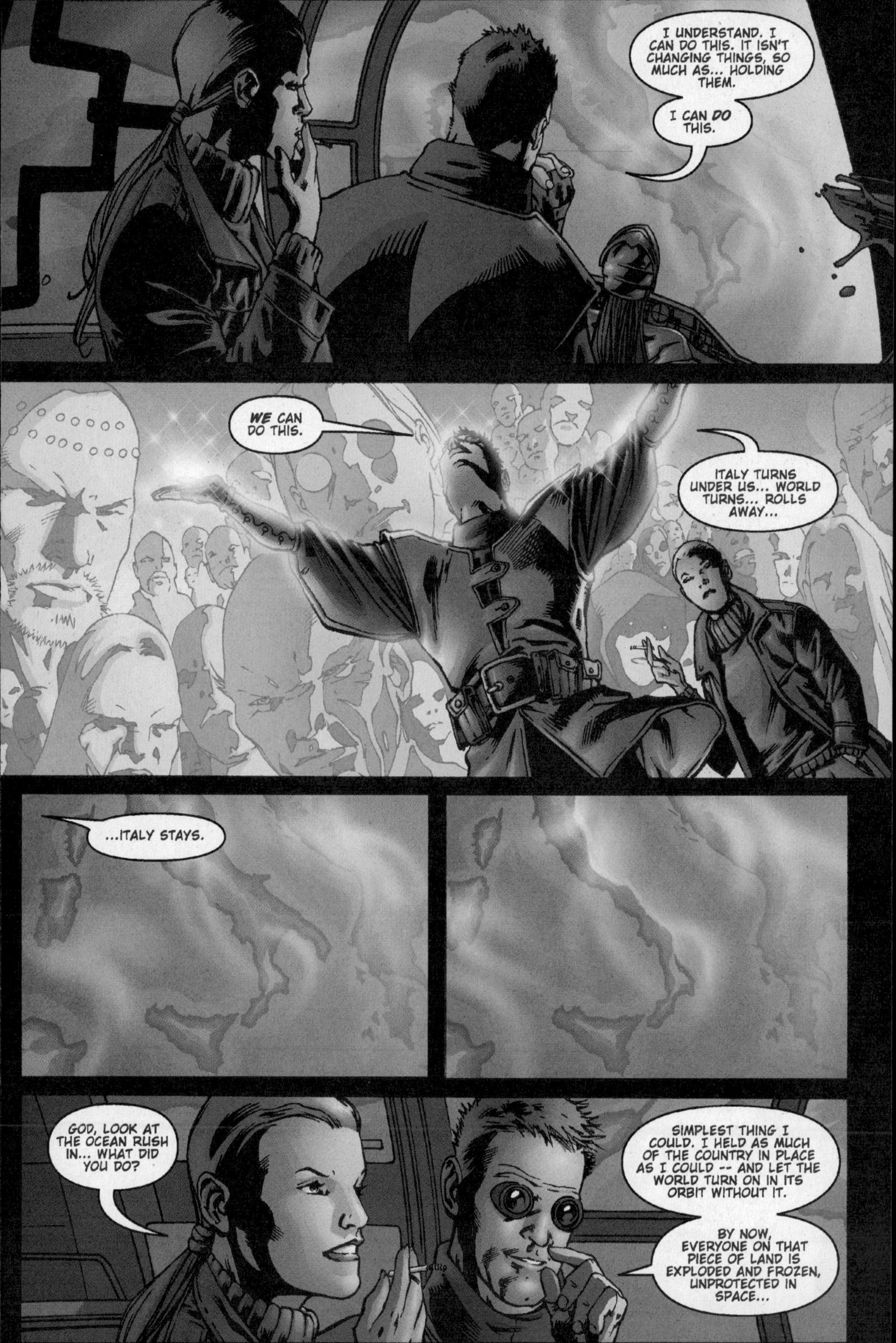
I UNDERSTAND. I CAN DO THIS. IT ISN'T CHANGING THINGS, SO MUCH AS... HOLDING THEM.
I CAN *DO* THIS.
WE CAN DO THIS.
ITALY TURNS UNDER US... WORLD TURNS... ROLLS AWAY...
...ITALY STAYS.
GOD, LOOK AT THE OCEAN RUSH IN... WHAT DID YOU DO?
SIMPLEST THING I COULD. I HELD AS MUCH OF THE COUNTRY IN PLACE AS I COULD -- AND LET THE WORLD TURN ON IN ITS ORBIT WITHOUT IT.
BY NOW, EVERYONE ON THAT PIECE OF LAND IS EXPLODED AND FROZEN, UNPROTECTED IN SPACE...

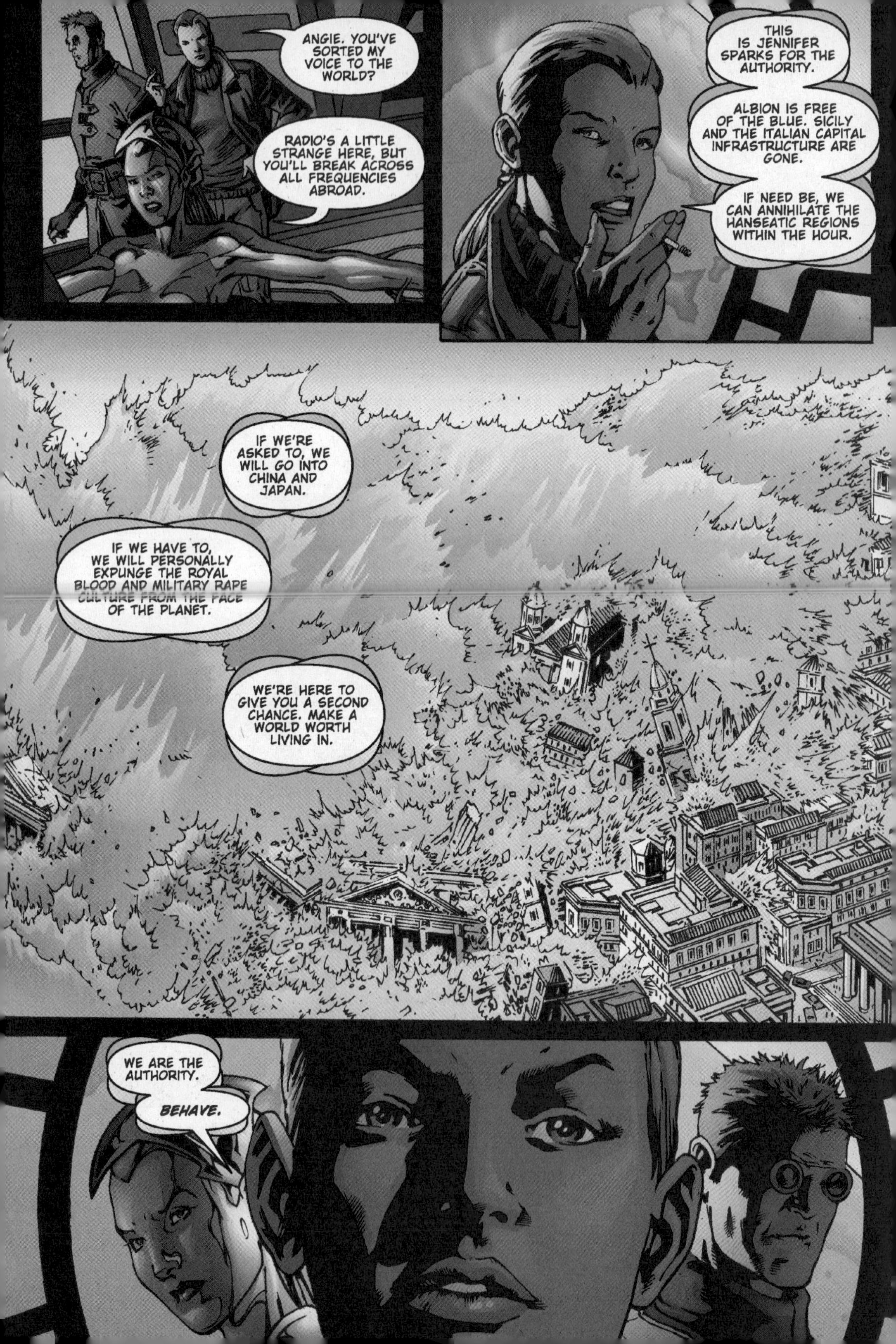
ANGIE. YOU'VE SORTED MY VOICE TO THE WORLD?
RADIO'S A LITTLE STRANGE HERE, BUT YOU'LL BREAK ACROSS ALL FREQUENCIES ABROAD.
THIS IS JENNIFER SPARKS FOR THE AUTHORITY.
ALBION IS FREE OF THE BLUE. SICILY AND THE ITALIAN CAPITAL INFRASTRUCTURE ARE GONE.
IF NEED BE, WE CAN ANNIHILATE THE HANSEATIC REGIONS WITHIN THE HOUR.
IF WE'RE ASKED TO, WE WILL GO INTO CHINA AND JAPAN.
IF WE HAVE TO, WE WILL PERSONALLY EXPUNGE THE ROYAL BLOOD AND MILITARY RAPE CULTURE FROM THE FACE OF THE PLANET.
WE'RE HERE TO GIVE YOU A SECOND CHANCE. MAKE A WORLD WORTH LIVING IN.
WE ARE THE AUTHORITY.
BEHAVE.

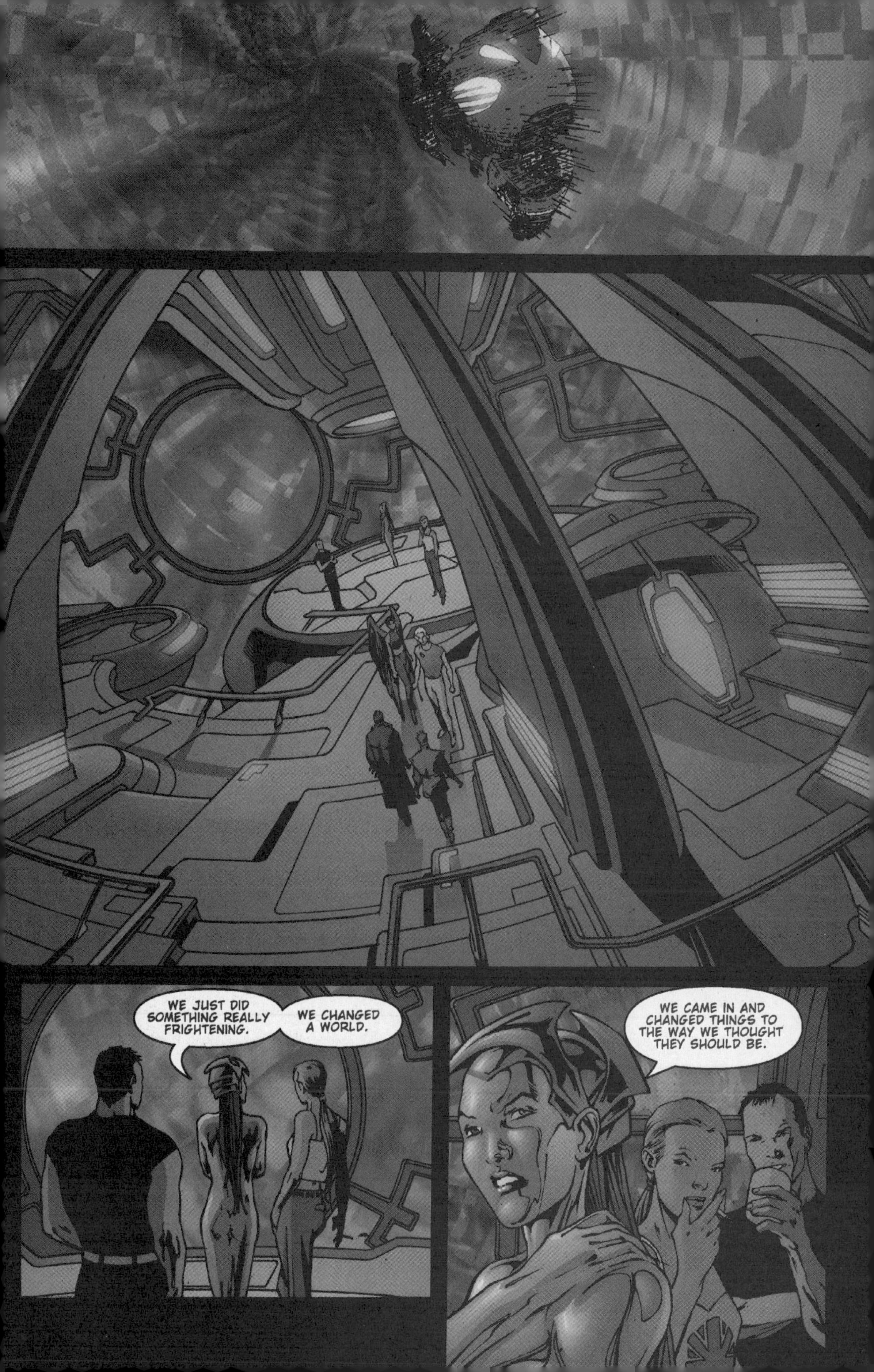
WE JUST DID SOMETHING REALLY FRIGHTENING.
WE CHANGED A WORLD.
WE CAME IN AND CHANGED THINGS TO THE WAY WE THOUGHT THEY SHOULD BE.

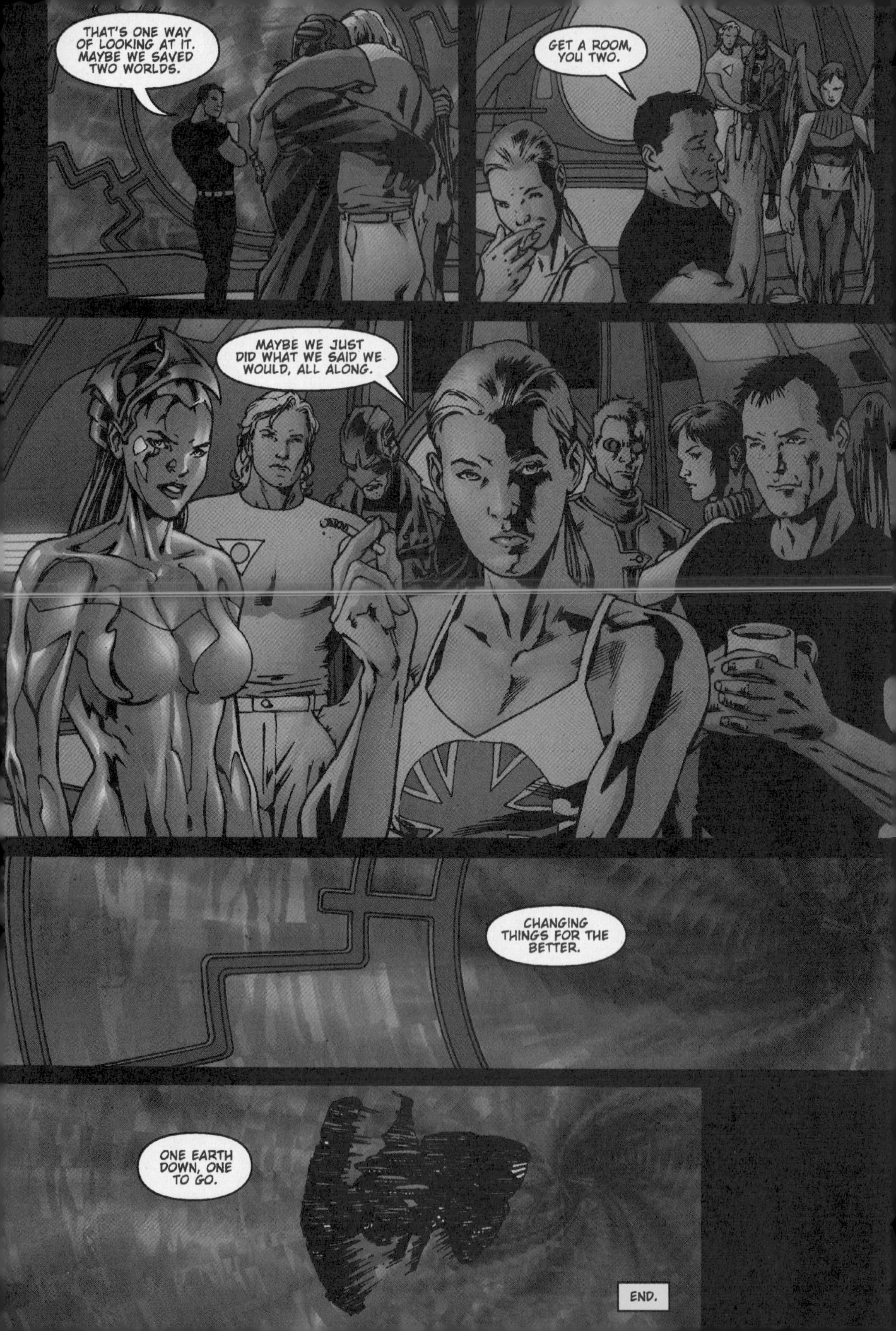
THAT'S ONE WAY OF LOOKING AT IT. MAYBE WE SAVED TWO WORLDS.
GET A ROOM, YOU TWO.
MAYBE WE JUST DID WHAT WE SAID WE WOULD, ALL ALONG.
CHANGING THINGS FOR THE BETTER.
ONE EARTH DOWN, ONE TO GO.
END.

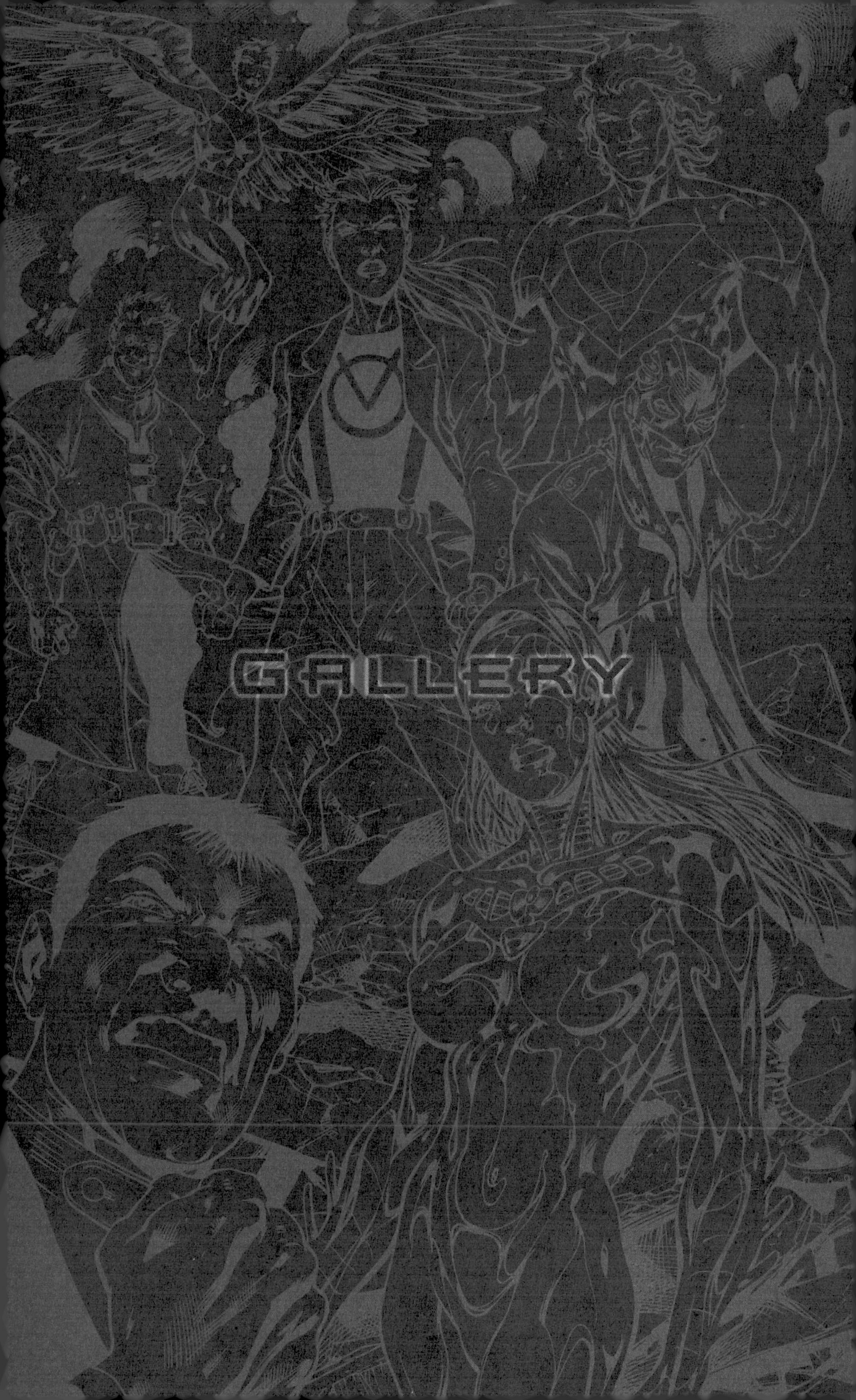
GALLERY

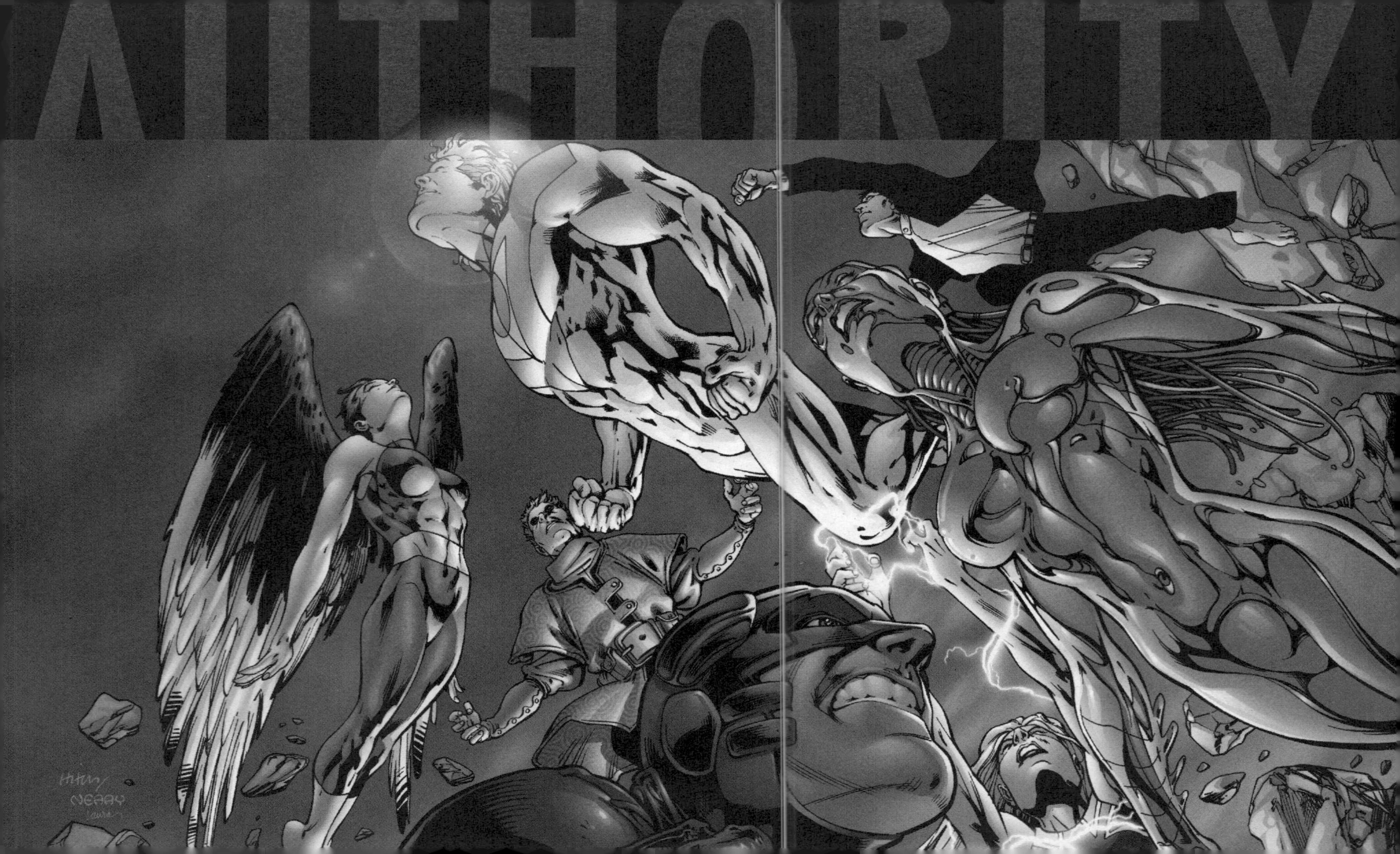
AUTHORITY

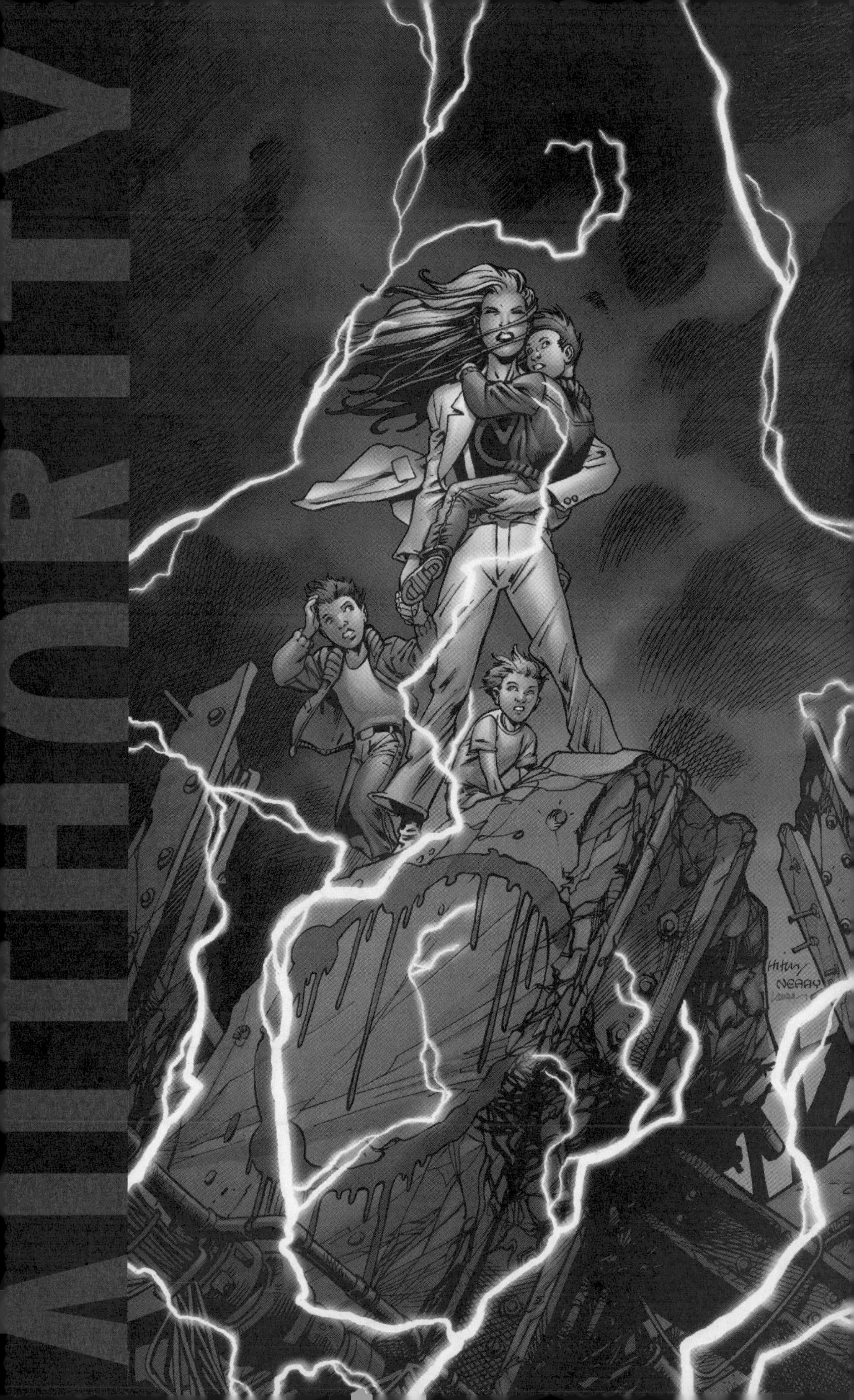

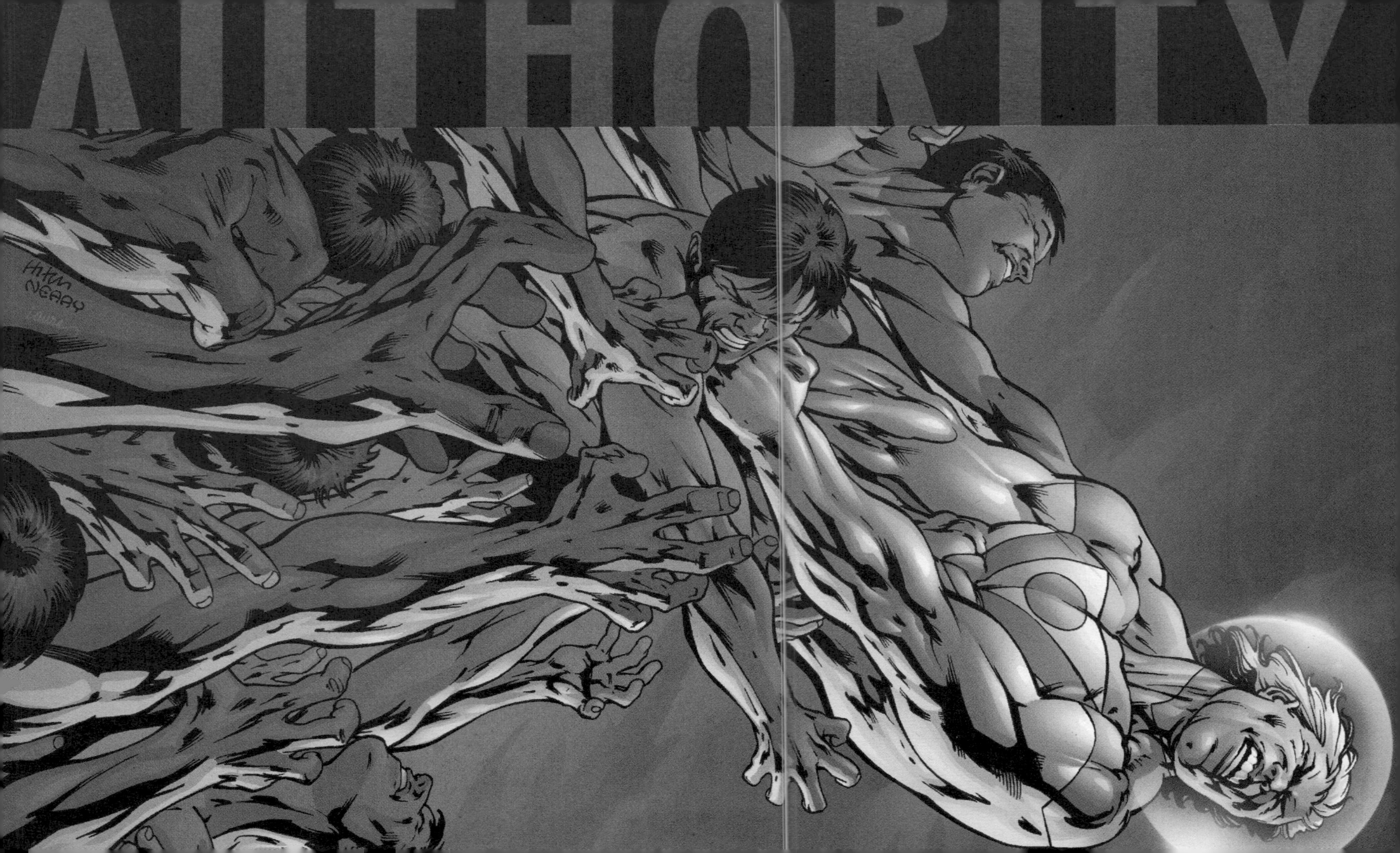
AUTHORITY

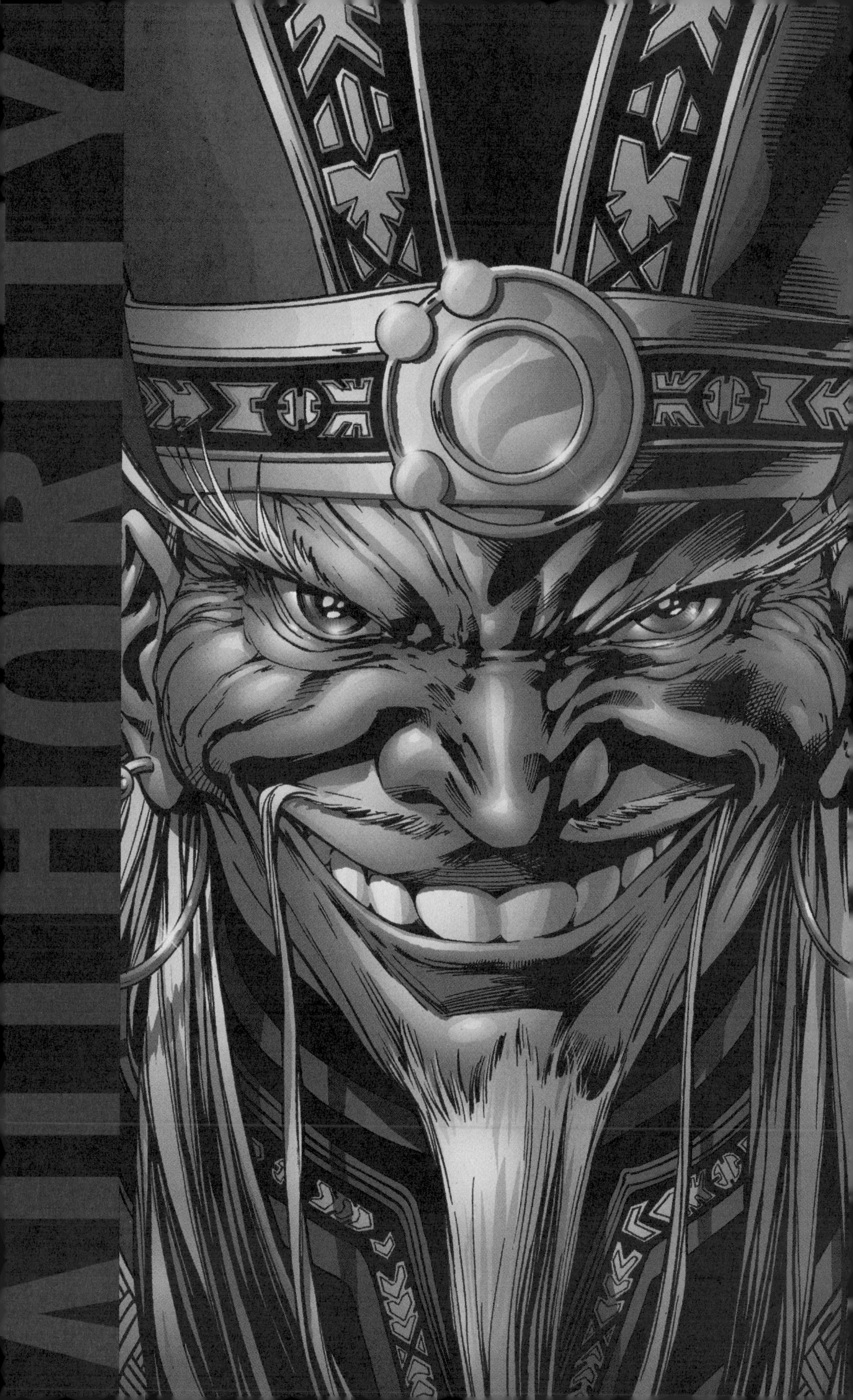
AUTHORITY

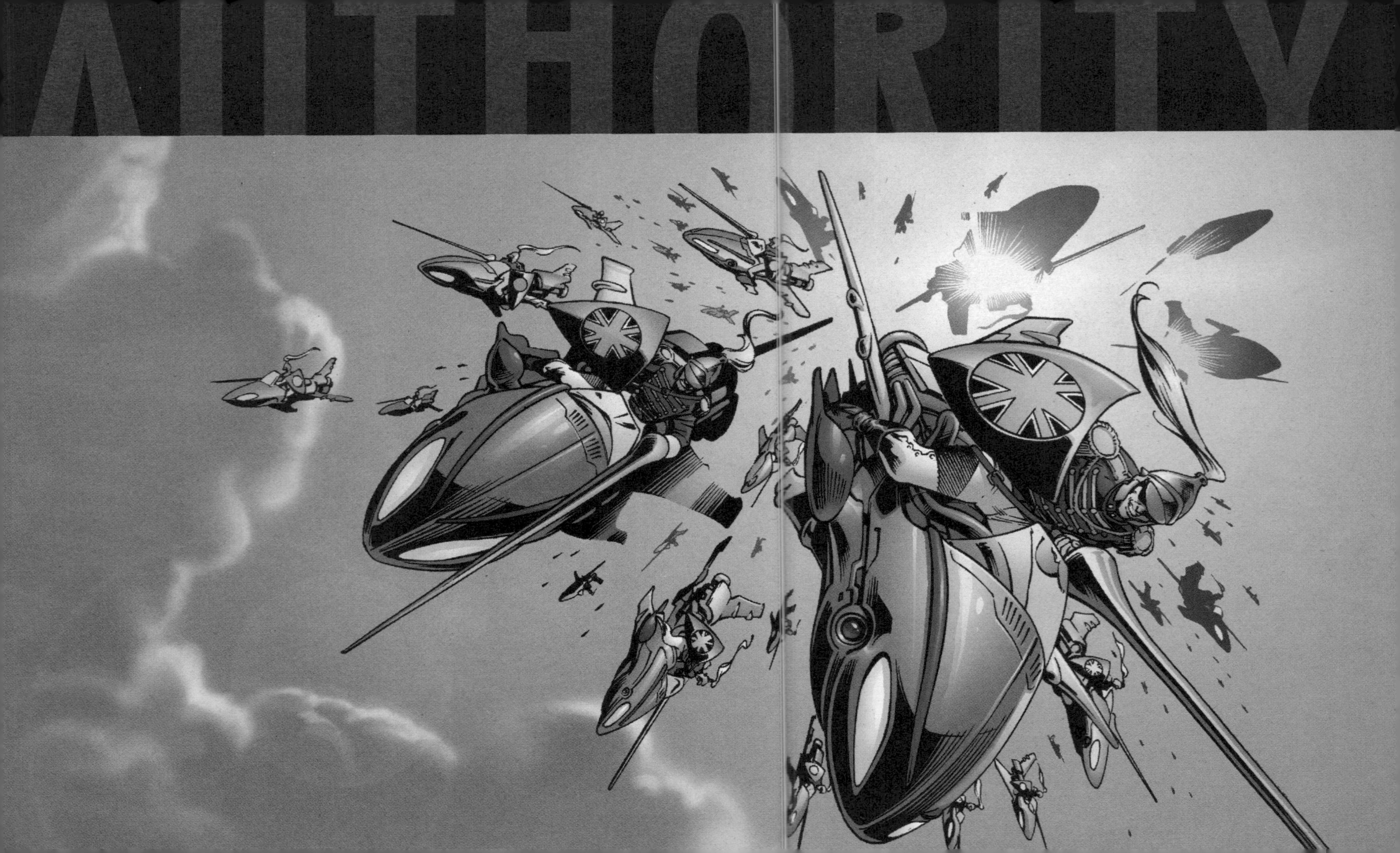
AUTHORITY

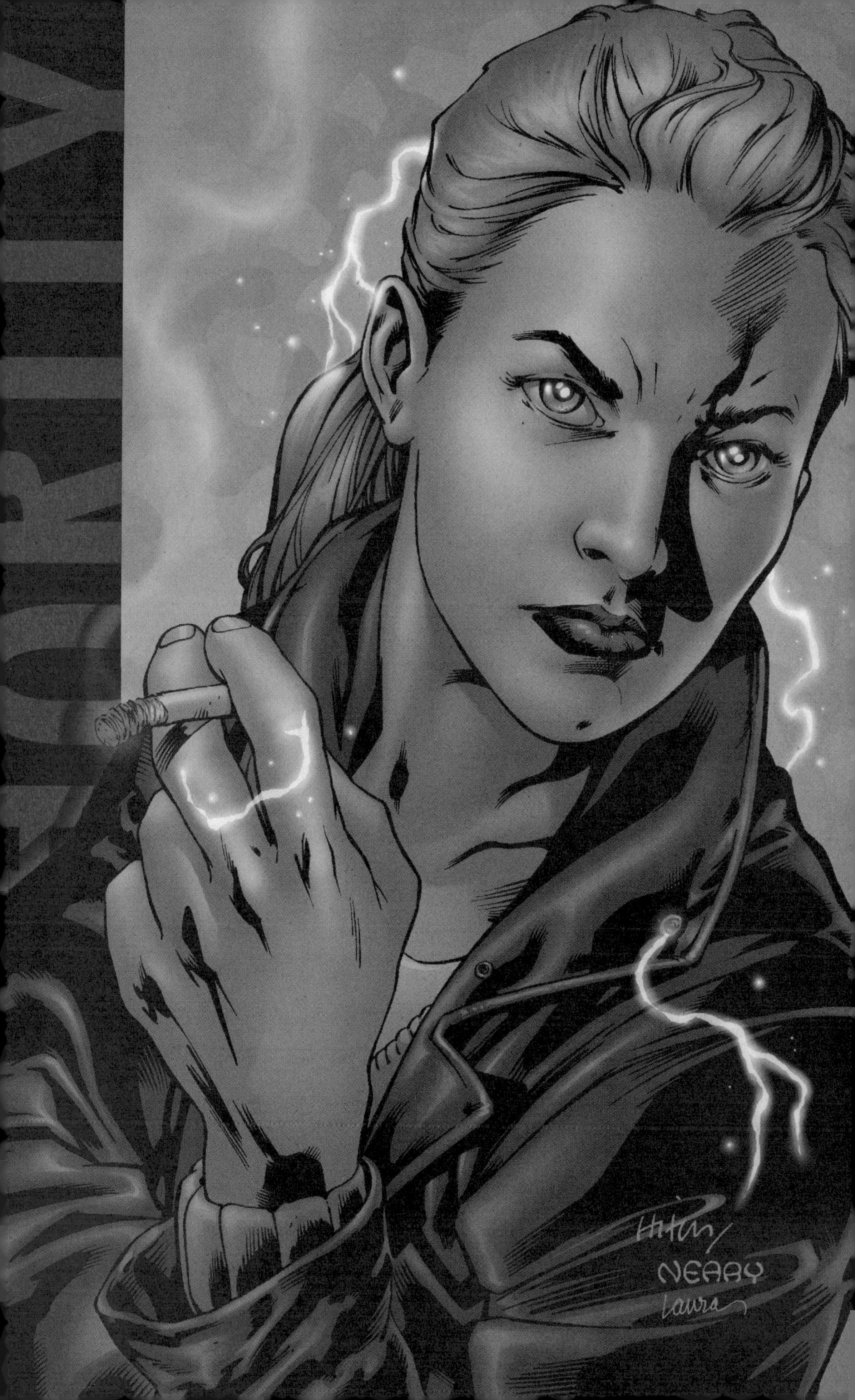
Hitch/
NEARY
Laura

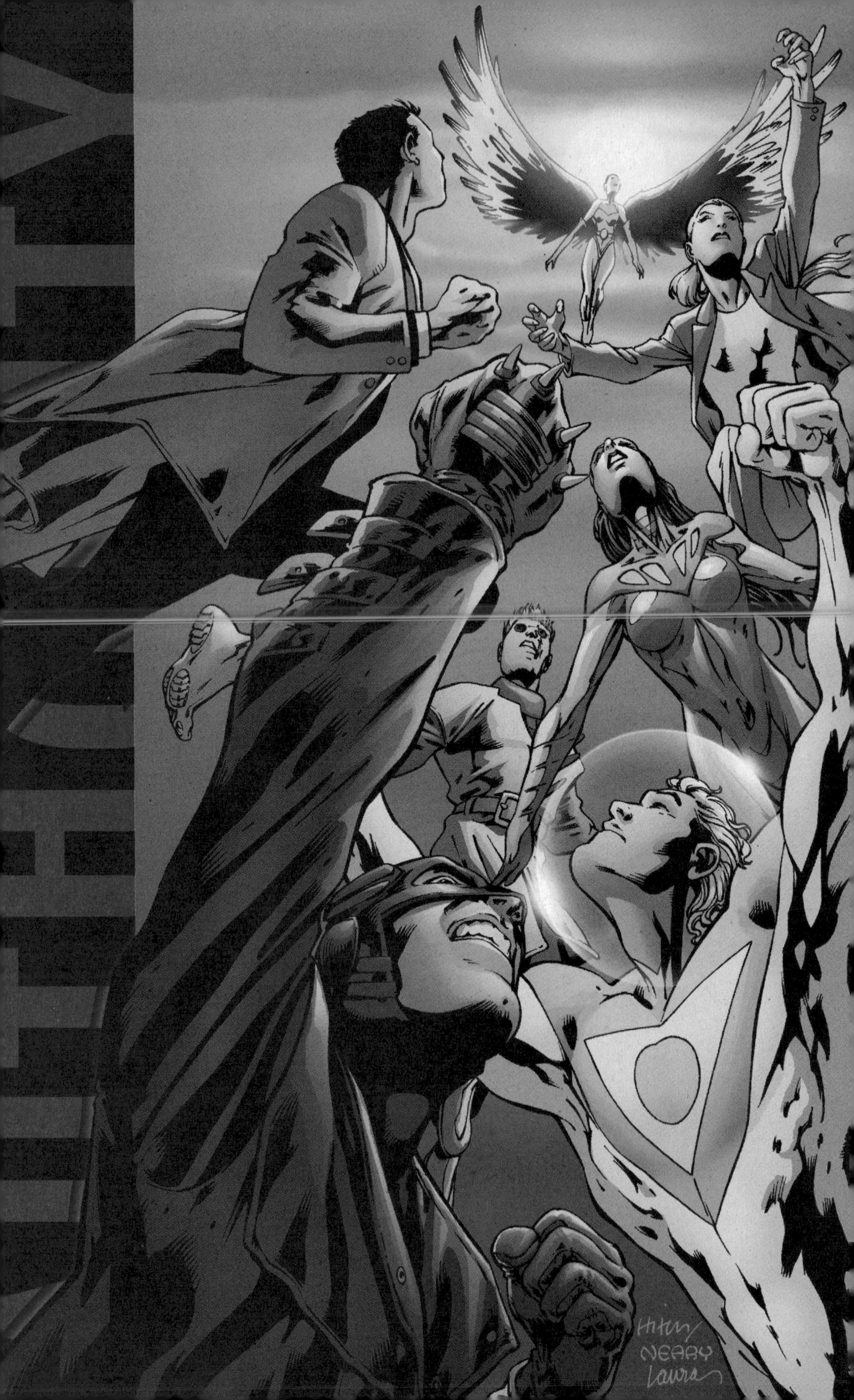
Hitch/
NEARY
Laura

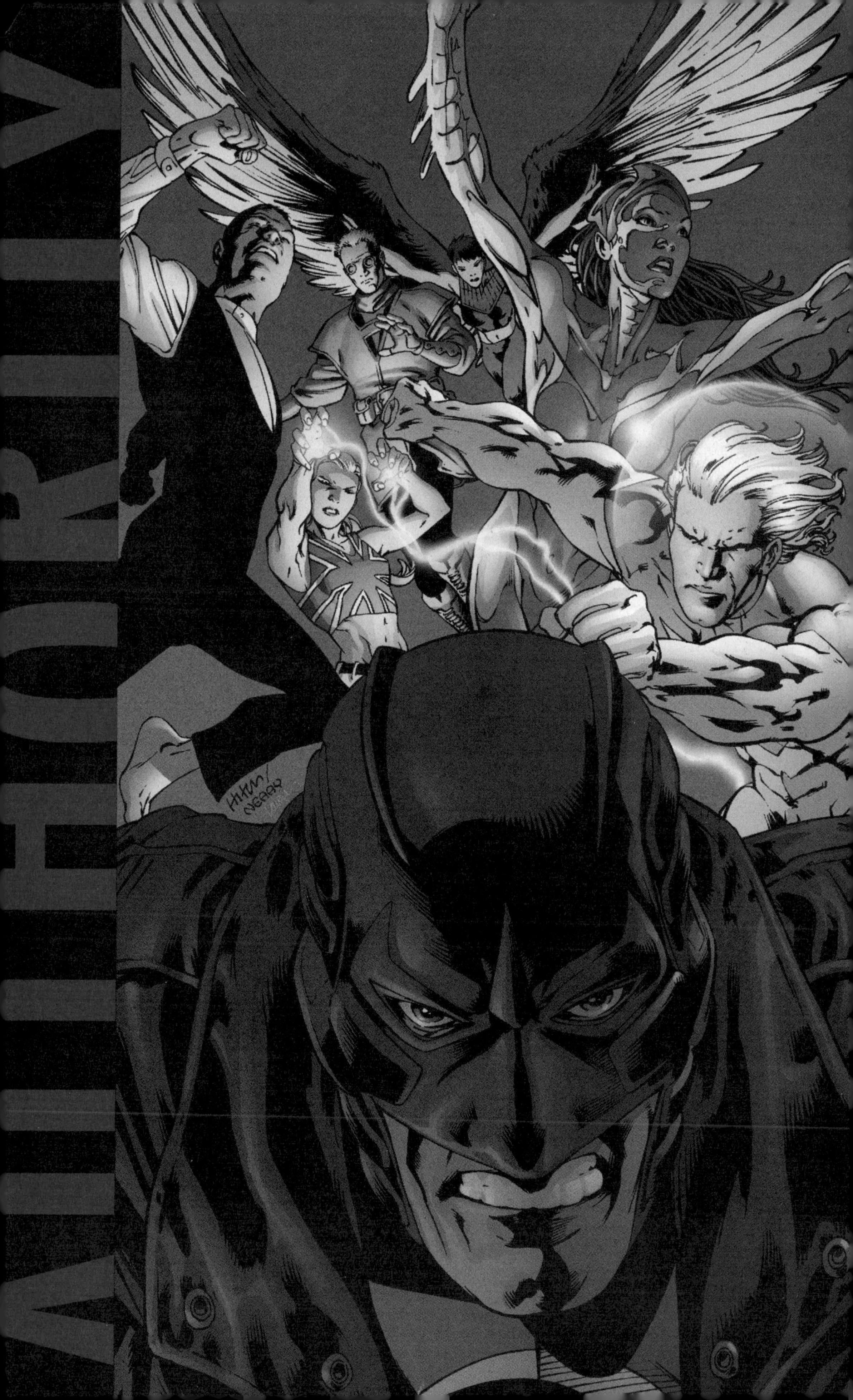
AUTHORITY

WILDSTORM COLLECTIONS

The Authority: Relentless
Ellis/Hitch/Neary

The Authority: Under New Management
Ellis/Millar/Hitch/Quitely

The Authority:
Earth Inferno and Other Stories
Millar/Quitely/Weston/Scott/Leach

Crimson: Loyalty & Loss
Augustyn/Ramos/Hope

Crimson: Heaven & Earth
Augustyn/Ramos/Hope

Crimson: Earth Angel
Augustyn/Ramos/Hope

Crimson: Redemption
Augustyn/Ramos/Hope

Deathblow: Sinners and Saints
Choi/Lee/Sale/Scott

Danger Girl: The Ultimate Collection
Campbell/Hartnell/Garner

Divine Right:
Book One
Lee/Williams

Gen13
Choi/Lee/Campbell/Garner

Gen13: #13 ABC
Choi/Lee/Campbell/Garner

Gen13: Bootleg Vol. 1
Various writers and artists

Gen13: Grunge the Movie
Warren

Gen13: I Love New York
Arcudi/Frank/Smith

Gen13: Interactive Plus
Various writers and artists

Gen13: Starting Over
Choi/Lee/Campbell/Garner

Gen13: We'll Take Manhattan
Lobdell/Benes/Sibal

Gen13: Superhuman Like You
Warren/Benes/Andrews

Gen13/ Superman
Hughes/Bermejo/Nyberg

Kurt Busiek's Astro City: Life in the Big City
Busiek/Anderson

Kurt Busiek's Astro City: Confession
Busiek/Anderson/Blyberg

Kurt Busiek's Astro City: Family Album
Busiek/Anderson/Blyberg

Kurt Busiek's Astro City:
Tarnished Angel
Busiek/Anderson/Blyberg

Leave It to Chance: Shaman's Rain
Robinson/Smith

Leave It to Chance: Trick or Threat
Robinson/Smith/Freeman

The Monarchy
Bullets Over Babylon
Young/McCrea/Leach/Pleece

Mr. Majestic
Casey/Holguin/McGuinness/D'Anda

Out There: The Evil Within
Augustyn/Ramos/Hope

Planetary/Authority: Ruling the World
Ellis/Jimenez/Lanning

Planetary:
All Over the World and Other Stories
Ellis/Cassaday

Planetary: The Fourth Man
Ellis/Cassaday

Steampunk: Manimatron
Kelly/Bachalo/Friend

StormWatch: Force of Nature
Ellis/Raney/Elliott

StormWatch: Lightning Strikes
Ellis/Raney/Lee/
Elliott/Williams

StormWatch: Change or Die
Ellis/Raney/Jimenez

StormWatch: A Finer World
Ellis/Hitch/Neary

StormWatch: Final Orbit
Ellis/Various

Wetworks: Rebirth
Portacio/Choi/Williams

WildC.A.T.s: Gang War
Moore/Various

WildC.A.T.s: Gathering of Eagles
Claremont/Lee/Williams

WildC.A.T.s: Homecoming
Moore/Various

WildC.A.T.s/X-Men
Various writers and artists

Wildcats: Street Smart
Lobdell/Charest/Friend

Wildcats: Vicious Circles
Casey/Phillips

Wildcats: Serial Boxes
Casey/Phillips

Zero Girl
Kieth

AMERICA'S BEST COMICS

ABC Special
Moore/ Various

League of Extraordinary Gentlemen
Moore/O'Neill

Promethea: Book One
Moore/Williams III/Gray

Promethea: Book Two
Moore/Williams III/Gray

Promethea: Book Three
Moore/Williams III/Gray

Tomorrow Stories: Book One
Moore/Nowlan/Veitch/Baikie/Gebbie/Barta

Tom Strong: Book One
Moore/Sprouse/Gordon

Tom Strong: Book Two
Moore/Sprouse/Gordon

Top Ten: Book One
Moore/Ha/Cannon

Top Ten: Book Two
Moore/Ha/Cannon

STAR TREK COLLECTIONS

Star Trek: Other Realities
Various

Star Trek:
The Next Generation
Enemy Unseen
Various

Star Trek:
The Next Generation
Forgiveness
Brin/Hampton

Star Trek:
The Next Generation
Gorn Crisis
Anderson & Moesta/Kordey

Star Trek: Voyager
Encounters With the Unknown
Various

Star Trek: New Frontier
Double Time
David/Collins/Roach

To find more collected editions and monthly comic books from WildStorm and DC Comics, call 1-888-comicbook for the nearest comics shop or go to your local book store.

JIM LEE Editorial Director JOHN NEE VP & General Manager SCOTT DUNBIER Group Editor JOHN LAYMAN Editor-Original Series
RACHELLE BRISSENDEN and ERIC DeSANTIS Collected Edition Editors PAUL LEVITZ President & Publisher
GEORG BREWER VP-Design & Retail Product Development RICHARD BRUNING VP - Creative Director
PATRICK CALDON Senior VP - Finance & Operations CHRIS CARAMALIS VP - Finance TERRI CUNNINGHAM VP - Managing Editor
DAN DIDIO VP - Editorial JOEL EHRLICH Senior VP - Advertising & Promotions ALISON GILL VP - Manufacturing
LILLIAN LASERSON Senior VP & General Counsel DAVID MCKILLIPS VP - Advertising
CHERYL RUBIN VP - Licensing & Merchandising BOB WAYNE VP - Sales & Marketing